LSAT®

LAW SCHOOL

ADMISSION TEST®

JAY B. CUTTS, M.A.
Director
Cutts Graduate Reviews
Albuquerque, New Mexico

JOHN F. MARES, J.D., M.B.A., M.A.
Attorney at Law
Founder, Mares LSAT Review
Lansing, New York

BARRON'S

DEDICATION

To the memory of our dear friend and LSAT colleague, Jack Oberst

ABOUT THE AUTHORS

Jay Cutts is a test preparation and admissions specialist who has helped several thousand applicants get accepted to law school, medical school, and graduate school since 1990. He specializes in advanced, personalized strategies for test-taking, timing, logical patterns, problem-solving, and test anxiety.

John Mares is a practicing attorney and business professional with an M.B.A. in Finance and International Management and an M.A. in Latin American Studies. He founded the Mares LSAT Review and is a successful inventor.

All inquiries should be addressed to:
Barron's Educational Series, Inc.
250 Wireless Boulevard
Hauppauge, New York 11788
www.barronseduc.com

ISBN: 978-1-4380-0232-3
ISBN (with CD-ROM): 978-1-4380-7335-4

ISSN: 1936-0185
ISSN (with CD-ROM): 1943-3786

PRINTED IN THE UNITED STATES OF AMERICA
9 8 7 6 5 4

10% POST-CONSUMER WASTE
Paper contains a minimum of 10% post-consumer waste (PCW). Paper used in this book was derived from certified, sustainable forestlands.

CONTENTS

PRACTICE TESTS

Preface

This book is a fresh, up-to-date approach to the LSAT. It is designed to help you, today's law school applicant, master the LSAT and get accepted to law school. We'd like to share with you some of the elements that make this book uniquely effective.

First, Barron's *LSAT* is founded on critical, unique, and highly advanced strategies. These strategies draw on our thirty-plus years of combined experience working hands-on with thousands of successful law school applicants. These strategies address timing, test taking, problem solving, test anxiety, the writing sample, and highly systematic and in-depth tools for correctly answering each and every type of LSAT question.

Second, the Barron's staff and the authors share the conviction that this book can best serve the prelaw community by listening to you. We asked a team of nearly fifty current prelaw students to review the book before publication, and their feedback has helped us make sure that the book meets your needs.

If we can personally offer any guidance to you on your path to law school, or if you have any feedback on this book, please feel free to contact us through Jay's website: *www.cuttsreviews.com/prelaw*. At that site, you can also take advantage of free materials to support your prep, such as our Solution of the Week program and our prelaw forum.

On behalf of all of us involved with this book, we wish you success in your pursuits.

Jay B. Cutts, MA
John F. Mares, JD, MBA, MA

Visit here for our free LSAT support materials.

ACKNOWLEDGMENTS

We would like to thank the following people: Wayne Barr, Bob O'Sullivan, and Linda Turner at Barron's for their kind and wise guidance; and our professional consultants Leigh Deusinger (adviser at Washington University), Sara Faradji (Carnegie Mellon), Crystin Immel, Michael Jasso (University of New Mexico), Brein Millea (Harvard), Randy Mink, Catherine Oliver (Oliver-Editorial.com), and Ronak Shah (University of Illinois at Chicago) for contributing according to their areas of expertise.

We would like to express our heartfelt appreciation to our families for their patient support during the long process of researching and writing this book. We both also want to express our gratitude for the support of two people who have encouraged and supported us over many years: Janelle Campbell, founder of Creative Learning Center, and Ethel Ortenburger, retired head administrator for the University of New Mexico School of Law, who first encouraged John to share his LSAT expertise with others.

Finally, we also want to thank the prelaw student review panel for their generous feedback: Janelle Alisuag, Matthew Allen, Brian Anderson, Gino Campana, Jessica Candelaria, Mary Casale, Ben Chalfin, Daniel Daragjati, Joshua Eastby, Sundous Eddeb, John Fleet, Timothy Charles Floro, Emily Furnish, Brooke Hamilton, Sarah-Marie Horning, Rob Iversen, Anthony Johnson, Kelsey Kolb, Hannah Loo, Chris Malafis, Derek Markle, Katy Mason, Nicole Massiah, Morgan Moone, Cale Numinen, Emily Patterson, Mark Perez, Amanda Pipik, Evan Rahn, Kelly Reed, Jean Roof, Matthew Russo, Wilma Rutherford, Katherine Shepardson, Chad Sibley, David Simiele, Teresa Sutton, Russ Terman, Bret Thixton, April Vivino, Brent Wajdowicz, and Kathryn Wickline.

Introduction to Mastering the LSAT

ORIENTATION TO THE LSAT

Getting into Law School

The goal of this book is to help you get accepted to law school. The Law School Admission Test (LSAT) is one of the most critical factors for admissions. In fact, if your grade point average (GPA) is strong enough, a superior LSAT score can guarantee your acceptance. The information here is based on the authors' multiple decades of hands-on LSAT instruction. The LSAT is learnable. For every LSAT question, there is a specific strategy for answering that question correctly. This book teaches all the strategies that you need, whether you are aiming for a 160 or a 180.

The LSAT

The LSAT is a half-day, paper-based test with four administrations per year: October (or in some years, late September), December, February, and June. The first three are given on Saturday mornings. Saturday Sabbath observers only may register for a non-Saturday test given within a few days after the Saturday test. The June test is on a Monday afternoon. The LSAT is required for admission to all law schools approved by the American Bar Association (ABA). Most Canadian law schools require the LSAT, and many non-ABA-approved law schools also require it. The Law School Admission Council (LSAC), which manages the LSAT, provides extensive information on the LSAT on its website at *www.lsac.org*. Review the information there, including test dates and deadlines.

The LSAT claims to measure comprehension of complex reading selections, organization of complex information, logical and critical thinking, and the ability to evaluate logical arguments. Except for the essay, all questions are multiple-choice, with five answer choices. There is no penalty for wrong answers, so fill in an answer for each question, even if you have not worked on it.

The LSAT contains the following elements, not necessarily in this order:

THE ELEMENTS OF THE LSAT
2 scored Logical Reasoning (LR) sections—35 minutes each
1 scored Reading Comprehension (RC) section—35 minutes
1 scored Analytical Reasoning (AR) section—35 minutes
1 unscored and unreported section of any of the three above types—35 minutes
1 unscored but reported Writing Sample—35 minutes

LOGICAL REASONING

Each of the two scored LR sections has the following characteristics:

> **LOGICAL REASONING**
>
> 25–26 questions
>
> 35 minutes
>
> Short passages with 1 question per passage

Each passage includes a partial or complete logical argument that may be valid or faulty. The questions may ask you to strengthen or weaken an argument; identify a flaw, an assumption, or a conclusion; or resolve a paradox. There are other types of questions that an LR passage may ask, and these are covered in Chapter 2.

READING COMPREHENSION

Each RC section presents four sets of long passages drawn on topics from the natural sciences, humanities, or social sciences. One of the four sets consists of two moderate-length passages.

> **READING COMPREHENSION**
>
> 27 questions
>
> 35 minutes
>
> 3 sets of a single passage with 6–8 questions
>
> 1 set of two shorter passages with
>   6–7 questions (Comparative Reading)

Each of the three single passages consists of about a half page of text followed by six to eight questions. The Comparative Reading set consists of two shorter passages, each about a quarter of a page, followed by six or seven questions.

ANALYTICAL REASONING

Each AR section includes four game setups, followed by questions.

> **ANALYTICAL REASONING**
>
> 23 questions
>
> 35 minutes
>
> 4 game setups followed by 5–7 questions

THE ESSAY (WRITING SAMPLE)

The essay has a 35-minute time limit. The essay requires you to (1) evaluate a brief statement, (2) understand two sides of an issue, (3) understand the criteria used to evaluate a solution, (4) apply the criteria in order to defend one solution as superior, (5) compose a coherent and grammatically correct essay using standard English, and (6) demonstrate a familiarity with the basic elements of legal writing.

LSAT Scores

You receive one total score that reflects your performance on all four scored multiple-choice sections of the LSAT. The unscored section does not contribute to your score. The essay does not receive a score but is forwarded to each school to which you send your LSAT score.

Your score is based on the total number of questions you answer correctly (raw score). There is no penalty for wrong answers and all correct answers are worth the same amount. The raw score is converted to a 120–180 scale (scaled score) according to a curve based on the scores of recent test takers. Table 1 gives an approximate conversion chart for converting raw scores to scaled scores. The actual scale changes slightly from test to test. Notice that one more correct answer often results in a higher scaled score.

Table 1. Converting Raw Scores to Scaled Scores

Raw Score Range	Scaled Score	Raw Score Range	Scaled Score	Raw Score Range	Scaled Score	Raw Score Range	Scaled Score	Raw Score Range	Scaled Score
0-15	120	30	133	48-49	145	68-69	157	87	169
16	121	31-32	134	50	146	70-71	158	88	170
17	122	33	135	51-52	147	72-73	159	89	171
18	123	34-35	136	53	148	74	160	90	172
19	124	36	137	54-55	149	75-76	161	91-92	173
20	125	37-38	138	56-57	150	77	162	93	174
21	126	39	139	58	151	78-79	163	94	175
22-23	127	40-41	140	59-60	152	80	164	95	176
24	128	42	141	61-62	153	81-82	165	96	177
25	129	43-44	142	63-64	154	83	166	97	178
26	130	45	143	65	155	84-85	167	98	179
27-28	131	46-47	144	66-67	156	86	168	99-101	180
29	132								

Score requirements for admission vary widely from school to school. In general, scores of 149 or below are not competitive, though schools may accept a small number of students in this range. Scores in the 150 to 160 range may be competitive at some schools but will not be competitive at many others. Scores of 161 and above will most likely be considered strong by many schools. Students applying to the most competitive schools, however, may need scores above 170.

Canceling Scores and Nonstandard Conditions

At the end of your official LSAT administration you have the option of canceling your test. If you do cancel, you will not find out how you scored. In specific circumstances that have caused you to perform poorly, such as illness, it may be helpful to cancel. However, you also have six calendar days from the date of your test to request a score cancellation. Because test takers' impressions of how they performed are often highly inaccurate on the actual test day, give yourself a day or two to consider whether or not you should cancel.

If you end up with a lower score on record because you did not cancel, most schools do not hold that against you, as long as your score is strong on your next test. In this case you should address, in your personal statement, any reasons that led to your lower score. If you are taking the LSAT on the last acceptable administration for an application year, it may be important to *not* cancel your score, even if the score may not be your best, because getting an official score for that administration will allow you to meet the LSAT requirement for your school. You can then usually take a subsequent LSAT and submit that score as a supplement to your first score. In such a case, send a written note to the schools to which you are applying so that they know to wait for your second score.

If you feel that the testing conditions at your testing center were substandard, you can file a complaint with LSAC. Substandard conditions can include excessive noise, overly cold or hot rooms, failure of a monitor to correctly keep track of time or to enforce quiet in the room, or other actions of the monitor that result in substandard testing, such as not allowing you to use a permitted watch or cutting a break short. If LSAC decides that you were not given standard conditions, it may submit a note to the schools where you are applying. In this case, the schools may take into account that your score was negatively affected.

THE ADMISSIONS PROCESS

LSAT Scores

LSAC provides a database of law schools. You can access the database from the LSAC home page under the link "*Searchable Law School Data and Descriptions.*" Many schools publish a grid showing the likelihood of admissions based on LSAT score and undergraduate GPA. Find the school in which you are interested and select the link that says "*LSAC Law School Description.*" If the school publishes a grid, it will appear on the last page of the description. Below is an example of part of a grid. For each GPA range, there are two columns. The first shows how many applications (Apps) were received in that range. The second shows how many people in that range were admitted (Adm).

Table 2. Sample Admissions Grid

LSAT Score	3.75+ Apps	3.75+ Adm	3.50–3.74 Apps	3.50–3.74 Adm	3.25–3.49 Apps	3.25–3.49 Adm
175–180	0	0	0	0	0	0
170–174	0	0	1	1	3	3
165–169	2	2	5	4	8	7
160–164	20	16	18	13	16	11
155–159	34	26	54	26	46	21
150–154	29	9	42	11	52	8

Find the column that matches your undergraduate GPA. In calculating your GPA do *not* include any graduate coursework. Then, for each LSAT range, you can determine the relative odds of being accepted. For example, in Table 2, if your GPA is 3.6 and your LSAT score is 156, fifty-four people applied in that range and twenty-six of them were admitted. The relative odds of being accepted in that range, then, were about 50 percent. In other words, one out of two applicants was admitted, and you will be competing with one other person for a spot.

In Table 2, for the top GPA range and for LSAT scores above 154, the school accepted nearly all applicants. If you have a strong GPA, aim for an LSAT score that gives you greater than 90 percent odds of being accepted. Even if you get into this range, take the rest of the application process seriously. A halfhearted application can earn you a rejection despite good test scores.

Acceptance is based on many factors in addition to LSAT score and GPA. However, calculating your odds based on LSAT score and GPA can help you determine how much harder you need to work—both on the LSAT and the rest of the admissions process.

Importance of the LSAT

Law school admissions committees typically make their decisions based on LSAT scores, undergraduate GPA, your personal statement, letters of recommendation, and your academic and professional experience, including graduate-level coursework, internships, and volunteer experiences.

Think of the LSAT and GPA as your first hurdles. If you have a low LSAT score and a low GPA, the committee may not look seriously at the rest of your application. Because the GPA is difficult to increase, a strong LSAT score may be your best chance to be competitive.

Other Aspects of the Admissions Process

During the summer before you apply to law school, as you are preparing for your LSAT, you also need to prepare for other parts of the admissions process. These include a personal statement and letters of recommendation. Check with your adviser to be sure you will graduate on time. Identify the schools to which you will apply and determine the LSAT score you will need to be accepted.

> **WHAT ADMISSIONS COMMITTEES CONSIDER**
>
> LSAT score
> GPA
> Personal statement
> Letters of recommendation
> Experience: graduate coursework, volunteer work, internships, and paid work

TEST DAY SCHEDULE

The typical test day consists of three sections, a fifteen-minute break, and then two test sections and the essay, in that order. Every test taker receives one test section that is not scored and is not reflected in the score report. This test section is used by LSAC to test and develop new questions. By the end of the test, you will have received either a second section of RC or AR or a third section of LR. However, it is not possible to determine which section is the unscored one, so it is important to work equally well on each section. Typically, you will not receive a second RC or AR section or third LR section until after the break. However, the unscored section has historically been one of the sections given before the break.

HOW TO USE THIS BOOK

You will get the most out of this book if you study the chapters in the order in which they are presented. There is information in some chapters that is important for you to know when you reach subsequent chapters.

 TIP

STAY INFORMED ABOUT THE LSAT

Be sure to consult the LSAC website— *www.lsac.org*— for important details about the test.

Read through the book once, practicing what you learn. This will introduce you to all the insights and strategies that you need. However, you will probably not absorb everything on your first time through the book. Learning the LSAT is like learning a new language. It requires practice, repetition, and review. In order to master the LSAT, review this book three, four, or even five times. Each time you will absorb more of the strategies.

Some of the strategies that you will learn are powerful and intricate. They may not come naturally to you the first time you use them. Some, especially the strategies for logic, require patient practice for you to become comfortable and proficient with them. Read the instruction, practice slowly and carefully with test questions, and then come back and read through the instruction again.

Reference Lists

REFERENCE INFORMATION

Identify the information in this book that you can use as a reference resource.

There are a number of lists and tables in the book that thoroughly break down some of the important complex patterns of the test, such as the types of AR games, patterns for solving games, and types of if/then logic. These lists are *not* meant for you to memorize or read through thoroughly. Treat these lists as you would a dictionary. Glance at them briefly. Then use them as reference tools, coming back to them as you need them when you work on practice problems.

The Practice Tests

BONUS

Test 65 is an actual LSAT from 2012.

The answer explanations in the practice tests give step-by-step instruction on how to apply the strategies. They reinforce what you learn in the chapters. Read through the answer explanations carefully to learn more strategy.

Getting Started

Begin your prep by taking the diagnostic test on the following pages. Take your diagnostic test under timed conditions. Be sure to stop at thirty-five minutes for each section. If you take even a minute more, your score will not be accurate. After taking the diagnostic test, read Chapter 1, General Strategies, to learn the critical timing and test-taking strategies that apply to the entire LSAT. Each subsequent chapter refines and deepens these strategies for you. Hold off on reading the explanations for the diagnostic test until after you have read all of the chapters. You will get more out of the explanations then.

KEEP A REALISTIC EYE ON YOUR PROGRESS

At least once a month do another test to see how you are scoring. If your scores are not going up steadily, redo your study plan. Evaluate what you are getting wrong. Are you missing points because of poor timing? Are you lacking strategies for certain questions? Use the following three-month study plan to help organize your schedule.

THREE-MONTH STUDY PLAN

Here is a plan to organize your studying over three months. The actual LSATs referred to below are the LSAT exams published by LSAC and available at *www.lsac.org* or at a bookstore. It is not necessary to do all sections of an assigned test at the same time, except when a full mock test is assigned. After completing a test section, review both your timing and testing strategy. For a six-month study plan, go through the three-month plan twice.

Table 3. Three-Month Study Plan

	BARRON'S CHAPTERS	PRACTICE TESTS
FIRST MONTH		
Week 1	Read the Table of Contents, Introduction, and Chapter 1 (General Strategies).	Barron's Diagnostic Test. All sections timed.
Week 2	Read the Logical Reasoning chapter.	Barron's LR end-of-chapter test timed.
Week 3	Read the Reading Comprehension chapter.	Barron's RC end-of-chapter test. Actual LSAT untimed.
Week 4	Read the Analytical Reasoning chapter.	Barron's AR end-of-chapter test. Actual LSAT untimed.
SECOND MONTH		
Week 5	Read the Essay chapter.	Barron's Essay end-of-chapter test. Actual LSAT timed.
Week 6	Review the Introduction and General Strategies chapter.	Barron's Practice Test 1 untimed.
Week 7	Review the Logical Reasoning chapter.	Actual LSAT untimed.
Week 8	Review the Reading Comprehension chapter.	Barron's Practice Test 2 untimed. Actual LSAT timed.
Week 9	Review the Analytical Reasoning chapter.	Actual LSAT untimed.
THIRD MONTH		
Week 10	Review the Essay chapter.	LSAT Test 65 in Barron's book timed.
Week 11	Final review of the Introduction, General Strategies chapter, and Logical Reasoning chapter.	Barron's CD Practice Test 1 untimed. Actual LSAT untimed.
Week 12	Final review of the Reading Comprehension and Analytical Reasoning chapters.	Barron's CD Practice Test 2 timed. Actual LSAT timed.
Week 13	Review as needed.	Actual LSAT as a full mock test.

ANSWER SHEET
Diagnostic Test

SECTION I

1. Ⓐ Ⓑ Ⓒ Ⓓ Ⓔ	8. Ⓐ Ⓑ Ⓒ Ⓓ Ⓔ	15. Ⓐ Ⓑ Ⓒ Ⓓ Ⓔ	22. Ⓐ Ⓑ Ⓒ Ⓓ Ⓔ
2. Ⓐ Ⓑ Ⓒ Ⓓ Ⓔ	9. Ⓐ Ⓑ Ⓒ Ⓓ Ⓔ	16. Ⓐ Ⓑ Ⓒ Ⓓ Ⓔ	23. Ⓐ Ⓑ Ⓒ Ⓓ Ⓔ
3. Ⓐ Ⓑ Ⓒ Ⓓ Ⓔ	10. Ⓐ Ⓑ Ⓒ Ⓓ Ⓔ	17. Ⓐ Ⓑ Ⓒ Ⓓ Ⓔ	24. Ⓐ Ⓑ Ⓒ Ⓓ Ⓔ
4. Ⓐ Ⓑ Ⓒ Ⓓ Ⓔ	11. Ⓐ Ⓑ Ⓒ Ⓓ Ⓔ	18. Ⓐ Ⓑ Ⓒ Ⓓ Ⓔ	25. Ⓐ Ⓑ Ⓒ Ⓓ Ⓔ
5. Ⓐ Ⓑ Ⓒ Ⓓ Ⓔ	12. Ⓐ Ⓑ Ⓒ Ⓓ Ⓔ	19. Ⓐ Ⓑ Ⓒ Ⓓ Ⓔ	26. Ⓐ Ⓑ Ⓒ Ⓓ Ⓔ
6. Ⓐ Ⓑ Ⓒ Ⓓ Ⓔ	13. Ⓐ Ⓑ Ⓒ Ⓓ Ⓔ	20. Ⓐ Ⓑ Ⓒ Ⓓ Ⓔ	27. Ⓐ Ⓑ Ⓒ Ⓓ Ⓔ
7. Ⓐ Ⓑ Ⓒ Ⓓ Ⓔ	14. Ⓐ Ⓑ Ⓒ Ⓓ Ⓔ	21. Ⓐ Ⓑ Ⓒ Ⓓ Ⓔ	28. Ⓐ Ⓑ Ⓒ Ⓓ Ⓔ

SECTION II

1. Ⓐ Ⓑ Ⓒ Ⓓ Ⓔ	8. Ⓐ Ⓑ Ⓒ Ⓓ Ⓔ	15. Ⓐ Ⓑ Ⓒ Ⓓ Ⓔ	22. Ⓐ Ⓑ Ⓒ Ⓓ Ⓔ
2. Ⓐ Ⓑ Ⓒ Ⓓ Ⓔ	9. Ⓐ Ⓑ Ⓒ Ⓓ Ⓔ	16. Ⓐ Ⓑ Ⓒ Ⓓ Ⓔ	23. Ⓐ Ⓑ Ⓒ Ⓓ Ⓔ
3. Ⓐ Ⓑ Ⓒ Ⓓ Ⓔ	10. Ⓐ Ⓑ Ⓒ Ⓓ Ⓔ	17. Ⓐ Ⓑ Ⓒ Ⓓ Ⓔ	24. Ⓐ Ⓑ Ⓒ Ⓓ Ⓔ
4. Ⓐ Ⓑ Ⓒ Ⓓ Ⓔ	11. Ⓐ Ⓑ Ⓒ Ⓓ Ⓔ	18. Ⓐ Ⓑ Ⓒ Ⓓ Ⓔ	25. Ⓐ Ⓑ Ⓒ Ⓓ Ⓔ
5. Ⓐ Ⓑ Ⓒ Ⓓ Ⓔ	12. Ⓐ Ⓑ Ⓒ Ⓓ Ⓔ	19. Ⓐ Ⓑ Ⓒ Ⓓ Ⓔ	26. Ⓐ Ⓑ Ⓒ Ⓓ Ⓔ
6. Ⓐ Ⓑ Ⓒ Ⓓ Ⓔ	13. Ⓐ Ⓑ Ⓒ Ⓓ Ⓔ	20. Ⓐ Ⓑ Ⓒ Ⓓ Ⓔ	27. Ⓐ Ⓑ Ⓒ Ⓓ Ⓔ
7. Ⓐ Ⓑ Ⓒ Ⓓ Ⓔ	14. Ⓐ Ⓑ Ⓒ Ⓓ Ⓔ	21. Ⓐ Ⓑ Ⓒ Ⓓ Ⓔ	28. Ⓐ Ⓑ Ⓒ Ⓓ Ⓔ

SECTION III

1. Ⓐ Ⓑ Ⓒ Ⓓ Ⓔ	8. Ⓐ Ⓑ Ⓒ Ⓓ Ⓔ	15. Ⓐ Ⓑ Ⓒ Ⓓ Ⓔ	22. Ⓐ Ⓑ Ⓒ Ⓓ Ⓔ
2. Ⓐ Ⓑ Ⓒ Ⓓ Ⓔ	9. Ⓐ Ⓑ Ⓒ Ⓓ Ⓔ	16. Ⓐ Ⓑ Ⓒ Ⓓ Ⓔ	23. Ⓐ Ⓑ Ⓒ Ⓓ Ⓔ
3. Ⓐ Ⓑ Ⓒ Ⓓ Ⓔ	10. Ⓐ Ⓑ Ⓒ Ⓓ Ⓔ	17. Ⓐ Ⓑ Ⓒ Ⓓ Ⓔ	24. Ⓐ Ⓑ Ⓒ Ⓓ Ⓔ
4. Ⓐ Ⓑ Ⓒ Ⓓ Ⓔ	11. Ⓐ Ⓑ Ⓒ Ⓓ Ⓔ	18. Ⓐ Ⓑ Ⓒ Ⓓ Ⓔ	25. Ⓐ Ⓑ Ⓒ Ⓓ Ⓔ
5. Ⓐ Ⓑ Ⓒ Ⓓ Ⓔ	12. Ⓐ Ⓑ Ⓒ Ⓓ Ⓔ	19. Ⓐ Ⓑ Ⓒ Ⓓ Ⓔ	26. Ⓐ Ⓑ Ⓒ Ⓓ Ⓔ
6. Ⓐ Ⓑ Ⓒ Ⓓ Ⓔ	13. Ⓐ Ⓑ Ⓒ Ⓓ Ⓔ	20. Ⓐ Ⓑ Ⓒ Ⓓ Ⓔ	27. Ⓐ Ⓑ Ⓒ Ⓓ Ⓔ
7. Ⓐ Ⓑ Ⓒ Ⓓ Ⓔ	14. Ⓐ Ⓑ Ⓒ Ⓓ Ⓔ	21. Ⓐ Ⓑ Ⓒ Ⓓ Ⓔ	28. Ⓐ Ⓑ Ⓒ Ⓓ Ⓔ

SECTION IV

1. Ⓐ Ⓑ Ⓒ Ⓓ Ⓔ	8. Ⓐ Ⓑ Ⓒ Ⓓ Ⓔ	15. Ⓐ Ⓑ Ⓒ Ⓓ Ⓔ	22. Ⓐ Ⓑ Ⓒ Ⓓ Ⓔ
2. Ⓐ Ⓑ Ⓒ Ⓓ Ⓔ	9. Ⓐ Ⓑ Ⓒ Ⓓ Ⓔ	16. Ⓐ Ⓑ Ⓒ Ⓓ Ⓔ	23. Ⓐ Ⓑ Ⓒ Ⓓ Ⓔ
3. Ⓐ Ⓑ Ⓒ Ⓓ Ⓔ	10. Ⓐ Ⓑ Ⓒ Ⓓ Ⓔ	17. Ⓐ Ⓑ Ⓒ Ⓓ Ⓔ	24. Ⓐ Ⓑ Ⓒ Ⓓ Ⓔ
4. Ⓐ Ⓑ Ⓒ Ⓓ Ⓔ	11. Ⓐ Ⓑ Ⓒ Ⓓ Ⓔ	18. Ⓐ Ⓑ Ⓒ Ⓓ Ⓔ	25. Ⓐ Ⓑ Ⓒ Ⓓ Ⓔ
5. Ⓐ Ⓑ Ⓒ Ⓓ Ⓔ	12. Ⓐ Ⓑ Ⓒ Ⓓ Ⓔ	19. Ⓐ Ⓑ Ⓒ Ⓓ Ⓔ	26. Ⓐ Ⓑ Ⓒ Ⓓ Ⓔ
6. Ⓐ Ⓑ Ⓒ Ⓓ Ⓔ	13. Ⓐ Ⓑ Ⓒ Ⓓ Ⓔ	20. Ⓐ Ⓑ Ⓒ Ⓓ Ⓔ	27. Ⓐ Ⓑ Ⓒ Ⓓ Ⓔ
7. Ⓐ Ⓑ Ⓒ Ⓓ Ⓔ	14. Ⓐ Ⓑ Ⓒ Ⓓ Ⓔ	21. Ⓐ Ⓑ Ⓒ Ⓓ Ⓔ	28. Ⓐ Ⓑ Ⓒ Ⓓ Ⓔ

Diagnostic Test

SECTION I

Time: **35 minutes**

27 Questions

> **DIRECTIONS:** Each set of questions in this section is based on one passage or on a pair of passages. Answer the questions based on what is <u>stated</u> or <u>implied</u> in the passage or in the pair of passages. More than one answer choice could conceivably answer the question in some cases. However, you should choose the <u>best</u> answer. The best answer is the response that answers the question most accurately and completely. When you have chosen the best answer, fill in the space on your answer sheet that corresponds to your answer.

The issue of who owns a particular item is generally a straightforward one in mainstream society. Anyone who creates an object *Line* is recognized as owning that object. If the (5) owner sells the object, the person who has purchased it is recognized as the new owner. If someone takes an object without the consent of the owner, that person is recognized, both by law and by society, as not being the (10) true owner of the object. In short, the creation of an object conveys ownership and the economic contract between seller and purchaser transfers ownership. No application of force or coercion can succeed in wresting owner- (15) ship away from the recognized owner.

Suppose the creator of an object has sold that object willingly and then regrets the sale. Suppose this person claims to be the rightful owner, by virtue of having created the object, (20) and demands that the new, "false" owner return the object. Is it not true that society, and the law, would give precedence to the

contract between consenting seller and purchaser? Just as *Caveat emptor—Let the buyer* (25) *beware*—applies to transactions in our society, so does *Caveat venditor—Let the seller beware.* Once the contract between seller and buyer is completed, it cannot be reversed without the consent of both parties. Such is (30) the expectation in our mainstream society.

This value may not apply, however, when members of the mainstream society deal with societies with different values. Consider, for example, certain Native American artifacts (35) that were recently confiscated by the federal government from a museum owned by non-Native Americans. The confiscated items included medicine bundles, war bonnets, and other items with cultural and spiritual sig- (40) nificance to the Native American tribes that originally created the items. Admittedly, the museum owner's inability to provide records documenting the legal purchase of the items is troubling from the mainstream perspec-

GO ON TO THE NEXT PAGE

(45) tive. So are the discredited claims of a Native American tribal member whose photographs that were intended to establish his ownership turned out not to match the confiscated objects. However, aside from these techni-
(50) calities, there is a deeper issue.

The cultural director of one of the tribes claiming ownership of the artifacts states the issue plainly. These articles have spiritual importance, he asserts, to the tribal members
(55) who owned the articles and to their families. Regardless of how the museum obtained the articles, they belong to the Native American people who created them and to the tribe. They are not for a museum to display or to
(60) profit from. The distinction between this view and the mainstream view of the sanctity of the seller/buyer contract is perhaps a simple one. From the Native American standpoint, there are some objects that are so spiritually
(65) significant that no one person can own them, and if no one owns them, no one has the right to sell them. The question the rest of us must ask ourselves is what treasure our mainstream culture has lost that it holds no object
(70) holy enough to rise above buying and selling.

1. Which one of the following most accurately expresses the main point of the passage?
   (A) Ownership of an object is established by a contract between a seller and a buyer.
   (B) Some Native American tribes do not recognize the selling of an object as conveying ownership.
   (C) The mainstream view of ownership is not held by some nonmainstream cultures, whose values call mainstream values into question.
   (D) Spirituality is a quality that should not be bought and sold.
   (E) The view that no one really owns any object calls into question the spirituality of mainstream values.

2. The author of the passage would be most likely to agree with which one of the following statements?
   (A) A society that considers one object so spiritually significant that no one has the right to sell that object may possess something of value that a society that considers no object spiritually significant in the same way does not possess.
   (B) A society that considers no object so spiritually significant that it cannot be bought or sold is culturally inferior to a society that has at least one object that it considers so spiritually significant that it cannot be bought or sold.
   (C) If an object does not have such spiritual significance that no one person can own it, then the culture that produced that object may have lost a spiritual treasure that it formerly possessed.
   (D) Mainstream society does not consider even one object to have spiritual significance.
   (E) A museum should only be allowed to purchase a particular Native American artifact if the members of the tribe that created the artifact agree to the sale.

GO ON TO THE NEXT PAGE

3. Which one of the following describes the author's primary purpose in mentioning the fact in the second paragraph that a contract between buyer and seller cannot be reversed without the consent of both parties?

(A) to state a conclusion that is defended in the rest of the passage

(B) to introduce a fact that is later proven to be untrue

(C) to defend an assertion made earlier in the second paragraph

(D) to summarize a point of view that is in contrast to a point of view introduced in the third paragraph

(E) to establish a general expectation of mainstream society

4. As described in the passage, the distinction between the mainstream view of the seller/buyer relationship and the view expressed by the cultural director of the tribe in question is most closely analogous to which one of the following distinctions?

(A) On island X, the parents of a young woman initiate the arrangement of her marriage by negotiating with the parents of an eligible partner. On island Y, the same custom applies but in some cases the parents of a young man can initiate the arrangement of his marriage by negotiating with the parents of an eligible partner.

(B) On island X, the parents of a young woman initiate the arrangement of her marriage by negotiating with the parents of an eligible partner. On island Y, the same custom applies but in cases in which the two partners are too incompatible to live together, the parents of the young couple can subsequently agree to nullify the marriage by mutual consent.

(C) On island X, the parents of a young woman initiate the arrangement of her marriage by negotiating with the parents of an eligible partner. On island Y, the same custom applies but there are some young women who are considered to have such potential for educational advancement that the parents are not allowed to arrange their marriages.

(D) On island X, the parents of a young woman initiate the arrangement of her marriage by negotiating with the parents of an eligible partner. On island Y, the same custom applies but in cases in which the parents believe their daughter has great spiritual potential, they are allowed to decide not to arrange a marriage for her.

(E) On island X, the parents of a young woman initiate the arrangement of her marriage by negotiating with the parents of an eligible partner. On island Y, the custom has been lost and young people often are not able to find a marriage partner.

GO ON TO THE NEXT PAGE

5. The author uses the word *treasure* in the last sentence most likely in order to refer to
   (A) the unique value of an object that has spiritual significance
   (B) cultural artifacts that were created by mainstream culture at an earlier time but have been lost since then
   (C) the fact that some objects are spiritually cheapened when they are bought or sold
   (D) a cultural quality that may have been lost by a society that does not recognize exceptions to the contractual relationship between seller and buyer
   (E) the fact that spiritual objects are just as valuable economically as other objects, even if spiritual objects do not have a practical use

6. According to the passage, which one of the following is true about the artifacts that were confiscated from the museum?
   (A) The museum from which they were confiscated specialized in Native American artifacts.
   (B) The museum had not legally purchased the artifacts that were confiscated.
   (C) The artifacts all originated with one specific tribe.
   (D) The federal government confiscated the artifacts based on technicalities.
   (E) The ownership claims of one tribal member are now considered unsubstantiated.

7. Which one of the following statements is most strongly supported by information given in the passage?
   (A) If the seller of an object decides that the object should not have been sold, the seller does not have a legitimate argument for the buyer to return the object if the buyer does not consent to returning the object and if the buyer is a member of the mainstream culture.
   (B) If the seller of an object decides that the object should not have been sold, the seller may have a legitimate argument for the buyer to return the object, even if the buyer does not consent to returning the object.
   (C) A belief in the sanctity of the seller/buyer contract is a simplistic view.
   (D) The sanctity of the seller/buyer contract has a spiritual value in Native American culture that it does not have in mainstream culture.
   (E) Native Americans should ask themselves if they have not lost something valuable, given the fact that mainstream values differ significantly from their own.

GO ON TO THE NEXT PAGE

Passage A

There are numerous techniques that can be used to create a work of abstract art. The basis of an abstract artwork can consist of
Line a pattern of shapes and colors, including
(5) lines, geometrical figures, and free-form areas of color or texture. Alternatively, the same elements can be applied without any pattern.

To begin a composition, apply the basic patterns or shapes to the canvas. Unless you
(10) are creating a totally abstract expression, your piece will include references to real-world objects or shapes. This is where both the agony and the ecstasy of abstract creation begins. To what extent will your images
(15) conform to the shapes of their real-world counterparts? To what extent will you simply follow the demands of convention and to what extent will you travel the path of your own perceptions?
(20) To answer this question, you must turn to, and trust, your inner eye. When you look at the sunflower in the garden, what does your *inner* eye see? How tall is the flower compared to its neighbors? The measuring tape may say
(25) the difference is three feet. The inner eye may place the head of the sunflower among the constellations. It is the development of this inner eye that will determine your success with abstract art, along with your ability to let
(30) your inner eye control your hand.

Passage B

The current crisis in the art world is not founded, as some artists would have us believe, in the low value that our society places on art, with the resulting inability of
(35) young artists, or old ones for that matter, to earn a living through their art. Rather, it is that there are not enough young artists. The direct cause of the dearth of young people interested in creating art is that children are
(40) no longer given the chance to create art in the public schools.

A recent survey of parents found that as many as 90 to 99 percent of parents thought that instruction in art should be required in
(45) the schools and should be allotted as much as four hours a week. These feelings were the same across all cultural and economic boundaries.

Are the intuitions of parents correct?
(50) Does the application of fingerpaint to paper in random shapes and colors at the whim of the imagination really bring benefit to the student in the long run? Regardless of the answer to these questions in terms of
(55) academic performance, one fact is clear. Both our intuitions and the research conducted on the topic indicate that the more opportunity a person is given as a young student to experiment with the joyful process of artistic
(60) creation, the more likely the person is to continue to create art as an adult. And the more adults there are who themselves create art, the greater the market will be for people who are trying to earn a living as an artist.

GO ON TO THE NEXT PAGE

8. It is most likely that both authors would agree with which one of the following statements about creating art?
   (A) A majority of people believe that creating art is a worthwhile activity.
   (B) Being successful with art requires training.
   (C) It is possible for a person to learn to enjoy creating art through in-person instruction with an experienced artist.
   (D) Creating good art requires trusting your own perceptions.
   (E) Creating a work of art has the potential for bringing joy to the artist.

9. Both passages are primarily concerned with examining which one of the following topics?
   (A) in what way the creation of art can be personally rewarding
   (B) in what way art can be an expression of inner vision
   (C) in what way the creation of art can have beneficial effects
   (D) in what way art can transcend the restrictions of patterns
   (E) in what way artists can more easily earn a living through their art

10. Which one of the following most accurately describes a relationship between the two passages?
   (A) Passage B expands on a distinction for which Passage A provides a background.
   (B) Passage B addresses in a generalized way a topic that Passage A addresses in a personalized way.
   (C) Passage B reconciles a conflict that Passage A introduces.
   (D) Passage B rejects on both intuitive and scientific grounds a position that Passage A defends solely on intuitive grounds.
   (E) Passage B proposes a solution to a problem that Passage A poses but leaves unanswered.

11. It can be inferred that the argument made in Passage B relies on which one of the following assumptions?
   (A) The current crisis in the art world is the result of the low value that our society places on artistic creation.
   (B) There are some artists who believe that the current crisis in the art world is not the result of the low value that our society places on artistic creation.
   (C) Art education for children, regardless of whether it is formal or intuitive, improves children's performance in their academic work.
   (D) The more opportunity a young person is given to experiment with art, the more likely that person will be able to earn a living as an artist when the person is an adult.
   (E) Adults who themselves create art are more likely to buy works of art than are adults who do not create art.

12. Which one of the following describes the author's primary purpose in mentioning the distance measured by the measuring tape, in the last paragraph of Passage A?
   (A) to describe a technique for accurately representing perspective in an abstract painting
   (B) to present a metaphor for how inner vision operates
   (C) to provide objective evidence that is then used to support a conclusion
   (D) to emphasize the distinction between conventional perception and inner vision
   (E) to present an example of a simple strategy that children can use in creating art

GO ON TO THE NEXT PAGE

Alien life has been hypothesized to exist in the solar system and throughout the universe. Whereas science fiction typically depicts most
Line extraterrestrial life forms as having humanoid
(5) and/or reptilian forms, it is more accurate to say that alien life would encompass a wide range of life forms, from bacteria-like through plant and animal forms, to humanoid forms. The main question that faces exobiologists,
(10) scientists concerned with extraterrestrial life, is to what extent the characteristics of life on other planets would be similar to life as we know it.

Exobiologists have posited a distinction
(15) between universal and parochial (narrowly restricted) characteristics of life. Universals are features that are thought to have evolved independently more than once on Earth (and thus, presumably, are more likely to appear)
(20) and are so intrinsically useful that species, even extraterrestrial ones, will inevitably tend toward them. The most fundamental of these is probably bilateral symmetry, but more complex characteristics include flight, sight,
(25) photosynthesis, and limbs, all of which are thought to have evolved independently several times on Earth. Although these characteristics are highly likely to evolve in any life form, the specific forms that these character-
(30) istics take can vary greatly. The types of eyes that have evolved, for example, exhibit radically different working schematics and different visual foci: the visual spectrum, infrared, polarity, and echolocation.
(35) Parochials, in contrast to universals, are essentially arbitrary evolutionary characteristics. These often have little inherent utility (or at least have a function that can be equally served by dissimilar morphology) and
(40) probably will not be replicated. Communicating by means of vibrating vocal cords is a parochial characteristic. Intelligent aliens could communicate through gestures, as deaf humans do, by sounds created from struc-
(45) tures unrelated to breathing, which happens on Earth when, for instance, cicadas vibrate their wings or crickets stridulate their wings, or visually through bioluminescence or chromatophore-like structures.

(50) Attempting to define parochial features challenges many taken-for-granted notions about morphological necessity. Skeletons, which are essential to large terrestrial organisms according to the experts in the field of
(55) gravitational biology, are almost certain to be replicated elsewhere in one form or another.

The question of the extent of diversity among extraterrestrials is by no means settled. Whereas many exobiologists do stress that the
(60) enormously heterogeneous nature of life on Earth foretells an even greater variety in outer space, others point out that convergent evolution—the phenomenon by which the common requirements of life itself cause divergent life
(65) forms to develop similar characteristics—may dictate substantial similarities between life on Earth and extraterrestrial life. These two schools of thought are called "divergionism" and "convergionism," respectively.

Adapted from *http://en.wikipedia.org/wiki/ Extraterrestrial_life* (accessed August 13, 2012).

GO ON TO THE NEXT PAGE

13. Which one of the following most accurately expresses the main point of the passage?
    (A) There are certain factors that would cause extraterrestrial life to have some similarities to life on Earth but the extent of similarity is unknown, as is the extent of variation among different forms of extraterrestrial life.
    (B) Although there are certain factors that would cause extraterrestrial life to have similarities to life on Earth, it is unlikely that we will ever find extraterrestrial life.
    (C) The fact that certain characteristics of life are universal leads exobiologists to conclude that life must exist in other parts of the universe, even though the exact characteristics of extraterrestrial life would vary.
    (D) The forces of divergence and convergence are likely to cancel each other out, resulting in a moderate degree of diversity among extraterrestrial life forms.
    (E) Exobiologists are mainly concerned with the potential extent of diversity among all extraterrestrial life forms and are roughly equally divided between those who favor divergionism and those who favor convergionism.

14. The passage most strongly suggests that exobiologists would agree with which one of the following statements?
    (A) Alien life is more likely to exist in our solar system than in more distant parts of the universe.
    (B) An extraterrestrial life form that has universal characteristics is unlikely to have parochial characteristics.
    (C) The study of extraterrestrial life has the potential to refine the understanding of concepts about life on Earth.
    (D) Because of the vastness of the universe compared to Earth, extraterrestrial life is almost certain to exhibit an even greater diversity of life forms than does life on Earth.
    (E) The extraterrestrial life forms depicted by science fiction are not realistic.

15. Which one of the following most accurately describes the organization of the passage?
    (A) Two hypotheses about an issue are discussed with details and explanations and a conclusion is arrived at that introduces two additional hypotheses.
    (B) A hypothesis is introduced, two different methods for testing the hypothesis are discussed, and one is concluded to be better than the other.
    (C) An hypothesis is introduced, two different methods for testing the hypothesis are discussed, and then two more methods are discussed.
    (D) A question is posed, a theoretical framework for answering the question is introduced, detail is provided to explain the theoretical framework, and a related question is introduced.
    (E) A question is posed, a distinction useful for addressing the question is explored, and an answer to the question is offered.

16. The passage most strongly suggests which one of the following about parochial characteristics?
    (A) Some life forms are likely to have predominantly parochial characteristics.
    (B) Skeletons are a parochial feature that almost certainly would be found among extraterrestrials.
    (C) A predominance of parochial features would lead to substantial similarities between extraterrestrial life and life on Earth.
    (D) Communication is not a parochial characteristic, but the biological structures used for communicating are typically parochial.
    (E) A parochial feature is more decorative than utilitarian, and life forms are likely to have some decorative features.

GO ON TO THE NEXT PAGE

17. Suppose that an extraterrestrial life form were discovered that had two eyes, one on the left side and one on the right side, that processed visual information based on the polarity of the light. Which one of the following statements would most likely be put forth by exobiologists who favor divergionism?

(A) This discovery supports divergionism because, even though the presence of eyes is a feature that is common on Earth, the use of polarity to process visual information is rarely found on Earth.

(B) This discovery supports divergionism because, even though bilateral symmetry is expected in extraterrestrial life, having bilateral eyes that use polarity to process visual information does not occur on Earth.

(C) This discovery supports divergionism because, even though having a left and right eye is not enough to establish bilateral symmetry, the presence of eyes is a universal characteristic expected in extraterrestrial life.

(D) This discovery supports divergionism because, even though the extraterrestrial life form has substantial similarities to life on Earth, it could not actually survive on Earth.

(E) This discovery supports divergionism because, even though the extraterrestrial life form has some characteristics that are rare on Earth, it has no characteristics that fail to appear on Earth.

18. According to the passage, each of the following is an example of a universal characteristic EXCEPT:

(A) a skeleton
(B) communication
(C) bioluminescence
(D) photosynthesis
(E) sight

19. In the context of the passage, the description of a parochial characteristic as having "little inherent utility" is most clearly expressed by which one of the following statements?

(A) Stridulating the wings helps crickets develop greater flight endurance.

(B) The flexibility of the tongue, which is essential to human speech, is an inherited trait.

(C) Communicating through gestures is less practical than communicating through speech.

(D) It takes little physical effort for humans to vibrate the vocal cords.

(E) Vibrating the vocal cords does not serve a critical biological function.

20. Based on the passage, which one of the following statements is most likely to be true?

(A) Intelligent extraterrestrial life is most likely to be either humanoid or reptilian.

(B) The primary issue in exobiology is whether there are planets capable of sustaining life that are close enough to Earth that exobiologists could study these extraterrestrial life forms.

(C) Bilateral symmetry evolved independently more than once in Earth life forms.

(D) Given that life forms on Earth share many universal characteristics, convergionism is probably more valid than divergionism.

(E) Communication has no actual biological utility.

GO ON TO THE NEXT PAGE

What factors determine to which country a particular territory rightfully belongs? The case of the Falkland Islands, as they are known to Britain, which claims ownership (5) of them, or Las Islas Malvinas, as they are known to Argentina, which also claims ownership of them, is an example of a question of ownership that seems impossible to resolve.

The British claim is based on the fact that (10) nearly the entire population of three thousand are of British descent, consider themselves British, and are opposed to any Argentinean claim of ownership. At first glance this would seem to be an airtight case for British (15) nationality. After all, should not the nationality of a territory be defined by the inhabitants, and if, as is in rare circumstances the case, nearly all of the inhabitants are in agreement, should not that be the end of the discussion? (20) It would seem that real conflict over nationality would only be an issue in those sad parts of the world in which the population is divided into distinct camps that are in unresolvable conflict.

(25) The Argentinean argument, however, is based on the assertion that the British illegitimately populated the islands with their own countrymen in order to establish a claim of ownership. The Argentinean interest in the (30) islands predates the settlement by the British and apparently predates the settlement by any people at all. There is precedent for the claim that a government has flooded a region with people sympathetic to it. Some (35) Hawaiians argue that, although the vote for Hawaiian statehood was a democratic one, the results were distorted by the presence of large numbers of non-Hawaiian natives who had been encouraged by the United States to (40) settle in Hawaii. Similarly, some historians claim that the British intentionally inundated the northern part of Ireland with non-Irish settlers from Scotland and England.

The case of the Falklands is distinct from (45) these examples, however, because there were no indigenous people there in the first place. This raises the question of whether, and on what basis, a government can claim ownership of a piece of land that is unoccupied, (50) and whether doing so before another government does the same lends any credibility to the claim.

An historian can only wonder if all of the international law that supposedly governs (55) such events is simply a way to give a semblance of dignity to what is fundamentally a schoolyard brawl, in which the biggest bully walks away the winner. Perhaps it would be a more civilized act to declare that no one can (60) have the Falklands and to turn the land back over to the penguins, petrels, and passerines that were there before we were.

21. Which one of the following most accurately expresses the main point of the passage?
    (A) The nationality of a territory should be determined by the majority of the inhabitants of the territory.
    (B) Only in cases in which the inhabitants of a territory are divided by irresolvable conflict should the nationality of the territory be considered unresolvable.
    (C) The international criteria used to determine the ownership of a territory are not sufficiently clear to determine ownership.
    (D) Flooding a territory with people sympathetic to the interests of a particular country is not a legitimate means of establishing ownership.
    (E) Both Britain and Argentina should withdraw their citizens from the Falklands.

GO ON TO THE NEXT PAGE

22. Which one of the following, if true, would most weaken the position that the passage attributes to the British government?

(A) Britain sent British citizens to other New World colonies in order to bolster the British claim to those colonies.

(B) Argentina has never populated a territory with its own citizens in an attempt to establish a claim of ownership.

(C) The people of British descent who settled in the Falklands did so without any encouragement from the British government.

(D) Before any settlers from Britain arrived, there were fifty people on the Falklands who were of Argentinean descent, considered themselves Argentinean citizens, and were opposed to any British claim of ownership.

(E) Nearly 85 percent of the people who consider themselves Argentinean citizens believe the Falklands belong to Argentina and are opposed to any British claim of ownership.

23. As it is presented in the passage, the relationship between Britain and Argentina is most similar to the relationship in which one of the following?

(A) Country X declares independence from Country Y. Country Y rejects Country X's declaration of independence because the majority of people in Country X were born in Country Y.

(B) Team X claims they should be awarded the trophy for top team in their league because they have won more games than any other team. Team Y claims that Team X's claim is illegitimate because some of the teams that Team X beat were not from the same league as Team X and Team Y.

(C) Contestant X in a spelling bee spelled more words correctly than did Contestant Y. Contestant Y claims that the contest was not legitimate because Contestant X received many words with a Spanish origin and Contestant X is a native speaker of Spanish.

(D) Company X claims they should be given the exclusive contract for selling hamburgers on campus because most students on campus like Company X's hamburgers. Company Y claims that students like Company X's hamburgers only because Company X distributed free samples of hamburgers to students on campus in violation of the school's policies.

(E) Senator X filibusters a bill so that it cannot be brought to a vote. Senator Y claims that Senator X's actions are unethical because the majority of the senators present were in favor of the bill and the majority should prevail.

GO ON TO THE NEXT PAGE

24. The primary purpose of the second paragraph in relation to the rest of the passage is to
   (A) present a plausible claim that is later shown to be questionable
   (B) present a hypothesis that the author uses to support a conclusion
   (C) report a position that the author believes is without merit
   (D) provide the historical background for a discussion that is presented in subsequent paragraphs
   (E) establish which of two arguments is the more defendable

25. The author would most likely consider which one of the following as an example of a "more civilized" act, as described in line 59?
   (A) A less powerful nation defeats a more powerful nation in a battle to determine the ownership of a territory that both claim.
   (B) A more powerful nation agrees with a less powerful nation that the ownership of a territory that both claim will be decided by the outcome of a single battle between the two nations.
   (C) A less powerful nation suggests to a more powerful nation that the issues concerning the ownership of a territory that both claim be decided by a third, impartial nation that is even more powerful.
   (D) A more powerful nation threatens to invade a less powerful nation over the ownership of a territory that both claim, but instead of invading, attends a meeting arranged by the less powerful nation to negotiate the issues of ownership.
   (E) A more powerful nation maintains control of a territory that is also claimed by a less powerful nation but offers a generous compensation to any citizens of the less powerful nation who live in the disputed territory and wish to move away.

26. With which one of the following statements would the author of the passage be most likely to agree?
   (A) If two countries both claim ownership of a territory that has never been inhabited, the claim of the country that has the greater resources for developing and protecting the territory is the more legitimate claim.
   (B) If two countries both claim ownership of a territory that has never been inhabited, the claim of the country that agrees to leave the territory unpopulated is the more legitimate claim.
   (C) If a country claims ownership of a territory that has never been inhabited, the claim is not legitimate if citizens of the country subsequently settle in the territory.
   (D) If a country claims ownership of a territory that has never been inhabited, the claim is more legitimate if that country is the first to make such a claim.
   (E) If a country claims ownership of a territory that has never been inhabited, it is unclear whether the claim is legitimate.

GO ON TO THE NEXT PAGE

27. The passage provides information sufficient to answer which one of the following questions?

(A) What factors legitimately determine to which country a particular territory rightfully belongs?

(B) In what way is the situation in the Falklands different from the situation in Hawaii?

(C) Are there any current inhabitants of the Falklands whose ancestors were born in Argentina?

(D) Are there any current inhabitants of the Falklands who were born in Britain?

(E) Do a majority of Argentineans believe that Las Islas Malvinas belong to Argentina?

Time: 35 minutes
   23 Questions

> **DIRECTIONS:** The groups of questions in this test section are each based on specific sets of conditions. Making a rough diagram may be useful for answering some of the questions. For each question choose the answer choice that is most accurate and complete. Fill in the space on your answer sheet that corresponds to your answer.

QUESTIONS 1–5

Seven volunteers—Kelly, Li, Morton, Nuanez, Ostrowsky, Palluca, and Rifkin—are to visit with a patient in the hospital on a specific afternoon. Each time slot for a visit is thirty minutes and the time slots start at 4 P.M. and on each subsequent half hour consecutively, with no gaps. Each volunteer visits exactly once. The volunteers appear according to the following conditions:

   Rifkin visits after Morton.
   Nuanez visits before Palluca
   Palluca visits immediately after Rifkin.
   There are exactly two time slots between Li's visit
      and Kelly's visit.
   Morton's visit starts on a half hour.

1. Which one of the following is an acceptable schedule of visitors, starting with the first visitor and proceeding consecutively?
   (A) Kelly, Morton, Ostrowsky, Li, Nuanez, Rifkin, Palluca
   (B) Li, Morton, Ostrowsky, Kelly, Rifkin, Palluca, Nuanez
   (C) Nuanez, Kelly, Morton, Ostrowsky, Li, Rifkin, Palluca
   (D) Nuanez, Li, Rifkin, Palluca, Kelly, Morton, Ostrowsky
   (E) Nuanez, Morton, Kelly, Ostrowsky, Rifkin, Palluca, Li

GO ON TO THE NEXT PAGE

2. Which one of the following must be false?
   (A) Ostrowsky's visit is immediately after Li's visit and immediately before Morton's visit.
   (B) Morton's visit is immediately after Ostrowsky's visit and immediately before Kelly's visit.
   (C) Kelly's visit is immediately after Ostrowsky's visit and immediately before Rifkin's visit.
   (D) Ostrowsky's visit is immediately after Palluca's visit and immediately before Kelly's visit.
   (E) Nuanez's visit is immediately after Morton's visit and immediately before Li's visit.

3. If Palluca visits at 6:30, which one of the following could be true?
   (A) Morton visits at 5:30.
   (B) Nuanez visits at 4:00.
   (C) Li visits at 4:30.
   (D) Ostrowsky visits at 5:30.
   (E) Nuanez visits at 4:30.

4. Exactly how many volunteers are there any one of whom could visit sixth?
   (A) one
   (B) two
   (C) three
   (D) four
   (E) five

5. If Kelly visits before Li, which one of the following must be true?
   (A) Ostrowsky visits after Li visits.
   (B) Palluca visits after Li visits.
   (C) Either Nuanez visits first or Kelly visits first.
   (D) Either Palluca visits last or Ostrowsky visits last.
   (E) Either Morton visits second or Kelly visits second.

GO ON TO THE NEXT PAGE

QUESTIONS 6–10

The marketing department at a grocery store will choose four items to put on sale from among eight popular items—grapes, lettuce, mayonnaise, napkins, orange juice, paper plates, steak, and tomatoes. The following conditions apply:

If grapes are chosen, neither steak nor paper plates are chosen.

If mayonnaise is not chosen, tomatoes must be chosen.

If lettuce is not chosen, paper plates are not chosen.

Either lettuce is chosen or mayonnaise is chosen but not both.

6. Which one of the following could be a complete and accurate list of the items chosen to be put on sale?
(A) grapes, lettuce, napkins, orange juice
(B) grapes, lettuce, napkins, tomatoes
(C) napkins, orange juice, steak, tomatoes
(D) grapes, mayonnaise, steak, tomatoes
(E) mayonnaise, napkins, paper plates, tomatoes

GO ON TO THE NEXT PAGE

7. If paper plates are chosen, which one of the following could be true?
   (A) Neither grapes nor lettuce are chosen.
   (B) Neither grapes nor tomatoes are chosen.
   (C) Both napkins and steak are chosen.
   (D) Both steak and tomatoes are chosen.
   (E) Both napkins and orange juice are chosen.

8. If tomatoes are not chosen, then which of the following statements must be true?
   (A) Steak is chosen.
   (B) Steak is not chosen.
   (C) Napkins are chosen.
   (D) Oranges are not chosen.
   (E) Mayonnaise is not chosen.

9. If grapes are chosen, which one of the following, if true, would completely determine the list of items to be put on sale?
   (A) Tomatoes are not chosen.
   (B) Tomatoes are chosen.
   (C) Oranges are chosen.
   (D) Oranges are not chosen.
   (E) Napkins are not chosen.

10. Which one of the following, if substituted for the condition that, if lettuce is not chosen, then paper plates are also not chosen, would have the same effect in determining which items are chosen to be placed on sale?
    (A) If mayonnaise is chosen, then either grapes are chosen or exactly one of napkins, oranges, steak, and tomatoes is not chosen.
    (B) If paper plates are chosen, then tomatoes must also have been chosen.
    (C) If grapes are chosen, then lettuce is not chosen.
    (D) If grapes are chosen, then tomatoes are also chosen.
    (E) If grapes are not chosen, then paper plates are not chosen.

GO ON TO THE NEXT PAGE

QUESTIONS 11–16

Six students—Foster, Giang, Hernandez, Kovac, Morris, and O'Donnell—are to participate in debates on Saturday. There are three debates—one in the morning, one in the afternoon, and one in the evening. In each debate exactly two students will participate. Each student participates exactly once during the day. The participation of the students is governed by the following conditions:

> If Giang debates in the morning, then O'Donnell debates in the evening.
>
> If Morris does not debate in the afternoon, then Kovac debates in the evening.
>
> Hernandez debates in either the morning or the afternoon.
>
> Hernandez and Foster do not participate in the same debate.

11. Which one of the following could be an accurate assignment of students to debate teams?
    (A) Morning: Hernandez, Kovac
        Afternoon: Morris, O'Donnell
        Evening: Giang, Foster
    (B) Morning: Giang, Hernandez
        Afternoon: Morris, O'Donnell
        Evening: Foster, Kovac
    (C) Morning: Foster, Hernandez
        Afternoon: Morris, O'Donnell
        Evening: Giang, Kovac
    (D) Morning: Hernandez, O'Donnell
        Afternoon: Foster, Kovac
        Evening: Giang, Morris
    (E) Morning: Foster, Giang
        Afternoon: Kovac, Morris
        Evening: Hernandez, O'Donnell

GO ON TO THE NEXT PAGE

12. If Foster debates in the morning, which one of the following could be true?
   (A) Kovac debates at the same time as Hernandez.
   (B) Morris debates at the same time as O'Donnell.
   (C) Morris debates in the evening and O'Donnell debates in the afternoon.
   (D) Morris debates in the morning and O'Donnell debates in the afternoon.
   (E) Kovac debates in the morning and O'Donnell debates in the afternoon.

13. If Giang debates in the morning, which one of the following must be true?
   (A) Hernandez and Morris debate at the same time.
   (B) Foster and Morris debate at the same time.
   (C) Foster and O'Donnell debate at the same time.
   (D) Kovac debates in the morning.
   (E) Morris debates in the afternoon.

14. Which one of the following must be true?
   (A) Either Hernandez debates in the morning or Foster debates in the morning.
   (B) Either Hernandez debates in the morning or Giang debates in the morning.
   (C) Either O'Donnell debates in the evening or Giang debates in the morning.
   (D) Either Giang does not debate in the morning or O'Donnell does not debate in the morning.
   (E) Either Morris does not debate in the afternoon or Kovac does not debate in the afternoon.

15. Which one of the following is a pair of students who cannot debate together in the morning?
   (A) Giang and Hernandez
   (B) Hernandez and Morris
   (C) Hernandez and Kovac
   (D) Morris and O'Donnell
   (E) Kovac and Morris

16. Each of the following could be true EXCEPT:
   (A) Foster and O'Donnell debate in the morning and Giang and Morris debate in the afternoon.
   (B) Giang and Kovac debate in the morning and O'Donnell and Foster debate in the evening.
   (C) Foster and Kovac debate in the morning and Hernandez and Morris debate in the afternoon.
   (D) Hernandez and Kovac debate in the morning and Giang and O'Donnell debate in the evening.
   (E) Hernandez and Morris debate in the afternoon and Foster and O'Donnell debate in the evening.

GO ON TO THE NEXT PAGE

QUESTIONS 17–23

Six artists—Lambert, Montoya, Ping, Reuben, Sokolov, and Tranh—are to present a sampling of their works to a panel of judges. Each artist has a twenty-minute presentation period. One artist presents per period and the periods do not overlap. The order in which the artists present is determined by the following conditions:

   Montoya presents after Lambert.
   Ping presents either first or third.
   Montoya presents after Reuben but before Sokolov.

17. Which one of the following is an order in which the artists could present, from first to last?
   (A) Reuben, Lambert, Montoya, Ping, Tranh, Sokolov
   (B) Ping, Lambert, Reuben, Montoya, Tranh, Sokolov
   (C) Ping, Lambert, Montoya, Reuben, Sokolov, Tranh
   (D) Lambert, Reuben, Ping, Sokolov, Montoya, Tranh
   (E) Ping, Tranh, Reuben, Montoya, Lambert, Sokolov

18. If Tranh presents first, which one of the following could be true?
   (A) Montoya presents immediately after Ping.
   (B) Reuben presents immediately after Lambert.
   (C) Lambert presents immediately after Ping.
   (D) Reuben presents fifth.
   (E) Sokolov presents fifth.

GO ON TO THE NEXT PAGE

19. Which one of the following must be true?
    (A) The second presentation is given by either Lambert or Reuben.
    (B) The first presentation is given by either Ping, Lambert, or Reuben.
    (C) The fourth presentation is given by Montoya.
    (D) Tranh presents in either second, third, or sixth place.
    (E) Sokolov presents in either fifth or sixth place.

20. Which one of the following CANNOT be true?
    (A) Lambert presents immediately after Tranh.
    (B) Montoya presents immediately before Tranh.
    (C) Ping presents immediately after Tranh and immediately before Montoya.
    (D) Sokolov presents immediately after Montoya and immediately before Tranh.
    (E) Tranh presents immediately after Lambert and immediately before Ping.

21. If Tranh presents before Montoya, which one of the following CANNOT be true?
    (A) There are exactly two presenters between Lambert's presentation and Reuben's presentation.
    (B) There are exactly two presenters between Ping's presentation and Tranh's presentation.
    (C) Lambert presents after Tranh but before Ping.
    (D) Tranh presents immediately before Montoya.
    (E) Ping presents immediately after Tranh and immediately before Montoya.

22. Which one of the following must be false?
    (A) There is exactly one presenter between Tranh and Montoya.
    (B) Tranh presents second and there are exactly two presenters between Lambert and Reuben.
    (C) Tranh presents sixth and there is one presenter between Ping and Sokolov.
    (D) Tranh presents sixth and there is one presenter between Lambert and Reuben.
    (E) Montoya presents fourth and there are exactly four presenters between Tranh and Ping.

23. If Reuben presents before Lambert, the order of the presentations is completely determined if which one of the following is true?
    (A) Sokolov presents sixth.
    (B) Tranh presents fifth.
    (C) Ping presents first.
    (D) Montoya presents fifth.
    (E) Tranh presents third.

 STOP If you finish before the 35-minute time period is over, you may go back and check your answers in this section only. You may not work on any other test section.

Time: **35 minutes**

26 Questions

DIRECTIONS: The questions in this section are based on the reasoning contained in brief statements or passages. More than one answer choice could conceivably answer the question in some cases. However, you should choose the <u>best</u> answer. The best answer is the response that answers the question most accurately and completely. You should avoid making any assumptions that, by commonsense standards, are implausible, superfluous, or incompatible with the passage. When you have chosen the best answer, fill in the space on your answer sheet that corresponds to your answer.

---

1. Francine: People are often unconsciously influenced by the people around them. When Robert served as a judge at the recent dog show, he did not notice that the owners of four out of the five dogs he was judging were surly and did not look up, whereas the owner of one dog smiled broadly at Robert. Even though all of the dogs performed equally well, Robert awarded the blue ribbon to the dog whose owner smiled at him. Clearly Robert was influenced by the smile.

Which one of the following, if true, most strengthens Francine's argument?
   (A) Most observers of the show felt that the dog that earned the blue ribbon performed better than the other four dogs.
   (B) Most observers of the show felt that the five dogs performed equally well.
   (C) Robert felt that the five dogs performed equally well.
   (D) Robert had decided which dog would receive the blue ribbon before the owner of the winning dog smiled at him.
   (E) Robert does not enjoy watching any particular type of dog more than other types.

2. Senator: The bill that is coming up for a vote is troubling to me. I have promised my constituents that I will not vote for it. However, I also will not vote against it. Further, I believe that no senator should ever abstain from a vote and I always follow that principle.

   Journalist: Then I can write in my article that you are going to filibuster the bill to prevent it from coming to a vote.

Which one of the following most accurately describes the method of reasoning used in the journalist's argument?
   (A) A conclusion is made about the value of a proposal based on the opinions of a person who is an authority on the subject matter of the proposal.
   (B) An argument is rebutted by showing that a generalization used in the argument does not apply to the specific situation in the argument.
   (C) A conclusion about an outcome is arrived at by eliminating other possible outcomes.
   (D) A claim is accepted as true solely on the basis that the opposing claim was not well defended.
   (E) A fact that is true of one phenomenon is concluded to be true of a similar phenomenon.

GO ON TO THE NEXT PAGE

3. Without regular exercise of some form, whether indoors or outdoors, most people do not feel as energetic as they would like to feel. People who exercise regularly have a lot of willpower. In today's health conscious society there are at least some people who do feel as energetic as they would like to feel and it must be true that these people have a lot of willpower.

Which one of the following arguments is most parallel in reasoning to the argument above?

(A) If a member of the track team cannot attend a practice session, the member can exercise alone, as long as the exercise is documented by an adult. Gretchen has attended every practice session this season, so she has not had to practice alone.

(B) Without universal health care insurance, many people are unable to afford the care that they need. However, universal health care insurance requires that everyone pay at least a small amount in insurance premiums. Therefore, either some people will need health care that they cannot afford or everyone will pay insurance premiums.

(C) We cannot change our habits if we do not make a conscious attempt to do so. However, making a conscious attempt to change habits requires repeated practice and anything that is practiced repeatedly can become a habit.

(D) No artist can become accomplished, and certainly there are accomplished artists today, if the artist is overly concerned with the details of daily life. However, an artist who is not overly concerned with the details of daily life has a chaotic existence. Therefore, there are some accomplished artists today who have a chaotic existence.

(E) Without adequate vitamin D intake, children can suffer from impaired bone mineralization and in severe cases develop rickets. Vitamin D is necessary for bone development and rickets is a disease resulting from impaired bone development.

4. Some years ago the Johnsville city council voted to increase the annual salary paid to any mayor of the city. After Cedarville doubled the salary paid to their mayor, they were able to attract a candidate for mayor who was much more qualified than previous candidates. Even though an independent study established that Johnsville's salary increase was not enough to attract better mayoral candidates, Johnsville's recently elected mayor is far more qualified than any other mayor in recent history.

Which one of the following is most strongly supported by the information in the passage above?

(A) Johnsville's current mayor was attracted to the mayoral position by something other than the salary.

(B) Cedarville attracts more mayoral candidates than does Johnsville.

(C) Johnsville is unlikely to attract a candidate in the future who is as qualified as the current candidate.

(D) Cities that offer high salaries to their mayors have better-qualified mayors than cities that offer lower salaries.

(E) Johnsville's mayors are likely to serve fewer terms than Cedarville's mayors.

GO ON TO THE NEXT PAGE

5. New red-light cameras that take pictures of drivers who run red lights have recently been installed at ten critical intersections in the city. As a result, we can expect an increase in "rear-ending" accidents, in which a motorist drives into the rear-end of the car directly in front of him or her. Red-light cameras cause drivers to become overly careful about running red lights. When a driver stops quickly to avoid running a red light, it is likely that the driver's car will be rear-ended.

The claim that new red-light cameras will result in an increase in rear-ending accidents plays which one of the following roles in the argument?

(A) It is a premise without which the conclusion would be invalid.

(B) It is an intermediate conclusion that is used to support the claim that when a driver stops quickly to avoid running a red light, a rear-end accident is likely.

(C) It is background information that is used to support the argument but is not itself a premise that supports the conclusion.

(D) It is cited as evidence that drivers tend to stop too quickly at red lights that are monitored by red-light cameras.

(E) It is a conclusion that is in part supported by the claim that red-light cameras cause drivers to be overly careful about running red lights.

6. Professor: I fail to understand the principles of my students. All of my students believe that it is unethical to cheat on an exam and none of them have cheated on my exams. However, when a fellow student is caught cheating on an exam in another class, they fail to condemn that student.

Each of the following, if true, most helps to resolve the apparent paradox described above EXCEPT:

(A) When students condemn another student, they do it only among themselves.

(B) Students are unlikely to condemn someone who has committed an ethical breach that they themselves have committed at one point.

(C) Only teachers, who invariably maintain the confidentiality of a student/teacher relationship, are in a position to discover that a student has cheated on an exam.

(D) The professor's students believe that it is unethical to condemn a fellow student.

(E) The professor's students believe that condemning a student is different from condemning an action of that student.

GO ON TO THE NEXT PAGE

7. No business that plans to maintain its productivity should be forced by law to hire people who are incompatible with the current employees. When there is incompatibility among employees, the amount of stress in the workplace increases. It has frequently been proven that employees are less productive when there is stress in the workplace.

Which one of the following principles, if valid, most helps to justify the reasoning in the argument above?

(A) If a business wants to hire people who are compatible with the current employees of the business, no law is needed to ensure that they can do so.

(B) No law should force a business to reduce the amount of stress in the workplace, if doing so would hinder the business in fulfilling its plans.

(C) No business should be forced by law to do something that hinders it in fulfilling its plans.

(D) No business should be forced by law to hire people who are less productive than the current employees.

(E) A business should hire people who support the business's plans, if doing so does not increase the amount of stress in the workplace.

8. Astronomer: Of the planets in our solar system, the only planets that indicate the possible existence of surface water are the small planets.

Student: Then you are saying that if a planet in our solar system does not indicate the possible existence of surface water, it is a large planet.

The reasoning in the student's argument is flawed in that

(A) the student fails to consider that it is the geological characteristics of small planets that allow for the possibility of the existence of surface water

(B) the student accepts that the astronomer's statement is true solely on the basis that it has not been proven false

(C) from observations that no large planet exhibits the possible existence of surface water, the student infers that all small planets exhibit the possible existence of surface water

(D) the student fails to apply a generalization about all planets to a set of specific planets

(E) the student falsely assumes that because large planets are alike in one way, they are alike in a different way

GO ON TO THE NEXT PAGE

9. The laws that protect the endangered silvery minnow should be left in place. The presence of the silvery minnow helps stabilize many other aspects of the river's ecology. In addition, if the laws were removed, the silvery minnow population would inevitably decline, and as a result, many other species that are critical to the river's ecology would begin disappearing.

Which one of the following, if assumed, allows the argument's conclusion to be properly drawn?

(A) The number of silvery minnows does not affect the population of any of the game fish in the same waters.

(B) Certain other species that are beneficial to the health of the river's ecological system in which the silvery minnows live are thriving.

(C) Only silvery minnows that are native to a particular ecological system are beneficial to that system.

(D) There are no factors other than ecological ones that are relevant to the laws protecting the silvery minnow.

(E) When the ecology of the river is disturbed, the population of many fish species declines.

10. Principle: If the people in a society share a uniform set of ethical values, the children of that society should be taught those values at an early age.

Application: The people of Borunat Island hold a diverse set of ethical values. Therefore, the children do not need to be taught values at an early age.

The application of the principle is most vulnerable to criticism on the grounds that it

(A) confuses a claim that is sufficient for an event to occur with a claim that is necessary for an event to occur

(B) assumes as a premise a claim that it incorporates in its conclusion

(C) fails to consider that possibility that the diverse values held by the people of Borunat Island are not in conflict

(D) falsely generalizes from a claim about one set of people to a claim about all people

(E) treats a stated hypothesis as a proven fact

GO ON TO THE NEXT PAGE

11. Patients who are recovering from knee surgery have traditionally been advised to avoid any pressure on their knee for three weeks in order to avoid injuring the repaired knee. Recently, however, some studies have shown that patients who begin putting mild pressure on their knee as soon as two days after surgery develop more strength in the supporting muscles than do patients who wait three weeks to put pressure on their knee. Therefore, patients should now be advised to start putting mild pressure on their knee soon after surgery.

Which one of the following is an assumption required by the above argument?

(A) Patients who started putting pressure on their knee soon after surgery did not have more serious knee problems before surgery than patients who waited three weeks to start applying pressure to their knee.

(B) The physician, not the patient, should decide when to start applying mild pressure.

(C) The fear of injuring the repaired knee does not keep patients from walking soon after surgery.

(D) Strong supporting muscles play an important role in preventing knee injuries.

(E) Most patients are willing to endure an activity that causes them pain if the activity helps them recover more quickly.

12. Journalist: Some journalists base their stories on secondhand information that they have gotten from news services, from the Internet, or from other journalists. News from these sources may be accurate. It may even be insightful. It is not, however, honest news. A journalist's role is to be personally involved in each story, writing out of his or her experience, feelings, and values.

Which one of the following most accurately expresses the conclusion in the argument above?

(A) There can be insightful news that is not honest.

(B) To write from personal experience does not require the use of secondhand information.

(C) A journalist who writes from a personal bias is not being honest.

(D) A journalist should be personally involved in each story.

(E) When a journalist bases stories on information that has not involved the journalist's experience, feelings, and values, the result is not honest news.

GO ON TO THE NEXT PAGE

13. The municipal court is one of the most efficient courts in the entire county. The county manager's report states that the municipal court has virtually no backlog of cases and few complaints of unfair judgments or of citizens being treated poorly. The court even has enough money left over in their budget to provide coffee and doughnuts to people appearing before the judges.

The statement that the municipal court is one of the most efficient courts in the county plays which one of the following roles in the argument?

(A) It is a claim that the argument attempts to support by citing the county manager's report.

(B) It is an intermediate conclusion that is used to support the main conclusion of the argument.

(C) It is an explicit premise.

(D) It is background information that is not used as a premise.

(E) It is a condition that is necessary for the main conclusion to be valid.

14. Some health care professionals are concerned that the recent emphasis on preventive medicine will result in a reduction in the effectiveness of curative medicine. This seems to be a self-contradictory view. It is true that funds devoted to research in preventive medicine may reduce the funds available for research in curative medicine. However, research in preventive medicine cannot help but give physicians far more effective preventive tools than they have ever had.

Which one of the following, if true, best indicates how the above argument resolves the self-contradiction referred to in the passage?

(A) A person must be cured first before preventive treatment can bring the person back to good health.

(B) Effective preventive treatment greatly reduces the need for curative treatment later on.

(C) Curative medicine research already receives far more funding than preventive medicine research.

(D) Preventive treatment and curative treatment can be used together in many medical conditions.

(E) Effective preventive tools will create more equality between preventively oriented physicians and curatively oriented physicians.

GO ON TO THE NEXT PAGE

15. The architect's plan for landscaping the new school calls for the use of thirty Norway maple trees. However, the Norway maple is hardly suited for use in our area, as the leaves burn easily and it is too sensitive to alkaline soil. The proof of this unsuitability is readily seen in the fact that only 5 percent of people who buy trees at our local nurseries choose a Norway maple.

The reasoning in the argument above is flawed in that the argument

(A) fails to provide an explanation for why the leaves would burn easily on the site in question

(B) rejects a view merely because the argument made for the view is inadequate

(C) distorts the argument for planting Norway maples and then attacks the distorted view

(D) is based on the actions of people who have not been shown to be experts in the relevant area

(E) infers that something cannot occur simply from the fact that it is unlikely to occur

16. Manager: It is my job to make sure that the average productivity of our factory does not drop and, if possible, that it increases. To that end, we take a daily measure of the number of units each worker completes in a day and divide that number by the number of hours for which the worker is paid. This provides us with an average number of units produced per worker per hour. However, I am concerned that this number is misleading, because _____ .

Which one of the following best completes the manager's statement?

(A) some workers are more productive than others

(B) problems on the assembly line can temporarily change the number of units produced per hour

(C) the productivity on some days is higher than the productivity on other days

(D) a number for average productivity does not indicate what the lowest and highest productivity rates are

(E) our definition of productivity includes the quality of the items that have been produced

GO ON TO THE NEXT PAGE

17. Although overmanaging a natural area is usually not helpful for our goal of maintaining an ecological balance, the prairie reserve outside of town should be completely mown at least three times during the growing season. It is true that excessive mowing can eliminate some less aggressive species, thus reducing the diversity that is part of an ecological balance. However, without regular mowing, the population of bindweed increases.

Which one of the following, if assumed, most helps justify the above argument?

(A) Mowing three times a season does not constitute overmanaging.

(B) Mowing fewer than three times a year does not result in as many less aggressive species being eliminated.

(C) Bindweed is more harmful to a good ecological balance than is mowing.

(D) Even though there are many less aggressive species and only one species of bindweed, there are more bindweed plants than there are plants of the less aggressive species.

(E) Bindweed is not a native prairie plant.

18. Many teenagers have difficulty interpreting the emotions of other people. This is not their fault. The parts of the brain that are responsible for the understanding of emotional states do not fully develop until after the teen years. By the time people have entered their mid-twenties, their brains have developed further and they are able to have more satisfying relationships.

Which one of the following, if true, most strengthens the reasoning in the above argument?

(A) Some teenagers are better than other teenagers at interpreting the emotions of other people.

(B) Being able to interpret the emotions of other people is a skill that leads to more satisfying relationships with others.

(C) Having satisfying relationships helps people learn to understand the emotions of others.

(D) The parts of the brain that are responsible for the understanding of emotional states are not the same parts of the brain that are responsible for having satisfying relationships.

(E) People who have gone through the same emotional difficulties are more likely to have satisfying relationships with each other.

GO ON TO THE NEXT PAGE

19. It is well known that attorneys who win a high-profile case can charge high rates for their services. Frank is an attorney who has handled hundreds of cases and has never lost a case. Unfortunately, Frank is not able to charge high rates for his services.

The statements above, if true, most strongly support which one of the following?

(A) If Frank continues winning cases, he will eventually be able to charge high rates for his services.

(B) Frank values service to his clients more than earning a high wage.

(C) Charging high rates does not correlate with the quality of clients that an attorney serves.

(D) Frank only accepts cases that he knows he can win.

(E) Of the cases that Frank has handled, none has been a high-profile case.

20. Educator: If you read to your children when they are young, your children will learn to read at an early age. Parents who are overworked do not have the time or energy to read to their young children. Yet, any parent who learned to read at an early age reads to his or her own young children.

If the statements above are true, which one of the following must be true?

(A) The children of any parent who learned to read at an early age will also learn to read at an early age.

(B) Any child who learns to read at an early age was read to when young.

(C) Any child who is not read to while young will not learn to read at an early age.

(D) Any child who is read to while young has a parent who learned to read at an early age.

(E) Any child whose parents are overworked will not learn to read at an early age.

21. Manager: If employees have a choice between using their old computer versus using one of our new computers with enhanced technology for producing more accurate results, they should use the old computer. Most people can work more quickly on their old computer.

Which one of the following principles, if valid, provides the most support for the manager's argument?

(A) The best technology is the technology that produces the best results.

(B) People should use a technology with which they are the most comfortable, even if that technology does not produce the best results.

(C) A technology that provides faster results is preferable to a technology that provides slower results, even if the slower technology produces more accurate results.

(D) The more that an older technology is used, the sooner it can be replaced with a newer technology.

(E) New technology should not replace old technology unless the new technology produces a better result.

GO ON TO THE NEXT PAGE

22. Three hundred people diagnosed with acute depression were asked whether they preferred outdoor social activities or indoor social activities. Eighty percent of the people reported that they preferred indoor social activities. Three hundred people diagnosed with hyperthyroidism were asked the same question. Only 20 percent reported that they preferred indoor social activities. Therefore, people with hyperthyroidism prefer outdoor social activities to a much greater degree than people with acute depression.

The reasoning in which one of the following arguments is most similar to the reasoning in the argument above?

(A) In 1994 there were a little over a million nonmelanoma skin cancers reported in the United States. Eighteen years later, there were over 3 million nonmelanoma skin cancers reported in the United States. Therefore, in another eighteen years there will be over 9 million nonmelanoma skin cancers reported in the United States.

(B) Any dancer who prefers modern dance to traditional dance has a background in jazz dance. Dancers who have a background in jazz dance prefer jazz music to classical music. Therefore, dancers who prefer modern dance to traditional dance also prefer jazz music to classical music.

(C) People with schizophrenia share many psychological characteristics with very young children. Both have an active and complex fantasy life and both have difficulty distinguishing the elements of their fantasy life from the elements of reality. Children are easily distracted by sensory input. Therefore, it is likely that schizophrenic people are also easily distracted by sensory input.

(D) One hundred yellow daisies and one hundred purple daisies were treated with a solution of liquid iron. Over half of the yellow daisies developed a deeper flower color within a week of treatment. Of the purple daisies only fifteen developed a deeper color within a week of treatment. Therefore, yellow daisies respond to liquid iron by a change in flower color much more than do purple daisies.

(E) Eighty-five percent of the tornadoes that occurred last year were preceded by a period of very hot weather and a complete absence of wind. In the previous year, over 70 percent of the tornadoes were preceded by these same conditions. Therefore, it is likely that a hot period with an absence of wind somehow causes tornadoes to form.

GO ON TO THE NEXT PAGE

23. The causes of the El Niño weather pattern, a warming that occurs over the Pacific Ocean and that can cause extreme weather, including floods, are not well understood. Increased air pressure over the western Pacific can sometimes cause an El Niño. Currently there is increased air pressure over the western Pacific, and the flooding from an El Niño could begin as early as next month on the California coast. Therefore, coastal communities in California should immediately begin taking precautions against flooding.

The argument depends on assuming which one of the following?

(A) The severity of the effects of an El Niño is in proportion to the degree of increased air pressure over the western Pacific.

(B) There is more than one significant cause of El Niños.

(C) There are no places other than California that could experience flooding next month if there is an El Niño.

(D) The event described in the argument as causing an El Niño in some cases will do so in this case.

(E) There has not been flooding from an El Niño in California in recent years.

24. An experiment was done with two large groups of kindergarten students to determine which strategies best helped develop early math skills. Both groups were given very simple addition problems. One group was instructed to use their fingers to add up the numbers, for example 3 + 2, by counting out loud "One, two, three, plus one, two," holding out three fingers and then two more, and then counting the total number of fingers that were held out. The other group was instructed to silently put three marks on paper, to then add two more marks, and finally, to count the total number of marks. The groups were monitored to ensure that the students followed the instructions. The group that used their fingers had significantly more correct responses than the other group. Clearly, then, at least for young children, using their fingers to add improves accuracy in addition.

The reasoning in the argument is most vulnerable to criticism on the grounds that it

(A) assumes that the instructors did not give subtle clues to the children they were instructing

(B) fails to consider the possibility that speaking out loud while adding improves accuracy

(C) fails to specify how many children were in each group

(D) neglects to consider whether there might be other strategies that are more effective than either counting on the fingers or using marks on paper

(E) infers that something is true of the whole simply from the fact that it is true of each of the parts

GO ON TO THE NEXT PAGE

25. Author: Many adults today simply do not pick up a full-length novel to read. It is too easy to fill one's time reading bits and pieces of gossip on the Internet. Admittedly, there is worthwhile information available via computer and perhaps even snippets of creative writing and fiction, but all of these are quite different from the experience of reading a full-length novel. Publishers should put small excerpts of full-length novels on the Internet in the hopes of enticing people to read the rest of the novel.

Which one of the following, if true, would most weaken the author's argument?

(A) As many full-length books that are not novels are sold today as were sold before the advent of the Internet.

(B) It has always been true that the majority of full-length novels that are published never achieve a wide readership.

(C) It is unwise for a publisher to invest time and money in a project for promoting sales if the project has no possibility of producing a profit.

(D) If publishers put many small snippets of novels on the Internet, the result would be an increase of the amount of time that people spend reading small bits and a decrease in the time people would have to read a full-length novel.

(E) Most authors of full-length novels do not consider making a profit to be their primary goal.

26. Nearly 80 percent of the Ponderosa pines in a sixty-square-mile area of national forest have been affected by a blight that causes yellowing of needles and premature needle drop. The residents of the town just south of the national forest claim that emissions from the coal-burning power plant in their town are responsible for weakening the health of the trees. However, although such emissions can undoubtedly cause the kind of tree damage observed, emissions are highly unlikely to be the cause of the damage occurring in the national forest, considering the limited amount of emissions from the plant and the vast area that is affected.

Which one of the following, if true, most weakens the reasoning?

(A) Prevailing winds typically blow from the town toward the affected area.

(B) Many of the trees had become affected before the power plant first began operating last year.

(C) Many trees near the power plant have symptoms of yellowing leaves and premature leaf drop.

(D) There is no other factor that has been identified as a possible cause for the damage to the Ponderosa pines.

(E) The quality of emissions from coal-burning plants is closely regulated by the federal government.

STOP If you finish before the 35-minute time period is over, you may go back and check your answers in this section only. You may not work on any other test section.

Time: 35 minutes
25 Questions

DIRECTIONS: The questions in this section are based on the reasoning contained in brief statements or passages. More than one answer choice could conceivably answer the question in some cases. However, you should choose the <u>best</u> answer. The best answer is the response that answers the question most accurately and completely. You should avoid making any assumptions that, by commonsense standards, are implausible, superfluous, or incompatible with the passage. When you have chosen the best answer, fill in the space on your answer sheet that corresponds to your answer.

1. When Dr. Lovato performed surgery on Patient X's leg, Patient X suffered a serious drop in blood pressure that resulted in complications requiring Patient X to spend an extra week in the hospital. If Dr. Lovato had anticipated the drop in blood pressure, she could have responded to it more quickly. However, the drop was due to Patient X's dependence on alcohol, which Patient X failed to disclose. For this reason, Dr. Lovato should not have her medical license suspended.

   Which one of the following principles, if valid, most helps to justify the conclusion of the argument?

   (A) A medical practitioner is only at fault if the practitioner has been given all of the available medical records in advance of the procedure that the practitioner is performing.

   (B) The license of a medical practitioner should not be suspended if the only harm suffered by a patient is loss of time or money.

   (C) If a medical practitioner fails to respond to a medical situation as quickly as possible, the practitioner's license should be suspended if the patient provided all relevant information in advance.

   (D) If a medical practitioner fails to respond to a medical situation as quickly as possible, the practitioner's license should not be suspended if the patient failed to provide information that would have allowed the practitioner to be better prepared.

   (E) If the actions of a medical practitioner result in increased recovery time for a patient, the practitioner's license should be suspended only if the patient informs the practitioner in advance that increased recovery time is unacceptable.

GO ON TO THE NEXT PAGE

2. Business incubators are programs that specifically support start-up businesses with a range of services and resources. One such resource is low-interest loans. These loans provide a new company with cash reserves. The failure rate for all start-up businesses is over 50 percent but the failure rate for start-up businesses that are supported by an incubator program is less than 13 percent. Part of the reason for the success of incubator-supported businesses is that it is easier for a new company to weather a difficult period if the company has cash reserves.

The statements above, if true, most strongly support which one of the following?

(A) If a start-up business has successfully weathered a difficult period, the business has access to low-interest loans.

(B) Start-up businesses that are not supported by a business incubator do not have access to low-interest loans.

(C) If a start-up business does not have cash reserves, it is unlikely to successfully weather difficult periods.

(D) Businesses without access to low-interest loans are less likely to succeed than businesses with access to low-interest loans.

(E) Access to low-interest loans helps start-up businesses succeed by making it easier for them to weather difficult periods.

3. Herman: Our experiment requires the brightest possible dog. Of the two dogs that are available to us, we should choose the Golden Retriever over the Norfolk Terrier because Golden Retrievers are far more intelligent.

Jaclyn: But this Norfolk Terrier has performed far better on our tests of intelligence than has this Golden Retriever.

Jaclyn's reply suggests that Herman's error in reasoning is which one of the following?

(A) He makes a conclusion about a group without providing evidence that his conclusion is valid.

(B) He infers that because something is unlikely to occur, it will not occur.

(C) He improperly presumes that what is true of the whole of a category is true of each member of the category.

(D) He falsely assumes that there are no other options.

(E) He fails to apply a generalization to all cases to which the generalization was meant to apply.

GO ON TO THE NEXT PAGE

4. A wide variety of plant and animal species makes a natural habitat particularly flexible. If the number of plants that a particular herbivore consumes for food decreases, a wide variety of plants ensures that there is probably another species of plants that the herbivore can eat while the first species recovers. If there is enough diversity, any change in the balance of species, either a large increase or a significant decrease in numbers, can be offset by another species.

Which one of the following best expresses the main conclusion drawn in the argument above?

(A) A wide variety of plant and animal species in a natural habitat allows one species to offset an imbalance that arises in other species.

(B) A wide variety in the species of plants and animals that live in a natural habitat results in the habitat being particularly flexible.

(C) A wide variety of plant and animal species in a natural habitat ensures that herbivores will have something to eat, even if their preferred food is diminished.

(D) A flexible natural habitat allows the species in that habitat to flourish.

(E) There are usually many plant species that an herbivore can eat, even if it favors a particular species.

5. Physician: In Country X the average citizen receives medical attention, including visits to the doctor, emergency treatment, and hospitalization, two hundred times in a lifetime. In Country Y the average citizen receives the same medical attention only forty times in a lifetime. The average life expectancy is the same in both countries and in both countries the government pays virtually all medical expenses, but in Country Y the amount of money spent on medical attention is five times the amount spent in Country X.

Which one of the following, if true, most helps to resolve the apparent discrepancy between the two countries described above?

(A) The average citizen in Country Y is healthier than the average citizen in Country X.

(B) The government of Country Y pays doctors five times more than the government of Country X pays their doctors.

(C) There are many people who are not citizens of Country Y but come to Country Y for medical treatment.

(D) The more regular medical attention received by citizens of Country X identifies medical problems at an early stage, which helps prevent more expensive treatments later.

(E) Whereas the average number of lifetime visits per person for medical treatment in Country X is two hundred, the actual number varies greatly and can be as low as ten for some people.

GO ON TO THE NEXT PAGE

6. Physicist: Time travel is clearly not feasible. Any phenomenon that cannot be explained within an existing theoretical framework cannot be replicated in the laboratory and time travel certainly cannot be explained within any existing theoretical framework. Time travel may exist in the world of fantasy but not in the real world.

The argument proposed by the physicist follows logically if which one of the following is assumed?

(A) Any phenomenon that exists only in the world of fantasy cannot be replicated in the laboratory.

(B) Phenomena in the real world can be explained within an existing theoretical framework.

(C) If a phenomenon is feasible, then it can be replicated in the laboratory.

(D) Unless a phenomenon is feasible, it cannot be replicated in the laboratory.

(E) Unless a phenomenon cannot be explained within an existing theoretical framework, it can be replicated in the laboratory.

7. Fresh fruit and vegetables eaten directly out of the garden probably provide better nutrition than similar foods bought from a store. Although the fruits and vegetables at some stores have been harvested as recently as twenty-four hours before being stocked on the shelves, many vitamins, enzymes, and other nutrients found in freshly harvested foods are greatly diminished within two hours of harvesting.

Which one of the following most accurately describes the role played in the argument by the claim that the fruits and vegetables at some stores have been harvested as recently as twenty-four hours before being stocked on the shelves?

(A) It is a statement that could be used as an objection to the conclusion drawn in the argument.

(B) It is a statement that counteracts a possible objection to the argument.

(C) It is a premise that is used to create an intermediate conclusion.

(D) It is a hypothesis that the argument rejects.

(E) It is a statement that is supported by a study.

GO ON TO THE NEXT PAGE

8. Schizophrenia occurs at the same rate among people from nearly all cultures, environments, and socioeconomic levels. If there were an environmental factor that caused this disease, schizophrenia would be expected to occur more frequently under certain environmental conditions than others. Because it does not, it is more likely that schizophrenia is caused by genetic factors.

Which one of the following, if true, most strengthens the argument?

(A) Each culture consists of a unique psychological, emotional, and physical environment.

(B) Some environmental factors increase the incidence of schizophrenia and other environmental factors decrease the risk.

(C) It is a consistent fact across all cultures and environments that if one identical twin has schizophrenia, the other does not.

(D) Genealogy has shown that nearly all family trees include either no members with schizophrenia or multiple members with schizophrenia.

(E) Many mental illnesses other than schizophrenia have been proven to have environmental causes.

9. Engineer: It is an acknowledged fact of highway building that a road bed that slopes more than 2 degrees creates dangerous driving conditions. The 12-mile stretch of state highway between Oakville and Titusville slopes 3 degrees. However, that stretch of road has fewer accidents than stretches of state highway that do not slope. Therefore, the stretch of state highway between the two towns should not be rebuilt.

The answer to which one of the following would be LEAST useful to know in order to evaluate the strength of the engineer's argument?

(A) For the stretch of highway in question, is it the road bed that slopes 3 degrees?

(B) What is the average number of accidents on the stretch of highway in question?

(C) Would rebuilding the stretch of highway in question reduce the rate of accidents below the current level?

(D) How many vehicles per week travel the stretch of highway in question and how many vehicles per week travel an average 12-mile stretch of the level state highway?

(E) Is there an alternate route between Oakville and Titusville that is safer?

GO ON TO THE NEXT PAGE

10. In the past century there was a dramatic population migration away from rural areas to urban areas. This migration would not have taken place if the development of industry had not been concentrated in urban areas. Whereas the loss of rural population has led to lower wages in rural areas, the current high standard of living enjoyed by middle-class urban dwellers would not have come about without the mass migration from rural areas into the cities.

Which one of the following can most properly be inferred from the information in the passage above?

(A) The high standard of living of middle-class urban dwellers establishes that during the last century the development of industry was concentrated in urban areas.

(B) If the development of industry during the last century had been concentrated in suburban areas, people migrating from rural areas would have settled in suburban areas.

(C) The fact that middle-class urban dwellers in some areas do not have a high standard of living establishes that there was not a migration from rural areas to those urban areas.

(D) People who moved from rural areas to urban areas earned more money in the urban area than they had earned in the rural area.

(E) Most of the descendants of people who migrated from rural areas to urban areas in the last century have middle-class jobs, whereas most of the people who originally migrated took jobs in industry when they arrived in the urban areas.

11. There are vaccinations available for most common childhood diseases. For all diseases for which there is a vaccination available, the vaccination is 100 percent effective in preventing the disease. This year all twenty instances of illnesses that kept a child out of school for more than a week were common childhood diseases. Therefore, most of the twenty instances could have been prevented.

The flawed pattern of reasoning in which one of the following is most closely parallel to the flawed pattern of reasoning in the argument above?

(A) Most people who have diabetes visit their doctor regularly. Everyone who visits their doctor regularly can feel confident that they are receiving good care. Of the two hundred patients who visited Dr. Jones regularly last year, most of them had diabetes. Therefore, the patients with diabetes who visited Dr. Jones regularly last year can feel confident that they are receiving good care.

(B) There are youth summer camps for most types of sports activity. Any child who attends a youth summer camp for a sport will show measurable improvement. Last year when Greg returned to school in the fall he showed measurable improvement in his soccer skills. Therefore, Greg must have attended a summer youth camp for soccer.

(C) All of the poems submitted for this year's literary magazine are sonnets. Most sonnets are written with a regular meter. Any poem with a regular meter is likely not to appeal to literary audiences that prefer free verse. If the literary magazine publishes all of the poems that have been submitted, most of those poems will not appeal to literary audiences that prefer free verse.

(D) All of the applicants for medical school at the state university last year had majored in chemistry. Most chemistry majors also take advanced math classes. Recruiters from the state university medical school gave presentations to the advanced math classes last year before the application process. Therefore, the presentations by the recruiters must have caused chemistry majors to apply to medical school.

(E) Smallpox has been completely eradicated in the last fifty years. Most people who have smallpox-like symptoms actually have chicken pox. For most people, chicken pox is uncomfortable but has no lasting negative effects. Therefore, the parents of children who have chicken pox do not need to have their children tested for smallpox.

12. Attorney: The past twenty years have seen a change in procedural rules for courts dealing with people charged with driving under the influence of alcohol. As a result of these changes, 30 percent of all such cases are now dismissed for procedural reasons. This is a shockingly high figure, given the seriousness of the offense, and given that many of the defendants are repeat offenders, and that there is often enough evidence to successfully convict the defendant if the case comes to trial. Even among murder cases the rate of dismissal for procedural reasons is barely 8 percent. We should roll back the changes of the past twenty years and return to a system that convicts the guilty.

The answer to which one of the following would be most relevant in determining the validity of the lawyer's conclusion?

(A) Are there at least four times as many people charged with driving under the influence of alcohol as are charged with murder?

(B) Are more people convicted of driving under the influence of alcohol now than were convicted twenty years ago?

(C) What percentage of the cases of people charged with driving under the influence of alcohol that go to trial result in convictions?

(D) What percentage of cases of people charged with driving under the influence of alcohol were dismissed for procedural reasons twenty years ago?

(E) Was the percentage of murder cases thrown out for procedural reasons twenty years ago higher or lower than the percentage of cases of people charged with driving under the influence of alcohol that were dismissed for procedural reasons twenty years ago?

GO ON TO THE NEXT PAGE

13. Archaeological excavations of the ancient city-state of Babylon have revealed that a large number of trees in the area surrounding Babylon were cut down during a certain thirty-year period, which resulted in a significant deforestation. This deforestation in turn resulted in erosion of topsoil and a permanent desertification of the area. This indicates that the rulers at the time—who were responsible for setting agricultural policy—were particularly shortsighted, as rulers with farsighted plans would never purposely institute policies that would destroy the land that supported their civilization.

The reasoning in the argument is flawed in that the argument

(A) infers that because something is true of a group as a whole, it is true of individual members of the group

(B) infers the intentions of certain individuals from the behavior of those individuals

(C) treats information that supports a conclusion as information that proves a conclusion

(D) fails to consider that an element that is considered to be a cause of a phenomenon may actually be the result of the phenomenon

(E) accepts a fact as true solely on the basis that the fact has not been proven to be false

14. Motivation is one of the most important factors determining how much a student learns, and the amount that a student learns is directly correlated with how happy the student is. Whereas some students are inherently motivated by the learning of new facts, many students are motivated primarily by the personal feedback that they receive from their teachers. Most teachers currently have so many students in their classes that they cannot give personal feedback. It follows, then, that _____ .

Which one of the following most logically completes the above argument?

(A) students who are happy either are inherently motivated by the learning of new facts or have a teacher who provides personal feedback

(B) a teacher who has too many students in class does not have students who learn

(C) a teacher who does not have too many students in class has students who learn

(D) an administrator who wants students to be successful should hire additional teachers

(E) an administrator who wants students to be happy should reduce the number of students that each teacher has in class

GO ON TO THE NEXT PAGE

15. Small businesses in Country X are not incorporated and are not allowed, by law, to have more than fifty employees. However, the business Rado's Tropical Designs has two hundred employees.

Which one of the statements below follows logically from the information above?

(A) Rado's Tropical Designs is not in Country X if it does not have more employees than are allowed by law.

(B) If Rado's Tropical Designs is not incorporated, it is probably not a small business.

(C) If Rado's Tropical Designs is a small business in Country X, it has more employees than are allowed by law.

(D) If Rado's Tropical Designs is in Country X, it is either incorporated or has more employees than are allowed by law.

(E) If Rado's Tropical Designs does not have more employees than are allowed by law, it either is not in Country X or is incorporated.

16. Physician: Recent studies have shown that the most significant factor in a weight loss program is the patient's ability to resist cravings for carbohydrates in order to eat a diet high in protein, fruits, vegetables, and oils. These studies disprove the claims of health gurus, who for years have claimed that regular exercise is the key to permanent weight loss.

The physician's argument is flawed in that it fails to consider the possibility that

(A) health gurus do not necessarily understand the medical aspects of weight loss

(B) any activity that a person undertakes simply because the person was advised to undertake it by an authority is unlikely to have long-term benefit

(C) eating a diet high in proteins, fruits, vegetables, and oils makes it easier for a person to exercise regularly

(D) many people are unable to resist cravings for carbohydrates despite their best intentions

(E) regular exercise stimulates metabolic processes that make it easier for a person to resist cravings for carbohydrates

GO ON TO THE NEXT PAGE

17. Anthropology is defined as the science of human beings. Any scientific field that sheds light on the various aspects of humanity throughout time is essentially a branch of anthropology. Cultural ecology, then, is a branch of anthropology because it deals with humanity's effect on the environment. The people who claim that because cultural ecology is concerned with ecosystems, cultural ecology is a branch of biology, are ignoring the definition of anthropology and mistakenly categorizing cultural ecology.

Which one of the following most accurately expresses the main conclusion of the argument above?

(A) Cultural ecology is best classified as a branch of anthropology, not a branch of biology.

(B) People who claim that cultural ecology is not a branch of anthropology are mistakenly categorizing cultural ecology.

(C) Cultural ecology should be classified on the basis of its primary focus rather than on subject areas that are peripheral to its focus.

(D) Any scientific field that deals with effects on the environment is essentially a branch of anthropology.

(E) Anthropology and biology deal with different aspects of life but overlap in their scope.

18. Voice recognition technology is a highly accurate alternative to typing that allows a person to control the characters that appear on a computer screen, such as in a word processing program, while avoiding repetitive wrist and hand injuries. Nevertheless, most businesses strongly discourage their employees from using voice recognition technology at work as a substitute for traditional typing.

Which one of the following, if true, most helps to account for the position of businesses mentioned in the argument above?

(A) The rate at which voice recognition technology produces text increases dramatically with practice.

(B) There are a number of mechanical devices that can prevent or reduce repetitive injuries while typing.

(C) Voice recognition technology costs more to set up per person than do other alternatives to traditional typing.

(D) Voice recognition technology is more accurate with nontechnical text than with technical text.

(E) Even the best voice recognition technologies produce text at less than half the rate of the average person typing by hand.

GO ON TO THE NEXT PAGE

19. Art critic: On one particular day, the visitors at a well-known art museum were asked to rank the paintings displayed in a monthlong exhibit. All visitors were given a form to complete at the end of their visit. The form asked them to rank each painting according to specific criteria, such as organization, use of technique, and lighting, and to rank the paintings' overall appeal. It is, however, a well-known fact that negative moods affect people's evaluation of art in unpredictable ways. For this reason, any results that the museum derived from the rankings are most likely unreliable.

Which one of the following, if true, most strengthens the art critic's conclusion?

(A) People who are in a negative mood evaluate a work of art in a more negative way than they do when they evaluate the same work of art when they are in a positive mood.

(B) People who are in a positive mood evaluate art in a predictable way.

(C) On the day on which the rankings were collected, most of the visitors to the museum were in neither a positive nor a neutral mood.

(D) On the day on which the rankings were collected, most of the visitors to the museum gave below-average rankings to all of the paintings.

(E) The visitors who were asked to rank the paintings spent less time viewing each painting than was average for all visitors to the monthlong exhibit.

20. A basic tenet of political science is that without an informed populace, the mere fact that each citizen has one vote does not constitute a democracy. This explains why, despite overwhelming exposure to the media, our political system, which grants each citizen one vote, is not in fact a democracy.

The conclusion of the argument above is most strongly supported if which one of the following is assumed?

(A) Our populace is informed only on those issues on which the media choose to report.

(B) The basic tenet of political science mentioned in the passage does not apply in all cases.

(C) The definition of what constitutes an informed populace differs among political scientists.

(D) Despite overwhelming exposure to the media, our populace is not informed.

(E) A political system that does not grant each citizen one vote cannot be a democracy.

GO ON TO THE NEXT PAGE

21. Jankowski's latest composition is a beautiful waltz inspired by a melody that she heard in a dream. The main melody of Jankowski's waltz is virtually identical to the main melody of a composition by Li. Jankowski does not recall ever having heard Li's waltz. Nevertheless, Jankowski must have heard it and should be considered guilty of plagiarism.

Which one of the following principles most helps justify the conclusion in the argument above?

(A) Lack of intention to plagiarize does not exempt an artist from being fined for plagiarism if it can be proven that part of the artist's work is virtually identical to part of an earlier work by another artist.

(B) If works of art created by two artists are virtually the same, even in part, the work created last should be considered a plagiarism.

(C) A musician whose melody is virtually the same as a melody created previously by another musician should be considered guilty of plagiarism even if both musicians independently created the melody without being influenced by the other.

(D) A musician whose composition is virtually identical to another musician's composition should be considered guilty of plagiarism even if the plagiarizing musician does not recall being exposed to the other musician's work.

(E) Artists who copy part of another artist's work in their own work should be considered guilty of plagiarism even if they were not consciously aware that their work included such copying.

22. Josep: Wolfberry is a good plant for wide-open spaces because it is a tough grower and its fruit is tasty. However, I completely disagree with growing it in a city backyard. It spreads far too much and is difficult to manage.

Montse: Although wolfberry is very manageable with only a little effort, even in a city yard, I disagree that it is a good plant. Its thorns make it difficult to pick the fruit and it rarely sets enough fruit to make the effort worthwhile.

Josep and Montse disagree over whether wolfberry

(A) has tasty fruits

(B) is a bad plant for a city yard

(C) is easy to manage in a city yard

(D) is a tough grower

(E) rarely sets fruit

GO ON TO THE NEXT PAGE

23. Author: One wonders whether the novels of the next generation will consist primarily of emoticons and abbreviations borrowed from the world of texting and e-mail. Whereas every generation creates valuable and exciting innovations on the language that they inherit, the language of electronic communication should not become the language of literature. Electronic communication serves the function of sending short messages with a minimum investment of time and hand movements. Literature need not be constrained by these criteria. The novelist has the luxury of crafting a paragraph of beautiful prose to express her joy, rather than inserting a smiley face.

The example above best illustrates which principle below?

(A) The values of one generation should not be expected to apply to a different generation.

(B) A form of communication that is faster than another form is often not the best form if it sacrifices clarity.

(C) There should be some cultural institutions whose purpose is to preserve traditional cultural elements so that the good elements from the past are not completely replaced by new innovations.

(D) Some innovations should not be used in a given situation, even when the innovations are positive, if the circumstances for which the innovations were developed differ from circumstances of the given situation for which their use is proposed.

(E) People generally do not like to change how they use language even if the changes are valuable or exciting.

24. As our society becomes more complex, the ethical dilemmas that we face also become more complex. No individual person has the time or energy to formulate ethical guidelines for all of the complex, new situations that are constantly arising. For this reason, an impartial committee should be appointed and funded to develop ethical guidelines and distribute them to the rest of us.

Which one of the following is an assumption required by the argument above?

(A) People currently do not share new ethical guidelines with each other.

(B) The ethical standards of the committee members would be the same as the ethical standards of the rest of us.

(C) There are no ethical dilemmas for which an ethical guideline cannot be developed.

(D) The members of an impartial committee for developing ethical guidelines should have higher ethical standards than the rest of us.

(E) It is unlikely that individual people will formulate ethical guidelines for new situations.

GO ON TO THE NEXT PAGE

25. Principle: In the case when a publicly owned building is in poor repair, the city should demolish it if the cost of demolition is less than the cost of repair. However, the city should not demolish any building unless that building has no historic value.

Application: The old Endicott Building is in poor repair and is a hazard to people walking near it. It would cost $30 million to repair it. Therefore, the old Endicott Building should be demolished.

Which one of the following, if true, most justifies the above application of the principle?

(A) The old Endicott Building has no historic value and the cost of demolishing it is less than the cost of repairing it.

(B) The old Endicott Building is a publicly owned building whose historical value is unknown.

(C) The old Endicott Building is a publicly owned building with no historical value and it would cost $40 million to demolish it.

(D) The old Endicott Building is a former courthouse with no historic value and it would cost $10 million to demolish it.

(E) The old Endicott Building is a former courthouse with no historical value and it is in worse repair than other buildings that have been demolished by the city.

 **STOP** If you finish before the 35-minute time period is over, you may go back and check your answers in this section only. You may not work on any other test section.

WRITING SAMPLE

Time: 35 minutes

> **DIRECTIONS:** You will have thirty-five minutes to organize and write an essay on the topic described on the next page. Read the topic and all of the directions carefully. It is generally best to take a few minutes to organize your thoughts before beginning to write. Be sure to develop your ideas fully and leave time at the end to review what you have written. **Do not write on any topic other than the topic given. It is not acceptable to write on a topic of your own choice.**
>
> No special knowledge is needed or expected for this essay. Admission committees are interested in your reasoning, clarity, organization, use of language, and writing mechanics. The quality of what you write is more important than the quantity.
>
> Keep your essay in the blocked and lined area on the front and back of the separate Writing Sample Response Sheet. That is the only area that will be reproduced and sent to law schools. Be sure to write legibly.

Scratch Paper
Do not write your essay here. Scratch work only.

DIAGNOSTIC TEST

DIRECTIONS: The situation described below gives two choices. Either one of the choices can be supported based on the information given. In your essay, consider both choices and then argue in favor of one over the other. Base your argument on the two specified criteria and on the given facts. There is no "right" or "wrong" choice. Either choice can be reasonably defended.

Max Builder is growing and hiring rapidly and needs to expand its business space in Faberg. While Max Builder's current building is functional, it is located in a rundown section of Waerout, which is Faberg's rail-and-warehouse district. Using the facts given below, compose an essay in which you argue in favor of choosing one alternative over the other on the basis of the two criteria below:

- The appearance of success is a key to Max Builder's ability to attract and retain clients in order to grow its business.
- Max Builder prefers to use a single facility in order to strengthen cohesion between its union and management.

The Far Green district on the outskirts of Faberg is quickly becoming the city's new destination for high-rise buildings and outdoor shopping malls. Far Green's raw land prices are escalating and premium building lots are selling fast. Max Builder could build a visually stunning and compact building on a corner lot in Far Green with beautiful offices, limited locker rooms and a small auditorium. However, Far Green's zoning and lot sizes preclude warehouses, workshops, and external material storage areas. Even though Far Green is distant from Waerout, and Max Builder's employees would spend considerable time and fuel commuting between the two locations, Far Green's value would likely double within five years.

Faberg's city council has offered Max Builder the opportunity to build a large new building on Waerout's edge, close to the center of Faberg. Max Builder could build the new complex with a lawn and waterfall, spacious offices, large locker rooms, a massive workshop, and an outside storage area, and still have room to grow. The Waerout location is located on an old smelter site that was notorious for its environmental infractions. Because Waerout is a rundown and possibly dangerous section of Faberg, some of Max Builder's best customers already do not want to drive into Waerout to visit Max Builder's current office.

Scratch Paper
Do not write your essay here. Scratch work only.

Use the lined area below to write your essay. Continue on the back if you need more space.

ANSWER KEY
Diagnostic Test

SECTION I: READING COMPREHENSION

1.	C	8.	E	15.	D	22.	D
2.	A	9.	C	16.	D	23.	D
3.	D	10.	B	17.	A	24.	A
4.	C	11.	E	18.	C	25.	C
5.	D	12.	D	19.	E	26.	E
6.	E	13.	A	20.	C	27.	B
7.	B	14.	C	21.	C		

SECTION II: ANALYTICAL REASONING

1.	A	8.	C	15.	E	22.	D
2.	D	9.	A	16.	A	23.	E
3.	B	10.	A	17.	B		
4.	D	11.	A	18.	C		
5.	E	12.	D	19.	E		
6.	B	13.	E	20.	C		
7.	D	14.	D	21.	E		

SECTION III: LOGICAL REASONING

1.	C	8.	C	15.	D	22.	D
2.	C	9.	D	16.	E	23.	D
3.	D	10.	A	17.	C	24.	B
4.	A	11.	D	18.	B	25.	D
5.	E	12.	E	19.	E	26.	A
6.	B	13.	A	20.	A		
7.	C	14.	B	21.	C		

SECTION IV: LOGICAL REASONING

1.	D	8.	D	15.	C	22.	C
2.	E	9.	B	16.	E	23.	D
3.	C	10.	A	17.	A	24.	B
4.	B	11.	C	18.	E	25.	C
5.	D	12.	D	19.	C		
6.	C	13.	B	20.	D		
7.	A	14.	E	21.	E		

CALCULATING YOUR SCORE

1. Check your answers against the Answer Key on page 63.
2. Use the Score Worksheet below to calculate your raw score. Your raw score is the total number of questions that you answered correctly.
3. Use the Conversion Table below to convert your raw score into a score on the 120–180 scale. Remember that these scores are approximate.

Score Worksheet

Section	Number of Questions	Number Correct	Number Incorrect	Number Not Answered*
Section I: Reading Comprehension	27			
Section II: Analytical Reasoning	23			
Section III: Logical Reasoning	26			
Section IV: Logical Reasoning	25			
Total:	101			

*You should not leave any questions unanswered. There is no penalty for guessing.

Conversion Table

Raw Score Range	Scaled Score	Raw Score Range	Scaled Score	Raw Score Range	Scaled Score	Raw Score Range	Scaled Score	Raw Score Range	Scaled Score
0–15	120	30	133	50	146	72–73	159	90	172
16	121	31–32	134	51–52	147	74	160	91–92	173
17	122	33	135	53	148	75–76	161	93	174
18	123	34–35	136	54–55	149	77	162	94	175
19	124	36	137	56–57	150	78–79	163	95	176
20	125	37–38	138	58	151	80	164	96	177
21	126	39	139	59–60	152	81–82	165	97	178
22–23	127	40–41	140	61–62	153	83	166	98	179
24	128	42	141	63–64	154	84–85	167	99–101	180
25	129	43–44	142	65	155	86	168		
26	130	45	143	66–67	156	87	169		
27–28	131	46–47	144	68–69	157	88	170		
29	132	48–49	145	70–71	158	89	171		

DIAGNOSTIC EXAM ANALYSIS

Every practice section that you take is an opportunity for you to evaluate your testing strategy. If you take a section under timed conditions, that also gives you an opportunity to evaluate your timing strategy. The last section of Chapter 1 provides a detailed worksheet and plan for reviewing your performance and identifying exactly what strategy error led to each wrong answer. The sections of Chapter 1 on timing explain how to evaluate your timing strategy. Be sure to evaluate your timing strategy for every section that you take under timed conditions.

Use the plan in Chapter 1 to review every question that you answered incorrectly. The plan lists twenty-two specific errors. For each question that you answered incorrectly, you should review the parts of Chapter 1 and the other relevant chapters that cover the strategies with which you had trouble. The key to success is identifying your errors and reviewing again and again.

Use the following chart to summarize your performance based on four main categories of error. Enter the number of incorrect answers in each column. Some questions may fall under more than one category.

Summary of Incorrect Answers

Section	Total Incorrect	Didn't Take Enough Time	Misread Information	Got Down to Two Answers	Didn't Have a Strategy
I: RC					
II: AR					
III: LR					
IV: LR					
Total:					

After you have reviewed your timing strategy, enter the results in the following chart. The questions for which you simply filled in a bubble without working on the question should be counted under Cold Guesses. If you spent more than fifteen seconds working on a question, do *not* count it under Cold Guesses. Under Number Correct and Number Incorrect, do not include Cold Guesses. The number in the Cold Guesses column, then, includes both incorrect and correct answers. In the final column, enter the number of incorrect answers on which you spent under two minutes.

Analysis of Timing Strategy

Section	Number Correct (not cold guesses)	Number Incorrect (not cold guesses)	Cold Guesses	Number of Incorrect Under 2 Minutes
I: RC				
II: AR				
III: LR				
IV: LR				
Total:				

If most of your incorrect answers took under two minutes, you should plan to spend more time on questions. If you have more than two or three questions incorrect—excluding cold guesses—you can increase your score by working on fewer questions but spending a little more time on the questions that you do work on. See the example below.

Example of Revised Timing Strategy

Section	Number Correct (not cold guesses)	Number Incorrect (not cold guesses)	Cold Guesses	Number of Incorrect Under 2 Minutes	Total Correct (including cold guesses)
First attempt	11	6	7	5	12
Revised attempt	11 + 2	0	7 + 4	0	15

By guessing cold on four more questions, the test taker in the example above had time to work the remaining two questions correctly. Approximately one out of five cold guesses results in a correct answer.

ANSWERS EXPLAINED

Section I: Reading Comprehension

1. **(C)** This is a *main idea* question. Choice C correctly captures the comparison between the mainstream culture and a specific nonmainstream culture in terms of how owner-ship is viewed and includes the author's conclusion that the nonmainstream view raises questions about the spiritual values of the mainstream culture.

   Choices A and B fail to take into account the comparison between two distinct cultural views. In addition, Choice B is not a true statement. To be true, it would need to add "in some situations." Choice D is a value that is implied as being held by some people but it does not constitute the main point of the passage. Choice E is incorrect because it is not true that the passage discusses the view that no one owns any object. The view stated in the passage is that some people believe that no one owns certain objects that have spiri-tual value.

2. **(A)** This is an *agree with a view* question. The correct answer is a view with which the author of the passage must agree. Choice A correctly reflects the author's comparison of two cultures. If a culture meets the criteria of *not* having any object that is considered so spiritually significant that it is above buying and selling, it may be missing something valuable that a society that does have such an object may have.

   Choice B is incorrect in that it goes too far. The society without the object may be miss-ing something of value but the author would not necessarily agree that such a culture is inferior. Choice C is incorrect because it implies that every object in a culture must have such spiritual significance that it transcends buying and selling in order for the culture to have the "treasure" referred to in the passage. The author only claims that a culture must have at least one such object.

   Choice D may seem too extreme at first glance. On further consideration, though, its extreme view may be justified. The author does imply that mainstream culture does not have even one object that meets the criterion of being so holy that it is above buying and selling. Choice D falls short not in being extreme but in failing to specify that the object with spiritual significance to which it refers *is beyond buying and selling.* Choice E is incorrect because it does not specify whether the object in question has any spiritual significance.

3. **(D)** This is a *function* question. Choice D is correct. The author has a reason for pointing out that mainstream culture considers the contract between seller and buyer irreversible without consent of both parties. The reason is to contrast that view with the view in the next paragraph. The view in the next paragraph is that the sale of an object may be con-sidered invalid if the object has such spiritual significance that the seller had no right to sell it.

   Choice A is incorrect because, whereas the statement is a conclusion, that conclusion is not one that is defended in the rest of the passage. Choice B is incorrect in that, whereas the statement is contrasted with something else, it is never proven to be an untrue statement.

   Choice C is incorrect. Although the quoted phrase does defend the earlier assertion that, if a seller had regrets, society would honor the seller/buyer contract over the feel-ings of the seller, this is not the author's primary purpose for making the statement. The primary purpose is to set up a contrast with the statement in the following paragraph.

Choice E is incorrect for the same reason. The statement in choice E is a correct statement but it does not reflect the author's primary purpose.

4. **(C)** This is an *analogous situation* question. The two islands are analogous to mainstream culture and nonmainstream culture. The two sets of parents are analogous to a buyer and a seller. The young people are analogous to the objects that are bought and sold. In each answer choice, island X represents a situation in which a specific contractual process is established. To create a valid analogy, island Y must involve a situation that transcends the contractual process based on special qualities of the young person. Choice C correctly involves a situation in which the young woman has such special qualities that she is not subject to the marriage negotiation contract.

Choice A is incorrect because island Y simply has a variation on the contract. There is no situation on island Y that transcends the rules of the contract because of special qualities of the young person. Choice B is incorrect because it merely expands on the contract, allowing it to be reversed by mutual consent. This is analogous to a seller and buyer both agreeing to reverse a sale but it is not analogous to a special situation that transcends the contract.

Choice D is close. There is an exception to the rules of the contract that is allowed if the daughter has special significance. The fact that the significance is spiritual is a distractor. The real problem with choice D is that both the evaluation of the daughter's specialness and the decision not to arrange a marriage for her is allowed to be made by the parents. To be analogous to the original passage, the evaluation and the decision must be made by the society as a whole, or at least by members who represent the interests of the society as a whole. This is defended by the quote "*they belong to the Native American people who created them and to the tribe.*" This reflects a collective evaluation, not an individual one. Choice D is incorrect.

Choice E is incorrect. The implication is that island Y has lost something valuable. However, in this analogy it is island X that is analogous to mainstream culture and so it would have to be island X that has lost something. Choice E is analogous to a situation in which the nonmainstream culture has no rules at all for buying and selling objects.

5. **(D)** This is a *use of a word/phrase* question. Orient yourself to the question stem by determining how the cited word is used. Choice A is incorrect because the word *treasure* does not refer to the value of objects of spiritual significance but rather to a quality that may have been lost in mainstream society. Choice B is incorrect because it refers directly to an object (unlike in choice A, which refers to the value of an object) rather than to the quality that may have been lost in mainstream society.

Choice C is incorrect because the statement in choice C, though consistent with the passage, does not refer to the word *treasure.* Choice E is incorrect because it is not a statement that can be defended by the passage. The passage does not claim that spiritually significant objects have economic value.

Choice D is correct because it identifies the word *treasure* as referring to a valuable quality of mainstream culture that may have been lost because mainstream culture does not have any objects spiritually significant enough to transcend the seller/buyer relationship.

6. **(E)** This is a *specific detail* question. Choice E is correct because the passage states that one tribal member submitted documentation to back up a claim of ownership and that the member's claim was "discredited."

Choice A is incorrect because there is no evidence in the passage that would establish that the museum specialized in Native American artifacts. Choice B is incorrect. Even though the owner of the museum was not able to establish proof of legal ownership, this does not constitute proof that the owner purchased the artifacts illegally. Choice C is incorrect because the passage specifically states that the objects were from Native American *tribes* and that the cultural director was from *one of the tribes claiming ownership*. Choice D is incorrect because the word *technicalities* refers to the fact that the museum owner could not provide proof of ownership and that the tribal member's proof turned out to be invalid. The word does not refer to the original reasons that the federal government had for confiscating the items.

7. **(B)** This is an *implied detail* question, with elements of extension and application. Choice B can be defended as being implied in that a member of a Native American tribe holding views such as those expressed in the passage may have a legitimate argument for transcending the seller/buyer contract of the mainstream culture. In other words, a Native American tribal member may be able to legitimately argue that the object was not available for sale in the first place.

Choice A is incorrect because the seller may have a legitimate argument, as described for choice B, regardless of the culture to which the buyer belongs. Choice C is incorrect. It distorts a quote from the passage. It is the distinction between the Native American view and the mainstream view that is described as being simple. The passage does not present any evidence that the belief in the sanctity of the seller/buyer contract is simplistic.

Choice D is incorrect because the sanctity of the seller/buyer relationship is described as an aspect of mainstream culture, not Native American culture. The word *sanctity* is a distractor, designed to confuse the test taker between the apparently mundane values of mainstream culture versus the apparently spiritual values of the nonmainstream culture.

Choice E attempts to state the reverse of the final sentence of the passage. However, the statement in choice E cannot be defended as being supported by information in the passage. The nonmainstream culture is described as having the same elements as the mainstream culture (the seller/buyer relationship) with an additional element (the fact that some spiritually significant objects transcend this relationship). Thus, the mainstream culture lacks something in comparison with the nonmainstream culture. It cannot be concluded that the nonmainstream culture, therefore, also lacks something.

8. **(E)** This is a Comparative Reading passage and the question is a *CR–agree* question, meaning that the answer is a statement with which both authors would agree. Choice E is correct because the author of Passage A believes that there is the possibility of the "ecstasy of abstract creation" and the author of Passage B states that the process of artistic creation is "joyful."

Choice A is incorrect because, although the author of Passage B would agree with the statement, the author of Passage A does not address the issue. Choice B is incorrect for a number of reasons. Neither author directly discusses success. Even though the author of Passage B does refer to training for children, it cannot be defended that the author of Passage A believes that training is necessary.

For choice C, the author of Passage B refers to the in-person instruction that children should receive. However, Passage B does not state that the instructor would be an experienced artist. Passage A does not refer to in-person instruction at all. Although the statement in choice C could be considered a commonsense truth, it cannot be defended that either author believes it to be true. Choice C is incorrect.

Choice D is incorrect. The author of Passage A would believe the statement but the author of Passage B does not address the issue of trusting one's own perceptions, so it cannot be defendably concluded that the author of Passage B would believe the statement.

9. **(C)** This is a *CR–in common* question. The correct answer is a statement that is true of both passages and also reflects a common primary theme of the two passages. Both passages discuss the potential benefits of the creation of art (choice C) and for both passages, the creation of art is the central theme. Choice C is the correct answer.

Choice A is incorrect. Passage A is primarily concerned with the personal joy of creating art but Passage B is primarily concerned with artists earning a living through their art. Choice B is incorrect. Passage A is primarily concerned with art as an expression of inner vision. Passage B mentions inner vision but this is not the primary concern of the passage.

Choice D is incorrect. Both passages mention creating images without the use of pattern. In Passage B this is peripheral to the main point. Passage A does not consider the use of patterns to be negative. The passage presents two equal options—either use shapes based on patterns or use shapes without patterns. In choice E, Passage B is primarily concerned with artists earning a living through their art, but Passage A is not concerned with this aspect. Choice E is incorrect.

10. **(B)** This is a *CR—relationship between passages* question. Choice B is correct because Passage A discusses the benefits of art strictly in terms of the benefit to an individual, whereas Passage B discusses the benefits of art in terms of the community of artists as a whole.

Choice A is incorrect because Passage B does not expand on a distinction. There are several distinctions introduced in Passage A, such as inner vision versus conventional vision. While Passage B does refer to this distinction, Passage B does not expand on it. Choice C is incorrect in that the only conflict introduced in Passage A is the conflict between inner vision and conventional vision, and Passage B does not reconcile this conflict.

Choice D is incorrect. The only position that Passage A could be said to defend is that an artist should rely on the inner eye. Passage B does not reject this. Choice D is a distractor in that Passage A is written from an intuitive standpoint and Passage B includes references to both intuition and scientific research. Choice E is incorrect. Passage A poses the question *To what extent will you simply follow the demands of convention and to what extent will you travel the path of your own perceptions*? However, Passage A does not leave this question unanswered, nor does Passage B present an answer to it.

11. **(E)** This is an *assumption* question and is similar to an LR question. The author's conclusion is that people who have been given the opportunity to experiment with art as children are more likely to create art as adults and that, as a result, the market for art will expand. The assumption is that the people who create art as adults are more likely to also

buy art. Choice E is correct. If choice E were negated—*Adults who themselves create art are not more likely to buy works of art than are adults who do not create art*—the conclusion does not hold.

Choice A is incorrect because it is the opposite of what the author claims. Choice B is incorrect. The author states that some artists *believe* that the art crisis is the result of the low value but it does not follow that there are some artists who do *not* believe it. If choice B is negated—*There are no artists who believe that the current crisis in the art world is not the result of the low value that our society places on artistic creation*—the conclusion is not affected.

Choice C is incorrect because the author does not state whether art education for children improves academic performance. If the statement is negated—that art does *not* improve academic performance—the conclusion is not affected. Choice D is incorrect because the author's argument is based on the premise that people who have had experience with art as children will *buy* art, not that they will make money from their own art.

12. **(D)** This is a *function* question that focuses on Passage A. Objectively measuring the height of the sunflower—three feet—using a measuring tape serves to create a contrast to the "inner" measurement of the sunflower—reaching up to the constellations. Choice D correctly expresses this.

Choice A is incorrect. Although the measuring tape does create an accurate measurement, the author does not refer to the tape as a tool for representing perspective. Choice B is incorrect because the measuring tape is not used as a metaphor. It is a literal statement. Choice C is incorrect. Although the measurement is objective information, the author does not use the information as a premise to support the conclusion. Choice E is factually incorrect in that it confuses Passage A with Passage B. The author of Passage A does not refer to children.

13. **(A)** This is a *main idea* question. Choice B is incorrect because the passage does not assert that it is unlikely that we will find extraterrestrial life. Choice C misconstrues the meaning of the word *universals* in the passage. The existence of universal characteristics does not imply that life exists elsewhere. Universal characteristics are characteristics that are likely to apply wherever life is found.

Choice D is incorrect because the assertion in choice D is not stated in the passage and because divergence and convergence do not constitute the main idea of the passage. Choice E is incorrect for the same reasons. Choice A is correct because it is consistent with the passage and because it captures the main idea.

14. **(C)** This is an *agree with* question. Choice C is correct because the passage indicates that the attempt to define parochial features in the study of exobiology has led to a reevaluation of issues in mammalian biology, for example, the role of the skeleton.

Choice A is incorrect because there is nothing in the passage that defends that any exobiologist holds this view. Choice B is incorrect in that the passage does not state that universal and parochial characteristics cannot appear in the same being. Choice D is incorrect because there is a difference of opinion between exobiologists as to whether extraterrestrial life would diverge toward great variation or converge toward a limited range of forms. Choice E is incorrect. The passage states that the portrayal of extraterrestrial life by science fiction is limited, not unrealistic.

15. **(D)** This is an *identify the structure* question. Choice D is correct. The question that is posed is *to what extent the characteristics of life on other planets would be similar to life as we know it.* The theoretical framework is to identify characteristics of life that are universal, as well as those that are parochial. The passage supplies detail to explain this framework. The related question is stated in the final paragraph: *The question of the extent of diversity among extraterrestrials is by no means settled.* This is different from the first question because it compares one form of extraterrestrial life with another form of extraterrestrial life. The first question compares Earth life with extraterrestrial life.

Choice A is incorrect because the passage does not include two hypotheses. Choice A confuses the two aspects of characteristics—universal and parochial—with two hypotheses. Choice B is incorrect because the passage does not begin with a hypothesis and because the breakdown of traits into universal and parochial does not constitute two different methods.

Choice C is incorrect for reasons similar to choice B. In addition, the two more methods mentioned at the end of the passage relate to a different but related topic. Choice E is accurate except for the final clause. There is no answer offered to the question concerning the extent to which extraterrestrial life differs from life on Earth.

16. **(D)** This is an *implied detail* question. Choice D is consistent with the information in the passage. Communication occurs in a wide range of life forms and thus can be considered a universal characteristic. The passage states that the structures used for communicating are an example of a parochial characteristic.

Choice A is incorrect because the passage does not address this issue. Choice B is incorrect in that skeletons are given as an example of a feature that would be replicated, making skeletons a universal characteristic.

Choice C confuses parochial characteristics with the distinction between divergent and convergent evolution. Choice C is incorrect. Choice E misconstrues the statement that parochial characteristics have little inherent utility as meaning that parochial characteristics are decorative. This is not a valid assumption. Choice E is incorrect.

17. **(A)** This is an *application/extension* question. Choice A is correct because, even though the presence of eyes would support the theory of convergionism—in which diverse life forms are expected to have similar characteristics—the presence of vision based on polarity is an example of diverse life forms having diverse characteristics, which is consistent with divergionism.

Choice B is incorrect because the passage states that vision based on polarity *does* occur on Earth. Choice C is incorrect because the presence of a universal characteristic supports convergionism, rather than divergionism.

Choice D is incorrect because the issue of whether the life form could survive on Earth is irrelevant to divergionism. Choice E is incorrect because divergionism does not necessarily depend on the existence of characteristics that do not appear on Earth at all, even though the appearance of such traits would support divergionism. The statement that extraterrestrial life might have an "even greater variety" than life on Earth could in theory refer to a more frequent occurrence of traits that are rare on Earth, as well as a more varied distribution of traits that are found on Earth.

18. **(C)** This is a *specific detail* question, in an EXCEPT format. Four of the answer choices are stated in the passage as examples of universal characteristics. One choice is not. Choice

C, bioluminescence, is given as an example of an arbitrary (parochial) characteristic that could be used for communication. Communication itself is a universal characteristic. The other answer choices are also specifically mentioned as universal characteristics. The presence of a skeleton is discussed in a paragraph about parochial characteristics, but it is cited as an example of a trait that is almost certain to be replicated in other life forms (universal).

19. **(E)** This is a *use of a word/phrase* question. The quoted phrase refers to the fact that a particular characteristic does not have much practical purpose in terms of the biological needs of the organism. Choice E exemplifies this. Speech is produced by vibrating the vocal cords but the activity of vibrating the vocal cords does not serve any significant biological need of the organism.

Choice A is incorrect because it states that a parochial function, crickets stridulating their wings, *does* have a biological function. Choice B is incorrect in that it does not address the absence of a critical biological function. The reference to inheritance is a distractor, as it confuses the concept of inheritance with the concept of an inherent quality.

Choice C is incorrect because a lack of utility does not refer to how practical or impractical a trait is. Communicating through gestures lacks inherent utility because moving the hands to convey meaning does not by itself serve any biological function. Choice D is incorrect for a similar reason. Vibrating the vocal cords meets the criterion of lacking of inherent utility for the reason stated in choice E, not because it takes little effort to vibrate the vocal cords.

20. **(C)** This is an *implied detail* question. Choice C is correct because the passage identifies bilateral symmetry as an important universal characteristic and also states that universal characteristics are thought to have evolved independently more than once.

Choice A is incorrect. The passage only mentions humanoid and reptilian forms as the forms most frequently used to represent extraterrestrial life in science fiction. Choice B is incorrect because the passage identifies the primary concern of exobiology as determining the extent to which extraterrestrial life differs from life on Earth.

Choice D is incorrect because the passage states that conflict between convergionist views and divergionist views is "by no means settled" and gives no evidence to support one view over the other. Choice E is incorrect because it confuses the parochial characteristics of the means of communicating (voice, wings, and so on) with the universal characteristic of communication itself.

21. **(C)** This is a *main point* question. Choice C correctly captures the essence of the passage. Choice A is incorrect because it is not a point that the author believes to be the most valid criterion for determining ownership. It is a point that the author says incorrectly appears to be a possible criterion but does not hold up as a criterion.

Choice B is incorrect because, even though the point in choice C is mentioned in the passage, it is not the main idea. Choice D is incorrect for the same reason. It is a statement that is consistent with the passage but is not the main point. Choice E is based on the author's query about whether it would be more civilized if no one inhabited the islands. The comment is not meant to be a recommendation, nor is it the main point of the passage.

22. **(D)** This is a *weaken* question. Choice D is correct because it is based on Britain's own criteria for ownership. If the fact that most of the citizens are of British descent, consider themselves British, and reject non-British claims of ownership establishes that Britain

does own the Falklands, then, if at one point most of the citizens were of Argentinean descent, considered themselves Argentinean, and rejected non-Argentinean claims to ownership, this argument equally would have established Argentinean ownership.

Choice A is incorrect because the passage implies that the British do not dispute that they sent settlers to the islands. They dispute that doing so is not a basis for claiming ownership. Choice B is incorrect for a similar reason. The fact that Argentina has not sent settlers anywhere does not make Britain's doing so illegitimate.

Choice C is incorrect because Argentina did not argue that the settlers were coerced into settling the Falklands. Argentina implied that regardless of how the settlers came to the Falklands, the presence of British settlers does not constitute a legitimate claim to ownership.

Choice E is incorrect. It confuses the beliefs of the people living on the islands with the beliefs of Argentinean citizens. This fact would not weaken the British argument, which is based solely on the preferences of the current residents.

23. **(D)** This is an *analogous relationship* question. Choice D correctly matches the relationship in the passage because Company X claims a right based on the preference of a group of people and Company Y claims that the act of establishing that group of people was itself illegitimate.

Choice A is incorrect because Country X would be analogous to the Falklands, when the correct answer requires that Country X and Country Y be analogous to Britain and Argentina, respectively. Choice B is incorrect because, if "more games" is presumed to be analogous to more British residents, the league would be analogous to the Falklands, but the claim that some of the games were with teams from other leagues does not have any clear analog in the original passage.

Choice C is incorrect because, if "more words" is considered analogous to more British residents, then the claim that Contestant X had an unfair advantage is not analogous to anything in the original passage. Choice E is incorrect because, if Senator Y is assumed to be analogous to Argentina, Argentina's argument is not based on the principle that the majority opinion should be the one that prevails.

24. **(A)** This is a *function* question. Choice A is correct because the second paragraph describes the British rationale, which the author says seems reasonable, but which in the next paragraph is shown to be questionable. Choice B is incorrect because the second paragraph does not contain a hypothesis.

Choice C is incorrect because the author does believe the British rationale has some merit. Choice D is incorrect because the second paragraph does not primarily provide historical background. Rather, it presents the British rationale and then presents the author's response to that rationale. Choice E is incorrect because the second paragraph does not establish one argument as more defendable. In fact, the passage does not at any point establish one argument as more defendable.

25. **(C)** This is an *application/extension* question. The phrase "more civilized" is used in the passage as a contrast to decisions that are made based on "bullying." Bullying refers to the use of force or the threat of the use of force to determine an outcome. A more civilized action, then, must be one in which force or the threat of force is not used. Choice C is correct because both parties agree to a nonviolent solution, namely, the arbitration of an impartial party. It is irrelevant whether the most or least powerful nation initiated the

suggestion, and the potential power of the arbitrating country is also irrelevant because that country has no vested interest in the outcome and so has no reason to use its force. Even though the least powerful nation initiates the request to negotiate in choice C, this does not imply that the nation does so because of intimidation.

Choice A is incorrect because, even though the "underdog" wins, the outcome is still based on force. Choice B is incorrect for a similar reason. Even though there is a "civilized" discussion of how the decision will be made, the outcome is still determined by force.

Choice D is incorrect because, even though the more powerful nation does not attack, its threat of attack will certainly influence the outcome of the negotiations. Choice E is incorrect because, even though the more powerful nation voluntarily offers generous compensation, that nation refuses to reconsider its ownership and the effect of the generous compensation is to consolidate its ownership by removing people from the territory who may oppose that ownership. The more powerful nation is using its wealth (power) to consolidate its ownership.

26. **(E)** This is an *implied detail* question. Choice E is correct because the author states that there are many criteria that could be, and have been, used to establish ownership, but that it is unclear which criteria, if any, are valid.

Choice A is incorrect because the claim is based on power (resources). The author questions whether power is a legitimate criterion for ownership. Choice B is incorrect and attempts to confuse the test taker by referring to the author's statement that it might be more civilized to abandon the Falklands. The author's suggestion is based on both countries relinquishing a claim to ownership, whereas in choice B, one nation maintains ownership but does not allow people to settle the territory.

Choice C is incorrect because the author does not claim that certain actions negate a claim of ownership, only that there are many actions that fail to clearly constitute a claim of ownership. Choice C seems to refer to the Argentinean claim about the British but in that claim, the settlement by British citizens was actively promoted by the British and was done so for the purpose of establishing a claim of ownership. Choice C does not state that the settlement was promoted by any government for any purpose. Choice D is incorrect because the author specifically states that it is not clear that being the first to claim a territory lends legitimacy to the claim.

27. **(B)** This is a *helps to answer* question. Choice B is correct, as the question can be answered with the statement that the Falklands were not inhabited by an indigenous people at the time that they were settled by nonindigenous people, whereas Hawaii was inhabited by indigenous people at the time that nonindigenous people began to settle there.

Choice A is incorrect because, although the passage poses this question, it does not provide an answer to it. Choice C is incorrect because there is no information in the passage about inhabitants of the Falklands who are of Argentinean descent. The passage does say that "nearly" all are of British descent but it does not indicate the descent of the others.

Choice D is incorrect because, although the passage states that most of the inhabitants are of British descent, it does not indicate whether any of them were actually born in Britain. Choice E is incorrect because the passage does not provide any information about the percentage of Argentineans who believe that the Malvinas belong to Argentina.

Section II: Analytical Reasoning

QUESTIONS 1–5

Below is the setup for questions 1–5. The game is a sequence (one-to-one correspondence, ordered). There are seven fixtures with no branches.

K   4:00   4:30   5:00   5:30   6:00   6:30   7:00
L
M
N
O
P
R

      M
       \
    N – RP
    L – – K
    K – – L
    M = :30

NOTE: Refer to Chapter 4 for an explanation of the problem-solving tools (shown in bold).

1. **(A)** This is the typical first question. Use **Eliminate—apply rules, four violations**. The condition *Rifkin must visit after Morton* is violated by choice D. The rule *Nuanez must visit before Palluca* is violated by choice B. The rule that there are two time slots between Li and Kelly is violated by choice E. The rule that Morton's visit starts on the half hour is violated by choice C.

2. **(D)** This is a *must be false* question. One answer choice violates rules. The others can be true or may be forced to be true. There is no new information and so nothing to diagram. Previous correct diagrams do not eliminate any answer choices. Use **Scan**. None of the answer choices stand out as being more likely to violate rules. Use **Test answers—prove a violation**, starting with choice A. Try to create a valid order using the sequence LOM. Morton can only go in 5:30 but it seems possible to create a valid order. Move on to choice B. Try to create a valid order around OMK. The order used to test choice A does this. Move on to choice C. Try to create a valid order using OKR. Fill in this sequence as L–OKRP or OKRP–L, using a temporary diagram. Place one of these sequences in the diagram in a way that leaves a half hour for Morton. It seems to work, so move on to choice D. Try to create an order using POK. Fill in the sequence as RPOK. The third position before Kelly is taken by Rifkin, which means that Li must come after Kelly: RPOK–L. This would force Morton and Nuanez to come after RP, which is a violation. You can quickly double-check that choice E is valid by placing Morton in second place and filling in an order that seems to work.

3. **(B)** This *could be true* question presents new information that goes in the diagram. Four answer choices violate rules. Start with **Diagram—put in new information**, putting RP in 6:00 and 6:30. Use **General—options for fixture**. What are the options for 7:00? They

are Kelly, Li, and Ostrowsky. Nuanez must appear before RP. Use **Diagram—parallel universes**. Because Kelly and Li are interchangeable, there are only two options for 7:00: K/L or O. Create two universes and fill in what must be true and then what could be true (**Diagram—apply rules, musts** and **Diagram—apply rules, with options**). In the universe with K/L in 7:00, Morton must go in 4:30. In the universe with O in 7:00, K and L must go in 4:00 and 5:30 (K/L and L/K). Morton must again go in 4:30.

4:00	4:30	5:00	5:30	6:00	6:30	7:00
N/O	M	O/N	K/L	R	P	L/K
K/L	M	N	L/K	R	P	O

Use **Eliminate—check answers against diagram**. You can quickly see that choices A, C, D, and E are not possible. Choice B represents one of the possibilities in the top universe.

4. **(D)** This is a *how many* question, specifically *how many players can be assigned to a specific fixture*. There is no new information. Use **General—count places in sequence**. Both Morton and Nuanez must be followed by two players and are thus out. The remaining players are K/L (they are interchangeable), O, P, and R. Using **Eliminate—check previous valid assignments**, the answer to question 1 shows that Rifkin can be in 6:30. Make a temporary list showing the players that you have proven can be in 6:30 and enter Rifkin. If you have other valid orders in your diagram that show other players that can be in 6:30, enter them. The remaining players to be tested are K/L, P, and O. Test K/L by putting one of them in 6:30. The other must go in 5:00. RP must go between them, O must go in 7:00 and M in 4:30, with N in 4:00. Test P. You have to prove definitely whether or not P can go in 6:30. Create a viable order and test it against all of the conditions. Add Palluca to the list of possible players for 6:30. Test O. Put O in 6:30. Use **General—options for fixture.** What are the options for 7:00? They are only K/L. **Diagram—apply rules, musts**: 5:30 is L/K; M must go in 4:30. Use **General—options for player**. What are the options for RP? There are none. O cannot go in 6:30. There are four players that can: K, L, R, and P. The correct answer choice is D.

4	4.5	5	5.5	6	6.5	7
	M		L/K		O	K/L

5. **(E)** This is a *must be true* question with new information that does not go directly into the main diagram. Use **Diagram—supplemental diagram or rules** and make a temporary diagram that shows K– – L, with two players between K and L. Use **General—options for player**. There are four options for the K – – L pair. K can be in 4:00, 4:30, 5:00, or 5:30. Use **Diagram—parallel universes** to create four universes. Use **Diagram—apply rules, musts** to fill in what is known for each universe and **Diagram—apply rules, with options** to fill in options. Use **Eliminate—check previous valid assignments** to eliminate choice A, because the correct answer to the previous question contradicts A. Use **Eliminate—check answers against diagram** to check all of the answers. Choice B is incorrect because in the universe with K in 5:30, P visits in 6:30. Choice C is incorrect because O and N are interchangeable in two universes. Choice D is incorrect because L visits last in the

universe with K in 5:30. Choice E must be true. In three universes M visits in 4:30. In the remaining universe K visits in 4:30. Note that the universe in which K visits in 4:00 can be broken into two versions—one with RP in 6:00 and 6:30 and one with RP in 6:30 and 7:00.

QUESTIONS 6–10

Below is the setup for this game.

```
G                      1    2    3    4  |  _  _  _  _
L
M
N
O
P      If G →  -S, -P
S      If -M → T
T      If -L → -P

       Either L
          or M
          bnb
```

6. **(B)** This is the typical first question. Use **Eliminate—apply rules, four violations**. The rule *If G → -S, -P* is violated by choice D. The rule *If -M → T* is violated by choice A. The rule *If -L → -P* is violated by choice E. The rule *Either L or M but not both* is violated by choice C.

7. **(D)** This is a *could be true* question. Four answers violate rules. One does not. There is new information so use **Diagram—put in new information** and put P in the main diagram. Use **Diagram—apply rules, musts**. The rule *If G → -S, -P* indicates that G cannot be in. Put G in the discard pile. The rule *If -M → T* does not apply because we do not have information on M. The rule *If -L → -P* indicates that L cannot be out (because P is already in). Put L in the "in" pile. The final rule indicates that M must be out. Go back to the top of the rules and go through them again. Now the rule *If -M → T* indicates that T must be in. The diagram so far is below.

```
1    2    3    4  |  _  _  _  _
P    L    T          G   M
```

What is known to be true.

Use **Eliminate—check answers against diagram** to check each of the answers against this diagram. Choice A cannot be true because L must be chosen. Choice B cannot be true because T must be chosen. Choice C cannot be true because there is only one remaining place in the main diagram. Choice E is incorrect for the same reason. Choice D could be true. T is already chosen, there is room for S to be chosen, and choosing S does not violate any rules.

8. **(C)** This is a *must be true* question. Four answer choices could be true or might be false. One choice is forced to be true. There is new information that goes in the diagram. Use **Diagram—put in new information** and put T in the discard pile. Use **Diagram—apply rules, musts**. If T is out, M cannot be out. Put M in the main diagram. Then L must be in the discard pile. Finally, P must also be in the discard pile. Use **Diagram—apply rules, with options**. Read the first rule carefully. The fact that P is out does not mean that G is out. G can be in or out. Use **Diagram—parallel universes**, creating one universe with G in and one with G out. In both universes the discard pile is full and the remaining players appear in the main diagram. Use **Eliminate—check answers against diagram.** N is chosen in both universes. Choices A and B are possibilities but are not required. Choices D and E cannot be true.

9. **(A)** This is a *completely determined if* question that gives new information that can be put in the diagram. Use **Diagram—put in new information** and put G in the main diagram. Use **Diagram—apply rules, musts**. S and P must go in the discard pile. Use **Diagram—parallel universes**, one with L in the main diagram and one with M. Applying the rules, the universe with L in must have M out and vice versa. The universe with M out must have T in. Use **General—options for fixture**. In the universe with L in, the options for the last remaining fixture are N and O. In the universe with M in, the remaining players are N, O, and T. Use **Eliminate—check answers against diagram**. Choices B through E could be true in either universe. Choice A is only true when the order specifically includes G, M, N, and O.

10. **(A)** This is an *equivalent condition* question, with no new information. In *equivalent condition* questions, there is nothing to put in the main or temporary diagrams. Test each answer to see if it replicates the condition that it replaces without leaving off or adding any restrictions. Choice B can be written as $P \therefore T$. Its contrapositive is $-T \to -P$. It is also true that $If -T \to M$ and $If M \to -L$, which can be combined as $If -T \to -L$. However, the two statements $If -T \to -L$ and $If -T \to -P$ cannot logically be combined to get $If -L \to -P$. In choice C if G is present, then P and L will both be absent. However, this is more restrictive than the original because it requires G to be present in order for $If -L \to -P$ to be true. In choice D, if G is present, T is chosen. This is a distractor. The absence of T would require the presence of M, which triggers the absence of L, but even if choice D had said the absence of T, it has the same flaw as choice C. Choice E, along with the original conditions, results in P not ever being chosen. This, of course, includes P not being chosen when L is not chosen, but is too broad. In choice A, the presence of M means the absence of L. There are only two possibilities for L being absent. Either G is chosen or it is not. When G is chosen, then P is out, satisfying the original condition. When G is not chosen, choice A requires that three of N, O, S, and T be chosen, which means that P must be out and at the same time no new restrictions are imposed.

QUESTIONS 11–16

This game has one-to-one correspondence (each player is used exactly once) and is ordered (it matters to which team a player is assigned). This is not a sequence game because it does not show the order in which three or more players appear, making it an ONS-A game. There are three fixtures (the three debates), each with two branches. The branches are not ordered (it does not matter to which branch a player is assigned). The setup is shown below.

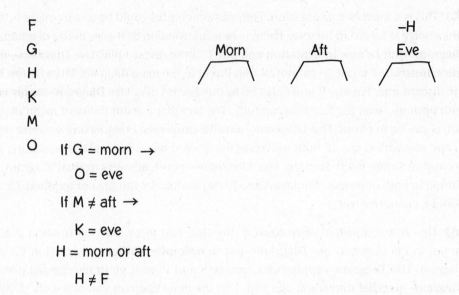

F
G
H
K
M
O   If G = morn →

           O = eve

       If M ≠ aft →

           K = eve

       H = morn or aft

           H ≠ F

11. **(A)** This is a typical first question. Choices B through E each violate one of the four conditions. Choice A does not violate any conditions.

12. **(D)** This is a *could be true* question with new information that goes into the main diagram. Use **Diagram—put in new information** and put F in the morning. Use **Diagram—apply rules, musts** and put H in the afternoon. Use **Diagram—parallel universes** to create three universes around the three possibilities for M. When M is not in the afternoon, K must go in the evening. For the universe with M also in the evening, G must go in the afternoon to avoid triggering the "G in the morning" rule. For the universe with M in the morning, G/O and O/G go in the remaining afternoon and evening slots.

   This leaves the universe with M in the afternoon. There are two options for K (morning or evening) and so this universe must be split into two. The universe with K in the morning can be filled in completely. With K in the evening, G/O and O/G are in the remaining morning and evening slots.

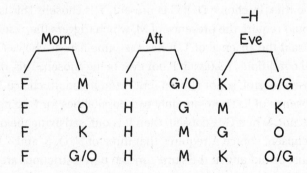

   Use **Eliminate—check answers against diagram** to find the correct answer. Note that this process does not require you to understand exactly why, for example, K cannot debate at the same time as H. The diagram simply shows that that is not one of the options. The alternative approach to creating parallel universes is to test the answer choices.

13. **(E)** This is a *must be true* question with new information that goes in the main diagram. The question can be solved in the same way as question 12, with four universes. Alternatively, test the answer choices. To test a *must be true* answer choice, try to show that it is impossible to create an order in which the answer choice is not true. Start with the basic diagram of G in morning and O in evening. For A, put H in morning and M in afternoon. The remaining players, K and F, seem to be able to go in either morning or evening. Similarly, choices B through D do not seem to be necessary. For choice E, putting M in the morning or evening results in a rule violation.

14. **(D)** This is a *must be true* question with no new information. Because there is nothing new to diagram, test the answers. No answer choice stands out as being best to start with, so start with choice A. To test a *must* answer choice, negate it. Create an order in which H is not in the morning (thus is in the afternoon) and F is not in the morning. F must go in the evening because H is in the afternoon. Try to create viable options by avoiding placements that trigger rules. For example, do not put G in morning and do put M in afternoon. The order seems viable. Go on to choice B. The negation of choice B is to put H in the afternoon and G any place other than morning. A seemingly viable order can be created. The negation of choice C is to put O in either morning or afternoon and to put G in the morning. With O NOT in evening, G cannot go in morning, so choice C cannot be true. To negate choice E, have M debate in the afternoon and K debate in the afternoon. There seem to be viable options. To test choice D, put G in the morning and in the morning. This violates the rule that if G is in the morning, then O must be in the evening. It must be true that one or the other of G and O must be someplace other than morning. In other words, G and O cannot both debate in the morning.

15. **(E)** This is a *cannot be true* question with no new information. There is nothing new to put in the main diagram, so test the answers. Use **Eliminate—check previous valid assignments** to eliminate choice C, based on the answer to question 11. No other answers stand out as being better to test first, so begin with choice A. To test the answer choice, put G and H in the morning and show that there is no violation. There seem to be lots of possible valid assignments, so move on to choice B and then choice D. Both seem to lead to viable assignments. Test choice E. Put K and M in the morning. Apply the rules. This assignment is a direct violation of the rule that if M is not in the afternoon, then K must be in the evening.

16. **(A)** This is a *could be true EXCEPT* question with no new information. Four answer choices could be true. The correct answer cannot be true (violates rules). Because there is nothing new to go into the diagram, test the answer choices. Start with choice A. Put F and O in the morning and G and M in the afternoon. This leaves H and K to go in the evening. However, H cannot go in the evening. Choice A violates the rules.

QUESTIONS 17–23

This is a sequence game. It has six players and six fixtures with no branches. In the figure below, the sketch in parentheses combines the first and third conditions.

L
M
P
R
S
T

$$\underline{1} \quad \underline{2} \quad \underline{3} \quad \underline{4} \quad \underline{5} \quad \underline{6}$$

L – M

P = 1 or 3

R – M – S

$$\left(\begin{array}{c} L \\ R - M - S \end{array} \right)$$

17. **(B)** This is the typical first question. Answer choice A and answer choices C through E each violate one of the original conditions. Choice B contains no violations.

18. **(C)** This is a *could be true* question with new information that goes in the diagram. Use **Diagram—put in new information** to put T in 1. Use **Diagram—apply rules, musts** to put P in 3. Use **General—count places in sequence** to find the options for M. Two players must come before M and one must come after. M must go in fifth and S in sixth. Places 2 and 4 are taken by L/R and R/L. Use **Eliminate—check answers against diagram**. Only choice C can be true.

19. **(E)** This is a *must be true* question with no new information. One of the answer choices must be true based on the original conditions. Because there is no new information, the answers must be tested. Start with **Eliminate—check previous valid assignments**. Choice D can be eliminated because in the answer to question 17, T presents in fifth place. Use **Test answers—negate a must**, starting with choice A. Put someone besides L and R in 2. The most likely person is T, who has no restrictions. A viable order seems likely here. Go on to choice B. Again, T is a likely player to work in 1. The same strategy applies to choice C. Test choice E by counting places in the sequence. L, R, M, and P must come before S. S cannot present before the fifth place and can present in either 5 or 6.

20. **(C)** This is a *CANNOT be true* question with no new information. There is nothing specific to diagram, so test the answer choices, starting with choice A. Try to create a viable order with L immediately after T. Because T has no restrictions, it seems like there are many options, so go on to choice B. M does have many restrictions and tends to go toward the end. Put M in 4, T in 5, and S in 6. There seem to be options for assigning the other players in a viable order. Go on to choice C. Putting P after T requires putting P in 3 and so T goes in 2. M must go in 4. However, there are not enough places left for L and R to go before M. Choice C cannot be true.

21. **(E)** This is a *CANNOT be true* question with new information that does not go in the diagram. Use **Diagram—supplemental diagram or rules** to notate T – M. There are four

positions in which T can present before M: – 1, 2, 3, and 4. Create four parallel universes. In all of them, M and S must be in 5 and 6, respectively. The universes with T in 2 and T in 4 have to each be broken into two more—one with P in 1 and one with P in 3. This makes six total universes, a fairly large number. However, all the players fall into place by using L/R and R/L where needed. You can now use **Eliminate–check answers against diagram** to find the correct answer.

22. **(D)** This is a *must be false* question with no new information. One answer violates rules. The other four could be true (or must be true). Because there is no new diagrammable information, test the answers, starting with choice A. Try to create a viable order with one player between T and M. M tends to go toward the end. Put M in 5 and T in 3. It seems likely that you can arrange the remaining players to make a viable order. Go on to choice B. Put T in 2. Create a universe with P in 1 and a universe with P in 3. The universe with P in 3 allows L and R to be separated by two players. Test choice C. With T in 6, M and S must go in 4 and 5, respectively. Create two universes based on P in 1 or 3. When P is in 3, there can be one presenter between P and S. Use the same diagrams to test choice D. In both universes L and R must be adjacent. Choice D must be false. Choice E can be checked by using the universe with P in 1.

23. **(E)** This is a *completely determined* question with new information that does not go in the diagram. With the correct answer choice, all of the presentation slots will be exactly determined. Use **Diagram—supplemental diagram or rules** to make the notations R–L and R–L–M–S. This can be expanded into two temporary notation universes, based on Ping: P–R–L–M–S and R–L–P–M–S. T has many options, though P must always be in either 1 or 3. It would take too many diagrams to write out all the options when T is included. Instead, test the answer choices, beginning with choice A. Put S in 6. What are the options for T? There are still many. Go on to choice B. Putting T in 5 determines where T is but there are still two options for P. Go on to choice C. Putting P in 1 still leaves multiple options for T. In choice D, M in 5 forces S into 6 but still leaves options for P and T. In choice E, putting T in 3 determines both where T and P go and the other players all fall into place.

Section III: Logical Reasoning

1. **(C)** This is a *strengthen* question based on cause and effect. Francine's argument is that the smile caused Robert to choose a particular dog. To strengthen the argument, a premise is needed that reinforces that conclusion. Choice C eliminates the possibility that Robert actually felt that one dog performed better than the others and strengthens the possibility that his vote was based on another factor, namely, the smile.

Choice A is irrelevant when considering which factors influenced Robert, as is choice B. Choice D would weaken the argument. If he made his decision before the smile, the smile could not have been the cause of his decision. Choice E goes in the direction of indicating that Robert's choice was not based on a personal preference and so might have been caused by the smile. However, awarding the blue ribbon is not based on enjoying the dogs but rather on their performance. Thus, choice E is incorrect.

2. **(C)** This is a *type of reasoning* question. The senator eliminates three possible courses of action and the journalist concludes that a fourth possibility will occur. Choice C correctly states that the journalist arrives at the conclusion by eliminating other possibilities.

Choice A is incorrect because, even though the senator makes claims about the value of the proposal, the journalist's conclusion does not involve the value of the proposal, and the question stem refers to the journalist's conclusion.

Choice B is incorrect. The senator makes a generalization about never abstaining from voting but the journalist does not rebut that viewpoint. Choice D does not apply, as there is no opposing claim in either argument. Choice E refers to arguing by analogy. The journalist does not use an analogy.

3. **(D)** This is a *parallel reasoning* question. The deductive logic in the passage is

$$If -exercise \rightarrow -energetic$$
$$If exercise \rightarrow willpower$$

The argument says that there are people who feel as energetic as they would like (*energetic*). The contrapositive of the first if/then statement is

$$Energetic \rightarrow exercise$$

Which can be combined with *Exercise* → *willpower* to conclude

$$Energetic \rightarrow willpower$$

This is the conclusion of the passage. In symbols, the logic can be represented as

$$If -A \rightarrow -B$$
$$If A \rightarrow C$$
$$B \rightarrow A \rightarrow C$$

The logic in answer choice D is

$$If concerned \rightarrow -accomplished$$
$$If -concerned \rightarrow chaotic$$
$$Accomplished \rightarrow -concerned \rightarrow chaotic$$

Choice A is incorrect. Its logic is

$$If -track\ practice \rightarrow practice\ alone$$
$$Track\ practice \therefore -practice\ alone$$

Choice B is incorrect. Its logic is

$$If\ not\ universal\ insurance \rightarrow -afford$$
$$If\ universal\ insurance \rightarrow everyone\ pays$$
$$Therefore\ either\ -afford\ or\ -everyone\ pays$$

Choices C and E are not deductive arguments.

4. **(A)** This is a *conclusion—what can be inferred* question. The setup establishes the premises that in some cases (e.g, Cedarville) an increased mayoral salary attracts a better-qualified candidate, that Johnsville increased their salary, that Johnsville attracted a better-qualified candidate, but that an independent study showed that Johnsville's salary increase was not enough to attract a better-qualified candidate. The gap in the argument is that it could not have been the salary increase that attracted the new mayor. Choice A correctly concludes that the current mayor was attracted by something other than the salary.

Choice B is incorrect because there are no premises in the argument that establish that a higher salary attracts more candidates. Choice C also cannot be defended. In fact, because something other than money attracted the current candidate, it is possible that the other factor will attract an equally qualified candidate in the future.

Choice D is incorrect because, even though the argument establishes a tentative correlation between salary and quality of candidates, the argument also demonstrates the existence of other factors that could attract a new candidate and provides an example of an increased salary that is not large enough to attract a better-qualified candidate. Choice E is incorrect. It is based on assuming a correlation between the mayoral salary and the number of terms that the mayor serves. There is no evidence in the argument to support that assumption.

5. **(E)** This is a *role of a claim* question. The premises are

> *Premise: red-light cameras have been installed*
> *Premise: red-light cameras cause drivers to be overly careful*
> *Premise: drivers stop too quickly at intersections with red-light cameras*
> *Premise: stopping quickly causes rear-end accidents*

The conclusion is that red-light cameras cause rear-end accidents, which is the same as the statement in the question stem. The correct answer is choice E.

Choices A, C, and D do not correctly identify the statement as a conclusion. Choice B is incorrect because, although the statement is a conclusion, it is not an intermediate conclusion. The statement that when a driver stops quickly to avoid running a red light, a rear-end accident is likely to occur, supports the first statement, not the other way around, as proposed by choice B.

6. **(B)** This is a *resolve a paradox* question presented in an EXCEPT format. Four of the answer choices resolve the paradox. One does not. Choice A explains how the professor might not be aware of the fact that the students do condemn the student who cheated. Choice A is out. Choice C explains why the professor's students would not know if a student cheated in another class. Choice C explains the paradox and is out.

Choice D provides an ethical principle that explains why the professor's students do not condemn a student who has cheated, even though they believe cheating is wrong. Choice D is out. Choice E distinguishes between condemning the student who cheated versus condemning the cheating. It explains the paradox and is out.

Choice B is irrelevant to explaining the paradox because it is not known whether or not the professor's students cheated at one point. Choice B does not explain the paradox and thus is the correct answer.

7. **(C)** This is a *strengthen by applying a principle* question. The argument to be strengthened is

$$\textit{If incompatibility} \rightarrow \textit{stress}$$
$$\textit{If stress} \rightarrow \textit{less productive}$$

The business plans to maintain its productivity. Therefore, it should not hire incompatible people. The conclusion states that the business should not be forced by law to hire incompatible people. The gap in the argument is that the law should not force the business to do something that violates its plan (to maintain productivity). Choice C accomplishes this and is the correct answer.

Choice A is irrelevant to the argument, as the issue is not about laws allowing the business to hire compatible people. Choice B is incorrect in that the principle needed to strengthen the argument concerns laws that force the business to increase the amount of stress. Choice D is incorrect because the new employees may be as productive as the current employees but the presence of the new employees may cause an overall drop in productivity. Choice E is incorrect because whether or not the new employees support the plan to maintain productivity is irrelevant. It is their presence that causes the drop in productivity.

8. **(C)** This is a *flaw* question. The argument sets up a dichotomy between the small planets in our solar system and the large planets. The astronomer states that none of the large planets show the existence of water and that some of the small planets do. The student incorrectly infers that all of the small planets show the existence of water. Choice C accurately expresses this and is the correct answer.

Choice A is incorrect because it is not necessarily a flaw and because the student has not necessarily failed to consider the fact mentioned in choice A. Choice B refers to an argument in which one claim is attacked but not proven false and an arguer then concludes the claim must be true. This does not match the setup and choice B is incorrect.

For choice D, the student's error is in making a generalization about all small planets from characteristics of some small planets. The student failed to understand the exceptions to a generalization. Choice D is incorrect. Choice E refers to an argument by analogy. A case can be made that the student falsely assumed that because two planets are both small and one shows the existence of water, the other must show the existence of water. However, this is an analogy about the small planets, not the large ones. Choice E is incorrect.

9. **(D)** This is a *sufficient assumption* question. The question stem asks for a new premise that is sufficient to make the conclusion valid. The argument is

> *The presence of the silvery minnow is good for the ecology.*
> *The absence of the silvery minnow is bad for the ecology.*
> *Therefore the laws that protect the silvery minnow are good (should be left in place).*

Because the argument for keeping the laws in place is based on the ecological value of the silvery minnow, choice D is the correct answer. It establishes that ecological issues are the only ones that are relevant. Choice D is both a sufficient and a necessary assumption. If choice D is negated—*There are factors other than ecological ones that are relevant to the laws protecting the silvery minnow*—the argument falls apart. It would no longer be possible to determine which factors were the most important, ecological or other factors.

Choice A is irrelevant because the argument is not concerned with game fish and because it does not imply either a reason for or against keeping the law. Choice B is incorrect because it goes in the wrong direction, implying that the silvery minnows are not important. Choice C is irrelevant because the issue of whether the silvery minnows are native or not is outside the scope of the argument. Choice E is incorrect because it discusses the effect of the river ecology on the fish population rather than the effect of the fish population on the ecology.

10. **(A)** This is a *flawed application of a principle* question. The logic in the principle is

$$If\ uniform\ values\ \rightarrow\ teach\ at\ early\ age$$

The application states

$$-uniform\ values\ \rightarrow\ -teach\ at\ early\ age$$

The negation of both sides of an if/then statement does not result in a valid statement. *Uniform values* is a sufficient condition. It is enough to cause *teach at early age*. The application implies that *uniform values* is a necessary condition. In other words, without *uniform values*, there could be no *teach at early age*. The flaw in the application is confusing a sufficient condition with a necessary condition. Choice A is correct.

Choice B incorrectly refers to circular reasoning. In choice C, the issue is not whether or not the values are in conflict but whether or not they are uniform. Diverse values cannot be uniform. Choice D is incorrect in that the application reasons from a claim about all people to a claim about one set of people. Choice E is incorrect because the principle is not a hypothesis. It is a premise that must be accepted as true.

11. **(D)** This is a *necessary assumption* question. The essence of the argument is

> *Injury of knee is bad.*
> *Early mild pressure develops supporting muscles.*
> *Therefore, early mild pressure is good.*

The gap in the argument is the connection between *supporting muscles* and *avoid injury*. Choice D directly states that the supporting muscles play an important role. When choice D is negated, the result is

> *Supporting muscles play no role in preventing injury.*

This negation would destroy the argument. If the supporting muscles play no role, then developing them does not prevent injury. Choice D is an assumption that is necessary to make the argument work and thus is the correct answer. Without choice D, the argument falls apart.

The negation of choice A is that the patients who started applying mild pressure soon were in worse condition to start with. If anything, this would strengthen, not destroy, the argument. Choice A is out. The negation of choice B is that the patient should decide when to apply mild pressure. This does not weaken the argument. The negation of choice C is that fear of injury keeps some patients from walking. However, the application of mild pressure does not necessarily require walking. Thus, the negation of choice C does not weaken the argument.

The negation of choice E is that patients are not willing to perform an activity that causes pain, even if it would help them recover. This does not weaken the argument because the argument does not claim that applying mild pressure causes any pain.

12. **(E)** This is a *main conclusion* question. The first sentence is a premise, not a conclusion. The second and third sentences qualify the first sentence. The fourth sentence states a conclusion: *It is not honest news.* The word *it* refers to the first sentence, that some journalists base stories on secondhand information. The conclusion, then, is that when journalists base stories on secondhand information, it is not honest journalism. The final sentence explains why it is not honest journalism, and is thus a supporting premise. Choice E correctly states the main conclusion.

Choice A is a true statement and is a conclusion but it is not the main conclusion. Choice B cannot be concluded from the argument. Choice C confuses writing from personal involvement, which is good, with writing from a personal bias, which is bad. Choice D goes in the right direction. When compared with choice E, however, choice D is missing the part of the conclusion that states that not writing from personal involvement is not honest.

13. **(A)** This is a *role of a claim* question. The argument is

> Premise: no backlog
> Premise: fewer complaints
> Premise: money left over
> Conclusion: the municipal court is efficient

Choice A is the correct answer. The statement quoted in the stem is supported by all of the other statements. In other words, the quoted statement is the main conclusion.

Choice B is incorrect because the quoted statement is not used to support another conclusion. Choice C is incorrect because the quoted statement is a conclusion, not a premise, and is not used to support a further conclusion. Choice D is incorrect because the quoted statement is not background information. Choice E refers to a necessary assumption. The quoted statement is not an assumption.

14. **(B)** This is a *resolve a paradox* question but it is unusual in that the passage provides a partial resolution. The correct answer must complete the resolution. The paradox involves an implication that directing resources toward preventive medicine will harm the development of curative medicine and that patients may then suffer from inadequate curative treatment. The arguer states only that directing resources toward preventive medicine will result in more effective preventive tools. The argument is not complete.

Choice B bridges the gap. More effective preventive treatment greatly reduces the need for curative treatment later on, so the fear that effective curative treatment will not be available is unfounded. Choice B is the correct answer.

Choice A is irrelevant. Choices C, D, and E seem to address a reconciliation or equality between preventive and curative therapies but they do not address the concern that curative treatment will fall behind.

15. **(D)** This is a *flaw* question. The argument concludes that Norway maples are not suitable. It supports its conclusion with the fact that only 5 percent of tree buyers buy Norway maples. The gap in the argument is the issue of whether the tree buyers' preferences accurately reflect whether or not the Norway maple grows well in the area in question. Choice D addresses this issue by pointing out that people who buy trees are not necessarily experts in horticulture.

Choice A condemns the argument for failing to provide supporting evidence for a premise. Because a premise must be accepted as true, failing to support a premise is not a logical flaw. Choice B is incorrect because the arguer does not refer to a case made for the use of Norway maples and thus does not reject such a case on the basis of an inadequate support. Choice C is incorrect for the same reason. There is no argument presented for the Norway maples.

Choice E seems possible at first glance. Using the adversarial approach, the defense for choice E is that the arguer says Norway maples are *unlikely* to grow well and then infers that they *will not* grow well. Pursuing the adversarial approach, the attack on choice E is that the argument does not actually say the Norway maples are *unlikely* to do well. It starts from the premise that they *will not* do well. In addition, choice E says that the conclusion is based "simply" from the fact, meaning that the fact is the only reason. The argument provides a different reason. Even if the inference from unlikely to impossible is partially valid, it is not the only, or even primary, way that the arguer defends the conclusion. Choice E is incorrect.

16. **(E)** This is a *complete the sentence/argument* question. The blank at the end of the sentence requires a reason why the average is misleading. According to choice E, if productivity is defined as including the quality of the items, the average units per hour per worker is misleading in that it does not take into account quality. Choice E is correct.

Because the manager's concern is average productivity, as stated in the first sentence, choices A, B, and C are incorrect. Even though they may be true statements, that fact does not make the number for average productivity misleading. An average assumes that there are individuals who are above or below the average. Choice D is incorrect because the goal of measuring the average productivity does not require that the maximums and minimums be reported, and thus choice D, though true, does not make the average misleading.

17. **(C)** This is a *sufficient assumption* question. The argument is

> *negatives of mowing: reduce diversity*
> *positives of mowing: reduce bindweed*
> *Assumption: positives outweigh negatives*
> *Conclusion: mow*

The argument does not state why reducing bindweed outweighs reducing diversity. However, choice C supplies the missing assumption. In other words, choice C is sufficient to conclude that mowing should be done. The negation of choice C is that mowing is more harmful than letting bindweed grow, with the result that the conclusion (mow) falls apart.

Choice A is incorrect because the argument does not depend on avoiding overmanaging. The argument acknowledges that overmanaging may be necessary. Choice B is irrelevant because the argument does not propose mowing fewer than three times a year. Choice D makes an interesting distinction between number of species and number of plants, but the argument does not depend on the number of plants. The argument is concerned with the elimination of species. Choice E is irrelevant. Even if bindweed were a native plant, it could still be true that it is more harmful to a good ecological balance than is mowing.

18. **(B)** This is a *strengthen* question. It is based on matching the terms *interpreting the emotions of others* and *having more satisfying relationships*. The logic is

> *Premise: teens not interpret emotions*
> *Premise: older people do interpret emotions*
> *Unstated assumption: interpret emotions → more satisfying relationships*
> *Conclusion: older people have more satisfying relationships*

Choice B strengthens the argument by explicitly supplying the premise *interpret emotions → more satisfying relationships*.

Choice A is irrelevant. It does not support the argument in any way. Choice C implies that having satisfying relationships is the cause of understanding emotions. However, the argument claims that having satisfying relationships is the effect, not the cause, of understanding emotions.

Choice D goes in the wrong direction. The argument would be more compelling if the same part of the brain were responsible for both interpreting emotions and having good relationships. Choice E implies that people who have experienced the emotional difficulties of not understanding the feelings of others might form more satisfying relationships.

However, there is no basis for assuming that the people with whom those in their mid-twenties are having relationships have gone through the same emotional difficulties. Choice E is incorrect.

19. **(E)** This is a *conclusion—what can be inferred* question. The premises are

Premise: Attorneys who win a high profile case can charge high rates.
Premise: Frank is an attorney who has won every one of his hundreds of cases.
Premise: Frank cannot charge high rates.

Frank does not meet the criterion for charging high rates. Based on the contrapositive of the first premise, the following is true of Frank:

–can charge high rates ∴ –attorney who won a high-profile case

Frank cannot have won a high-profile case. If he had, he could charge high rates. The premise indicates that even one high-profile case is enough to guarantee that the attorney can charge high rates. Choice E correctly concludes that Frank could not have won any high-profile cases.

Choice A is incorrect because no matter how many non-high-profile cases Frank wins, there is no guarantee that he can charge high rates. Choice B may be a true fact but it is not a fact that can be concluded from the premises. Choice C cannot be concluded from the premises because the premises do not discuss the quality of clients. Choice D could be a true fact but there are no premises in the argument that could lead to choice D as a conclusion.

20. **(A)** This is a *must be true* question. The premises are

Premise: If read to child when young → child learn to read at early age

$$(If B → C)$$

Premise: If parent learned to read at early age → read to child when young

$$(If A → B)$$

Premise: If overworked → –read to child when young

$$(If D → –B)$$

The first two premises can be combined to create

If parent learned to read at early age → child learn to read at early age

$$(If A → C)$$

Choice A states this conclusion and is the correct answer.

Choice B is equivalent to *If C → B*. This is not a true statement, based on *If B → C*. Choice C is equivalent to *If –B → –C*. This is also not a true statement. Choice D is equivalent to *If B → A*. This does not follow from *If A → B*. Choice E is equivalent to *If D → –C*. The relationship between conditions D and C cannot be derived from the premises.

$$If D → –B$$
$$If –B → –A$$

But neither –*B* nor –*A* has a relationship with C. Therefore, choice D is incorrect.

21. **(C)** This is a *strengthen by applying a principle* question. The information in the argument is

   Old: faster, less accurate results
   New: slower, more accurate results

   To strengthen the argument, a principle is needed that leads to choosing the old computer over the new one. Choice C indicates choosing faster over slower, even when slower is more accurate. Choice C is the correct answer.

   Choice A is incorrect because choosing the best results would lead to choosing the new computer. Choice B is incorrect because it is not known whether the people are more comfortable with the old computer or the new one. It cannot be assumed that they are more comfortable with the old computer. Choices D and E are incorrect because the argument is not concerned with replacing technologies.

22. **(D)** This is a *parallel reasoning* question. The argument in the setup is a statistical argument. Group A and Group B are the same size but have different characteristics (depression vs. hyperthyroidism). A large percentage of Group A prefers *indoors*. A small percentage of Group B prefers *indoors*. Choice D has two groups (yellow and purple). A large percentage of the yellow group changes color. A small percentage of the purple group changes color. Choice D is parallel in reasoning to the original.

   The other choices are incorrect because they use specific types of logic that are not statistical arguments. Choice A uses the logic of predicting the future from a past pattern. Choice B is incorrect because it uses if/then logic. Choice C uses an analogy and is therefore incorrect. Choice E is incorrect because it uses a cause-and-effect argument.

23. **(D)** This is a *necessary assumption* question. The argument states that high pressure can, in some cases, cause an El Niño. It then concludes that coastal communities should immediately begin preparing for flooding. The assumption is that there will actually be an El Niño. Choice D captures this assumption by saying that the event that *can* cause an El Niño *will* cause one. The negation of choice D is *The event that can cause an El Niño will not cause one*, in which case the argument falls apart.

   The negation of choice A is that the severity of the El Niño is not proportional to the degree of increased air pressure. This does not affect the argument. The negation of choice B is that there is only one cause of El Niños. If anything, this would strengthen the argument.

   The negation of choice C is that there are other places besides California that could experience flooding. This does not weaken the argument. The negation of choice E is that there has been recent El Niño flooding in California. This does not affect the argument. Even if there has been recent flooding, there is still a need to prepare for the upcoming flooding.

24. **(B)** This is a *flaw* question that uses the wording *vulnerable to criticism*. Choice B is correct. There are two factors that distinguish the first group of children from the second group—counting on the fingers and saying the numbers out loud. The conclusion identifies the counting on the fingers as the significant factor. However, it would have been equally valid to conclude that counting out loud was the significant factor.

   Choice A is incorrect because, even if true, it would affect both groups in the same way. Choice C is irrelevant. The passage specifies that the groups were large, which is enough to allay concerns that the groups were too small to be representative. Choice D is irrelevant. The conclusion is not based on what constitutes the most effective possible strategy but rather on which of the two strategies tested was more effective. Choice E, if analyzed carefully, does not apply. If the "two parts" refers to the two groups, there is nothing that is inferred to be true of the two groups.

25. **(D)** This is a *weaken* question. The problem set forth in the argument is that people do not read full-length novels. The cause is that they read short bits of various kinds of information on the Internet. The solution is to put short bits of full-length novels on the Internet in the hopes that people will then be interested in reading the full novel. Choice D points out a way in which the author's solution could actually make the problem worse.

Choice A is irrelevant to the argument about full-length novels. Choice B is incorrect because it is not the stated goal of the argument for any novel to achieve wide readership. The goal is for more people (the amount is not specified) to read full-length novels.

Choice C is incorrect because it does not match the situation in the argument. It is not known whether or not the author's suggestion has the possibility of producing profit. Choice E is irrelevant because the author's conclusion is not based on making a profit.

26. **(A)** This is a *weaken* question based on a *cause-and-effect* argument. A problem is established (diseased pines) and a cause is proposed (emissions). The argument rejects the proposed cause (emissions) on the grounds that the emissions are too spread out to have a significant effect. Choice A weakens the argument by providing a mechanism (prevailing winds) that would regularly concentrate the emissions over the affected area.

Choice B is incorrect because it strengthens the argument that there is no correlation between the power plant and the affected trees. Choice C goes in the right direction (emissions cause disease) but does not weaken the argument because the argument does not take issue with the fact that the emissions can cause the symptoms but rather that the quantity of emissions reaching the large area that is affected would be too small to cause symptoms.

Choice D goes in the right direction by suggesting that the only proposed cause is the emissions. However, stating that no other causes have been identified is not the same as establishing that there are no other causes. Choice E goes in the wrong direction. It implies that emissions are not harmful, which strengthens the argument.

Section IV—Logical Reasoning

1. **(D)** This is a *strengthen by principle* question. Test the answer choices by matching the principle to the original setup. Choice D is correct because it is an exact match. Choice A is incorrect because the issue is not whether or not the physician received all of the medical records, but whether the patient withheld information. Choice B is incorrect because, even though the patient did only suffer a loss of time and possibly money, this is not the reason that the argument presents for not suspending the doctor's license and so does not strengthen the argument.

The logic in choice C is *If provide → suspend.* The logic in the passage is *–provide ∴ –suspend.* These two statements are not equivalent. Choice E is incorrect because the critical point is not the patient's failure to tell the physician that increased recovery time is unacceptable but rather the patient's failure to disclose medical information.

2. **(E)** This is a *conclusion—what can be inferred* question. The setup contains premises that can be combined to defend a conclusion. Choice E is correct because the passage

states *If access → reserves* and *If reserves → weather* and choice E correctly concludes *If access → weather*.

Choice A is incorrect because it states *If weather → access*, which does not follow from *If access → weather*. For choice B, the passage states that start-up businesses that are supported by incubators do have access to low-interest loans but this does not imply that other businesses do not.

For choice C, having cash reserves helps weather difficult periods but *not* having reserves does not necessarily mean that a business will *not* weather difficult periods. Choice D is incorrect for several reasons. The passage discusses start-up, or new, businesses but choice D refers to businesses in general. In addition, although the passage states that access to low-interest loans increases the chances of survival, lack of access does not necessarily lead to failure, because the business may have access to other resources.

3. **(C)** This is a *flaw* question. Choice C is correct because Herman presumes that because Golden Retrievers as a group are more intelligent than Norfolk Terriers as a group, the individual Golden Retriever must be more intelligent than the individual Norfolk Terrier.

Choice A is incorrect because failure to back up a premise with evidence is not considered a logical flaw. Choice B is incorrect because nothing that Herman infers is unlikely to occur. Choice D is incorrect. Although Herman assumes the two dogs are the only options, this assumption is correct and not a flaw. Choice E goes in the wrong direction. Herman over-applies a generalization.

4. **(B)** This is a *main conclusion* question. The conclusion of the passage is stated in the first sentence. The other sentences support the first sentence. Choice B is the only answer choice that paraphrases the first sentence. Choice D goes too far by making new conclusions about a flexible habitat. The remaining answer choices are true statements but are premises, rather than conclusions.

5. **(D)** This is a *resolve a paradox* question. Identify the fundamental paradox. It is a numerical one. The average number of visits is given. Make up numbers for costs in order to clarify the paradox, following the restriction that the cost for Country Y must be five times the cost for Country X.

	# of Visits	Cost
Country X	200	10,000
Country Y	40	50,000

The paradox is now clear. A greater number of visits should correlate with a higher cost, not a lower cost. Choice D effectively explains the paradox by stating that the more regular attention that citizens of Country X receive prevents them from needing more expensive care later.

Choice A explains why citizens of Country Y need fewer medical visits but does not explain the higher costs. Choice B would account for higher costs per visit in Country Y but falls short of a convincing explanation in two ways. First, mathematically, Country Y would have to pay their doctors twenty-five times more to make the expenses come out as described. Second, the explanation does not take into account that medical expenses include fees other than doctors' fees.

Choice C is irrelevant because the numbers cited only apply to citizens. Choice E does not change the numbers at all because, in citing an average, it is understood that some people receive more than the average number and some people receive fewer.

6. **(C)** This is a *sufficient assumption* question. The logic in the setup is deductive.

$$If -explained\ within\ framework \rightarrow -replicable$$

The conclusion of the passage is that time travel is not feasible. To make a bridge from the if/then premise above to the conclusion, the following premise is necessary:

$$If -replicable \rightarrow -feasible$$

Choice C is the contrapositive of the above if/then and is sufficient for reaching the conclusion that time travel is not feasible.

Choices A, B, and E do not create a link to the element *feasible*. Choice D does use the element *feasible* but does so incorrectly. The logic in choice D is

$$If -feasible \rightarrow -replicable$$

with the contrapositive

$$replicable \therefore feasible$$

whereas the required premise is

$$If -replicable \rightarrow -feasible$$

7. **(A)** This is a *role of a claim* question. Choice A is correct because the fact that fruits and vegetables in a store may have been fresh twenty-four hours ago could be used to argue that there is not much difference between produce eaten directly out of the garden and produce bought from a store.

Choice B is incorrect because the quoted claim *is* a possible objection, not a rebuttal of a possible objection. Choice C is incorrect because the quoted claim is not used to derive a conclusion. Instead, it is rebutted by the claim that even two hours results in a loss of nutrients. Choice D is incorrect because the quoted claim is not a hypothesis. A hypothesis states a theory. Choice E is incorrect because there is no evidence that the information in the quoted claim came from a study. It could have come from another source.

8. **(D)** This is a *strengthen* question based on a cause-and-effect passage. In addition, the cause-and-effect argument is based on a genetic cause. This is a common pattern in LR. A primary way to strengthen the claim of a genetic cause is to show that other blood relatives have the same condition. Choice D is correct for this reason. Choice D also shows that *absence* of schizophrenia runs in families, which strengthens the argument even further.

Choice A is incorrect because it does not reinforce the genetic aspect of schizophrenia. Choice B is incorrect for the same reason. Choice C is incorrect because it goes in the wrong direction. With a genetic cause, identical twins should both have schizophrenia. Similarly, choice E is incorrect because it goes in the wrong direction, implying that schizophrenia, like similar diseases, has an environmental cause.

9. **(B)** This is a *relevant information* question presented in the *LEAST* format. For four of the answer choices, the response to the question posed would be relevant, meaning that the response would either weaken or strengthen the engineer's argument. The correct answer choice contains a question, the response to which would be least relevant or irrelevant.

Choices A, C, D, and E all raise relevant questions. For choice A, knowing whether it is the road bed that is sloped, as opposed to the surface of the road, for example, would help determine whether the road met the acknowledged standard mentioned in the first sentence. Choice C is relevant because the engineer's argument is based on whether the road could be made safer by rebuilding it and safety is reasonably measured by the rate of accidents.

Choice D is relevant because it provides a comparison of the rate of accidents between the sloped section and unsloped sections of state highway. The engineer's argument mentions only the number of accidents, which is not the same as the rate. Rate is a more appropriate measure of safety than is number of accidents. Choice E is relevant because if there were a safe alternate route, the stretch of highway in question might not need to be rebuilt.

Choice B is left. It is not relevant because the *number* of accidents on the stretch in question is not enough by itself to determine the safety of the road. The rate (number of accidents per total number of cars) must be compared with the rate for non-sloping stretches, because presumably the rebuilt road would be level.

10. **(A)** This is a *conclusion—what can be inferred* question. The setup is based on deductive logic.

$$\text{If } -industry\ concentrated \rightarrow -migration, \text{ and}$$
$$\text{If } -migration \rightarrow -high\ standard\ of\ living\ for\ middle\text{-}class\ urban\ people$$

The logical conclusion is

$$\text{If } -industry\ concentrated \rightarrow -high\ standard\ of\ living\ for\ middle\text{-}class\ urban\ people$$

This conclusion is captured by choice A, which states the contrapositive of the statement above.

Choice B infers, without any supporting evidence, that because concentration of industry in urban areas led to migration to urban areas, concentration of industry in suburban areas would have led to migration to suburban areas. Although this could have been true, it cannot be concluded from facts in the passage.

Choice C states

$$-high\ standard\ of\ living\ for\ middle\text{-}class\ urban\ people \therefore -migration$$

This statement switches the two sides of the logical conclusion left to right, which does not necessarily create a true statement. Choice C is not defendable.

Choices D and E seem consistent with the passage and could be true but cannot be defended as true. These answer choices are not based on deductive logic.

11. **(C)** This is a *parallel flaw* question. The setup is a deductive argument based on sets, rather than if/then arguments. The first set is *common childhood diseases*. The second set is *diseases for which vaccinations are available*. For the first set, most of the members also belong to the second set. The second set overlaps more than half of the first set. The second set has the characteristic that for all of its members, the vaccinations are 100 percent effective. Finally, the setup establishes a group of twenty instances that all belong to the first set and then concludes that most of those instances would fall in the overlap area. The flaw in logic is that, whereas for most (more than half) of common childhood diseases there are vaccinations that would prevent them (the overlap area), it is not true

that for any particular set of instances of common childhood diseases more than half will fall in the overlap area. Of twenty instances, theoretically, all could fall in the smaller part of Circle 1.

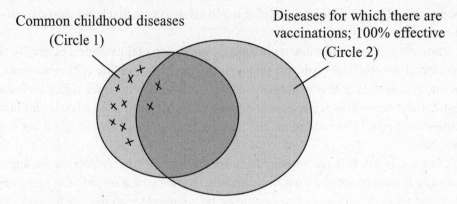

Common childhood diseases
(Circle 1)

Diseases for which there are vaccinations; 100% effective
(Circle 2)

X's represent a set of specific instances of childhood disease

Choice C captures the same pattern as the setup.

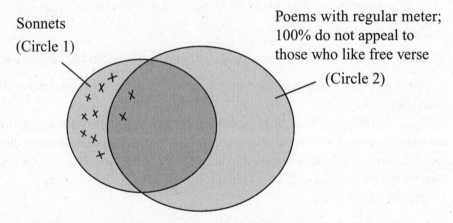

Sonnets
(Circle 1)

Poems with regular meter; 100% do not appeal to those who like free verse
(Circle 2)

X's represent the set of sonnets that were submitted

Choice A is incorrect because it is a valid argument. Choice B is based on the logic

If camp → improvement
(Greg showed) improvement ∴ camp

This is invalid logic, but it is not the same type of flaw as in the setup.

Choice D is incorrect because it is a cause-and-effect argument, not a deductive argument. Choice E is incorrect because it is not a deductive argument.

12. **(D)** This question is based on a statistical argument. The attorney compares a period twenty years ago with today and claims that today's dismissal rate of 30 percent is too high and that the situation of twenty years ago should be restored. However, the attorney does not cite the dismissal rate twenty years ago. If, twenty years ago, the dis-

missal rate were higher than 30 percent, the attorney's argument would be destroyed. Choice D correctly asks about the dismissal rate twenty years ago.

Choice A is incorrect. It attempts to address the attorney's point that the dismissal rates for murder, a more serious offesnse, are lower than 30 percent. Choice A addresses the number of cases of murder and driving under the influence of alcohol but it is the rate, not the actual number, that is relevant.

Choice B is incorrect because it is not the rate of conviction but the rate of dismissal with which the attorney is concerned. In addition, choice B addresses actual numbers, not a ratio. Choice C is incorrect because it also addresses the people who are convicted rather than the cases that are dismissed, even though choice C does correctly refer to ratio, in contrast to choice B.

Choice E is incorrect. It discusses the relative rate of dismissals twenty years ago for murder and drunken driving cases. The relevant issue is the comparison of dismissal rates for drunken driving cases twenty years ago and today.

13. **(B)** This is a basic *flaw* question. Choice B is correct because it identifies that the author has established only that the rulers *carried out* an action that had certain results and incorrectly infers that the rulers intended for those results to take place.

Choice A is incorrect. An example of the flaw in choice A would be saying that because the Babylonians as a group cut down trees, certain individuals must have cut down trees. Choice C is incorrect because the passage does not contain any information that supports the conclusion. There is only evidence of what the rulers did. There is no evidence that supports what the rulers' intentions were. Choice D is incorrect. The only cause-and-effect information in the passage is that cutting down trees caused desertification. However, the flaw in the argument is not that the desertification could have caused the cutting of trees. Choice E is incorrect in that there is no fact in the passage that is accepted as true because it has not been proven false.

14. **(E)** This is a *complete the sentence/argument* question. Choice E correctly captures the relationship that lower class size leads to more personal attention, which leads to more learning, which leads to more happiness.

Choice A is incorrect because students may be happy for reasons other than those mentioned in the passage. Choice B is incorrect because it is too absolute. Even if the teacher can give no personal attention, there may still be students in the class who learn. Choice C is incorrect for a similar reason. Even if a teacher does not have too many students, the teacher still might not give personal attention. In addition, even if the teacher gives personal attention, there might be other reasons why the students do not learn. Choice D is close but is incorrect because of the word *successful*. The passage does not define what constitutes success. It only defines happiness as a goal, as in choice E.

15. **(C)** This is a *conclusion* question that asks *what can be inferred*. The correct answer can be defended as being true, based on the premises in the setup. The premises are deductive:

If small business in X → not incorporated
If small business in X → not allowed more than fifty employees

Choice C is correct because it establishes Rado's as a small business in Country X, which is sufficient to trigger the result that Rado's is not allowed more than fifty employees.

Choice A is incorrect because Rado's could be in Country X and not have more employees than allowed by law if it is not a small business. Choice B is incorrect because if Rado's is not in Country X, none of the conditions apply. Choice D is incorrect because even if Rado's is in Country X, if Rado's is not a small business, none of the conditions apply. Choice E is incorrect because Rado's could be in Country X but not be a small business.

16. **(E)** This is a *flaw—fails to consider* question. The information that the arguer fails to consider is information that would weaken the argument. The conclusion of the argument is that recent studies disprove the claim that exercise is the key to permanent weight loss. The conclusion is based on one premise, namely that recent studies show that it is the ability to resist cravings for carbohydrates that is the key to weight loss. The flaw is the failure to consider that exercise might assist in resisting cravings. This fact would destroy the arguer's conclusion. Choice E correctly points to this flaw.

   Choice A is not the flaw in the argument because choice A would make the physician's argument stronger. Choice B is not the flaw in the argument because it would apply equally to the physician's recommendation and the health gurus' recommendation. Choice C is not the flaw because the information in choice C, if true, does not weaken the argument. It still maintains that diet is the primary weight loss factor. Choice D, if true, would not weaken the argument. The physician's argument does not depend on most people being able to resist carbohydrate cravings.

17. **(A)** This is a *conclusion* question that asks you to identify the main conclusion. The third sentence states the main conclusion. The first two sentences support the third sentence and the final sentence reinforces the third sentence. Choice A correctly paraphrases the third sentence.

   Choice B is incorrect for two reasons. First, it refers to the final sentence, which is a premise that supports the conclusion. Second, choice B is not accurate. The passage refers to people who claim that cultural ecology is a branch of biology. This is not the same as claiming that cultural ecology is *not* a branch of anthropology.

   Choice C is incorrect because the argument does not claim that cultural ecology should be classified as anthropology because humanity is its main focus. Rather, the logic states that if a science deals with humanity *at all*, it is a branch of anthropology. Choice D is incorrect because the passage does not make this claim. Choice E is incorrect because it is not stated in the passage and is not the main point.

18. **(E)** This is a *resolve a paradox* question that does not use the word *paradox* in the question stem. There are two statements that appear mutually contradictory. On the one hand, voice recognition technology is accurate and helps avoid injury. On the other hand, businesses discourage its use. The correct answer must resolve this apparent contradiction. Choice E correctly resolves the paradox by stating that, whereas the technology is highly accurate, it is slower.

   Choice A is incorrect because it simply reinforces the benefits of the technology. Choice B is incorrect. It implies that the technology may not be necessary because there are other ways to avoid repetitive injury. However, this is not enough to explain why businesses actively discourage its use.

   Choice C is incorrect because it compares this technology to other technologies that are alternatives to traditional typing. To resolve the paradox, voice recognition technology must be shown to be inferior to traditional typing in some way. Choice D is incorrect for a similar reason. It does not establish a drawback in comparison with traditional typing.

19. **(C)** This is a *strengthen* question based on a miscellaneous type of logic. The art critic's argument is that negative moods result in unreliable rankings and therefore the rankings of the visitors were unreliable. The missing bit of logic is that the visitors who ranked the paintings were in a negative mood. Choice C correctly expresses this.

Choice A is incorrect because the argument is that negative moods result in unreliable rankings, *not* negative rankings. If all the rankings were negative, that would be predictable. Choice B is incorrect because it is irrelevant unless it were known that the visitors who gave the rankings were in a positive mood, in which case it would *weaken* the argument.

Choice D is incorrect because if all the visitors gave below-average rankings, the rankings would be predictable. This does not support the art critic's conclusion that the rankings were unreliable. If the rankings were consistently low, the museum could still determine relative preferences, for example, more people liking painting A than painting B. Choice E is incorrect because the amount of time spent viewing the paintings does not necessarily mean that the rankings were less predictable. Some people might be able to give a reliable ranking with a shorter viewing.

20. **(D)** This is a *sufficient assumption* question. The argument is deductive.

$$If-informed \rightarrow -democracy$$

The conclusion of the argument is that our system is not a democracy. The only statement that can lead to that conclusion is that our populace is not informed (*–informed*). Choice D correctly states this. The statements in the other answer choices cannot lead to the conclusion *not democracy*.

21. **(E)** This is a *strengthen by principle* question. Choice E correctly matches the facts that Jankowski copied part of another artist's work and was not consciously aware that she was copying. Choice A is incorrect because the conclusion of the passage does not involve fines. Choice B is incorrect because it fails to include the fact that the artist was not aware of copying. Choice C is incorrect because the implication in the passage is that Jankowski did *not* independently create the melody but rather had heard it somewhere and subconsciously copied it, and thus had been influenced by Li.

Choice D is incorrect because it refers to an entire composition, rather than part of a composition. Jankowski's and Li's compositions are not identical in total, so this principle does not match the passage.

22. **(C)** This is a *committed to agree/disagree* question in which the two arguers must disagree. Choice C is correct because Josep is committed to the fact that wolfberry is difficult to manage in the backyard, and Montse is committed to the fact that wolfberry is very manageable in the backyard.

Choice A is incorrect because Josep states that wolfberry has tasty fruits and Montse does not say whether it does or does not, so she is not committed to an opinion. Choice B is incorrect because both are committed to the fact that wolfberry is a bad plant for the city backyard. Choice D is incorrect because Montse does not express an opinion on this and thus is not committed. Choice E is incorrect because Montse is committed to the truth of choice E but Josep does not express an opinion. He only states that the fruit is tasty, not that the fruit is set frequently.

23. **(D)** This is a *match a concrete example to a principle* question. The passage provides the concrete example. The answer choices represent principles. The author's reason for not wanting the shortcuts of electronic communication to be used in novels is that these shortcuts were designed to address specific circumstances, namely, the need to type quickly and to reduce hand motions, and that these constraints do not apply to literature. Choice D matches this.

Choice A is incorrect because the issue is not a generational one but an issue of the communication requirements. Choice B is incorrect because the passage does not state that electronic communication shortcuts are less clear. Choice C is incorrect because this is not the basis of the author's argument. Choice E is incorrect because the author does not argue for the use of traditional literary language on the grounds that it is too hard to change.

24. **(B)** This is a *necessary assumption* question. Use negation to test the answer choices. Choice B is correct because if negated (*The ethical standards of the committee would not be the same as the standards of the rest of us*), the argument falls apart. The point of the argument is that the committee would create standards that the rest of the people would find appropriate.

Choice A is incorrect because, if negated (*People now do share guidelines with each other)*, the argument is not affected. Even with sharing, it is possible that not all of the needed ethical guidelines are covered. Choice C is incorrect. The negation of choice C is *there may be some ethical dilemmas for which guidelines cannot be developed*. This statement does not undermine the argument that a committee could create and disseminate guidelines for many dilemmas.

The negation of choice D reads *The members of the committee do not necessarily have higher standards than we do*. This does not affect the argument. Presumably the committee would be effective if the members had the same standards as others. Choice E is incorrect in that it implies that people cannot create any guidelines. The passage says that people do not have the time or energy to deal with *all* of the dilemmas. It does not say that people cannot deal with some dilemmas.

25. **(C)** This is an *application of a principle* question. The criteria for demolition that are identified in the principle are:

> *publicly owned*
> *poor repair*
> *If demo cost < repair cost* → *demolish*
> *If historic value* → *−demolish*

The contrapositive of the last statement is: *Demolish* ∴ *− historic value*

To match the principle, a building must be a publicly owned building in poor repair. Because the application calls for the demolition of the building, the building cannot have historic value. Once it is established that the building has no historic value, then if its demolition cost is less than its repair cost, the building *must* be demolished. However, if the demolition cost is not less than its repair cost, it might or might not be demolished, so it is not necessary that the demolition cost be less than the repair cost.

Choice C meets all of the necessary conditions: poor repair, publicly owned, and not of historic value. It is irrelevant that the demolition costs are higher than the repair costs. This does not prevent demolition. An answer choice that included the three necessary conditions *and* the condition that the demolition costs were lower than the repair costs would be a stronger answer than C but there is no such answer choice.

Choice A is incorrect because it does not establish that the building is publicly owned. Choice B is incorrect because it leaves open the possibility that the building has historical value. The building cannot be demolished until the historical value is determined. Choice D is incorrect because the fact that the building is a former courthouse does not establish that it is currently publicly owned. The low demolition cost is a distractor. It only results in demolition if the building is publicly owned and has no historic value. Choice E is incorrect because being a former courthouse does not establish it as a publicly owned building. The comparison with other buildings is irrelevant.

Writing Sample: Example of a Superior Response to the Essay

Max Builder ("MB") chooses the Waerout location ("WL") over the Far Green location ("FG") because WL allows MB the opportunity to keep its workforce together and WL's new facility will impress its clients. MB uses two criteria, which are MB wants a new building that will impress its customers, and MB wants to enhance the relationships between its managers and workers. WL is MB's superior alternative because WL's large new facility allows MB to simultaneously attract clients and bond its employees together in a single location. FG is MB's inferior alternative because FG splits MB's management and union into separate camps and its luxury could create a negative impression on MB's clients. WL is therefore MB's superior alternative because WL better meets MB's selection criteria.

MB uses two criteria to choose between WL and FG. One criterion says MB wants to appear successful in order to attract clients and thereby grow its business. The other criterion says MB wants a single location in order to strengthen its employee bonds. These criteria may be combined into a single rule that says MB desires to build the relationships between its employees while impressing its clients. Because MB is already an established business, MB's need to forge the bond between its employees is more important than MB's need to impress its customers.

WL is MB's superior choice because WL's single location facilitates the relationships between MB's workers. WL is a large, functional, and beautiful building that will appeal to MB's customers. Unfortunately, WL could pose environmental problems and WL's value is unlikely to appreciate. However, WL is MB's superior alternative because WL allows MB to unify its employees, and the new building will impress its clients.

FG is MB's inferior choice. FG's lavish location could offend MB's customers by appearing overly costly. FG is expensive, might not appreciate, and could drive a wedge between MB's management and union. While FG's value could appreciate, FG's distant and expensive location points away from FG. Therefore, MB rejects FG as MB's less desirable alternative.

WL is MB's superior alternative. WL's single location strengthens MB's employee relationships. WL will impress its clients by building a functional and relatively inexpensive building. FG's distant, luxurious location could split MB's employees and negatively impact MB's client relations. In conclusion, MB chooses WL because WL strengthens the bonds between MB's employees and WL will impress MB's customers more than FG will.

General Strategies

1

→ **YOUR PLAN OF ATTACK**
→ **TIMING STRATEGY**
→ **TESTING STRATEGY**
→ **ANALYZING ERRORS**

This chapter introduces important strategies that apply to the entire LSAT. The later chapters review in-depth strategies specific to each section.

YOUR PLAN OF ATTACK

There are two tasks that you must accomplish to get a top score on the LSAT:

1. Master timing strategy.
2. Learn the patterns for each type of test section and master the strategies for getting to the correct answer.

Timing strategy is extremely important for improving your score. Timing strategy is covered in depth below and is reviewed at the beginning of each chapter. Many people underestimate the importance of good timing. Timing strategy involves learning how to use your time as effectively as possible.

In addition to timing, the essence of improving on the LSAT is learning the behind-the-scenes agendas and patterns for each of the three types of LSAT sections and then learning the powerful strategies that help you get to the correct answer more quickly and more accurately. This introduction teaches important strategies that apply to the entire LSAT. Each chapter of this book teaches you the specific strategies that you need to master each type of LSAT question.

Mastering Strategy

All LSAT questions require strategy. LSAT questions do not test knowledge of the real world, law, or any other academic subject. If you miss a question, there is a strategy that you could have used to answer that question correctly. Carefully review every question that you get wrong to make sure you understand the patterns in the question and the strategies you could have used.

Many people, when they review a question, feel that they made a careless error. In fact, most errors that seem "careless" are *not* the result of being "sloppy" but rather are the result of (1) not using time well, such as rushing or quitting too soon; (2) missing an important distinc-

> **ARE THESE OBLIGATIONS SABOTAGING YOUR EFFORTS?**
>
> Are you spending too much time on work, school, travel plans, family obligations, extracurricular activities, volunteer positions?
> Cut back for success.

tion; or (3) having misunderstood the question stem. Look beneath the surface to determine the cause of your error.

Test Anxiety and Learning Disabilities

If test anxiety affects your performance on tests, you will find that mastering the timing strategies and testing strategies will eliminate much of the anxiety. For many people, anxiety is centered around the conflict between wanting to speed up to get to more questions and needing to slow down to be more accurate. A good timing strategy tells you how much time to spend on a question and when to move on. You can work this out and perfect it before going into your actual LSAT.

Another common aspect of test anxiety is that you, the test taker, feel that you do not think in the same way as the test writers. You have your own reasons for choosing your answer over theirs. Testing strategy helps you understand exactly why one answer must be correct and the other answers are inherently wrong, meaning that they contain fatal flaws. You *can* learn to think like the test writers!

If you have a physical or learning disability that affects your ability to get through the test quickly and accurately, you can inquire about taking the test under special conditions. Do this at least four to six months before your test, as the process for receiving special accommodations can be lengthy.

How to Practice

There are several ways to practice LSAT questions. The main way is to practice untimed. Untimed practice lets you experiment with strategies. It allows you to push your abilities by working on a question for ten or fifteen minutes, or more. Untimed practice is the best way to analyze the test and build your strengths.

As you become more skilled, you will also do occasional timed sections. After you have studied timing strategy, do a timed section just for the purpose of trying out your new timing approach. Later on, you can do timed sections to see how you are scoring and to evaluate your timing strategy. Eventually, you can challenge yourself by doing several timed sections at a sitting, or by doing a full, timed test. You may also wish to build your stamina by testing under distracting conditions or with a reduced time limit.

As you get closer to your test, plan on at least one full, timed test. Even up to your test day, though, continue to do untimed practice to build your skills.

LSAC has many previous actual LSATs available for sale. These are extremely valuable to study. Be aware, however, that tests more than four or five years old may have slightly different patterns than the current test.

TIMING STRATEGY

What does "timing strategy" mean? You may say, "I need to learn how to go faster to get to all the questions. That's the only way I can get more points." Consider this view carefully to see whether it is valid.

Everyone develops certain strategies for taking tests over the years, and these strategies operate on a subconscious level. As you take a test, you continually make decisions about how to use your time without being aware of these decisions. For example, when a test section begins, what do you do first? Most people begin with the first question. That may not be the best way to start a section, but it is an assumption that you may have developed from your past test-taking experience. This, and other assumptions, can be analyzed carefully to determine what is actually the best approach on the LSAT.

How many questions do you hope to work on? Should you be pushing yourself to work faster or letting yourself relax and work more carefully? When you finish one question, on which question should you work next? If you are having trouble with a question, should you guess and move on now or spend more time on it? How much time is acceptable to spend on a question? If you get stuck on a question and cannot think of anything else to do with it, should you guess and move on or do something else?

If you were to take the LSAT right now, you would have to make the above decisions, but your decisions would probably not be the best ones for the LSAT. Study the strategies below so that you can test and adjust your assumptions about timing strategy.

Step 1: Test Layout

The first step in developing a good timing strategy is to know the "geography" of each test section—how many questions there are and how many problem sets, as well as how much time you have for the entire section.

Step 2: Keeping Track of Time

You will need to keep track of time during the test. You are allowed to bring one watch into the testing room but it cannot be digital. In other words, it can only be a watch with hands (analog) and it *cannot* have any functions other than keeping time, such as a calculator or stopwatch.

Your watch should be large enough so that you can see the hands clearly and can easily pull out the stem. It is not necessary for the watch to have a second hand because you will only use the minute hand for timing.

HOW TO USE YOUR LSAT WATCH

During each test section, you need to know when the thirty-five minutes for the section is almost up. Because your watch will be used for keeping time for each question, rely on the monitor to give a five-minute warning. At this time, fill in the bubbles for any questions that you have left blank up to this point—without actually looking at the questions to which the bubbles correspond—and then continue to work on questions until the monitor calls time. If there is a wall clock in the test room, you can also use that to know how much time is left on the section. However, if the clock is behind you, the monitor may not allow you to turn around frequently.

As you begin each question, set the two hands of the watch to 12 o'clock. The minute hand will act as a stopwatch, showing how many minutes have elapsed. The minute hand will never go further than five minutes. Ignore the hour hand, as it will stay on 12. You only need to keep track of the time that you spend on an individual question. It is not necessary to keep track of the time setting up an RC or AR passage. For most questions, you will arrive at an answer within a minute or two and will not need to refer to your watch. You will simply enter your answer, go on to your next question, and reset the watch to 12. However, on a few critical questions, you may need to spend extra time, and then it is important to know how much time you have already used.

On most questions, you will not need to know how much time you spent. However, because you cannot know in advance for which questions you will need to know the time, you must reset your watch at the beginning of every question. Once you are used to resetting the watch, it takes only a second to do so. Although this process may use a minute of a section, there is no alternative. If you do not know the time you have spent on a critical question, you will either cut your time short and miss a question that you otherwise could have gotten, or you will spend too much time on the question.

Some people can keep track of time in their head but this comes at a price. When part of the brain is keeping track of time, you are partly distracted from the problem-solving process. In addition, there is a tendency to rush. Free up your problem-solving abilities by using an external device (your watch) to keep track of time. If you find this distracting at first, stick with it! Most people, even those who at first become very anxious by keeping track of time, find that with some practice, the watch gives them a sense of control over time and reduces anxiety.

When you practice, whether timed or untimed, keep track of time for each question and write the time down. On the actual exam, you do *not* write the time down. By doing this when you practice, though, you can review your results to see whether you spent enough time on certain questions or if you tended to rush.

Step 3: Understanding Timing

The test-taking assumptions that you have developed over the years make up a mental test-taking model that is counterproductive on the LSAT. To help you develop a more effective mental framework, consider the following hypothetical model. This model is for instructional purposes. Do *not* take this model literally!

During an LSAT there are many factors that will determine how you will do on each question. These include how much practicing you have done, how well you have learned testing strategies, how well you slept the night before, how alert or tired various systems of your body are, and how many or few distractions are in your mind. Imagine that, if you were going to take the LSAT tomorrow, you had an all-knowing perspective, an omniscient viewpoint, and could determine exactly how long it would take to get the correct answer for each question. An omniscient viewpoint might tell you, for example, that for question 17 you would get the right answer after 4 minutes and 17 seconds and not a second before. (This is hypothetical! In real life you clearly cannot know this.)

With this knowledge, see if you could plan the perfect timing strategy. The purpose of this exercise—given that you clearly cannot do this on a real test—is to understand the elements that lead to your best score. To keep things simple, suppose a test section had ten questions and you had fifteen minutes to complete it, and suppose that you could determine the following times (in minutes and seconds) needed to get each question right.

Table 1.1. Hypothetical Test Section

QUESTION	TIME	QUESTION	TIME
1	4:03	6	0:29
2	0:47	7	2:26
3	7:38	8	1:40
4	1:12	9	2:30
5	3:55	10	3:15

Which question would you do first? Would you start with question 1 or would you start somewhere else?

Which question would you do second? Third?

Do you see that you should do the quickest question first? That is question 6 at 0 minutes and 29 seconds. Because every question is worth one point, regardless of how difficult it is, to get the most points, just choose the quickest questions.

Following this logic, the second question is question 2 at 0 minutes and 47 seconds, then question 4, and so on. Here is a chart of the best timing strategy:

Table 1.2. Best Strategy for the Hypothetical Test

QUESTION	TIME USED	TIME LEFT
6	0:29	14:31
2	0:47	13:44
4	1:12	12:32
8	1:40	10:52
7	2:26	8:26
9	2:30	5:56
10	3:15	2:41
5	3:55 not enough time	

This would give you seven correct answers and you would guess cold on the remaining three questions. Notice that after question 10, there is not enough time left to get the next easiest question, question 5.

Suppose you need to get eight questions right in order to get the score you want. The above result is one short. How could you tweak it? Consider this carefully. What different way could you use your time to get one more correct?

If you try to save time on certain questions by going faster, you will get those questions wrong. For example, if, on question 9, you only spend 2 minutes, you will not get it correct. According to the omniscient viewpoint, question 9 requires a full 2:30. Do you see that there is no way to get more points?

Most of the elements of this hypothetical model *cannot* be applied to the actual test. You obviously will not know how long it will take you to do a question, nor can you compare all the questions and figure out definitively which one will take the least time. However, this exercise brings out several important points that you can use to your advantage. This strategy can be *simulated* in two steps: (1) choose the best (quickest) question to work on next, and (2) give each question the full time that it needs.

It *is* possible to simulate choosing the next quickest question. For each type of section, you will learn a specific strategy for doing so. The strategy is only an approximation. It would be too time-consuming to evaluate each question precisely. However, without a strategy for choosing, most people do the questions in order. They work on some difficult questions and leave some easy questions undone.

To approximate choosing the next quickest question, you need a strategy for quickly assessing questions. The strategy varies with the type of section. In RC and AR, you can choose by passage. In LR, you have to choose on a question-by-question basis. Because choosing questions is an approximation, you may find that you have chosen some hard questions. This is inevitable. It does not mean that your system for choosing is wrong.

It is also possible to approximate giving each question the time that it needs. Without a strategy for doing so, most people quit on hard questions too soon, leaving a trail of ten or fifteen wrong answers in their wake. Throughout this book, you will learn strategies for giving questions the time that they need.

Another lesson of the omniscient viewpoint model is that you do not need to decide how many questions you are going to attempt. If you set a goal, you will inevitably rush to meet it. Let the test tell you how far you can get. In the preceding example, the test told you that you could do seven questions and get all of them correct. If you tried to do eight questions, you would have gotten only six correct, at most. If you choose what to work on next and give each question the time that it needs, you can be confident that you are using your time in the best way.

TWO STEPS TO PERFECT TIMING

1. Choose the next easiest passage to work on.
2. Give each question the time that it needs.

The strategy of choosing what to work on and giving it the time that it needs is effective even for people aiming for scores in the upper 170s. This strategy does not *require* you to skip certain questions. It simply allows you to do so if necessary. The strategy of giving each question the time that it needs helps ensure that you do not lose even one point through a careless error.

STRATEGY FOR RC AND AR SECTIONS

There are some general strategies for choosing what to work on that are successful for both RC and AR, in which each passage is followed by multiple questions. These strategies are expanded upon in the RC and AR chapters. (For choosing what to work on in LR sections, see Chapter 2.) Scan through the test section before you begin working on it to identify which passages seem to be the most difficult. This can be done in 20 seconds or less. These are the passages you will do last, if at all. Choose whole passages, not individual questions. Within a passage there are some easy questions and some hard questions. However, it would be far too difficult and time-consuming to pick only the easy questions from all of the passages. Doing so would force you to work on even the hardest passages. Choosing passages that are easier and then working on all of the questions in that passage seems to work better for most people. In both RC and AR, there is a general tendency for the first passage to be easier and the last harder, but there are many exceptions.

Once you have ranked the four sets in terms of difficulty, start with the easiest set, and work every question in it before going on to the next easiest set. As you continue, it is important not to put an expectation on how many questions you will be able to do. Let the test tell you how far you can get.

As you approach the end of the time for a section, avoid the pressure to rush. If you start a new set with limited time left, it is important to choose the easiest questions within that set. A common error is to try to get to all of the questions in the set before time is called. Inevitably, if you do this, you will get most of the questions wrong. There are no extra points awarded for finishing a set! Continue to work carefully and to give each question the time that it needs. Be prepared to leave a set unfinished. Of course you will put cold guesses down for any question that you do not actually work.

STRATEGY FOR ALL SECTIONS

What about giving each question the time that it needs? (This applies to LR, as well as RC and AR.) In our example of the omniscient viewpoint, you knew exactly what that time was. In reality, you do not. Obviously, spending ten minutes on a question is too long, even if you get it right. Spending only one minute is too short. Many questions cannot be answered in one minute. How long is acceptable to spend on a question?

Many people get an internal warning when they have spent more than a minute and a half on a question. This is probably based on college exams. For the LSAT, a cutoff of a minute and a half or two minutes is too short. The exact amount of time that will optimize your score varies among people. However, experience suggests that you should allow at least three minutes on hard questions and sometimes four or five. You will only have to do this on a handful of questions, but those are the very questions that will increase your score.

Here is another hypothetical model for understanding timing. It is not *literally* true but is a helpful approximation. On a particular test section there may be, for example, ten questions that you can get right in two minutes or less. The remaining questions cannot be gotten right in two minutes, no matter how hard you try. They require more time. If you limit yourself to two minutes per question, you will get your first ten right but every question after that will be wrong. This may sound unrealistic but in fact it is typical of timed sections for beginning LSAT students—twelve questions right and fourteen questions wrong. All of the time spent on those fourteen missed questions—possibly twenty minutes or more—was wasted. In fact, the test taker could have gotten three of them right by chance in thirty seconds of filling in answers. In reality you cannot know in advance which question may take more than two minutes. This model is helpful because it reminds you that if you do not give at least some questions extra time, you may not be able to increase your score, even if you work on many questions.

Assuming you are willing to spend some extra time on a question, how do you know when you have given a question the time that it needs? If you are getting close to four or five minutes and still have no inkling, guess and move on. However, if you guess and move on at two or three minutes, you will cheat yourself out of points. If necessary, rest your eyes for a few seconds, take a breath, and then do what it takes to be certain of your answer.

If you are spending three or four minutes on questions but still not getting them correct, you need to learn more patterns and strategies. Do this by reviewing the chapters and working untimed on practice questions.

Cold Guesses

There is no penalty for wrong answers on the LSAT, so put an answer down for all questions, including the ones on which you do not have time to work. On all sections of the test, stop when the monitor gives a five-minute warning and fill in all remaining bubbles. When you fill in bubbles, do not spend time looking at the questions. Some people are tempted to spend a few seconds trying to eliminate some answers on the questions for which they are putting a cold guess. This is not a good use of time. Either give a question the time that it needs to get it right or else fill in the bubble without looking at the question.

When filling in bubbles, choose one letter and stick with it. The odds for any of the five answer choices are virtually the same, although on some sections there may be a miniscule statistical advantage to D or E. Do not try to second-guess patterns of answers on the bubble sheet, such as whether there seem to be too few Cs, for example. Also, do not use a different letter for each answer in hopes of "shot gunning" your way to more answers. Stick with one letter.

After filling in the bubbles, there will be time left. Continue choosing questions and working on them until time is called. Working under such time pressure may seem hopeless but one more point can increase your scaled score, so make use of the last few seconds. Be ready to fill in the bubble for the final question the instant that the monitor announces the end of the section.

If the monitor calls time and you have not filled in the remaining bubbles, you must put your pencil down. When the next section begins, you *cannot* turn to the previous section but you can fill in unmarked bubbles on the answer sheet.

TIP

DON'T RUSH!

Let the test tell you how many questions you can do correctly.

Perfect Timing Strategy Versus Perfect Testing Strategy

If you choose the next easiest passage to work on and give each question the time that it needs, you might not get the score you were hoping for but you will get the best score that is possible for you that day. Your goal is to become 100 percent efficient, meaning that you get every question that you work on correct. This is, of course, an ideal toward which you can aim, even though in reality you might not achieve it. It is very important to realize that you cannot increase your score by going faster or trying to get to more questions. If you save time on a question but get it wrong, you have wasted all the time you spent on it.

Suppose that you achieve close to 100 percent accuracy in timing but are only scoring a 155 and you want to score 165. Going faster will not gain extra points but learning the patterns of the test more deeply and practicing the strategies for getting correct answers will improve your performance and increase your score.

Step 4: Evaluating Your Timing

To evaluate your timing, look at the questions on which you actually worked, as opposed to questions on which you guessed cold. If you answered any of the questions on which you worked incorrectly, check how much time you spent on the question. If you spent fewer than three or four minutes, you may have stopped too soon. If you got three, four, five, or more questions wrong (on which you worked), you may have been able to get more questions right by working on fewer questions and taking more time on the remaining questions.

Below is an example of how typical students might use their time before studying strategy. The example breaks down all the factors that help you improve your score. Notice how much improvement can be made by strategy alone!

TIP

THE POWER OF TIMING STRATEGY

It is theoretically possible to go from a score of 141 to a score of 160 just with better timing strategy!

TYPICAL PERFORMANCE AND POSSIBLE IMPROVEMENT

A test taker's first attempt at a timed section resulted in working on 22 of the 27 questions in a section and not working on the other 5. Of the 22 questions that the student actually worked on, 10 were correct and 12 incorrect. The student did not put cold guesses down for the 5 questions that were not worked. The student got a total of 10 questions right. Expanded to a full test, the score would be 141.

Table 1.3. First Attempt at Timing

27 Total Questions			SCORE	
ATTEMPTED 22		LEFT 5		
10 right	12 wrong	0 right	Total right = 10	Score = 141

In the next attempt, the student simply takes time to put guesses down for the five questions not worked on. By chance, the student would get one more point. This is enough, if applied to a full test, to move the score to 143.

Table 1.4. Results with Guesses Put Down for Unworked Questions

27 Total Questions			SCORE	
ATTEMPTED 22		LEFT 5		
10 right	12 wrong	1 right	Total right = 11	Score = 143

Below, the student *chooses* which 22 questions to work on instead of just doing the first 22. As a result, the 5 questions left are harder ones and some of the questions worked on are now easier. The student can now get 13 of 22 right. The total correct is now 14, for a scaled score of 151.

Table 1.5. Results with Choosing Which Passages to Work On

27 Total Questions			SCORE	
ATTEMPTED 22		LEFT 5		
13 right	9 wrong	1 right	Total right = 14	Score = 151

By adding these two strategies, the student's score has gone from 141 to 151. Now the student adds the strategy of taking more time on some of the 9 questions that were wrong. To do so requires cutting 6 of the 9 questions and using the time saved to get the other 3 correct. This means that the student works on 16 questions instead of 22 and leaves 11 questions instead of 5. The student still gets the original 13 correct, plus three more by spending more time. Because the student is guessing cold on 11 questions, instead of 5, the student will get one more correct answer by chance. The total correct is now 18, for a scaled score of 160. The student's best score comes from doing fewer questions but spending more time on them.

Table 1.6. Results When Some Questions
Are Sacrificed to Work Longer on Others

27 Total Questions			SCORE	
ATTEMPTED 16		LEFT 11		
16 right	0 wrong	2 right	Total right = 18	Score = 160

You can evaluate your timing strategy through the variables we just considered.

Notice that at first this student missed a lot of the questions that had been worked on. By the end, everything that was worked on was correct, even though fewer were attempted. One hundred percent of 16 is a higher score than 45 percent of 22!

Table 1.7. Higher Accuracy on Fewer Questions
Results in More Points

	Attempted	Right	Wrong	% right
1st attempt	22	10	12	45
2nd attempt	22	10	12	45
3rd attempt	22	13	9	59
4th attempt	16	16	0	100

WRITE DOWN YOUR TIME

Whether practicing timed or untimed, always write down the amount of time you spend on a question. Use the information to evaluate your timing as you prepare for the actual test.

Write down the time you spend on each question for both untimed and timed practice. Look at each question you got wrong. How much time did you spend on it? If you spent only one to three minutes, you are stopping too soon. For questions that you answer incorrectly, consider what strategy you could have used to get the question right. The more comfortable you are with your strategies, the more likely you will allow yourself the extra time to get an answer correct.

On your official LSAT you *should* keep track of time but you should *not* write down times. When you do a practice test, you *should* write down your times for *each* question so you can evaluate your timing strategy.

Applying Timing Strategy

A good timing strategy for the LSAT is very different from a timing strategy in an academic class. On the LSAT, you are *not* trying to beat the clock. The difference between getting your average score and getting your best score depends on how you perform on one, two, or three more difficult questions on each section. Getting those questions right requires taking extra time with them. How do you know which questions those will be? You can recognize them because they will feel difficult; you will feel frustrated with them; you will feel as though you do not know how to answer the question; and you will feel pressured to move on to another, easier question. These are the signs that the very question you are working on is the one that can push your score up!

When you run into such a question, check your watch. If you have only spent a minute or two, take more time. If you cannot answer the question after four minutes, make your best guess. There is no guarantee that by working on a tough question you will get it right. However, if you work on five such questions, you may get two or three right, which is enough to increase your scaled score. Working longer on some difficult questions may mean cutting four or five others. However, you will get one point by guessing cold on the questions you cut.

As paradoxical as it may seem, many test takers learn to forget about time for the three to five minutes that they might need on some questions. This allows them to feel more relaxed and to think more clearly. This approach has been described as creating a "timeless five-minute bubble" around each question. While you are in the bubble, you do not need to think about time. When you are finished with the question you are working on, you can move on to the next question and create a timeless bubble around it. Put in terms of neuropsychology, concern about time tends to lock the brain into detail thinking mode and, in this mode, it is difficult for the brain to effectively problem solve. Learning to work from a global (big-picture) perspective allows the brain to set aside thinking about time and problem solve creatively.

If Your Watch Is Not Allowed

Monitors have the final say in what is allowed in the testing room. There is a small chance that, even though your watch meets the requirements, a monitor may not allow it. If a polite discussion does not change the monitor's mind, use a backup plan. Your backup plan is to use the clock in the testing room to keep track of time for each question. This can be hard if the clock is behind you. Explain to the monitor what you will be doing so he or she knows you are not cheating.

To keep track of time for each question, write down the time when you start working on the question. To figure how much time you have spent, you have to look at the clock and compare the current time to the starting time.

Summary of Your Timing Strategy

1. Set your watch to 12 o'clock to keep track of time for the whole section.
2. For RC and AR sections, in about twenty seconds scan the whole section and rank the passages from easiest to hardest. For LR, apply the timing strategy taught in Chapter 2.
3. For RC and AR, go to the easiest passage first. Do all of the questions in that passage— even the ones that are difficult—before going on to the next passage. Skip the passages you had agreed to cut.
4. For LR, go to the first question that you choose to work on and give it the full time that it needs.
5. Each time you begin a question, set your watch to 12 o'clock. As you are working on the question, if you start feeling that it is taking too long, glance at the clock. If you have spent less than four minutes, take more time with the question. If you believe you have done everything possible, you can guess and move on, even if it is less than four minutes. However, if in doubt, always err on the side of spending more time. At five minutes, if you are not close to an answer, guess and move on.
6. You do not need to keep track of time used for reading or setting up a passage. You only keep track of time while you are working on a specific question.
7. For RC and AR, if there is enough time to start a new passage but not enough to finish it, do not read the setup. Skim the questions and look for any that can be answered with only a quick reference to the setup.

8. When the monitor gives the five-minute warning, fill in bubbles for everything on which you have not worked, without spending time trying to work the questions. You will get one in five right by chance.

9. Use the remaining time to keep working till the end. Even one more right answer could increase your score.

LSAT STRATEGY

Why Is Strategy Important?

Mastering the LSAT is primarily a matter of strategy. Strategy involves learning how the LSAT is put together—the hidden patterns and agendas—and learning tools for getting even the most difficult questions correct. The LSAT does not test factual knowledge in any area. All questions are answerable solely based on understanding what the LSAT writers are looking for and on having the tools to critically compare and contrast answer choices that seem potentially correct.

THE FUNDAMENTAL AGENDA OF THE LSAT

Most LSAT takers report that they can narrow answers down to two possibilities and then have difficulty finding the correct answer. Many test takers assume that the test writers think one answer is somehow better, more clever, or more elegant than the other answer. It may seem that the test writers simply like their answer better. None of these impressions is accurate. In reality, the LSAT is designed so that one answer is correct and the other answer that you are considering is dead wrong. A wrong answer is wrong because it has a fatal flaw. A correct answer is correct because it can be *proven* to be correct.

The fundamental agenda of the LSAT is that a correct answer must be defendable—in court, if necessary—by specific words in the passage. If a person were to sue LSAC over a credited answer, the writers of the LSAT would be able to point to specific words in the passage to prove that their answer was indeed correct. Similarly, the writers of the LSAT could point to the fatal flaw in your answer choice. As you begin to study the LSAT, you may not at first spot the information that defends a certain answer and you may not spot the fatal flaw in the wrong answers. Once you become more familiar with the test, you will find that the defenses and the fatal flaws are easier and easier to spot. The primary goal of this book is to help you learn exactly this, both through the instruction in the chapters and through the thorough explanations of each test question.

The exact nature of defenses and fatal flaws varies among the three section types. Each chapter teaches the strategies you need for that section of the LSAT.

Below are important strategies that apply to the LSAT in general. Detailed strategies for each section type are covered in the chapter for each section.

Do All the Questions in a Set

When working on a passage with multiple questions, in RC and AR, do all of the questions in the set, even if some are difficult. Even in easier passages, some questions are hard. If one question in a passage stumps you, go on to others in that passage. After you have worked the

> **LEARNING TO WORK QUICKLY WITH STRATEGIES**
>
> At first, new strategies can seem to take a lot of time. By giving yourself plenty of time to experiment with new strategies now, they will become second nature by the time you take your test, and you will be able to apply them quickly.

other questions, it may be easier to answer the harder one. It is not necessary to do questions within the passage in order. Do not go on to the next passage until you have worked on every question in the current passage. Do not plan to come back to a passage later to finish it.

When to Guess

For all section types, if, at five minutes, you are not close to an answer, put down your best guess. Do not leave it blank. In guessing, be careful not to choose an answer just because it "seems" good. You will probably be falling for a distractor.

What is a distractor? The test writers build at least one wrong answer choice into most questions that is designed to mislead you. This distractor may look better than the real answer for various reasons. It may just make sense. It may use wording from the passage that seems familiar. It may contain numbers or patterns that seem related to the passage. It may draw on emotionally charged issues (e.g., *C. Everyone should have affordable legal representation*).

Unless you have a clear reason to choose one answer over another when you are down to two, it is safer to use a rule of thumb. A good rule is to choose the answer that is lowest on the page. Then you have a true 50:50 chance of being right. If you look for an answer that "feels" better, you will pick the distractor.

It should be very rare that you have to guess. Only guess if (1) you have used your full four to five minutes, or (2) you have exhausted all of your strategies. Never guess just because the question is hard and you want to save time. You need to give each question the full amount of time that it requires.

TIP

TESTING STRATEGY

Do all the questions in a set before going on to the next set!

Use Your Eyes, Not Your Memory

Most test takers have a strong habit of reading the setup and a question and trying to work out the answer in their head, using their memory of what they read and their memory of what the question is asking. Your memory is not accurate enough to do a good job of this, especially during a long test.

Train yourself to continually look back at the printed information to get the facts you need. This takes a burden off of the processing functions of your memory. Sometimes people complain that they have to continually go back and forth between the questions and the passage, reminding themselves of what they have already read. In fact, this is the *best* way to process information accurately.

The minute you finish reading something and turn your eyes away, the memory of what you read begins to change. Details become blurred and the brain starts interpreting what it remembers. You can notice that you sometimes miss a question because you remembered information from the passage inaccurately.

After reading a question and considering the first answer choice, it is possible that you no longer remember accurately what the question was asking, especially if it is a complex

> ### DON'T TRUST YOUR MEMORY
>
> The LSAT overwhelms your ability to accurately remember what you have read. Go back and reread as often as necessary to make sure you have the facts correct.

question. Get in the habit of going back and briefly looking at the **question stem** (the statement of the question, not including the answer choices) again before going on to the next answer choice. The habit of relying on memory is a strong one and a difficult one to change. You may feel that answering the question from memory is faster or easier than going back and rereading again. It may be faster but it is also less accurate.

When reviewing a question you got wrong, look for signs that you remembered things inaccurately or did not go back and look for the facts. Notice if you misconstrued the question or the answer choice. These indicate a reliance on memory instead of real facts.

Orienting

Each LSAT question is based on certain information—either a long passage (RC), a short paragraph (LR), or a game setup (AR). It is important to orient yourself to this information. For each LSAT section there are specific ways to orient. Do not simply read the information superficially and then try to answer the questions. At the same time, a good orientation often means that you have not bogged down in reading too much detail. Orienting means letting the information "sink in."

Similarly, when you read a question stem, take time to orient to it. Ask yourself if you understand the question. Identify any confusion that you may have about the question. Consider what your strategy is going to be. Many errors are the result of not having oriented well to the passage and/or the question stem. Look for this error in your practicing and take more time to orient.

Use Visual Aids

This strategy is a corollary of "Use your eyes, not your memory." Memory is not very effective at keeping distinct categories separate, whereas a picture can compare and contrast two categories clearly. Much LSAT strategy depends on keeping two categories distinct, so using visual aids is a critical tool.

EXAMPLE

Consider the following confusing information about two vehicles owned by Maria. Her truck is red. She also has a Subaru. The Toyota has a camper top. Maria could sleep in the back of the Subaru if she sleeps sideways. The four-wheel drive is great for camping in the desert. The silver vehicle is cooler in the desert than the red one, even if it only has all-wheel drive. What Maria likes most about her oldest vehicle is that when she sleeps in it in the desert, which she does without being sideways, it has an air conditioner in case she needs it.

Answer this question without looking back. Does the four-wheel drive vehicle have air-conditioning? Even if you go back and review the words in the above paragraph, you will probably have to do a lot of mental work to keep the two categories—truck versus car—straight. Now let's look at how much clearer it is to organize this same information visually and graphically.

Use two columns to compare and contrast the two vehicles. A contrast between two categories is a fundamental pattern in the LSAT. The first sentence says the truck is red, so "truck" and "red" go in the same column.

truck	
red	

The next sentence shows that in contrast to "truck" and "red" there is "Subaru." This goes in the contrasting column. Notice that each line so far represents a certain quality. The first line represents body style. The line for Subaru represents make. This helps show what is known about each category. So far the body style and color of Subaru are not known.

truck	
red	
	Subaru

The next fact is "The Toyota has a camper top." Because "Toyota" cannot be "Subaru," this information goes in the first column.

truck	
red	
Toyota	Subaru
camper top	

The next fact tells us that it is possible to sleep in the Subaru, but only sideways.

truck	
red	
Toyota	Subaru
camper top	
	sleep only sideways

"The four-wheel drive is great for camping in the desert." This information is not related to anything else that is already known so far. Scan the rest of the facts for clues. The next sentence says that the silver vehicle is all-wheel drive. Because silver is not red, the sentence must refer to the second column. Because all-wheel drive is not four-wheel drive, four-wheel drive goes in the first column.

truck	
red	silver
Toyota	Subaru
camper top	
	sleep only sideways
four-wheel drive	all-wheel drive
great for camping in desert	cooler in desert

Does the last sentence provide anything new? "What Maria likes most about her oldest vehicle is that when she sleeps in it in the desert, which she does without being sideways, it has an air conditioner in case she needs it." Fill in the blank rows.

truck	
red	silver
Toyota	Subaru
camper top	
	sleep only sideways
four-wheel drive	all-wheel drive
great for camping in desert	cooler in desert

Using two-column visual organizer allows you to sort the information more reliably than doing it by memory. At the same time, a visual organizer allows you to compare and contrast information quickly and effortlessly. Can you now answer the question "Does the four-wheel drive vehicle have air conditioning?"

The visual aid also shows us what is not known. This is particularly helpful because memory tends to fill in blanks based on assumptions. Is the Subaru a sedan? You might have assumed so. You might have assumed it was not. The truth is that this information is unknown. The space in the second column that represents body type is blank. What else is unknown about the Subaru? The Toyota?

Whenever information needs to be compared or contrasted, use a visual aid, making use of the limited scratch space in your test booklet. Making columns is one of the most powerful organizing tools, but you can experiment with other ways of visually organizing information, such as using sketches and making circles to represent sets. If you make an error because you did not have the information organized well enough, do the problem again using visual aids.

Big-Picture Thinking Versus Detail Thinking

These are two distinct mental modes of processing information—detail thinking and big-picture thinking. These modes correspond roughly to left-brain and right-brain processing, respectively. Detail thinking is linear. It focuses narrowly on the problem and forges straight ahead, using calculations. Big-picture thinking is global and holistic. It does not focus on a goal but rather tries to see as much as possible. It steps back from the situation and looks at it freshly. For many people, the brain is not able to operate in these two modes at the same time.

Both of these processing styles are necessary for the LSAT. In fact, part of what the LSAT is testing is your ability to use these two styles at the appropriate times. Problem solving requires the ability to use both. Because the two modes typically cannot be used together, problem solving requires learning when to use each and how to switch between them.

Most people have a preference for one of these styles over the other. Even if you are naturally an intuitive thinker, you may find that because the LSAT involves logic, time pressure,

 TIP

A PICTURE REALLY IS WORTH A THOUSAND WORDS

Pictures are much better at keeping distinctions straight.

 TIP

LEFT BRAIN VS RIGHT BRAIN

Testing strategy teaches you how to use both for success.

and psychological pressure, you automatically switch into detail thinking. This may prevent you from using your greatest asset—the ability to do big-picture thinking.

Try to discover which of these modes comes most naturally to you. Notice when you are using big-picture thinking and when you are using detail thinking. Notice how you switch, or have difficulty switching, from one to the other.

ARE YOU STUCK IN DETAIL MODE?

One sign that you are stuck in detail mode is that you have failed to see the obvious. Consider this problem: Two pizzas are to be divided among seven people, while leaving a third of the total pizza for the next day. On the next day the remainder of the pizza is divided among five people but only after a quarter of the original amount is thrown away. How much is left? Suppose a test taker comes up with the answer of 2.17 pizzas. This person's detail thinking may have followed all of the details and come up with an answer. A big-picture perspective, however, indicates that there were only two pizzas to start with, so there cannot possibly be 2.17 pizzas left! There must have been a calculation error at some stage. Big-picture thinking is a reality check on detail thinking.

A person locked into detail thinking often speeds ahead and does not want to slow down, look around, or change directions. If you feel this way, try switching to big-picture thinking to make sure you are on the right track.

ARE YOU STUCK IN BIG-PICTURE MODE?

It is also possible to be stuck in big-picture mode. One sign of this is not having the focus to deal with details. The person stuck in big-picture mode has a general sense of the passage but would rather guess on a challenging question and move on than deal with having to crunch numbers, organize information, and problem solve. Many of the testing strategies presented in this introduction are good tools for helping you dig more deeply into the details.

THE BIG-PICTURE SANDWICH

How can you coordinate these two modes? Do not expect to use them at the same time. Most people find that this is not possible. You can, however, switch between them. One powerful tool for doing this is the big-picture sandwich. Start each problem from a big-picture perspective. Understand what you are dealing with and organize your plan of attack. Then switch to detail thinking to analyze the data. Finally, before leaving the problem, switch back to big-picture thinking to make sure your answer makes sense. During the process of solving the problem, you may also need to switch back and forth several times.

Consider this more closely. When orienting to a passage or question, use the big picture to see if you understand the situation, to see where there is some confusion, to consider what the plan of attack should be, and to organize the information. These are orienting steps. Then switch to detail mode, comparing facts, doing calculations, and reorganizing information. (If you get to a dead end or lose track of what you are doing, you can temporarily switch back to big-picture mode.) When you have solved the problem, switch back to big-picture mode to see if your answer makes sense. Big-picture mode allows you to monitor how confident you are in the answer. If your confidence is low, you are not done.

TIP

DETAIL THINKING

Good at cranking out details.

Bad at remembering why.

TIP

BIG-PICTURE THINKING

Good at planning.

Bad at doing the detail work.

THE BIG-PICTURE SANDWICH

Start with the big picture.

Deal with the details.

Double-check using the big picture.

Using the big-picture sandwich teaches your left brain and right brain how to work hand in hand.

CONFIDENCE LEVEL

When you decide on a correct answer, you always have some sense of how confident you are in your answer, even if you are not consciously aware of that sense. As you come back to the big picture at the end of a question, monitor your confidence level. If you are not confident in your answer, you are not yet done with the question! One of the most common causes of wrong answers is ignoring your lack of confidence in the answer and moving on. To look at it the other way around, one of the most powerful tools you can use to pick up a point that you would otherwise have lost is to notice that your confidence level is low and to continue working on the problem.

Sometimes your confidence in your answer is low but you have eliminated all of the other answers. If you cannot defend your answer with confidence, that answer cannot be correct. In such cases, you have most likely already eliminated the correct answer and are left with two answers, neither of which is correct. By starting from scratch, you can win back an extra point.

Your Plan of Attack

On a typical question you will orient yourself to the information and then you will read the question stem and orient yourself to it. At this point, rather than simply diving into the answer choices, take a moment to strategize. Consider what your plan of attack is going to be. In some cases you need to go back to the passage to review information. In other cases you need to refresh your memory as to the main idea of a passage. Some problems require you to sketch out logical arguments. In some cases you will evaluate the answer choices in order and in other cases you will not. Taking a moment to consider your plan of attack is an orienting step. Do this after you have oriented to the question stem but before you start going through answer choices.

The Generic Way to Answer a Question

Use a systematic approach on every question. Many people simply read through a question quickly and then look at the first answer choice. This is not necessarily the best way to problem solve. Here is how the process can be broken down and made more systematic. The systematic process described below applies to the RC and LR sections of the test. The AR section has its own systematic approach, described in depth in Chapter 4.

> **HOW TO ANSWER A QUESTION**
>
> **STEP 1** Orient yourself to the question.
> **STEP 2** Decide on a plan of attack.
> **STEP 3** First pass through the answers. Quickly eliminate answers that are clearly wrong.
> **STEP 4** Second pass through the remaining answers. Carefully and thoroughly apply strategies.

STEP 1. ORIENT TO THE QUESTION STEM

After you have oriented yourself to the passage, read the question stem carefully, without yet looking at the answer choices, and orient to it. Is there anything confusing or ambiguous about it? Is it clear what the question is looking for? It is sometimes helpful to take a moment to mentally picture the situation that the question deals with. Many people feel that they should get through the question quickly in order to get to the "important" part—the answer choices. In fact, taking the time to be well oriented to the question can help you avoid many errors.

STEP 2. PLAN OF ATTACK

Consider how to start working on the question. Do not simply start reading choice A. There is often a better way to start. Sometimes it is best to go back to the setup and clarify concepts and facts. Often it is helpful to create a sketch, or organize the information graphically. Sometimes there is specific information stated in the passage that will determine the answer. Find this first before looking at the answer choices.

STEP 3. FIRST PASS THROUGH THE ANSWERS—PROCESS OF ELIMINATION

After completing Step 2, make a first pass through the answer choices, eliminating only those answers that are clearly out. You are learning strategies that will allow you to evaluate answers in depth, but do not use those in-depth strategies during this pass. In-depth strategies require extra time. You might, for example, spend a lot of time carefully evaluating answer choices A through D, only to find that answer choice E is obviously the right one. The time spent on A, B, C, and D would have been wasted. The first pass gives you a quick overview of the answer choices. Save in-depth analysis for the second pass.

Be conservative about eliminating answer choices at this point. Only eliminate answer choices that are clearly out. If there is any uncertainty, leave the answer in until the second pass. Answers can often be categorized as going in the right direction or the wrong direction. For example, if a question asks what would be true about Einstein, then the answer choice "He never came up with any original ideas" goes in the wrong direction. The statement "He was very smart" would go in the right direction but still might not be the correct answer because of other factors. Answers that go in the wrong direction are clearly out.

STEP 4. SECOND PASS WITH IN-DEPTH ANALYSIS

For the remaining answer choices, use your strategies to determine the correct answer. There may only be two choices left at this point or there may be more. For each type of LSAT section there are many specific strategies that you can use to compare and contrast two answer choices. For AR questions, you will learn a complete system of logic that allows you to accurately find the correct answer. For RC and LR, the most powerful way to apply your strategies is through the **adversarial approach**, described below.

Use the two-pass approach on all RC and LR questions. For instructional purposes, the explanations of RC and LR questions in this book do not usually go through a two-step process but rather focus on the essential problem-solving strategies that you would use in either the first or second pass.

MARKING ANSWER CHOICES

As you work through the answer choices in your two passes, use marks to indicate which answer choices are out, which ones are in but are weak options, and which answer choices are likely. Draw a line through the letter of answer choices that are out, use plusses or double plusses, and question marks, as shown below:

Once you have determined a correct answer, circle it, as with answer choice E, and then write the letter of the correct answer next to the question number. This helps you be accurate as you transfer answers to the bubble sheet.

(E) 17. ... clearly been an accurate observer of human behavior.

Which one of the following statements best represents the main conclusion of the argument?

(A) Dr. Manning is probably better adjusted emotionally than most people.

(B) Too much emotional discomfort can be harmful in the long run.

(C) Dr. Manning's claim fails to consider that painful emotional experience may have results that negatively affect our lives.

(D) A highly traumatic experience would make a person emotionally stronger than a mildly uncomfortable experience.

++ (E) Dr. Manning's claim is valid.

Figure 1. Examples of marks for answer choices.

The Adversarial Approach—The Secret Weapon for Finding the One Correct Answer

There are probably five, ten, fifteen, or more questions that you are getting wrong now but which you can get right with good strategy. These are the questions that will raise your score. These questions probably all have one thing in common. You get down to two possible answers but then choose the wrong one.

The adversarial approach is the most powerful tool for finding which of two answers is correct, particularly on the RC and LR sections. Here is how the strategy works.

When there are two answers left, most people like one answer better than the other and, at first, simply pick the answer that they like. When it becomes clear that they are often wrong, test takers begin to look more carefully at the two answers, comparing them and trying a little harder to evaluate them. When you find yourself doing this, notice that there is still a bias toward the answer that you liked in the first place. This bias often prevents you from being objective, so, despite your effort, you still get many wrong answers.

Even when you want to be more objective, it is difficult to do so. The power of our biases cannot easily be overcome. It takes a specific, active strategy to achieve objectivity. The strategy for this—the adversarial approach—is drawn from the American legal system.

> **THE ADVERSARIAL APPROACH**
>
> To overcome your own blind spots, defend to the death the answer you don't like and attack to the death the answer that you do like.

In some legal systems, one attorney argues both sides of a case before the judge. It is that attorney's responsibility to understand both sides, evaluate them, and present a balanced perspective. In America, an adversarial system is used. Each side is represented by its own attorney. Each attorney focuses only on his or her perspective—either attacking or defending a position. By eliminating the constraint of being balanced, the system allows each side to aggressively pursue one point of view. It is then the judge's responsibility to synthesize both sides. In theory, the adversarial system results in a clearer picture of each side of the issue.

How does this apply to RC and LR? Suppose that you have eliminated choices B, C, and E. Choice A seems strong to you. Choice D seems unlikely. You can now apply the four steps of the adversarial approach. They do not have to be applied in a specific order.

(STEP 1) Attack the answer you like.

(STEP 2) Defend the answer you do not like.

(STEP 3) Defend the answer you like.

(STEP 4) Attack the answer you do not like.

Step 1 requires you to attack choice A, but choice A is the answer choice that you like. Similarly, Step 2 requires you to defend choice D, but you do not really believe that choice D is correct. Steps 1 and 2 are the most counterintuitive, but this also makes them the most powerful. If you can conscientiously attack the answer choice that you like and conscientiously defend the answer choice that you do not like, you will see the aspects of the issue that you missed before. It may or may not turn out that you were correct in the first place.

In Steps 3 and 4 you justify your original bias, which may turn out to be correct. However, you now do so in more depth. As you try to prove that choice A is correct, you may discover that it is difficult to do so. As you try to prove that choice D is incorrect, you may discover some merits to it. These steps, then, are also valuable. However, the most powerful aspect of the adversarial approach is in reversing your mental bias so that you can see what before was hidden by your blind spots.

It is not easy to reverse your bias. There is a strong tendency to slip back into defending the choice that you like and attacking the choice that you do not like. It may help to imagine that you are an attorney who will be paid a million dollars if you can prove that someone is innocent. You may deeply believe that the person is guilty but you have a strong incentive to prove him or her innocent. You may have to dig very deeply to find any basis for a defense but that is exactly what your job is.

One unexpected obstacle to effectively using the adversarial approach is the possibility of falling into a neutral position. Neutrality may sound "fair" but in this case it is not effective. If you try to see both the pros and cons of an answer choice, you will miss the extremes. To pursue the analogy above, you must leave "fairness" to the judge, whose role you will take on only after you have presented the extremes. Your first job is to be extreme.

By focusing all your attention on finding the defense for an answer, you see elements that you could not have seen before. The same holds true for the attack. By doing all four steps, you have the best chance of seeing all the points. As you apply this approach, you are not yet in the judge's position of weighing the pros and cons. That will come at the end. The most common error in applying the adversarial approach is falling back into the judge's position too soon, and therefore failing to attack from the extreme standpoint and defend from the extreme standpoint. If you continue to get wrong answers, work harder at attacking and defending from the extremes.

Ambiguity

Sometimes the wording in a question or answer choice is confusing. The wording may have two different interpretations.

EXAMPLE

You are responsible for collecting research information from three hospitals, two clinics, and five universities. Each institution must have its own unique data collection form.

Do you see the ambiguity? Are there three institutions or ten? It is important to identify ambiguity or confusion if it exists. Many people are resistant to feeling confused. They may hope they will catch on later. In fact, it is very helpful to notice confusing wording, identify why it is confusing, and then find a way to resolve the confusion.

In the above example, does creating a unique form for each institution require making ten forms or three forms? The word *institution* is ambiguous. "Hospital" could be an example of one institution. Alternatively, the sentence could mean that Hospital A is one institution and Hospital B is another. How is the test taker supposed to know the correct interpretation?

The LSAT cannot contain a question that is truly ambiguous. There must be some evidence that shows which interpretation is intended. To deal with an ambiguity, first identify the two interpretations. Then ask which interpretation would be defendable based on the information given in the test.

Consider the rest of this passage.

EXAMPLE

Data must be collected within a week of the time it is compiled and must be delivered directly to the office of the research coordinator. Each of the ten institutions is responsible for double-checking the accuracy of its form. You are responsible for getting the signature of the head of staff at each hospital and clinic, but the universities do not need to have their forms signed.

The phrase "each of the ten institutions" defines how the word *institution* is being used.

The Default Multiple-Choice Question

A common cause of errors is misinterpreting the question stem. You may have understood the question stem when you started working on the question, but as you proceed, your brain can easily drift from what the question stem actually said to what can be called the default multiple-choice question.

Find the correct answer to the following:

(A) The moon is made of green cheese.

(B) Three plus five is nine.

(C) Earth revolves around the Sun.

(D) Spinach is delicious.

(E) All lawyers make more money than any doctors.

Most likely you chose answer choice C. What question were you answering? The default multiple-choice question is "Which answer choice is true in the real world?" Sometimes an LSAT question asks this but often LSAT questions are *not* asking the default question. As you orient to a question stem, ask yourself whether it is asking for a fact that is true or for something else. If it is asking for something else, be on guard not to slip into the default question.

Working Backward from Answer Choices

This is similar to the adversarial approach but not quite as rigorous. Test an answer choice by temporarily assuming it is correct. Would that result in any contradictions? Would the answer fit the information in the passage? Testing an answer choice can help you see things about it that you would not see otherwise.

Answers That Seem Too Easy

Some people eliminate an answer choice because it seems too easy or obvious. However, if the answer choice is defendable, it must be the correct answer. There *are* easy questions on the test.

The Voices in a Passage

RC and LR passages reflect the attitude and opinions of the author of the passage but they may also refer to the attitudes of other parties. The emotional and logical stance of a person is referred to as the person's voice. For example, if an author is excited about a new theory and feels that all of the evidence supports that theory, there will be wording in the passage that reflects these emotions and beliefs on the part of the author. If the author then quotes from a scientist who feels negatively about the new theory, then the scientist's voice is different from the author's. Some RC and LR questions require you to distinguish the voices in a passage.

Put Cold-Guess Answers for Any Question That You Do Not Work

As described earlier under Timing, there is no penalty for wrong answers, so fill in a bubble for each question, including ones that you do not have time to work.

Filling in Bubbles

When you fill in bubbles for questions that you *have* worked on, you can use one of several approaches. The approach you choose should be the one that prevents you from mistakenly filling in a wrong bubble.

Some people have to fill in the bubble immediately after getting an answer. This lowers the chances that you will fill in the wrong bubble, because you only have to keep one letter in mind. On the other hand, it is more time-consuming because you have to go back and forth between the test booklet and the answer sheet many times.

On the other extreme, some people transfer all of their answers to the bubble sheet toward the end of the time for the section. This has the advantage of only going from the test booklet to the answer sheet once. It has the disadvantage that transferring so many answers at a time may lead to inaccuracy.

A middle ground is to do a certain number of questions, such as those on one or two pages, and then transfer answers. If you find yourself filling in the wrong bubble, transfer your answers more frequently.

TIP

TESTING ANSWER CHOICES

Let the answer choices work for you. Testing out answers gives you valuable information.

If, on your actual LSAT, you find that you have transferred a block of answers incorrectly—in other words all of your answers are one or two lines off of where they should be—you have some options. If there are only a small number of answers involved, you may need to take the time to thoroughly erase your original answers and reenter them on the correct line. If you need to do this, it will be important that you have written the letter of the correct answer next to the question number in your test booklet.

If there are so many answers off that taking the time to correct them would hurt your score, you can ask to have your answer sheet hand scored. If possible, make a note on the answer sheet to indicate where the numbers got off and where you got back on the correct numbers. As soon as the section is over, raise your hand to inform the monitor. The monitor may not respond to you until the end of that half of the test day, namely, at the break or at the end of the day. Let the monitor know what happened and that you would like to have your answer sheet hand scored. There have been cases in which the monitor has allowed a test taker to correct the bubbling right then, though you should not expect this. If your bubbling error is so severe that the sheet cannot be adequately hand scored, it may significantly lower your score. You may then need to retake the test, and you should inform the schools to which you are applying about the reason for your low score.

Always Look at All of the Answers

One of the most common causes of wrong answers is choosing an answer that looks good without having considered all of the answers. Even if you are confident in an answer, you should at least quickly look at the remaining answers. Otherwise, you may fall for a distractor. This is one of the most important strategies for avoiding errors. Train yourself to do this on every single question.

Questions with EXCEPT and LEAST

Questions that use the words "EXCEPT" or "LEAST" are logically complex. Consider the question "All of the following are brown EXCEPT . . ." Your attention will focus on the quality of being brown but the correct answer is something that is not brown. It is easy to get confused and choose something brown. When an LSAT question asks for an exception—for the opposite of what the test taker would normally look for—the word EXCEPT or LEAST is capitalized to draw your attention to it.

Orient to exception questions by reminding yourself that you are looking for four of whatever is expected, such as four brown things in the example above, and that these four are the wrong answers. The correct answer will be whatever is remaining when you identify the four (incorrect) brown answers. You can hold out four fingers to remind yourself. Use this strategy in conjunction with going back and skimming the question stem before looking at each answer choice. Notice if you have a tendency to stumble on exception questions.

Consider a question that asks "All of the following are good EXCEPT . . ." You might think that the correct answer must be something that is bad but this is not necessarily true. Four of the answer choices are good but the remaining choice may be neutral. The exception is not necessarily the opposite of the quality that defines the four other answer choices. It may just be the absence of that quality.

TIP

ALWAYS LOOK AT ALL OF THE ANSWERS

Always.
Every time.
It pays off.

"DON'T LOOK AT THAT ELEPHANT" QUESTIONS

Questions with EXCEPT or LEAST point you away from what you would normally focus on. Be prepared!

Stamina

The LSAT is a very long test. There is no question that you will get tired and that your brain will not be at its optimum at all times during the test. There are some simple things that you can do to maximize your endurance during the test.

Intense brain activity consumes oxygen. Combined with sitting still for hours, your brain will become oxygen-deprived. When you feel tired and your thinking is foggy, you can stretch and flex your arms and legs and yawn and breathe deeply. During the test you need to be moderately unobtrusive about this but frequent mild stretching and deep breathing will help you think more clearly.

Your eyes will also become overworked in the test. The eyes are involved not only in seeing what is on the page but in mental processing as well. When you have trouble focusing your attention, try closing your eyes, blinking them rapidly, or covering them with the cupped palms of your hand. Shifting your focus to a point in the far distance also can relax the eye muscles.

When you are tired, you may be more bothered by distractions. You should assume that you will have distractions during your test day and be prepared for them. It may help you practice for distractions by occasionally working on questions in a noisy or distracting environment.

An often unrecognized symptom of physical and neurological fatigue is an emotional one. Some people, partway through the test, start to feel discouraged. They may find themselves thinking "I don't care about this any more. I'm probably not supposed to go to law school anyway, so just please let this be over so I can go home and eat chocolate." If you start to have negative, discouraged thoughts, recognize it as a sign of fatigue. Stretch, flex, breathe deeply, blink your eyes, and keep going. It may help to tell yourself, "Of course, I'm supposed to go to law school. Get with it!"

During the week before your test, simulate the schedule of the test day. Keep a note card with approximate times of day that each section will start and finish, along with break times. No matter what you are doing—working, shopping, going to class, or actually working on the test—during the time that will be devoted to a test section on your actual test day, do not eat, drink, or use the bathroom. If you find that you have trouble following that schedule, such as needing to use the bathroom, getting hungry, or having low blood sugar, adjust your eating and drinking patterns.

Identify any areas of anxiety that you have, such as a fear of not finding the test center, of not waking up on time, or of not getting the score you need, and come up with a backup plan for each concern. Dealing with these concerns in advance may help you get a good night's sleep before your test.

Analyzing Your Testing Strategy

After completing a section, either timed or untimed, go over each wrong answer to determine which strategies you could have used to avoid the error. On the following pages is a list of possible errors to which you can refer, along with a worksheet for keeping track of your errors.

If you get a question wrong, look at it carefully. Although some errors may strike you as "careless," errors are usually not because of carelessness. They are the result of incorrect timing or testing strategy. Every error gives you a chance to learn how to approach the test more effectively. Use the checklist on page 130 to review the causes of errors. As you review an error, go back to the chapters in this book and look for the information that would help avoid that particular error.

TIP

THE KEY TO GOOD TIMING

Always analyze your timed test sections carefully to see how you could have improved timing and strategy.

LIST OF REASONS FOR ERRORS

1. **DID NOT USE BIG PICTURE.** Got lost in details. Did not step back to see the big picture. Missed obvious information because focus was too narrow.

2. **TIME PRESSURE.** Not careful enough because of feeling rushed to get on to other questions. Tried to do too many questions.

3. **COULD NOT ORGANIZE INFORMATION.** Confused by complex details, facts, and concepts. Lacked tools to organize the information. Got lost partway through. Did not use visual aids—drawing, charts, columns—when needed. Did not create a systematic road map of how to solve the problem.

4. **ELIMINATED THE CORRECT ANSWER.** Crossed out the correct answer.

5. **MISREAD QUESTION OR FACTS.** Misinterpreted part of the question or information. Did not apply strategy for ambiguous questions. Did not orient to the question. Read something into the problem or made an unwarranted assumption.

6. **SPENT LESS THAN THREE MINUTES.** Chose a wrong answer on a question that could have been gotten right with more time. Did not keep track of time. Felt hesitant to spend four or five minutes.

7. **REMEMBERED SOMETHING INACCURATELY.** Did not double-check the facts. Used memory instead of eyes. Rushed.

8. **THOUGHT YOU HAD IT RIGHT.** Did not take an extra moment to see if you missed anything. Did not challenge your answer or defend other answer choices.

9. **DID NOT READ ALL ANSWER CHOICES.** Chose an answer without using the other answers as a double check. Tried to save time by not reading all answer choices.

10. **DID NOT CHECK YOUR CONFIDENCE LEVEL.** Did not notice that you were not confident about the answer. Unsure of answer but did not want to take more time. Did not use double checking or big picture to increase confidence. Chose an answer you did not like because all of the others seemed wrong. Did not go back and start from scratch with all answer choices.

11. **DID NOT KNOW WHAT STRATEGIES TO USE ON QUESTION.** Did not step back to see the big picture. Did not use diagram to organize the information. Did not use the adversarial approach. Did not work backward from answer choices. Did not use imagination or intuition to get new insights into the problem. Did not check whether some answers were too big or too small.

12. **GOT UNCOMFORTABLE OR ANXIOUS AND QUIT QUESTION TOO SOON.** Let physical/psychological discomfort level dictate your timing strategy instead of controlling time yourself. Did not use the tension between two answers to help you analyze more deeply (adversarial approach.)

13. **FELL FOR A DISTRACTOR.** Chose an answer that felt right or that seemed good for a vague reason. Did not use the adversarial approach. Did not give the question enough time. When guessing, tried to justify one answer instead of using a random rule of thumb.

14. **PICKED RIGHT ANSWER BUT PUT WRONG LETTER.** Do not yet have perfect strategy for transferring answers to the bubble sheet.

15. **GOT DOWN TO TWO ANSWERS AND PICKED WRONG ONE.** Did not use the adversarial approach. Tried the adversarial approach but did not argue all the way to the end. Not able to turn energy of frustration into energy for analysis. Did not give the question a

full four to five minutes. Did not use estimation. Did not focus on what the difference was between the two answer choices.

16. **DID NOT USE PROCESS OF ELIMINATION.** Could have gotten closer to an answer by eliminating the wrong answer choices.

17. **MISTAKE ON GAME SETUP.** Misinterpreted or missed game conditions, other than if/thens.

18. **IF/THEN ERRORS.** Incorrectly interpreted if/then conditions.

19. **MADE LOGIC ERRORS ON AR.** Was not accurate in diagramming options.

20. **COULD NOT RESOLVE AN AMBIGUITY.** Did not identify the two (or more) possible interpretations and ask which interpretation was defendable.

21. **DID NOT GET THE MAIN IDEA.** Did not analyze the setup clearly enough for the big picture. Did not find the main dichotomies. Got too bogged down in detail. Not enough practice scanning for structure. Thrown off by a difficult topic.

22. **MISSED AUTHOR'S TONE QUESTION.** Did not see answers in terms of continuum.

23. **OTHER.** Describe.

Analysis of Wrong Answers

Use a worksheet like this to evaluate your wrong answers every time you do a test section. For each question you got wrong, put down the time you spent on it and the reasons you got it wrong. Choose your reason from the master list of reasons. If you choose "other," explain. For each error, review the strategy for avoiding that error. You do not need to include questions on which you guessed cold.

> ### SUMMARY
>
> This chapter described how to practice and the four steps of a good timing strategy—knowing the test layout, keeping track of time, understanding timing for each section, and evaluating your timing. The chapter reviewed twenty specific strategies for the LSAT and described how to analyze your errors.

Note: This page may be photocopied.

ANALYSIS OF ERRORS

Example: Q #15   Time: 3:30   Reason: Eliminated correct answer. Time pressure

Test # _____   **Section:** _____

Q # _____   Time: _____   Reason: _____

Q # _____   Time: _____   Reason: _____

Q # _____   Time: _____   Reason: _____

Q # _____   Time: _____   Reason: _____

Q # _____   Time: _____   Reason: _____

Q # _____   Time: _____   Reason: _____

Q # _____   Time: _____   Reason: _____

Q # _____   Time: _____   Reason: _____

Q # _____   Time: _____   Reason: _____

Q # _____   Time: _____   Reason: _____

Q # _____   Time: _____   Reason: _____

Q # _____   Time: _____   Reason: _____

Q # _____   Time: _____   Reason: _____

Q # _____   Time: _____   Reason: _____

Q # _____   Time: _____   Reason: _____

Q # _____   Time: _____   Reason: _____

Q # _____   Time: _____   Reason: _____

Q # _____   Time: _____   Reason: _____

Q # _____   Time: _____   Reason: _____

Q # _____   Time: _____   Reason: _____

Q # _____   Time: _____   Reason: _____

Q # _____   Time: _____   Reason: _____

Q # _____   Time: _____   Reason: _____

Q # _____   Time: _____   Reason: _____

Logical Reasoning $\quad$ 2

The Logical Reasoning (LR) chapter teaches you the skills that you need to quickly and accurately answer LR questions. You will learn all of the elements listed above. This chapter includes breakdowns of sample LR passages and questions with complete explanations, so that you can put into practice the information that you learn in the chapter. At the end of the chapter is a practice LR section with complete explanations of answers.

Some tables in this chapter have complex breakdowns of important LR patterns. These tables are reference tools. It is not necessary to memorize them. Glance through them now. Return to them as you work on questions.

Read through the chapter carefully now. Then, as you work on questions, come back to the chapter to review the applicable strategies and patterns.

INTRODUCTION TO LOGICAL REASONING

There are two scored LR sections on every LSAT. If you get a third LR section, one of the three is an unscored, experimental section. There is no way to know which of the three is unscored. Do your best on all three. An LR section typically consists of twenty-five or twenty-six **passages**. Older practice tests may have sections with twenty-four.

Each passage begins with the **setup**, usually a short paragraph or a short dialogue between two people. The setup is followed by one **question stem**—a sentence that states the question. This is followed by five **answer choices**, labeled A through E (See Figure 2.1). Older tests may have setups followed by two question stems.

Frank: Anyone who does not like fruit must not like people either.
Shannon: You are wrong. I like fruit but I do not like people.
Therefore, people who do not like fruit, do like people.

Frank's and Shannon's statements provide the most support for the
claim that they disagree over the truth of which one of the following?

(A) People who do not like people also do not like fruit.
(B) People who do not like people do like fruit.
(C) People who like people also like fruit.
(D) People who like fruit may like people.
(E) People who do not like fruit like people.

Figure 2.1. Anatomy of an LR passage

The subject matter for the setup comes from a wide range of areas. Certain unusual topic areas appear with an unexpected frequency, such as "traffic" and "city council/municipal issues." A list of major topic headings is found in Table 2.1:

Table 2.1. Major Topics That Appear in LR Setups
and Their Relative Frequency

	Percent of LR Setups in Which Each Topic Appears
Physical Science (animals, anthropology, archaeology, astronomy, biology, ecology, garden/botany, geology, paleontology, physics/chemistry, weather)	21
Health (diet, food, health, medicine)	16
Social Science (ethics, history, philosophy, political science, psychology, sociology)	15
Business/Government (business, city council/municipal issues, employees) NOTE: city council/municipal = 5%; other business/government topics = 9%	14
Arts (art, literature, music, performing arts)	7
Transportation (aircraft, traffic, transportation)	7
Technology (technology)	5
Legal (legal)	4
Education (education)	4
Journalism (journalism, media)	3

To master LR, you need to learn four skills:

1. Understand the structure of logical arguments.
2. Understand the types of questions that the stems ask.
3. Understand the types of arguments that LR tests.
4. Master the strategies for determining exactly why one answer is correct and the other answers are incorrect.

TIMING STRATEGY

A strong LR timing strategy helps you (1) gain points by working efficiently, (2) avoid errors caused by working too quickly, and (3) reduce anxiety.

Adapting Timing Strategy to the Logical Reasoning

Review the general timing strategy described in the General Strategies chapter (Chapter 1). The timing strategy for LR is a little more complex than for RC and AR. Because LR is not divided into four passages, you cannot simply choose certain passages. Instead you must choose on which of the twenty-five or twenty-six questions to work.

To control your time on the LR, make two passes through the section. When timing begins, start on the first page and go through to the end of the section *choosing only a modest number of questions on which to work* (deciding the exact number is described below). You will pick a small number of the easiest questions and you will skip the rest. By the time you have finished this first pass, you have seen every page of the section, done the easiest questions, and left the hardest. Then, on your second pass through the section, go back to the first page of the section and pick the next easiest of the remaining questions, going page by page until the five-minute warning. At that time, you will put a cold guess down (choose one letter and fill in the bubble for that letter) for every question that is left and then continue working on a problem until time is called.

When you choose which question to work on or to skip, do so at a glance, using only a few seconds. When you fill in cold guesses for questions on which you have not worked, do not take time to look at the question or to try to eliminate answers. For each question, either work it thoroughly or fill in a bubble randomly.

How many questions should you work on in your first pass? How do you choose which questions to work on? Consider Sheila, a fictitious but otherwise typical prelaw student. Sheila usually scores from ten to fifteen questions correct on a timed LR section. She has never gotten fewer than ten questions correct under timed conditions. Sheila sets a **target** of eight questions for her first pass. Sheila's target is low enough that even on the most difficult LR section, and even when she is having a bad day, she can still get her target of eight questions. This allows her to work in a relaxed and careful way during her first pass.

When the timing for an LR section begins, Sheila starts with the first page. Because there are usually eight pages on the LR section, Sheila plans to work on an average of one question per page during her first pass. Sheila quickly scans the first page and chooses one question that seems relatively easy.

There is no guarantee that Sheila has in fact chosen the easiest question. She chooses at a glance and it is possible that the question may be harder than she thought. With practice, Sheila will be more accurate at finding easy questions.

When Sheila finishes with her first question, she turns the page and is looking at pages 2 and 3. She picks the two easiest questions on these pages. They may be on the same page. She keeps up her average pace of one question per page. Sheila knows that the first five questions of an LR section are typically easier than questions at the end. She may choose some extra questions from the first three pages. She also knows that the last five questions are usually the hardest. She may not choose any from the last five. By her eighth question, she has looked at every page of the section. She knows she has made an effort to work the easiest questions and avoid the hardest ones.

After her first pass, Sheila has time remaining, because she chose a low enough target number. She goes back to the first page, choosing the next easiest question, and continues page to page choosing the best question to work on. When the monitor gives the five-minute warning, Sheila fills in choice D on the bubble sheet for each question that she has not answered. Then she goes back to the test and keeps working. Using the last minutes well may raise her score.

When Sheila starts her second pass, she does not have any preconceived idea of how many more questions she will do. If the section is difficult and/or if she is having a slow day, she may only get to a few more questions. If the section is easy and/or she is having a great day, she may get to many more questions. Sheila lets the test and the testing conditions tell her how far she can get. If she rushes to get more questions, she gets many wrong and lowers her score.

If, as Sheila practices, she improves and is always getting at least fifteen questions right, she will change her target. Making her target twelve, instead of eight, allows her to choose one question from one page and two from the next, one from the third, and two from the fourth, and so on. It is not important exactly how many she does per page. She simply needs a simple plan for working on twelve questions during her first round.

Sheila may eventually be able to answer twenty or more questions correctly. Choosing twenty questions during her first pass is cumbersome. Instead, she changes her strategy. She will *cut* one question per page during the first pass, for a total of about eight questions. This guarantees that she can work in a relaxed way during the first pass. During her second pass, she goes back to the eight questions that she cut and chooses one more on which to work. Once she has carefully solved that question, she chooses another.

People who are untrained in timing typically start at the beginning and work every question in order until time is called. They are working on many difficult problems and leaving many easy ones. In theory, by making two passes, you choose the easiest, and leave the hardest, questions. In practice, you may end up working some hard questions and leaving some easy ones, but you will have greatly improved your efficiency.

Even though, statistically, the questions start out easier and become harder, it is not a good idea to simply start at the beginning and work questions in order. There are many difficult questions toward the beginning and many easy questions later. Get your best score by choosing for yourself.

How Much Time Should You Spend on Each Question?

Another difference between Sheila and untrained test takers is that untrained test takers rarely spend more than a minute and a half on a question. They rush to get to all of the questions and, as a result, get many questions wrong. Sheila has learned that, even though the average time she spends on a question is about a minute, she can increase her score by spending more time on a handful of more difficult questions, thus getting them right.

How you make decisions about the amount of time you spend on a question is probably the most important part of your timing strategy. Carefully review the general instructions on timing strategy in the "General Strategies" chapter (Chapter 1). Beware of the "average time per question" trap! Many people calculate that, for thirty-five minutes and twenty-five questions, there is a minute and a half per question, and they then allow themselves only that much time. This approach is based on several erroneous assumptions. One such assumption is that you are going to attempt every question in the section. For over 90 percent of LSAT takers, that is not the best strategy. Another assumption is that each question should be given the same amount of time. In reality, many questions take less than a minute and a half, so there is extra time left over for those questions that do take longer.

To implement a successful timing strategy, you have to know how much time you have spent on a question. This requires that you use a watch. Review the guidelines for using a watch given in the "General Strategies" chapter (Chapter 1). Also, review the guidelines for evaluating your timing strategy.

SUMMARY OF TIMING STRATEGY FOR LR

1. Scanning the first page of the section, choose an easy question and work on it. Most questions take about a minute but on some questions, you will take up to three or four minutes if necessary. Do not exceed five minutes.

2. Use your watch to keep track of time on each question by setting the hands to noon when you start each question.

3. Depending on your target number, choose another question on the first page or go on to the next page.

4. If you are looking at two facing pages, it is all right to choose more questions from one page than the other. It is all right to choose slightly more from among the first five questions and fewer or none from among the last five.

5. Continue working your target number of questions until you have gotten through the last page of the section.

6. If there is time left, go back to the beginning and choose one easy question. Continue this process as long as there is time left.

7. At the five-minute warning, fill in bubbles for questions not already answered.

8. Continue working on a question until time is called.

THE STRUCTURE OF AN ARGUMENT

The LR section tests your ability to understand and manipulate logical arguments. LR questions are *not* a test of your world knowledge, your ethics, your values, or your opinions about issues.

Before you study the types of LR arguments, it is important to understand the basic elements of any logical argument. Consider the following exchange:

George: All white cats are deaf, right?
You: Sure, I guess so.
George: And Little Binky is white, right?
You: Yes, Little Binky is white.
George: Aha! Then Little Binky is deaf.
You: OK. You win.

An arguer is trying to convince you of something that you do not already believe to be true. The arguer starts with facts that you already believe to be true (*all white cats are deaf* and *Little Binky is white*) and then establishes that if those facts are true, something else—something that you had not previously thought of—must, by virtue of the principles of logic, also be true (*Little Binky is deaf*).

Every logical argument must include both facts that are accepted as true by all parties and some new fact that is derived from the established facts.

Premises

The established facts that all parties must agree are true are called **premises**. In the argument above, the premises (P1 and P2) are:

> P1: *All white cats are deaf.*
> P2: *Little Binky is white.*

When George presents these premises and asks "Right?" you have to say, "Right." If you question a fact, for example by saying, "Wait. Who told you all white cats are deaf?" there is no longer a basis for an argument. This is an important principle. When a question stem says, for example, "Which one of the following, if true . . ." the stem is indicating that the answer choices are to be considered as premises. You cannot question them. It can be very tempting to cross out an answer choice that says something like "It is good for children to eat lots of candy" or "People should never say hello to a lonely person." However, when the answer choices are premises, you cannot evaluate whether they are true or not. You must accept them as true and consider how they affect the argument.

Likewise, if a question stem reads, "If the above are true, . . ." the stem indicates that the statements in the setup are to be considered as true premises. You cannot decide that some of the statements are not true.

Conclusions

When George applies logic to the two premises on which you and he both agree and comes up with a new fact, he is creating a **conclusion**. In the argument above, the conclusion (C) is:

> C: *Little Binky is deaf.*

Many LR questions ask what can be concluded. To be concluded, a statement must follow from the premises and from valid principles of logic.

Assumptions

For LR, an **assumption** is a premise that is necessary to make an argument work but which is not stated. Test out the following possibilities. Which one is an assumption in George's argument?

> A. *All white cats are in fact deaf.*
> B. *You have seen Little Binky.*
> C. *Little Binky belongs to George.*
> D. *Little Binky is in fact deaf.*
> E. *Little Binky is a cat.*

Choice A is not an assumption. The fact that all white cats are deaf is a stated premise, not an unstated one. Choice B is irrelevant. It does not matter whether you have seen Little Binky or not, as long as you agree that Little Binky is white. Test choice C. Suppose Little Binky does *not* belong to George but rather belongs to Jacki. Does this destroy the argument? No. Therefore, choice C is not an unstated fact that is necessary to the argument.

Choice D is a stated premise. Test choice E. Suppose Little Binky were not a cat but a rhinoceros. What happens to the argument? It falls apart completely. The argument depends on Little Binky being a cat, a fact which was not stated. Choice E is an assumption in George's argument. When a real assumption is negated (e.g., making Binky *not* a cat), the argument is destroyed.

When an LR question stem asks "Which one of the following is an assumption in the above argument?" the word *assumption* is being used with the technical meaning described above. Note that this technical meaning is different from the meaning of *assumption* as used in casual conversation.

Inference

The term **inference** is also used in a technical sense in LR. Inference refers to a process, specifically the process of moving through premises and assumptions to a conclusion. In other words, the process of making a logical argument is *inference*.

The word *inference* also refers to the end product of the inference process, namely the conclusion. To infer means to arrive at the conclusion. Therefore, when an LR question stem asks "Which one of the following can be inferred?" it is asking what can be concluded. Do *not* apply the casual meaning of the word *infer* when working LR questions. In a casual sense, infer could mean "What might you read into this?" or "What else might be true?" In LR, the word *infer* must refer only to what can be concluded through valid logic based on given premises. An inference is a statement that can be defended as being true. An inference need not be the *main* conclusion of an argument— only *a* conclusion.

> **THE COMPONENTS OF A LOGICAL ARGUMENT**
>
> Arguments are built from **premises and assumptions**. They arrive at **conclusions** through the use of **inference**. Logical arguments can be **valid** or **invalid**.

Valid Logic

There is a small but critical step between George's establishment of the premises and his presentation of the conclusion. George applied logic to the premises. Specifically, George used the principle that if all members of a set have characteristic C and if individual M is a member of that set, then individual M also has characteristic C.

There are many forms of valid logic. Consider the argument:

> Staci: I played a wide variety of sounds while Little Binky was playing in the living
> room and Little Binky did not respond to any of them. Therefore, there is a
> significant chance that Little Binky is deaf.

The conclusion is similar to George's but follows different logic. Staci's logic is based on the definition of deafness and on experimental results.

When you evaluate a logical argument, consider not just the conclusion of the argument but also the premises upon which it is based and the type of logic that is used to move from the premises to the conclusion. Two arguments may reach identical conclusions and yet proceed in completely different ways.

Flawed Logic

The LR section also tests your ability to identify when an argument is *not* valid and why. Many LR questions present flawed arguments. There are two ways that an argument can be flawed. The argument may use a valid type of logic but apply it incorrectly. Alternately, the argument may use logic that is inherently flawed.

Consider George's argument about Little Binky. Without the assumption that Little Binky is a cat, George's argument is flawed because he does not establish that Binky is a member of the set of white cats. His logical principles are still valid, but he would not be applying them appropriately.

In the following argument, the logic itself is flawed:

> *Jason: My cat was named Little Binky and was deaf, so your Little Binky is also deaf.*

Jason's underlying logic is that if two individuals have the same name, they must have the same characteristics. This is not a valid logical principle.

TYPES OF ARGUMENTS

This section breaks down the types of valid and flawed logic. You will learn diagramming tools and common logic concepts—such as cause and effect and analogy—that are tested in LR questions.

Valid Arguments

There are two broad categories of logical arguments—deductive and inductive. You need to use different tools for working with these different categories.

DEDUCTIVE ARGUMENTS

For the LSAT, deductive arguments are arguments that present absolute rules:

> *If you go to the store, you will be late for school.*
> *All baseball players have red sports cars.*

Do you see how the above arguments are absolute? If you go to the store, there are no options. You *will* be late. If someone meets the condition of being a baseball player, that person *does* have a red sports car. Deductive arguments are meant to be taken as inviolable rules.

Deductive arguments deal with an idealized universe in which certain relationships are true with absolute certainty. Deductive logic is almost mathematical. Deduction is not concerned with your opinion, with alternate options, or with what is fair. Deductive arguments require you to understand and apply absolute rules in a logically precise way.

Compare the previous arguments with these nondeductive statements:

> *If you go to the store, you might have a hard time catching the bus to school.*
> *A lot of baseball players seem to like fancy cars.*

These nondeductive statements do not make an absolute prediction. You may or may not make it to school on time if you go to the store. A baseball player may or may not have a fancy car. These statements are about the real world, not about the idealized world of absolute rules to which deductive arguments refer. Even though the above examples are fairly obvious, it can sometimes be difficult to distinguish a deductive argument from a nondeductive (inductive) one. Consider:

> *My friends and I go to the lake on the Fourth of July. We play tennis or volleyball but we never play football.*

This sounds like a conversational, real-world inductive setup. In fact, though, it presents absolute rules, which can be expressed in a condensed notation:

> Rule 1: *If "Fourth of July," then "lake"* and
> Rule 2: *If "Fourth of July," then "tennis or volleyball and not football."*

To work with deductive arguments you often need to diagram or symbolize them. The two main types of deductive arguments require two different diagramming systems. The two types are **set** arguments and **if/then** arguments.

Set Arguments

Set arguments establish groups, or sets, of people or objects and then state certain characteristics of members of the set. In the argument *All baseball players have red sports cars,* the set is *baseball players* and all members of that set have the characteristic of owning a red sports car.

A set argument can be diagrammed by drawing a circle to represent the set, as shown in Figure 2.2. The arrow points to the characteristic that is true for all members of the set. The rectangle around the diagram represents the boundaries of the logical "universe." In other words, the diagram can be interpreted as saying that baseball players are a subset of the universe. You do not need to draw the rectangle in your diagrams but the rectangle is useful for learning purposes.

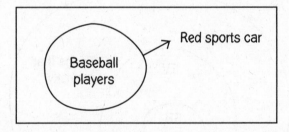

Figure 2.2. Circle diagram representing a set argument

Set arguments may show complex relationships between two or more sets:

> *Any small business is an entrepreneurial venture. All entrepreneurial ventures are risky. John's business is a small business. Therefore, John's business is risky.*

In this example, *small business* is a set and so is *entrepreneurial venture.* What is the relationship of these two sets?

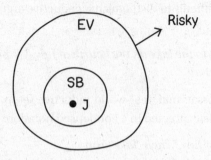

Figure 2.3. Small business (SB) is a subset of entrepreneurial
venture (EV). John (J) is a member of SB and therefore of EV.

Small business is a subset of entrepreneurial venture. In Figure 2.3, the circle representing
small business falls completely within the circle representing entrepreneurial venture. John's
business falls in the category *small business* and is represented by a dot in the SB circle. Thus,
John's business has the characteristic *risky*. Consider:

> *Any small business is an entrepreneurial venture. All entrepreneurial ventures
> are risky. Greta's business is risky.*

How would you diagram this? The two circles are the same as in Figure 2.3. Where would
you put the dot for Greta's business? What do you know about Greta's business? Because it
is risky, it is *possible* that it is a small business, in which case Greta's business can be placed
within the small business circle. However, it is also possible that Greta's business is not a
small business.

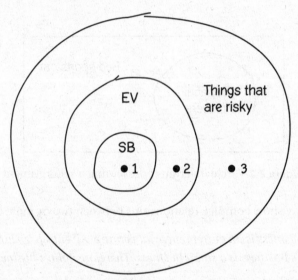

Figure 2.4. Circle diagram representing Greta's business. Dots 1, 2,
and 3 represent the three possible locations for Greta's business.

In Figure 2.4, the circles for small businesses and entrepreneurial ventures are shown as
a subset of all things that are risky. Dot 1 represents the case in which Greta's business is a
small business. Dot 2 represents the case in which Greta's business is not a small business
but is an entrepreneurial venture. Dot 3 represents another possibility—that Greta's business
is neither a small business nor an entrepreneurial venture. It is simply something else that
is risky.

In actuality, the argument does not provide enough information to determine where Greta's business should be placed. It is important to know that you do *not* know where Greta's business goes. An LR question might ask the following:

EXAMPLE

Which one of the following statements can be inferred about Greta's business?

(A) It is a small business.

(B) It is an entrepreneurial venture but not a small business.

(C) It is not an entrepreneurial venture.

(D) It is a small business but not an entrepreneurial venture.

(E) It might be a small business.

Choices A through C could be true but do not have to be. Choice D cannot be true. All small businesses are entrepreneurial ventures. Choice E might strike you as being a nonanswer. Anything *might* be a small business. However, choice E is the only defendable answer. The question tests your ability to distinguish what is known, what is not known, and what might be true.

With any set argument, remember that, whereas all members of a set may have a certain characteristic, it is possible that other elements in the universe may also have that characteristic. Just because Greta's business is not a member of EV does *not* mean that it is not risky.

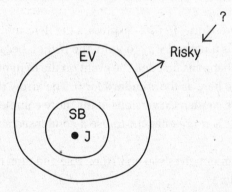

Figure 2.5. Remember that there can be other elements in the universe (shown by the question mark) that have the same characteristics as a set.

Set arguments are not very common on the LR but are easy to diagram. Diagram a set argument in a question that asks you to find a parallel argument with the same structure.

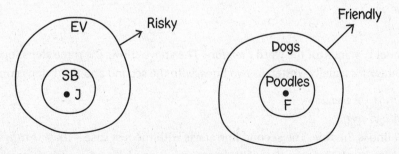

Figure 2.6. Parallel set arguments with different content but the same structure.

In Figure 2.6, the diagram on the right represents the statement *All dogs are friendly. All poodles are dogs. Fido is a poodle. Therefore, Fido is friendly.* The structure of the two arguments is the same, though the content is different.

If/Then Arguments

If/then arguments are the second type of deductive argument used in LR questions. If/thens are used in many LR questions, as well as in the Analytical Reasoning section, so it is important to study them carefully. If/then arguments are not diagrammed with circles but rather by symbolizing the if/then statements, for example, *If A, then B.*

The anatomy of an if/then argument. An if/then argument states an absolute rule about the universe. *If it rains, the sidewalk will be wet.* The if/then argument relates two events:

1. raining, and

2. the sidewalk being wet

One of the two events is the **determining factor**. The other is the **result** that must occur if the determining factor takes place. The determining factor usually occurs first in time and the result usually occurs later in time. In the above example, the determining factor is *raining* and the result is *the sidewalk being wet.* Remember that this is an absolute rule. If the determining factor occurs, the result *must* occur.

The if/then argument above can be symbolized as:

> *If rain* → *wet*

The left side of this expression—*If rain*—expresses the determining factor. The right side expresses the result. This is a natural way to write the if/then because, reading from left to right, the event on the left happens first and the event on the right happens second. This left-to-right order is referred to here as the **standard** form. The arrow represents the word *then*. The words *rain* and *wet* are condensed versions of the more complex statements *it rains* and *the sidewalk will be wet.* It is more efficient to use a condensed shorthand rather than the entire statement.

A complete if/then argument gives you an if/then rule and then tests you to see if you can apply the rule. For example:

> **The rule:** *If it rains, the sidewalk will be wet.*
> **The test:** *It is raining. What must be true?*
> **The answer:** *The sidewalk will be wet.*

Symbolically, a complete if/then argument might look like this:

> *If rain* → *wet*
> *Rain*
> ∴ *wet*

The symbol ∴ stands for the word *therefore.* The above shows the three steps separately but such a statement is usually written as two lines, with the second and third steps combined:

> *If rain* → *wet*
> *Rain* ∴ *wet*

The first line is the rule. The second line starts with the test case—*there is rain*—and ends with the result—*wet.* The complete if/then argument can be read as *If it rains, the sidewalk will be wet. It is raining. Therefore, the sidewalk will be wet.*

TIP

IF/THEN ARGUMENTS

If/then arguments are critical to both Logical Reasoning and Analytical Reasoning. Practice if/thens until you have them mastered.

Valid and invalid variations on an if/then. The previous argument is clearly valid. Given the rule that if it is raining, then the sidewalk will get wet, and given the fact that it is raining, the sidewalk will get wet. However, what if the test case is not so simple? Try the examples below:

> **The rule:** *If it rains, the sidewalk will be wet.*
> **The test:** *It is <u>not</u> raining. What must be true?*
> **The answer:** *?*

Or

> **The rule:** *If it rains, the sidewalk will be wet.*
> **The test:** *The sidewalk is wet. What must be true?*
> **The answer:** *?*

Or

> **The rule:** *If it rains, the sidewalk will be wet.*
> **The test:** *The sidewalk is <u>not</u> wet. What must be true?*
> **The answer:** *?*

Do you feel confident in your answers? It is extremely important to be able to distinguish which variations on an if/then statement are valid and which are invalid. Both the LR and the Analytical Reasoning sections test you on this.

Consider the above examples, using symbols. The first example says:

> **If rain** → **wet**
> *–rain ∴ ?*

Note the negative sign in front of the word *rain*, indicating *not rain*. You may be tempted to say "*–rain ∴ –wet*." Is this valid? In this universe in which rain must result in the sidewalk being wet, is it true that if it does not rain, the sidewalk will not be wet? It is *not* true. There can be other factors that cause the sidewalk to be wet. Perhaps the sprinkler was on.

What about the next statement?

> *Wet ∴ ?*

It is tempting to say that if the sidewalk is wet, it must have previously rained. However, this is not valid, for the same reason. If the sidewalk is wet, it could have been because of a different cause, such as the sprinkler.

Finally, there is the third statement:

> *–Wet ∴ ?*

If the sidewalk is not wet, is it true that it did not rain? In this case the answer is yes. If the sidewalk is not wet, it could not have rained because if it had rained, the sidewalk would be wet. This final variation on the original if/then statement *If rain* → *wet* is a valid variation and in fact is the only valid variation.

The variations that you just read about can be represented generically as:

1. *If A* → *B*

   A ∴ B (Valid)

2. *If A* → *B*

   –A ∴ –B (Invalid)

3. *If A → B*

   B ∴ A (Invalid)

4. *If A → B*

   –B ∴ –A (Valid)

Look carefully at these four variations. In the first one, the second line simply repeats the first line, and is thus valid. In the second variation, both sides of the first line are negated in the second line. The *A* in the first line becomes *not A* (*–A*) in the second line, and similarly for the *B*. This is not valid logic. It may sound reasonable to say that if rain makes the sidewalk wet, then not raining makes the sidewalk dry but this is not valid and the LSAT tries to trap you into this error.

In the third example, the two sides of the original are switched in the second statement. The *B* is moved to the left side and the *A* to the right side. This is also an invalid variation. *If the sidewalk is wet, it must have rained, right?* Wrong. Do not fall into the trap.

So far the variations have either negated the elements or switched them from left to right. The final variation does both. In moving from the first line to the second line, it switches the elements from left to right and it also negates each of them: *–B ∴ –A*. This is a valid argument. To summarize, when you start with an if/then statement in standard form, negating both sides is not valid. Switching the sides is not valid. However, doing both does result in a valid statement:

> **If A → B**
> *–B ∴ –A*

This variation is called the **contrapositive**. Every if/then statement has a contrapositive and the contrapositive is also a valid statement. The contrapositive reverses the two sides of the standard if/then and negates them. Consider:

> *If you don't eat, then you will be hungry.*

Or written symbolically:

> *If –eat → hungry.*

Create the contrapositive. *Hungry* must go on the left and *eat* must go on the right. Negating *hungry* results in

> *–hungry ∴*

but how do you negate *–eat*? It already has a negative in front of it. To negate a statement that originally is negative, turn it into a positive:

> *–hungry ∴ eat*

If you are not hungry, you must have eaten because if you had not eaten, you would be hungry.

If you have trouble remembering which variations are valid and which are invalid, try using a real-world if/then statement, such as *If you do not take the LSAT, you will not get into law school.* If you test out the variations on this statement, you should find that it is intuitively obvious whether they are true or not. For example, if you do not remember whether negating both sides is valid or not, test the statement *If you do take the LSAT, you will get into law school.* This is intuitively untrue and so you have proven to yourself that negating both sides does not create a valid statement.

Creating a standard if/then. The LSAT presents if/then statements in words, not in symbols. Sometimes the wording is easy to understand, such as *Anyone who takes physics in the fall must take organic chemistry in the spring.* However, in other cases the wording is very complex and difficult to understand, for example, *The empire will crumble only if the educated become complacent,* or *The Tigers will win the tournament unless the Coyotes replace their team captain.* For the untrained test taker such wording can be intimidating, if not impossible, to analyze. However, you can use a simple, three-step process to easily break down any if/then statement. Apply the following three steps to the statement *The empire will crumble only if the educated become complacent.*

STEP 1 **IDENTIFY THE TWO ELEMENTS THAT ARE BEING RELATED.** The two elements, in abbreviated form, are *empire crumble* and *educated complacent.*

STEP 2 **DETERMINE WHICH ONE HAPPENS FIRST (OR IS THE DETERMINING FACTOR) AND WHICH ONE HAPPENS SECOND (THE RESULT). CREATE AN IF/THEN STATEMENT WITH THE DETERMINING FACTOR ON THE LEFT AND THE RESULT ON THE RIGHT, LEAVING A LITTLE SPACE BEFORE EACH.** The complacency of the educated seems to be the cause and the crumbling of the empire seems to be the result:

> If (blank) educated complacent → (blank) empire crumble

STEP 3 **DETERMINE WHETHER IT IS THE PRESENCE OR THE ABSENCE OF THE DETERMINING FACTOR THAT IS IMPORTANT. COMPLETE THE IF/THEN BY ENTERING ANY NEEDED NEGATIVE SIGNS.** At this point you must determine whether the statement is saying that the fact of the educated becoming complacent guarantees that the empire will crumble or that as long as the educated do not become complacent (the absence of *educated complacent*) the empire will not crumble. If the answer is not clear, use the example of the LSAT and law school by creating parallel language. In other words, create a true statement about the LSAT and law school using the wording *only if.* You would have to say something like *You will get into law school only if you take the LSAT.* Does this imply that if you take the LSAT, you will get into law school? No. Therefore, it is the absence of the LSAT and the absence of *educated complacent* that determines *not law school* and *not empire crumble:*

> If –educated complacent → –empire crumble
> (compare with If –LSAT → –law school)

We have taken the statement from Step 2 and entered in negative signs. The result is a valid if/then statement in standard form. Create the contrapositive:

> Empire crumble ∴ educated complacent
> (compare with law school ∴ LSAT)

The empire crumbled, therefore the educated must have become complacent. You got into law school. Therefore, you must have taken the LSAT.

Special if/then wording. In the example above you analyzed an if/then statement that used the wording *only if.* There are two other wording variations with which you should be familiar—the wording *unless* and the wording *if and only if.* Try to memorize the interpretation of these wording variations. However, if you do forget how to interpret them or become confused about their interpretation, you can (1) apply the three steps and (2) use a parallel example, such as the law school and LSAT example, to figure out the meaning.

The word *unless* is easy to interpret. Simply translate *unless* into *if not*:

> *You will not get into law school **unless** you take the LSAT.*
> *You will not get into law school **if** you do **not** take the LSAT.*

The word *unless* indicates that it is the absence of the determining factor that predicts the result. The absence of taking the LSAT guarantees that you will not be accepted. This strategy will work for all instances of *unless*. The *unless* statement above does not predict what happens if you *do* take the LSAT.

The expression *only if* also indicates the absence of the determining factor. However, an *only if* statement has a different construction from an *if not* or *unless* statement. Compare:

> *You will **not get into** law school **if** you do **not take** the LSAT.*
> *You will **not get into** law school **unless** you **take** the LSAT.*
> *You will **get into** law school **only if** you **take** the LSAT.*

All of the statements say *The absence of LSAT leads to the absence of law school* but use different forms:

> *If absence of A, then absence of B.*
> *Unless presence of A, absence of B.*
> *Only if presence of A, presence of B.*

Do not worry if the wording variations seem confusing. Use the three-step approach and the example of LSAT and law school to understand any complexly worded if/then statement. For *only if* statements, you can also use an easy strategy. When you read a statement such as *Only if you eat your dinner will you get dessert*, think of it as being followed by the statement "Otherwise, not."

> *Only if you eat your dinner will you get dessert. Otherwise (if you do not eat your dinner), not (you will not get dessert).*

This is the same as saying

> *If not eat dinner* → *not dessert,*

which is the correct interpretation.
In terms of *A* and *B*, the statement *Only if A, then B* is equivalent to

> *Only if A, then B. Otherwise (if not A), then not B,*

which is equivalent to

> *If –A* → *–B.*

The logic becomes a little more challenging if the *only if* statement itself already contains a negative. Consider *Only if you do not fail the exam will you graduate.* Break this down using the "otherwise" method:

> *Only if you do not fail the exam will you graduate. Otherwise (fail the exam),*
> *not (not graduate).*
> *If fail the exam, then not graduate.*

Notice that the *otherwise* phrase negates the negative expression *not fail* and turns it into the positive, *fail.* In this complex logic, it is the absence of *not failing* that is the determining factor. Using the *otherwise* method is easier if you put the *only if* part of the sentence first.

The third wording variation for if/thens is *if and only if*. Consider the statement *If, and only if, you are accepted to law school will you start law classes in the fall*. This statement includes an *only if* but also includes an *if*. It is equivalent to saying:

> Only if you are accepted to law school will you start law classes in the fall

AND

> Getting accepted to law school DOES guarantee that you will start law classes in the fall.

In other words, *If you do not get accepted, you will not start* AND *If you do get accepted, you will start.*

Thus, an *if and only if* statement actually consists of two distinct if/then statements. In symbols, an *if and only if* statement reads:

> If –A → –B

AND

> If A → B

These two statements cover all the possibilities. If A occurs, you know what happens. If A does not occur, you know what happens.

Compare the three wording variations in Table 2.2.

Table 2.2. Special If/Then Wording

	Wording	Symbols	Logic
unless	Unless A, then not B	If –A → –B	Absence of determining factor predicts absence of result.
Only if	Only if A, then B	If –A → –B	Absence of determining factor predicts absence of result.
If and only if	If, and only if, A, then B	If –A → –B If A → B	Absence of determining factor predicts absence of result. Presence of determining factor predicts presence of result.

If/then logic can quickly become overwhelming and confusing. If you find yourself becoming lost in the words, go back to the three steps and identify:

1. What are the two factors?
2. Which one is the determining factor?
3. Is it the presence or the absence of the determining factor that predicts the result?

Also, you can use the relationship between taking the LSAT and law school to figure out *unless* and *only if* statements and you can use the relationship between being accepted to law school and starting classes in the fall to figure out *if and only if* statements.

Triggers. The determining factor was defined earlier as the one element (of the two elements that are being related in the if/then) that determines the result. In the LSAT and law school example, LSAT is the determining factor. In order for you to put this determining factor to use, though, you have to know whether it is the presence of the LSAT or absence of the

LSAT that leads to a result. Because it is the absence of the LSAT that leads to the absence of being accepted to law school, we can call the absence of the LSAT (*–LSAT* or *not LSAT*) a **trigger**. A **trigger** is an expression in an if/then statement that guarantees a certain result. In the statement

     If –LSAT → *–law school*

the term *not LSAT (–LSAT)* is a trigger. It guarantees the result *not law school*. Now consider the contrapositive:

     law school ∴ *LSAT*

ABOUT IF/THEN NOTATION

The *therefore* sign (∴) may be used instead of the *then* sign (→) when the element on the left occurs **after** the element on the right. The statement *B* ∴ *A* can be read as *B, therefore A must have previously taken place.*

In this statement, *law school* is a trigger. If you are accepted to law school, it is guaranteed that you have taken the LSAT. For any if/then statement, if you write out both the statement and the contrapositive, the elements on the left side are always triggers and the elements on the right side are *not* triggers (Table 2.3).

Table 2.3. Triggers and Non-Triggers

Triggers	NOT Triggers
Not LSAT	LSAT
Law school	Not law school

If you feel comfortable with the following shortcut, you can determine the triggers just from the standard if/then statement, without writing out the contrapositive. The element on the left is a trigger. The negation of the element on the right is a trigger. (Remember that the negation of a negative is a positive.) The element on the right is not a trigger and the negation of the element on the left is not a trigger. In the statement and contrapositive below, the triggers are shown in bold:

     If **A** → *B*
     –B ∴ *–A*

Triggers: *A, –B*
Non-triggers: *–A, B*
Use triggers to your advantage. Consider a passage that begins:

     Anyone who eats cheese regularly does not have a calcium deficiency. John does not eat cheese regularly.

The first sentence gives you the rule. The second sentence gives you additional information. You may need to determine what, if anything, can be validly concluded about John, given that he does not eat cheese regularly. The standard statement and the contrapositive are:

If cheese → *–calcium deficiency*
Calcium deficiency ∴ *–cheese*

The two triggers (bolded) are on the left: *cheese* and *calcium deficiency*. Is the information given about John a trigger? No. Not eating cheese does not match either of the triggers. This tells you that there is no further conclusion you can derive about John. Now consider the variation:

> *Anyone who eats cheese regularly does not have a calcium deficiency. John does not have a calcium deficiency.*

This new statement about John (*not calcium deficiency*) is still not a trigger. You still cannot conclude anything else about John. Next consider:

> *Anyone who eats cheese regularly does not have a calcium deficiency. John has a calcium deficiency.*

Calcium deficiency is one of the triggers. It predicts that John has not eaten cheese regularly. Consider the following:

> *Anyone who eats cheese regularly does not have a calcium deficiency. John eats cheese regularly.*

Eats cheese is a trigger. You can conclude that John does not have a calcium deficiency. To summarize, the elements on the left of the if/then and the left of the contrapositive are triggers. If you are given a trigger, you can come to a new conclusion. The elements on the right are not triggers. You cannot conclude anything new from them.

Practice Exercise 1

For each if/then statement below, identify the two elements that are triggers. The answers are below.

1. If rain → wet

2. If clean plate → dessert

3. If –homework → fail

4. If –work → –money

5. If *A* → *B*

For an *if and only if* statement—which contains two distinct *if/thens*—all of the elements and their negations are triggers:

> *If A* → *B*
> *If –A* → *–B*

Do you see why *A, not A, not B,* and *B* are all triggers when both of the statements above are given?

A trigger can predict forward or backward in time. If you are accepted to law school, you must have previously taken the LSAT.

Answers to Practice Exercise 1:

1. rain, –wet

2. clean plate, –dessert

3. –homework, –fail

4. –work, money

5. *A*, –*B*

Necessary conditions versus sufficient conditions. You will see the terms **necessary conditions** and **sufficient conditions** on some LR questions. In questions that ask you to identify a logical flaw, an answer choice may say:

> *takes a condition necessary for X to be a condition sufficient for X*

or

> *treats a condition sufficient for X as a condition necessary for X*

Consider the statement *If you eat ice cream, you will gain weight.* Eating ice cream is sufficient to guarantee that you will gain weight. However, is eating ice cream necessary for you to gain weight? No. You could gain weight in other ways. Consider the general statement:

> *If A → B*

The element *A* is sufficient to guarantee that *B* will take place. However, the element *A* is not necessary for *B* to take place, because other factors could cause *B*. Consider the example *If it rains, the sidewalk will get wet:*

> *If rain → wet*

Rain is sufficient to make the sidewalk wet. However, it is not necessary for it to rain for the sidewalk to be wet. The sprinkler may have run. A sufficient condition is a condition, the presence of which guarantees a result.

If the *absence* of the determining factor guarantees the result, then the determining factor is a *necessary* condition. The result cannot happen without that determining factor. Can you get into law school without the LSAT? No. Taking the LSAT is a necessary condition for *getting accepted to law school* to occur. However, taking the LSAT is not sufficient for getting into law school:

> *If –LSAT → –law school*
> *If –A → –B*

LSAT is necessary for *law school* and *A* is necessary for *B*.

If the terms *necessary* and *sufficient conditions* are a bit confusing for you, use the concept of whether it is the presence or the absence of the determining factor that guarantees a result. If the absence of *X* guarantees the absence of *Y*, then *X* is necessary for *Y*. If the presence of *Q* guarantees the presence of *Z*, then *Q* is sufficient to produce *Z*.

If Aurelia says, "I took the LSAT, so I'm going to get into law school," what logical flaw has she made? She has *taken a condition necessary for getting accepted to be a condition sufficient for getting accepted.* Without the LSAT, she cannot get accepted, but she has mistaken this for a different condition that says that the LSAT alone is sufficient for getting accepted.

Necessary and sufficient conditions can also work backward in time. If Aurelia says, "Jocelyn didn't get into law school, so she must not have taken the LSAT," she is confusing the necessary condition—taking the LSAT—for a sufficient condition. She is looking at the result—not getting into law school—and then looking back in time and assuming that taking the LSAT would have been sufficient for (it would have guaranteed) getting in.

If an if/then statement gives you a sufficient condition, then the contrapositive of that statement is a necessary condition, and vice versa. Consider the statement:

If rain → *wet*

The element *rain* is sufficient to guarantee the occurrence of *wet*. By writing the contrapositive

–wet ∴ *–rain*

you can see that without wet, *rain* could not have occurred. In other words, *wet* is necessary for *rain* to have previously taken place. The absence of *wet* guarantees the absence of *rain*.

If the original statement gives a necessary condition

If –LSAT → *–law school,*

then the contrapositive

law school ∴ *LSAT*

indicates that getting into law school is sufficient to prove that you had previously taken the LSAT. The presence of *law school* guarantees the previous presence of *LSAT*.

In some situations a certain element may both be necessary and sufficient. If you have a ticket for a movie, you will get in. If you do not, you will not. Having a ticket is necessary and having a ticket is also sufficient. (Remember that if/then logic is deductive and deals with an idealized, absolute universe. In the real world there may be other factors that would keep you from getting into the movie.) The movie scenario can be expressed by an *if and only if* statement: *You will get into the movie if, and only if, you have a ticket.*

Table 2.4 summarizes the characteristics of necessary and sufficient conditions.

Table 2.4. Necessary and Sufficient Conditions

	Sufficient or Necessary	Presence or Absence	Basic Wording	Alternate Wording
If $A \rightarrow B$	A is sufficient for guaranteeing that B will occur.	The presence of A is the determining factor.	If A occurs, B will occur.	
If $-A \rightarrow -B$	A is necessary for B to occur.	The absence of A is the determining factor.	If A does not occur, B cannot occur.	B does not occur unless A occurs. B occurs only if A occurs.
If $A \rightarrow B$ If $-A \rightarrow -B$	A is necessary for B to occur and A is sufficient for guaranteeing that B will occur.	Both the presence and absence of A are determining factors.	If A occurs, B will occur and if A does not occur, B will not occur.	B occurs if, and only if, A occurs.

If/then arguments that test a rule. Some arguments present a rule and then test your understanding of the rule by giving you a case and asking you to come to a conclusion. Consider the following argument:

> *Every current employee who has worked at AAA Storm Door for at least three years gets two weeks of vacation. Jurgen started working at AAA Storm Door in 2009 and has worked there without interruption since that time.*

The if/then statement in the first sentence can be symbolized as:

> *If 3 years → 2 weeks of vacation*

What do you know about Jurgen? Because the year 2009 is more than three years ago and he has worked at AAA Storm Door continually since then, he must meet the criterion *has worked at AAA Storm Door for at least three years.* The argument now reads:

> **Rule:** *If 3 years → 2 weeks of vacation*
> **Case:** *Jurgen = 3 years*
> **Conclusion:** *Jurgen = 2 weeks of vacation*

The argument presents a rule, *If A → B,* and then gives you a test case: *A.* Your task is to determine what can be concluded. In order to derive a valid conclusion, you must know what the triggers are for the argument. Consider:

> *Nura told us that if she is accepted to the study abroad program, she will go to Qatar for next semester. Unfortunately, Nura was not accepted to the study abroad program.*

What can be concluded? Symbolize the if/then statement and write down the two triggers. Then read the explanation below.

For the above argument, the first sentence gives the if/then statement (the rule) and can be symbolized in standard form as:

> *If accepted → Qatar*

The triggers are (1) the element on the left side of the standard form (*accepted*) and (2) the negation of the element on the right side (*–Qatar*). The test case that you are given is that Nura is not accepted. *Not accepted* is *not* one of the triggers. There is nothing that follows from the fact that Nura is not accepted.

Combining if/thens to create an argument. Some arguments present two if/then statements and test your understanding of the relationship between them. You have probably seen arguments such as:

> *If Jason goes to the party, Mariah will go.*
> *If Mariah goes to the party, Sara will go.*
> ∴ *If Jason goes to the party, Sara will go.*

A deductive argument that includes two premises and then draws a conclusion based on the premises is called a **syllogism**. You should be prepared to draw conclusions from syllogisms and to evaluate whether or not they are valid.

In the argument above, the two if/then statements have a common element. Mariah appears in both. For a syllogism to be valid, there must be a common element between the if/thens:

$If A \rightarrow B$
$If B \rightarrow C$
$\therefore If A \rightarrow C$

Is there a common element in the following if/then statements?

> *If Eduardo orders spaghetti, Jessica orders lasagna. If Olivia orders salad, Jessica orders lasagna.*

The statements can be symbolized as:

$If A \rightarrow B$
$If C \rightarrow B$

The common element is *B*, Jessica orders lasagna. However, the argument does not function as a valid syllogism. If *A* occurs, you know that *B* occurs, but what follows from *B* occurring? Nothing. In order to make a valid syllogism, you would need to have another if/then rule in which *B* is a trigger for some other event, *C*. In the statement If $C \rightarrow B$, *B* is not a trigger. You can think of each element as a stepping stone across a stream. You need to step from *A* to *B* and then from *B* to *C*. In the above argument you can step from *A* to *B* but then cannot step anywhere from *B*. You can step from *C* to *B* but this does not help you get across the stream (Figure 2.7).

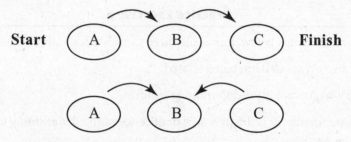

Figure 2.7. The top diagram shows *If A then B, If B then C*.
The bottom diagram shows *If A then B, If C then B*.

Now consider the following argument:

> *If Eduardo orders spaghetti, Jessica orders lasagna. If Olivia orders salad, Jessica does not order lasagna.*

The two statements can be symbolized as:

$If A \rightarrow B$
$If C \rightarrow -B$

This looks very much like the previous example, which was not a valid syllogism. Look carefully. What is the common element? There are two occurrences of *B* but one is positive and one is negative. Rewrite the second if/then so that it is positive. Do this by writing the contrapositive:

$B \therefore -C$

If *A* occurs, you know that *B* occurs. If *B* occurs, you know that *not C* occurs. Now there is a valid syllogism:

$If A \rightarrow B$
$B \therefore -C$
$\therefore If A \rightarrow -C$

Note that the *therefore* symbol is used in two different ways. In the second line, it represents the fact that *B* happened second and therefore *−C* must have occurred previously. In the third line it represents a conclusion.

Just as a single if/then statement may present a rule and then give you a test case, a syllogism can present rules and then give you a test case. Consider the argument in the following exercise:

Practice Exercise 2

If Jill goes to school in Montana, Kerri goes to school in Nebraska. If Lou goes to school in Pennsylvania, Jill goes to school in Montana. If Hank goes to school in Ohio, Kerri does not go to school in Nebraska. If Lou does not go to school in Pennsylvania, Jill does not go to school in Montana.

List all of the statements that must be true if Kerri does not go to school in Nebraska. Use your tools to work out all of the if/then relationships. Then check your answers against the explanation at the end of this section.

Practice Exercise 3

For each of the statements below, follow the three steps for evaluating if/thens.

1. List the two events that are being related.

2. Identify which event is the determining factor.

3. Determine whether it is the presence or absence of the determining factor that determines the result.

Write out an if/then statement in standard form, first as a complete sentence and then using symbols. Then write the contrapositive. Finally, write down the two triggers. The answers and explanations are given at the end of this section.

1. Mushrooms pop up overnight whenever it rains.

2. Trees that are not fertilized annually will not grow properly.

3. If you do well on the test, you must have studied for three hours.

4. Unless you finish your dinner, you cannot have dessert.

5. The shuttle launch will take place Saturday only if it does not rain.

6. Acme Corporation will file for bankruptcy if, and only if, they are not approved for a loan.

For each of the following statements, tell whether each conclusion is valid or invalid. The answers are at the end of this section.

1. Kurt does not take a vacation unless Fiona takes a vacation. Fiona takes a vacation. Therefore, Kurt takes a vacation.

2. Kurt does not take a vacation unless Fiona takes a vacation. Kurt does not take a vacation. Therefore, Fiona takes a vacation.

3. Taylor signs up for Philosophy only if Reggie signs up for Linguistics. Reggie signs up for Linguistics. Therefore, Taylor signs up for Philosophy.

4. Taylor signs up for Philosophy only if Reggie signs up for Linguistics. Reggie does not sign up for Linguistics. Therefore, Taylor does not sign up for Philosophy.

5. If Ken goes to the baseball game, Sandra goes to the hockey game. If Greg goes to the football game, Sandra does not go to the hockey game. Ken goes to the baseball game. Therefore, Greg does not go to the football game.

Answers to Practice Exercises 2–4:

Practice Exercise 2

Symbolize the statements in standard form:

$$If\ J = M \rightarrow K = N$$
$$If\ L = P \rightarrow J = M$$
$$If\ H = O \rightarrow K = -N$$
$$If\ L = -P \rightarrow J = -M$$

The test case is that Kerri does not go to school in Nebraska. Look for $K = -N$ as a trigger (on the left side). It does not occur on the left side in the standard forms, so rewrite one of the statements with K as a contrapositive. Rewriting the first if/then would give $K = -N \therefore J = -M$. Rewriting the third if/then would give K in N, rather than K not in N.

The only trigger with K not in N, then, results in J not in M. Add this to the list of true statements that follow from K not in N. Now find what must be true if J is not in M. $J = -M$ does not appear as a trigger in the left side of any of the standard if/thens. Check the contrapositives. Look to see if the negation of $J = -M$, namely $J = M$, occurs on the right side of any of the standard forms. It is in the second if/then statement. The contrapositive of the second statement is $J = -M \therefore L = -P$.

Add $L = -P$ to the list of true statements. Now look for instances of $L = -P$ as a trigger. It occurs on the left side of the last standard if/then statement, with the result that $J = -M$, which is already listed as a true statement. Double-check to see if the negation of $L = -P$, namely $L = P$, occurs on the right side of any of the standard if/then statements. It does not, so all of the results of K not in N have been found.

True statements:

$$J = -M$$
$$L = -P$$

Practice Exercise 3

1. *Mushrooms pop up overnight whenever it rains.*
   - **STEP 1** Mushrooms pop up. Rain.
   - **STEP 2** The determining factor is rain.
   - **STEP 3** It is the presence of rain that determines mushrooms popping up.

   If it rains, mushrooms pop up. If R → mushrooms.

   Contrapositive: –mushrooms ∴ –R

   Triggers: R, –mushrooms

2. *Trees that are not fertilized annually will not grow properly.*
   - **STEP 1** Fertilize. Grow properly.
   - **STEP 2** The determining factor is fertilize.
   - **STEP 3** It is the absence of fertilize that determines not grow properly.

   If trees are not fertilized annually, they will not grow properly. If –fertilize → –grow.

   Contrapositive: grow ∴ fertilize

   Triggers: –fertilize, grow

3. *If you do well on the test, you must have studied for three hours.*
   - **STEP 1** Do well. Studied.
   - **STEP 2** The determining factor is studied.
   - **STEP 3** It is the absence of studied that determines the absence of doing well.

   If you do not study for three hours, you will not do well on the test. If –study → –do well.

   Contrapositive: do well ∴ studied

   Triggers: –study, do well

   NOTE: It may not have been obvious to you that it is the absence of studying that results in not doing well. You can avoid making an error by double-checking the contrapositive. When the standard form for this example is written as the absence of studying causing not doing well, the contrapositive conforms exactly to the original statement.

4. *Unless you finish your dinner, you cannot have dessert.*
   - **STEP 1** Finish dinner. Get dessert.
   - **STEP 2** The determining factor is finishing dinner.
   - **STEP 3** It is the absence of finishing dinner that determines not getting dessert.

   If you do not finish your dinner, you do not get dessert. If –finish → –dessert.

   Contrapositive: dessert ∴ finish dinner

   Triggers: –finish, dessert

   NOTE: Convert the word *unless* to the expression *if not*. It will then be clear that it is the absence of finishing that is the determining factor.

5. *The shuttle launch will take place Saturday only if it does not rain.*
   - **STEP 1** Launch. Rain.
   - **STEP 2** The determining factor is rain.
   - **STEP 3** It is the absence of *not rain* that determines the absence of launch.

   If it rains, the shuttle launch will not take place on Saturday. If R → –launch.

   Contrapositive: launch ∴ –R

   Triggers: R, launch

NOTE: This is an example of a complex *only if* in which the original statement contains a negative. Apply the *otherwise* strategy. *Only if it does not rain will the shuttle launch take place on Saturday. Otherwise (does rain), not (not launch).*

6. *Acme Corporation will file for bankruptcy if, and only if, they are not approved for a loan.*

An *if and only if* statement should be broken into two parts. Both are true. In this example, the first part is *Acme Corporation will file for bankruptcy if they are not approved for a loan.*

(STEP 1) Bankruptcy. Approved.

(STEP 2) The determining factor is *approved.*

(STEP 3) It is the absence of *approved* that determines *bankruptcy.*

If they are not approved for a loan, the corporation will file for bankruptcy. If –approved → bankruptcy.

Contrapositive: –bankruptcy ∴ approved

Triggers: –approved, –bankruptcy

The second part of the statement is *Acme Corporation will file for bankruptcy only if they are not approved for a loan.*

(STEP 1) Bankruptcy. Approved.

(STEP 2) The determining factor is *approved.*

(STEP 3) It is the absence of *not approved* (= the presence of *approved*) that determines the absence of *bankruptcy.*

If they are approved for a loan, the corporation will not file for bankruptcy. If approved → –bankruptcy.

Contrapositive: bankruptcy ∴ –approved

Triggers: approved, bankruptcy

Note: Use the *otherwise* method. *Only if they are not approved for a loan will Acme Corporation file for bankruptcy. Otherwise (are approved), not (not bankruptcy).*

Practice Exercise 4

1. *Kurt does not take a vacation unless Fiona takes a vacation. Fiona takes a vacation. Therefore, Kurt takes a vacation.*

   Solution: If –Fiona → –Kurt. The only triggers are –Fiona and Kurt. The presence of Fiona is not a trigger, so the conclusion is invalid.

2. *Kurt does not take a vacation unless Fiona takes a vacation. Kurt does not take a vacation. Therefore, Fiona takes a vacation.*

   Solution: As in number 1, the absence of Kurt is not a trigger, so the conclusion is invalid.

3. *Taylor signs up for Philosophy only if Reggie signs up for Linguistics. Reggie signs up for Linguistics. Therefore, Taylor signs up for Philosophy.*

   Solution: If –R = Linguistics → –T = Philosophy. The only triggers are Reggie not signing up for Linguistics and Taylor signing up for Philosophy. The presence of Reggie signing up for Linguistics is not a trigger. The logic is invalid.

4. *Taylor signs up for Philosophy only if Reggie signs up for Linguistics. Reggie does not sign up for Linguistics. Therefore, Taylor does not sign up for Philosophy.*

Solution: The standard form of the if/then is *If −Reggie = Linguistics → −Taylor = Philosophy*. As in number 3, Reggie not signing up for Linguistics is a trigger and it predicts that Taylor will not sign up for Philosophy. The logic is valid.

5. *If Ken goes to the baseball game, Sandra goes to the hockey game. If Greg goes to the football game, Sandra does not go to the hockey game. Ken goes to the baseball game. Therefore, Greg does not go to the football game.*
   Solution: The logic is valid. It can be derived from:
   If Ken = baseball → Sandra = hockey
   and
   Sandra = hockey ∴ Greg not = football, which is the contrapositive of *If Greg = football → Sandra not = hockey*.

TIP

INDUCTIVE ARGUMENTS

For LSAT purposes, an inductive argument is any argument that is not deductive.

INDUCTION

On the LSAT, an **inductive** argument can be defined as any argument that is not deductive. Whereas deductive arguments are built on absolute rules, inductive arguments are not limited to absolute rules. An inductive argument may contain rules but usually also contains information that is not absolute. Rather than being based on *must* statements, inductive reasoning may include *should* or *might* statements. Where deductive arguments refer to an absolute universe, inductive arguments refer to "real-world" situations. Compare:

Deductive argument: *If a species is endangered, it cannot be hunted.*

Inductive argument: *If a species becomes so rare as to be endangered, it would be helpful if society agreed to stop or limit the hunting of that species.*

The inductive argument above sounds more like a real-world discussion than a logical proposition. This is true for most inductive arguments. Beware, however, of arguments that sound like real-world discussions but which in fact contain absolute rules.

> No one wants to see a species become extinct. Today, species are becoming extinct at an alarming rate. Any species that becomes so rare as to be on the endangered species list must be protected by law from being hunted. In addition, any animal that is illegal to hunt is worthy of respect. The Mexican gray wolf is on the endangered species list. Therefore, the Mexican gray wolf is worthy of respect.

Do you see that the above argument, even though it sounds like a real-world discussion, actually presents absolute rules?

Rather than worrying about the term *inductive*, think of LR arguments as either deductive or not deductive. If an argument is deductive, you must be careful to identify the absolute rules and interpret them correctly. You may need to diagram a deductive argument, either using sets or if/then statements. If an argument is not deductive, you do not need to apply these steps.

Major Types of Valid Inductive Logic

There are six common types of inductive logic that you should be familiar with on the LR. They are:

1. Analogy
2. Cause and effect
3. Elimination of other options
4. Generalization
5. Statistical arguments
6. Tautology

Analogy. An argument by **analogy** arrives at a conclusion about situation A by establishing that situation A is similar in some respects (is analogous) to situation B and therefore situation A must be similar in another respect to situation B.

> *Dogs are very similar to wolves in their genetic makeup and in their temperament. Wolves are healthiest when they eat freshly killed meat. Therefore, we can assume that the best diet for dogs would consist primarily of freshly killed meat.*

Table 2.5 below shows the analogy between wolves and dogs that is established by two known similarities. When a new fact is introduced about wolves, a conclusion about dogs is drawn based on the analogy.

Table 2.5. Analogy Between Wolves and Dogs

	Wolves	Dogs
Similarity	Fact: genetics	Fact: genetics
Similarity	Fact: temperament	Fact: temperament
Similarity	Fact: freshly killed meat is healthy	*Conclusion by analogy: freshly killed meat is healthy*

Cause and effect. Cause-and-effect arguments are based on the logic that if event A often occurs before event B, event A might be the cause of event B.

> *Many people who smoke cigarettes later develop lung cancer. Therefore, smoking cigarettes contributes to the development of lung cancer.*

The argument above establishes that (1) smoking cigarettes takes place before the development of lung cancer and (2) there is a significant **correlation** between smoking and developing lung cancer.

Cause-and-effect arguments are based on a **correlation** between two events. There is a correlation between two events if one event regularly occurs after the other or if the two events regularly occur at the same time. A correlation may indicate a **causal relationship** between the two events. A cause-and-effect argument makes the claim that the correlation proves a causal relationship.

Elimination of other options. An argument by **elimination** identifies all possible options and proves that one option is the correct one by showing that the other options must be eliminated.

The Turkey Trot Restaurant offers a choice of mashed potatoes, wild rice, or mixed vegetables with their entrees. However, the restaurant has run out of both mashed potatoes and wild rice. Therefore, the restaurant will serve mixed vegetables with their entrees.

Generalization. An argument by **generalization** relates information about specific examples to information about a general category.

I have had five pit bulls over the years and every one of them was friendly and loyal. It must be that all pit bulls are friendly and loyal.

The argument establishes that something is true of many members of a group and then concludes that the same thing must be true about all members of a group.

Conversely, an argument by generalization can start with a fact that is true about a group in general and conclude that the same fact must be true for a particular member of the group.

It is a well-known fact that people from warm climates are typically gregarious. The ambassador is from a warm climate. We can therefore expect the ambassador to be gregarious.

Statistical arguments. A **statistical** argument is an argument that bases its conclusion on statistical evidence.

Over 40 percent of the sedans produced by Company X last year had serious problems with their brakes. Therefore, it is likely that your sedan, which was produced by Company X last year, will have brake problems.

A variation on statistical arguments involves surveys. These arguments sample a representative subgroup.

In a telephone survey, over 85 of 100 homeowners in the metropolitan area said they would vote for Senator Jackson in the upcoming election. Therefore, it is probable that Senator Jackson will get most of the metropolitan homeowner vote.

Tautology. A **tautology** is an argument that is true by definition.

All bachelors are unmarried men.

A tautology is valid. A bachelor is by definition a man who is not married.

MAJOR TYPES OF INDUCTIVE LOGIC

The most common types of inductive logic on the LSAT are analogy, cause and effect, eliminating other options, generalization, statistical arguments, and tautology.

Additional Tools for Inductive Logic

In addition to the specific types of inductive argument presented above, there are a number of tools that inductive logic can use to support conclusions.

Application of a moral principle. A conclusion can be supported by citing a moral principle. For example, *It is better to choose a plan that benefits many people a small amount than a plan that benefits a few people greatly. Therefore, the city should choose the plan that reduces the sales tax slightly rather than the plan that creates a lottery.*

Argument by facts. A conclusion can be supported simply through relevant facts. *Everyone needs calcium and sesame seeds have calcium. Therefore, if people want to get more calcium, they can eat sesame seeds.*

Citing an authority. Quoting the opinion of an authority in a relevant field is a tool for supporting a premise. *Albert Einstein said that studying physics can help people improve their memory.*

Comparison and contrast. Establishing similarities or differences between two phenomena can help establish or disprove qualities that the two phenomena share, strengthening or weakening an analogy. *Even though Weimaraners and Dachshunds are members of the same species, they have very different temperaments. The fact that Weimaraners are long-lived does not mean that Dachshunds are long-lived.*

Predict the future from an established pattern. This tool uses an established pattern of events to predict that another event will occur in the future. It is a type of generalization. *Every year for the past ten years it has rained on the Fourth of July. Therefore, we are canceling the outdoor picnic that is scheduled for the Fourth of July this year because it is almost certain to rain.*

What is true for a group must be true for each member of the group. This type of logic argues that if a group as a whole has a certain characteristic, the members of the group also have that characteristic. *Dogs are smarter than sheep. Therefore, my dog is smarter than your sheep.*

Flawed Arguments

So far this chapter has discussed types of valid arguments. The LR section also tests your ability to identify types of flawed arguments. Some flawed arguments are simply the result of incorrectly applying a valid type of logic. Other flawed arguments are based on reasoning that is inherently flawed. In the sections below you will first learn the most common types of flawed arguments. Then you will review the less common types.

MOST COMMON FLAWED ARGUMENTS

There are over fifty types of flawed arguments that have appeared on recent actual LSATs. The most common ones are listed here. There are so many possible flawed argument types that no particular type shows up very often. By carefully studying all of the types listed here, you will be prepared for whichever types are used on your test.

Confusing Necessary and Sufficient Conditions

This is one of the three most frequently used types of flawed arguments. In your review of if/then arguments you learned that a sufficient condition is one that guarantees a result. *Raining guarantees that the sidewalk will be wet.* A necessary condition is a condition without which something cannot happen. *Taking the LSAT is necessary for you to get accepted to law school (if you do not take the LSAT, you will not get into law school).*

Table 2.6. Necessary and Sufficient Conditions

	Condition	Result
Sufficient condition	Rain	Wet
Necessary condition	Taking LSAT (without this condition) →	Getting into law school (not this result)

Confusing necessary and sufficient conditions can mean either (1) starting with a necessary condition and mistakenly thinking it is sufficient, or (2) starting with a sufficient condition and mistakenly thinking it is necessary. Consider:

I took the LSAT. Why didn't I get accepted to law school?

Even though taking the LSAT is necessary for getting accepted, it is not enough (sufficient) to guarantee acceptance. The arguer above has taken a necessary condition as sufficient. The arguer below mistakenly takes a sufficient condition to be necessary:

My professor said that if I missed any more classes, I would fail the course. I didn't miss any more classes. Therefore, the professor should not have failed me.

Missing classes was sufficient for failing the course but it was not a necessary condition for failing. Failing could occur without missing any more classes.

Inferring That What Is True of the Parts Must Be True of the Whole

This is another one of the three most common flawed arguments.

None of the berries on this plant would make me sick, so if I eat all of the berries, I will not get sick.

The living room and kitchen are decorated in a Mediterranean motif, so we can assume that the entire house is designed in a Mediterranean motif.

This flawed reasoning mistakenly attributes properties that are true of part of something (each berry is non-toxic) to be true of the entire thing (if I eat all of the berries, the combination will not be toxic). In a variation, this type of flaw attributes characteristics of members of a group to the group as a whole.

False Cause

False cause is the third of the three most common types of flawed argument. A valid cause-and-effect argument correctly infers that a certain event that often comes before another event is a cause of the second event. In many cases, however, the simple fact that one event comes first and another comes later —or that two events often occur together—does not mean there is a causal relationship. False cause arguments see a correlation between two events and incorrectly assume a cause-and-effect relationship. In some cases, the fact of two events occurring together is a coincidence. In other cases, it may be that they are both caused by a third factor.

People with lung cancer often have discolored teeth. Therefore, discoloration of the teeth must lead to lung cancer.

The argument is flawed because it fails to consider the possibility that smoking leads to both discolored teeth and lung cancer.

In another type of false cause argument, event A and event B frequently occur together and the argument concludes that A causes B, when in fact it is equally possible that B causes A.

Whenever Viet drives fast, he feels the urge to use the bathroom. Driving at high speeds must cause him to have to empty his bladder.

The argument is flawed because it fails to consider that having a full bladder may cause Viet to start driving at high speeds.

Ambiguity

In the LR section, **ambiguity** refers to a word that is used in two contexts with two different meanings.

> *Martha claims to have a lot of energy. She runs, plays tennis, bicycles, and dances. Ed claims to have a lot of energy but all he does is lift weights, which requires only the most minimal of movement.*

Martha and Ed are using the word *energy* in two different ways. For Martha, energy refers to movement. For Ed, energy refers to muscle power.

A special instance of ambiguity is with the use of pronouns.

> *Union member: We will benefit if the company matches the retirement contributions of the workers.*

> *Manager: On the contrary. We will not benefit at all if we have to pay the additional amount.*

The word *we* is being used to refer to two different groups. In the first case it refers to the workers. In the second case it refers to management. Pronouns are inherently ambiguous. They refer to different people depending on the context.

Circular Reasoning

A **circular** argument is one in which the conclusion is a restatement of one of the premises. In other words, the arguer has slipped in a premise that states the very conclusion that the arguer hopes to prove.

> *People who do not eat meat do not die as soon as people who do eat meat. Such people also have fewer diseases. Therefore, vegetarians live longer and healthier lives than meat eaters.*

The premises contain all of the information that the arguer puts in the conclusion. The argument is circular. It ends up where it started.

Unrepresentative Sample

An argument based on an **unrepresentative sample** relies on data from individuals who may not be representative of the group about which the argument is trying to draw a conclusion.

> *I asked a dozen people at the mall if they planned to buy the latest teen fashion and none of them did. Therefore, the latest teen fashion is unlikely to sell well.*

The argument is flawed because the people who were questioned may not have been representative of the teenagers who are the market for the latest fashion.

Assuming There Are No Other Options

An argument may falsely assume that there are only certain options in a situation, when in fact there may be other options that the argument fails to consider.

> *Jefferson and Ortega are both running for mayor but Ortega's support has all but disappeared. Therefore, Jefferson will be the next mayor.*

The argument fails to consider that there may be other candidates for mayor.

Argument Against the Person

Known in formal logic as an ad hominem (Latin: to the person) argument, this type of flawed reasoning attacks the character of the person whom the arguer is trying to rebut, instead of addressing the person's argument. To be a flawed argument, the attack on the person's character must be irrelevant to the argument.

> *Fred says that we should all tighten our belts during this time of recession, but Fred has been convicted three times of driving while impaired, so I hardly think we should listen to his advice.*

Unreliable Source

An argument that uses an **unreliable source** draws its premises from a source that for some reason is questionable, perhaps because the source is biased or perhaps because the source is uninformed.

> *According to John, his opponent does not have the necessary skills to serve as chair of the board of directors. Therefore, I will vote for John.*

Applying a Generalization to an Inappropriate Case

This flawed argument applies a generalization to a situation that the generalization was not meant to cover.

> *One should be polite to one's elders. Olivia was in the wrong, then, when she spoke harshly to the older man who tried to grab her purse.*

The generalization of being polite to one's elders was not meant to apply to people who are trying to commit a crime.

False Appeal to Authority

An argument that falsely appeals to authority is one in which an authority is cited to support a conclusion but the authority is not an expert in the field with which the argument deals.

> *Albert Einstein recommended that we wash our hair every day.*

Albert Einstein was an authority on physics, not on hair care.

Distorting a View to Make It Vulnerable to Criticism

In this type of flawed argument, the arguer distorts the view of another person in such a way that the other person's view can be more easily attacked.

> *Ferguson: There are so many unwanted pets suffering on the streets that the city ought to set up a new shelter to accommodate these pets until homes can be found for them.*

> *Petrick: If the city were to take in every stray dog, cat, ferret, and python, the costs of food, shelter, and medical attention would be crippling to our budget.*

Petrick distorts Ferguson's argument. Ferguson argues for a shelter to accommodate some of the stray pets. Petrick portrays Ferguson's argument as calling for a shelter for all such pets, an argument that is easier to attack.

Disproving a Claim That Was Not Made

In this flawed argument, the arguer attacks a certain claim but the claim that is attacked was in fact never made by the person whom the arguer is trying to rebut.

> *Ferguson: There are so many unwanted pets suffering on the streets that the city ought to set up a new shelter to accommodate these pets until homes can be found for them.*

> *Petrick: It is not true that the city has enough money left over from last year's budget to create a new shelter. In fact, there was a shortage last year.*

Ferguson did not claim that there was money left over from last year's budget.

Concluding That Something Is True Because Most People Believe It to Be True

This type of reasoning is clearly not valid.

> *Everyone feels that Pacheco will win the election. Therefore, Pacheco's only opponent should save money by withdrawing now.*

The argument assumes that Pacheco will win, based on the beliefs of most people.

Accepting a Fact as True Because It Has Not Been Proven to Be Incorrect

In this type of flawed argument the arguer shows that there is no evidence against a certain proposition and concludes that therefore the proposition must be true.

> *No one has yet proven definitively that time travel is impossible. Therefore, scientists should accept that time travel is a reality and should begin work on developing the technology to achieve it.*

The argument is flawed because it fails to consider the possibility that even though there is no proof that time travel is impossible, it may turn out to be.

Rejecting a View Because It Has Not Been Proven

This type of flawed argument is the inverse of the previous one. Here a view is thrown out because it has not been proven definitively to be true.

> *Despite years of attempts, no one has yet proven the existence of the purported yeti. Therefore, scientists should admit that the Abominable Snowman is a myth.*

The argument is flawed because it fails to consider that even though there is no proof of the yeti's existence, the yeti may still prove to be real.

Inferring That Because Something Is Possible, It Must Occur

Consider the following:

> *Spending twenty minutes a day under a sun lamp in the winter sometimes cures seasonal depression. Therefore, if Ferenc spends twenty minutes a day under a sun lamp this winter, his usual seasonal depression will not occur.*

The argument is flawed because it fails to consider that, even though the treatment can cure depression, it is not guaranteed to cure depression.

Inferring That Because Something Is Unlikely to Occur, It Will Not Occur

This is the inverse of the previous type of flawed argument.

> *There are hardly ever any accidents on Route 147. Sandy is driving Route 147 tonight, so she will not have an accident.*

The fact that accidents are unlikely does not warrant the conclusion that an accident cannot happen.

Assuming That Because a Conclusion Is False, All of the Premises Are False

This type of flawed reasoning fails to consider the possibility that even though a conclusion is not valid, some of the premises in the argument may be correct.

> *Jason argues that the moon is a celestial body and that some celestial bodies host life. Jason has concluded that the moon hosts life, which is clearly incorrect. Therefore, we must conclude that the moon is not a celestial body.*

The fact that the conclusion of Jason's argument is incorrect does not imply that the premises of his argument are incorrect.

LESS COMMON FLAWED ARGUMENTS

There are many types of flawed arguments that only appear on the LSAT occasionally. Even though any given type occurs rarely, every LR section has less common flawed arguments. Become familiar with all of the types listed below.

Accepting a Claim Because an Opposing Claim Was Not Well Defended

> *Forbes claims that most people prefer coffee to tea but Forbes's argument is inconclusive. Therefore, most people prefer tea to coffee.*

Analogy

Although argument by analogy is valid, it is easy for an analogy to be incorrect. Simply because two things are similar in one way does not mean that they are similar in all ways. The following is an example of a false analogy:

> *Both church services and baseball games take place on Sunday. Eating ice cream in church on Sunday is considered inappropriate, so John should not eat ice cream at Sunday's baseball game either.*

Assuming There Are No Additional Necessary Factors

This flawed argument states that A is necessary for B to occur and that A occurs and thus B occurs. If fails to consider that A is not sufficient for B to occur and that there may be other factors that must occur along with A in order to guarantee the occurrence of B.

> *For a seed to sprout, it must have water. I have regularly watered the seeds I am trying to grow, so the seeds will sprout.*

Biased Language Used Against Opponents

This argument uses language that reflects poorly on people who may disagree with the arguer.

> *Statistics clearly show that most people want LaVail to win the election. The supporters of Sterling, then, must be either ignorant, stubborn, or both.*

Contradictory Premises

An argument that contains premises that are mutually contradictory is flawed.

> *Inez plays tennis every Saturday. Tomorrow is Saturday and Inez sometimes does not play tennis on Saturday. Therefore, there is a chance that Inez will not play tennis tomorrow.*

Failure to Apply a Generalization to All Cases

In this type of flawed reasoning the arguer cites a generalization but does not apply it to all applicable cases.

> *It is widely believed that people with red hair have fiery tempers. Edward has red hair, but there is no reason to believe that he has a fiery temper.*

Fails to Consider

This category includes several types of flawed reasoning. In all of these types the arguer fails to consider a certain possibility and thus the arguer's conclusion is flawed.

Fails to consider whether a specific situation meets a definition. Consider the example:

> *Most people believe that entertainment without any redeeming value is a waste of time. Therefore, most people believe that watching television reality shows is not a productive use of a person's time.*

The argument fails to consider whether *watching television reality shows* meets the definition of *entertainment without any redeeming value.*

Fails to consider that there may be an exception to a rule and that the exception would negate a recommendation.

> *Drug X grows new hair on bald heads in 90 percent of bald men. Therefore, any man who is bald and who wishes to grow new hair should take drug X.*

The argument is flawed because it fails to consider that there may be some men who can grow new hair only if they do *not* take drug X.

Fails to consider that if A causes B, something else other than A can cause B.

> *Drug X and drug Y both reliably grow new hair on bald heads. Henry is bald and wants to grow new hair. If he does not take drug X or drug Y, he will not grow new hair.*

The argument is flawed because the arguer fails to consider that there may be other ways in which Henry can grow new hair.

Fails to Establish

Similar to *fails to consider,* this category also includes a number of variations.

Fails to establish that an alternate approach is viable. In this flawed argument the arguer proposes an alternate approach but does not establish that the approach would work.

> *The Johnson firm has studied the feasibility of building a bridge across the river in the middle of town and has found that the project would be costly. Therefore, the city should plan to establish a ferry service to carry people and cars across the river.*

The argument is flawed because the arguer does not establish that the ferry service would be viable.

Fails to establish that the evidence presented is relevant to the conclusion.

> *We clearly need a ferry service to shuttle people and cars across the river in the middle of town. Both Eudora and Plainsville have had ferry service across the rivers in their towns for many years.*

The argument is flawed because the arguer fails to show that the information about the ferries in the other towns is relevant to the conclusion that the arguer's town should have a ferry. This flaw is not the same as citing irrelevant evidence because the evidence in this argument may or may not be relevant. The arguer has simply failed to establish that the evidence is relevant.

False Appeal to Fear

In this flaw the arguer tries to persuade the listener by appealing to fear rather than through logic.

> *Vote for Sanders for mayor. I hate to think of the terrible consequences that will follow if Sander's opponent wins the election.*

False Assumptions About Groups

This type of flawed argument assumes that every member of a group has a certain quality that most members of the group have. Alternately, this flawed argument attributes the characteristics of one group to another group that does not necessarily have those characteristics.

> 1. *It is well known that Labrador retrievers are gentle with children. For that reason, it is not possible that my Labrador retriever attacked your child, as you claim.*
> 2. *Surely fish must be among the cruelest of animals. They show no affection whatsoever for their young, abandoning them completely or, even worse, eating them.*

The second argument is flawed because it attributes certain emotions about offspring to animals that do not necessarily hold those emotions.

Hasty Generalization

This flawed argument takes a narrow premise and makes a generalization that is overly broad.

> *Marek did not eat any meat for breakfast today and he feels unusually good. Therefore, vegetarians must live long, healthy lives.*

Invalid Inferences

There are a number of types of flawed arguments in which the arguer infers (concludes) something incorrectly.

Infers from most similar situations to the current situation. This flawed argument concludes that because most similar situations have a certain characteristic, the current situation has the same characteristic.

At most baseball games, hot dogs are sold. Therefore, if Lon goes to the baseball game tomorrow, he will be able to buy a hot dog.

Infers from behavior to intention. This argument considers a behavior and makes an invalid conclusion about the intention behind the behavior.

The citizens of Riverdale voted overwhelmingly for the new mayor, who promptly raised the city's sales tax. It must be that the citizens wanted to pay higher taxes.

Infers from a person holding a belief to the person holding an implication of that belief. This flawed argument makes the unwarranted conclusion that if a person holds a certain belief, the person also believes an implication of that belief.

> *Ernesto believes that children should not be spanked. It is clear that if a child is never spanked, he or she will grow up to be spoiled. Apparently, Ernesto believes that children should grow up to be spoiled.*

Irrelevant Considerations

An argument is flawed if the premises on which it relies are irrelevant to the conclusion.

> *Drug Z has had a successful record of curing depression in young adults and particularly in women. Sandra is an overweight middle-aged woman. She should try drug Z. It might help her.*

Drug Z is only known to cure depression in young people. Sandra is not young and has not been shown to be depressed. The information about drug Z is irrelevant to the conclusion that Sandra should try it.

Treats One Element as Something Else

There are a number of flawed arguments that misinterpret one element of the argument.

Treats a rebuttal of an argument as proof that the argument is false.

> *John cited a report that claimed that 60 percent of town residents favored a property tax increase in order to fund the proposed new high school as proof that the high school should be built. John's citation was incorrect. In fact, the report claimed that 40 percent of town residents favored the property tax increase. Therefore, the new high school should not be built.*

The arguer rebuts the original argument by pointing out a factual error. However, it is not valid to then infer that the conclusion of the original argument was flawed. There may be other reasons why the high school should be built.

Treats a proof as merely a reinforcement of an argument.

> *It is true that all members of this year's graduating class have gotten job offers and that Una is a member of this year's graduating class. However, that does not prove that she received a job offer. It simply makes it likely that she did.*

The arguer refuses to admit that the premises prove the conclusion and instead tries to persuade the listener merely that the conclusion could be true.

Treats supporting information as information that proves the conclusion. This is the reverse of the previous flaw. The arguer tries to make supporting information seem sufficient to prove the conclusion.

> *Many of the members of this year's graduating class have received job offers. More women than men have received job offers. Una is a woman and is a member of this year's graduating class. Therefore, Una must have received a job offer.*

Treats an unjustified assertion as an intentionally false assertion.

> *Francesca claimed in her argument before the Senate subcommittee that the Mexican gray wolf was not an endangered species. In fact, it is an endangered species. Clearly, Francesca attempted to mislead the members of the subcommittee.*

The argument fails to consider that Francesca's error was unintentional.

Treats the existence of an effect as proof of intention to produce the effect.

> *As a result of Norman's decision to invest his company's retirement plans with Acme Investments, 40 percent of the value of the funds was lost and several employees were forced to postpone their retirement. Because intentionally losing employees' money is a crime, Norman should be charged with a crime.*

The argument establishes that Norman's action had a certain result but errs in asserting that Norman intended for that result to happen.

Treats a hypothesis as a fact. In this flawed argument a hypothesis is presented as an unsupported possibility but is then taken to be a fact.

> *Although there is no evidence for it, one possible explanation for Thompson's sudden departure from the law firm is that he was embezzling money from the firm. Therefore, an audit should be done immediately and Thompson should be required to pay any missing sums.*

The arguer first admits that there is no evidence to support a hypothesis that Thompson embezzled but the conclusion assumes that Thompson did embezzle.

Treats a main factor as a necessary condition. This flawed argument misconstrues a factor that is important for a certain result as a factor without which the result cannot happen.

> *A strong personal statement is an important factor in the admissions committee's decisions for accepting students into law school. Mario does not have a strong personal statement. Therefore, Mario will not be accepted.*

The personal statement is defined as an important factor but the arguer misinterprets the definition as stating that the personal statement is a necessary factor.

ARGUMENTS THAT REFUTE OTHER ARGUMENTS

Recognize arguments that refute other arguments. They involve more complex logic. If you master these arguments, you can gain points.

Refuting Arguments

Many LR questions involve an argument that attempts to refute a previous argument. Some more complex arguments may involve refuting a previous argument that attempted to refute an even earlier argument. You may be asked to identify the type of reasoning that the second arguer uses to refute the first argument or to identify reasoning that would weaken the first argument.

A refutation can involve simply pointing out a logical flaw in the first argument. The flaws may be any of the types of flawed arguments that you reviewed above. A refutation is *not* a type of flawed argument. Rather, refutations are valid arguments that point out flaws or drawbacks in the argument that the refutation is trying to attack. Below are specific tools for refuting arguments.

CHALLENGE AN ARGUMENT BY PROVIDING ADDITIONAL EVIDENCE

The arguer brings in new information that then changes the conclusion without having to challenge the original information or the original logic.

> *Ned: Emissions from the Jones factory are well below the national standards, so there is no reason to believe the emissions are the cause of the increase in asthma among our children.*

> *Tamara: The increase in asthma is much greater among children who live downwind of the Jones factory than it is among children who live upwind of the factory. If Ned is looking for evidence to link the emissions to asthma, there it is.*

CHALLENGE AN ARGUMENT BY PRESENTING AN ALTERNATE EXPLANATION

> *Paula: Last winter there was twice as much rain as in any of the previous twenty years. Undoubtedly the rain must have weakened the foundations of the dam and that must be what caused the dam to break.*

> *Rajesh: Last winter there were two serious earthquakes centered within miles of the dam. It is more likely that the earthquakes were the cause of the dam's failure.*

Rajesh's argument provides a different cause for the effect that Paula discusses, thus weakening Paula's argument.

CHALLENGE AN ARGUMENT BY SHOWING THAT ITS CONCLUSION WOULD LEAD TO UNDESIRABLE RESULTS

The arguer acknowledges the strengths of the original argument but points out an undesirable result that the original arguer did not address.

> *Granted the penalty on factory emissions proposed by city hall would significantly decrease pollution and increase the health of our residents. However, the penalty would also cause many factories to move to more lenient locations, with the result that many of our residents would lose their livelihoods.*

A related rebuttal points out that the conclusion of the original argument would lead to a logical absurdity.

> *The city has proposed a policy that no one can water their yards more than three times a week. According to the proposal, residents can request a waiver but only if they can show that the plants in their yard have died from lack of water. This policy is absurd. The point of watering is to keep your plants alive.*

CHALLENGE A GENERALIZATION

This type of rebuttal attempts to show that a generalization made in an argument does not apply or is not valid.

> *Frank claims that no one needs three weeks of vacation a year but studies have shown that most people work better if they do have three weeks of vacation.* (Challenges by showing that the generalization is false.)

It's true that most books say that parakeets are friendly but my parakeet is clearly unfriendly. (Challenges by showing an exception to the generalization.)

ESTABLISH A GENERALIZATION AND USE IT AGAINST AN ARGUMENT

This tool sets up a generalization that can then be used to rebut another argument.

Everyone on my block is opposed to the new trash collection schedule. Nearly everyone on the adjacent block is opposed to it. Clearly the vast majority of people in our neighborhood are opposed to the new schedule, so the city should drop the proposed change despite the advantages the city cited.

CHALLENGE BY ANALOGY

This attacks an argument by showing that an analogous argument is flawed.

The mayor says that if we all tighten our belts, we'll be back in prosperous times within six months. That is exactly what the previous mayor convinced us to do, and it was three years before prosperous times returned.

CHALLENGE THE VALIDITY OF AN ANALOGY

This type of rebuttal points out that two phenomena that are supposedly similar are in fact not similar in an important way.

Mr. Anderson claims that our city would benefit from a new convention center just as our neighboring city Oakville did. What Mr. Anderson did not mention was that Oakville has five times the population of our city. Our small city could never support such a center.

UNDERMINES AN APPARENT COUNTEREXAMPLE TO A GENERAL CLAIM

In this type of rebuttal, the first arguer cites a claim made by another party—either the second arguer or another party not present in the argument—and then attacks the claim by citing a counterexample to the stated claim. The second arguer rebuts the first arguer by showing that the counterexample does not apply.

Valeria: University policy states that plagiarism is a serious offense punishable by expulsion. However, the university president herself, in her recently published book on academic principles, borrowed extensively from better-known authors. The university president has not been expelled so the policy should be abandoned.

Zack: Plagiarism is the use of previously published material without attribution or permission from the author. The university president has written permission from all of the authors whom she quoted and attributes her quotes to them. Therefore, the university president did not commit plagiarism.

Valeria attacks the policy on plagiarism by attempting to show that the university president was not subjected to the university policy. Zack challenges Valeria's argument by showing that the university president's case does not constitute an exception to the university policy.

QUESTION TYPES

This section teaches you to recognize and understand the types of question stems that LR items use. There are five categories of question types that account for over 75 percent of all LR questions. There are an additional ten question types that are less frequent but that are important for you to understand.

MOST COMMON QUESTION TYPES

The effect of a new premise (strengthen, weaken, or resolve a paradox)—29% of LR questions

Assumption—13% of LR questions

Identify a conclusion—13% of LR questions

Identify the flaw—13% of LR questions

Parallel reasoning—7% of LR questions

LESS COMMON QUESTION TYPES

Application of a principle

Committed to disagree/agree

Complete the sentence/argument

Consistent with both arguments

Identify an element of an argument

Match a principle to a concrete example

Must be true

Relevant information

Role of a claim

Type of reasoning

Most Common Question Types

The following five categories of questions are listed in the order of how frequently they occur. Most of the categories encompass several distinct question types or variations.

THE EFFECT OF A NEW PREMISE

This is the most common category of LR question. In nearly 30 percent of LR questions, the answer choices are new premises and you must find the one that—depending on the specific question stem—strengthens the conclusion, strengthens the conclusion by applying a principle, weakens the conclusion, or resolves a paradox presented in the argument.

The premises in the answer choices *must* be accepted as true. You cannot throw out an answer choice simply because you do not think it is true or consistent with the passage. Assume each answer choice is a true statement and then test whether it accomplishes the goal stated in the stem (strengthens, weakens, or resolves the paradox). This advice may sound straightforward but most test takers initially find themselves falling into the trap of throwing out an answer choice because it seems untrue. On most multiple-choice questions

---

> **EFFECT OF A NEW PREMISE QUESTION TYPE**
>
> Strengthen the conclusion
>
> Strengthen by applying a principle
>
> Weaken the conclusion
>
> Resolve a paradox

on exams that you have taken, you have to evaluate whether an answer choice is true or false, so you must train yourself *not* to do this on questions that test the effect of new premises.

Because all *effect of a new premise* questions require you to assume that the answer choices are true, the question stems nearly always use wording such as *Which one of the following, if true; which one of the following, if valid;* or *which one of the following, if assumed.* Be particularly careful when you see the wording *if assumed.* Such a question is *not* an *assumption* question.

To solve an *effect of a new premise* question, first identify the structure of the original argument. Identify the premises. Identify the conclusion. Identify the type of reasoning that the arguer uses. These may sound like simple steps but in fact it can be difficult to identify these elements of the argument. Take the time to carefully identify the elements of the argument and write them down in the scratch area of your test.

Strengthen a Conclusion

Nearly half of the *effect of a new premise* questions ask you to find the new premise that **strengthens** the argument. To solve a *strengthen* question, identify the structure of the argument and test the answer choices to see which one makes the argument more convincing. Such arguments typically involve cause-and-effect arguments, matching of terms, or matching of two events. These are explained below.

Strengthen questions based on cause-and-effect arguments. The majority of *strengthen* questions involve cause-and-effect arguments, in which two or more factors have a correlation and the conclusion states that one factor causes another.

Consider an argument that states that many people who snore also suffer from insufficient sleep. The statement establishes a correlation between snoring and lack of sleep. The argument may then conclude that snoring causes people to lose sleep. A cause-and-effect argument typically starts with a correlation and then concludes that one factor causes the other. A correlation between two events is not enough to prove that event A caused event B. It is possible that event B caused event A, that another factor caused both A and B, or that B was caused by a factor that has no relationship to A. Consider the ways in which the following statements strengthen the conclusion that snoring causes loss of sleep. In terms of A and B, in which A is snoring and B is sleeping, the original argument says

A leads to not B. Therefore, A causes not B.

   1. *Before John started snoring, he slept well.*

This premise shows that lack of snoring is correlated to sleeping well or *not A leads to B.* Combined with the original premise, the argument now reads

A leads to not B. Not A leads to B. Therefore, A causes not B.

The method of strengthening, then, is based on the logic that if a certain event causes a second event, then if the first event does not occur, the second event should not occur either.

   2. *John is not kept awake by noisy neighbors.*

This premise eliminates an alternative explanation for John's lack of sleep. Eliminating alternative explanations strengthens the case that it was snoring that prevented John from sleeping, not some other factor.

   3. *When John's snoring worsened, he began to sleep even less.*

The logic in this premise is that if a little of A causes a little of B, then a lot of A should cause a lot of B.

4. *John's lack of sleep does not cause him to snore.*

This premise strengthens the argument by eliminating the possibility that it is B that causes A.

5. *Snoring is known to disrupt deep sleep brain rhythms and cause the sleeper to briefly wake up.*

This premise strengthens the argument by providing an explanation for the mechanism by which A causes B.

The examples above include the most common methods for strengthening a cause-and-effect argument. They are listed below.

THE MOST COMMON METHODS FOR STRENGTHENING A CAUSE-AND-EFFECT ARGUMENT (A CAUSES B)

1. The absence of A causes the absence of B.
2. Eliminate other possible causes of B.
3. More of A causes more of B.
4. B does not cause A.
5. Provide an explanation for the mechanism by which A causes B.

Practice Exercise 5

Create five premises that strengthen the following cause-and-effect argument, using each of the methods above.

Many people who jog regularly have fast metabolisms. Therefore, jogging must cause people's metabolisms to speed up.

The arguments above, relating snoring and lack of sleep and relating jogging and metabolism, are relatively simple, with one A factor and one B factor. Other cause-and-effect arguments in a *strengthen* question may be more complex. Below are examples of variations on cause-and-effect arguments, along with the methods for strengthening the arguments.

1. **Argument:** *Snoring is not associated with lack of sleep. Therefore, people who do not sleep well probably have an underlying medical problem other than snoring.*
   A is not associated with B. Therefore, a different factor, C, is the cause of B.
   Strengthening premise: *People who snore usually sleep longer than people who do not snore.*
   The premise strengthens by presenting more evidence that A does not cause B.

2. **Argument:** *Snoring physically disrupts the sleep cycle but in fact most people who snore sleep better than the general population. Therefore, people who snore are probably genetically predisposed to sleep well.*
   There are reasons why A does not cause B but in fact A is associated with B in this case, so there likely are genetic factors that override A's usual effect on B.
   Strengthening premise: *People who snore usually report that at least one of their parents slept well.*
   The premise strengthens the argument by showing that a blood relative has the trait identified as genetic.

3. **Argument:** *People who sleep only during the day often snore. These same people often do not sleep well. This indicates that there is something about sleeping during the day that leads to not sleeping well.*

   A and B are found together. A, B, and C are also found together. Therefore, A must cause C.

   Strengthening premise: *People who sleep only during the day but do not snore and otherwise sleep in conditions similar to people who sleep only during the day who do snore, sleep well.*

   The premise strengthens the argument by showing that when A occurs without B but all other conditions are equal, C does not take place. This eliminates B as a cause of C and strengthens A as the cause.

4. **Argument:** *Many people injure themselves exercising. However, proper exercise can help people avoid injuries, so it is not necessary to avoid exercising in order to avoid injuries.*

   A factor that might seem to cause a negative result actually occurs along with a positive result, so it is not necessary to avoid the seemingly negative factor.

   Strengthening premise: *Proper exercise strengthens tendons that otherwise might tear under strain induced by exercise.*

   The premise strengthens by showing the mechanism by which a seemingly negative factor actually accomplishes a positive result.

5. **Argument:** *Snoring leads to lack of sleep. Snoring also leads to general medical complaints. Therefore, snoring accounts for an increase in the number of visits to physicians.*

   A causes B. A also causes C. Therefore, A causes a consequence (visits to physicians) of both B and C.

   Strengthening premise: *Many people consider lack of sleep to be a condition that they should discuss with their physician.*

   The premise strengthens the argument by showing how B leads to the same consequence to which C leads.

6. **Argument:** *Snoring leads to loss of sleep, which is unhealthy. Sleeping on your side can prevent snoring. Therefore, if you tend to snore, you should make a resolution to sleep on your side whenever you get into bed.*

   A (sleeping on one's side) is desirable. Therefore, one should resolve to do A.

   Strengthening premise: *Resolving to take an action during sleep is often effective in actually performing the action.*

   The premise strengthens by stating that a resolution actually leads to the desired action.

SUMMARY OF STRATEGIES FOR MORE COMPLEX STRENGTHENING BASED ON CAUSE AND EFFECT

1. Provide further evidence for one of the premises.
2. Strengthen a genetic argument by establishing that a blood relative has the trait in question.
3. State additional relationships between the events in such a way as to strengthen the argument.
4. Explain the mechanism by which a seemingly negative event is actually positive.
5. State that a prelude to an event, as suggested by the argument, actually leads to the event.

Strengthen questions based on matching terms. In these questions there are two distinct terms that are used to establish a correlation. To strengthen the argument, find a premise that shows that the terms refer to the same phenomenon.

1. **Argument:** *In the past, American politicians lacked an in-depth understanding of both the history and political philosophies of European countries. Fortunately, this is no longer the case today. As a result, American politicians make better judgments about foreign policy issues.*

   Strengthening premise: *An understanding of the history and political philosophy of a country leads to making better judgments in foreign policy decisions.*

   The original argument uses two distinct phrases—*in-depth understanding of history and political philosophy* and *make better judgments*. The argument implies that the one leads to the other but does not state it. The new premise strengthens the argument by stating that the two terms are related.

   Strengthen questions based on matching events. This type of question is similar to the matching of two terms but instead of matching specific terms, the argument attempts to match broader events.

2. **Argument:** *Maria has refused to attend every sporting event to which we have invited her. Her husband, Greg, dislikes most sporting events, so clearly Greg is convincing Maria not to attend.*

   The argument tries to tie Maria's behavior to Greg's behavior.

   Strengthening premise: *The only sporting events that Maria has refused to attend have been in a field of sports that Greg dislikes.*

   The new premise makes a closer connection between Greg's dislikes and Maria's behavior.

Strengthen questions based on miscellaneous types of logic. Some *strengthen* questions are not based on either cause and effect or matching two events or terms.

1. **Argument:** *Acme Corporation will be hiring college students for summer jobs. In the past, Acme has only hired students with high grade point averages. If you want to get a job at Acme, it is important to keep your grades up.*

   Strengthening premise: *Acme has stated that the only criterion needed for a college student to get a job is a high grade point average.*

   The original argument implies that grade point average is important for getting a job. The new premise documents that a high grade point average is the only criterion needed for getting a job.

2. **Argument:** *The black locust is a faster-growing tree than the pinyon pine. Therefore, the black locust makes a better shade tree.*

   Strengthening premise: *A tree that grows faster develops a thicker canopy than a slower-growing tree, thus blocking out more sunlight.*

   The original argument implies that there is a relationship between rate of growth and shading properties. The new premise specifies this relationship.

3. **Argument:** *In the past ten years many universities have eliminated general studies degrees. At the same time, there has been an increase in the number of universities offering computer science degrees. Therefore, the number of students earning degrees in computer science must now be larger than the number of students earning degrees in general studies.*

Strengthening premise: *In general there are many more students enrolled in any computer science degree program than there are students enrolled in any general studies degree program.*

The original argument compares the number of degree programs in one area with the number of degree programs in a different area. However, the original argument's conclusion refers to the number of students. The new premise makes a connection between the number of students and the type of program.

In this type of question you must distinguish the number of categories from the number of members of a category. Table 2.7 illustrates two scenarios. In both scenarios there are more computer science programs (500) than general studies programs (300). In scenario 1, there are fewer students enrolled on average in a general studies program (50) compared to the average number of students enrolled in a computer science program (200). As a result, the total number of students enrolled in all computer science programs is larger than the total number of students enrolled in all general studies programs.

In scenario 2, the average number of students in a general studies program is 200, whereas the average number of students in a computer science program is 50. As a result, there are fewer total students enrolled in all computer science programs, even though there are many more computer science programs than general studies programs.

Table 2.7. Distinguish Number of Categories from Number of Members of a Category.

	# of Students per Program	# of Programs	# of Students
Scenario 1 General studies	50	300	15,000
Scenario 1 Computer science	200	500	100,000
Scenario 2 General studies	200	300	60,000
Scenario 2 Computer science	50	500	25,000

4. **Argument:** *The New Daily Times movie critic gave the same star rating to both the latest vampire movie and the new documentary on the Mexican gray wolf. Therefore, the two movies must have the same value to society.*

   Strengthening premise: *The New Daily Times movie critic assigns star ratings based on a movie's value to society.*

   The original argument implies that there is a relationship between the star rating and the social value of a movie. The new premise documents the relationship.

There can be many variations in *strengthen* questions. In addition to studying the examples above, carefully review the *strengthen* questions that you encounter in your practice exams.

Wording variations for strengthen arguments. The basic wording for a *strengthen* question stem is:

> *Which one of the following, if true, most strengthens the argument?*

Below are some examples of variations on this basic wording. To recognize a *strengthen* question stem, first look for wording such as *which one of the following, if true.* Then, look for wording that indicates that the argument or conclusion above is to be strengthened, supported, justified, or correctly drawn.

┌───┐

WORDING VARIATIONS FOR *STRENGTHEN* QUESTIONS

Which one of the following, if true, most strengthens the politician's argument?

Which one of the following, if true, most strengthens the reasoning in the above argument?

└───┘

Strengthen by Applying a Principle

The second type of *effect of a new premise* question type also involves strengthening the argument, but in this case, your task is to identify the principle that strengthens the original argument. The number of *strengthen by applying a principle* questions is about equal to the number of *strengthen* questions.

A principle is an abstract statement, as opposed to a concrete statement. For example, *Shanelle is a history major and she loves sushi* is a concrete statement about a specific person. On the other hand, *College students in the social sciences often prefer ethnic food* is an abstract statement, referring to categories of people and food. Abstract statements can be more difficult to understand than concrete statements.

Most questions that ask you to strengthen an argument by applying a principle are quite similar. The setup presents an argument. The argument may have a logical gap or a missing bit of information necessary to make the argument valid. The answer choices are stated in abstract terms. The correct answer matches the concrete details of the setup and strengthens the argument.

1. **Argument:** *It is true that Inez included in her thesis a statement that was virtually an exact quote from an essay by Jonathan Swift published in an anthology of essays. However, she should not be expelled for plagiarism because she got the statement from her roommate, who claimed to have made it up herself that morning.*

   Strengthening premise: *The inclusion in an academic work of previously published material without permission from the author cannot be considered plagiarism unless the person including the disputed material knows that the material was previously published.* The principle is an abstract one. It does not address Inez's situation specifically. However, it exactly matches her situation. In addition, the principle establishes that Inez is not guilty of plagiarism, because she thought the material was made up by her roommate.

Be careful not to confuse this type of question with a question that includes principles in the setup and then asks you to identify an answer choice that can be concluded based on the original principle. Such a question is a *conclusion* question. *Conclusion* questions are covered below.

Wording variations for arguments that strengthen by applying a principle. Basic wording for these questions is:

> *Which one of the following principles, if valid, most helps to justify the argument above?*

Below are variations for arguments that strengthen by applying a principle.

WORDING VARIATIONS FOR ARGUMENTS THAT STRENGTHEN BY APPLYING A PRINCIPLE

Which one of the following principles, if valid, most helps to justify the reasoning in the scientist's argument?

Which one of the following principles, if valid, provides the most support for the scientist's argument?

Which one of the following principles, if valid, most helps to justify the reasoning in the scientist's response to the journalist?

Which one of the following principles, if valid, most helps to justify the reasoning in the scientist's argument?

EFFECT OF A NEW PREMISE QUESTION TYPES

These types—including strengthen, strengthen by applying a principle, weaken, and resolve a paradox—account for 30 percent of all LR questions!

Weaken

The third type of *effect of a new premise* question is a question in which you must find a new premise that weakens the argument. *Weaken* arguments are inverses of *strengthen* arguments. The two share common elements. About 40 percent of *weaken* questions involve cause-and-effect arguments. About 20 percent involve statistical or survey arguments. About 10 percent involve analogies. The other 30 percent include miscellaneous types.

Weaken based on cause and effect. Just as in *strengthen* arguments, *weaken* arguments based on cause and effect present a correlation between events and then conclude that one event caused the other. In *weaken* arguments, look for a new premise that *weakens* the cause-and-effect relationship stated in the setup.

1. **Argument:** *One batch of jelly was made with artificial sweetener and a second batch was made with sugar. The batch made with artificial sweetener had a greater amount of spoilage. Because sugar does not have any preservative properties, it must be that the artificial sweetener actually caused spoilage.*

   Weakening premise: *The jars used for the second batch were sterilized longer than the jars for the first batch.*

   The new premise introduces an alternate explanation by pointing out an additional difference between the two batches. Providing an alternate plausible explanation is a significant method of weakening a cause and effect argument.

2. **Argument:** *The crack in the dam has all the markings of damage from freezing. However, the water in the dam has not frozen during the past ten years. Therefore, the cause of the crack must be minor earthquakes.*

   Weakening premise: *The only earthquakes that have occurred in the area of the dam in the last ten years have been too small to cause the type of crack that has appeared.*

   The new premise eliminates the cause suggested in the original argument.

3. **Argument:** *The recent explosion at the gravel pit occurred shortly before the increase in emergency room visits for asthma attacks among children. However, the explosion cannot be the cause of the attacks because a child would have to have been within a half mile of the explosion to be affected by it.*

   Weakening premise: *The area immediately around the gravel pit is heavily populated by families with children.*

   The new premise negates an assumption in the argument that there were few children in the vicinity of the explosion.

4. **Argument:** *In a recent experiment one group of asthma sufferers was asked to exercise vigorously for 30 minutes, whereas the control group was not asked to exercise. The group that exercised experienced fewer symptoms than the control group, so exercise must reduce asthma symptoms.*

   Weakening premise: *People who are asked to do a potentially helpful activity may experience a decrease of symptoms just from believing the activity may help them.*

   This type of question requires you to spot a flawed control group experiment. In this experiment the treatment group knew they were being treated.

5. **Argument:** *In a recent experiment one group of asthma sufferers was asked to exercise vigorously for thirty minutes, whereas a second group was asked to exercise for only five minutes. The two groups had exactly the same number of asthma attacks during the study, so the amount of exercise must not affect the frequency of asthma attacks.*

   Weakening premise: *The people in the group who exercised for thirty minutes had five times the number of asthma attacks as the people in the second group before the study began.*

   The new premise shows that the two groups were not equivalent. The premise relies on a measure of improvement (for example, from five attacks per day to one attack per day), as opposed to a simple count of the number of attacks. In Table 2.8, the number of attacks in each group is the same but the improvement (change in the number of attacks) is greater in group 1.

Table 2.8. Number of Attacks Versus Change in Attacks

	Number of Attacks	Change in Attacks
Group 1	1 per hour	From 5 attacks per hour to 1 attack per hour
Group 2	1 per hour	From 2 attacks per hour to 1 attack per hour

6. **Argument:** *John switched his overweight dog from commercial dog food to a special healthy dog food but despite three months on a strict diet of the healthy food, his dog has not lost any weight. Therefore, the special healthy dog food is not effective in reducing weight in dogs.*

   Weakening premise: *In most cases it takes a minimum of six months for a change in diet to have an effect on a dog's weight.*

   The new premise attacks the timeline that is assumed in the original argument.

7. **Argument:** *All of Marek's cousins like to play soccer. Marek also likes to play soccer. Therefore, the interest in playing soccer must be genetic.*

   Weakening premise: *Most of Marek's cousins attend schools that have active programs of encouraging children to participate in soccer.*

   The new premise presents an environmental (nongenetic) reason why all of Marek's cousins like to play soccer. Introducing a nongenetic cause of a behavior is a common method of weakening a genetic cause-and-effect argument.

SUMMARY OF STRATEGIES FOR WEAKENING BASED ON CAUSE AND EFFECT

1. Provide an alternate explanation.
2. Eliminate a cause suggested in the original argument.
3. Negate an assumption in the original argument.
4. Point out a flawed control group experiment.
5. Show that two groups that were assumed to be equivalent in the original argument differ in a significant way.
6. Show that the timeline on which the original argument is based is not realistic.
7. Establish a nongenetic (environmental) cause as an alternate explanation for a cause that is implied as genetic in the original argument.

Weaken based on statistical or survey arguments. In these arguments the logic is based on numerical evidence. The numerical evidence may be given as specific numbers, specific percentages, or as a statement that more people met a certain criterion than another. The evidence may come from a measurement (statistical information) or from asking people about their preferences (a survey).

1. **Argument:** *In surveys, most people do not list attending sporting events as an important priority. Despite this, some experts claim that entertainment is a top priority for people. Clearly, these experts are incorrect.*

   Weakening premise: *There are many forms of entertainment other than attending sporting events.*

   The new premise shows that the terms *sporting events* and *entertainment* do not match. This is the reverse of a *strengthen* argument that shows that two terms do match.

2. **Argument:** *The results of Josh's survey of incoming freshmen included three times as many completed surveys from freshmen who were unhappy with their courses as from freshmen who were happy with their courses. It is apparent that Josh's results are biased by his own dislike of his courses.*

   Weakening premise: *An independent study of freshmen determined that nearly four times as many freshmen were unhappy with their courses as were happy with their courses.*

   In this argument an unequal representation is taken to show a bias. The argument is weakened by showing that the unequal representation matches the actual occurrence of opinions as measured impartially.

3. **Argument:** *A new test for diabetes has a 90 percent success rate in identifying people who have diabetes, compared to the 75 percent success rate for the current test. Therefore, the current test should be replaced by the new test.*

   Weakening premise: *The current test has a 95 percent success rate in identifying people who do not have diabetes, whereas the new test has only a 60 percent success rate.*

   This method of weakening depends on understanding that a diagnostic procedure must be evaluated on four criteria: true positive results (correctly identifying people who do have diabetes), true negative results (correctly identifying people who do not have diabetes), false positive results (determining that someone has diabetes when he or she does not), and false negative results (determining that someone does not have diabetes when he or she does). Evaluating a diagnostic procedure on only one of these criteria is flawed and the argument can be weakened by showing that one of the other criteria favors the alternative diagnostic procedure.

4. **Argument:** *Your plan for reducing our company's shortfall recommends reducing vacation time but that will only save $10,000. My plan identifies ten workers who can be eliminated without reducing productivity. Because the average worker earns $20,000, my plan saves the company $200,000 and should be implemented.*

   Weakening premise: *All the workers who have been identified for elimination are interns who are working without pay.*

   The new premise shows that the group that the arguer is identifying (workers to be eliminated) does not in fact fall into the category that the arguer defined (earning $20,000).

5. **Argument:** *Of thirty-five reported small airplane crashes, only seven of the ninety-eight people involved survived. Small airplanes are clearly very dangerous. In fact, the statistics are worse than they appear because there are many unreported airplane crashes in which no one survived.*

   Weakening premise: *If an airplane crash is unreported, there is no way to know how many people did or did not survive.*

   The new premise does not necessarily destroy the original argument. The original statistics still document that small airplanes are not particularly safe. However, the new premise weakens the argument by pointing out a flaw in the argument's logic. Nothing can be known about an event that is unknown.

6. **Argument:** *Ben's Grocery has recently expanded their selection of gourmet coffees in an attempt to increase profits. The managers of Ben's apparently believe that wealthier people will buy more gourmet coffee if there is a larger selection. However, only 10 percent of Ben's customers buy gourmet coffee, whereas over 90 percent buy milk. Ben's should expand their selection of milk rather than their selection of gourmet coffee.*

   Weakening premise: *Ben's earns a much higher profit from the sale of gourmet coffee than they do from the sale of milk.*

The new premise attacks the original conclusion mathematically, showing that a smaller number of sales of product A can lead to a higher profit if the profit per sale for product A is larger by enough of a margin than the profit per sale for product B. The logic in this attack is similar to the logic in Argument 5 on page 181, under "Weaken Based on Cause and Effect."

Table 2.9. The Fallacy of Percentages. A smaller percentage may yield a higher profit when the profit per sale is higher.

	% of All Buyers	Actual Number of Buyers	Profit per Sale	Total Profit
Gourmet coffee	10	50	$3.00	$150
Milk	90	450	$0.10	$ 45

The lesson of this example is to not be misled by percentages or by any other ratio (percentage is simply a specific type of ratio.) A higher ratio may not mean a larger result. The following argument gives a further example of the need to distinguish ratios from actual numbers.

7. **Argument:** *Three-quarters of the residents of Poplar City have BMW autos. Only one-tenth of the residents of New Madrid drive BMW autos. Clearly the total number of BMWs owned by residents of Poplar City is far greater than the number of BMWs owned by residents of New Madrid.*

Weakening premise: *Poplar City has a population of 10,000 and New Madrid has a population of 800,000.*

Beware of ratios (including percentages). Do not confuse ratios with actual numbers. *One out of ten* is a ratio. *Fifty BMWs* represents a number. When you see ratios in premises, look for the actual numbers in the conclusion. In the above argument, the conclusion implies that the actual number of BMWs is higher in the town that has the ratio of 3:4 versus the town with the ratio of 1:10.

Table 2.10. The Difference Between Ratio and Actual Number

	Ratio of Residents Who Have BMWs	Total Number of Residents	Total Number of BMWs
New Madrid	1:10	800,000	80,000
Poplar City	3:4	10,000	7,500

SUMMARY OF STRATEGIES FOR WEAKENING BASED ON STATISTICAL OR SURVEY ARGUMENTS

1. Show that two terms that are equated in the argument are not equivalent.
2. Establish that an unequal sampling in a survey is in fact representative.
3. Show that a diagnostic procedure that is effective in one mode of diagnosis (true positive, true negative, false positive, false negative) is not effective in another mode.
4. Show that a phenomenon that the arguer claims will lead to a benefit because of certain criteria does not actually match the criteria.
5. Point out a logical flaw in the original argument.
6. Show that a lower ratio (including percentage) results in a higher actual number, or vice versa.

Weaken based on an analogy. About 10 percent of *weaken* questions are based on analogy. An analogy states that two phenomena are similar in one way and, thus, are probably similar in a second way. To weaken such an argument, you must show that the two phenomena are not alike in some relevant way.

1. **Argument:** *Sharmain likes to play chess and she also excels at math. Hank plays chess, so he most likely excels at math as well.*

   Weakening premise: *Francesca plays chess but performs poorly at math.*

   The original argument establishes that Sharmain has two characteristics and then concludes that Hank is analogous to Sharmain through one characteristic (chess) and must therefore also have the second characteristic. The new premise establishes that there are examples of people who share the first characteristic (chess) without also sharing the second characteristic (math).

2. **Argument:** *Viet should probably add a nitrogen fertilizer to his vegetable garden. Karen added nitrogen fertilizer to her garden and it stimulated plant growth, which resulted in better fruit. If Viet fertilizes his garden with nitrogen, he will have better fruit too.*

   Weakening premise: *Viet's garden has much more nitrogen in the soil than Karen's garden had before she fertilized it, and too much nitrogen can result in poorer fruit.*

   The new premise shows that the two gardens are different in a critical way.

3. **Argument:** *The previously unidentified fossil in the local museum can now be identified as a juvenile tyrannosaurus. The proportions of the skull match nearly exactly the unique proportions of tyrannosaurus skulls. In addition, the foot bones also show characteristics that are unique to the tyrannosaurus.*

   Weakening premises: *Tyrannosaurus hands typically have two clawed digits, which are not present in the fossil.*

   No tyrannasauri lived in the region in which the fossil was found.

   The first new premise weakens by establishing that a tyrannosaurus had qualities not present in, or different from, the fossil. The second premise weakens by showing why the fossil could not be a tyrannosaurus.

SUMMARY OF STRATEGIES FOR WEAKENING BASED ON ANALOGY ARGUMENTS

An analogy argument states that one phenomenon has certain characteristics, that a second phenomenon is similar to the first phenomenon, and that therefore the second phenomenon has the same characteristics. The primary ways of weakening an analogy argument are to (1) show that the two related phenomena are different in an important way, or (2) give a reason why the second phenomenon could not have the characteristics.

Types of Strategies:

1. Argument: Phenomenon 1 has characteristics A and B. Phenomenon 2 has characteristic A. Conclusion. Phenomenon 2 must have characteristic B. Weaken by an example of another phenomenon with characteristic A but without characteristic B.

2. Show that two phenomena that the arguments claim are analogous are different in a significant way. (Phenomenon 2 has characteristics that Phenomenon 1 does not have, or Phenomenon 2 lacks characteristics that Phenomenon 1 has.)

3. Provide a reason that supports that Phenomenon 2 cannot have the qualities that the analogy argument implies it has.

Weaken based on miscellaneous arguments. About 20 percent of *weaken* arguments have miscellaneous types of logic. Often the arguments simply present facts and make a conclusion. Below are examples of common *weaken* questions with miscellaneous logic, along with the strategies for weakening them.

1. **Argument:** *Our city could increase its water supply to meet future needs either by extending our existing wells down an additional 100 feet or by entering into a complex agreement with our nearest neighboring city that would require building miles of new pipeline. Extending our existing wells would cost far less, be completed more quickly, and involve less legal planning than an agreement with our neighboring city. Therefore, we should choose the option of lowering our existing wells.*

   Weakening premise: *Lowering the existing wells would introduce toxic minerals into the drinking water.*

   The original argument claims that choice A is better than choice B for a number of reasons. The new premise weakens the argument by establishing that choice A introduces negative effects not considered by the original argument. A variation on this type of weakening would be to show that choice B has positive qualities that were not anticipated by the original argument.

2. **Argument:** *Liam recently bought a new grill, a large supply of hot dogs, and a chef's hat and apron. Apparently, Liam is planning to grill hot dogs.*

   Weakening premise: *Liam's father is having a birthday next week and his father has expressed an interest in taking up grilling.*

   The original argument cites a series of events and states a conclusion that explains the events. The new premise provides an alternative explanation for the same events.

3. **Argument:** *According to recent theories of astrophysics, any astronomical body that is smaller than Pluto would not have a detectable gravitational effect on a star the size of our sun. No comet larger than Pluto has been detected in our solar system, so it is unlikely that a comet would ever affect the sun's gravity.*

   Weakening premise: *Astronomers have documented that a comet in a nearby part of our galaxy has had a gravitational influence on a star the size of our sun.*

   The original argument cites a theory. The new premise presents a documented fact that contradicts the conclusion of the theory. The argument below also weakens an argument by citing facts, but in this case the facts are statistical rather than observed.

4. **Argument:** *Many raw foods have antitumor properties. People who eat a lot of raw foods can reduce their risk of cancer.*

   Weakening premise: *A recent study shows that the rates of four common types of cancer are slightly higher in people who report eating raw foods as 30 percent or more of their diet than the rates of cancer of people who report eating raw foods as 10 percent or less of their diet.*

   This new premise uses a statistical correlation, rather than an observed fact, to weaken the argument.

5. **Argument:** *Long-term fasting can lead to exhaustion and depression. People who want to lose weight should not resort to long-term fasting.*

   Weakening premise: *The type of fasting used by nearly all weight loss programs does not last long enough to induce exhaustion or depression.*

   The new premise weakens the original argument by showing that a premise of the original argument is irrelevant to the conclusion. The situation that the original argument is addressing, fasting for weight loss, does not match the criteria that make fasting harmful. The original premise would only be valid if the weight loss program lasted three months, for example. The original premise was correct in principle but its time frame was off.

An original premise might also be inherently irrelevant. Consider:

Weakening premise: *No modern weight loss program uses extended fasting of any kind.* In this example the original premise is not correct even in principle. It is in error and thus is irrelevant to the conclusion.

A new premise cannot negate a premise in the setup. All premises in the setup have to be accepted as true. (*All white cats are deaf, right?*) In the above examples the new premise does not say that the original premise is false. It says, rather, that the original premise does not apply to the conclusion.

SUMMARY OF STRATEGIES FOR WEAKENING BASED ON MISCELLANEOUS ARGUMENTS

1. Show that a choice favored by the conclusion has additional negative qualities.

2. Show that a choice rejected by the conclusion has additional positive qualities.

3. Provide an alternative explanation for a series of events.

4. Attack the conclusion of a theory by citing an observed event or fact that contradicts the conclusion.

5. Provide statistical evidence that contradicts the conclusion.

6. Show that a premise is irrelevant, either because it does not match the conclusion at all or because it partially matches the conclusion but does not match the time frame or quantities involved in the conclusion.

Wording variations for weaken arguments. The basic wording for a *weaken* question stem is:

> *Which one of the following, if true, most weakens the argument?*

Study the variations below to learn the elements that indicate a *weaken* question.

WORDING VARIATIONS FOR *WEAKEN* ARGUMENTS

Which one of the following, if true, most seriously weakens the scientist's argument?

Which one of the following, if true, would most weaken the scientist's argument?

Which one of the following, if true, most weakens the reasoning?

Which one of the following, if true, most seriously calls into question evidence offered in support of the scientist's conclusion?

Which one of the following, as a possible challenge, most seriously weakens the scientist's argument?

Which one of the following, if true, constitutes the logically most compelling rebuttal to the scientist's argument?

Which one of the following, if true, would provide evidence against the scientist's theory?

Which one of the following, if true, most seriously undermines the reasoning in the argument?

Resolve a Paradox

The final category of question types involving the effect of a new premise is that of **resolving a paradox**. In *resolve a paradox* questions, the setup includes seemingly contradictory statements. The first step in solving such a question is to identify which statements constitute the paradox and what the nature of the paradox is. The paradox usually involves two premises.

The correct answer for a *resolve a paradox* question is a new premise that explains how each of the premises that constitute the paradox can be true despite the fact that the premises appear to be contradictory. Often the correct answer is something unexpected that you would not necessarily have thought of but once you consider it, it makes sense. For this reason, the best way to solve a *resolve a paradox* question is to read each answer and test whether it resolves the paradox.

Solving these questions is like solving a mystery. A piece of the puzzle that will explain everything is missing. Fortunately, the missing piece is one of the five answer choices.

Nearly any topic that is otherwise used in LR questions can be used in a *resolve a paradox* passage, though there are slightly more physical science questions than average, and fewer passages on the arts. *Resolve a paradox* questions do not have the large number of variations that *strengthen* and *weaken* questions have. Most can be solved using the same tools.

TIP

RESOLVING A PARADOX

To resolve a paradox, first identify what it is about the information presented that is contradictory or paradoxical.

1. **Argument:** *The Flix21 movie complex responded to complaints about long waits in the ticket line by setting up three new ticket sales stations and hiring additional employees to staff the new stations. Nevertheless, on the first weekend that the new stations were in operation, the average wait in the ticket line was five minutes longer than before the new stations were implemented.*

    Resolving premise: *Flix21's ads before the weekend promised "More ticket sellers. Faster lines." As a result the number of people attending Flix21's complex greatly increased.*

    The original argument is paradoxical in that three new ticket stations should logically result in faster ticket sales and shorter waits in the ticket line. The new premise provides additional information that explains how the facts in the original argument can all be true and yet do not result in a paradox.

Wording of the question stem. About half of *resolve a paradox* question stems refer to a discrepancy, paradox, or conflict. Of these, the vast majority use the wording *apparent discrepancy*.

> *Which one of the following, if true, helps explain the apparent discrepancy in the above argument?*

In addition, you will also see a small number of questions with the wording *discrepancy, apparent paradox, paradox,* and *conflict.* About half of *resolve a paradox* questions use the wording *explains the facts,* without referring to a paradox.

> *Which one of the following, if true, most helps to explain the facts given above?*

Some such questions may hint at a paradox with wording such as *a significant difference* or *an unexpected fact.*

> *Which one of the following, if true, most helps to explain the unexpected result that the dolphins that were not hand-fed grew larger?*

In most cases these questions function in exactly the same way as the questions that use the wording *discrepancy, paradox,* or *conflict.* In some cases the facts in the passage may not be quite as contradictory.

The wording of the stem for all types of *resolve a paradox* questions is consistent. The wording usually includes *Which one of the following, if true* and asks which answer choice *helps to* or *most helps to* either explain or resolve.

ASSUMPTION

For purposes of the LSAT, an **assumption** is a premise that is not stated in the setup. An assumption question asks you to identify a new premise that either is necessary or sufficient to make the argument valid. Assumption questions account for a little under 15 percent of all LR questions. Just as in *effect of a new premise* questions, the answer choices consist of five premises. The answer choices must be accepted as true. You cannot eliminate an answer choice simply because you do not believe it is a true statement.

The wording for a basic *assumption* question stem takes one of two forms:

> **Necessary assumption:** *Which one of the following is an assumption required by the argument?*
>
> **Sufficient assumption:** *Which one of the following, if assumed, allows the argument's conclusion to be properly drawn?*

The phrase *if assumed* serves the same function as the phrase *if true* that is found in *effect of a new premise* questions. It reminds you that you must consider the premise to be true. Additionally, it lets you know that the question is an *assumption* question.

All assumption questions are based on a logical argument that makes a strong case for its conclusion but leaves out at least one important point. In other words, the argument has a gap, a missing piece of the puzzle. The correct answer identifies the missing piece. The correct answer either supplies a new bit of information that makes the argument work, or it points out an unstated premise without which the argument cannot work.

Necessary Versus Sufficient Assumptions

The two forms of question stem above represent two distinct types of *assumption* questions: **necessary** and **sufficient**. The distinction between these two types is similar to the distinction between sufficient and necessary conditions, described in this chapter's section on if/then arguments. A sufficient assumption is a premise that is enough (sufficient) to make the conclusion work. A necessary assumption is a premise that is required (necessary) to make the conclusion work. In other words, a necessary assumption is a fact that, if it were not true, would cause the conclusion to be invalid.

In part, the distinction between necessary assumptions and sufficient assumptions is one of perspective. A sufficient assumption adds something that makes the conclusion stronger. A necessary assumption, if taken away, makes the conclusion weaker (or destroys it).

There are no *assumption* question stems that combine the two types. The question stems for *assumption* questions pose either a *sufficient assumption* question or a *necessary assumption* question. When you see the word *assume* in a question stem, be prepared to identify whether the question is asking for *sufficient* or *necessary*. Below are wording variations for each type.

WORDING VARIATIONS FOR *NECESSARY ASSUMPTIONS*

Which one of the following is an assumption required by the scientist's argument?

The argument depends on assuming which one of the following?

Which one of the following is an assumption on which the scientist's argument depends?

The argument relies on the assumption that . . .

The scientist's argument depends on which one of the following?

In the above wording variations, *necessary assumptions* include the words *required, depends,* or *relies on*. Most include the wording *which one of the following* but that wording is sometimes left off, as in the fourth example above. Nearly all include the words *assumption* or *assume* but that may also be left off, as in the final example.

WORDING VARIATIONS FOR *SUFFICIENT ASSUMPTIONS*

Which one of the following, if assumed, allows the argument's conclusion to be properly drawn?

Which one of the following, if assumed, most helps justify the politician's argument?

The conclusion of the politician's argument is most strongly supported if which one of the following is assumed?

The conclusion follows logically from the premises if which one of the following is assumed?

Which one of the following, if assumed, enables the scientist's conclusion to be properly drawn?

The conclusion is properly drawn if which one of the following is assumed?

The conclusion drawn follows logically from the premises if which one of the following is assumed?

The argument's conclusion is properly drawn if which one of the following is assumed?

The conclusion drawn is most strongly supported by the premises in the argument if which one of the following is assumed?

Question stems for *sufficient assumptions* nearly always include the phrase *which one of the following*, along with a clause that is equivalent to *if assumed*.

To distinguish the two types of *assumption* questions, use the following summary:

Necessary assumptions: *The argument depends on/relies on/requires one of the below.*

Sufficient assumptions: *If one of the below is assumed, the conclusion will be strengthened/be properly drawn/be justified/be supported/follow logically from the premises.*

Identify whether the stem represents a necessary or sufficient assumption. You can refer to the previous information. The answers are given below the exercise.

1. The scientist's argument relies on which one of the following?

2. Which one of the following is an assumption on which the scientist's argument depends?

3. Which one of the following, if assumed, enables the scientist's argument to be properly drawn?

4. The scientist's argument requires that . . .

5. The conclusion follows logically from the premises in the argument if which one of the following is assumed?

6. The conclusion drawn is most justified if which one of the following is assumed?

Answers:

1. necessary	3. sufficient	5. sufficient
2. necessary	4. necessary	6. sufficient

Necessary assumptions. In a *necessary assumption* question, there is a gap in the logic presented in the setup. The gap represents information that was not stated but must be true for the argument to work.

1. **Argument:** *Jenna loves Weimaraner dogs and has always wanted one. Until recently she has not been able to afford owning a pet, but now that she is earning enough money to support one pet, she will undoubtedly get a Weimaraner.*

   The gap in the above argument is not readily apparent. The argument seems to be valid and well supported by its premises.

   Necessary assumption: *There is not another pet that Jenna would rather own than a Weimaraner.*

   The assumption points out a gap in the argument. If there were another pet that Jenna would rather own, she would get that pet instead of a Weimaraner, given that the argument states that she can afford only one pet.

   Because a necessary assumption is required for the argument to work, the best way to test whether an answer choice is a necessary assumption is to negate the answer choice. For the above example, negate the necessary assumption:

   Premise: *There is not another pet that Jenna would rather own than a Weimaraner.*

   Negated premise: *There is another pet that Jenna would rather own than a Weimaraner.*

   What would happen to the argument if the negated version of the assumption were true? If there is a pet that Jenna would rather own, she would get that pet instead of the Weimaraner. The conclusion—that Jenna will now get a Weimaraner—is destroyed. Consider the possible answer choice below and test it by negating it:

   Premise: *Jenna is not allergic to any dogs.*

   Negated premise: *Jenna is allergic to some dogs.*

   How does the negated assumption affect the conclusion? The fact that Jenna may be allergic to some dogs does not mean that she is allergic to Weimaraners, and even if she were, she may still want to own a Weimaraner. The negated premise fails to destroy the conclusion. Therefore, the original premise could not be an assumption of the argument. Only a true assumption destroys or seriously undermines the conclusion when removed from the argument (negated).

The primary strategy for solving a necessary assumption question, then, is to test the answer choices by negating them. Practice this as you work on assumption questions.

Sufficient assumptions. *Sufficient assumption* passages also have a gap in the logic of the argument. The correct answer inserts a new fact into the gap and thereby strengthens the argument. A *sufficient assumption* question is similar in this way to a *strengthen* question. You can use many of the strategies that apply to *strengthen* questions to solve *sufficient assumption* questions.

Compared to *necessary assumption* questions, *sufficient assumption* questions are more frequently based on deductive logic. Because deductive arguments are based on absolute rules, it is easier to pinpoint the missing element.

1. **Argument:** *Anyone who does not either graduate from high school or earn a high school equivalence degree will have a hard time finding a well-paying job. Victor withdrew from high school before graduating and never returned to finish his degree. Therefore, Victor will have a hard time finding a well-paying job.*

    The argument is deductive. It states that *If –graduate and –equivalence → –well-paying job.* Victor's case meets the criterion of *–graduate (not graduate)*. In order to make the conclusion, it is clear that the missing piece is whether or not Victor earned a high school equivalence degree.

    Sufficient assumption: *Victor did not earn a high school equivalence degree.*
    With this fact, the conclusion of the argument is properly drawn.

    Unlike in *necessary assumption* questions, it is not necessary to negate the answer choices. Simply plugging in the answer choice as it is stated is enough to strengthen the conclusion. However, in some questions it can also be helpful to use the strategy of negating premises. If the correct answer is not clear from plugging premises into the argument, negating answer choices and testing how that affects the argument might reveal the correct answer. In fact, for many *assumption* questions—whether the question stem is stated as *necessary* or as *sufficient*—the correct answer may be both necessary and sufficient. In other words, for many *assumption* questions, the correct answer actively strengthens the argument *and* if the correct answer is negated, the argument is destroyed. In the above example, what happens if you negate the correct answer?

    > **Premise:** *Victor did not earn a high school equivalence degree.*
    > **Negated premise:** *Victor earned a high school equivalence degree.*

    If Victor earned a high school equivalence degree, he does not meet the criterion of the first if/then statement and the argument falls apart. The correct answer in this case is both sufficient (it is enough to make the argument work) and necessary (without it, the argument falls apart).

Do not be overly concerned if the line between *sufficient* and *necessary assumptions* seems blurry. You can easily identify the intent of the question stem, because all *assumption* questions stems fall either into one category or the other, with no overlap. However, as you work a question, if plugging the answer choice into the argument (the strategy for *sufficient assumptions*) does not seem to help, try negating the answer choice (the strategy for *necessary assumptions*).

CONCLUSION

The next most common major question type is **conclusion**. *Conclusion* questions ask you to identify a conclusion of an argument. *Conclusion* questions account for a little under 15 percent of LR questions. In some *conclusion* questions you are asked to find the one main conclusion, the main point, of the argument. More often, however, a *conclusion* question asks you to find a statement that can be concluded based on the premises in the passage. In other words, it may be possible to conclude a certain fact even though that fact is not the main point of the argument and may even be peripheral to the argument as a whole. With *conclusion* questions, then, it is necessary to distinguish *main conclusion* questions from *what can be inferred* (anything that can be concluded) questions.

In a *conclusion* question, the five answer choices represent possible conclusions. This is in contrast to the question types that have been covered earlier in this chapter, in which the answer choices represented possible premises. *Conclusion* question stems never say *Which of the following, if true,* because *if true* only applies to premises. The stems may, however, say *If the above statements are true* because the above statements include premises.

TIP

CONCLUSION QUESTIONS

For *conclusion* questions, prove that the facts in the passage lead to one of the answer choices.

What Can Be Inferred

The majority (60 percent) of *conclusion* questions ask you to identify the answer choice that can be inferred from the premises in the setup. Remember that inference is the process of moving through premises to a conclusion, applying valid logic. Do not interpret the word *infer* in the ordinary sense of something that could be true. To infer that an answer choice is logically valid means that the premises in the argument can be combined to *prove* the truth of the answer choice. An inference is identical to a conclusion.

1. **Argument:** *Cottonwood trees are fast-growing trees frequently used to create shade in a residential lot. There are a number of slower-growing trees that have the advantages of bright fall color and edible fruit, neither of which the cottonwood possesses. Most landscapers, however, avoid planting trees that they do not consider to be cost-effective for the size of the tree. Landscapers generally consider a slow-growing tree not to be cost-effective for its size.*

   Correct conclusion: *Many landscapers will continue to plant less decorative, non-fruiting trees as shade trees, even though more decorative and useful trees are available.* The argument presents a number of premises. It does not arrive at a conclusion. Your task is to identify the answer choice that can be proven to be true, given the premises in the argument. Below is a proof of the correct premise:

   > *Premise: Landscapers do not plant non-cost-effective trees.*
   > *Premise: Landscapers consider slow-growing trees to be non-cost-effective.*
   > *Intermediate conclusion: Landscapers will not plant slow-growing trees.*
   > *Premise: Cottonwoods are not slow-growing trees and they are good shade trees.*
   > *Premise: Cottonwoods are less decorative and do not fruit.*
   > *Conclusion: Landscapers who need to plant a shade tree will plant a less decorative, non-fruiting tree.*

   What can be inferred questions are relatively straightforward to solve. Identify the premises in the passage. These are your "raw materials" for defending an answer. Test the answer choices to determine whether or not a particular answer choice can be defended using the premises in the passage and valid logic.

Must Be True

This type of *conclusion* question is a slight variation on *what can be inferred* questions. In *must be true* questions, the correct answer is forced to be true because of rigorous deductive reasoning or absolute mathematical arguments. The setup generally consists of deductive premises, typically without a stated conclusion. The question asks you to identify an answer choice that must be true, given the premises in the conclusion.

1. **Argument:** *Anyone who owns a Gabby Natty doll also owns a Tubby Tow Truck. However, anyone who owns a Tubby Tow Truck does not own a water cannon. Sandi owns a water cannon.*

   Correct conclusion: *Sandi does not own a Gabby Natty doll.*

   The deductive statements are:

   If Gabby → Tubby

   If Tubby → –Water

   Water ∴ –Tubby

   –Tubby ∴ –Gabby

The question stem for a *must be true* question is typically *If the statements above are true, which one of the following must be true?*

Identify the Main Conclusion

This type of *conclusion* argument is significantly different from a *what can be inferred* question. It accounts for 40 percent of *conclusion* questions. In this type it is not enough to prove that an answer choice can be proven correct. Instead, you must defend that the answer choice states the main conclusion, or main point, of the argument. This is similar to a Reading Comprehension question that asks you to identify the main point.

To answer a *main conclusion* question you must understand the premises and the conclusions that are stated in the argument. You must also identify the intent of the argument. What is the arguer trying to prove?

In some questions, the main conclusion is explicitly stated in the argument. In other questions, the main conclusion is created by combining two or more explicit statements. In a small number of questions, the main conclusion is not given in the passage, and you must infer it.

1. **Argument:** *Animal shelters in most cities have no choice but to put down hundreds of animals yearly. Shelters simply do not have the money available to maintain all of the unwanted animals for which they are responsible. However, an alternative—no-kill shelters—is likely to become prevalent in the near future. A number of cities have proven that no-kill shelters can be economically viable and have no drawbacks compared to traditional shelters.*

   Correct conclusion: *No-kill animal shelters are likely to become prevalent in the near future as an alternative to traditional animal shelters.*

   Scanning the argument, determine that the intent of the passage is to establish that no-kill shelters will become prevalent. You can defend this by showing that the other statements all support the proposal that no-kill shelters will become prevalent. The first two sentences establish that the traditional shelter has certain drawbacks and that an alternative is needed. The final sentence shows that no-kill shelters have been viable in some locations and supports the conclusion that no-kill shelters will become more prevalent. The correct answer choice is a close paraphrase of the explicitly stated conclusion.

2. **Argument:** *Economists have predicted that if gas prices drop next summer, people will drive to more distant locations on their summer vacations. However, people are more likely to stay home. Once people have experienced sharply increased gas prices, they are likely to develop habits of frugality that persist even when the price hikes that created the habits have reversed.*

   Correct conclusion: *If gas prices drop next summer, people will most likely stay home.*

   The correct conclusion in this case combines information explicitly stated in the first and second sentences of the argument. Neither sentence alone captures the full conclusion. The statement in the second sentence, *people are more likely to stay home,* by itself provides only part of the information needed to state a conclusion. In many *main conclusion* questions, you must combine information from two or more sentences to accurately state the full conclusion.

3. **Argument:** *Economists have predicted that if gas prices drop next summer, people will drive to more distant locations on their summer vacations. However, once people have experienced sharply increased gas prices, they are likely to develop habits of frugality that persist even when the price hikes that created the habits have reversed.*

   Correct conclusion: *A prediction about economic activity in the face of fluctuating prices is likely to prove incorrect.*

   This argument is a modification of the previous one. It contains all of the premises of the original but does not include the sentence that states the conclusion. The correct answer choice provides a conclusion that can be defended as being the main point, even though it is stated in general terms.

If you are unclear about what the conclusion of a passage is, examine each statement and ask yourself if that statement is meant to support another statement or concept. Statements that support another concept are premises, not the main conclusion. Two premises can be combined to create an intermediate conclusion that is then used to support the main conclusion.

> **Premise:** *All fruit contains vitamin C.*
> **Premise:** *Pawpaws are a fruit.*
> **Intermediate conclusion:** *Therefore, pawpaws contain vitamin C.*
> **Main conclusion:** *If John needs to get more dietary vitamin C, he should eat pawpaws.*

CONCLUSION TYPES

The four types of conclusion questions are *what can be inferred*, *what must be true*, *identify the main conclusion*, and the rare *which conclusion can be rejected*.

Which Conclusion Can Be Rejected?

There is a rare type of *conclusion* question that asks you to identify a conclusion that violates the premises in the argument. The correct answer choice is one that can be proven to be incorrect.

FLAW

Flaw questions make up about 13 percent of LR questions. A *flaw* question asks you to identify the logical flaw in the argument. A logical flaw is an error in reasoning. Earlier in the chapter you reviewed the categories of logical flaws that have appeared on recent LSATs. The five answer choices to a *flaw* question are often based on these categories. There can also be answer choices that are based on flawed reasoning unique to the particular setup.

For *flaw* questions, the setup contains an argument with premises and at least one conclusion. However, just as in *weaken* arguments, the argument has a gap. For *flaw* questions, the gap hints at something that is erroneous in the logic of the argument. When you read the setup for a *flaw* question, ask yourself if you "buy" the argument on an intuitive level. Does the argument sound reasonable to you? Even though you know the argument has a flaw, in some questions the flaw is so well hidden that the argument sounds viable. It is helpful in this case to acknowledge that you do not see a flaw. On the other hand, if you intuitively feel that something is wrong with the argument, try to identify what bothers you about it. If you are not able to pinpoint the error quickly, move on to analyzing the answer choices. Having focused briefly on the error, even if you cannot identify it explicitly, may help you recognize the correct answer when you see it.

Flaw questions can occur in a basic form, in which the answer choices may include any type of logical flaw, or in a specialized form, in which the stem uses the wording *fails to consider the possibility*. In the *fails to consider* form, the flaw in the argument is that there is an element that the argument has failed to consider. Your task is to identify which answer choice represents that element.

Basic "Flaw" Questions

The question stem for a basic *flaw* question can include wording such as:

> *Which one of the following most accurately describes a flaw in the argument?*
> *The reasoning in the argument is flawed in that the argument . . .*
> *The reasoning in the argument is vulnerable to which one of the following criticisms?*
> *The argument is most vulnerable to criticism on the grounds that . . .*

A more comprehensive list of wording variations is given at the end of this section. Notice that in some of the examples above, the correct answer completes the sentence. The wording *vulnerable to criticism* and its variations occurs in about half of the *flaw* questions. *Vulnerable to criticism* stems do *not* indicate a separate type of question. The wording *vulnerable to criticism* is simply an alternative way to indicate that the question is a *flaw* question.

To solve a basic *flaw* question, read through the setup to get a sense of what is missing or erroneous. Then move on to the answer choices. Scan the answer choices first to see if one answer choice seems to match your intuitive sense of the logical flaw. For easier questions, this will lead you to the answer. Harder questions, however, have one or more incorrect answer choices designed to trick you. In most *flaw* questions, then, you will have to apply a more advanced problem-solving strategy.

As you evaluate an answer choice, consider first whether it is a true statement. If it is not, then it cannot be the correct answer. Even if it is a true statement, it still might not be correct. Consider the following example:

SAMPLE PASSAGE 1

At the city's upcoming summer festival, both fruit and hot dogs will be given away. Most people like to eat fruit in the summer. Therefore, most people will choose fruit over hot dogs.

The argument is most vulnerable to criticism in that it

(A) presumes, without warrant, that people will take free food even if they are not hungry

(B) infers that because people behave a certain way in one situation, they will behave the same way in a different situation

(C) fails to consider whether people who like to eat fruit in the summer also like to eat hot dogs in the summer

(D) presumes, without warrant, that people only eat fruit in the summer

(E) fails to address the possibility that food other than fruit and hot dogs will be given away at the festival

---

Solution: Which answer choices are factually correct? For choice A, the passage does not address what might happen if people are not hungry. For choice B, the passage's premise that people like to eat fruit in the summer presumably refers to situations other than the summer festival, so it is true that the argument infers that people will behave the same way at the festival as they do in other situations. Choice B, then, is a true statement but is it the flaw in the argument? No. It is not a logical flaw to believe that people's food preference in other situations will be the same at the festival. Choice B is a true statement but does not represent the logical flaw in the argument.

Is choice C a true statement? The argument does "fail" to do what choice C describes. Choice C, then, is a true statement. Does choice C represent a flaw in the argument? If people who like to eat fruit also equally like to eat hot dogs, then the conclusion falls apart. Choice C does represent a flaw in the argument. Choice C is a possible correct answer.

Is choice D a true statement? There is no evidence that the argument assumes that people only eat fruit in the summer. Choice D is not a true statement and can be eliminated.

Is choice E a true statement? Yes. The argument does fail to do what choice E describes. Does choice E represent the flaw in the argument? Choice E seems to be irrelevant. Even if other food is available, people will still prefer fruit. The correct answer is choice C.

Remember that the default multiple-choice question—the question to which your brain is likely to revert—is *Which one of the following is true?* *Flaw* questions often try to trap you into falling for an answer choice that is true but does not represent the flaw in the argument. Beware!

Fails to Consider a Possibility

In Sample Passage 1, answer choices C and E use *fails to consider* wording. One of the categories of flawed reasoning is failing to consider a certain possibility. *Fails to consider a possibility* questions are a specialized form of *flaw* question in which all of the answer choices fall into the category of failing to consider a certain possibility. Whereas other categories of flawed reasoning point out an error in logic, the answer choices in *fails to consider* questions usually refer simply to information or possibilities that the arguer did not consider and, as a result, came to an incorrect conclusion. The difference between a logical error and an informational error (a fact that the arguer failed to consider) is illustrated below:

1. **Argument:** *Any student who does not have an official score on the LSAT will not be accepted to law school. Greg recently took the LSAT and has received his official score. Therefore, Greg will be accepted to law school.*
   Logical error: *The argument confuses a condition that is necessary for a student to get into law school with a condition that is sufficient for getting into law school.*
2. **Argument:** *Any student who does not have an official score on the LSAT will not be accepted to law school. Greg recently registered to take an official administration of the LSAT. Thus, he will have an official score on the LSAT.*
   Informational error: *The argument fails to consider that Greg might not take the exam for which he is registered.*

In the first example, confusing a necessary condition with a sufficient condition is an error in logic. In the second example, the arguer's error is in not taking into account a fact: the possibility that Greg will not actually take the exam. Most of the answer choices in *fails to consider* questions are based on facts.

> Martina: Striped bass are attracted to live bait. I see you just cast your fishing line and that you used live bait. You already have a fish tugging on your line, so most likely you have caught a striped bass.
>
> Martina's reasoning is questionable in that it fails to consider the possibility that
> (A) some live bait is more effective than other live bait in attracting striped bass
> (B) some striped bass are equally attracted to lures and live bait
> (C) fish other than striped bass are more attracted to lures than to live bait
> (D) fish other than striped bass are attracted to live bait
> (E) the ability to catch fish depends on the amount of experience of the person fishing

Solution: The answer choices above are all based on facts. The logical error is that Martina has failed to consider one of these facts. All of the answer choices except D are irrelevant. Choice D is correct because it indicates that the fish on the line may be something other than a striped bass. Martina's logic is flawed because she ignored a possible fact that would have altered her conclusion.

Takes for Granted

In Sample Passage 2, Martina failed to consider a fact that could be true. Another rare type of *flaw* question involves taking for granted that something is true when in fact it might be false. It uses wording such as *The logic in the argument is questionable in that the argument takes for granted that . . .*

Wording Variations of Answer Choices

It is often difficult to recognize the type of a flawed logic to which an answer choice is referring. Sometimes the wording of an answer choice is so complex as to obscure the type of logic, so it is important for you to carefully analyze the answer choices. The lists below show you the variations of wording for specific types of logical flaws. Also review the flawed logic types that are described earlier in the chapter if necessary.

WORDING VARIATIONS FOR MAJOR CATEGORIES OF FLAWED LOGIC AS THEY ARE DESCRIBED IN *FLAW* QUESTION ANSWER CHOICES

Necessary versus sufficient conditions

Takes a condition necessary for trees to set fruit to be a condition sufficient for trees to set fruit.

Treats a condition sufficient for trees to set fruit as a condition that is required for trees to set fruit.

True of the parts versus true of the whole

Infers, from a claim that no individual within a group has a certain characteristic, that the group as a whole does not have that characteristic.

Infers that something is true of the whole simply from the fact that it is true of each of the parts.

Infers that because something is true of a group as a whole, it is also true of each member of the group.

False cause

Fails to consider that a number of different effects may be produced by one single cause.

Does not provide evidence that the tree's blooming is the result, not the cause, of the tree's infection with fungi.

Draws a conclusion about a cause simply on the basis of a statistical correlation.

It takes what is probably the effect of an event to be its cause.

Ignores the possibility that one cause may have different effects in different circumstances.

Fails to consider that two events are independent effects of a common cause.

Incorrectly infers a cause from a correlation.

Ambiguity

Fails to consider the possibility that the author is referring to two distinct uses of the word "bloom."

Uses the word "bloom" in a nontechnical way, whereas Fred uses the word in a botanical sense.

It uses the term "bloom" with one meaning in the premises and with a different meaning in the conclusion.

Circular reasoning

Draws a conclusion that simply restates a fact that was stated in one or more of the argument's premises.

Relies on an assumption that is equivalent to assuming that the conclusion is valid.

Relies on a premise that presupposes the truth of the conclusion.

Unrepresentative sample

It relies on the testimony of a group that is not likely to be representative of the group identified in the conclusion.

Assuming there are no other options

Fails to consider that there may be other explanations for the birds' behavior.

Fails to address the possibility that there are requirements for a tree to bloom other than the presence of sunlight and carbon dioxide.

Takes for granted that there are only two possible explanations for a particular event.

Argument against the person

Attacks Fernando's character rather than his argument.

Unreliable source

Relies on evidence from a source that there is no reason to believe is reliable.

Relies on statistical evidence that is not likely to be reliable.

Relies on the truth of claims made by a source that is likely to be biased.

Takes for granted the truth of a claim made by a person who had a motive to be untruthful.

Applying a generalization to an inappropriate case

The argument applies a generalization to a case to which it was not intended to apply.

Fails to apply a general rule to all relevant cases. (This is the inverse of the above.)

False appeal to authority

The conclusion in the argument is based on statements by people who have not been shown to be experts in the appropriate area.

Distorting a view to make it vulnerable to criticism

The argument distorts the scientist's view in a way to make that view appear more vulnerable to criticism.

It distorts the scientist's argument and then attacks the distorted view.

Disproving a claim that was not made

Attacking an argument that was not actually put forth.

Concluding that something is true because people believe it to be true

Concludes that something must be true, because most people believe it to be true.

Defends a view on the basis that the view is broadly held.

Accepting as true because not proven incorrect

Infers that a claim is true merely on the basis that the view has not been proven to be incorrect.

Rejecting a view because it has not been proven

Confuses an absence of evidence supporting the scientist's argument with the existence of evidence against the argument.

Rejects a view merely because the argument made for the view is inadequate.

Repudiates a conclusion simply on the grounds that an inadequate argument has been made for it.

Inferring that because something is possible, it must occur

Draws a conclusion about what must be true merely based on evidence of what is likely to occur.

Infers that something will be successful simply because it could be successful.

Fails to consider that what is probable is not necessarily inevitable.

Inferring that because something is unlikely, it will not occur

Infers that something cannot occur simply from the fact that it is unlikely to occur.

Assuming that because a conclusion is false, all the premises are false

Fails to consider that, although the conclusion of an argument may be false, some of the assumptions used to support the conclusion may be true.

Non-flaws

There is a category of incorrect answer choice in which the answer choice, though true, is not a logical flaw and therefore cannot be the correct answer. These **non-flaws** typically state that the argument has failed to support a premise in some way. Failing to support a premise cannot be a logical flaw because premises must be accepted as true.

SAMPLE PASSAGE 3

At the city's upcoming summer festival, both fruit and hot dogs will be given away. Most people like to eat fruit in the summer. Therefore, most people will choose fruit over hot dogs.

The argument is most vulnerable to criticism in that it

(A) provides no evidence to support the assertion that most people like to eat fruit in the summer

(B) does not indicate how many people will attend the festival

(C) fails to consider whether people who like to eat fruit in the summer also like to eat hot dogs in the summer

(D) fails to adequately define what constitutes fruit

(E) fails to provide support for the assertion that there will be no charge for the fruit and hot dogs at the festival

Solution: In this variation of Sample Passage 1, answer choices A, B, D, and E are all non-flaws. Each of them is a true statement. For example, the argument does not provide evidence to support the assertion that people like to eat fruit in the summer. In a real-life discussion, evidence to support a fact makes the fact more believable, but in LR it is not necessary to support a premise. Failure to do so is not a flaw in logic.

Similarly, the argument does not tell how many people will attend the festival. Telling the attendance of the festival would be information that would bolster the premise. If many people come to the festival, it is more likely that statistical correlations (such as people's preference for fruit) will hold true. However, failing to bolster a premise is not a logical flaw.

Choices D and E are also true statements that might bolster the argument. Neither is a logical flaw because it is not necessary to support or further bolster a premise. Choice C is correct because if people who like fruit also like to eat hot dogs, the argument falls apart.

Wording Variations for "Flaw" Question Stems

Below is a comprehensive list of variations. (Be careful to distinguish wording variations of question stems from wording variations of answer choices.)

NON-FLAWS

Beware of the non-flaws. If a question asks you to identify a flaw in the argument, failing to support a premise with statistics or examples is *not* considered a logical flaw.

WORDING VARIATIONS FOR *FLAW* QUESTION STEMS

Basic *flaw* questions

Which one of the following most accurately describes a reasoning flaw in the argument above?

The reasoning in the scientist's argument is flawed in that the argument . . .

Which one of the following most accurately expresses the scientist's error in reasoning?

A questionable technique used by the scientist in making her argument is that of . . .

The scientist's reasoning is flawed in that the scientist . . .

The journalist's response to the scientist suggests that the scientist commits which one of the following flaws in reasoning?

Basic *flaw* questions with *vulnerable to criticism*

The reasoning in the argument is most vulnerable to criticism on the grounds that it . . .

The scientist's argument is most vulnerable to the criticism that she . . .

The journalist's reply to the scientist's argument is most vulnerable to criticism on the grounds that the journalist . . .

The journalist's reasoning is vulnerable to which one of the following criticisms?

The reasoning in the scientist's argument is most vulnerable to criticism on which one of the following grounds?

Fails to consider

The scientist's reasoning is questionable in that it fails to consider the possibility that . . .

The reasoning in the scientist's argument is most vulnerable to the criticism that the scientist fails to consider which one of the following possibilities? (This variation contains both *vulnerable to criticism* and *fails to consider*.)

The scientist's argument is flawed in that the argument fails to consider the possibility that . . .

The scientist's argument is flawed because it fails to take into account that . . .

Takes for granted

The reasoning in the scientist's argument is questionable in that she takes for granted that . . .

PARALLEL REASONING

Parallel reasoning arguments present an argument and ask you to identify an answer choice that contains an argument that has the same (parallel) structure as the original. About 7 percent of LR passages involve parallel reasoning.

Parallel reasoning questions present five answer choices, each of which is a complete argument. For this reason, an entire parallel reasoning question can be quite long, sometimes taking up most of a column. These long passages can seem intimidating, and many people, if they are going to skip any questions at all, skip parallel reasoning questions. Some more difficult parallel reasoning questions *can* be time-consuming. However, many, even if lengthy, can be solved quickly.

In a parallel reasoning question, first identify the type of logic in the original passage. If the type of logic is one that you can readily recognize—in other words, if the logic is one of the types of logic that you have studied in this chapter—then you may be able to find the correct answer quickly.

SAMPLE PASSAGE 4

All folk music is based on recurring themes. Kerry claims that her new composition is folk music, although it is not based on recurring themes. Therefore, Kerry's new composition is not folk music.

Which one of the following is most similar in reasoning to the above argument?

(A) Classical music often draws on themes from the folk music of the composer's native country. Critics claim that Beethoven's music reflects themes from Hungarian folk music, even though Hungary was not Beethoven's native country. Therefore, Beethoven's music was not classical music.

(B) It must be true that Isaiah is not in law school. All law students spend at least twenty hours a week in the library at this time of year. Even though Isaiah has many homework assignments, he is only spending fifteen hours a week in the library at this time of year.

(C) All modern art uses abstract designs to create impressions. Li's art uses abstract designs to create impressions, even though Li has not studied modern art. Therefore, Li's art is modern art.

(D) Everyone in our building who came down with the flu last month has small children at home. Hannah came down with the flu, although she believes she did not get it from her children. Nevertheless, having small children at home must have caused her to get the flu.

(E) Michael recently choreographed a new dance and claimed that it was a folk dance. Michael's journalism professor saw the dance and claimed that it did not have any of the qualities that are necessary to make it a folk dance. Therefore, Michael's new dance is not a folk dance.

Solution: Because a parallel reasoning question requires that you match the logical structure of the original passage with the structure in an answer choice, first identify the structure of the original passage. This can be easy, moderately easy, or difficult, depending on the passage. Following is the hierarchy that correlates with the difficulty of identifying the structure of the original passage:

**HIERARCHY OF DIFFICULTY IN
PARALLEL REASONING ORIGINAL PASSAGES**

Easiest: deductive arguments (if/then or sets)

Moderately easy: one of the other types of logic categories described in this chapter

Difficult: an argument that is not based on deduction or any other specific category of reasoning described in this chapter

---

If the original passage is a deductive argument, you are in luck. It will be quick and easy to identify the structure. If the argument is not deductive but is recognizable as one of the other categories of logic that you have studied, you may still find that it is easy to identify the logic and match it to an answer. If none of the above hold true, then the question will probably take more time.

In Sample Passage 4, what type of reasoning does the original passage use? Is it (1) deductive, (2) a recognizable nondeductive logic category, or (3) something else? The first sentence is an absolute rule. The argument is deductive. Now analyze the logic. Is the deductive argument an if/then or a set argument? It is difficult to tell from the first sentence. Try it first as an if/then. If that does not work, you can try organizing it as a set argument.

Taking the first sentence, create a standard if/then statement. The two phenomena being related are:

1. folk music
2. recurring themes

Which is the determining factor (comes first)? *Recurring themes* seems to be what leads to folk music.

> *If (blank) recurring themes → (blank) folk music*

The blanks indicate that we have not yet determined whether it is the presence of recurring themes or the absence of recurring themes that determines the result. It is not true that anything with recurring themes is folk music. It must be the absence of recurring themes that determines the result.

> *If −recurring themes → −folk music*

How does this statement relate to the rest of the passage? Kerry's composition does not have recurring themes.

> Rule: *If −recurring themes → −folk music*
> Case: *−recurring themes*
> Conclusion: *−folk music*

More concisely stated this would be:

> *If −recurring themes → −folk music*
> *−recurring themes ∴ −folk music*

You can write the logic in an even more generalized form simply as:

If A → B
A ∴ B

It does not matter whether A is a negative or positive statement, as long as A is the same in both the first and second line of the logic.

Now that you have isolated the structure of the logic, test the answer choices. Try testing all the answer choices in the Sample Passage.

Explanation: In choice A, the main premise (first sentence) is not an absolute statement, so choice A is not deductive and cannot be the correct answer. In choice B the first sentence does not seem to be a premise. In fact, the first sentence is the conclusion. The main premise is the second sentence, that *all law students spend at least twenty hours a week in the library.* As an if/then statement, this becomes:

If –twenty hours → –law student

The third sentence tells us:

(Isaiah) – twenty hours

because Isaiah only spends fifteen hours. The conclusion follows exactly as in the original.

(Isaiah) – twenty hours ∴ (Isaiah) – law student

Choice B is an exact match for the original. It must be the correct answer. You can quickly skim the rest of the answer choices to make sure you have not made an error. On a timed test it would not be advisable to actually work out the other answer choices because they are so long.

For learning purpose, consider choices C through E. Choice C can be diagrammed as

If –abstract → –modern
Abstract ∴ modern

This is not the same logic as the original and in fact is not valid logic. Choice C is out. Scanning choice D, you can quickly spot that it is a cause-and-effect argument. It is out. Choice E is a false appeal to authority argument. It is out.

There are three common misconceptions about parallel reasoning questions. First, a correct answer in a parallel argument question does *not* need to have subject matter that is similar to the original passage. If the original passage discusses music, be careful not to choose an answer choice simply because it also discusses music. The correct answer can be on a completely different topic.

Second, a correct answer does *not* need to have the same sentence structure as the original. Do not choose an answer choice simply because it has similar wording, phrases, or sentences. The correct answer may have completely different phrasing or sentence structure. Third, a correct answer does not have to have the logical elements in the same order as in the original. In the example above, the correct answer had the conclusion in the first sentence, whereas the original had the conclusion in the third. The order is not important.

The only thing that you must match is the logic itself. If the original passage is an if/then statement, the correct answer must have the same if/then logic. If the original passage is a cause-and-effect argument, the correct answer must be a cause-and-effect argument. Consider the following:

Francesca and Nick were both tested for hand/eye coordination and spatial ability and scored in the 99th percentile. Francesca has begun taking golf lessons and is already playing exceptionally well. Nick is also interested in learning golf. It is likely that he will also play exceptionally well.

The reasoning in which one of the arguments below is most similar to the reasoning in the argument above?

(A) Anyone who plays golf well has excellent hand/eye coordination. Martin and Olivia both play golf well. It is likely that both Martin and Olivia have excellent hand/eye coordination.

(B) Patricia and Tomas both scored in the 99th percentile on the same intelligence test. Patricia studied logic puzzles for three months before taking the test. Tomas also studied logic puzzles. It is likely that studying the puzzles caused him to score high on the test.

(C) Sandra and Hugh are both realtors. Sandra's sales have equaled Hugh's for the last five years. It is likely that Hugh uses many of the same sales strategies that Sandra uses.

(D) Jennifer and Louis have both submitted proposals to the city council for the development of a new sports complex. Jennifer's proposal has the support of several architecture professors at the university. Louis's proposal does not have support from any professors, so it is likely that his proposal is not well designed.

(E) It is likely that dolphins experience sadness. Dolphins and humans have similar social needs and emotions. Humans are sometimes isolated and experience sadness.

Solution: Identify the type of logic in the original argument. Is it deductive? No. Is it a type that you have studied? Yes, it is an analogy. Two people are alike in one way. Therefore, they will be alike in another way. Scan the answer choices. Do you see one that is an analogy?

Choice A is a distracter in that it talks about golf. This does not mean that it is a wrong answer, only that you must evaluate it further. What type of logic does it use? The first sentence is an absolute statement. Choice A is a deductive, if/then argument and cannot be the correct answer.

Choice B is a distracter because it has a sentence structure that is nearly identical to the original. However, it is a cause-and-effect argument and cannot be the correct answer.

Choice C does not use any particular type of logic. It is clearly not an analogy and cannot be the correct answer. Choice D is a logical flaw that infers that Louis's project is not valid because it has not been documented as being valid.

Choice E discusses a topic that is different from the original. It also begins with its conclusion. Nevertheless, it is an analogy—dolphins and humans are alike in one way so they must be alike in a second way—and is the correct answer.

A little over half of parallel reasoning questions involve deductive arguments, generally if/then statements, although occasionally sets. The remaining are likely to be based on the most common types of reasoning.

Parallel Flaw

A special type of parallel reasoning question tells you that the original argument is flawed and asks you to identify an argument that is flawed in the same way. This type of question can be solved in virtually the same way as other parallel reasoning questions. Any answer with valid logic is wrong.

Wording Variations

The wording for parallel reasoning and parallel flaw question stems is easy to identify. The stems usually say "parallel" or "similar."

WORDING VARIATIONS FOR *PARALLEL REASONING* AND *PARALLEL FLAW* QUESTIONS

Parallel reasoning

Which one of the following arguments is most similar in reasoning to the argument above?

The reasoning in which one of the following arguments is most similar to the reasoning in the argument above?

Of the following arguments, which one illustrates a principle that is most similar to the principle illustrated by the passage above?

Parallel flaw

The flawed pattern of reasoning in which one of the following is most parallel to the reasoning in the argument above?

The pattern of flawed reasoning in which one of the following is most similar to the reasoning in the argument above?

The questionable reasoning in the scientist's argument is most similar in its reasoning to which one of the following?

Less Common Question Types

The most common question types, covered above, account for more than 75 percent of LR questions. The remaining question types, although less common, are important and account for nearly 25 percent of LR questions. No particular type accounts for more than 3 or 4 percent—some account for much less—but as a group they represent types of questions that you must master. There are ten specific less common question types that are covered below. They are listed from the most frequent to the least frequent.

> **MOST COMMON AND LESS COMMON QUESTION TYPES**
>
> The most common question types include *effect of a new premise (strengthen, weaken, resolve a paradox), assumption, conclusion, flaw,* and *parallel reasoning.* Also study the less common question types. They can gain you points!

PRINCIPLE

Two types of questions have to do with principles. In one type, ***application of a principle***, both a principle and an application of the principle are given. In the second type, ***match a concrete example to a principle***, one or the other is given, and you must match a principle with a concrete example of the principle.

Application of a Principle

In this question type the setup consists of two distinct statements, as shown below:

SAMPLE PASSAGE 6

Principle: One should only donate money if one does not expect either praise or favors in return.

Application: It was acceptable for Henry to donate money to the Red Cross, even though after he did so, he received a warm letter of thanks and a discount coupon.

Which one of the following, if true, most justifies the above application of the principle?

The principle states absolute rules that dictate whether or not a certain action is valid. In other words, the principle contains a deductive argument, usually an if/then. The application part of the setup then applies the principle to a specific situation. The application does not completely take into account all of the conditions that are required by the principle's deductive statement. Your task is to identify the missing part. *Application of a principle* questions may either ask you to identify a new premise that strengthens the argument or to identify a flaw in the argument. This type of question, then, is a specialized form of either a *strengthen* question or a *flaw* question. You can use the strategies you have learned for those two types as you work *application of a principle* questions.

Because the principle is typically a deductive, if/then statement, start by diagramming the deductive rules. For the sample passage above, what are the premises in the principle?

The two elements of the if/then statement are *expecting praise/favor* and *donating*. The determining factor (the one that comes first) is *expecting praise/favor*. It is the presence of *expecting praise/favor* that determines that you should not *donate*.

> *If expect praise OR If expect favor → –donate*

Match this to the application. Did Henry expect praise? Did he expect favor? Do you see the gap in the argument? The application tells us that Henry *received* both praise and favor but this does not match *expecting* praise or favor. To justify the application of the principle, a statement is needed that shows that Henry did not *expect* to receive either the praise or the coupon.

Correct Answer Choice: Before making the donation, Henry did not expect to receive either the letter or the coupon.

Now the argument is complete. All of the conditions in the principle have been addressed.

> *If expect praise OR If expect favor → –donate*
> *Donate ∴ –expect praise AND –expect favor*

The second statement is the contrapositive of the first and therefore is a valid statement. *Henry donated, which is valid because he did not expect either praise or favor.*

Flawed application of a principle. In some *application of a principle* questions, the application contains an error. The question stem asks you to identify the flaw in the reasoning, in exactly the same way as for *flaw* questions. The stem is worded to the effect *The application of the principle is most vulnerable to criticism on the grounds that it . . .*

Principle: Plagiarism is a serious breach of the trust between a student and a teacher. Any student whose work has been declared a plagiarism by an impartial committee should be expelled.

Application: The committee that evaluated Sinead's thesis contained several faculty members who had nonacademic reasons for wanting her to be expelled. Even though all the committee members agreed that her work was a plagiarism, she should not be expelled.

The above application of the principle is most vulnerable to criticism on the grounds that it

(A) fails to consider the possibility that Sinead knowingly committed plagiarism

(B) fails to provide evidence that a faculty member had nonacademic reasons for wanting Sinead expelled

(C) applies a principle that contradicts the principle stated in the passage

(D) confuses a claim that is sufficient for an event to take place with a claim that is necessary for that event to take place

(E) assumes without warrant that the committee members are able to accurately determine whether or not a statement is a plagiarism

Solution: First identify the logic in the principle and then try to spot the gap in the argument. The first sentence of the principle is merely an introduction. The second sentence contains the principle.

If declared a plagiarism by an impartial committee → expel

In order to meet the qualifications for leading to *expel*, the situation must include a committee, impartiality, and a declaration of plagiarism. Compare this with the application. There is a committee and a declaration of plagiarism. There is *not* impartiality. Therefore, Sinead's situation must be described as *not declared a plagiarism by an impartial committee*. The conclusion of the application is *not expel*. Consider the application's entire argument, then:

If declared a plagiarism by an impartial committee → expel
–declared a plagiarism by an impartial committee ∴ –expel

or

If A → B
–A ∴ –B

Do you see that this is not a valid argument? Whereas the presence of A must lead to B (plagiarism is sufficient to lead to expulsion), the absence of A does *not* necessarily lead to B (it is not necessary to have been declared a plagiarist by an impartial committee to be expelled). There may be other factors that lead to B, even when A is absent. It is not valid to conclude that Sinead should not be expelled because there may be other reasons that would lead to her expulsion.

If the real-world explanation of why the logic is flawed does not work well for you, stick with the symbolic logic. It is clear that the A/B logic above is not valid. That is all you need to know and is sometimes much easier to understand than the real-world explanation.

Now that you understand the logic, which answer choice is correct? Choice D points out that the application incorrectly turns a sufficient condition into a necessary one. Choice D is the correct answer.

Choice A is irrelevant because the conditions that lead to being expelled do not require that the person knowingly plagiarized. Choice B refers to a failure to defend a premise. This is never a logical flaw. Premises are accepted as true without proof. The argument does not do what choice C describes. Just as in choice A, choice E goes beyond the conditions that define when expulsion must take place. The principle does not require that the committee be correct, only that the committee members are impartial and declare the work a plagiarism.

Wording variations. There are only a few possible variations for the wording of the question stem in *application of a principle* questions. You can recognize an *application of a principle* question most easily by its format:

> *Principle:*
> *Application:*

Occasionally the word *application* is replaced by *conclusion*.

WORDING VARIATIONS FOR *APPLICATION OF A PRINCIPLE* QUESTIONS

Basic form

Which one of the following, if true, justifies the above application of the principle?

From which one of the following sets of premises can the conclusion be properly drawn using the principle?

Flawed form

The application of the principle is most vulnerable to criticism on the grounds that it . . .

Match a Principle to a Concrete Example

Be careful not to confuse this type of question with the *application of a principle* question type described above. (See Table 2.11.) In a *match a principle* question the setup gives you either a principle or an application but not both. The setup is *not* labeled *Principle:* or *Application:* as in *application of a principle* questions, so you must refer to the question stem and the answer choices to determine which of these the setup represents.

Table 2.11. Distinguishing *Application of a Principle* Questions from *Match a Principle to a Concrete Example* Questions

	Setup	Answer Choices
Application of a principle	A principle and an application	Strengthen or find the flaw in the application
Match a principle to a concrete example	Either a principle or an application, but not both	Find an application that matches the initial principle, or find a principle that matches the initial application

A *match a principle to a concrete example* question either (1) gives you an initial principle and asks you to find a concrete example that correctly matches the principle, or (2) gives you a concrete example and asks you to identify a principle that matches the example. In either case the task is essentially the same. In the first case, the five answer choices are concrete examples. In the second case, the five answer choices are principles.

Principle to concrete examples. These questions start with a principle in the setup and then ask you to choose which of the five answer choices matches the principle. The principle may be deductive, with absolute rules, or not.

SAMPLE PASSAGE 8

A high-quality pair of shoes may cost many times more than the low-quality alternative. However, because high-quality shoes last longer, the person who consistently buys only high-quality shoes may spend less on shoes in a ten-year period than the person who consistently buys low-quality shoes.

Which one of the following most closely conforms to the principle illustrated in the passage above?

(A) A low-price table saw may perform just as well as a high-price table saw.

(B) Many people find that the enhanced picture quality of an expensive television screen is worth the extra cost.

(C) Buying a used car costs less up front, but the cost of repairing and replacing used cars adds up over time to more than the cost of buying a new car.

(D) A high-quality suit may cost more than a lower-quality suit, but in a business environment, a high-quality suit can make the difference between getting a job offer and not getting a job offer.

(E) People who buy low-quality kitchen appliances spend more time replacing items when the items break down prematurely than if they had bought higher-quality appliances in the first place.

Solution: In this example, the setup represents a principle. Identify the principle. *Over time, one $200 expenditure costs less than five $85 expenditures.* Which answer choice illustrates the same principle? Focus on the elements of time and expense. Over a longer time, one alternative costs less, even though over a shorter time it appeared to cost more.

Choice A does not involve time. It discusses expense but then goes on to compare quality. The original principle does not directly address quality. Choice B does not involve time. It discusses money and appreciation. Choice C discusses the short term and the long term, as well as money. It matches exactly the criteria in the principle. Choice C is most likely the answer. Quickly evaluate the remaining choices.

Choice D does not include time and adds in a different criterion—getting a job. Choice E refers to saving time, not money. Choice C is the correct answer.

Concrete example to principles. In this type of question, the setup includes a concrete example and the answer choices represent five principles. You must find the principle that matches the example. As you saw in the Sample Passage above, matching means finding the rules or criteria in the principle and proving that the example is based on the same rules or criteria.

Thirty regular customers of a restaurant petitioned the manager to institute a smoking area on the outdoor patio. Two of the twenty-five waitstaff protested, claiming they would be exposed to secondhand smoke. The manager decided not to institute a smoking area.

Which of the following principles is illustrated by the situation described above?

(A) The opinion of a majority of employees takes precedence over the opinion of a minority of customers.

(B) In a disagreement between management and employees, the opinion of employees takes precedence over the opinion of the management when health issues are involved.

(C) The laws of a municipality take precedence over the requests of even a large number of customers.

(D) The opinion of even a single employee takes precedence over the opinions of a large number of customers when health issues are involved.

(E) The health of even a single employee takes precedence over the health of a large number of customers.

Solution: Because the setup is a concrete example and not a principle, it is generally not possible to identify the principle in advance. Instead, test the answer choices by comparing them with the original example.

For choice A, the setup does not refer to a majority of employees. In fact, it refers to a minority of employees. Choice A is out. Choice B is flawed in that it is not clear that there is a disagreement between management and employees. Management does not necessarily have an opinion. The disagreement is between some customers and a few employees. Choice B is out.

Choice C is irrelevant because we do not have any information on whether there are local laws governing smoking on the patio. Choice D accurately captures all of the elements of the example. Choice E is flawed because the issue does not concern the health of customers but rather the preferences of customers.

The wording of the question stem for *match a principle to a concrete example* questions is typically similar to what is used in the examples above. Read the stem to determine whether the setup is a principle or a concrete example.

ROLE OF A CLAIM

Role of a claim questions are based on a complete argument set forth in the setup. The question stem then cites a statement from the argument and asks you to identify the role that that statement plays in the argument. You can recognize a *role of an argument* question by its wording. The main wordings of the stem are:

> The claim that . . . plays which one of the following roles in the argument?
> Which one of the following most accurately describes the role played in the
> argument by the claim . . .

The wording variations for these stems are listed at the end of this section.

The word *claim* in the question stem, along with its variations *statement* and *contention*, can refer to any information that the argument asserts to be true. You are asked to identify the role that the claim plays in the argument. There are a number of specific types of roles that are tested in LR.

Types of Roles

The answer choices in a *type of roles* question consist, naturally, of descriptions of certain types of roles, a role being the function that the statement performs. Functions fall into two categories. The first category consists of the fundamental logical elements, including premises, assumptions, and conclusions. The function of a premise, for example, is to provide evidence that leads to the conclusion. The second category of functions consists of more complex relationships involving the fundamental elements. For example, an element may be a premise in an argument that the original argument is attempting to attack.

Fundamental logical elements. The fundamental logical elements are the building blocks of an argument. They can be used alone to create a valid argument or they can be used in more complex logical roles. Review the elements and their roles listed below.

Premise: *an explicit (stated) fact that is accepted as true without the need for proof. A premise's function is to support the conclusion.*

Necessary premise: *a premise without which the conclusion would be invalid.*

Sufficient premise: *a premise that by itself is enough to guarantee that the conclusion is valid.*

Assumption: *an implicit (unstated) fact that is accepted as true without the need for proof. An assumption functions as a premise but is not stated.*

Conclusion: *a fact that is proven to be true by applying logic to accepted facts (premises, assumptions). A conclusion can also be proven by applying logic to previously established conclusions.*

Main conclusion: *the conclusion that it is the ultimate purpose of the argument to establish.*

Intermediate conclusion: *a conclusion that is arrived at by applying logic to accepted facts (premises, assumptions) and is then used to support the main conclusion.*

Background information: *facts that help establish the context of the argument but are not used in the logic itself. In other words, background information is not used to prove conclusions.*

Hypothesis: *a proposed conclusion that the argument attempts to prove.*

Example: *information that illustrates another element of the argument. An example is typically not used in the logic itself.*

Generalization: *a statement that takes facts about a specific situation and attempts to create a prediction about situations that fall into a general category.*

Complex logical roles. Fundamental logical elements can be used to create more complex logical roles. The following are examples of complex relationships that are tested in *role of a claim* questions. For each of the following relationships, try creating an argument that includes the relationship.

COMPLEX LOGICAL RELATIONSHIPS THAT ARE TESTED IN *ROLE OF A CLAIM* QUESTIONS

A premise in an argument that the main argument is attempting to attack

Evidence that supports another premise, such as a reason to believe a fact or an explanation of a fact

A premise that is used to create an intermediate conclusion

A premise that follows from another premise

A premise that proves the truth of a conclusion

A fact that is taken for granted by the argument as false

A statement that counteracts a possible objection to the argument

A claim that is inconsistent with the evidence presented in the argument

A statement that is refuted by the argument

A statement that illustrates a principle

A statement that qualifies a conclusion

A statement that is supported by a study

A statement that is the basis for an analogy that supports the conclusion

A statement that establishes the importance of a conclusion but is not evidence for the conclusion

A statement that sets out a problem to resolve

A statement that is compatible with both accepting and rejecting a conclusion

A hypothesis that the argument rejects

A conclusion that is a generalization

A conclusion that is supported by an intermediate conclusion

The answer choices for *role of a claim* questions may consist of descriptions of the fundamental logical elements or of the more complex logical roles. There are many other combinations of logical relationships that could be tested, although the examples above cover most of the relationships that actually have been tested on recent LSATs. You may find that the wording of an answer choice obscures the real relationship. As you work through practice LSAT questions that test *role of a claim*, refer to the lists above. This will help you be able to recognize the role relationships.

SAMPLE PASSAGE 10

Unfortunately, voters today have little real information to go on when choosing the best candidate for office, and as a result, voters often end up with officials whose values do not represent those of the voters. Studies have shown that traditional debates reveal a candidate's values better than staged debates or brief television ads. If candidates are required to participate in traditional debates, the values of elected officials will better match the values of the people who voted them into office.

The statement that voters often end up with officials whose values do not represent the voters' values plays which one of the following roles in the argument?

(A) It is a conclusion that is proven by another premise.

(B) It is a premise on which the argument relies.

(C) It is a premise that is used to create an intermediate conclusion.

(D) It sets out the problem that the argument hopes to solve.

(E) It is a hypothesis that the argument rejects.

Solution: Read the setup and identify the premises and conclusion. If you are able to understand how the statement in the question stem relates to the argument, scan the answer choices to find an answer that matches your understanding. If you are not clear on how the statement in the stem relates to the argument, begin by testing the answer choices.

Choice A refers to an intermediate conclusion. The cited statement is not an intermediate conclusion. For choice B, is the cited statement a premise? A premise is used later in the argument to support the conclusion. Choice B does not seem to be used later. Choice B can be left as a weak possibility. Choice C also takes the cited statement as a premise, one that is used to create an intermediate conclusion. The cited statement does not seem to be used to create another premise. Leave choice C in as a weak possibility. For choice D, is the cited statement a description of the problem that the argument hopes to solve? Yes, this seems to exactly describe the role of the cited statement. This is most likely the best answer. Quickly glance at choice E. The argument does not reject the cited statement. Choice D is the correct answer.

Some *role of a claim* questions may not test logical relationships directly but rather may test information that is specific to the argument. For example, an answer choice might read *helps explain why pigs are more intelligent than dogs*. Such a statement can be evaluated on its meaning rather than its logical elements.

WORDING VARIATIONS FOR *ROLE OF A CLAIM* QUESTIONS

The claim that . . . plays which one of the following roles in the scientist's argument?

The statement that . . . plays which one of the following roles in the scientist's argument?

The contention that . . . plays which one of the following roles in the scientist's argument?

The claim that . . . figures in the argument in which one of the following ways?

That Mars contains water figures in the argument in which one of the following ways?

The point of the geologist's discussion of the ice age in the argument is to present . . .

The point that Mars contains frozen water is offered in the argument as . . .

Which one of the following most accurately describes the role played in the argument by the claim that Mars contains water?

COMMITTED TO DISAGREE

This question type involves two arguers and asks you to make determinations about the logic to which each arguer is committed and to what extent the two arguers are committed to the same or different logic.

TIP

COMMITTED TO DISAGREE QUESTIONS ON READING COMPREHENSION

Learning the *committed to disagree* questions on LR will help you with the Comparative Reading passage on the Reading Comprehension section.

Frank: Anyone who does not like fruit must not like people either.

Shannon: You are wrong. I like fruit but I do not like people. Therefore, people who do not like fruit, do like people.

Frank's and Shannon's statements provide the most support for the claim that they disagree over the truth of which one of the following?

(A) People who do not like people also do not like fruit.

(B) People who do not like people do like fruit.

(C) People who like people also like fruit.

(D) People who like fruit may like people.

(E) People who do not like fruit like people.

Solution: Frank is committed to the if/then statement

> *If –like fruit → –like people*

Frank must also be committed, then, to the contrapositive

> *Like people ∴ like fruit*

These are the only two logical statements to which Frank is committed. For any other logical statement, Frank would have no opinion. In *committed to disagree* questions it is important to know both the arguments to which the arguer is committed and the arguments to which the arguer is *not* committed (about which the arguer has no opinion).

Shannon is committed to the if/then statement

> *If –like fruit → like people*

along with its contrapositive

> *–like people ∴ like fruit*

Table 2.12. Summary of the Situations for Which Each Arguer Has an Opinion and Does Not Have an Opinion

	Committed	Not Committed*
Frank	If –like fruit → –like people Like people ∴ like fruit	If like fruit If –like people The White Sox are great
Shannon	If –like fruit → like people –like people ∴ like fruit	If like people If like fruit The White Sox are great

*This column can include *anything* other than the elements to which the arguer is committed, including elements that are irrelevant to the argument, such as the White Sox.

The information in Table 2.12 is a good start but a *committed to disagree* question does not simply ask you to identify what Frank believes or what Shannon believes. You must identify a statement about which Frank and Shannon disagree. This is a very important concept to understand thoroughly because (1) it is complex; (2) if you do grasp the concept well, the questions are easy to answer; and (3) this same type of logic appears in the Comparative Reading passage in the Reading Comprehension section.

What does it mean that Frank and Shannon *disagree* about a statement? It means that one of them is committed to believing that the statement is true and the other is committed to believing that the statement is false. If one of the two does not have an opinion about the statement, then the two do *not* disagree and the statement *cannot* be the correct answer.

Table 2.13. Chart of Frank's and Shannon's
Responses to the Five Answer Choices

	Committed to Believing the Statement Is True	Committed to Believing the Statement Is False	Not Committed
(A) People who do not like people also do not like fruit.		Shannon	Frank
(B) People who do not like people do like fruit.	Shannon		Frank
(C) People who like people also like fruit.	Frank		Shannon
(D) People who like fruit may like people.	Frank Shannon		
(E) People who do not like fruit like people.	Shannon	Frank	

Table 2.13 shows that the correct answer is the one for which one arguer is committed to believing the statement is true and the other arguer is committed to believing that the statement is false. In the table this is represented by one person being in the second column and the other person being in the third column (the final answer choice). If either arguer is in the "Not Committed" column, the answer choice cannot be correct. Test out each of the five statements above for yourself so that you are clear on why each arguer is committed to its truth, committed to its falsehood, or not committed.

There are several cases that potentially can trick you. No matter how vehemently one arguer may feel that a particular statement is false, there can be no disagreement if the other arguer does not have an opinion (is not committed to a position). Similarly, no matter how strongly one arguer feels that a statement is true, there can be no disagreement if the other arguer is not committed to a position. Finally, be careful in cases in which both arguers are committed to an opinion but it is the same opinion, as in the fourth statement in Table 2.13. In order for there to be a disagreement, the two arguers must be committed to the *opposite* opinions. One believes the statement is false and the other that it is true.

Some committed to disagree questions are based on deductive logic, such as in Sample Passage 11. Questions may be slightly more challenging when the arguments are not deductive, as in Sample Passage 12.

Andrea: Independence is a valuable quality for all children to develop. Simple art such as finger painting is an ideal activity for children because they can create a finished artwork without needing help from an adult. Because they did the project by themselves, their sense of independence is enhanced.

Ted: But when children complete a finger painting, even if they did not get help from an adult, they have not done it by themselves. There can be no finger painting without the people who made the paints and the paper, the plants and minerals that the paints and paper are made from, the people who pay the taxes that make the school building and the teachers available, and so on. Adults should help children develop a sense of interdependence, rather than an exaggerated sense of self-importance.

The statements above provide the most support for concluding that Andrea and Ted disagree about whether

(A) finger painting is an activity that children can do without help from an adult

(B) when children do work without help from an adult, they have done the work by themselves

(C) interdependence is a valuable quality for children to develop

(D) when children do work by themselves, their sense of independence is enhanced

(E) adults should help children develop valuable qualities

Solution: With the inductive arguments above, it is not as easy to summarize each arguer's belief as it was with the deductive argument in the previous Sample Passage. Start with the answer choices and work backward, determining for an answer choice what each arguer's position would be. In choice A, both Andrea and Ted would be committed to the truth of the statement. Andrea specifically makes the statement given in choice A and Ted admits that it is possible. For choice B, Andrea is committed to its truth. Ted explicitly states that even though a child may have done the work without the help of an adult, the child has not done the work by himself or herself. Thus, Ted explicitly finds the statement in choice B false. Andrea and Ted are committed to disagreeing on the truth of choice B, so B must be the answer.

Look quickly at the remaining choices. Ted is committed to the truth of choice C. Andrea does not state an opinion about interdependence. Presumably, she could think interdependence and independence are both valuable qualities. Because Andrea's position is unclear, choice C cannot be the answer.

Andrea clearly is committed to the truth of choice D. Ted's position is unclear. Choice D cannot be the answer. Both Andrea and Ted are committed to the truth of choice E, so the two arguers do not disagree.

WORDING VARIATIONS FOR *COMMITTED TO DISAGREE* QUESTIONS

The statements above provide the most support for holding that Sandra and Tomas disagree about whether . . .

Frank's and Shannon's statements provide the most support for the claim that they disagree over the truth of which one of the following?

Frank's and Shannon's statements commit them to disagreeing on whether . . .

Frank and Shannon disagree over whether . . .

COMPLETE THE SENTENCE/ARGUMENT

This type of question is based on a setup that establishes most of an argument but leaves the last sentence incomplete. You are to identify the answer choice that best fills in the blank at the end of the setup. You can easily identify this type of question by the blank line at the end of the setup paragraph.

For all questions in this category, the last line—the line that is incomplete—is the conclusion. The setup, then, gives you the premises and part of the conclusion and asks you to identify the answer choice that correctly completes the conclusion. The arguments are typically *not* deductive.

SAMPLE PASSAGE 13

Raising vegetables in the garden requires a delicate balance. If the gardener does not apply enough fertilizer, the plants will be stunted and unproductive. If the gardener applies too much fertilizer, the plants will become lanky and tasteless. The gardener must keep a constant eye on how plants are responding to the gardener's attention. This is not dissimilar to raising children. Parents must _____.

Which one of the following most logically completes the argument?
- (A) be careful not to overfeed their children
- (B) not withhold their attention from their children, even when parents are busy
- (C) give both positive and negative attention to their children
- (D) provide their children access to a wide variety of experiences
- (E) carefully balance giving their children too much attention and giving their children too little attention

---

Solution: Because you have to complete the conclusion, your first task is to understand the premises and how the argument attempts to create a conclusion. In this example, the conclusion is based on an analogy. Raising plants is similar to raising children. Identify exactly in what way the two are similar. The gardening part of the analogy is laid out first and more thoroughly in the setup. Gardening requires a "delicate balance" of applying too little fertilizer and too much fertilizer. Parenting, then, must be a "careful balance" of applying too little attention and too much attention. Choice E is the correct answer.

Choice A is a distracter, confusing feeding plants with feeding children. Choice B discusses only too little attention. In choice C, positive and negative attention is not the same as too much or too little attention. Choice D is somewhat off the mark, though if anything, it only addresses too much attention.

WORDING VARIATIONS FOR *COMPLETE THE SENTENCE/ARGUMENT* QUESTIONS

Which one of the following most logically completes the argument?

Which one of the following most logically completes the last sentence of the passage?

The conclusion of the argument above is most strongly supported if which one of the following completes the passage?

Of the following, which one most logically completes the argument in the passage?

TYPE OF REASONING

This type of question asks you to identify the specific type of logic used in the argument. The arguments may be valid or flawed, although questions that specifically ask you to identify the flaw in an argument fall under the category of *flaw* questions. The answer choices refer to the types of reasoning that you reviewed in the "Types of Arguments" section of this chapter. The answer choices might include examples of flawed reasoning as well as valid types of reasoning. The answer choices also often include types of refutations, which are also covered under "Types of Arguments" earlier in this chapter.

To solve a *type of reasoning* question, review the setup, identify premises and conclusions, and try to get a sense of what type of logic the arguer has used. Then test the answer choices.

SAMPLE PASSAGE 14

When Europeans first began colonizing the New World, they thought of it as a paradise of wide open spaces, in contrast to the congested living conditions of many of the European cities of the time. However, the New World is now as congested as Europe. Similarly, the claims that we should colonize Mars because of its vast open spaces should be rejected. After a short while, Mars will be just as congested as Earth.

The argument proceeds by

(A) rejecting a proposal on the basis that the proposal has not been proven to be valid

(B) treating an assertion that is not correct as an assertion that is intentionally misleading

(C) challenging an assertion by providing additional evidence

(D) establishing a conclusion by eliminating alternative possibilities

(E) defending one argument by showing that the argument is similar to another, presumably valid argument

---

Solution: Compare each answer choice with the passage. For choice A, the argument rejects the proposal to colonize Mars, but not on the basis that the proposal has not been proven to be valid. For choice B, the argument does not imply that the people who say we should colonize Mars are being intentionally misleading. For choice C, the argument does challenge the assertion that we should colonize Mars. The argument does not provide additional direct evidence that Mars colonization would fail. Instead, it argues through an analogy. Go on to choice D. The argument does not eliminate other possibilities. For choice E, the argument does defend the argument against colonizing Mars by showing that it is similar to an argument for colonizing the New World. Choice E *describes* an analogy without using the word *analogy*. Choice E is the correct answer.

RELEVANT INFORMATION

This rare type of question presents an argument and then asks you to identify information that would be useful for evaluating the effectiveness or validity of the argument. Relevant information does not necessarily strengthen or weaken an argument. It is simply information that would be relevant.

SAMPLE PASSAGE 15

Only people who have worked for Company X for at least ten years and have not taken more than three consecutive days of sick leave in the last year will be allowed to take three weeks paid vacation next summer. John has worked at Company X for eleven years and has taken four days leave in a row in the last month. Therefore, John is not eligible for taking three weeks paid vacation next summer.

Evaluating the validity of the above argument requires a clarification of which one of the following?

(A) whether John took three weeks of vacation last year

(B) whether the leave John took last month was the only leave of more than three days that John took in the last year

(C) whether John's leave last month was for illness

(D) whether Company X can afford to pay for the vacations of all of the employees who are eligible

(E) whether John will be allowed to take unpaid vacation

Solution: Only answer choice C is relevant to the conclusion of the argument. If John's leave was for illness, then the conclusion is valid. If his leave was not for illness, then the conclusion is not valid. The answer to the issue posed in choice C completely determines whether the conclusion is valid or not. In addition to the wording of the stem in the example, typical wording of the stem for these questions include the phrase *useful in evaluating*.

IDENTIFY AN ELEMENT OF AN ARGUMENT

This rare type of question asks you to identify an answer choice that represents a certain element of the argument. The examples in recent tests include asking you to identify a comparison that is made and asking you to identify which element of an analogy corresponds to another element of the analogy.

CONSISTENT WITH BOTH ARGUMENTS

In this rare type of question, two arguers present arguments, just as in the *committed to disagree* questions, but in this case you are asked to find an answer choice that is consistent with both arguments.

SAMPLE PASSAGE 16

Kendra: All applicants who have less than three years of experience must submit at least three letters of recommendation.

Ursula: Any applicant who applies from out of state must submit a birth certificate.

Which one of the following scenarios is consistent with both the principle given by Kendra and the principle given by Ursula?

Solution: An answer choice that is consistent with both is:

Peter is applying from out of state, has four years of experience, and is submitting two letters of recommendation and a birth certificate.

An answer choice that is *not* consistent with both is:

Tammi has two years of experience, is applying from in state, and is submitting two letters of recommendation.

Whereas Tammi is not required to submit a birth certificate under Ursula's conditions, she is required to submit at least three letters of recommendation under Kendra's conditions. Thus, the answer choice is *not* consistent with both sets of conditions.

Question Formats

You have now reviewed all of the types of questions that appear in LR. There are also several special formats in which questions of any type can be presented.

"EXCEPT" QUESTIONS

Consider the following possible question stem:

All of the following strengthen the argument EXCEPT

For such a question there are four answer choices that strengthen the argument. The one remaining answer choice—the one that does *not* strengthen the argument—is the correct answer.

EXCEPT questions require careful attention. First, the correct answer in the example above is *not* necessarily one that weakens the argument. It may be an answer choice that has no effect or is irrelevant. Prove which answer choices *do* strengthen the argument and cross them off.

Second, an EXCEPT question is logically confusing in that you have to keep a certain criterion in mind, such as *strengthening*, and yet you are looking for an answer that is *not strengthening*. This situation is a bit like someone telling you, "Don't think about elephants." All you can think about is elephants. It is very easy to get confused and end up choosing an answer choice that strengthens (or whatever the criterion for the question is). To avoid this, as you orient yourself to the question stem, make a notation in the scratch area of the test that there will be four *strengthens* and one *not strengthen*.

Only a few percent of LR questions use EXCEPT. On recent tests they have historically appeared only in questions based on *resolve a paradox*, *strengthen*, and *weaken* (all *effect of a new premise* questions), as well as *conclusion* and *consistent with both arguments* questions.

"LEAST" QUESTIONS

You may rarely find a question stem like the following:

> *Information on which of the following topics would be LEAST useful in evaluating the argument?*

As with EXCEPT questions, four answer choices would be useful and the one remaining answer choice would be correct. LEAST questions have the same logical pitfalls as EXCEPT questions. LEAST questions appear on some of the older practice LSAT material. In recent tests they have become rare.

ONE-LABELED ARGUER

Many setups are labeled with a name or description of the arguer.

> *Ethel: John says we should all take nice vacations this year. However, John was once found cheating on checkers. Why should we take the advice of a cheater?*

> *Researcher: Our experiments show that Earth's rotation is slowing. At this rate, we will all need to find a new home in 14 billion years.*

The fact that the arguer is labeled does not affect the logic of the passage or the process that you use to answer the question. The label can be completely ignored, although some people may find the passage to feel "friendlier" when there is a label. Labeling a one-person argument has become more common in recent exams. Nearly a third of passages have a one-person label.

Do not confuse a one-label argument with an argument in which two elements are labeled. Two-label arguments have unique properties.

TWO-LABELED ARGUERS

Just under 10 percent of LR questions have setups with two distinct arguments. Each argument is preceded by a label. The labels may be names or they may be descriptions of the arguer (such as researcher, scientist, journalist). In *application of a principle* questions, the labels are "Principle" and "Application."

> *Olivia: Average temperatures around the world have increased by at least several degrees during my lifetime. Clearly, we can expect temperatures to continue to rise.*

> *Patrick: I disagree. Last summer was the coolest that I remember. I barely had any opportunities to go swimming.*

More than two-thirds of the questions with two-labeled arguers occur in passages with either *application of a principle* questions or *committed to disagree* questions. Both types involve comparing two distinct arguments.

Of the remaining passages with two-labeled arguers, half are *flaw* questions. The flaw involves how one arguer responds to or misunderstands the other. Other passages with two-labeled arguers involve *type of logic* questions, asking you to identify the logic that one arguer uses in responding to the other.

Occasionally a *strengthen* or *relevant information* question uses a format with two-labeled arguers. You can use the same strategies for such questions in this format as you would for the same type of question in the normal format.

OBSOLETE: TWO QUESTION STEMS FOR ONE SETUP

Passages of this type have not appeared on the LSAT in several years but you will find them in older practice material. In this format, one passage was followed by two distinct questions, each with its own stem and answer choices. It is possible that a few such questions may reappear occasionally on current LSATs.

HOW TO SOLVE LOGICAL REASONING QUESTIONS

Chapter 1, "General Strategies," reviews the most common testing strategies for solving questions on the LSAT, including the LR section. Review Chapter 1 now to refresh your memory. Below you will learn how to apply these strategies to LR.

Starting an LR Question

When you start a new timed LR section, apply the timing strategies that you have studied in Chapter 1 and at the beginning of this chapter. Pick a question to work on first, set your watch to noon, and follow the steps below.

Problem-Solving Steps

There is a specific set of steps for working through a complex LR problem. On easy problems, it is not necessary to use all the steps. However, if you are getting questions wrong because of what seem like "careless errors," or if there are questions that you cannot get right even when you work them carefully, then learning the systematic set of steps will help you gain points.

GLANCE AT THE QUESTION STEM

When you start a new LR question, glance quickly at the question stem. You do not need to analyze the stem at this point. The purpose of glancing at the stem is to get a quick sense of which type of question the stem represents. You may catch the word *weaken* or notice that the stem is asking for a conclusion, or you may notice the wording *Which one of the following, if true*, which gives you a general orientation to what the stem is asking for.

If the meaning of the stem is not too clear, go directly to the passage. You will come back to the stem later. However, if you do not at least glance at the stem, you will not have any sense of what you are looking for.

READ THE PASSAGE

Next, read through the passage to get a sense of the argument. If you have understood the stem, look for elements that you will need to identify in order to solve the question. You will come back to the passage again after orienting yourself to the question stem.

ORIENT TO THE QUESTION STEM

After reading the passage the first time, come back to the question stem. At this point, it is vital that you understand the question stem thoroughly. This stage is one of the two most critical stages of problem solving. Being thorough here often makes the difference between a correct answer and an avoidable error.

Orienting to the question stem includes two specific steps. The first step is to ask yourself if you clearly understand what the question stem means. What type of question is it? Are there any aspects of the question that do not make sense?

Many question stems are worded in a complex way that disguises the type of question. Break the stem down carefully to make sure you understand it. If you have trouble breaking down a complex question stem, refer to the lists of wording variations for all of the question types listed in this chapter.

When a question asks you about an argument, you must distinguish to which argument it is referring. Many setups contain only one argument. Other setups, however, either include two or more arguments or refer to another argument that is not presented.

SAMPLE SETUP 1

Philosopher: Scientists recently hypothesized that the lifespan of the sun is a billion years shorter than they had previously thought. I have gone through their evidence and do not find it convincing. Therefore, I conclude that the sun will survive as long as scientists had previously thought.

Which one of the following, if true, would most seriously weaken the scientists' argument?

The stem asks you to weaken the scientists' argument, *not* the philosopher's.

Plan of attack: Once you have clearly understood the question stem and to which argument it refers, the second step is to consider what your plan of attack will be. It is often not a good idea to simply read the question stem and start evaluating the first answer choice. Generally, you need to review the setup to look for more specific information. The information that you need depends on the type of question.

REVIEW THE PASSAGE

Having oriented yourself carefully to the question stem and considered what information you need from the passage, come back to the passage a second time. You may need to clarify what the conclusion is, what the premises are, what type of logic is being used, and if there are gaps in the argument. A gap indicates that there may be unstated assumptions or errors in the logic. Ask yourself if you "buy" the argument. On an intuitive level, does it make sense to you? Even if you know the argument is valid, it may strike you as flawed. This is important to notice. Similarly, even when you are told that an argument is flawed, it may sound perfectly valid. In both cases, this discrepancy is a clue as to what is going on.

SCAN THE ANSWER CHOICES

Once you have read the passage for a second time, you are ready to scan the answer choices. Scanning means to quickly glance at all five answer choices. There are several purposes for doing this. First, the answer choices might change how you understand the question. Second, you may spot an answer choice that seems to closely match your intuitions about the question. This does not mean that you should automatically choose that answer. Often intuition leads you in the wrong direction and equally often an answer choice is partially correct but has a fatal flaw that requires more careful analysis to detect. However, an answer choice that seems to match your understanding of the question is certainly a good place to start. Finally, scanning the answer choices helps refine your sense of what tools you will need for answering the question.

TEST THE ANSWER CHOICES

In most cases, scanning the answer choices does not lead directly to the correct answer. Your next step is to test the answer choices carefully. Starting with the first answer choice, apply a two-pass approach, described below.

The Two-Pass Approach

Make two passes through the answer choices. The first time you go through the answers, spend only enough time to determine for each answer choice whether that choice can be eliminated or must be left as a possibility. Do not be too quick to eliminate answers. If you find that you are missing many questions because you initially eliminated the correct answer, become more conservative. Only eliminate a choice if it is clearly wrong. If it seems wrong but you are not sure, leave it in and put a question mark next to it.

Ask yourself if an answer choice goes in the right direction or wrong direction. If an answer choice is consistent with the passage, it goes in the right direction. If an answer choice is inconsistent with or contradicts the passage, it goes in the wrong direction and can be eliminated. The fact that an answer choice goes in the right direction does not, of course, mean that it is the correct answer, but it must be left in, to be evaluated more carefully in the second pass.

SAMPLE PASSAGE 17

Dr. Manning claims that psychological challenges help keep us emotionally flexible and healthy. According to Dr. Manning, even though a difficult emotional experience may be uncomfortable or even have unfortunate results, the very fact of facing the situation with courage builds our repertoire of emotional tools and makes our lives better in the long run. Dr. Manning has clearly been an accurate observer of human behavior.

Which one of the following statements best represents the main conclusion of the argument?

(A) Dr. Manning is probably better adjusted emotionally than most people.

(B) Too much emotional discomfort can be harmful in the long run.

(C) Dr. Manning's claim fails to consider that painful emotional experiences may have results that negatively affect our lives.

(D) A highly traumatic experience would make a person emotionally stronger than a mildly uncomfortable experience.

(E) Dr. Manning's claim is valid.

Solution: Does choice A go in the right direction or the wrong direction? Choice A is consistent with the passage, even though it is probably not defendable. During the first pass, leave choice A in, though you can mark it with a question mark to show that it does not seem likely. This allows you to come back later to double-check it. It is not unusual for a correct answer to seem unlikely at first.

Choice B goes in the wrong direction. It contradicts the passage. Cross it out. Choice C is also inconsistent with the passage. Dr. Manning does consider the possibility mentioned in C. Cross off choice C.

Choice D seems an extreme statement but it is consistent with the passage in that it maintains a correlation between emotional pain and emotional growth. It is an unlikely answer but you cannot eliminate it without further testing. Mark it with a question mark. Choice E is consistent with the passage. The last sentence indicates that the author of the passage believes that Dr. Manning's observations are valid. Though this answer may seem too simple or obvious, it fits as the main point that the arguer is trying to convey. Choice E is the correct answer.

As you make your first pass through the answer choices, use marks to indicate answer choices that are out, that are in but unlikely, and that are in and seem to be good (one plus mark) or strong (two plus marks).

(E) 17. ... clearly been an accurate observer of human behavior.

Which one of the following statements best represents the main conclusion of the argument?

(A) Dr. Manning is probably better adjusted emotionally than most people.

? (B) Too much emotional discomfort can be harmful in the long run.

✗ (C) Dr. Manning's claim fails to consider that painful emotional experience may have results that negatively affect our lives.

(D) A highly traumatic experience would make a person emotionally stronger than a mildly uncomfortable experience.

+ + (E) Dr. Manning's claim is valid.

Figure 2.8. Marks showing answer choices that have been eliminated (crossed out), are unlikely ("?"), are possible ("+"), or are strong ("++"). The correct answer is circled and then written by the question number.

The second pass. After completing the first pass through the answer choices, review what is left. How do the remaining answers compare and how do they differ? In some cases, simply reviewing the remaining answers leads to the correct answer. In other cases, you need to apply advanced strategies for examining each remaining answer choice and proving which one is correct. The most powerful strategy for finding the correct answer when you are down to two or three possibilities is the adversarial approach.

ADVERSARIAL APPROACH

The adversarial approach is described in detail in Chapter 1. Review it now. Below is a description of how to use it in LR.

When left with two, or sometimes three, answer choices, untrained test takers guess and move on. Such a strategy is not productive. If you are not able to get some of these more complex questions correct, you will have a hard time increasing your score. It *is* possible to figure out exactly why one answer choice is correct and exactly why the other answer choices are incorrect. It may take another thirty seconds to four minutes to get the correct answer but this strategy allows you to get many more correct answers.

The adversarial approach is based on the fact that, when there are two or three answer choices left, you have most likely developed a bias for one answer and against the others. This bias prevents you from seeing information you may have missed. To counteract your bias, start with an answer choice that you think is probably not correct and *defend* it. This forces you to look for evidence that the answer choice is correct. Similarly, when you come to the answer choice that you believe is probably correct, *attack* it. Prove that it must be wrong. The key to applying the adversarial approach effectively is that when you are defending, you must defend wholeheartedly and when you attack, you must attack wholeheartedly.

After applying the adversarial approach, you usually have a clearer picture of the strengths and weaknesses of each answer. Even if you run out of time (after three to four, or even five minutes) on a question without proving one answer correct, your guess is more likely to be correct.

WHAT TO DO IF THERE IS NO CLEAR ANSWER

If you have used the three to five minutes that are reasonable to spend on a single question and still do not have a clear answer, put your best guess. If you have only spent one or two minutes on the question and do not have a clear answer, continue working on the question.

In some cases, you may have worked carefully through all of the remaining answer choices and found that no answer choice seems to work. In other cases, it may seem that more than one answer choice can be defended. Assuming that you have not exhausted your allotted time for the question, it is *not* a good strategy in such cases to guess and move on. You have most likely made an error or missed important information. Start the question from scratch, using the remaining time. You may well be close to a correct answer if you can undo your error. Study the list of common errors discussed later in this section, so that you can more quickly identify what you may have missed.

ANSWER THE QUESTION

Once you have proven why one answer choice is correct and the others are wrong, you are ready to indicate your answer. Chapter 1 discusses strategies for marking the bubble sheet. Review those strategies. Once you have chosen the correct answer, circle the letter of your answer *and* write the letter next to the number of the question. As you bubble in your answers, your markings next to the answer choices might be difficult to read. Putting the letter of the correct answer next to the number gives you a clear reminder of which bubble to fill in.

Common Errors

Many test takers, when they review questions they have gotten wrong, feel that they have made a "careless error," which implies that they did not pay enough attention, and they resolve to be "more careful." In actuality, virtually all errors are the result of not applying a valid strategy or of applying a strategy incorrectly. Review *each and every* incorrect answer and determine the real reason why you got the question wrong. Below are the most common errors.

TOO LITTLE TIME

For a question that you got wrong, did you spend enough time on it? Check your notes. Remember that you should write down the time that you spend on each question even when you are working untimed. If you only spent one or two minutes on the question, consider why you did not take more time. If you attempted the question under timed conditions, you could have taken three to five minutes on it. If you attempted the question under untimed conditions, then you could have worked on the question longer. In untimed practice it is sometimes helpful to spend even fifteen or twenty minutes or more wrestling with a question.

One typical reason for stopping too soon on a question is that you may have been convinced that you had the correct answer. If this happens regularly, start to monitor your confidence level on each question more carefully. If you are only 90 percent confident in your answer, then you still have some doubt and should take a little more time on the question. If you find that you really do feel completely confident in answers that turn out to be wrong, then you may be eliminating answer choices too quickly or not reading all of the answer choices.

Another common reason for stopping too soon is that you think you have done everything possible. In some cases, that may be true. In most cases, however, you could have pushed the adversarial approach further.

A third major reason for stopping too soon, especially on a timed section, is that you feel rushed for time. You feel that you should be getting on to other questions in the section. If you feel this way, you may not yet have worked out exactly what your timing strategy is. If you are convinced in theory that it is worth your while to spend two, three, or four minutes on certain difficult questions, but in practice you are feeling rushed after two minutes on a question, there is a gap between your theory and your practice. When you are in a timed section, you may be unconsciously reverting to old test-taking patterns.

TOO FRAZZLED

Even if you are actually spending three to five minutes on some questions, if you are getting questions wrong, it may be because your brain is still worrying about time. See the comments in Chapter 1 on creating a "timeless four-minute bubble" around each question.

NOT ORIENTED TO THE QUESTION STEM

A very common cause of mistakes is that the test taker has not taken the time to orient well to the question stem. If this happens to you, you may find that you have misunderstood the question stem or interpreted it as a different type of question. If this happens regularly, take more time—even just a few seconds may be enough—to make sure you are clear on the question stem.

THE DEFAULT MULTIPLE-CHOICE QUESTION

As discussed in Chapter 1, if you were given a set of five answer choices, without any setup or any question stem, and asked to choose the correct answer, you would naturally assume that you are looking for the answer choice that is a true statement. This is the default multiple-choice question, namely, *Which one of the following is a true statement?*

Some LR questions actually ask this. Many, however, ask something very different. Your brain, however, can easily forget what question it is trying to answer and, without your noticing, revert to the default multiple-choice question. If you get a question wrong and find that the answer you chose represents a true fact, whereas the question stem asked for a premise that would weaken the argument, you have most likely reverted to the default multiple-choice question.

A good strategy for preventing both reverting to the default question and getting confused as to what question you are answering is to periodically go back to the question stem and refresh your brain as to what you are looking for. When you move to the next answer choice, briefly glance back at the stem.

INADEQUATE APPLICATION OF THE ADVERSARIAL APPROACH

The adversarial approach is your most powerful tool but you need to train yourself to use it most effectively. The most common error in applying the adversarial approach is to mix attacking and defending. Consider that you are trying to attack the answer choice C, which you liked, and your inner dialogue goes as follows:

> *What could be wrong with C? Hmm. I really like it. It seems to work. It matches the setup. OK, what could be wrong with it? Maybe it's too extreme. I don't think so, though. It seems all right to me.*

Are you *really* trying to attack choice C? Your brain cannot get out of the "I like C" rut. When you do spot a possible weakness, your thinking immediately goes back to saying that you like C, instead of mercilessly pursuing your attack. The same, of course, is true of halfhearted defending. It may help to think of an attorney who is being paid a million dollars to prosecute someone, even though the attorney believes that the person is innocent. The more you can avoid mixing attacking and defending, the more effective your use of the adversarial approach.

In many cases, when you try to attack an answer choice, there is actually nothing wrong with it. Similarly, you may try to defend an answer choice for which there are no points of defense at all. However, you cannot know this in advance for an answer choice. You still must attack, attack, attack and defend, defend, defend. It may only take thirty seconds of attacking to determine that there is no point of attack and then you can be more confident in your findings.

FAILURE TO USE YOUR EYES INSTEAD OF YOUR MEMORY

The strategy of using your eyes, not your memory, is described in Chapter 1. If you find that you have gotten confused on information from the setup or the question stem, you might have tried to use your memory to fill in facts, instead of going back with your eyes to review the information.

FAILURE TO USE VISUAL AIDS

This error is similar to the previous one. If you are getting confused on information or remembering it incorrectly, you may need to use some visual aids. This means making notes in your scratch area or in the passage itself. Even doodling can help some people organize their thoughts. Visual information functions very differently from information in short-term memory. Learn to make more use of visual aids.

DISTRACTERS

As described in Chapter 1, a distracter is an incorrect answer that has been designed to appear correct because it contains elements that superficially seem to match what the question stem is asking for. Because many questions contain distracters, you cannot answer a question solely on the intuitive feeling that an answer choice seems correct.

FAILURE TO CHECK ALL THE ANSWER CHOICES

If you find that you are choosing an incorrect answer that is higher in the list of answer choices than the real answer, you might have decided your answer was correct when you saw it and then did not check the rest of the answers after it. The test writers hope that you will become vested in the distracter before you get to the correct answer.

Even if you feel very confident that you have found the correct answer before looking at all the answer choices, it is still a good idea to glance briefly at the remaining answers. A few extra seconds will either confirm that the remaining answers do not need to be examined or will indicate that there may be something in one of the remaining answers that you should consider.

ELIMINATING AN ANSWER THAT SEEMS TOO EASY

Some correct answer choices may seem too easy or too simplistic. Remember that there *are* easy questions on the LSAT. If you eliminate an answer choice only because it seems too simplistic and instead choose one that is more convoluted, you may well be wrong. If an answer choice meets the criteria that the question stem sets forth, it is the right answer, even if it seems too easy. If you are not convinced that an easy answer is the correct one, work through the other answer choices carefully to prove that they are not defendable.

RATIO VERSUS ACTUAL NUMBER

Consider the following problem. In town X, 30 percent of the people own BMWs. In town Y, 5 percent of the people own BMWs. In which town are there more BMWs? Do you see why the question cannot be answered? If town X has 10,000 people and town Y has 4 million people, then town Y will have more BMWs.

A ratio, such as 30 percent or two-fifths, is not the same as an actual number, such as twelve BMWs. Many LR questions give you ratios, including percentages, and try to trick you into making a conclusion about actual numbers.

HOW TO PRACTICE

Chapter 1 discusses several distinct ways of practicing, each of which helps you develop different skills. Review this information.

For LR, most of your studying should be untimed, so that you can learn as much as possible on each practice question. As you work on problems, refer back to the lists and descriptions in this chapter. When you do a timed section, use the guidelines in Chapter 1 to evaluate your timing strategy.

RATIO OR ACTUAL NUMBER

Be careful. Would you rather have 3 percent of Person A's income or 80 percent of Person B's income?

As you get closer to your official test, do several timed sections at a sitting, working up to doing full mock tests. Whenever you do a timed section, evaluate it for timing strategy. Then review each question that you got wrong.

To make maximum improvement, review this entire chapter periodically. Each time you go through it, you will learn more and improve your skills.

PRACTICE PASSAGES WITH EXPLANATIONS

The following six questions represent some of the important most common and less common question types for LR. Work each question, taking as much time as you need to apply the strategies that you have learned. Refer back to the descriptions and strategies that are explained in the chapter. Then read the complete explanation that follows each question.

Practice Passage 1

1. In reporting political news, the news media should be fair and unbiased. The news media today are anything but fair and unbiased. They only report the most controversial political stories, leaving the community in ignorance of the myriad day-to-day events that make up the true political climate.

   Which one of the following, if true, most strengthens the argument above?
   (A) Most people in the community have access to sources other than the news media for learning about the day-to-day events of politics.
   (B) Some people do not realize that the news media are not being fair and unbiased.
   (C) Election results are often influenced by the information that people in the community have received from the news media.
   (D) Reporting on the day-to-day events of politics constitutes a fair and unbiased perspective.
   (E) Most people who access the news media find the details of controversial stories more interesting than the details of day-to-day events.

EXPLANATION FOR PRACTICE PASSAGE 1

Glance at the question stem. It is a *strengthen* question. Read the setup, looking for the conclusion, premises, and type of reasoning. Read the question stem carefully to confirm that it is a *strengthen* question and to orient to it. The question stem is straightforward. Go back to the setup. There are only three sentences. Determine which one is the conclusion. The first sentence is the point that the argument is trying to prove. Organize the premises and logic.

> Premise: *media not fair/unbiased*
> Premise: *media report controversial; media not report day to day*

The arguer claims that the media is currently *not* doing what it should. What they *are* doing is *report controversial*. What they *should* be doing, then, must be *report day to day*. Compare this with the conclusion:

> Conclusion: *media should be fair/unbiased*

The premise says media should *report day to day*. The conclusion says the media should be *fair/unbiased*. For the argument to work, these two terms must be equated. *Report day to day* has to be equal to *fair/unbiased*. Scan the answer choices. Choice D meets this criterion and completes the argument.

The other answer choices are irrelevant to the argument. Neither choices A, B, C, nor E provide information that supports the conclusion.

Practice Passage 2

2. Music teacher: In a survey of the 126 students in our school district's music program, each of the students reported that their parents were supportive of their study of music. Yet, a survey of all households in which students in the district's music program live revealed that only fifty-five of those households provided a quiet time and space for practicing music.

   Each of the following, if true, helps to explain the discrepancy described above EXCEPT:
   (A) Many music students live in the same household as a sibling who is a music student.
   (B) Many students in the district live in a household with only one parent.
   (C) Many music students do all of their practicing outside of the home.
   (D) Some students are not able to accurately evaluate their parents' intentions.
   (E) Many students in the district live with a relative other than a parent.

EXPLANATION FOR PRACTICE PASSAGE 2

Glance at the question stem. The word *discrepancy* indicates a *resolve a paradox* question. Read the setup, looking for a gap. Go back to the question stem and read it carefully. Orient to it. The question involves resolving a paradox but it is an EXCEPT question. Four answer choices resolve the paradox. The correct answer is the remaining one. To avoid forgetting the stem, make a note in your scratch area, such as "4 resolve, 1 not resolve = correct."

Go back to the passage and try to identify exactly what is paradoxical. There are 126 students who claim their parents are supportive, but only fifty-five homes allow the students a quiet time and place to practice. This is paradoxical because providing a quiet time and place to practice seems to be a significant way that parents can support their child. Consider any explanations that might explain the discrepancy. If nothing comes to mind, test the answer choices.

What is the effect of choice A on the paradox? If the 126 students consisted solely of pairs of siblings who lived together, there would only be sixty-three households. If some households included three siblings studying music, there could be only fifty-five households. Choice A resolves the paradox and is out.

What is the effect of choice B? It is not clear. There may be some relationship between some children living with only one parent and the number of households but it is not obvious what the relationship is. Leave choice B in.

What is the effect of choice C? Students who do all of their practicing outside of the home do not require a quiet time and place for practicing and yet their parents may be supportive in another way. Choice C resolves the paradox and is out.

What is the effect of choice D? Students who cannot effectively evaluate their parents' intentions may believe their parents are supportive when in fact the parents may not be. Choice D resolves the paradox and is out.

What is the effect of choice E? The students were asked about the attitude of their parents, not of the person who is the head of their household. If many students do not live with their parents, the discrepancy is explained. Choice E is out. Only choice B remains and it must be the correct answer. Choice B does not explain the paradox in any direct way.

Practice Passage 3

3. Traffic engineer: Eliminating most car traffic from the downtown area has the support of many city council members, but to do so would require increasing the amount of bus service between downtown and the rest of the city. The city does not have the money to buy new buses and the current buses are generally in poor repair. Increasing the number of hours that these buses are on the road would only result in mechanical breakdowns that would reduce service even further. Therefore, we cannot eliminate car traffic from most of the downtown area.

Which one of the following is an assumption on which the traffic engineer's argument depends?

(A) City council members would not support buying new buses.

(B) None of the current buses are in good mechanical condition.

(C) No people who work downtown also live downtown.

(D) There are enough current buses to provide the increased service as long as none are out of service at any given time.

(E) The city does not have enough money to repair the current buses to such an extent that the buses become equivalent in condition to new buses.

EXPLANATION FOR PRACTICE PASSAGE 3

Glance at the stem. The stem seems to be an *assumption* question. Read the setup. Note whether there is a gap that might indicate an unstated assumption. Read the stem carefully and orient to it. Confirm that this is an *assumption* question. The fact that the argument "depends" on the assumption tells you that the assumption is a necessary one, as opposed to a sufficient one. The correct answer is such that without it, the argument will fall apart. Your plan of attack is to negate each answer choice and evaluate the extent to which the argument is affected. Return to the setup to look again for any gaps. The argument seems sound. There is no readily apparent gap. Test the answer choices.

Test choice A by negating it. If the city council members *did* support buying new buses, would that destroy the argument? No. They may support the idea but still not have the money to implement it.

Negate choice B. *At least one of the current buses is in good condition.* This does not significantly change the fact that most are in poor condition. The traffic engineer's argument does *not* depend on the fact that all of the buses are in bad shape. Choice B is out.

Negate choice C. *At least one person who works downtown lives downtown.* A handful of people living and working downtown does not change the given premise that more bus service is needed between downtown and the rest of the city. Choice C is out.

Choice D is somewhat difficult to analyze. It is OK during this first pass to leave it in with a question mark.

Negate choice E. *The city does have enough money to repair the current buses to such an extent that the buses become equivalent in condition to new buses.* If this were true, it seems as though the problem would be solved and the engineer's objection would fall apart. To be sure, reevaluate choice D.

Negate choice D, simplifying the wording to better understand it. *There are not enough current buses to do the job.* If anything, this would strengthen the engineer's argument. Choice D is out. Choice E is the correct answer.

Practice Passage 4

4. The increased use of multiple food additives in the prepared foods that make up the bulk of our diet today has been accompanied by an increase in certain rare forms of cancer. The cause of this increase in cancer remains a mystery. Of the ten food additives that are commonly found together in over 80 percent of prepared foods, none was sufficient for causing cancer when tested in the laboratory in the quantity in which the additive typically occurs in prepared foods.

Which one of the following most accurately describes a flaw in the argument's reasoning?

(A) The argument fails to provide documentation that the laboratory tests on the food additives did not reveal a potential for causing cancer.

(B) The argument treats a statistical correlation between two events as a cause.

(C) The argument presumes, without justification, that two phenomena that are similar in one respect are similar in another significant respect.

(D) The argument concludes from a claim that no member of a set has a certain characteristic that the set as a whole does not have that characteristic.

(E) The argument treats a condition that is sufficient for causing cancer as a condition that is necessary for causing cancer.

EXPLANATION FOR PRACTICE PASSAGE 4

Glance at the question stem. It appears to ask for a flaw. Read the setup, looking for a gap in the logic. Orient to the stem more carefully. It is a *flaw* question. Consider your strategy. You will go back to the setup to look more carefully for a gap in logic. If you can identify a gap, scan the answer choices for it. Otherwise, test the answer choices.

Making your first pass through the answers, which are in and which, if any, can be eliminated? The answer choices, on first glance, all seem to have some relevance to the argument. For the second pass, evaluate each more carefully.

Is choice A a true statement? Yes. The argument does not provide any documentation. Is choice A the flaw in the argument then? No. Failing to provide evidence to support a premise is never a logical flaw in LR. Choice A is out.

Is choice B a true statement? Try to defend that it is. Identify the two events to which choice B refers. The easiest events to defend are probably the increase in the use of food additives and the increase in certain cancers. The argument does establish a statistical correlation between these. Does the argument leap from the correlation to saying that the additives are the cause for the cancer? No. In fact the argument does the opposite. It claims that despite the correlation, the additives do not cause cancer. Choice B has been proven incorrect.

Choice C refers to an analogy. Do not be mislead by the abstract wording. The wording in choice C is simply the definition for an analogy, without using the word *analogy*. Is the flaw in the argument that it creates a false analogy? No. The argument is not based on saying that one thing is like something else.

Try to make a case for choice D. The argument does refer to members of a set. The set is the group of ten additives that are often found together. The characteristic of the individual members of the set is that they do not cause cancer. The flaw is that the set as a whole—all the members together—may in fact cause cancer. It is not logically valid to assume that the set as a whole has the same properties as the individual members. Choice D seems very likely to identify the flaw in the argument. Briefly test choice E.

Try to defend choice E. Find something in the passage that is identified as sufficient to cause cancer. There is nothing. Choice E is a distracter. It refers to a type of logical flaw that is common on LR—confusing sufficient and necessary conditions—but it is not the flaw that occurs in this argument. Choice D is confirmed as the correct answer.

Practice Passage 5

5. History professor: In the past, serious students of history traveled to the parts of the world that they were interested in studying. Today's students are pressured to produce research results as quickly as possible. Information on the Internet is much more quickly available than is information buried in libraries in remote countries. Today's students, then, are pressured to use the Internet for their research. We can presume that these students will have neither the need nor the time to travel to the parts of the world that they are studying.

The claim that today's students are pressured to produce research results as quickly as possible plays which one of the following roles in the history professor's argument?

(A) It is the main conclusion of the argument.
(B) It is an intermediate conclusion that supports the main conclusion.
(C) It is a claim on which an intermediate conclusion is based.
(D) It is a hypothesis that the argument attempts to prove.
(E) It is a conclusion that is supported by an intermediate conclusion.

EXPLANATION FOR PRACTICE PASSAGE 5

Glance at the question stem. It is lengthy, so you may or may not spot the word *roles*. Read the setup, and try to get an overall sense of the argument. Read the question stem carefully and orient to it. The stem asks you to consider a specific claim from the passage and identify the role of that claim. Review the setup, analyzing how the particular claim fits in. If your analytical skills are good, you may be able to scan the answer choices and find the correct answer. Otherwise, test the answers.

For choice A, is the claim the main conclusion? No. The conclusion is the last sentence. For choice B, first test whether the claim supports the conclusion. It clearly does. Second, test whether the claim is an intermediate conclusion. To be an intermediate conclusion, a claim must follow from stated premises. The claim does not follow from other premises but is given as a premise that is to be accepted as true. The claim is not an intermediate conclusion and choice B is out.

Choice C, at first glance, may seem to be very similar to choice B. On closer inspection, choice C says that the claim is used to arrive at an intermediate conclusion. To prove this, find a statement that is derived from the claim that students are pressured. The second sentence and the third sentence are combined to conclude the fourth sentence. The fourth sentence is not the main conclusion but is used to support the main conclusion, so the fourth sentence is in fact an intermediate conclusion. Choice C appears to be correct. Briefly check the remaining choices.

Choice D is incorrect because the claim is given as an accepted premise. There is no attempt to prove it. Choice E is also incorrect because the claim is not a conclusion.

Practice Passage 6

6. To successfully grow a garden requires, above all else, patience. True, a certain amount of nitrogen, phosphorus, and other elements is necessary for plants to survive. True, a certain amount of weeding helps plants grow larger. But having plants that survive and grow larger _____ .

Which one of the following most logically completes the argument?

(A) requires, above all else, patience

(B) requires certain elements, weeding, and patience

(C) can contribute to having a successful garden

(D) is not as important as having a successful garden

(E) is not the primary measure of a successful garden

EXPLANATION FOR PRACTICE PASSAGE 6

The blank at the end of the setup, along with the wording of the stem, indicate that this is a *complete the argument/sentence* question. Read the setup, trying to get a sense of where the argument is going.

To test the answer choices, it is necessary to clearly understand the structure of the argument. The first statement is the conclusion. All of the other statements support it.

> Conclusion: *without patience not successful*
> Premise: *certain elements are necessary for surviving*
> Premise: *weeding is necessary for growing large*
> Premise: *but, surviving and growing . . .*

The word *but* in the third premise is a contrast word. It shows that there is a contrast between "surviving and growing" and something else.

> *(survive and grow) versus (patience)*

Patience is the only other quality in the argument that can stand in contrast to surviving and growing.

Test the answer choices against this analysis. For choice A, do surviving and growing require patience? The passage states that surviving and growing can be accomplished with certain elements and weeding. Choice A is unlikely. Choice B includes certain elements and weeding, along with patience, as the elements needed for surviving and growing. However, choice B does not capture the sense of contrast between surviving/growing and patience. Choice B is also unlikely.

Choice C is undoubtedly a true statement but again there is no element of contrast. Choice C is unlikely. Choice D does capture contrast. This is in the right direction. Choice D presents the contrast

> *(survive and grow) = not important versus (patience) = important*

Leave choice D in as a possibility, marked with a plus.

Choice E is similar to choice D. How do they differ? Choice E simply says that surviving and growing are not the criteria that determine whether a garden is successful. This is more defendable than choice D. Attack choice D. Nothing in the argument establishes which is more important. The argument states only that success is distinct from survival and growth. Choice D goes too far. Choice E is the correct answer.

SUMMARY

In this chapter, you learned how to control your time on LR. The chapter went on to describe the structure of logical arguments and the premises, conclusions, and assumptions that constitute arguments. Inference, valid logic, and flawed logic were defined.

You learned the various types of arguments. Arguments can be either deductive or inductive. Deductive arguments can be based on sets or on if/then logic. Inductive arguments include analogy, cause and effect, elimination of options, generalization, statistical arguments, tautology, application of a moral principle, argument by facts, citing an authority, comparison and contrast, and predicting the future from an established pattern.

The most common flawed arguments are confusing necessary and sufficient conditions; inferring that what is true of the parts must be true of the whole; false cause; ambiguity; circular reasoning; unrepresentative sample; assuming there are no other options; argument against the person; unreliable source; applying a generalization to an inappropriate case; false appeal to authority; distorting a view to make it vulnerable to criticism; disproving a claim that was not made; concluding that something is true because most people believe it to be true; accepting a fact as true because it has not been proven to be incorrect; rejecting a view because it has not been proven; inferring that because something is possible, it must occur; inferring that because something is unlikely to occur, it will not occur; and assuming that because a conclusion is false, all of the premises are false.

The less common types of flawed arguments include accepting a claim because an opposing claim was not well defended, analogy, assuming there are no additional necessary factors, biased language used against opponents, contradictory premises, failure to apply a generalization to all cases, failure to consider, failure to establish, false appeal to fear, false assumptions about groups, hasty generalization, invalid inferences, irrelevant considerations, and treating one element as something else.

The chapter reviewed the elements used for refuting arguments, namely to challenge an argument by providing additional evidence, challenge an argument by presenting an alternate explanation, challenge an argument by showing that its conclusion would lead to undesirable results, challenge a generalization, establish a generalization and use it against an argument, challenge by analogy, challenge the validity of an analogy, and undermine an apparent counterexample to a general claim.

You learned the various types of questions. The most common types are the effect of a new premise including strengthening, strengthening by principle, weakening, and resolving a paradox, as well as assumption, conclusion, flaw, and parallel reasoning types. The less common types include principle, role of a claim, committed to disagree, complete the sentence/argument, type of reasoning, relevant information, identify an element of an argument, and consistent with both arguments.

The special question formats reviewed in the chapter include EXCEPT questions, LEAST questions, one-labeled arguer, two-labeled arguers, and the obsolete format of two questions per passage. Strategies for solving LR questions were described. These strategies taught you to glance at the question stem, read the passage, orient to the question stem, review the passage, scan the answer choices, test the answer choices, and use the adversarial approach, as well as teaching what to do if there is no clear answer.

Common errors to avoid include taking too little time, being too frazzled, not orienting to the question stem, falling for the default multiple-choice question, inadequate application of the adversarial approach, failure to use the eyes instead of the memory, failure to use visual aids and distracters, failure to check all answers, and eliminating an answer that seems too easy. Finally, the chapter discussed how to practice and presented practice passages with explanations.

Time: 35 minutes

25 Questions

> **DIRECTIONS:** The questions in this section are based on the reasoning contained in brief statements or passages. More than one answer choice could conceivably answer the question in some cases. However, you should choose the <u>best</u> answer. The best answer is the response that answers the question most accurately and completely. You should avoid making any assumptions that, by commonsense standards, are implausible, superfluous, or incompatible with the passage. When you have chosen the best answer, fill in the space on your answer sheet that corresponds to your answer.

1. Along with the increase in average global temperatures over the past two centuries, there has been a parallel increase in volcanic activity. This leads to the conclusion that increased temperatures cause increased volcanic activity.

   Which one of the following, if true, most strengthens the argument?
   (A) Sunspots can cause an increase in volcanic activity.
   (B) Increased global temperatures have caused an increase in average summer rainfall.
   (C) During a previous thousand-year period during which global temperatures did not change, volcanic activity decreased.
   (D) Volcanic activity does not cause an increase in global temperatures.
   (E) There is more volcanic activity in the Southern Hemisphere than in the Northern Hemisphere.

2. Student: I recently installed both spreadsheet program Q and spreadsheet program Z—produced by competing companies—on my computer, and the installation for each program was successful. Program Z runs perfectly. Program Q runs perfectly unless program Z is open, and in that case program Q causes my system to crash. Clearly, program Q is not compatible with my operating system.

   Which one of the following, if assumed, allows the student's conclusion to be properly drawn?
   (A) Any program that is incompatible with the operating system of the computer on which it is running will cause a system crash if it is run when another program is open, assuming that both programs were installed successfully.
   (B) Any program that was installed successfully and causes a system crash when another program is open is not compatible with the operating system of the computer on which it is running.
   (C) If two programs are successfully installed on the same computer and both programs have the same function, it is unlikely that both can be run at the same time without causing a system crash.
   (D) Any company that produces software and is aware that a competing company builds similar software builds a mechanism into their software such that if similar software from the competing company is successfully installed on the same computer, the computer's system will crash.
   (E) The company that produces program Q also produces other software that is incompatible with the operating system of the student's computer.

GO ON TO THE NEXT PAGE

3. Human skin produces vitamin D when exposed to sunlight. Because heavily pigmented skin can block the production of vitamin D, a study was conducted with two groups of people, one group consisting of people with dark skin pigmentation and one group with light skin pigmentation. The groups were similar in age, socioeconomic status, diet, and overall health. Vitamin D blood levels were measured daily for both groups. The group with more heavily pigmented skin had higher average vitamin D levels than the other group.

Which one of the following, if true, most helps to explain the findings of the study above?

(A) People in the group with lighter skin got more exposure to sun than did people in the group with darker skin.

(B) Half of the people in the group with darker skin had vitamin D levels lower than average for the group.

(C) Sunscreen lotions do not provide the same protection for people with lighter skin as they do for people with darker skin.

(D) Some people with light skin develop darker skin when exposed to the sun.

(E) People who are aware that they have a factor that might limit their intake of a necessary nutrient are more likely to take active measures to supplement that nutrient.

4. Certain business leaders have suggested to the state legislature that small businesses be exempted from sales tax. The leaders' rationale is that such a change would make the prices at small businesses more competitive compared to the prices at larger businesses. It is just as likely that small businesses would raise their prices to compensate for the lack of sales tax and pocket the difference. Clearly, business leaders who would mislead the legislature in such a way should be barred from further lobbying.

Which one of the following best describes the flaw in the argument above?

(A) It distorts a view to make the view more vulnerable to criticism.

(B) It confuses a condition that is necessary for an event to occur with a condition that is sufficient for the event to occur.

(C) It treats an unjustified assertion as an intentionally false assertion.

(D) It fails to document that small businesses are just as likely to raise their prices and pocket the difference as to leave their prices low.

(E) It relies on the opinions of a group that is unlikely to be representative of the group to which the conclusion applies.

GO ON TO THE NEXT PAGE

5. Most people have a lot of experience testing the ripeness of peaches in the store. Store X has many peaches available. It also has a variety of exotic fruits with which most people have no experience. Most of the exotic fruits are riper than most of the peaches. However, most people will buy a fruit only if they trust their assessment of the fruit's ripeness. At the same time, most people only trust their assessment of a fruit's ripeness if they have a lot of experience testing the ripeness of that fruit.

If the above statements are true, which one of the following can most strongly be supported?

(A) Some of the people who buy the exotic fruits at Store X do not realize that there are peaches that are riper than the exotic fruits.

(B) A ripe exotic fruit tastes better than an unripe peach.

(C) Those people who do have a lot of experience testing the ripeness of the exotic fruits in Store X will buy the exotic fruits rather than the peaches.

(D) The fact that the exotic fruits are riper than the peaches will not prevent most people from buying peaches.

(E) Most people will buy apples rather than peaches if the apples are riper and if the people have a lot of experience testing the ripeness of apples.

6. Picasso should be honored for inspiring future generations to think creatively. By viewing Picasso's works, with their powerful flow of fresh creativity, young people of later generations have been moved to create new directions, not just in art, but in politics, food, religion, and in fact every area of modern life.

Which one of the following is an assumption required by the above argument?

(A) Picasso believed that future generations would benefit from his art.

(B) Picasso also inspired people of his own generation.

(C) A person can be honored for the future result of an action that the person performed earlier.

(D) A person working in a certain field should not be honored if that person only inspires others working in the same field.

(E) A person can be honored for an unintentional result of that person's actions.

GO ON TO THE NEXT PAGE

7. Fernandez: Newspapers are a better source of news than television because people can review the information in the newspaper at their own leisure. Television can supplement the news but should never replace newspapers as a news source.

Osman: Newspapers clearly serve a valuable need by virtue of their comprehensive coverage. However, there are many news events that people need to know about as quickly as possible and only television can deliver news as it happens.

Fernandez's and Osman's statements provide the most support for the claim that they disagree over which one of the following issues?

(A) In some cases television should replace newspapers as a news source.

(B) In some cases newspapers are a better source of information than is television.

(C) There are many events about which people need to know as quickly as possible.

(D) Newspapers are valuable because people can review the information in the newspaper at their leisure.

(E) The information on television is more likely to be biased than the information in a newspaper.

8. Physician: On a daily basis 60 percent of our clinic staff's time is spent taking care of the 10 percent of our patients who have the most serious medical needs. If we were to refer these patients to the nearest urgent care facility, we could use the time we save to see many more patients with less serious medical needs.

Which one of the following, if true, most seriously weakens the physician's argument?

(A) There are on the average only fifteen patients a day who would qualify for being referred to an urgent care facility.

(B) The physician's plan would save the physician more time than it would the rest of the staff.

(C) Most urgent care facilities are so busy that patients must wait several hours for treatment.

(D) Because of the paperwork involved, it takes more staff time to transfer a patient to an urgent care facility than it does to actually treat the patient.

(E) Most of the physician's patients would like to have more time with the physician during an office visit.

GO ON TO THE NEXT PAGE

9. Veterinarians know that if a dog has been abused by a previous owner, the current owner must establish a high level of trust with the dog if the dog is ever to become a truly loving pet. The kind of activity that establishes a high level of trust varies from dog to dog. Oddly, there are some dogs that best establish trust with their owner if they are reprimanded sharply when they displease the owner. Any owner who has such a dog, then, should reprimand the dog sharply when it misbehaves, even if the owner would rather treat the dog with kindness.

Which one of the following principles, if valid, most helps to justify the conclusion in the above argument?

(A) If a pet best establishes trust with its owner by being treated with kindness when the pet displeases the owner, the owner should treat the pet with kindness, even if the pet's misbehavior was serious.

(B) Training a dog requires treating the dog consistently in all situations.

(C) An owner sometimes knows better than a veterinarian how to help a dog become a truly loving pet.

(D) If there is a method for preventing a dog from being abused, everyone who is involved with the dog should apply that method.

(E) If there is a method for helping a dog become a truly loving pet, the owner should apply that method.

10. The newly independent nation of Khazarsko just held a popular election to determine the future form of government. Only two options—democracy and constitutional monarchy—were listed on the ballot, though write-in options were allowed. Constitutional monarchy was rejected and there were few write-in votes cast. Therefore, we should congratulate the people of Khazarsko for choosing democracy.

Which one of the following most accurately describes the method of reasoning used in the argument?

(A) It assumes that what is true for most members of a group is true for all members of the group.

(B) It concludes that an event is likely to occur because the only other realistic option has been eliminated.

(C) It treats a claim that is virtually inevitable as a claim that is merely possible.

(D) It infers from a claim that one of two possible options for an outcome is likely, that the other option will not occur.

(E) It concludes that one of two possible outcomes will not occur based on a sampling of a group that is not representative of the group as a whole.

GO ON TO THE NEXT PAGE

11. Children at day care centers where loud music is played regularly often develop the ability to concentrate on a specific task by shutting out external interference. Many such children also develop advanced artistic skills, which can be seen in their drawing and crafts. It must be that the exposure to loud music somehow improves artistic ability.

Which one of the following, if true, most strengthens the argument above?

(A) Children at day care centers where loud music is never played do not usually exhibit greater than normal artistic skills or the ability to concentrate on a specific task by shutting out external interference.

(B) There are many children who do not attend day care who have both the ability to concentrate by shutting out external interference and have advanced artistic skills.

(C) There are many children who do not listen to loud music who have the ability to concentrate by shutting out external interference and have advanced artistic skills.

(D) Most children who do not have advanced artistic skills also do not have the ability to concentrate by shutting out external interference.

(E) Children at day care centers where soft music is played regularly learn to concentrate but not as well as do children exposed to loud music.

12. Physician: John will continue to gain weight unless he replaces his carbohydrate consumption with fruits, nuts, vegetables, and protein or embarks on a daily routine of at least thirty minutes of aerobic exercise. Because John has indicated that he will not embark on a daily routine of at least thirty minutes of aerobic exercise, it is clear that he will continue to gain weight.

The conclusion of the argument is properly drawn if which one of the following is assumed?

(A) John will not consider reducing his total calorie intake.

(B) John will not do regular anaerobic exercise on a daily basis for at least thirty minutes.

(C) John continues to consume the same amount of carbohydrate and does not consume any additional fruits, nuts, vegetables, or protein.

(D) John has an allergy to most nuts and to some fruits.

(E) John is unwilling to consider lifestyle changes other than diet or exercise that have helped other people lose weight in the past.

GO ON TO THE NEXT PAGE

13. If a fruit tree bears a heavy crop of fruit in the early summer, it is likely that it will begin to lose its leaves prematurely in the fall. The pear tree in Greta's yard is beginning to lose its leaves prematurely this fall. Therefore, it is likely that it bore a heavy crop of fruit early in the summer.

The flawed pattern of reasoning in which one of the following is most closely parallel to that in the argument above?

(A) The new hardware store in town closed its doors after only three months in business. This indicates that the business was most likely undercapitalized, as new businesses that are undercapitalized are very likely to go out of business within the first four months.

(B) If a highway is resurfaced every three years, it will not require annual repairs. County Highway 72 has not been resurfaced for the past five years. Therefore, it most likely requires annual repairs.

(C) Greg recently chased a wild animal away from his campsite. The wild animal later developed a fear of humans. Therefore, Greg's chasing the animal probably caused the animal to fear humans.

(D) All fossils are imprints in rock. Most imprints in rock are of no scientific interest. This fossil is an imprint in rock, so most likely it is of no scientific interest.

(E) Unless telepathy can withstand the rigors of scientific testing, it cannot be considered a valid area of study. Foreman has concluded that telepathy is not a valid area of study, and therefore, telepathy cannot withstand the rigors of scientific testing.

14. Sociological studies have shown that the rate of domestic violence has not changed over the past thirty years. At the same time, the number of court convictions for domestic violence has increased by nearly 40 percent.

Which one of the following, if true, most helps to resolve the apparent discrepancy in the argument above?

(A) Sociologists only began to define domestic violence in the middle of the twentieth century.

(B) Many people are hesitant to discuss domestic violence if it is occurring in their family.

(C) Recent changes in domestic violence law have made it easier to acquit a person accused of domestic violence if his or her spouse is also violent.

(D) Juries are as likely to convict a woman of domestic violence as they are to convict a man.

(E) The population has increased by nearly 40 percent over the past thirty years.

GO ON TO THE NEXT PAGE

15. Long distance travel by plane is fast but filled with discomforts—large crowds, cramped seats, noise, and jet lag—to name a few. Long distance travel by train may have its discomforts, but they are gentler—spread out and interspersed with pleasant conversation, beautiful views, good meals, and lots of relaxation. For those who do not mind the extra time it takes to arrive at their destination, travel by train is more pleasant than travel by air.

The statement that the discomforts of long distance travel by train are gentler plays which one of the following roles in the above argument?

(A) It is a rebuttal to a possible argument against traveling by plane versus traveling by train.

(B) It is a premise given in support of the conclusion that travel by train is more pleasant than travel by air for those who do not mind spending the extra time.

(C) It is given as evidence that many people prefer to travel by train if they do not mind spending the extra time.

(D) It establishes an analogy that is used to support the intermediate conclusion that long distance travel by train has discomforts.

(E) It proposes a hypothesis that the argument then defends with examples.

16. People who play tennis experience certain physiological responses in their arms, legs, and cardiovascular system that lead to overall increased vitality. If you do not like to play tennis but want to increase your vitality, you should watch people playing tennis.

Which one of the following statements, if true, most strengthens the argument?

(A) Encouraging someone else to perform a healthful activity creates a positive feeling for the person who does the encouraging.

(B) Performing vigorous physical activity is not the only way to develop increased vitality.

(C) Observing someone exercising certain motor skills can increase the observer's ability to perform those motor skills.

(D) Refraining from exposure to physical activities can reduce the likelihood that a person will perform physical activities.

(E) The observer of an activity often experiences some of the physiological responses of the person performing the activity.

GO ON TO THE NEXT PAGE

17. Engineer: Unless a society has a widespread demand for energy resources, development of such resources cannot be economical. At the same time, there are many societies that have a critical need for energy resources without that need being widespread, and these societies have no choice but to develop energy resources. It follows then that some societies _____ .

Which one of the following most logically completes the sentence?

(A) have no choice but to forgo development of energy resources

(B) can develop energy resources economically without having a widespread demand

(C) develop energy resources uneconomically while meeting a critical need

(D) have a widespread demand for energy resources but are not able to develop such resources economically

(E) have a critical need for energy resources and also have a widespread demand

18. Scientist: Scientists have toyed with the concept of telepathy over the years but a serious study of telepathy has never been undertaken. Perhaps that is for the best. To seriously study telepathy would require hiring teams of specialists and funding research projects for years. We cannot afford that kind of expense. For this reason, telepathy should not be studied seriously by scientists.

The scientist's argument is most vulnerable to criticism on the grounds that it

(A) fails to define precisely what is meant by the term *telepathy*

(B) rejects a view solely on the basis that the view has not been proven

(C) treats a hypothesis as an established fact

(D) fails to establish that telepathy can be proven to exist

(E) fails to consider that there might be financial benefits derived from the serious scientific study of telepathy that might be greater than the costs

19. Owners of businesses that are not incorporated are vulnerable to litigation. Owners of businesses that are incorporated must report to a board of directors. Therefore, any business owners who must report to a board of directors are not vulnerable to litigation.

The pattern of flawed reasoning in which one of the following arguments is most similar to that in the argument above?

(A) It is clear that any deep-sea bacteria that can function in complete darkness can metabolize sulfur, because only bacteria that live near deep-sea vents can metabolize sulfur, and bacteria that live near deep-sea vents can function in complete darkness.

(B) Most lawsuits against businesses result from events that happen toward the end of the work week. Most employees are tired by the end of the work week. Therefore, the events that trigger most lawsuits result from employees being tired when they interact with customers.

(C) All patents on scientific inventions constitute intellectual property. All intellectual property is subject to the laws governing inheritance. Therefore, anyone who owns something that is subject to the laws governing inheritance holds a patent on a scientific invention.

(D) Elm trees are susceptible to Dutch elm disease. Trees that are not elm trees are not susceptible to Dutch elm disease. Therefore, any tree that is not susceptible to Dutch elm disease is not an elm.

(E) Poets who lack a formal education are limited in their range of expression. Poets who have a formal education have the ability to inspire. Thus, poets who have a formal education are not limited in their range of expression.

GO ON TO THE NEXT PAGE

20. Some people's eyes shift back and forth when they talk to others. These people are interpreted by others as being guilty of a misdeed, and yet some such people are not guilty of anything. At the same time, people who believe that they are talking with someone who is guilty of a misdeed invariably press the person with whom they are talking to confess to something, even if it is something that did not actually occur.

Which one of the following can be properly inferred from the claims above?

(A) There are people whose eyes shift back and forth when they talk to others who confess to misdeeds they did not do.

(B) There are people whose eyes shift back and forth when they talk to others who have committed the misdeeds that others think they have committed.

(C) There are people who do not believe another person if the second person claims to be innocent.

(D) There are people who are pressed to confess to something that they did not do.

(E) There are people who are interpreted as being innocent when in fact they are guilty of a misdeed.

21. Mayor: Over the past twenty years the city has acquired an additional 30,000 acre-feet of water rights. However, unless we acquire another 50,000 acre-feet, we will not be able to meet the water needs of our residents for more than thirty more years. Unfortunately, the current water resources for which we can negotiate only amount to 20,000 more acre-feet.

If the statements above are true, which one of the following must also be true?

(A) The city is unlikely to be able to meet the water needs of its residents beyond thirty years.

(B) Once the city has access to 80,000 acre-feet of water rights, it will be able to meet the water needs of its residents for thirty years.

(C) If the city acquires 50,000 additional acre-feet of water rights, it will be able to meet the water needs of its residents for more than thirty years.

(D) Unless the city finds new water resources for which it can negotiate, the city will not be able to meet the water needs of its residents beyond thirty years.

(E) The city currently has rights to less than half of the water that it needs to guarantee that it can meet the water needs of its residents for the next thirty years.

GO ON TO THE NEXT PAGE

22. Business leaders and politicians who have no personal appreciation of the delicate balance of nature will inevitably make decisions that result in the further degradation of our natural environment. For this reason, even though schools have become obsessed with test performance, school children should be given the opportunity to spend quiet time in a natural setting.

Which one of the following is an assumption required by the argument above?

(A) Business leaders and politicians are more concerned with test performance than with an appreciation of nature.

(B) People who have a personal appreciation of the delicate balance of nature will make decisions that prevent the further degradation of our natural environment.

(C) Spending quiet time in a natural setting leads to an appreciation of the delicate balance of nature.

(D) Spending quiet time in a natural setting is not something that can be evaluated by a test.

(E) It is possible to spend quiet time in a natural setting in a large group.

23. Authors who are well-known sell many more books than authors whose names are not recognized by the general public. The best-known authors hardly have to publicize their new books at all. The moment their new book is out, people are lined up to buy it. The best advice for a new author, then, is to become involved in as many publicity events as possible so that the public begins to recognize your name.

Which one of the following most accurately states a flaw in the reasoning above?

(A) It infers from the characteristics of similar situations that something will be true of a current situation.

(B) It treats a factor that is important for a result to occur as a factor that is necessary for a result to occur.

(C) It infers that because it is possible for an author to become well-known through publicity, it is inevitable that an author will become well-known through publicity.

(D) It falsely assumes that there are no other factors in addition to being well-known that are necessary for an author's work to sell well.

(E) It fails to rule out the possibility that the fact that people readily buy the books of a particular author is the cause of the author being well-known, rather than the effect.

GO ON TO THE NEXT PAGE

24. The early ancestors of birds were dinosaurs that branched off into a radically new direction from the mass of other dinosaurs, namely the ability to fly through the air. As a result, a relatively tiny group eventually evolved into a major new family with hundreds of widely varying species, the birds. Modern flying mammals, such as the bat, are in the same position as these early ancestors of birds. They are going in a radically new direction from their fellow mammals. It is likely, then, that some day there will be a vast family of widely varying flying mammals descended from bats.

Which one of the following, if true, most weakens the argument above?

(A) Many early species of flying dinosaurs eventually became extinct.

(B) During the time of the early ancestors of birds, there were no other flying animals with which the flying dinosaurs had to compete.

(C) It took millions of years for the early species of flying dinosaurs to evolve into the widely varied species of birds.

(D) The evolution of the early species of flying dinosaurs may have caused the extinction of other species that would have been at least as varied and innovative as the birds.

(E) The odds of any dinosaurs developing the ability to fly were miniscule.

25. A study of drivers approaching an intersection as the traffic light turned yellow found that the average driver of a passenger car would stop for the light if it turned yellow when the driver was more than 50 feet from the intersection and would go through the light if the light turned yellow when the driver was fewer than 50 feet from the intersection. The same study showed that drivers of commercial vehicles would go through the light unless the light turned yellow when the driver was 100 feet or more from the intersection. Clearly, drivers of passenger cars are more safety conscious than are drivers of commercial vehicles.

Which one of the following, if true, would most weaken the argument above?

(A) It requires more distance to safely stop the average commercial vehicle than it does the average passenger car.

(B) Drivers of commercial vehicles are more likely to signal that they are stopping than are drivers of passenger cars.

(C) Over 80 percent of tickets issued for running a red light are given to drivers of passenger cars.

(D) Drivers of commercial vehicles are often paid by the job rather than by the hour, so that the more quickly they complete a job, the more money they can earn.

(E) Many drivers of passenger cars will go through a light unless the light turned yellow when the driver was 100 feet or more from the intersection.

STOP If you finish before the 35-minute time period is over, you may go back and check your answers.

ANSWER KEY

1.	D	**8.**	D	**15.**	B	**22.**	C
2.	B	**9.**	E	**16.**	E	**23.**	E
3.	E	**10.**	B	**17.**	C	**24.**	B
4.	C	**11.**	A	**18.**	E	**25.**	A
5.	D	**12.**	C	**19.**	A		
6.	C	**13.**	A	**20.**	D		
7.	A	**14.**	E	**21.**	D		

ANSWERS EXPLAINED

1. **(D)** This is a *strengthen* question based on a cause-and-effect argument. The argument gives a correlation between increased global temperatures and increased volcanic activity and then concludes that the increased temperatures caused the increased volcanic activity. To strengthen the argument, an answer choice must either (1) support that the temperature causes the volcanic activity, or (2) show that the volcanic activity is not the cause for the increase in temperature. Choice D does the latter.

   Choice A is incorrect because it does not strengthen the causal relationship between temperature and volcanoes. Choice B is incorrect because rainfall has no relationship to volcanic activity. Choice C is incorrect because it goes in the wrong direction. It indicates that temperature does not correlate with volcanic activity. Choice E would only go in the right direction if it were true that the Southern Hemisphere is warmer than the Northern Hemisphere but this is not necessarily true.

2. **(B)** This is a *sufficient assumption* question. The correct answer must lead inevitably to the conclusion. The argument is deductive. Choice B matches the criteria that apply to Q, namely that it was installed successfully and that it causes a system crash when Z is open, and choice B provides an absolute if/then rule that in such cases the first program (Q) is not compatible with the operating system.

   If install successful AND causes crash when other program open → incompatible

   This condition is completely sufficient to arrive at the conclusion of the argument.
   Choice A is incorrect because it states

   If incompatible → crash

   This is not *sufficient* to lead to the conclusion. Choice C is incorrect because the word *unlikely* prevents it from being deductive. In addition, choice C only refers to the system crash, not the fact that Q is incompatible with the system.

   Choice D is incorrect for a similar reason. It only explains the system crash, not the incompatibility with the system. Choice E is incorrect because it is not <u>sufficient</u> to lead to the conclusion, even though it provides evidence that might support the conclusion.

3. **(E)** This is a *resolve a paradox* question that does not use the word *paradox* in the stem. The paradox is that people in the group with darker skin would be expected to have lower vitamin D levels, when in fact they had higher levels. Choice E correctly explains the apparent paradox by stating that if people are aware that they may be susceptible to a vitamin D deficiency, they may either take a supplement or get more sun exposure.

Choice A is incorrect because it goes in the wrong direction. It would result in the lighter-skinned group having higher vitamin D levels. Choice B is incorrect because the fact that some people in a group are below the average does not change the fact that as a whole, the average for the group is higher.

Choice C is incorrect because it only says there may be a difference in how sunscreen functioned for the two groups and does not say whether the difference would give more or less protection to a particular group. Choice D is irrelevant. It does not change the fact that the people in the lighter-skinned group had lighter skin on average than the people in the other group.

4. **(C)** This is a *flaw* question. Choice C is correct because the arguer assumes that the business leaders *intentionally* failed to mention the possibility that small businesses could raise prices and pocket the difference. There is no evidence that failing to mention the possibility was intentional.

Choice A is incorrect because the arguer did not distort the business leaders' view. Rather, the arguer showed that the view was limited or inaccurate. Choice B is incorrect because the argument does not involve necessary or sufficient assumptions. Choice D is incorrect because failure to document a premise is not a logical flaw. Choice E is incorrect because the argument does not rely on the opinions of a group (the business leaders) but rather on the arguer's opinion.

5. **(D)** This is a *conclusion: what can be inferred* question. The correct answer must be defendable as true based on the premises in the passage. The premises include

$$If -lots\ of\ experience\ testing \rightarrow -trust$$
$$If -trust\ assessment \rightarrow -buy$$

It can be concluded from the above premises that

$$If -lots\ of\ experience\ testing \rightarrow -buy$$

Because most people do not have lots of experience testing the exotic fruit, they will not buy it, regardless of any other positive qualities of the exotic fruit, such as ripeness. It is not true that people will necessarily buy a fruit that they have lots of experience testing, so it is not valid to conclude that people will buy peaches. They may not buy anything. It is, however, valid to conclude that the fact of the exotic fruit being ripe will not affect whether or not people buy peaches. Choice D is correct.

Choice A is incorrect because it cannot be defended as being true. Choice B is incorrect for the same reason. It may be true but cannot be proven to be true. Choice C is incorrect because the if/then statements in the passage only guarantee that if a person does not have experience testing the fruit, that person will not buy it. It does not guarantee that if that person has experience, he or she will buy it. It also does not guarantee that a person will buy the ripest fruit of the fruits that he or she is willing to buy. Choice E is incorrect for this latter reason.

6. **(C)** This is a *necessary assumption* question. The correct answer is a fact without which the argument falls apart. Choice C is correct because its negation—*A person cannot be honored for the future result of an action performed earlier*—would destroy the argument. The argument honors Picasso for the future result of an earlier action.

Choice A is incorrect because its negation—*Picasso did not believe future generations would benefit from his art*—does not affect the argument. The argument is not based on what Picasso believed. Choice B is incorrect. If he had not inspired people of his own generation, it would not affect the argument.

Choice D is incorrect. Its negation is irrelevant to the argument. Choice E is incorrect. Its negation—*A person cannot be honored for unintentional results*—is irrelevant because the argument does not depend on Picasso's results being unintentional.

7. **(A)** This is a *committed to agree/disagree* question that asks for a statement with which the two arguers are committed to disagreeing. Choice A is correct because Fernandez is committed to believing that television should never replace newspapers as a news source, and Osman is committed to believing that television should replace newspapers as a news source when there is news that people need to know about immediately.

Choice B is incorrect because both arguers agree with it. Choice C is incorrect because Osman is committed to the truth of choice C but Fernandez does not take a position. Choice D is incorrect because Fernandez is committed to its truth but Osman does not take a position. Choice E is incorrect because neither arguer is committed to a position.

8. **(D)** This is a *weaken* question based on a statistical argument. Choice D is correct because the argument is based on saving time, which could then be used for other patients. If it takes more time to transfer a patient than it does to treat the patient, the result is a loss of time.

Choice A is incorrect because it does not change the fact that those fifteen patients take up 60 percent of the staff time. Choice B is incorrect because it is irrelevant exactly which staff member saves the most time as long as the medical staff as a whole can see more patients. Choice C is incorrect because the physician's argument does not depend on the quality of care experienced by patients who are transferred to urgent care facilities. The argument depends only on the amount of time saved by the physician's staff. Choice E is incorrect because it is at best irrelevant and at worst tends to strengthen the argument.

9. **(E)** This is a *strengthen by principle* question. The setup establishes a specific example. The correct answer is a principle (general statement) that strengthens the conclusion. Choice E is correct because it establishes the principle that if there is a way to help, the owner should help. The principle overrides the owner's apprehension about being sharp with the dog. The answer may seem overly simplistic but it inevitably leads to the conclusion of the argument and it has no flaw, so it must be the correct answer.

Choice A is incorrect because it does not apply to the conclusion, which deals with dogs that best establish trust when they are reprimanded sharply. Choice B is incorrect because the original argument is not based on treating a dog the same way in all situations. Choice C is incorrect because the conclusion recommends following the veterinarian's advice even if doing so goes against the owner's intuitions. Choice D is incorrect because it deals with stopping abuse in the first place, whereas the original argument deals with a dog that has already been abused.

10. **(B)** This is a *type of reasoning* question. The argument establishes that there are only two possible options—the people of Khazarsko choose either democracy or constitutional monarchy. The third possibility, that another option will receive a sufficient number of write-in votes, is eliminated in the third sentence. The logic is that, of the two original options, one (constitutional monarchy) is eliminated. Therefore, the remaining option will be chosen. Choice B correctly identifies this reasoning.

Choice A is incorrect because the argument does not assume that all citizens voted for democracy, only that enough of them did for democracy to be chosen. Choice C is incorrect because it is backward. If anything, the argument treats an event that is likely as one that is inevitable. Choice D is incorrect because it implies that the arguer starts with the claim that democracy is likely and uses that fact to conclude that constitutional monarchy is unlikely. This is backward. Choice E is incorrect because, even though the argument does state that constitutional monarchy will not occur, that statement is not based on a sampling of a group but rather on the actual vote. Even if the vote is considered a sampling, there is no evidence that the sampling is *not* representative of the voters.

11. **(A)** This is a *strengthen* question based on a cause-and-effect argument. There are three factors that are found together—loud music, concentration, and being artistic. The argument concludes that loud music causes being artistic. To strengthen the conclusion, an answer choice must either show that a different possible factor does not cause being artistic, that there is another example of loud music causing being artistic, or that without loud music, being artistic does not occur. Choice A does the latter.

Choice B is incorrect because it does not mention loud music. Choice C is incorrect because it weakens the argument, showing that loud music is not necessary for artistic ability. Choice D is incorrect because it does not mention loud music. Choice E is incorrect because, although it strengthens the causation between music and concentration, it does not include artistic ability.

12. **(C)** This is a *sufficient assumption* question. The logic in the argument is deductive.

$$If -(replace\ or\ exercise) \rightarrow continue\ to\ gain\ weight$$

To trigger this rule, both *replace* and *exercise* must be absent. If either *replace* or *exercise* takes place, the rule is not triggered. To avoid triggering the rule, it is necessary to have at least one or the other. A good real-world rule for understanding this logic is that if you do not have either an LSAT score <u>or</u> an exemption from the LSAT, you will not get into law school.

$$If -(LSAT\ or\ exemption) \rightarrow -law\ school$$

One or the other is required to avoid triggering the rule.

The option *exercise* has been eliminated. For the conclusion (John will continue to gain weight) to be true, the option *replace* must also be eliminated. Choice C correctly eliminates *replace*.

Choice A is incorrect because it is irrelevant to the option *replace*, which specifies *how* he must change his diet. Choice B is incorrect for the same reason. Choice D is incorrect because it is not sufficient to lead to the conclusion that he cannot implement the dietary changes that are required. Choice E is incorrect because according to the logic in the argument, there are no other actions that will allow him to avoid continuing to gain weight.

13. **(A)** This is a *parallel flaw* question. The original argument is *not* an if/then, even though it looks similar to an if/then. If a tree bears a heavy crop, it is *likely* to lose leaves. This is a different argument from saying that it will lose leaves, and, therefore, you cannot use the contrapositive to evaluate the argument. To best understand the logic, use a set diagram. One set represents trees that bear a heavy crop in summer. The second set represents trees that lose their leaves prematurely. The second set overlaps most of the first

set because it is likely (more than 50 percent probability) that if a tree is a member of the first set, it is also a member of the second.

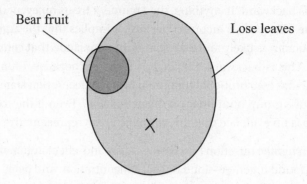

Ninety percent of the set *bear fruit* has the characteristic *lose leaves* but only ~15 percent of the set *lose leaves* has the characteristic *bear fruit*. The figure above shows why, for a tree that loses its leaves early, represented by the X, it is *not* likely that the tree bore fruit early.

Choice A is correct because it has the same structure as above. The small circle represents businesses that are undercapitalized and the large circle represents new businesses that go out of business within four months. Whereas there is a high likelihood of a member of the small set being a member of the large set, there is only a small likelihood that a member of the large set is also a member of the small set.

Choice B is incorrect because it is a deductive if/then. Choice C is incorrect because it is a cause-and-effect argument. Choice D is incorrect. It can be represented by sets but the small set (fossils) falls completely within the large set (imprints in rocks). In addition, the logic is valid. Choice E is incorrect because it is a deductive if/then.

14. **(E)** This is a *resolve a paradox* question. The paradox is that the rate of domestic violence has not changed in the past thirty years but the number of convictions for domestic violence has increased. Choice E is correct because an increase in population would by itself explain how the rate (number of occurrences of domestic violence per 100 people) could be the same but the actual number of occurrences could be higher.

Choice A is incorrect because the time period in the setup occurs after the middle of the twentieth century. Choice B is incorrect because it would have the same effect on assessments now and thirty years ago and so does not explain the discrepancy. Choice C is incorrect because it would result in fewer convictions. Choice D is incorrect because it would apply to cases now and to cases thirty years ago in the same way.

15. **(B)** This is a *role of a claim* question. Choice B is correct because the claim that the discomforts are gentler for travel by train is given as a fact (premise) and the fact is one of the elements that lead to the conclusion that travel by train can be more pleasant.

Choice A is incorrect because the arguer would support, not rebut, an argument against traveling by plane. Choice C is incorrect because the claim is not *evidence* (proof) that people might prefer trains but rather *explains* why they might do so.

Choice D is incorrect because the statement that long distance travel by trains has discomforts is not established by analogy with planes but is given as a fact. It is not a conclusion. Choice E is incorrect because the claim is not a hypothesis. A hypothesis proposes a theory. The claim is simply a stated fact.

16. **(E)** This is a *strengthen* question. Choice E is correct because it is the physiological responses of playing tennis that promote vitality and choice E establishes that merely watching people playing tennis can induce the same physiological responses.

Choice A is incorrect because a positive feeling does not necessarily translate into increased vitality. Choices B and D are incorrect because, although they are consistent with the passage, they do not present any new information that strengthens the conclusion. Choice C is incorrect because an increase in the observer's *ability* to perform certain skills does not increase vitality unless the observer actually *performs* the skills. There is nothing in choice C that leads to the observer actually playing tennis.

17. **(C)** This is a *complete the sentence/argument* question. The correct answer must be something that can be concluded from the premises. The premises include

If –widespread → –economical to develop
Some societies not widespread <u>and</u> must develop

The result is that there are some societies that will develop energy resources uneconomically, as is correctly stated in choice C.

Choice A is incorrect because the societies mentioned in the passage must develop energy resources. It cannot be defended from the passage that there are other societies that have no choice but to forgo development. Choice B is incorrect because it contradicts the first premise.

Choice D is incorrect because, although it is a possibility, it cannot be defended by the passage. Choice E is incorrect for the same reason. It is likely to be true but cannot be defended as a logical conclusion.

18. **(E)** This is a *flaw* question that uses the phrase *"vulnerable to criticism,"* rather than the word *flaw*. Choice E is correct because the argument is based on not being able to afford the research, and if the research were to generate more money than it costs, the argument would fall apart.

Choice A is incorrect because it falls into the category of failing to support a premise. It is not a logical flaw to fail to define terms in a premise. Choice B is incorrect because it is not true. The scientist does not reject the possibility of telepathy. Choice C is the inverse of choice B. Choice C is incorrect because the scientist does *not* claim that telepathy is an established fact. Choice D is incorrect. Even though the scientist does not prove that telepathy can be proven to exist, it is not necessary to do so.

19. **(A)** This is a *parallel flaw* question. The original passage consists of deductive if/then statements.

If –incorporated → vulnerable
If incorporated → report to board
∴ If report to board → –vulnerable

The logic is flawed because *report to board* is not a trigger. The erroneous logic implied by the conclusion is:

If report to board → incorporated and If incorporated → –vulnerable

All steps in the logic above are incorrect. In terms of A and B, the flawed logic is:

$$If -A \rightarrow B$$
$$If A \rightarrow C$$
$$\therefore If C \rightarrow A \text{ (which is not a valid statement)}$$
$$and \ If A \rightarrow -B \text{ (which is not a valid statement)}$$

Choice A is the correct answer because it has the same flaw as the original. Its logic is:

$$If -deep\text{-}sea \ vent \rightarrow -sulfur$$
$$If \ deep\text{-}sea \ vent \rightarrow operate \ in \ darkness$$
$$\therefore If \ operate \ in \ darkness \rightarrow deep\text{-}sea \ vent \ and \ If \ deep\text{-}sea \ vent \rightarrow sulfur$$

Choice B is incorrect because it is a cause-and-effect argument. Choice C is incorrect because it is based on sets. However, even if interpreted in terms of if/then statements, choice C does not match the original.

$$If \ patent \rightarrow IP$$
$$If \ IP \rightarrow inheritance$$
$$\therefore If \ inheritance \rightarrow IP \ and \ If \ IP \rightarrow patent$$

This structure is $If A \rightarrow B$, $If B \rightarrow C$, whereas the original
argument was $If -A \rightarrow B$, $If A \rightarrow C$.

Choice D is incorrect because it is a valid argument. Choice E is incorrect. Its logic is:

$$If -formal \rightarrow limited$$
$$If \ formal \rightarrow inspire \text{ (up to this point the argument is the same as the original)}$$
$$\therefore \ If \ formal \rightarrow -limited \text{ (this is flawed but not in the same way as the original)}$$

20. **(D)** This is a *conclusion: what can be inferred* question. Choice D is correct because the argument establishes that there exists at least one person who will be interpreted as guilty when the person is not. The passage further establishes that when such a person talks to others, the others will (this is an absolute rule) press the person to confess. Because the person did not commit a misdeed, the person is being pressed to confess to something that the person did not do.

Choice A is incorrect because the argument does not prove that any of the people whose eyes shift ever *does* confess. These people are only *pressed* to confess. Choice B is a statement that could be true but it is incorrect because it cannot be proven to be true by anything in the passage. Choices C and E are incorrect for the same reason.

21. **(D)** This is a *must be true* question. The correct answer is a conclusion that inevitably follows from the premises in the setup. Choice D is correct because the current resources are not enough to provide 50,000 more acre-feet, and without 50,000 more acre-feet, the city cannot meet the needs of the residents beyond thirty years.

Choice A is incorrect because the likelihood of finding additional water is not given in the passage. Choice B is incorrect because the math is wrong. The city has added 30,000 acre-feet recently and needs 50,000 acre-feet more, but this 80,000 must be added to the amount of water rights that the city owned before the 30,000 acre-feet were added.

Choice C is incorrect because the additional 50,000 acre-feet only guarantees enough water for the next thirty years, not necessarily beyond thirty years. Choice E is incorrect for the same reason as choice B.

22. **(C)** This is a *necessary assumption* question. The logic is

$$\text{If } {-appreciation} \rightarrow {-good\ decisions}$$
$$\therefore \ quiet\ time$$

To make the argument work, it is necessary to add

$$\text{If } quiet\ time \rightarrow appreciation$$

Choice C correctly states this condition. If choice C is negated—*Quiet time does not lead to appreciation*—the argument falls apart.

Choice A is incorrect. Its negation—*Business leaders are not more concerned with test performance than with nature*—does not weaken the argument. Choice B is incorrect because it is the incorrect negation of both sides of the original premise, from

$$\text{If } {-appreciation} \rightarrow {-good\ decisions}$$
$$\text{to}$$
$$\text{If } appreciation \rightarrow good\ decisions$$

The second statement is not valid.

Choice D is incorrect because it is irrelevant. Its negation—*spending time in nature can be evaluated by a test*—does not necessarily weaken the argument. Choice E is incorrect. Its negation—*it is not possible to spend quiet time in nature in a large group*—does not necessarily weaken the argument because the argument does not depend on children being in a large group.

23. **(E)** This is a *flaw* question. In the original setup, the arguer cites an author's being well-known and people buying an author's books readily as occurring together and then concludes that being well-known is the cause of people buying the books readily. The flaw is that the arguer fails to consider that the cause-and-effect relationship may be the reverse. Choice E correctly states this.

Choice A is incorrect. Even though the arguer does infer that new authors will be able to do what earlier authors have done, that is not a logical flaw. Choice B is incorrect because the arguer does not say that publicity (the factor that is important for selling books) is necessary for selling books. The arguer cites publicity as an important factor, not a necessary one.

Choice C is incorrect because the arguer does not state that becoming well-known through publicity is inevitable, only that it is possible. Choice D is incorrect. Even though the arguer does not cite any additional factors, this is not a logical flaw. The argument is based on a new author doing what a previous author has done. The flaw is that the arguer has possibly misconstrued what the previous authors did in order to make people buy their books.

24. **(B)** This is a *weaken* question based on an analogy. The analogy is between a small group of dinosaurs that developed a trait that distinguished them from other dinosaurs and a small group of mammals (bats) that similarly distinguish themselves from other mammals. Both groups are similar in the fact that they developed flight. To weaken an analogy, it must be shown that there is a significant difference between the two groups. Choice B weakens the argument by pointing out that when the first flying dinosaurs evolved, there were no other flying animals with which they had to compete. With bats, there is a vast family of flying animals (birds) with which they must compete. This makes

it unlikely that bats would expand to fill the ecological niche of flying in the way that early flying dinosaurs did.

Choice A is incorrect because it does not matter if some early flying dinosaurs became extinct because there were others that did not become extinct and eventually evolved into the vast family of birds. Choice C is incorrect because time is not an issue in the argument.

Choice D does not weaken the argument. If bats follow the analogy of early flying dinosaurs, choice D simply means that bats may outcompete other flying species, which strengthens the argument. Choice E is irrelevant because it is a fact that both the early flying dinosaurs and bats do exist, regardless of what the odds are of them existing.

25. **(A)** This is a *weaken* question. Choice A is correct because it explains that the reason the commercial drivers did not try to stop in less than 100 feet was because of safety, and it explains that the safe stopping distance is greater for commercial vehicles than for passenger cars.

Choice B is incorrect. Even though it gives evidence that in one way commercial drivers may be more safety conscious, it does not explain why the commercial drivers seem less safety conscious in the study. Choice C is incorrect because it is most likely the result of the fact that the majority of drivers on the road are drivers of passenger cars. In order to show that drivers of passenger cars are more reckless, it would be necessary to compare the percentage of passenger car drivers who get tickets with the corresponding percentage of commercial drivers.

Choice D is incorrect because, if anything, it makes the commercial drivers seem less cautious, which would strengthen, rather than weaken, the argument. Choice E is irrelevant. The figures cited were averages, so it does not change the average number to state that there were some drivers whose numbers were above average.

Reading Comprehension 3

→ **AN OVERVIEW OF READING COMPREHENSION**
→ **TACKLING THE PASSAGE**
→ **UNDERSTANDING THE QUESTIONS**
→ **GETTING THE ANSWER**
→ **PUTTING STRATEGIES TO WORK**
→ **FOUR SAMPLE PASSAGES**

This chapter helps you understand the patterns that the Reading Comprehension section is testing. You will learn strategies for organizing your time, for orienting yourself to the passage, and for getting to the correct answer. A sample passage will be analyzed in depth to help you learn how to apply the strategies. Finally, you will have a chance to take an LSAT-style Reading Comprehension section test and review the answer explanations.

INTRODUCTION TO READING COMPREHENSION

The Reading Comprehension (RC) section of the LSAT comprises four sets of passages and questions, with a total of twenty-seven questions. Each set typically has from six to eight questions, and rarely five questions. The time limit is thirty-five minutes.

VOCABULARY FOR READING COMPREHENSION

Set: A passage and the questions that go with it. There are four sets per section.

Regular set: The traditional RC set, consisting of one long passage, followed by questions. An RC section contains three regular sets and one Comparative Reading (CR) set.

CR set: A Comparative Reading set, in which there are two shorter passages, Passage A and Passage B, followed by questions that typically refer to the relationship between the two passages.

Passage: The paragraph(s) that make up the reading selection for a set. A passage is followed by a series of questions.

Question stem: The sentence that poses the question you are to answer. The question stem does not include the five answer choices.

Question: A question stem and the five answer choices that go with it.

Section: The grouping of four RC sets that constitutes a thirty-five-minute testing section. An RC section typically has twenty-seven questions.

Three of the four sets consist of one long passage. The other set consists of two shorter passages, labeled Passage A and Passage B. This type of set is called Comparative Reading (CR) and differs slightly from the other sets.

The subject matter of the passages is drawn from the natural sciences (30 percent), social sciences (30 percent), humanities (20 percent), and law (20 percent). A fifth of all passages refer to law. A sixth refer to literature. The next most common topics are history, biology, geology, and sociology, followed by archaeology, art, ecology, political science, psychology, and technology.

EXAMPLES OF SUBJECTS FOR RC PASSAGES

Natural sciences: astronomy, botany, computers, ecology, geology, meteorology, technology, zoology
Social sciences: anthropology, archaeology, economics, education, history, languages, political science, psychology, sociology
Humanities: architecture, fine art, literature, music, philosophy, popular culture, spirituality, theater
Law: various

The RC combines some elements from the other sections of the test. Some question types in RC are identical to question types in LR. In addition, RC is set up in four sets, just as AR is.

Is It Possible to Improve on RC?

If RC were just a test of how well people read, it would be difficult to improve on it. The good news is that RC is very learnable. There are hidden agendas and secret patterns to RC. By mastering these RC strategies and combining them with timing strategy, you can increase your scores significantly.

Mastering Timing

A strong timing strategy is critical for getting your best score. To get the most out of this section, review the section on timing strategy in Chapter 1, "General Strategies," now.

The first step in timing strategy is to rank the difficulty of the passages. The difficulty of a passage is subjective. What is easy for one test taker might be impossible for another. Simply glance at the passage. If the topic seems unpleasant, it will be harder to understand. Also consider the complexity of the language. Some passages might be on an interesting topic but be written in a way that makes it hard to understand. The opposite is also true. A passage may be on a difficult topic but may be relatively easy to follow.

If two passages are equally difficult but one has more questions, choose the one with more questions, as it offers more possible points for the same setup time. However, never choose a harder passage just because it has more questions. The "more questions" rule only applies for passages of equal difficulty.

After taking a timed practice section, evaluate the effectiveness of your timing strategy. To do this, you need to know how much time you spent on each question. After marking an answer, make a note on scratch paper of the time it took. Score the section and then review your strategy.

Count how many questions you got wrong, ignoring the questions that were blind guesses. If there are more than one or two wrong answers, then there is room for improvement. How? Suppose you have five wrong answers. In theory, you could have skipped two of those questions and used the time to get the other three correct. How much time did you spend on the questions you got wrong? If there are many on which you spent only one or two minutes, you may be rushing. Compare the person who works on twenty-seven questions and gets twelve right with the person who works on sixteen questions and gets all of them right. Who has the better score?

Work on timing strategy until you are missing no more than two or three of the questions on which you actually worked (that is, do not count the cold guesses you get wrong) on a timed section. If you find that you have spent two minutes or less on questions that you got wrong, you might find that you will get them correct by allowing more time. Do not worry right now if your score is not where it should be. Focus on accuracy. Look carefully at each wrong answer and try to determine why you were not able to get it correct. Was something confusing? Were there two answers that were close? The next step is to master the RC strategies that help you get more questions correct more quickly.

How to Practice

Most practice on the RC—maybe 80 percent—should be done untimed. Working untimed means practicing and perfecting strategies for getting the right answer, no matter how long it takes. It may take twenty or thirty minutes to thoroughly work on one question. This is beneficial. If a particular question becomes frustrating, rather than giving up, set it aside, take a break, and come back to it later.

Even when practicing untimed, write down the time spent on each question. On many questions, it may feel like you are taking too long; however, the watch might tell you that you solved the problem within three to five minutes. On the real test it is OK to spend that much time on the more difficult questions. Keeping track of time helps you adjust your internal sense of what is too much time and what is acceptable. It also shows, on questions that you get wrong despite your best efforts, whether you gave the question enough time.

Periodically do an RC section timed to evaluate your timing strategy under testing conditions. Do a timed section now as you begin your studying and then again every few weeks. Before starting a timed section, review your timing strategy. Use your watch to keep track of time on each question. During the last few minutes, put cold guesses for questions that there is not enough time to answer. Note which questions were cold guesses.

On your official LSAT your timing strategy will be exactly the same as on your timed practice except that you will not write down the time for each question on your official test.

Many LSAT takers get their best score by working on only two or three passages and guessing cold on the rest. The person who works on three passages and gets every question correct scores higher than the person who works on all of the questions but gets half of them wrong.

TACKLING THE PASSAGE

THE THREE STEPS FOR MASTERING RC

1. Set up the passage.
2. Analyze and understand the questions.
3. Prove the correct answer and find the flaws in the wrong ones.

How to Set Up the Passage

What is the most efficient way to set up a passage? What needs to be remembered, what needs to be understood, and what can be ignored? A typical RC passage contains twenty, thirty, or more specific facts. However, a passage tests only three or four of those facts. The rest of the questions test what can be called big-picture information, such as the main idea, the author's tone, or the function of a particular phrase. The test taker who tries to absorb all the facts is doing too much work. Consider a different approach: read for the big picture.

All questions are either big-picture questions or fact questions. For a fact question, even if you tried to remember the facts the first time through the passage, your memory will not be accurate enough to answer the question. A better, faster, and more accurate strategy is to go back and get facts as they are needed.

This means it is not necessary to memorize facts when reading the passage. Then why bother to read the passage at all? To answer a big-picture question, it is necessary to first have a clear sense of the big picture—the overall structure and movement of the passage. The real purpose of the initial skimming of the passage, then, is to find the big picture.

The big picture of a passage has certain predictable elements. Most RC passages—and perhaps all of them—are built around what can be called a dichotomy: a contrast or a tension between two opposing things, something "on the one hand" versus something else "on the other hand." Consider the discussion given in Chapter 1 about the two vehicles: the Toyota and the Subaru, one red and one silver, one a car and one a truck. This is a clear example of a dichotomy. Two things are compared and contrasted. There may or may not be similarities but there must be a fundamental contrast.

The dichotomy can take the form of a problem to be solved, a dilemma, a paradox, or a contradiction, as well as a simple contrast between two things.

SAMPLES OF DICHOTOMIES

1. Because the supply of petroleum is decreasing steadily, we will need increasingly more sources of energy in the future.
2. Until recently, scientists believed that asteroids traveled alone.
3. Whereas the inquisitorial system of law allows for more cooperation among all parties, the adversarial system often results in more information being brought to light.
4. The theory of evolution replaced earlier attempts to explain biological variations as remnants of primordial differences.
5. Beethoven believed that traditional standards of musical composition were not sacred, that they should be broken at the whim of the creative force, and yet today, many teachers of composition hold Beethoven's own standards up as guidelines to be rigorously learned and followed.

Identify the dichotomies in the above examples. Use expressions such as "On the one hand, there is a red Toyota pickup. On the other hand, there is a silver Subaru wagon."

LSAT passages use certain kinds of dichotomies regularly. One of the most common is the dichotomy between an old phenomenon and a new phenomenon. The theory of evolution is a new theory replacing an old theory. Beethoven's standards were new compared to the traditional (old) standards from before his time.

Another common type is a dichotomy between theories, such as in Sample 4 above. Very often, one theory is old and the other new. However, passages can also use contemporary theories that are being contrasted with each other. Because a new theory is usually not presented unless it corrects flaws in a previous theory, the author of a passage usually finds the new theory better.

DICHOTOMIES

Organize dichotomies visually in your scratch area.

On the one hand	versus	On the other hand

The big picture involves not just a dichotomy but what the passage does with the dichotomy. All of this together creates what we can call the structure of the passage. Here are three examples of structures.

STRUCTURE 1

- A theory is presented.
- Facts supporting it are given.
- A fact that weakens it is given.
- The author concludes that the theory is good, despite the weakness.

- An attitude or belief from the past is presented.
- The current belief about the same subject is presented.
- Support for the superiority of the current belief is given.
- Additional support for the current belief is given.
- The author concludes that the current belief is superior.

- A dilemma is presented.
- A solution is given.
- Evidence to support the solution is given.
- The author points out a new problem that the solution would create.
- A way to overcome the new problem is given.
- The author concludes that the original solution has merits but also has drawbacks, and states that further research is needed.

The passage establishes the dichotomy and then builds a structure by incorporating elements such as definitions, explanations, clarifications, and examples. From there, it goes on to present elements such as solutions, partial solutions that create new problems, support for a view, objections to or criticisms of a view, rebuttals to objections, similarities and differences between A and B, and interim conclusions.

The flow of the passage is often predictable. If a theory, belief, or solution is defended, there are only two ways the passage can continue. Either the defense holds up or there is a problem with it. If there is a problem with it, there are only two ways the passage can continue. Either the problem can be overcome and the defense holds up, or the problem is fatal and the defense does not hold up.

The ending of a passage is often particularly important. A passage often introduces something new at the end or gives insights into the author's main point. The ending can confirm that a particular view or theory is correct or that it is correct but with some qualifications. Alternately, the passage may conclude that the view or theory is incorrect or that it is incorrect with some redeeming qualities. The passage may conclude that a further line of investigation is needed. It may propose a new synthesis that provides an alternative to either of the original two elements of the dichotomy. It may even suggest a whole new area that could be investigated as a result of the passage's line of inquiry.

TIP

ENDINGS ARE IMPORTANT!

Notice how the passage ends. Often there will be a question about it.

Finding the Big Picture (Structure)

Skim the passage below in order to find the big picture. Start at the beginning of the passage and skim until you find something that could be a dichotomy.

EXAMPLE

Relationships between elements of the natural world are often more complex than we realize, so that our actions affecting one element may have unexpected, and often negative, effects on another. For example, under natural conditions *(Line)* grasslands are grazed by various animals, and yet in certain circumstances, this *(5)* grazing may harm the health of the grassland. When grazing takes place under the unnatural conditions that result when grazing patterns are altered by people, the potential for harm is much greater.

Many grasslands in the West have been grazed under conditions altered by people for well over a hundred years. Scientists recently have been studying the *(10)* effects of grazing the American bison, commonly known as the buffalo, because it has a less harmful effect on grasslands than most other domestic grazing animals. Two factors have been measured—the health of the grasses and the health of the range area in general. Health of the grasses is measured by counting the number of grass clumps per acre still alive at the end of the season. Health of the range is *(15)* measured by calculating the number of different species of plants per acre and the total mass of vegetation produced per acre for the season. By comparing bison-grazed range areas with ungrazed control areas, researchers found that the more palatable, fine-textured grasses, such as Indian Rice Grass, suffered significant damage, whereas less tasty, coarse grasses, such as Sacaton, showed virtually none. *(20)* Overall range health declined in areas dominated by Indian Rice Grass but not in those dominated by Sacaton.

It is still unclear whether a decrease in the health of grasses, even with the more vulnerable ones, necessarily results in a decrease in range health in the long run. Rangelands dominated by the slower growing, fine-textured species will obviously *(25)* be more susceptible to permanent damage, but the ultimate effect on a rangeland depends on four identifiable factors. Areas with these characteristics would be most adversely affected: a high ratio of fine grasses to coarse grasses, a high ratio of grasses to non-grass plants, low annual rainfall, and high average seasonal temperatures. It would be a good idea to identify range areas with a combination *(30)* of these characteristics and take special restorative measures with them, because they are most susceptible to being damaged by human-directed grazing.

The first paragraph does not contain any significant dichotomies. It gives a general statement and an example. It refers to a possible problem, but there is no binary choice—no choice between two distinct things.

The second paragraph starts with facts. Facts are not dichotomies. The passage does mention that bison are different from other domestic grazing animals. This fact could be the basis for a dichotomy but the passage does not pursue it. The passage goes on to mention two additional factors—the health of grasses and the health of rangeland. Whereas there are differences between these two factors, the passage does not pursue a conflict between them.

TIP

FACTS ARE NOT DICHOTOMIES

A dichotomy must involve a conflict or contrast between two things.

Only when the passage introduces the distinction between fine-textured grasses and coarse grasses is there a clear, black-and-white distinction. Fine grasses do not hold up to grazing. Coarse grasses do. The final paragraph does not pursue this dichotomy further but does return to the dichotomy between the health of grasses and the health of rangelands—a dichotomy that was mentioned earlier in the passage but not pursued at that time. Thus, health of grasses versus health of rangelands is also a significant dichotomy. The paragraph states that the solution is unclear. It identifies further factors that need to be considered.

The ending tells us that we can use information about the difference between fine- and coarse-textured grasses and the information about how the health of grasses influences the health of rangeland to help solve the problem of damage caused by human-directed grazing.

The big picture of the passage, condensed to its essentials, is:

> *Fine grasses are more susceptible to damage than coarse grasses in grazing conditions that have been altered by people. Damage to grasses alone doesn't determine whether the rangeland is damaged, but in conjunction with other factors, it can. We can use this information to protect vulnerable areas.*

Why is it important to identify dichotomies and the big picture? First, big-picture questions cannot be accurately answered without a clear grasp of the structure of the passage. Second, many of the detail questions are specifically designed to confuse the reader between the facts on opposite sides of the dichotomy. In the example in Chapter 1, what color was the vehicle that had four-wheel drive? Often the test uses terms that sound similar to create additional confusion. For example, a passage might contrast neurolinguistic therapy with linguistic neuropathology.

It is difficult to keep dichotomies clear in your memory. A diagram on paper, on the other hand, is an almost foolproof way of keeping two sets of data distinct. Once the dichotomy is clear, put it down on paper immediately.

Diagramming the Big Picture

Theoretically, it is possible to draw a complete diagram of the dichotomies and facts in a passage, along with their relationships. However, this is too time-consuming on the actual test. During the test, only the main dichotomies and basic facts need to be written down. Go back to the diagram of the differences between the two vehicles, the Toyota and the Subaru. It is a good example of a basic working diagram. Even though it is only a part of the whole setup, it is a complete diagram of that part. Such a diagram makes it impossible to become confused.

In order to develop a sense of how much to diagram and how much to leave out, start by fully diagramming one or two passages. After that, try cutting back to what feels like just the essentials. If you get questions wrong because the diagram was too incomplete, try diagramming a little more. If a diagram contains information that was never needed to answer the questions, try doing less.

Diagramming is similar to making an outline of a passage. However, instead of putting headings down the side of the page, make columns across the top. The columns are usually in pairs—one column versus the other column.

> **CARDINAL RULE!**
>
> Use your eyes, not your memory.
> Don't try to remember facts.
> Go back and check them.
> Don't organize information in
> your head. Put it on paper.

Below is an RC passage presented one sentence at a time in order to break down the process of identifying the structure.

Until 1959, most social scientists considered the family unit to be the only valid subject of sociological research.

Is there a dichotomy? At first glance, this example may seem only to give facts. However, the statement "Until 1959" actually creates a dichotomy: what was true before 1959 versus what was true after 1959. This is a very common kind of dichotomy. It may be introduced with wording such as "until recently," "up to now," or "before the fourth century A.D."

Here is the second sentence of the same passage:

In the 1960s, sociologists at several major universities began interviewing single adults about their work habits, social relationships, and personal goals.

This reveals the other half of the dichotomy—what was true after 1959. The dichotomy can be diagrammed:

Family unit   versus   Single adults

Additional information about each side of the dichotomy can be added:

Family unit   versus   Single adults

  <1960   >1960

If the passage gives more facts about the earlier studies, those facts can go under "Family unit," and likewise for the later studies.

The third sentence of the passage is:

Modern researchers are divided as to whether young single adults constitute a sociological reality distinct from single senior citizens.

This sentence introduces a new dichotomy between younger and older, but it falls under the "Single adults" column. It is a dichotomy within one-half of an existing dichotomy. One category splits into two:

Family unit   versus   Single adults

  <1960   >1960

                                  younger   older

The next sentence of the passage is:

Young singles typically can look forward to an increasing income and are more flexible in developing new friends and interests.

TIP

THE IMPORTANCE OF DICHOTOMIES

Nearly all RC passages are based on dichotomies, even though it might not seem so at first glance.

This sentence gives specific information about the "younger" category. It also gives implied information about the "older" category, because they are contrasted:

<u>Family unit</u>   versus   <u>Single adults</u>

<1960   >1960

                                           <u>younger</u>   <u>older</u>

                                   increasing $ fixed $

                                   more flexible,   less flexible

                                   friends/interests

The passage continues:

However, most sociologists now believe that these differences are insignificant compared with the similarities among all ages of single people in free time and amount of social contact.

What has happened here? The author has reconciled the dichotomy. The problem is solved, the two sides brought together and the tension resolved.

<u>Family unit</u>   versus   <u>Single adults</u>

<1960   >1960

                                           <u>younger</u>   <u>older</u>

                                   increasing $ fixed $

                                   more flexible,   less flexible

                                   friends/interests

To summarize, then, there is a basic dichotomy, a new dichotomy within a branch of the original dichotomy, and the coming together (merging or bridging) of the two sides of a dichotomy. All of these were diagrammed, along with the details that go into each category.

Dichotomies are often indicated by words or phrases like "however," "on the other hand," and "in contrast." These show a switch from one side to the other. *John is happy with his job. However, he is dissatisfied with his living situation.* Words or phrases such as "similarly," "likewise," "furthermore," and "in the same way" show that the author is continuing to talk about the same side. *John is happy with his job. Furthermore, he enjoys his living situation.*

Once a dichotomy has been introduced, there are usually only a few directions in which the passage could go next. It could give examples. It could explain theories. It could evaluate whether something is good or bad. It could bridge a dichotomy. It could create a dichotomy within a dichotomy. Keeping these possibilities in mind helps you recognize quickly where the passage is going.

Identifying dichotomies is such a powerful organizing tool that it can be used to understand the structure of a passage even when the content of the passage is too difficult or complex to follow. The next passage is based on the most complex recent theories in astrophysics. For most people, the

> **WHERE THE PASSAGE CAN GO WITH DICHOTOMIES**
>
> Give examples of each part of the dichotomy.
>
> Explain each part.
>
> Evaluate each part.
>
> Create a dichotomy within a dichotomy.
>
> Bridge two parts of the dichotomy.

details of the passage would be incomprehensible. To avoid being sidetracked by complex detail, skip the details and stick with the big picture. The passage has been modified below to simulate that. The actual details are replaced with simple variables, A and B.

EXAMPLE

Until 1956, people thought that stars generated their energy by A. New research, however, indicated that Theory A could not explain Observation O. Theory B was put forward to explain Observation O. Theory B was widely attacked because calculations based on it came up with a different estimate for the life span of our sun than those based on previous observations. Prof. X reviewed the previous observations and found that the observations themselves were inaccurate, and once corrected, the new calculations matched those predicted by Theory B. Theory B not only gives us a more consistent explanation of how stars produce their energy, but also reassuringly gives life on Earth an extra 15 million years before our sun dies.

Even though the topic is highly complex, the structure of the passage is easy to spot by simply sidestepping the details.

How to Skim

Start skimming for the big picture at the beginning of the passage. If the first few sentences contain only facts but no dichotomies, continue until you find a dichotomy. Identify the two parts of the dichotomy clearly. It is helpful to take extra time on this step in order to be accurate.

Passages can be thought of as "an analysis of an interesting something." This phrase contains four implied questions that help build the big picture. What is the "something?" What makes it interesting? In what way is it analyzed? How does the analysis end up?

In the astrophysics passage, the "something" being analyzed was two theories. It was the contrast and tension between them that made the topic interesting. The analysis showed problems posed by Theory A and a partial solution (Theory B) with its own problems. The analysis concluded by showing how the problems with Theory B had been overcome.

Here are common answers to the four questions.

1. What is the "something" that is interesting?
   Theory
   Event
   Action
   Definition
   Phenomenon (social, political, natural, etc.)
2. What is interesting about it?
   Contrast (A versus B, old versus new)
   Dilemma/problem/inadequacy/unknown
   Paradox/discrepancy/paradoxical contradiction

TIP

THE POWER OF THE BIG PICTURE

With the big picture, even you can understand a passage on advanced thermonuclear theory!

READ SELECTIVELY

If you are reading the whole passage, you are doing too much work and taking too much time!
Skim.
Look for the big picture.
Don't obsess over details.

AN ANALYSIS OF AN INTERESTING SOMETHING

What is the "something"?
What makes it interesting?
How is it analyzed?
How does it end up?

3. In what way is it analyzed?
    Definitions/explorations/clarifications/examples
    Solutions
    Partial solutions with additional problems
    Support for a view
    Criticisms of or objections to a view
    Similarities between A and B
    Differences between A and B
    Interim conclusions
4. How does it end up?
    A view or solution holds up.
    A view or solution holds up with qualifications.
    A view or solution does not hold up.
    A view or solution does not hold up but has some redeeming qualifications.
    Further inquiry is needed.
    A new synthesis is proposed.

Highlighting

Highlighting is not strictly necessary on an RC passage, though it helps some people focus. If you highlight information that you never use, cut back. If you do not highlight, you can feel confident that identifying the dichotomies and the movement of the passage, along with some brief diagramming, is enough.

Setting Up Comparative Reading Sets

Set up the CR set in the same way that you set up the regular sets. Each of the two passages in CR is shorter than a regular passage. In addition to getting a sense of the big picture for each passage, orient yourself to how the two passages are related. In what way are they similar? In what way do they differ? There is usually an important contrast between the two. Consider the points of view of each author. What does each author believe? To what points is each committed?

UNDERSTANDING THE QUESTION TYPES

RC questions fall into two categories—detail questions and big-picture questions. Detail questions ask for facts that are specifically stated in the passage or that can be implied from information specifically stated. Big-picture questions test an understanding of the overall purpose and structure of the passage. When you begin to work on a question, start by orienting yourself to the question. Identify whether the question is a big-picture or a detail question. The following sections cover the types of questions that occur in each category, along with strategies for solving that type.

It would be nice to think that there is just one strategy for each type. Unfortunately, it is not that simple. One *main idea* question, for example, may throw completely different obstacles at the test taker than another *main idea* question. To master strategy, work carefully with hundreds of questions. The good news, though, is that there are certain things that all questions of a particular type have in common.

RC tests three thinking skills that are reflected in the questions:

1. **COMPREHENSION:** Has the reader understood the facts presented in the passage?
2. **EVALUATION:** Can the reader identify the relationships among the various elements of the passage?
3. **APPLICATION/EXTENSION:** Can the reader apply information in the passage to other situations?

The first of these is a detail skill and the others are big-picture skills.

Big-picture Questions

Big-picture questions test your holistic understanding of the passage, as opposed to understanding of specific facts. There are six major types of big-picture questions, nine less common types, and six types exclusive to CR.

Question stems can have straightforward wording or obscure wording. Obscure wording makes it difficult to identify the question type. The examples below show you both the straightforward and more obscure common wording variations for question stems.

MAJOR BIG-PICTURE QUESTION TYPES

The most common big-picture questions and percentage of occurrence are:

1. Main idea (12%)
2. Use of a word or phrase (9%)
3. Function (8%)
4. Agree with a view (8%)
5. Application/extension (7%)
6. Analogous situation (5%)

Together these account for nearly 50 percent of all RC questions.

Main Idea

Main idea questions constitute about 12 percent of all RC questions. Below are common wording variations for the question stem of *main idea* questions. Some question stems typically appear only in a CR set.

1. *The author's main point is . . .*
2. *The author's major contention is . . .*
3. *The main idea expressed in the passage is . . .*
4. *The primary purpose of the passage is to . . .*
5. *Which one of the following most accurately expresses the main point of the passage?*
6. *Which one of the following most accurately expresses the central idea of the passage?*
7. *Which one of the following most accurately states the main function of the passage?*
8. *Which one of the following statements most accurately summarizes the content of the passage?*

For Comparative Reading:

1. *Which one of the following most accurately states the main point of Passage A?*
2. *Which one of the following is the central topic of each passage?*

Strategy for main idea questions. To be correct, the answer must (1) be a statement that is true and consistent with the passage, and (2) match the structure (big picture). Beware of choosing an answer that is true or consistent but is not the main idea. A *main idea* question requires you to understand what the dichotomy in the passage is, as well as how the author treats the dichotomy, and what the conclusion of the passage is.

Use of a Word or Phrase

This type accounts for 9 percent of RC questions. Examples of main wording variations for *use of a word or phrase* questions are:

1. *In the context of the passage, the description of a work of art as "uplifting" mainly refers to its . . .*
2. *In using the phrase "the bane of his existence" the author of Passage A most probably means to refer to . . .*
3. *Which one of the following most accurately describes the author's use of the word "enfranchise" in line 17 and "disenfranchise" in line 36?*
4. *The author uses the word "interminable" (line 14) most likely in order to express . . .*
5. *By referring to the scientist's argument as "highly suspect" (line 36), the author most clearly intends to emphasize . . .*
6. *The author most likely refers to the Magna Carta (lines 20–23) and the Declaration of Independence, mentioned in lines 43–44, for which one of the following reasons?*
7. *Which one of the following expressions most accurately conveys the sense of the word "paramount" as it is used in line 43?*
8. *The passage most strongly suggests that the business owner believed that "net profit" should be defined in a way that . . .*
9. *The author describes the coincidence mentioned in the last paragraph as "extraordinary" in order to suggest that the coincidence . . .*

Strategy for use of a word or phrase questions. It is not enough to simply understand the literal meaning of the word. Examine its context. Consider the author's intent in using the word. Look at several lines immediately before the word. Sometimes it is necessary to refer to a previous paragraph.

Function

Questions that ask you to identify the function of an element of the passage account for 8 percent of questions. Common wording variations are:

1. *The author provides an example of a contemporary issue in lines 14–15 primarily in order to . . .*
2. *The author's discussion of rites of passage serves primarily to . . .*
3. *Which one of the following describes the author's primary purpose in mentioning the fact that the Mexican gray wolf is endangered?*
4. *The first sentence of the passage functions primarily in which one of the following ways?*
5. *In discussing the opinions of the landlord, the author of Passage B seeks primarily to . . .*
6. *The main purpose of the first paragraph of the passage is to . . .*

Strategy for function questions. A *function* question is similar to a *use of a word or phrase* question in that you must identify how certain information functions in the passage, or, in other words, what role the information serves. For a *function* question, the information that you are to evaluate is not limited to a word or phrase. It is less likely that line numbers will be cited. Orient yourself to the information that is cited. Referring to the previous question stems, you may need to consider what the author actually says about the contemporary issue, rites of passage, and so on.

As with *use of a word or phrase* questions, it is not enough to understand the literal facts about the contemporary issue, for example. You must understand what the author's intentions were for including the information and how the information fits into the passage as a whole. Does the information provide background information? Does it support a point? Does it attack a view? Does it resolve an issue? Look for clues in the lines immediately before the part of the passage that introduces the information. If necessary, look earlier in the passage.

Agree with a View

These account for 8 percent of questions. Variations are:

1. *The author of the passage would be most likely to agree with which one of the following statements?*
2. *It can be inferred from the passage that Madame Curie would most likely have agreed with which one of the following statements about the fear that scientific discoveries can have negative consequences for humanity?*
3. *Given the information in the passage, the author would be most likely to agree with which one of the following statements about modern operas?*
4. *The passage most strongly suggests that pacifists would agree with which one of the following statements?*
5. *It can be inferred from the passage that Gandhi most likely held which one of the following views?*
6. *It can be inferred from the passage that the author would be most likely to view the "outlandish opinions" mentioned in line 15 as . . .*

Strategy for agree with a view questions. These question stems may or may not specify a particular issue. Some, such as examples 1, 4, and 5 above, simply ask what a certain person would agree with. If no particular issue is specified, you have to base your answer on your big-picture understanding of the author's point. Eliminate choices that go in the wrong direction. For example, Gandhi would be unlikely to agree with a view that the best way to resolve issues is through armed combat. The view that negotiations with one's opponent can sometimes break down could be in the right direction—it involves peaceful negotiation—but is not necessarily the correct answer.

The correct answer must be defendable by information stated in the passage. Test each remaining answer. Look for information in the passage that would defend or attack a particular answer choice. For this type of question the correct answer can hang on subtle and unexpected elements, so be careful!

If the question stem does specify an issue, first review the information in the passage that describes the author's belief about the issue. Then eliminate answers that go in the wrong direction and test the remaining answer choices.

Application/Extension

This type of question tests your ability to absorb information from the passage and apply it to new situations. These questions often require you to extend the application of information beyond the way that the information is applied in the passage. *Application/extension* questions account for 7 percent of RC questions. The common wording variations of the stems are:

1. *As it is described in the passage, an interactive research methodology would be best exemplified by a research project that . . .*
2. *Given the information in the passage, to which one of the following would magnetic resonance imaging likely be most applicable?*
3. *The ethical principle supported in the passage would be most relevant as a standard for deciding that which one of the following is ethically ambiguous?*
4. *The author's description of consensus decision making suggests that which one of the following would be least appropriately described as a valid response to a person who refuses to understand the opinions of others?*
5. *Based on the passage, Einstein's attitude toward the quantum physicists' view would be most softened if the quantum physicists were to . . .*
6. *The author most probably means to include which one of the following groups among the "supporters of a transformational agenda" referred to in line 32?*
7. *Suppose that a team of physicists has detected a particle that does not follow the laws of either relativity theory or quantum mechanics. Which one of the following actions by the international physics community would most closely meet Einstein's criteria for "the ability to reevaluate established theory" as described in lines 23–26?*

Strategy for application/extension questions. Because there are so many ways in which application and extension can be tested, the wording of the stems can vary greatly. Orient yourself carefully to the stem. What information is the question asking you to work with? What are you supposed to do with the information? In many such questions you need to understand the opinions and perspectives of either the author or of the people referred to in the passage.

Some application/extension questions ask you to identify an example of something that is described in general in the passage. Some ask you to match information in the passage with a situation in the answer choices, much in the way that *matching* questions function in LR. Some questions ask about the author's intentions. Some provide new information, such as example 7 above, and ask you to apply information from the passage to the new situation.

All of the *application/extension* questions require you to have a solid understanding of the relationships in the passage, as well as a clear understanding of what the question is asking. These questions require abstract thinking.

Analogous Situation

These ask you to identify a situation that is analogous to something in the passage. The answers represent situations and can be lengthy. This type accounts for 5 percent of questions. Variations are:

1. *Based on the passage, which one of the following scenarios is most similar to the way in which the early settlers attempted to establish security?*
2. *The passage indicates that the works of Plato and teachings of Socrates were similar in that . . .*

3. As described in the passage, the university's policy for dealing with plagiarism is most closely analogous to which one of the following situations?

4. The relationship between the tribes that depend on fishing and the tribes that depend on hunting, as described in the passage, is most analogous to the relationship between which one of the following pairs?

The second example does not ask you to identify an analogous situation but rather, asks you to identify why two situations are analogous.

COMPARATIVE READING QUESTION TYPES

The questions on CR sets can be drawn from any of the general question types. However, many of the question types are unique to CR. There are six specific CR-type questions.

In Common

About half of CR-type questions ask you to identify something that Passage A and Passage B have in common. The common elements can be premises, types of logic, main ideas, issues, or opinions, among other possibilities. Possible wording variations are:

1. The argument described in Passage A and the argument made by the author of Passage B are both advanced by . . .

2. Which one of the following is mentioned in both passages as evidence to support the view that young children should play outdoors regularly?

3. Each passage suggests which one of the following about wild horses?

4. Both passages are concerned with answering which one of the following questions?

5. The passages have which one of the following goals in common?

6. Both passages identify which one of the following as a factor that is necessary for ethical action?

7. Which one of the following most accurately describes a perspective on ethics present in each passage?

8. Both passages mention television primarily in order to . . .

Strategy for in-common questions. Orient yourself carefully to the question stem to understand what the question is asking. When you find an answer choice that you believe is correct, be sure to find the exact wording in each passage that proves that the answer is correct. Do not rely on your memory.

Agree

An *agree* question asks you to identify a statement that the authors of the two passages would both agree is true. This is similar to an *in-common* question in some ways but is a distinct type. Wording variations include:

1. It can be inferred from the passage that the author of Passage A and the author of Passage B would accept which one of the following statements?

2. It is most likely that both authors would agree with which one of the following statements about health insurance?

Strategy for agree questions. Correctly answering an *agree* question requires that you understand the concept of an arguer being *committed* to certain facts. The following abbreviated passages illustrate this concept.

EXAMPLE

Passage A: Most people prefer fresh fruits to either canned or frozen fruits.

Passage B: Most people prefer frozen foods to canned varieties of the same food.

With which one of the following statements would both authors agree?

(A) Most people would prefer fresh oranges to canned oranges.

(B) Most people would prefer frozen oranges to canned oranges.

(C) When choosing non-fresh food, most people choose frozen food.

(D) Most people would prefer fresh carrots to canned or frozen carrots but if they could not have fresh carrots, most people would choose frozen carrots.

(E) When choosing fruit, most people have a preference as to how the fruit has been handled from the point where it was harvested to the point at which the person receives it.

Try to answer the question. Defend your answer. The discussion is below.

Consider choice A. Choice A is completely consistent with Passage A. However, Passage B contains no information on preferences for fresh food. Arguer B is not committed to any conclusion about fresh food. Therefore, Arguer B cannot agree with the statement in choice A. It is not enough to say that Arguer B might agree with it. You have to prove that Arguer B is *committed to the truth* of choice A. That is not the case.

Choice B is completely consistent with Passage B. Oranges are a food and the frozen food in choice B is preferred over the canned variety of the same food. Arguer A, however, is not committed to any information about a preference between frozen and canned versions of a food. Passage A treats frozen and canned versions equally. Even though Arguer A might not disagree with the statement in choice B, Arguer A is not *committed* to the truth of choice B.

Choice C refers to non-fresh food. Arguer B is committed to the fact that when given a choice between frozen and canned food, people prefer frozen. However, Arguer B does not address the possibility that there are other types of processing that people might prefer over frozen. Arguer B is not committed to the truth of choice C. Arguer A is not committed to a viewpoint when it comes to choosing between different styles of processing, only between fresh and processed.

Choice D is closer to an answer that both arguers would agree on but it has a fatal flaw. It refers to a vegetable (carrots), whereas Arguer A only discusses fruit. Arguer B is committed to the truth of choice C because her argument is based on food, in general, not just fruit.

Choice E refers to fruit. It simply states that most people care about the state of the fruit. This is consistent with Passage A because people have a preference (they care) for fresh over frozen or canned. Choice E is also consistent with Passage B because people do not want canned fruit if they can have frozen. Both arguers are committed to agreeing with choice E.

Disagree

This question type is the opposite of *agree* questions. The two arguers are committed to *disagreeing* about the truth of a statement. *Disagree* questions can also ask about how the author of one passage would critique the other passage. *Disagree* questions are more common than *agree* questions. The wording variations are:

1. *The authors would be most likely to disagree over . . .*
2. *The author of Passage B and the kind of critical thinker described in Passage A would be most likely to disagree over whether . . .*
3. *Which one of the following is a statement that is true of scientific inquiry, according to Passage A, but that is not true of theological inquiry, according to Passage B?*
4. *It can be inferred that the author of Passage B would regard which one of the following as a logical error in the arguments made in Passage A?*

Strategy for disagree questions. The disagreement in these questions is typically between the authors of the two passages. However, the disagreement can also be between arguers who are referred to by the author of a passage, as in example 2 above. Also, the disagreement can be between two perspectives, without necessarily referring to the authors of the perspectives, as in example 3 above. In example 3, you are asked to find a statement that is consistent with one perspective and inconsistent with the other. Just as in disagreement between authors, in disagreement between perspectives, one perspective must be committed to the truth of the statement and the other perspective must be committed to the falsehood of the statement.

Difference Between Passages

These questions require you to identify a difference between the two passages. This is *not* the same as identifying a statement on which the two authors disagree. The wording variations are:

1. *Passage B differs from Passage A in that Passage B is more . . .*
2. *Which one of the following distinguishes the music students discussed in Passage B from the art students discussed in Passage A?*
3. *Which one of the following statements most accurately describes a difference between the two passages?*
4. *The perspectives on endangered species presented by the two authors differ in which one of the following ways?*

Strategy for difference between passage questions. As you orient yourself to the passages, look for the similarities and differences. There are often too many similarities and differences to list, so work backward from the answer choices, testing each one. Do *not* rely on your memory. Go back to the passages.

Relationship Between Passages

This type of question asks you about the relationship between the two passages. The question may simply ask you to identify the relationship, or it may ask you specific questions that require you to relate the two passages. Common wording variations are:

1. *Which one of the following most accurately describes a relationship between the two passages?*
2. *How does the content of Passage B relate to the purpose of Passage A?*
3. *The facts that are cited in Passage B relate to the generalization reported in Passage A in which one of the following ways?*

Strategy for relationship between passages questions. Orient carefully to the question and review the passages before looking at the answer choices. For example, in variation 3 above, you would review what the generalization is in Passage A. However, variations 1 and 2 are so general that there is nothing specific for you to review in advance. Go right to the answer choices and test them by finding the exact words in the passages that would defend the answer.

A Premise in One Passage Supports a Conclusion in the Other

Wording variations for this specific question type are:

1. *Which one of the following assertions from Passage B provides support for the view attributed to Einstein in Passage A, lines 23–25?*
2. *Which one of the following assertions from Passage A most closely exemplifies what the author of Passage B means in referring to eminent domain as "mass megalomania"?*

Strategy for a premise in one passage supports a conclusion in the other. Use the same strategies as for *relationship between the passages*. To support a conclusion, use the LR strategies for strengthening a conclusion. Identify the conclusion. Identify the premises that support the conclusion and identify the type of logic that the author uses to arrive at the conclusion.

LESS COMMON BIG-PICTURE QUESTION TYPES

There are nine specific types of less common big-picture questions. Each of these individually accounts for 2 percent or fewer of all RC questions. As a group, they account for about 13 percent.

Agreement Between People

This rare question type asks you to identify a statement that two people would agree is true. The two people can include the author and people whose views are described in the passage. Typical wording is:

> *Based on the passage, it can be concluded that the author and Einstein would have the same attitude toward . . .*

Strategy for agreement between people. The strategy for this type is similar to the strategy for identifying with what statement an author would agree. In this case you must understand the viewpoint of both people. Review the viewpoints first and then go to the answer choices, eliminating ones that are clearly wrong. Test the other answer choices.

Assumption

RC assumption questions are similar to LR assumption questions. This is a rare type on RC. Typical wording is:

> *It can be inferred that the argument for legalized euthanasia in lines 54–56 relies on which one of the following assumptions?*

Strategy for assumption questions. Apply the same strategies that you use on an LR assumption question. Identify the premises and the conclusion. Look for a gap in the argument. Test the answer choices by negating them.

Helps to Answer

In this question type, the answer choices consist of questions. You are to choose the question that the passage provides enough information to answer. Common wording variations are:

1. *The passage provides information sufficient to answer which one of the following questions?*
2. *The passage provides information that most helps to answer which one of the following questions?*
3. *The discussion of quantum mechanics in the second paragraph can most justifiably be taken as providing an answer to which one of the following questions?*

Strategy for helps to answer questions. Test the answer choices by considering what the answer to the question in the answer choice would be. It is not necessary to come up with a precise answer, but you must determine that the question in the answer choice can be answered by information in the passage.

Identify a Difference

This type of question asks you to identify a difference between two elements in the passage. Common wording variations are:

1. *According to the passage, one of the ways that relativity theory differs from quantum mechanics theory is that . . .*
2. *The passage suggests that one of the differences between relativity theory and quantum mechanics is that the relativity theory . . .*

Strategy for identify a difference. Most people find this type relatively easy. Look for the exact wording that shows that the two elements differ.

Identify the Structure

This question type asks you to recognize elements of the structure and organization of the passage. Wording variations include:

1. *Which one of the following most accurately represents the structure of the third paragraph?*
2. *Which one of the following most accurately describes the organization of the passage?*

Strategy for identify the structure. To answer this question you must have a good sense of the big picture of the passage. Understand the dichotomies and understand how the author develops the passage.

Strengthen

This question type is similar to its counterpart in LR. It is not a very common question type, though its mirror image, *weaken*, accounts for 3 percent of RC questions. Common wording variations are:

1. *Which one of the following, if true, would most strengthen Feldenberg's assertion that raw foods contain more nutrients than cooked foods?*
2. *Which one of the following would, if true, most help to support the raw food theory?*

Strategy for strengthen questions. Apply the same strategies that are used for *strengthen* questions in LR. The premises in the passage must be assumed to be true. Determine whether there is an apparent gap in the argument. Analyze how the argument is put together, what the conclusion is, and how the argument tries to support the conclusion. Test the answer choices by showing how each one would strengthen the argument.

Support a Generalization

This rare question type asks you to identify a generalization that can be supported by statements in the passage. Typical wording is:

> *Einstein's perspective on quantum mechanics, as it is described in the third paragraph, gives the most support for which one of the following generalizations?*

Strategy for support a generalization. This question type is similar to a *what can be concluded* question in LR, with answer choices that are generalizations. Find the generalization that can be concluded based on the information in the passage. This type of passage may also ask you to match the concrete information in the passage with an abstract expression. For example:

> *Concrete information: Apples have vitamin C. Hawthorn berries have vitamin E.*
> *Abstract generalization: Many fruits are excellent sources of necessary nutrients.*

Tone

This question type asks you to evaluate the author's tone or attitude toward a topic or issue. Common wording variations include:

1. *Based on the passage, the author's attitude toward the proponents of raw food is most accurately described as . . .*
2. *The author's stance toward the financial services industry can best be described as . . .*
3. *The tone of the passage is best described as . . .*

Strategy for tone questions. Each passage has at least one "voice," representing the viewpoint of a particular person. Each voice has a specific tone, or attitude. Consider the following:

> *Most politicians try to be tactful when they are talking to the public, but not good old Congressman Harry Paxton. Harry recently told a group of constituents that they had the brains of a banana slug when it came to understanding the federal budget. He told them that one of their fellow citizens complained that the government was giving too much money to people on welfare who weren't doing anything to earn it. But the complainer was himself living on disability payments. The country would be a better place if we had more politicians like Harry.*

What are the voices in this passage? Does the author have a voice? In any passage, the author either has an opinion about the information or is neutral. A neutral passage is like a newspaper article. It presents only the facts without expressing an opinion. If the author's voice is not neutral, it will be either positive, in support of the information presented, or negative, critical of the information.

On the LSAT, if the author's voice is positive, it will be either totally positive or positive with some qualifications or reservations. In the previous article, the author is totally positive about Harry Paxton. No reservations are expressed. Suppose the last line had read:

> *The country would be a better place if we had more politicians like Harry, but he would be wise to tone down his approach or he may not get reelected.*

Then the author's voice would be positive with qualifications. Note that the phrase *"but not good old Congressman Harry Paxton"* in the first sentence already indicates that the author is positive. If the author's voice is negative, it will likewise be either totally negative or negative with some positive qualifications.

LSAT tone questions ask about the tone of a particular voice. In the previous passage, there are three distinct voices. One is the author's. Whose voice is reflected in the statement "they had the brains of a banana slug when it came to understanding the federal budget?" Whose voice is reflected in the statement "the government was giving too much money to people on welfare who weren't doing anything to earn it"? The first is Harry's voice. The second is the voice of the person on disability. Be careful to identify the various voices in a passage and to keep them separate. Most tone questions ask about the author's voice.

In tone questions, answers are often on a continuum.

EXAMPLE

(A) bitter
(B) mildly annoyed
(C) unconcerned
(D) cautiously supportive
(E) ecstatic

Note that these answers start with a totally negative tone, move through a mildly negative tone to neutral to a moderately positive tone, and then move to a fully positive tone. First identify where on the above continuum the author's voice falls. If the author is positive but mentions some drawbacks, this is the qualifiedly positive position, which is answer choice D. It is not necessary to agree with the exact wording, *cautiously supportive*. Go by the place on the continuum even if the wording does not seem to be perfectly accurate.

Weaken

Like *strengthen* questions, these questions are very similar to their counterparts on LR. Typical wording variations are:

1. *Which one of the following would, if true, most undermine the author's claim about the value of early music training?*
2. *Which one of the following, if true, would most weaken the position that the passage attributes to opponents of preventive medicine?*
3. *Which one of the following, if true, most seriously undermines the author's criticism of the United Nations' proposal for redistribution of health resources?*

Strategy for weaken questions. Use the same strategies that you learned for such questions on the LR section. Identify how the argument is put together. Find the premises and the conclusion. Identify the type of logic that the author uses to support the conclusion. Look for gaps in the logic. Do you "buy" the argument? If not, identify what exactly seems to be wrong with it. Test the answer choices. The correct answer, when added to the original argument, causes the argument to fall apart or at least weaken.

Detail Questions

All detail questions ask for facts. These may be facts that are specifically stated in the passage (*specific detail* questions) or facts that follow logically from the information that is explicitly stated (*implied detail* questions). Correct answers do not depend on outside knowledge. If you choose an answer based on your own outside information, it cannot be correct unless it can also be defended by information in the passage. Detail questions account for 25 percent of all RC questions. There are more *implied detail* questions than *specific detail* questions.

SPECIFIC DETAIL

Specific detail questions account for about 9 percent of RC questions. The wording *according to the passage* indicates that the question may be a specific detail question, as about 60 percent of specific detail questions use this wording. However, the same phrase is also found in some other question types. Common wording variations are:

1. *The passage states which one of the following?*
2. *According to the passage, Einstein recommended that . . .*
3. *The passage states that the purpose of peer review in scientific research is to . . .*
4. *Which one of the following is given by the passage as a reason for the decision to stop burning coal?*

Strategy for specific detail questions. The correct answer must be defendable by words stated in the passage. The test of a correct answer is to be able to physically point to the specific words in the passage that undeniably prove that the answer must be true.

IMPLIED DETAIL

Implied detail questions account for 15 percent of questions. Variations include:

1. *The author suggests/implies that . . .*
2. *It can be inferred from the passage that . . .*
3. *If the author's claim about wild boars is true, which one of the following is most likely to be true?*
4. *Which one of the following statements is most strongly supported by information given in the passage?*
5. *Which one of the following is most supported by the passage?*
6. *Which one of the following is most strongly implied by the passage?*
7. *The passage most strongly suggests that the author holds which one of the following views?*
8. *The passage provides the most support for inferring which one of the following statements?*
9. *Based on the passage, which one of the following is most likely to be true of negotiations based on the mediation methods mentioned in the second paragraph?*
10. *The second paragraph most strongly supports the inference that Einstein made which one of the following assumptions?*

11. *The passage indicates that relying on the reactions of animals to impending earthquakes may be unreliable due to . . .*

Strategy for implied detail questions. As with *specific detail* questions, the answer must be defendable by pointing to specific words in the passage. However, the answer is derived from facts in the passage through the application of logic. It is not specifically stated in the passage.

> *Anyone who has worked at the XSQ Coal Mine during the past twenty years can participate in the upcoming class action suit. Jamie Peters began work at the mine five years ago.*

It can logically be concluded from the above two facts that Jamie Peters is eligible to participate in the suit. This fact is not stated in the passage, but it follows indisputably from the facts that are given.

There are two traps to watch out for with *implied detail* questions. First, a conclusion that goes too far beyond what is stated cannot be logically defended. In the above example, it cannot be defended that Jamie Peters suffered injuries or illness while working in the mine. That conclusion goes too far.

The other trap is to reject a conclusion because it seems to be explicitly stated rather than implied. It is highly unlikely that an LSAT question will ask you to distinguish between one answer choice that is explicitly stated and another that is derived through logic. If an *implied detail* answer choice is absolutely defendable, it must be correct, even if it appears to be a restatement of a fact in the passage. Generally, on closer inspection, it turns out that the answer is not an exact restatement. There is usually some small leap of logic.

Some answer choices may seem too obvious or too simple to be correct. However, if they can be defended by words in the passage, they must be the answer. There are many easy questions on the test. Do not try to make the question more difficult than it is.

Answers to detail questions are often highly literal. If an answer choice says *Most of the people in cities suffer from allergies,* it is necessary to prove by words in the passage that at least one more than half of the people in cities suffers from allergies. This is what "most" means literally—at least one more than half.

Because *implied detail* questions involve a certain amount of logical "leap," they can range from very literal, in which you are inferring something that almost seems to be stated, to very broad, in which the question almost becomes like an *application/extension* question. Orient yourself carefully to the question stem to determine how literal or how generalized you need to be.

TIP

TWO TYPES OF DETAIL QUESTIONS

Specific detail
Implied detail

EXCEPT and LEAST

Just as in the LR and AR sections, some RC questions are posed in terms such as *all of the following . . . EXCEPT* or *which of the following is the LEAST . . .* In both of these variations, four answer choices have a certain characteristic. The one answer choice that does not have that characteristic is the correct answer. These question variations can be tricky in two ways. First, you must keep a certain criterion in mind and then look for the opposite or lack of it. The second confusing aspect of these variations is that when, for example, a question sets up four answer choices that strengthen the argument and you are looking for the exception, the correct answer is not necessarily one that weakens the argument. Four answers may clearly strengthen and one may be neutral or irrelevant. In RC, EXCEPT and LEAST questions are rare, with LEAST questions being rarer.

GETTING THE ANSWER
Strategies for Answering Questions

The first step in getting an answer is to orient to the question stem. Orienting means taking time to make sure the meaning is clear or identifying what it is about it that may not be clear. Orienting includes getting a sense of which part of the passage the question relates to, how the question fits into the structure of the passage, and what might need to be done to answer it correctly. Orienting need not take more than fifteen to thirty seconds but it is a critical step. It is a big-picture strategy, in which you let the information in the question sink into your mind more thoroughly. Often, test takers get a question wrong because they were never clear from the start what the question meant or how it fit into the passage.

After orienting to the question stem, the steps for solving an RC problem are the same as those outlined under "The Generic Way to Answer a Question" in the strategies section of Chapter 1. Quite often in RC, the second step is to go back to the passage and look for information. For example, if the question asks, *Which of the following is a form of torture prohibited by the Geneva Convention*, the second step is to scan the passage for information about forms of torture and the Geneva Convention. What if there is nothing there? There must be, because the answer must be defendable by statements in the passage. If it does not seem to be there, look again. If there is only one reference to torture and the Geneva Convention, for example, *the rack is prohibited under the Geneva Convention*, the answer must be based on that reference.

In RC, the answers must be correct for very literal and specific reasons. Look carefully for the exact reason that one of the answers must be correct. Look for the fatal flaws in the other answers. It is almost never the case that one answer is better than another. One is right. The others are dead wrong. Usually an answer is wrong because it either violates what is actually stated or is not defendable.

THE FOUR STEPS FOR GETTING THE CORRECT ANSWER

- **STEP 1** Orient to the question stem.
- **STEP 2** Decide on a plan of attack.
- **STEP 3** Make one pass through the answer choices, using elimination.
- **STEP 4** Use the adversarial approach to evaluate the remaining answer choices.

Typically, answers are wrong because they violate logic or they contain one word that is not defendable. For example, consider a passage that states *many people in the United States do not like to eat liver.* Suppose a question asks:

Which of the following is consistent with the passage?

Evaluate the answer that says:

A. Most Americans find eating liver unpleasant.

First consider the phrase "find eating liver unpleasant." The information that we have is that people "do not like to eat liver." Is this the same as saying that people find it unpleasant? Yes. It can be defended from the dictionary definitions of these terms that they are interchangeable. The same can be said about the terms *American* and *people in the United States.*

The term *most*, on the other hand, is dead wrong. *Most* means at least one more than half. The passage only states that "many" people do not like to eat liver. It cannot be defended that at least one more than half (the definition of *most*) do not like to eat liver. The flaw is a logical and semantic one.

When there are two remaining possible answers, the most powerful tool for finding the correct answer is the adversarial approach, described in the strategy section of Chapter 1. Be careful to keep the defending and attacking stages completely separate. When test takers find they cannot use the adversarial approach successfully, it is usually because of mixing the two stages.

BEWARE THE DEFAULT MULTIPLE-CHOICE QUESTION!

Review the example given in Chapter 1. Sometimes an RC stem does ask the default question. However, if the question is something else, there is a danger that your brain will revert to the default question. Obviously, this would result in getting a wrong answer. Go back regularly to reread the question while working through the answer choices.

Important Tips for Better Reading

Be an active reader. Have a plan and have tools for implementing your plan. Here are some additional tools that will help you be a more effective active reader.

DO NOT READ THE QUESTIONS FIRST

Does it help to read all the questions first before reading the passage? People who do this may feel that they will be able to spot the answers to detail questions as they read the passage. Many detail questions, however, are so specific that unless you are focusing on the question, the answer will not be easy to find. Thus, reading all of the questions in advance may only waste time.

If you start a new passage with only a few minutes left in the test, it would be a waste of time to set up the passage. In this case, go directly to a detail question and then search the passage for the information to answer that question.

SIGNAL WORDS

As you skim the passage, look for words that show whether the author is continuing a line of thought or switching to a contrasting line of thought.

<table>
<tr><td colspan="2">

CONTINUATION WORDS

Adding more: Also, again, as well, further, moreover, in addition
Comparing: similarly, likewise, in the same way
Concluding: thus, therefore, then, hence, finally, in summation, in conclusion
Giving examples: for example, for instance, as an example, in other words

CONTRAST WORDS

However, nevertheless, but, on the contrary, on the other hand, although, despite, regardless

</td></tr>
</table>

ARE EXTREME ANSWERS WRONG?

Not necessarily! If the passage makes an extreme statement, such as *All Americans hate liver*, then an extreme answer can be correct. However, be suspicious of extreme answers. Often they are not defendable.

YOUR MOST POWERFUL STRATEGY

The Adversarial Approach is your most powerful tool for answering tough questions correctly.

STEP 1 Attack the answer you like.
STEP 2 Defend the answer you don't like.
When you attack, totally attack. When you defend, defend like your life depends on it!

TIP

ACTIVE READING

Active reading means analyzing what you see. Ask questions. Break it down. Diagram.

READING MORE QUICKLY AND ACCURATELY

Many test takers find that the language in RC passages is so complex that it is difficult to understand. For people who are struggling with understanding the complex sentences, there are some helpful strategies.

---

1. Take a friendly approach to the passage.
2. Avoid detail. Look for the big picture.
3. Study and use sentence diagramming.
4. Do lots of untimed practice.

Clearly, interesting topics are easier to "get into" than boring ones. However, even with a boring topic, it is possible to take a friendly attitude. Pretend that you are interested! It may make your mind a little more receptive.

The purpose of skimming the passage is to see the big picture. Only read enough detail to be able to follow the flow of the passage. As with the passage on the theories of how the sun generates energy, stepping back from the complex details helps improve both reading speed and comprehension. Avoid getting bogged down in details.

Sentence diagramming is a powerful tool for breaking down a highly complex sentence. Diagramming a sentence means identifying the basic parts of the sentence—the subject, the verb, the object, modifiers, and connecting words—and drawing a picture of the relationships among these parts.

The following example shows how even an extremely complex sentence can be broken down into simple relationships. Let's start simply with "the child."

What does the child do? The child eats.

What does the child eat? The child eats bread.

When does this happen? During the war, the child eats bread.

What child does this? During the war, the child who lost her family eats bread.

Which war was it? During the war between the two ethnic groups, the child who lost her family eats bread.

This process could continue to the following result:

> *During the last war between the two ethnic groups occupying the territory in the eastern region of what was formerly known as Herzegovina, the child who lost her family on the trek from the mountains to the sea coast during the evacuation of the most vulnerable populations eats bread that she found in an abandoned cow shed as a photographer from the western press, moved by the mixture of sorrow and wisdom in her expression, quietly and surreptitiously snaps her portrait for posterity.*

Is it clear that the basic sentence is still "the child eats" and that every new bit of information tells more about an earlier bit? Try answering the questions:

What kind of war?

Which ethnic groups?

Which region?

What specific trek?

When did she lose her family?

Evacuation of whom?

TIP

DIAGRAMMING SENTENCES

Sentence diagramming is a powerful tool that helps you break apart the grammatical structure and understand the real relationships in the sentence.

What do we know about the bread?
What do we know about the photographer's motivation?
In what manner did the photographer snap her picture?

Formal diagramming teaches specific strategies for quickly identifying parts of sentences and relationships. If you find many sentences too complex to follow, find a good guide to diagramming. Diagramming should be practiced untimed. Diagramming is time-consuming but you may be able to use it on one or two questions to gain extra points.

VOCABULARY

It is not necessary to study vocabulary. An unfamiliar word in a passage should not be an obstacle. There are almost always other clues in the passage to clarify what the word means. RC is not really a vocabulary-based task and studying hundreds of vocabulary words will not increase your score.

READING CHALLENGING ARTICLES

Some people read challenging material, such as articles in technical or scientific journals, to help them perform better on RC. RC passages are designed specifically on dichotomies. Other challenging material is not likely to be organized in this way but may help improve analytical skills. The test taker's first priority should be to master the strategies given here.

PUTTING STRATEGIES TO WORK
Sample Passage with Questions

Here is the passage that was introduced earlier, along with seven questions. Try using strategies on these. Then check the in-depth explanations.

VOCABULARY

RC is not designed to be a test of vocabulary. If you see a word you don't know, there are contextual clues that will help you get the answer.

> Relationships between elements of the natural world are often more complex than we realize, so that our actions affecting one element may have unexpected, and often negative, effects on another. For example, under natural conditions
> *(Line)* grasslands are grazed by various animals, and yet in certain circumstances, this
> *(5)* grazing may harm the health of the grassland. When grazing takes place under the unnatural conditions that result when grazing patterns are altered by people, the potential for harm is much greater.
>
> Many grasslands in the West have been grazed under conditions altered by people for well over a hundred years. Scientists recently have been studying the
> *(10)* effects of grazing the American bison, commonly known as the buffalo, because it has a less harmful effect on grasslands than most other domestic grazing animals. Two factors have been measured—the health of the grasses and the health of the range area in general. Health of the grasses is measured by counting the number of grass clumps per acre still alive at the end of the season. Health of the range is
> *(15)* measured by calculating the number of different species of plants per acre and the total mass of vegetation produced per acre for the season. By comparing bison-grazed range areas with ungrazed control areas, researchers found that the more palatable, fine-textured grasses, such as Indian Rice Grass, suffered significant

damage, whereas less tasty, coarse grasses, such as Sacaton, showed virtually none.
(20) Overall range health declined in areas dominated by Indian Rice Grass but not in those dominated by Sacaton.

It is still unclear whether a decrease in the health of grasses, even with the more vulnerable ones, necessarily results in a decrease in range health in the long run. Rangelands dominated by the slower growing, fine-textured species will obviously
(25) be more susceptible to permanent damage, but the ultimate effect on a rangeland depends on four identifiable factors. Areas with these characteristics would be most adversely affected: a high ratio of fine grasses to coarse grasses, a high ratio of grasses to non-grass plants, low annual rainfall, and high average seasonal temperatures. It would be a good idea to identify range areas with a combination
(30) of these characteristics and take special restorative measures with them, because they are most susceptible to being damaged by human-directed grazing.

Take as much time as necessary on these so you can try new strategies.

1. Which one of the following most accurately expresses the main idea of the passage?
   (A) Whereas natural relationships are complex, grazing is generally more beneficial for grazing animals than it is for plants.
   (B) Use of grasslands to raise bison has had a deleterious effect on Indian Rice Grass-dominated rangelands.
   (C) Human impact may be endangering the health of certain rangelands.
   (D) Grazing of bison can reduce the health of some grasses but probably does not affect the health of the rangeland in general.
   (E) The exact relationship between the health of grasses and the health of rangelands is still unknown.

2. Based on the passage, the health of a rangeland with a significant population of grasses, the health of which has been damaged by grazing, may not decline if which one of the following is true?
   (A) The rangeland has an above-average number of trees and shrubs.
   (B) Most of the precipitation the rangeland receives comes in the summer.
   (C) The rangeland is not subject to high winds.
   (D) Coarse textured grasses become more palatable.
   (E) Sacaton is replaced by Indian Rice Grass.

3. It can be inferred from the passage that the absence of a measurable decline in the health of rangelands dominated by Sacaton supports the conclusion that grazing can reduce the health of a rangeland because
   (A) Sacaton is grazed by more types of animals than are most grasses
   (B) Sacaton grows mostly in the control plots used in this research
   (C) in the absence of other grasses, grazing animals will eat Sacaton
   (D) Sacaton grows in areas similar to those in which Indian Rice Grass grows, but it is more tolerant of high temperatures
   (E) Sacaton is similar in many ways to Indian Rice Grass, but is known to taste bad to bison

4. It can be inferred from the passage that which one of the following would be true of range areas that had been grazed by domestic animals other than bison?
   (A) The health of some palatable grasses may have decreased even more than in areas grazed by bison.
   (B) Most of the grazing would have occurred on Sacaton plants.
   (C) The overall health of the rangeland would probably be about the same as on the rangeland grazed by bison.
   (D) They would produce a better profit per acre than rangeland grazed by bison.
   (E) The health of the range area would be similar to that of the ungrazed control areas mentioned in the passage.

5. Based on the definition of rangeland health in the passage, which one of the following is true?

   (A) All other factors remaining unchanged, if, on a rangeland, certain species die out without being replaced by species that previously did not grow there, the health of the rangeland has decreased.
   (B) All other factors remaining unchanged, if, on a rangeland, the total number of plants decreases, the health of the rangeland has decreased.
   (C) All other factors remaining unchanged, if the number of coarse grasses on a rangeland increases, the result will be that the health of the rangeland decreases.
   (D) All other factors remaining unchanged, if a rangeland that has never been grazed under conditions altered by people begins to be grazed under conditions altered by people, the result will be that the health of the rangeland decreases.
   (E) All other factors remaining unchanged, if the health of the grasses on a rangeland decreases, the result will be that the health of the rangeland decreases.

6. The phrase "unnatural conditions" in the first paragraph is most likely intended by the author to mean
   (A) under certain conditions wild grazing animals can harm a natural rangeland
   (B) the relationship between the "natural" world and the "human" world is more complex than we realize
   (C) it is unclear whether truly natural conditions really exist
   (D) under human-directed grazing, fewer species graze an area compared to grazing under natural conditions
   (E) in some circumstances people change the ways in which grazing takes place on rangeland

7. The relationship between the health of the grasses and the health of the rangeland, as described in the passages, is most analogous to which one of the following relationships?

(A) The more fish there are in a pond, the more likely that nitrogen will build up, resulting in a rapid increase in algae.

(B) The gravitational fields of the planets in the solar system interact in a complex way, with each planet affecting the movement of adjacent planets, which in turn affect the movement of their neighbors.

(C) Each individual in a society expects to receive more from the society than that individual expects to return to the society, with the result that society as a whole becomes poorer as its individual members become richer.

(D) Whereas the quality of a food store's offerings can be reduced if the store carries too many perishable products, the store's real success depends on carrying many more non-perishable items than perishable ones and on effective marketing.

(E) Although it is important for a basketball team to include enthusiastic new players, to be successful the team must have more experienced players than new players.

Explanations and Strategies

QUESTION 1

Let's review the systematic process for answering questions. The first step is to orient to the question. This question is straightforward. It is a *main idea* question. The second step is to consider what approach to take. In this case, quickly review the big picture. The next step is to review all the answer choices, crossing out ones that are clearly wrong, such as those that go in the wrong direction. During this step, it is not necessary to evaluate each answer choice in depth. Spending a few minutes carefully evaluating answer choices A, B, C, and D would turn out to be wasted time if choice E were clearly and obviously correct. After this first pass through all five answer choices, then, if the answer is not clear, use the adversarial approach to evaluate the answer choices that are left.

The correct answer to a main idea question has to meet two criteria. It must be true according to the passage and it must be the author's central point. It is not enough for it just to be true. Consider choice A. It is consistent with the passage, but it is not the central point. Choice A is out.

Is choice B true or consistent? Yes. By checking the passage, it is clear that Indian Rice Grass is one of the grasses that would be overgrazed. Is this the main idea? No. Choice B is out.

Is choice C true or consistent? Yes. Is it the main idea? Possibly. Leave it in for now.

Is choice D true or consistent? That is questionable. The first part is true but there is no evidence to defend that it is unlikely that bison would affect the health of rangeland. Choice D does not pass the test of being true according to the passage or consistent with it. Three answers are out.

Is choice E true or consistent? On the surface choice E looks like it is consistent with the passage. Could it be the main idea? It is not clear. Leave it in.

There are now two answer choices left. Use the adversarial approach to test them. Starting with choice E, attack it. First try to attack that it is a true statement. Examine choice E carefully word by word. The phrase "exact relationship" matches a statement made in the passage. The phrase "the health of grasses and the health of rangelands" correctly matches the two contexts discussed in the passage. The phrase "is still unknown" is *wrong*! The passage says that the relationship is still *unclear*. Regardless of whether choice E may be the main point, it is not a true statement and can be eliminated.

Choice C must be the correct answer. Double-check it. Is it the main idea? This step may seem unnecessary to you, but it is an important safeguard against careless errors. It takes only seconds to verify that this is indeed the main idea. However, if an error had been made and choice C were not the correct answer, the error would show up now. You would then reevaluate the other answer choices. Choice C holds up as the main idea.

Here is a very common error to watch out for. You eliminate four answers but are not happy with the remaining answer. You choose it anyway because everything else is out. Inevitably, it turns out that you had eliminated the correct answer. Avoid the temptation to go with the remaining answer. Go back and reevaluate each answer using the adversarial approach. If this happens often, be more conservative about crossing out answers. It is better to leave an answer in during the first pass through and then evaluate more carefully during the second.

QUESTION 2

The first step is to orient to the question. Does this question seem confusing? It should. Notice the complexity of the wording. It is critical to break down the meaning before going on. First, note that it is a *detail* question. Your understanding of the passage may tell you that it is probably not a *specific detail* but rather an *implied detail*, for which you will have to piece information together from the passage. Now, break the sentence down. Find the grammatical subject of the sentence and the verb that goes with it. "The health . . . may not decline . . ." This is followed by an "if" statement. Put the "if" statement first. "If one of the following is true, the health . . . may not decline." Note that the subject, "health," is vague. Clarify this by asking what kind of health? *Health of a rangeland.* Clarify further by asking what kind of rangeland. *Rangeland with a significant population of grasses.* Clarify even further. What about these grasses? *Their health has been damaged by grazing.* Does this clarify the sentence?

Step two is to consider a plan of attack. Before looking at the answer choices, go back and review the factors that cause a rangeland's health to decline. One of the dichotomies is health of grasses versus health of rangeland. These are separate. Certain things hurt health of grasses but that is not necessarily the same as what hurts health of rangeland. Use your eyes, not your memory. There are four factors: *a high ratio of fine grasses to coarse grasses, a high ratio of grasses to non-grass plants, low annual rainfall, and high average seasonal temperatures.*

An answer choice that includes one of these factors goes in the wrong direction. It will cause the rangeland to decline. If four answer choices go in the wrong direction, the remaining answer must be the correct one, even if it does not contain a factor that would make the health of the rangeland improve. In other words, an answer choice could be correct by virtue of not affecting the health of the rangeland at all.

Make a first pass through the answers. What about choice A? Trees and shrubs are non-grasses. It goes in the direction of a lower than average ratio of grasses to non-grasses, which is the opposite of one of the four factors of decline. This could be the answer.

What about choice B? It sounds like it would help the health of the rangeland. However, the correct answer has to be defendable based on the four factors. Choice B does not relate to the four factors. It would still be possible to have *low annual rainfall* even though that rainfall comes in the summer. On closer inspection, choice B is not defendable. Could it be the irrelevant answer that is right because the others are clearly wrong? Maybe. Leave it in.

Consider choice C. There is nothing about winds in the four factors. Note that choices B and C both contain irrelevant factors. This means it is highly unlikely that the correct answer could be an irrelevant one. It is more likely that the correct answer will contain a factor that will strengthen the rangeland.

Consider choice D. Palatability is a factor in the health of the grasses, not of the rangeland. Being clear on the dichotomy between the two helps to avoid an error on this answer. Even though it is not one of the four factors of range decline, be safe and evaluate it. Grasses that previously tasted bad now taste good. They will get grazed more. The health of the rangeland will, if anything, get worse. Choice D goes in the wrong direction.

Consider choice E. In terms of the health of the rangeland, Sacaton is a "good" grass and Indian Rice Grass is a "bad" grass. Replacing good with bad goes in the wrong direction.

Choice A is the only one that contains a factor that would increase the health of the rangeland. On the actual test, this would be enough evidence to choose choice A. However, as an exercise, try to attack choice A, using the adversarial approach. Even on the real test, it would be important to look briefly at choice A to make sure there are no significant concerns. Notice that looking for reasons to justify choice A only confirms your original prejudice. It is more helpful to see whether choice A can be attacked.

The only possible attack on choice A is that it does not prove that there will be a "high" ratio of non-grasses to grasses, only that it will be higher than average. Given the flaws in the other choices, this is not enough to question A's validity.

QUESTION 3

Orient to the question. Again, the wording is complex. The basic sentence is, "It can be inferred." What is it that can be inferred? Find just the simple subject, verb, and object. *It can be inferred that the absence (of something) supports the conclusion that (something)*. What is it the absence of? *A measurable decline*. Continue asking questions to get more detail.

Another way to organize a complex sentence is to work backward or outward from the middle. Start with the phrase "rangelands dominated by Sacaton." Expand this to *the health* of those rangelands. Expand that to *a decline* in that health. The LSAT tests is your ability to understand complex sentences.

The question, then, says, "Rangeland dominated by Sacaton does not decline." How does this support the conclusion that grazing can hurt rangeland. The question asks for an inference. This is a fact but not one that is specifically stated. Also notice that the question seems paradoxical. How can an example in which the rangeland is *not* hurt explain why grazing *can* hurt rangeland?

The plan of attack is to use the eyes, not the memory, to scan the passage for information on the relationship between Sacaton and the health of rangelands. Sacaton is a coarse grass and the term *grasses* appears in two of the four factors: *a high ratio of fine grasses to coarse grasses, a high ratio of grasses to non-grass plants*. Sacaton, then, is a "good" grass that is expected to correlate with little damage. This correlation is a clue. The argument is based on cause-and-effect reasoning. The cause-and-effect argument is that Indian Rice Grass is associated with decline. One proof of this is that its opposite, Sacaton, leads to no decline.

Having oriented to the question, consider choice A. In more complex questions, it is easy to forget exactly what the question is asking. If necessary, glance at the question again.

Choices A and B seem irrelevant. Choice C sounds like it could be a true statement. It also sounds like a factor that would lead to the decline of the rangeland. However, the question stem is not asking for that. It is asking for a way in which the fact that Sacaton does *not* lead to damaged rangeland supports the conclusion that some grazing *can* lead to damaged rangeland. Choice C fails to explain that.

Choice D compares the two types of grasses in terms of tolerance for high temperature. Leave D in for now. Choice E is true and consistent with the passage. It also highlights the fundamental difference between coarse grasses and fine grasses. Remember the dichotomy between health of grasses and health of rangeland? Within health of grasses there is an additional dichotomy—coarse versus fine—with coarse being unpalatable and fine palatable. Choice E is obviously relevant in some way but is it the reason why the scenario described in the question supports the conclusion?

Now compare choices D and E, using the adversarial approach. Attack the answer choice that at first seemed good and defend the answer choices that at first seemed poor. You can also look for the defense of the answer choices that looked good and the attack for the answer choices that looked bad.

Try to attack choice D. It says that Sacaton withstands heat. The conclusion that needs to be defended has to do with how grazing can hurt rangeland. Withstanding heat is not directly related to grazing.

Compare this with choice E. Palatability is directly related to grazing. If the grass tastes better, it will be grazed more. In addition, choice E strengthens the cause-and-effect argument that "bad" grasses hurt the rangeland and "good" grasses do not.

QUESTION 4

Orient to the question. This is an inferred fact. Create a plan of attack. This question refers to a dichotomy between bison and other grazing animals. Go to the passage to find any relevant information on this dichotomy.

> . . . the American bison, commonly known as the buffalo, because it has a less harmful effect on grasslands than most other domestic grazing animals.

There is only one fact. Other domestic grazing animals cause more damage than bison. The correct answer must reflect greater damage.

Choice A refers to the health of grasses rather than the health of rangeland, but it does go in the right direction, that palatable grasses will be worse off. Leave it.

In choice B, it may be true that heavier grazers might eat more Sacaton than less heavy grazers but the question asks about the rangeland in general. There may not be any Sacaton there. "Most" means more than half and even if it were known that the Sacaton comprised more than half of the rangeland, it cannot be proven that more than half of the grazed plants were Sacaton. Choice B is undefendable.

Choice C contradicts the only known difference between bison and other domestic grazing animals. It is out.

Choice D is a distracter. Some people, especially if they have experience with ranching, may think bison are a poor choice economically. However, this interpretation reads too much in. There is nothing in the passage that would defend this view, even if it might be true in the real world. Choice D is out.

Choice E refers to the dichotomy between the bison-grazed areas and the ungrazed control areas. On the surface, this is reminiscent of the dichotomy between bison and other domestic grazing animals. However, the control plots were not grazed at all. Choice E compares these ungrazed plots with plots that would be grazed by the heavy-grazing domestic animals. The latter would suffer much more damage. Choice E is out.

Everything is out except choice A. Double-check choice A. A possible attack on choice A is that it talks about the health of grasses rather than of rangelands and the question asks about the effect on rangelands. Now rebut this attack. Destroying the grasses on a rangeland would lead directly to a diminishing of the health of the rangeland.

QUESTION 5

Orient to the question. It is straightforward. It is a *specific detail* or, possibly, *implied detail* question. The plan of attack is to review what the passage says about rangeland health. The four factors have already been identified. Is there anything else? The second paragraph tells how to measure rangeland health:

> *Health of the range is measured by calculating the number of different species of plants per acre and the total mass of vegetation produced per acre for the season.*

Is this enough to answer the question?

Choice A introduces new information. However, it does make sense and is consistent with the passage. Do not eliminate an answer unless it is clearly out. Leave choice A in.

Choice B seems consistent with the passage. Leave it in.

Choice C goes in the wrong direction. An increase in coarse grasses correlates with better rangeland health. Choice C is out.

Choice D seems to go in the right direction, as human-directed grazing correlates with decline in rangeland health. Leave it in.

Choice E also seems to go in the right direction. Leave it in.

Four answer choices are left. Use the adversarial approach to analyze each answer choice more deeply. The original attack on choice A was that it seems to introduce new information. Try to defend choice A. To do so, it must be matched with one of the given factors that affect rangeland health. Choice A has no relationship to either the human-controlled grazing or the four factors of rangeland health.

There are, however, two factors for measuring the health of the rangeland that might apply to choice A: (1) the number of different species of plants per acre, and (2) the total mass of vegetation produced per acre for the season. As these are ways of measuring the health, an increase in these measures means that the health has increased. Try to relate choice A to these factors. If a certain species dies out without being replaced by a species that previously did not grow there, the total number of different species of plants will be reduced on that same acreage.

The concept described in the previous paragraph is an important one. The word *species* defines a category. For example, the species *dandelion* constitutes a category. If an acre contains only dandelions, there is only one species on the acre. The category *dandelion* stands in contrast to the actual number of plants. There may be a thousand plants on the acre but there is only one species. This contrast between the number of categories and the number of members of a category is one that is tested frequently on both RC and LR. It is similar to the contrast between a ratio and actual number.

To clarify the distinction between number of species and number of members of a species in choice A, quantify the argument. Start with fifteen species of plants. Three of those species die out. No new species are introduced. Twelve remain. If the plants of those twelve species spread, there are more plants but still only twelve species.

This is a strong argument for choice A. However, it is important to quickly make sure that choices B, D, and E do not hold up. Choice B states that the total number of plants has decreased. The fact that there are fewer plants gives the impression that there is "less" in general. To attack this impression, try to prove that there could be fewer plants and yet a greater number of species. The proof can be mathematical.

	Before	After
# of plants	1,000	400
# of species	8	30

Compare the two scenarios. Before the decrease in the number of plants referred to in choice B takes place, there may have been 1,000 plants but they may have all been of 8 species. After B takes place, there are only 400 plants but there is a broader variety of species. It may seem counterintuitive but there is nothing in the passage to prevent this scenario. The number of plants simply does not necessarily correlate to the number of species.

The same argument will hold up for the relationship between fewer plants and total mass of vegetation.

	Before	After
# of plants	1,000	1
Mass of vegetation in kg	350 kg	500 kg

In this example, an absurd situation has been used to make a point. Even if an area were reduced from a thousand plants to one, if that one plant were huge, the mass could be greater than before. Choice B is out.

Attack choice D. Does a change from natural conditions to human-altered conditions necessarily mean a decline in rangeland health? No. It may result in a decrease under certain conditions but does not necessarily result in a decrease.

Attack choice E. Similarly, the passage states that a decrease in the health of the grasses does not necessarily result in a decrease in the health of the rangeland. Choice E is out. Choice A remains as the correct answer.

QUESTION 6

Orient to the question. It is a *use of a word/phrase* question. Find the phrase in the passage and review how the author has used it. The phrase stands in contrast to the word *natural*, which refers to grazing without human involvement. *Unnatural*, then, is defined as *grazing patterns . . . altered by people*. Choice A is a true statement but the question does not ask for a true statement but rather asks you to identify the meaning that the author wants to convey by the wording *unnatural conditions*. Choice A does not match the author's intended meaning.

Choice B draws on wording from the beginning of the passage. Although the author makes a distinction between grazing with and without human intervention, choice B fails to capture the essence of *grazing patterns . . . altered by people.*

Choice C also draws on wording from the passage, which makes it sound appealing. However, it also fails to capture the essence of *grazing patterns . . . altered by people.*

Choice D directly addresses human-directed grazing. It provides one example of how people might make changes to a "natural" grazing system. However, there is no evidence that people reduce the number of species that graze an area. Even more importantly, a single example does not capture the essence of the author's meaning for using the term *unnatural conditions.*

Choice E is a close paraphrase of *grazing patterns . . . altered by people.* Changing the ways in which grazing takes place is equivalent to altering the patterns of grazing. Choice E is correct.

QUESTION 7

Orient to the question. It is an *analogous situation* question. Identify specifically what the relationship between the health of the grasses and the health of the rangelands is. The grasses are a constituent of the rangeland but the rangeland is made up of more than just grasses. The grasses that are most vulnerable to grazing may decrease the health of the entire rangeland, but the effect is only significant if other factors are present. Some of the factors include the ratio of vulnerable grasses to non-vulnerable grasses. Some include the ratio of grasses to plants in the rangeland that are not grasses. Some of the factors that affect the health of the rangeland do not directly involve grasses at all.

Choice A implies that fish are the only factor in the health of the pond and that the more fish, the worse the health of the pond. There is no distinction between more or less harmful types of fish. There is no discussion of the health of the fish. Choice A does not capture the essence of the relationship.

Choice B implies that planets are part of a larger system. However, there is no discussion of the health of the planets or the system of which they are part. Choice B is out.

In choice C the individuals are analogous to the grasses and society is analogous to the rangeland. The relationship is that the better the financial health of the individuals, the worse the financial health of society. This is the opposite of the relationship between grasses and the rangeland. Choice C is out.

In choice D, the health of certain products (perishable ones) affects the health of the store but is not the sole factor. Other factors include the ratio of perishable to nonperishable products and marketing. This is analogous to the ratio of fine to coarse grasses and to the presence of factors other than grasses, for example, temperature and rainfall. Choice D is a good match. Test choice E.

In choice E, the individual players are analogous to the grasses. The team is analogous to the rangeland. However, the team consists only of members. This is not analogous to a rangeland consisting of grasses and a wide range of other plants. Although the ratio of new to older players is analogous to the ratio of fine to coarse grasses, there are factors given that are based on something other than players. In the passage there are important factors other than those involving grasses. Choice E is not a complete analogy. The correct answer is choice D.

SUMMARY

Review the topics in this chapter regularly as you practice. The chapter covers how to improve on the RC, including how to master timing and how to practice. It describes how to tackle the passage by setting up the passage, finding and diagramming the big picture, and skimming.

You learned how to understand the questions through a review of big-picture questions—main idea, tone, logical organization, literary techniques, and extension—along with strategies for these types. Detail questions include specific detail and implied detail. The chapter provides strategies for answering questions and tips for better reading, including not reading the questions first, looking for signal words, how to read more quickly and accurately, the importance of vocabulary, and reading challenging articles. The chapter closes with a discussion of how to put the strategies to work.

Time: 35 minutes
27 Questions

> **DIRECTIONS:** Each set of questions in this section is based on one passage or on a pair of passages. Answer the questions based on what is <u>stated</u> or <u>implied</u> in the passage or in the pair of passages. More than one answer choice could conceivably answer the question in some cases. However, you should choose the <u>best</u> answer. The best answer is the response that answers the question most accurately and completely. When you have chosen the best answer, fill in the space on your answer sheet that corresponds to your answer.

In the world of fiction, the line between science fiction and fantasy sometimes seems thin. Time travel, spaceships, and multiple
Line dimensions are well-recognized components
(5) of science fiction. Fairies, mythical beasts, and wizards are elements of the fantasy realms. How, though, are we to classify a story in which a spaceship arrives on a planet inhabited by unicorns, for example? What is the proper des-
(10) ignation for a story of fairies in which a wizard travels through time? Are these two genres merely variations on one imaginative theme?

The argument can be made that the line between science fiction and fantasy, while
(15) thin, represents in fact a vast gulf, a seemingly fine barrier between two parallel universes, through which, with a single step, one travels unimaginable distances. The difference between science fiction and fantasy is not
(20) one of content but of intent. Science fiction is rooted in the realm of science. Its intention is to tell a logical story that draws on technologies, present or future. The technologies of science fiction are plausible. They obey the laws
(25) of nature, even if the laws they obey are ones that have not yet been discovered by today's scientists.

Science fiction is serious. Just as the intention of science is to solve problems by under-
(30) standing them, the intention of science fiction is to solve problems that have been extrapolated into other times, other worlds, other dimensions. The problems of the universe—present and future—are not to be taken lightly.

(35) There is work to be done. If a science fiction story contains a unicorn, the unicorn is merely an opportunity for understanding the genetic mechanisms that could have led to the development of a horn in the genus Equus.

(40) What, then, is the intention of fantasy? It can only be to entertain, to enjoy, to thrill, to amaze, and, ultimately, to dream. If there is a time machine in a fantasy, surely it is a magical and mysterious object of wonder. If one travels in
(45) the time machine, it is not for any purpose other than sheer adventure. The less one knows about where one will end up, the greater the amazement, the more brilliant the dream. The unicorn in a fantasy represents the manifestation of the
(50) impossible. It is a marvel in and of itself, without any explanation for its existence.

Fantasy is not serious. It is full of whimsy and humor and delight. Even if the story is a dark one, there is always light in a fantasy,
(55) even if it is only the light of hope. Technology has a significant role in a fantasy story but it is a different role than in science fiction. In a fantasy, technology may be the tool of the forces of evil but even when the heroes use it,
(60) it is not technology that wins the day but the power of the human—or nonhuman—spirit. In the final analysis, science fiction operates from the intention to expand human knowledge, whereas fantasy, with the wave of a wand,
(65) leaves knowledge far behind, as, like Peter Pan, it tries to carry us off to worlds beyond the imagination where life is greater than solving problems.

1. Which one of the following most accurately expresses the main point of the passage?
   (A) Despite their similarities, science fiction and fantasy also have many differences.
   (B) It can be difficult in some cases to determine whether a work should be classified as science fiction or fantasy.
   (C) Many authors intend to write either science fiction or fantasy but end up blending elements of both.
   (D) Science fiction and fantasy are based on radically different intentions.
   (E) Science fiction is able to explain elements at which fantasy can only hint.

2. Given the information in the passage, the author would be most likely to agree with each of the following statements about fantasy EXCEPT:
   (A) Fantasy is separated from science fiction by a fine line.
   (B) Fantasy fundamentally deals with different content than does science fiction.
   (C) Time travel is one of the elements that can be found in a work of fantasy.
   (D) Technology can play an important role in fantasy.
   (E) Dark fantasy stories are essentially not serious.

3. The passage most strongly suggests that which one of the following would be true about a science fiction story that involved witches who flew on brooms?
   (A) The witches would exist in a dimension or universe that is different from ours.
   (B) The witches would use technology to defeat evil.
   (C) The story would be a hybrid between science fiction and fantasy.
   (D) The author's intention would be to take the reader far beyond technology.
   (E) The author would describe the technology by which the brooms were able to fly.

4. The passage provides information sufficient to answer which one of the following questions?
   (A) According to science fiction, what is the technology behind time travel?
   (B) What does a unicorn represent in a fantasy?
   (C) How should a story be classified if it involves a spaceship landing on a planet with unicorns?
   (D) What genetic mutations could lead to a member of the horse family growing a horn?
   (E) If a story involves wormholes, in which genre does it belong?

5. Which one of the following most accurately describes the author's use of the words *thin* and *gulf* in line 15?
   (A) The former refers to the fact that the difference between science fiction and fantasy is difficult to distinguish, and the latter refers to the fact that the difference between science fiction and fantasy is large.
   (B) The two words indicate that there are only a few ways in which science fiction and fantasy differ but that those ways are readily identifiable.
   (C) The former refers to the fact that science fiction operates linearly, whereas the latter refers to the fact that fantasy operates multidimensionally.
   (D) The former refers to an analysis of the difference between science fiction and fantasy that the author rebuts, and the latter is the author's description of the difference between science fiction and fantasy.
   (E) The former refers to the fact that the difference between science fiction and fantasy is difficult to distinguish, and the latter refers to the fact that the scope of fantasy is large and vast.

6. Suppose that the author of the passage had written a fantasy story in which a wizard goes into the future in a time machine and finds a race of small, winged humanoids. Which one of the following would most likely be an explanation of this situation that the author would include in the story?

(A) Using magic, the wizard adjusted the quantum engine that operated the time machine to take her 1,000 years into the future and in microseconds found herself among a band of tiny humanlike beings who had evolved wings.

(B) Tapping the time machine with her wand, the wizard was flung 1,000 years into the future. The fairylike humanoids there appeared to have evolved wings from folds under their arms, a remarkably fast adaptation, leading the wizard to suspect intense radiation levels.

(C) The time machine mysteriously whisked the wizard far into the future, where she found a band of fairies frolicking in the sun.

(D) The time machine whisked the wizard 1,000 years into the future. Just as her calculations had predicted, the fairies there, if she could bring one back, might help unravel the genetic mutations that were slowly destroying humanity.

(E) The wizard stepped out of the time machine into a group of fairies, frolicking in the sun. Standing there in awe, she tried to imagine what genetic mutations could have reduced humans to such a small size.

7. According to the passage, one of the ways that technology in science fiction differs from technology in fantasy is that

(A) in fantasy, technology is a tool of the forces of evil, and in science fiction, technology is a tool of the forces of good

(B) in fantasy, technology is a tool of the human spirit, and in science fiction, technology is the force that wins the day

(C) in fantasy, technology is based on magic, and in science fiction, technology is based on science

(D) in fantasy, technology is used for solving human problems, and in science fiction, technology is used for expanding knowledge

(E) in fantasy, technology carries us to worlds beyond imagination, and in science fiction, technology is simply a tool for solving problems

In recent years it has become clear that the United States cannot indefinitely depend on petroleum as the main source of energy. Both the limited quantity of this nonrenew-able resource and the political and economic dependence on those countries that continue to provide petroleum products dictates the need, sooner or later, to achieve independence from petroleum.

As we gingerly approach this transition, many people have raised a voice for renew-able energy resources. Petroleum and coal are examples of nonrenewable resources. They are remnants of an earlier geological time. As far as we know, they are no longer being formed. Wood, of course, still grows. Trees can be planted and harvested. However, to supply the energy needs of a community through wood can lead to devastation of the natural environ-ment. There are many areas around the world in which every last bit of burnable material has long since been chopped down and used, leav-ing the landscape denuded and barren.

Solar energy and wind are truly renewable resources. The harvesting of sun and wind do not, as far as we know at this point, upset the ecology. In addition, they do not require burn-ing and so do not produce toxic waste products. Some critics hypothesize that the technologies used for harvesting wind and sun may, how-ever, be toxic. Other critics question the effect on the environment of large-scale interference with patterns of sunlight and wind.

Another possible energy source that is rather unique is nuclear fission. Nuclear power plants have existed for many years. Relatively small amounts of fissionable material can pro-duce vast amounts of energy. From this stand-point, fissionable material is probably the most energy-packed substance in human history. However, equally unique is the tremendous length of time that the waste products remain toxic. These waste products must be kept in special storage facilities and monitored vir-tually forever to ensure that the highly toxic material does not leak into the environment.

Monitoring for the presence of escaped, radioactive materials in the vicinity of per-manent transuranic waste-storage facilities is critical for early identification of possible leaks. One possible technique for accomplishing this monitoring is the Zone technique. The area surrounding the storage facility is divided into concentric circles, forming bands 500 meters wide. Each band is divided into eight sectors. At regular intervals, soil samples are taken from each sector, and qualitative and quanti-tative analysis of radioactive isotopes is made and recorded. Data is adjusted to reflect the distance of the sample from the facility, the strength and direction of atmospheric winds since the previous collection date, and the background radiation and previous radiation accumulations. If a sample shows a radiation level higher than the average background level for its band that cannot be accounted for by wind-blown materials from an adjacent area, a possible leak is indicated. With this kind of accuracy, it is possible that the Zone technique could be the key to safe storage of radioactive waste and a better future.

8. Which one of the following most accurately expresses the main point of the passage?
   (A) It describes an effective methodology.
   (B) It analyzes a controversial process.
   (C) It advocates a new alternative.
   (D) It reports an important discovery.
   (E) It rebuts a proposed solution.

9. It can be inferred from the passage that the Zone procedure might produce an inaccurate result if
   (A) soil samples varied in size
   (B) a soil sample were taken from a significantly different portion of its sector than the previous sample from that sector
   (C) the background radiation in a particular sector were higher than the average background level for its band
   (D) the radiation levels of all samples for a particular date were nearly identical
   (E) there was a significant leak of radiation that only affected one sector of a band

10. Which one of the following most accurately describes the organization of the passage?
    (A) Background information is given, a theory is proposed, and supporting evidence is given.
    (B) Background information is given, a technique is criticized, and an alternate approach is advanced.
    (C) Background information is given, an assertion is put forward, and a process is described.
    (D) A dilemma is presented, an explanation is analyzed, and some flaws are revealed.
    (E) A dilemma is presented, various alternatives are dismissed, and a new theory is introduced.

11. Based on the passage, the author's attitude regarding solar energy can be most accurately described as
    (A) ambivalence, in that the author believes solar energy has some drawbacks, but other people have pointed out benefits of solar energy
    (B) confidence that solar energy is better than coal but not as productive as petroleum
    (C) confidence that solar energy is better than coal and petroleum but not as good as wind
    (D) concern that solar energy is as good as nuclear fission but not as efficient
    (E) uncertainty, in that the author believes that solar energy has benefits but is also aware of criticisms of his beliefs

12. The passage indicates that wood, as a fuel, and nuclear fission are similar in that
    (A) both are examples of renewable resources
    (B) both can leave the landscape denuded
    (C) both require monitoring for the release of toxins into the environment
    (D) both can lead to damage to the environment
    (E) both are highly energy packed

13. The second paragraph of the passage functions primarily in which one of the following ways?
    (A) It presents a solution to a problem introduced in the first paragraph and gives a context for the solution, which is then defended in the third paragraph.
    (B) It introduces a possible solution that is discarded in a later paragraph.
    (C) It explains the basis for a problem introduced in the first paragraph.
    (D) It provides several examples of alternatives to nonrenewable resources and points out their drawbacks.
    (E) It reports on the destruction of the natural environment caused by an overdependence on wood.

Passage A

The American system of law could not have developed as anything other than male-dominated. Historically, virtually all legislators,
Line judges, and lawyers have been male. Even
(5) if the majority of men who were involved in shaping the legal system had wanted to accommodate the viewpoints of women, they would have been unable to do so, given the absence of women's voices in the legal field. It is unlikely,
(10) though, that many of the men so involved were even aware that there might be a difference between a male view of law and a female view of law.

Today there are many important voices
(15) speaking out for a feminist approach to law. There is a fundamental paradox in feminist law, though, that has yet to be resolved. Is equity under the law best achieved by treating women as equals to men or by recognizing
(20) fundamental differences between men and women? The argument for treating women as equals is based on the fact that, in the past, women have not been treated as equals. For example, in the past, the law has set different
(25) standards for women's right to vote, to serve in the military, and to earn the same pay as men. When women have been treated differently from men, the difference has nearly always been to the detriment of women.

(30) The argument for treating women differently under the law is based on recognizing that women's needs, values, social interactions, and lives as a whole are fundamentally different from those of men. The dilemma is
(35) that, if the law is allowed to treat women differently from men, who will ensure that such different treatment does not result in inferior treatment? If it is men, we are all in trouble.

Passage B

The battle of the sexes is rooted in the fact
(40) that men do not see women as women see themselves. Every man, when pressed, will admit that he is not sure what to make of women. This is not because women do not try to explain themselves. It is because the male
(45) psyche is deeply programmed to see women through a male filter.

Perhaps the biggest complaint about men is that they treat women differently from how they treat other men. However, this is only half
(50) of the problem. Men also get into trouble by not treating women as different from men. Consider the man who gets off of a heated phone conversation about politics with a male friend and says to his wife, "Those cookies sure smell
(55) good." The woman may be highly offended that he talks about important topics with male friends but talks about trivialities with her. However, if the man is working on a project and grunts at her, "Gimme that wrench," as he
(60) would to a male friend, she may be offended that he is treating her impersonally.

Eventually men realize that sometimes a woman wants to be treated in the same way that the man would treat another man and
(65) sometimes she wants to be treated differently. Most men are able to make this switch. The problem for them is that they are never able to determine when to do which and are almost always responding in the wrong way.

14. The author of Passage A and the author of Passage B would be most likely to agree on the truth of which one of the following statements?
    (A) Historically, women have not had the opportunity to voice their opinions about how they are treated.
    (B) Men typically are aware that women have viewpoints that are different from those of men.
    (C) It would be good if women were allowed to take the same combat positions in the military as are men.
    (D) It is unclear whether it is best for women to be treated as similar to men or as different from men.
    (E) When men treat women differently from how they treat men, men typically treat women as inferiors.

15. Which one of the following statements most accurately characterizes a difference between the two passages?

(A) Passage A considers the question of whether women should be treated in the same way as men or as different, in order to establish rules that men can follow for relating to women, whereas Passage B deals with the same question but concludes that men are unlikely to be able to know when to treat women one way or the other.

(B) Passage A considers the question of whether women should be treated in the same way as men or as different, from the perspective of the law, whereas Passage B treats the same question from the perspective of interpersonal relationships.

(C) Passage A is primarily concerned with achieving fair treatment of women under the law, whereas Passage B is primarily concerned with achieving fair treatment for men under the law.

(D) Passage A is primarily concerned with supporting the argument that women's needs are different from those of men, whereas Passage B is primarily concerned with supporting the argument that men sometimes treat women as they would treat men and sometimes treat women differently.

(E) Passage A is primarily concerned with supporting the argument that it is not possible for the current American legal system to become less male dominated, whereas Passage B is primarily concerned with supporting the argument that men would accommodate the needs of women if they knew how to do so.

16. Given the information in the passage, which one of the following would be most helpful to the type of man described in Passage B?

(A) guidelines from his wife as to what constituted, for her, being treated as a woman

(B) a nonverbal signal from his wife indicating whether, at that moment, she wished to be treated in the way that he would treat a man or in a different way

(C) a list of the laws that apply to interacting with a woman in a domestic situation

(D) a book describing the major differences between men and women

(E) counseling to help him learn to communicate with his wife in a nonviolent way

17. The authors would be most likely to disagree over

(A) whether or not the American system of law has historically been male dominated

(B) whether or not men see women as women see themselves

(C) whether or not there is a fundamental misunderstanding between men and women

(D) the extent to which men are generally interested in accommodating the ways in which women are different from men

(E) the kind of training that men need in order to understand the needs of women

18. Which one of the following most accurately describes a relationship between the two passages?

(A) Passage B considers an aspect of the argument in Passage A and then rejects the argument.

(B) Passage A provides support for a hypothesis, and Passage B provides additional support by expanding on a premise in Passage A.

(C) Passage A establishes the legal basis for a conclusion, and Passage B draws the same conclusion through a psychological basis.

(D) Passage B examines in detail a dilemma that Passage A establishes only in general terms.

(E) Passage A presents an unsolved dilemma, and Passage B expands on one aspect of the dilemma.

19. Which one of the following is mentioned in both passages as an example of the difficulty in communication between men and women?

(A) There are instances in which men treat women differently than they would treat other men.

(B) Most men are unaware that there is a difference between the male view and the female view.

(C) Feminists are not in agreement as to whether equity for women is best achieved through laws or through interpersonal relationships.

(D) When men treat women differently from the way they treat other men, they usually see women as inferiors.

(E) Many men want to accommodate women's differences but are not clear on how or when to do so.

Compared to countries outside of the Western Hemisphere, the United States is predominantly a nation of recent immigrants. Historically, many immigrant families quickly became integrated into the mainstream American culture, often by the second generation. While first-generation immigrants continued to speak the language of their homeland, eat the foods that they grew up with, and associate with others from their original country, their children very often did not speak the language of the parents, though they may have understood it, ate American food, and associated with native-born Americans from many backgrounds. By the third generation, the children typically understood little or nothing of their grandparents' language, had only a vague sense of life in the "old world," and most likely had one parent who was from a different cultural background.

In contrast to this typical pattern, some ethnic groups did not readily assimilate into the mainstream culture. In some cases this may have been partly by choice. Some ethnic groups maintained a strong cultural identity that relied on and preserved certain traits that were different from those of mainstream culture. In other cases, a group may have been involuntarily isolated by the attitudes of mainstream Americans. Such isolation typically kept the group impoverished and uneducated, which in turn reinforced in the minds of mainstream Americans the "inferiority" of the group.

Fortunately, the second half of the twentieth century saw a significant opening of opportunities for many of America's most severely discriminated-against groups. Educational opportunities, the ability to enter professions, housing opportunities, greater social acceptance by mainstream Americans, and prominent positive role models have all helped many people from disadvantaged groups move solidly into a middle-class existence. This has, in turn, changed mainstream perceptions of the disadvantaged group and created a class of leaders from within the group who can advocate for greater equality and can help facilitate change in their cultural community.

There are two issues that may trouble the consciences of members of disadvantaged groups who have solidly entered the middle class. The first is that there are still millions of members of disadvantaged groups who suffer from poor education, lack of opportunity, and ongoing discrimination based not only on their socioeconomic status but also on their membership in the group. To what extent do the "successful" members of such a group turn their efforts to helping the others, and to what extent do they leave the past behind and move forward with creating a new path?

The second issue is a personal one. Does the long-sought-for entry into mainstream culture result in losing one's long-cherished cultural identity—the unique language, the food, the religion, the sense of one's people? The two issues perhaps raise essentially the same question. Does acceptance into the mainstream culture mean losing one's identity, and does returning to one's identity in order to help others and for personal strength only lead back into the old ways of poverty and discrimination? Most likely, for such people a new identity will emerge that does not abandon the old identity but does not lead back to the isolation of prejudice.

20. Which one of the following most accurately expresses the main point of the passage?

(A) Most immigrant groups in the United States have been able to assimilate into the mainstream culture sooner or later.

(B) In the United States, members of immigrant groups who have been historically discriminated against may achieve education and professional careers but cannot escape from being discriminated against in their personal lives.

(C) Even though many immigrant groups in the United States have easily assimilated into mainstream culture, many have been involuntarily kept separate, and as they eventually enter the mainstream, they face new dilemmas that may lead to a revised sense of identity.

(D) In the United States, members of immigrant groups eventually assimilate into the mainstream culture but often involuntarily lose elements of their culture, such as language, that were originally important to them.

(E) No one outside of a disadvantaged group can advise members of a group to what extent they should assimilate and to what extent they should draw on the elements of their own culture.

21. It can be inferred that the comments about first-generation immigrants in lines 7–15 rely on which one of the following assumptions?

(A) The husband and wife in a first-generation immigrant family both spoke the same native language.

(B) It is possible to regularly speak one's native language at home and still learn to speak English well enough to earn a living.

(C) It is possible to understand what is being said in a language without being able to speak the language.

(D) The children of first-generation immigrants purposely distanced themselves from the habits of their parents that were different from the corresponding American habits.

(E) First-generation immigrants from a particular country lived in the same part of a town as other first-generation immigrants from that country.

22. By referring to middle-class members of a disadvantaged group as " 'successful' members" (line 59), the author most likely means to emphasize that

(A) using entrance into the middle class as a criterion for determining success may have only limited validity

(B) middle-class members of disadvantaged groups may not be financially successful

(C) for people from disadvantaged groups, entrance into the middle class may not be permanent

(D) even though people may have middle-class jobs and incomes, they may not be accepted as middle class by mainstream members of society

(E) people cannot be considered successful if they abandon the cultural background from which they came

23. According to the passage, which one of the following is likely to occur during the first three generations of an immigrant family?

(A) A family member will lose the ability to speak his or her native language, though the member may still be able to understand it.

(B) Children will refuse to eat food that they consider to be non-American.

(C) Members of younger generations will be uncomfortable socializing with first-generation immigrants.

(D) Children will not be able to understand the language that their parents speak with each other.

(E) A family member will marry someone from a different cultural background.

24. The passage most strongly suggests that the author would agree with which one of the following statements?

(A) Mainstream Americans should help members of disadvantaged groups learn mainstream cultural values.

(B) First-generation members of the middle class who come from a disadvantaged background may not be clear on how they want mainstream Americans to relate to them.

(C) People who speak a foreign language should teach their children to speak that language by using the language in the home.

(D) Middle-class Americans would benefit by reviving some cultural practices from their family background that have been lost over recent generations.

(E) The issue of members of disadvantaged groups entering the middle class may be troubling to mainstream Americans in several ways.

25. What is the author's primary purpose in referring to the fact that isolation kept cultural groups impoverished and uneducated, in lines 30–32?

(A) to establish a significant negative effect of isolation on a group

(B) to provide an example of a mechanism by which isolation is continually reinforced

(C) to provide a contrast with those members of the group who were able to move into the middle class

(D) to underscore the dangers facing middle-class members of a disadvantaged group who identify closely with their group

(E) to establish that mainstream Americans hold the primary responsibility for the low socioeconomic status of disadvantaged groups

26. Which one of the following, if true, would most strengthen the author's assertion that many second-generation children could not speak their parents' language, even though they could possibly understand it?

(A) Children of immigrants typically do not want to be seen as different by the children with whom they associate.

(B) Children of immigrants who attempt to speak their parents' native language usually speak with a pronounced American accent.

(C) If parents speak a foreign language between themselves but do not address their children in that language, the children will be unlikely to understand the language.

(D) If parents require their children to speak with the parents only in the parents' native language, the children will become fluent in the language.

(E) Children generally speak with their parents in the language that the children use with other children, rather than in the language that the parents speak to them.

27. Which one of the following is most strongly suggested by the passage?

(A) The experience of immigrants in the United States is significantly different from the experience of immigrants in other countries in the Western Hemisphere.

(B) Members of disadvantaged groups who want to enter the middle class will have to choose between mainstream cultural values and the values of the disadvantaged group.

(C) Members of disadvantaged groups who enter the middle class often use methods to do so that later trouble their consciences.

(D) Diet, languages spoken, and the people with whom one associates are important measures of the extent to which a person has become integrated into the mainstream culture.

(E) Even when people from a disadvantaged group become successful, the forces of discrimination tend to drive them back into their previous status.

STOP If you finish before the 35-minute time period is over, you may go back and check your answers.

ANSWER KEY

1.	D	**8.**	A	**15.**	B	**22.**	A
2.	B	**9.**	C	**16.**	B	**23.**	E
3.	E	**10.**	C	**17.**	D	**24.**	B
4.	B	**11.**	E	**18.**	E	**25.**	B
5.	A	**12.**	D	**19.**	A	**26.**	E
6.	C	**13.**	B	**20.**	C	**27.**	D
7.	B	**14.**	D	**21.**	C		

ANSWERS EXPLAINED

1. **(D)** This is a *main idea* question. Choice D is correct because the main point is that the two genres are radically different and that the difference has to do with their respective intentions.

    Choice A is incorrect because the point is not just that there are differences but that the differences are fundamental. Choice B is incorrect because, even though the statement is consistent with the passage, it is not the main point. Choice C is incorrect because it does not capture the radical difference between the genres. Choice E is incorrect for the same reason, as well as not necessarily being consistent with the passage.

2. **(B)** This is an *agree with a view* question in an EXCEPT format. Four of the answer choices are statements with which the author would agree. The author would agree with choice A because the passage specifically states that the line between the two genres is "fine," even though the fine line represents a "gulf." The author would agree with choice C because the passage cites an example of time travel in fantasy. Choice D is a close paraphrase of a sentence from the passage. The author would agree with choice E because the author describes fantasy as "not serious," even in instances of dark fantasy. The author would not agree with the remaining answer, choice B, because the difference between the two genres is defined by "intent" rather than "content." Choice B is the correct answer choice.

3. **(E)** This is an *implied detail* question. Choice E is correct because science fiction is concerned with describing and explaining technologies, as opposed to simply using magic to explain flying brooms.

    Choice A does not follow from the passage and does not address the witches' brooms. Choice A might imply that in another universe the laws of physics would be different, but to be correct, the answer must explain flight by brooms in scientific terms. Choice B is incorrect because it would more likely be an element of fantasy. Choice C is incorrect because the passage claims that the two genres are distinct and does not propose hybrids between them. Choice D is incorrect because it is an element of fantasy.

4. **(B)** This is a *helps to answer* question. The correct answer choice is a question that can be answered by information in the passage. Choice B is correct because the passage states that unicorns represent "the manifestation of the impossible."

    Choice A is incorrect because nothing in the passage discusses the technology of time travel. Choice C is incorrect. The passage poses the question in choice C as a rhetorical question, without answering it. Choice D is incorrect because the question is brought up but not answered. Choice E is incorrect because wormholes are not mentioned in the passage.

5. **(A)** This is a *use of a word/phrase* question. Choice A is correct because the author uses both words to refer to the difference between science fiction and fantasy in a paradoxical way. The difference is thin in one way and yet great in another way.

   Choice B is factually incorrect. Choice C cites a valid distinction between the two genres but does not match the use of the words *thin* and *gulf*. Choice D is incorrect because the author does not rebut the use of the word *thin*. The author purposely uses the word. Choice E is incorrect because "gulf" does not refer to the scope of fantasy but to the distance between science fiction and fantasy.

6. **(C)** This is an *extension/application* question. Choice C is correct because it does not include any explanations of how things work, accumulation of knowledge, or solving a problem, all characteristics of science fiction rather than fantasy.

   Choice A is incorrect because it explains how the time machine works. Choice B is incorrect because it explains the evolutionary mechanism that produced the fairies. Choice D is incorrect because it involves an accumulation of knowledge and solving a problem. Choice E is incorrect because it involves trying to find an explanation for the evolutionary change.

7. **(B)** This is an *identify a difference* question. Choice B is correct because the passage states that in fantasy it is not technology that wins the day but rather the power of the human spirit. The passage implies that in science fiction it *is* technology that wins the day.

   Choice A is incorrect because, in fantasy, technology can also be the force of good. Choice C is incorrect because the passage does not establish that technology must work by magic in fantasy. Choice D is incorrect because the passage does not support that fantasy is concerned with solving human problems. Choice E is incorrect because, even though according to the passage, fantasy takes us to worlds beyond imagination, it is not necessarily technology that accomplishes that.

8. **(A)** This is a *main conclusion* question. Choice A is the correct answer because the passage is concerned with describing a methodology for detecting radiation leaks. Choice B is incorrect because the Zone methodology is not controversial. Choice C is incorrect because the Zone methodology is not described as being an alternative. Choice D is incorrect because the passage is not primarily concerned with a discovery. Choice E is incorrect because the passage does not rebut a proposed solution.

9. **(C)** This is an *implied fact/inference* question. Choice C is correct because the sample from each sector is compared with the background radiation for the band as a whole. If a sector had a background radiation higher than the average for its band, the sample would appear to have high radioactivity.

   Choice A is incorrect because small variations in sample size are irrelevant. Choice B is incorrect because the procedure does not require that samples be taken from the same part of the sector each time. Choice D is irrelevant. Choice E is incorrect because a leak would result in an *accurate* reading.

10. **(C)** This is an *identify the structure* question. Choice C best matches the structure of the passage because the background information is followed by the assertion that there is a need to find alternate energy sources, and then the Zone process is described.

Choice A is incorrect because no theory is proposed. Choice B is incorrect because there is no technique that is criticized. Choice D is incorrect because there is no explanation analyzed or flaws revealed. Choice E is incorrect because there is no new theory introduced.

11. **(E)** This is a *tone* question that asks for the author's attitude and reasons for that attitude. Choice E is correct because the author believes that solar energy does not upset the ecology and does not produce waste products but is aware of the concerns of critics who question the author's beliefs.

Choice A is incorrect because it reverses the author's position and the position of critics. Choice B is incorrect because the author evaluates coal and petroleum as being equally negative. Choice C is incorrect because the author considers solar and wind as being equal. Choice D is incorrect because the author's preference for nuclear power is not based on it being more efficient than solar but on it avoiding possible drawbacks of solar.

12. **(D)** This is an *analogous situation* question, in which the similarity between two elements must be identified. Choice D is correct because the passage states that each of the two can lead to damage to the environment.

Choice A is incorrect because the passage does not state that nuclear fission is based on a renewable resource. Choice B is incorrect because the use of nuclear fission, although it can lead to environmental damage, does not lead to the denuding of the landscape. Choice C is incorrect because the passage does not mention that the burning of wood requires monitoring for toxins. Choice E is incorrect because only nuclear fuel is described as highly energy packed.

13. **(B)** This is a *function* question. Choice B is correct because the second paragraph introduces the possibility of renewable alternatives to dependence on petroleum but the use of renewable energy sources is discarded in the third paragraph.

Choice A is incorrect because the solution mentioned in the second paragraph is not defended in the third paragraph. Choice C is incorrect because the second paragraph does not do what is described in choice C. Choice D is incorrect because the second paragraph only mentions one alternative to nonrenewable resources, wood. Choice E is incorrect because, although the second paragraph does what is described in choice E, it is not the primary function of the paragraph.

14. **(D)** This is an *agree with a view* question in a CR passage. Choice D is correct because both passages acknowledge that there are advantages and disadvantages to men treating women as being the same versus being different.

Choice A is incorrect because the second passage describes women as speaking up about their opinions. Choice B is incorrect because the first passage states that many men are not aware that women have different viewpoints, and the second passages states that men are aware of it. Choice C is incorrect because, as an example of treating women the same as men, both passages see the pros and cons of this treatment as unclear. Choice E is incorrect because Passage A supports choice E but Passage B does not.

15. **(B)** This is an *identify the difference between CR passages* question. Choice B is correct because the focus in Passage A is on law and the focus in Passage B is on interpersonal relationships.

Choice A is incorrect because Passage A is not concerned with rules that men can follow but with the legal system, which applies to men and women. Choice C is incorrect because Passage B is not concerned with the law. Choice D is incorrect because the assertion that women's needs are different from those of men is not the primary focus of Passage A. The primary focus is that it is unclear whether women should be treated as equals or as different under the law. Choice E is incorrect because Passage A does not assert that the current system cannot become less male dominated. This is a misreading of the statement that in the past the American legal system could not help but develop in a male-dominated way.

16. **(B)** This is an *extension/application* question. Choice B is correct because the main problem is described as not knowing when to treat a woman in the same way as a man and when not to do so.

    Choices A and D are incorrect because the passage implies that men understand for the most part what is expected from them but do not know *when* to use the two different modes of communication. Choice C is incorrect because Passage B is not concerned with laws. Choice E is incorrect because violent communication is not an issue in the passage.

17. **(D)** This is a *disagree* question, asking for a point on which the two authors would be committed to opposite opinions. Choice D is correct because Passage A describes men as generally not being aware of differences between men's views and women's views, whereas Passage B describes men as being aware of the differences, even if they are not always able to respond to them.

    Choice A is incorrect because the author of Passage B is not committed to an opinion about the law. Choice B is incorrect because both authors would agree that men do not see women as women see themselves. Choice C is similarly incorrect because both authors would agree with the statement. Choice E is incorrect because neither author is committed to an opinion about this.

18. **(E)** This is a *relationship between the passages* question. Choice E correctly identifies the relationship. Choice A is incorrect because Passage B does not reject an argument from Passage A. Choice B is incorrect because Passage A does not present a hypothesis. Choice C is incorrect because the two passages do not draw the same conclusion. Choice D is incorrect because it is not true that Passage A argues only in general terms.

19. **(A)** This is an *in common* question that asks for an element that both passages have in common. Choice A is correct because Passage A discusses males within the legal system treating women as different and Passage B discusses men treating their wives differently than they would treat a male friend.

    Choice B is incorrect because the statement in B is found only in Passage A. Choice C is incorrect because this is not the disagreement among feminists. The disagreement is as to whether the law should deal with women in the same way as or differently from men. Choice D is incorrect because in Passage B the example of a man treating his wife differently from a man does not state that the man saw his wife as an inferior, even if she felt that she was being treated as inferior. Choice E is incorrect because it is stated only in Passage B.

20. **(C)** This is a *main point* question. Choice C is correct because it includes all of the elements of the passage.

Choice A is incorrect because, though consistent with the passage, it is not the main point. It does not include the difficulties of assimilation that are the emphasis of the passage. Choice B is incorrect because the passage does not say that successful members of such groups face personal discrimination.

Choice D is incorrect because, although consistent with the passage, it is not the main point. Choice E is incorrect because the passage does not state the information in choice E, and choice E is not the main point.

21. **(C)** This is an *assumption* question. It functions in the same way that a *necessary assumption* question does in LR. Choice C is correct because its negation —*It is not possible to understand a language without being able to speak it*—directly contradicts the statement that children of first-generation immigrants typically did not speak their parents' language, even though they may have understood it.

Choice A is incorrect because its negation—that the husband and wife had different native languages—does not conflict with the sentence in any way. Choice B is incorrect because the sentence does not require that the immigrants learned English well enough to earn a living, even though it is likely that some did.

Choice D is incorrect because the statement does not require that the children *purposely* distanced themselves. The distancing may have happened unconsciously. Choice E is incorrect because, even though the immigrants socialized with each other, the statement does not necessarily require that they lived near each other.

22. **(A)** This is a *use of a word/phrase* question. Choice A is correct because the author implies that entering the middle class is not the only measure of success.

Choice B is incorrect because the author is not implying that members of disadvantaged groups who have entered the middle class do not earn a middle-class income. Choice C is incorrect because the author does not imply that the middle-class members of disadvantaged groups are at risk of losing middle-class status.

Choice D is incorrect because the author does not imply that these middle-class people are not accepted by others. Choice E is incorrect because the author does not imply that these middle-class people cannot be considered successful unless they maintain their cultural roots.

23. **(E)** This is a *specific detail* question. It asks for information that is stated in the passage. Choice E is correct because the passage states that the children of the third generation most likely have one parent from a different cultural background.

Choice A is incorrect because the passage does not state that a native speaker of a language will lose the ability to speak that language. Choice B is incorrect because the passage only states that children will learn to eat American food, not that they will refuse other food.

Choice C is incorrect for a similar reason. The passage only suggests that younger generations will associate more with mainstream Americans, not that they will shun immigrants. Choice D is incorrect because the passage only states that children of the first-generation immigrants will not be able to *speak* their parents' language. By the third generation, the parents are speaking English.

24. **(B)** This is an *agree with a view* question. Choice B is correct because the author emphasizes the ambiguity involved in taking on a middle-class identity along with an identity as a member of one's ethnic group.

Choice A is incorrect because the author acknowledges that adopting mainstream values has pros and cons. Choice C is incorrect because the author does not reveal a personal opinion on this. Choices D and E are incorrect because there is no information in the passage to defend that the author believes this.

25. **(B)** This is a *function* question. Choice B is correct because the cited fact is followed by the statement that poverty and lack of education constitute a cycle by reinforcing the prejudices of mainstream Americans. Answer choices A, C, D, and E fail to identify this function.

26. **(E)** This is a *strengthen* question, which is rare in RC but functions in the same way as a *strengthen* question in LR. Choice E is correct because, if true, it explains why the children would not learn to speak their parents' language, even if they could understand it.

Choice A is incorrect because how the children speak with their peers does not explain why they would not be able to speak with their parents in the parents' language. Choice B is incorrect because it leaves open the possibility that the children could speak their parents' language well but with an accent.

Choice C is incorrect because the author's assertion is that the children often *can* understand the language. Choice D is incorrect because it gives a condition that would lead to the children speaking the language but does not explain why the children did not speak it. It does not follow from choice D that if the parents do *not* require the children to speak the language, that the children will *not* become fluent.

27. **(D)** This is an *implied fact/inference* question. Choice D can be correctly inferred because the passage states that many immigrant families are integrated into mainstream culture by the second generation and then cites diet, languages spoken, and people with whom one associates as the criteria for concluding that integration has occurred.

Choice A is incorrect because in the first sentence, the passage compares the populations in the United States to populations in other countries *outside* of the Western Hemisphere. Choice B is incorrect because the passage states that such people will blend their cultural experiences.

Choice C is incorrect because it distorts information from the passage. The passage states that such people may be troubled by the fact that others in their group are still in need, *not* because of what the individual did to achieve middle-class status. Choice E is incorrect because there is nothing in the passage to support it.

Analytical Reasoning

4

- → **INTRODUCTION TO ANALYTICAL REASONING**
- → **TIMING STRATEGY**
- → **ORGANIZING THE SETUP**
- → **UNDERSTANDING THE QUESTION TYPES**
- → **HOW TO SOLVE QUESTIONS—A SYSTEMATIC APPROACH**
- → **SAMPLE GAMES WITH EXPLANATIONS**
- → **A PRACTICE GAME WITH EXPLANATIONS**

This chapter teaches you the skills that you need to quickly and accurately answer Analytical Reasoning (AR) questions. In the chapter you will find a number of lists of detailed AR patterns. Use these lists as resources that you can refer back to as you practice. You do not need to memorize the lists. Glance at them now. As you work through actual problems and refer to the lists, the patterns will become increasingly familiar and useful for you.

INTRODUCTION TO ANALYTICAL REASONING

The AR section is one of the four scored sections (1 RC, 2 LR, 1 AR) on the LSAT. If there are two AR sections on your test, one of them will be unscored. Each AR section consists of four **games**, each of which contains a **setup**, including **conditions**, followed by five to seven questions, with twenty-three questions per AR section. There have been sections with twenty-two or twenty-four questions on older tests.

Many people initially find the AR to be intimidating. In actuality, the AR is very learnable. Once you have mastered the skills in this chapter, you will have clear, logical tools for systematically solving the questions.

> ### WHICH SECTION OF THE LSAT IS UNSCORED?
>
> On the test day you will have five sections—one scored RC, two scored LR, one scored AR, and one unscored section that could be RC, LR, or AR. There is no way to predict which section is unscored. Do your best on all sections.

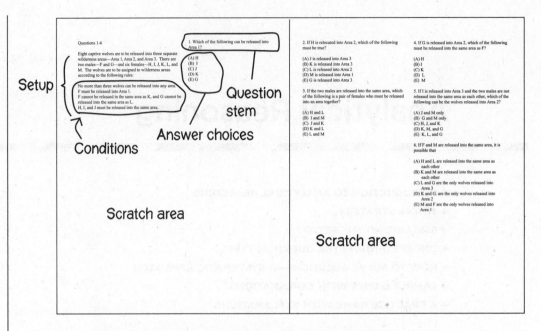

Figure 4.1. Anatomy of an AR game, showing the setup, conditions, questions, question stems, answer choices, and scratch area

The Three Necessary Skill Sets for Analytical Reasoning

The skill sets that you need to solve a game accurately and quickly are:

1. Organizing the Setup
2. Understanding the Question Types
3. Using a Systematic Problem-Solving Approach

Almost all errors that test takers make on the AR are the result of not having the right tools for one or more of the above skill sets. This chapter begins by reviewing general timing strategy and showing how to apply it to the AR.

TIMING STRATEGY

As on all sections of the LSAT, a strong timing strategy allows you to (1) gain points by working efficiently, (2) avoid errors caused by working too quickly or anxiously, and (3) reduce anxiety.

Adapting Timing Strategy to the Analytical Reasoning Section

General timing strategy is described in Chapter 1, "General Strategies." Review it now to refresh your memory. How should you adapt this strategy to the AR?

Rank the Games

As in RC, there are four sets (called games in AR). As soon as timing starts for a section, quickly glance at each of the four games and rank them in order of difficulty. There is a general tendency for the first game to be easiest and the last game to be hardest but because there are exceptions, you have to evaluate the games for yourself. Remember:

1. Do not try to read the setup or the questions. Judge the game at a glance.
2. The first game is often easy but do not fall into the trap of assuming that it is.

RANK THE GAMES

Always rank the difficulty of the games before you start a timed section. If you don't, you'll find yourself working on hard games and leaving easy ones undone.

3. Look for the complexity of the variables. A game with multiple sets of players in complex relationships is harder than a game with one set of players.

4. Take hints from the answer choices. Complex-looking answers may look intimidating but may indicate what the diagram should look like.

5. If two games appear equally difficult, choose the one with the most questions. Do not, however, choose a harder game just because it has more questions.

Ranking the order of the games is an approximation. It would take too much time to determine exactly which games are the most complex. By quickly ranking the games, you avoid working on the hardest ones.

Working Each Game

Once you have ranked the games, start with the easiest. Do not move on to the next game until you have worked *every* question on the current game. Even on an easy game, there will be some questions that are difficult.

JUMPING FROM GAME TO GAME

Trying to "cherry-pick" easy questions by jumping from game to game is not a good strategy. Once you start a game, stick with it!

Test takers sometimes wonder if they should skip a harder question in their current game and then use their time to answer an easier question in another game. The problem with such a strategy is that it may well force you to set up a game that you would not otherwise have worked and that will be harder than the current game.

If a particular question is tough, work on other questions in the current game first. These questions may give you enough insight into the game for you to be able to then answer the more difficult question. You can work on the easiest questions first and then tackle harder ones. Generally, a question that asks you which of five answer choices does not break rules is easy. Questions that give you new information are easier to solve than questions that do not.

HOW MUCH TIME SHOULD YOU SPEND ON EACH QUESTION?

This is the most important element of your timing strategy. Review the instruction on timing strategy in Chapter 1. Most test takers will get the most points by allowing themselves three, four, or sometimes five minutes on a difficult question. You may only need to do this for a few questions on a section, but doing so often makes the difference between getting a few more questions right or not.

Test takers who spend only a minute or two on a question typically leave a string of wrong answers in their wake. Certain questions simply cannot be solved in less than two, three, or even four minutes. If you always quit after one or two minutes, you will not get the more difficult questions right. On the other hand, it is not a good idea to spend more than five minutes on any one question.

To implement a successful timing strategy, you have to know how much time you have spent on a question. At the start of each question, set your watch to noon. If you start to feel that a question is taking a lot of time, look at your watch to see how much time you have spent. Do not try to keep track of time mentally. Even if you can, it prevents you from giving your full attention to the problems.

HOW MANY GAMES SHOULD YOU WORK ON?

The fatal flaw for most test takers is that they attempt to answer too many questions. Who comes out ahead—the person who works on twenty-four questions and gets twelve right, or the person who works on fourteen questions and gets all of them right (plus 2 points for the questions they guess on)? Actually, once you have developed a strong timing strategy, the test itself will tell you how far you can get. Let's look now at what to do once you have finished the easiest game.

After the easiest game, work on the next easiest game. If you are still having difficulty with the AR section, you may run out of time during the second game. If you are already performing strongly on the games, you will be able to get to a third and possibly a fourth game. When you get to the last game on which you will have time to work, do the easiest questions first. As

LET THE TEST TELL YOU HOW MUCH TO WORK ON

Don't try to decide in advance exactly how many questions you will do. Setting a specific goal causes you to rush and miss points. Choose the next easiest question and give it the time that it needs.

time runs out, be on guard against the urge to complete all the questions in the current game. Many people fall into this trap and attempt to cram in three or four questions in the last minutes. Usually they answer these questions incorrectly. Instead, pick the next easiest question in the game and give it the full time that it needs for you to be confident in your answer. There are no bonus points for completing a game!

If you (1) choose what to work on next and (2) give each question the time it needs, the test will show you how far you can get. If you are running low on time and try to go faster to answer additional questions, you risk answering many questions incorrectly. Why does this happen? You may have an expectation of how many questions you should answer. When you see that you are not going to get to that many in the remaining time, what happens? Untrained test takers get anxious and begin to rush. Trained test takers drop the expectation and stick with the reality. By working well on a few more questions, they maximize their score.

As you practice, you will get a more realistic sense of how many questions you can do. Of course, how many questions you answer in any particular section depends on many factors. Even if you work successfully on just two games, you can still achieve at least an average or above-average score.

When your timing is perfect, you get nearly every question that you work on right. Even so, you might find that you still are not at the score you would like. This means that you need to learn and master the strategies in this chapter. If you try to boost your score just by going faster, you will most likely lose points.

TIMING FOR SUPERIOR TEST TAKERS

If you are aiming for a near perfect score, note that we do not suggest that you *should* cut questions, only that, in some cases, you can get extra points by cutting some questions.

Consider a superior test taker who attempts all 23 questions, gets 20 correct, and spent an average of 90 seconds on each of the 3 incorrect questions. What would happen if the test taker cut 2 of those 3 questions and used the additional 3 minutes to get one more question correct? The total number correct would be 21, up one point from 20. In addition, there is approximately a 40 percent chance that one of the two answers that were guessed will be correct.

The suggestion to cut questions if necessary is not based on settling for an average score. On the contrary, it is an additional tool that the superior test taker can use to develop the absolutely most efficient timing strategy possible.

Guessing at the End

At the monitor's five-minute warning, put answers down for the questions you are not going to get to. Do not spend time looking at the questions. Simply fill in a bubble for each unanswered question randomly. Statistically there is no letter that is significantly more likely to be correct.

After filling in the remaining bubbles, go back to a question and continue to work on it until time is called. If you can eliminate even one answer choice, you will be a bit closer to another correct answer.

Summary of Timing Strategy for AR

1. Rank the difficulty of the games.
2. Work on the easiest game. Do all the questions in it before moving on. Take three to five minutes per question if necessary. Do not exceed five minutes per question. Use your watch to keep track of time on each question. There is no need to keep track of how much time you spend setting up the game or of how much time you spend on the entire game.
3. If time, go to the second easiest game. If time is running low, apply Step 6.
4. If time, go to the third easiest game. If time is running low, apply Step 6.
5. If there is time, go to the final game. If time is running low, apply Step 6.
6. If you start a game that there is not enough time to finish, choose the easiest questions. Do not rush to complete the game.
7. When the monitor gives a five-minute warning, fill in bubbles for questions that you have not already answered.
8. Continue working on a question until time is called.

ORGANIZING THE SETUP

The first and most important step in AR is to accurately organize the information in the **setup**. The setup consists of a paragraph, including a description of the game and some **conditions** that apply to the game, followed by a list of additional conditions. Conditions are **rules** that govern how the **elements** of the game can and cannot interact with each other. Elements consist of **players** and **fixtures**. The players, often people, are assigned to certain fixed positions (the fixtures).

Consider a game in which Freddie, Greta, Irene, Jason, and Kerry are each to perform during five specific time slots in a singing competition. The five people are the players. The five specific time slots are the fixtures. The sentence "Players are assigned to fixtures" can help you determine who are the players and what are the fixtures in a game. In the game above, "people are assigned to time slots." Players can be individual people, groupings of people, events, or objects, such as colors, flowers, fruit, or trees.

VOCABULARY FOR ANALYTICAL REASONING GAMES

Setup: the paragraph and following conditions that establish how the game works

Conditions (rules): the rules that determine how the elements relate to each other

Restrictions: a synonym for conditions that refers to the fact that conditions restrict the options that a player has

Elements: the players and fixtures of the game

Players: the elements that are assigned to fixed positions

Fixtures: the fixed positions to which players are assigned

Assignment: an attempted arrangement of players in the fixed positions. An assignment may be **valid**—it does not break rules—or it may be **invalid**—it breaks at least one rule

Why is organizing the setup so important? Many people rush through the setup so they can get on to answering questions. This is a common but disastrous pattern. If you have not accurately understood the setup and conditions, you will make mistakes, no matter how hard you work on the questions. If you have misunderstood even one of the conditions, you may well get several questions wrong or more! On the other hand, if you accurately understand the setup and conditions, create an effective diagram, and apply a systematic approach to solving questions, you can correctly answer every question on which you work.

STEP BY STEP APPROACH FOR ORGANIZING THE SETUP

1. Read the setup.
2. Identify the players and the fixtures. Use the template "(blank) is assigned to (blank)." The first blank represents players. The second blank represents fixtures.
3. Create the diagram. The diagram represents the fixtures. Create a supplemental diagram if needed.
4. List the players.
5. Going in order, identify each condition, make sure you understand it, and then rewrite it in an abbreviated form.
6. Briefly consider the relationships between conditions. For example, which conditions, if combined, would result in a new condition? Which elements have the most restrictions? Which elements have no restrictions?
7. Find any information that can be placed directly into the diagram.

The Setup and Conditions

Consider that the proctor has just announced, "You may now turn to the next section and begin." You have taken a deep breath to avoid rushing and to focus your mind. You have ranked the four games in order of difficulty. You have turned to the easiest game. Now apply the steps given in the previous chart.

Read through the setup so that you can identify the elements and can determine which elements are the players and which are the fixtures. Determining the players and fixtures helps you to create the diagram.

Using the blank margins of your test booklet—your **work space**—list the players. Use only the initial letter of each player in order to save space. There is never more than one player with the same initial letter. Use the separate list of players as a checklist when solving a question.

USING THE MARGINS OF YOUR TEST BOOKLET

The AR section requires more "scratch paper" space than the other sections of the LSAT. Because there is no scratch paper available, use the margins of your test booklet. This work space is limited. Practice condensing your scratch work. The diagramming strategies taught in this chapter are designed to use space efficiently. Write small but neatly. Do not take time to erase your scratch work unless you need that space. Current LSATs spread each game across two pages. Earlier LSATs put each game on one page.

Next consider each condition, in the order it is given in the setup. Look first for conditions that are given in the setup paragraph. When you are sure you understand a condition, summarize it. Write it in your work space, using symbols and abbreviations. Then do the same for the next condition. In theory, you could simply refer to the conditions on the test page, rather than repeating them in your work space. However, rewriting the conditions has two important advantages. First, it forces you to understand the condition clearly. Second, having the conditions listed in a concise form allows you to work with them more easily.

Once you have summarized all of the conditions, look for obvious relationships among conditions. For example, consider the two conditions:

> *If Kerry sings in the third time slot, Irene sings in the fifth time slot.*

And

> *If Freddie sings in the first time slot, Kerry sings in the third time slot.*

These conditions are related. Both conditions include Kerry. Combine these to derive a third condition:

> *If Freddie sings in the first time slot, Irene sings in the fifth time slot.*

If you do not spot any relationships among conditions at first glance, do not waste time looking more deeply. A game has many intricate relationships. These relationships will become apparent as you work the game. It is usually not productive to try to work out all of the relationships in advance.

Identify which players have the most restrictions. In the previous example, Kerry has more restrictions than Freddie or Irene. Also note which players have no restrictions. A player with many restrictions is more likely to create rule violations, whereas a player with no restrictions is less likely to do so. Although there are frequent exceptions to the above generalization, a good strategy is to first test players with the most restrictions when looking for rule violations.

The final step in organizing the setup is to identify any information that can go directly into the diagram. For example, if Greta must always sing in the second slot, you can put Greta into the diagram under 2 as permanent information.

Below is a diagram of a setup, showing the fixtures (1–7) across the top, some information about the game entered above the fixtures, the list of players on the left (F, I, M), and the list of rules, shown underneath the list of players. For the moment, do not be concerned about what the summaries of the rules mean.

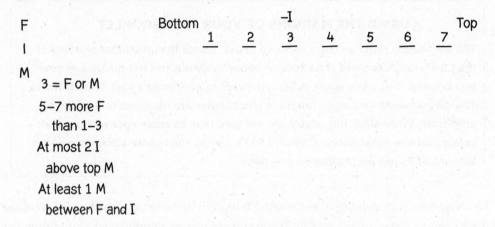

Figure 4.2. Example of the setup for a game

SYMBOLS FOR SUMMARIZING CONDITIONS

The symbols that you use to summarize the conditions should be concise and yet unambiguous. You will find the symbols presented in this chapter to be helpful for most conditions. You can also modify these symbols or create your own. If you find that you have misinterpreted your notation, refine your system. There are hundreds of variations on how conditions are expressed. These variations often require you to be creative with your symbols. This chapter goes over practice questions that will help you learn some common summarizing tools. The explanations for the sample section test at the end of this chapter and for the practice tests in this book will help you refine your set of symbols. The symbols for summarizing if/then conditions are rather standard.

TYPES OF CONDITIONS

Conditions define the relationships among players. For most games the conditions fall into one of the following categories:

MAIN CATEGORIES OF CONDITIONS

1. **Defining quantity.** Specifies quantities.

   Freda has at least one apple but not more than three apples.

   $$F = 1\text{--}3$$

   Roster contains exactly one document.

   $$R = ex\ 1$$

   There are at most seven squirrels.

   $$\text{at most } 7\ S \quad \text{or} \quad S = 0\text{--}7$$

   Defining quantity constitutes about 5 percent of all AR conditions.

2. **Comparing quantity.** Indicates quantities by comparison.

   Joggers has one more member than Hikers.

   $$J = H + 1 \quad \text{or} \quad J = 1 \text{ more than } H$$

   Group B has more members than group A.

   $$B > A \quad \text{or} \quad B \text{ more than } A$$

   Comparing quantity constitutes about 3 percent of conditions.

3. **Defining relative position in a sequence.** Indicates where a player fits into a sequence by comparing the player with another player.

   <u>**Sanders is immediately below Tanaka.**</u>

   $$S\ T$$

   Michael is below Nora but above Quincy.

   $$Q - M - N$$

   For the two diagrams above, "below" is defined as to the left.

   <u>**Randy is older than Teresa.**</u>

   $$R - T$$

   "Older" is defined as to the left.

   Defining relative position constitutes 40 percent of conditions. This type of condition predominates in **sequence** games (described later in this chapter).

4. **Assigning characteristics to a player.** Directly specifies characteristics that a certain player must have.

   Jordan has a computer.

   $$J = C \quad \text{or} \quad J = comp$$

   Shawn plays solitaire.

   $$S = sol$$

   Wozniak orders the chocolate cheese cake.

   $$W = cake$$

   Assigning characteristics constitutes 30 percent of conditions.

5. Defining two or more alternate options (either/or). One of two conditions must be true.

Either Francine has worked at Tetwiler's longer than Ian has or Susan has worked at Tetwiler's longer than Thomas has.

$$\text{Either} \quad F - I$$
$$\text{or} \quad S - T$$

"Longer" is defined here as to the left.

Either/or conditions constitute 6 percent of conditions. Either/or questions can contain any of the above condition types. They do not exclude the possibility that both statements could be true.

6. Defining two possible options but both cannot be true (either/or but not both). One of two statements must be true but they cannot both be true.

Either Tanaka goes to the meeting on Thursday or Garcia goes to the meeting on Friday, but not both.

$$\text{Either} \quad T = \text{Tues}$$
$$\text{or} \quad G = \text{Fri}$$
$$\text{bnb}$$

(Note the use of the abbreviation "bnb" for "but not both.")

Either/or but not both conditions constitute 5 percent of conditions. This is a variation on regular either/or conditions that expressly prohibits both conditions from being true.

7. If/then condition. The occurrence or absence of one event determines the occurrence or absence of another event, for example, *If Roger goes to the store, Sandra does not go to the store.*

If/then conditions constitute 25 percent of all conditions. If/then conditions are broken down into subtypes below. If/then statements may include components from the above condition types.

For each of the types of conditions described above, you will see many variations on how the condition is worded. Familiarize yourself with these variations. When you work with a condition in a practice test, analyze the wording to be sure you understand the condition. Use the following list of wordings as a reference. You do not need to memorize the variations. Glance through them now to become familiar with them and come back to the list as you are working on practice questions.

EXAMPLES OF WORDING VARIATIONS FOR THE SIX PRINCIPAL CONDITION TYPES (EXCLUDING IF/THEN CONDITIONS)

1. **Defining quantity.**

   Exactly three flowers are included.

   No more than four flowers are included.

   Prizes are given in all five categories.

   At least one adult must be selected.

   At least one math teacher, one science teacher, and one history teacher must be selected.

   Exactly one runner and one tennis player participate each day.

   Exactly two ingredients are added after the milk is added.

   In each race, at least one but not more than two members of the Hares participates.

   Each exhibit includes exactly three species of dogs.

2. **Comparing quantity.**

   There are more geraniums than petunias.

   The first row contains more viewers than the second row.

   The garden plot that Frank weeds on Tuesday must be the garden plot that Gennifer weeds on Friday.

   Team 1 and Team 3 must have exactly one runner in common.

3. **Defining relative position in a sequence.**

   Poker must take place before Hopscotch.

   Poker takes place at some time before Hopscotch but after Mahjong.

   Both Poker and Hopscotch take place after Mahjong takes place.

   The team that includes Jacobs must participate before the team that includes Nichols.

   The team that includes Jacobs cannot participate after any team that includes Nichols.

   A garden plot is weeded by both Frank and Karina exactly one time.

   H is faster than L.

   H is faster than each of K and M.

   Mario is in either the first or second race.

   Either Gerald or Lenora is the fourth fastest.

   The dental office is on a floor that is neither immediately above nor immediately below the floor on which the veterinary office is located.

   The fiction bookshelf is immediately below the history bookshelf.

   The fiction bookshelf is above the languages bookshelf but below the biography bookshelf.

   Inez cannot participate in two races in a row.

   If Inez participates in a race earlier than Javier, Inez participates in a race immediately before the race in which Javier participates.

   Neither Javier nor Mach races last.

   At least one team debates after the team from Hudsonville.

   There is a vase with a red rose that is on a lower shelf than any vase that contains a yellow rose.

There is a vase with a pink rose that is on a shelf immediately below a vase with a white rose.

At least two runners must participate between the races in which Inez and Javier participate.

Walter must perform in a time slot some time after the time slot in which Valeria performs.

All children must participate before any adult participates.

Any adult from Hudsonville participates before the adult from Jacksonville.

The first day that Inez participates is some day before the first day on which Javier participates.

There is at least one day on which both Rashanna and Tran participate.

Exactly one race separates the races in which Greg and Fiona participate.

4. **Assigning characteristics to a player.**

Vase 3 contains red roses.

The last performance includes only one performer.

Fernandez is a catcher.

Hanako cannot be a pitcher.

The first vase does not contain a geranium.

The first performance and the last performance are given by the same person.

Of the first four performances, exactly one is given by Ling.

Xena participates in the third performance.

The person who performed in the third time slot did not receive a scholarship.

Tanaka is not on a team that placed in the finals.

Tanaka, Vinetti, and Woida are the only players who can participate on the third team.

Singing must be assigned to slots 2, 4, 5, or 6.

R must be placed in the same drawer as N.

The performers assigned to the second and fourth time slots cannot be either Greg, Jamie, or Kahn.

Exactly one vase contains both a red and a yellow rose.

Tanaka participates in the first race in which Woida participates.

Running must take up an entire day by itself.

The petunia is pink and is included.

5. **Defining two or more alternate options (either/or).**

Fernandez is on the same team as either Grosz or Hamato.

Either T or V is the second fastest.

Neither Tan nor Ulibarri performs in the fifth time slot.

Either Fernandez or Gilliam must be the catcher on the team for which Jackson is the pitcher.

Either the saw is more expensive than both the router and the posthole digger or both the router and the posthole digger are more expensive than the saw.

Tanaka performs either immediately before or immediately after Ulibarri.

6. **Defining two possible options but both cannot be true (either/or but not both).**

Either Fernandez or Grosz, but not both, is a catcher.

Tanaka performs either some time before Ulibarri or sometime after Valeria, but not both.

Either R is heavier than M, or R is heavier than S, but not both.

Either Tanaka and Ulibarri perform consecutively or Tanaka and Valeria perform consecutively, but not both.

Each team member is either an outfielder or a pitcher, but not both.

He must sign up for either rhetoric or logic but cannot sign up for both.

In addition to the above six principal condition types, the seventh—if/then statements—defines more complex relationships. The powerful strategies for understanding and manipulating if/then statements are described in depth in Chapter 2, "Logical Reasoning" (LR). If/then statements are critical in AR. A quarter of the questions in AR involve if/then logic. The above condition types are often combined with if/then logic. Review the if/then strategies in Chapter 2 now.

If/Then Conditions in Analytical Reasoning

Below are common variations of if/then conditions that you will find in AR. Note that the wording of an if/then can often be confusing. Apply the rules given in Chapter 2 for converting an if/then relationship into its standard form. Use the information listed below as a resource. It is not necessary to memorize it. Glance through it now. As you work with if/then statements on practice questions, come back to this list to help you sort out the various types of if/thens.

IF/THEN CONDITIONS

If/then conditions are particularly important in AR. Be sure you know how to identify which is the determining factor and which the result. Be sure you can identify the contrapositive and can determine which conditions are triggers and which are not triggers. If/then conditions are described fully in Chapter 2.

TEN PRINCIPAL TYPES OF IF/THEN CONDITIONS

Percentages are out of the total number of if/then conditions and are approximate. If/then conditions account for about 25 percent of all conditions.

1. **If A → B** If A occurs, then B must occur.

   Example: If Williams attends the conference, Young also attends the conference. (If W → Y)

   This is NOT the same as saying that Williams and Young must go together. If Williams does not attend the conference, Young can still go. Frequency: Accounts for 15 percent of AR if/then conditions

2. **AB** A and B must appear together.

   Example: Williams attends the same conference that Young attends. (WY or W = Y) Frequency: Accounts for ~13 percent of if/then conditions

3. **Not AB (or –AB)** A and B cannot appear together.

   Example: Williams does not attend any conference that Young attends. (–WY or not WY or W ≠ Y) Frequency: ~13 percent

4. If A → not B (or –B) If *A* occurs, then *B* does not occur.

Example: If Williams attends the conference, Young does not attend the conference. (If W → –Y or not Y)

This IS the same as saying that Williams and Young cannot be at the conference together. However, it is NOT the same as saying that one or the other must go. It is possible for both not to go. Frequency: ~13 percent

5. If not A (or –A) → B If *A* does not occur, then *B* must occur.

Example: If Williams does not attend the conference, then Young attends. (If –W → Y)

This is NOT the same as saying that they cannot both attend. If Williams does attend, Young can still attend. Frequency: ~7 percent

6. If A → A = x If *A* occurs, then *A* occurs with a certain characteristic (*x*).

Example: If Williams attends the conference, then Williams attends on Saturday. (If W → W = Sat)

Williams may or may not attend but if Williams attends at all, it must be on Saturday. In this type of rule, both sides of the if/then have to do with the same person. Frequency: ~5 percent

7. If not A (or –A) → not B (or –B) If *A* does not occur, then *B* does not occur.

Example: If Williams does not attend the conference, then Young does not attend. (If –W → –Y)

If Williams does attend, Young may or may not attend. Frequency: ~2 percent

8. If A = x → either y or z If *A* occurs with a certain characteristic (*x*), then one of two other characteristics (*y* and *z*) must occur.

Example: If Williams attends the conference on Thursday, then Williams must be either the first or second presenter. (If W = Th, then W = 1 or 2)

This rare type of rule could also specify only one additional characteristic on the right side. This differs slightly from the previous type in that the previous type only required that Williams be "in" the game, whereas this type requires that Williams meet a specific condition (in the game on Thursday). Frequency: ~2 percent

9. If A = x → B = y If *A* occurs with a certain characteristic (*x*), then *B* occurs with a different characteristic (*y*).

Example: If Williams attends the conference on Thursday, then Young attends the conference on Saturday. (If W = Th → Y = Sat) Frequency: 26 percent

10. If A → B and If not A (or –A) → not B (or –B) *A* occurs if and only if *B* occurs.

Example: Young attends the conference if, and only if, Williams attends the conference.

The phrasing "if and only if" encompasses two different conditions. Young goes if Williams goes (if Williams goes, then Young must go) and Young goes only if Williams goes (if Williams does not go, then Young does not go.) Frequency: 2 percent

The most common variations in wording for if/then statements are shown in the following box. Glance through these now and come back to this list as a resource when you are working on practice questions.

EXAMPLES OF WORDING VARIATIONS FOR IF/THEN CONDITIONS

1. If A → B

If G is selected, then H must be selected.

Any vase that contains freesias also contains gaillardias.

If any of the catchers is chosen to attend the award ceremony, then the oldest pitcher must also be chosen to attend.

If either Franciscus or Jamison is chosen, both must be chosen.

He must take rhetoric if he takes journalism.

2. AB

Books by Twain must be on the same shelf as books by Vonnegut.

Garza attends the first lecture that Hamato attends.

Klein and O'Harrell will have the same major.

3. Not AB (or –AB)

No garden is weeded by both Thomas and Sylvia together.

Perkins and Washburn do not enroll in the same major as each other.

Greg and Janique are not on the same debate team.

Freddie does not sample the same food as Hannah; nor does Gerald sample the same food as Jong.

Greer cannot be assigned to the same committee as Montoya.

Sophia does not attend any of the three conferences that Uli attends.

4. If A → not B (–B)

If Tanaka performs, then Ulibarri does not.

If Tanaka performs, then neither Ulibarri nor Valeria can perform.

Ulibarri performs only if Tanaka does not.

He cannot take rhetoric if he takes debate.

If he takes debate, then he can take neither rhetoric nor journalism.

5. If not A (or –A) → B

If Tanaka does not perform, then Ulibarri does.

If a vase does not contain a rose, then that vase contains a geranium.

He must take rhetoric if he does not take journalism.

6. If not A (or –A) → not B (or –B)

If Tanaka does not perform, then Ulibarri also does not perform.

A rose is included in the arrangement only if it is red.

7. If A → A = x

If Koning participates, then Koning participates on Team 3.

If both Fernandez and Grosz participate, then at least one of them is a catcher.

8. If A = x → either y or z

If Fernandez is a catcher, he must play either Saturday or Sunday.

If a vase contains a red rose, that vase contains neither a red geranium nor a yellow freesia.

9. If A = x → B = y

If Francine orders the lobster, then Garrett orders the salmon.

If Francine does not order lobster, then Hanson orders goose.

If Fernandez is catcher in the third game, then Grosz is pitcher in the fourth game; otherwise Grosz is catcher in the fourth game.

If Johnson is third oldest, then Johnson is older than each of Kimball and Lovato.

If Poindexter majors in philosophy, then Valentino also majors in philosophy.

If Tanaka performs earlier than Ulibarri, then Sonntag performs earlier than Reynolds.

If Tanaka does not perform, then Ulibarri performs in the third time slot.

10. If A → B AND If not A (or –A) → not B (or –B)

(This type has appeared only in its basic form.)

Young attends the conference if, and only if, Williams attends the conference.

Standard form. As you learned in Chapter 2, the standard form of an if/then statement places the condition that happens first (the condition that is the determining factor) on the left side of the equation and the condition that happens second (the result) on the right side. Try the exercises below. In each exercise, rewrite each sentence in the standard form.

Practice Exercise 1

Example: *John does not go to the party if Frances goes.*

If Frances, then –John (or even more abbreviated: If F → –J)

Explanations follow each set of practice exercises.

1. If office R has a printer, it has neither a fax nor a copier.

2. If office R has a fax, then it also has a printer.

3. Either Ramon or Li must attend the party that Pearl attends.

4. Pearl must attend the same party that Li attends.

5. If Sandra attends the first meeting, then Liam attends the meeting immediately after the meeting that Sandra attends.

6. If Morgan does not perform, then Niles performs in the third time slot.

Answers:

1. If office R has a printer, it has neither a fax nor a copier.
   The logic: If *A*, then neither *B* nor *C*.
   The standard form: Write this as two separate statements. If R = printer, then –fax. If R = printer, then –copier.

2. If office R has a fax, then it also has a printer.
   The logic: If *A*, then *B*.
   This is already in standard form.

3. Either Ramon or Li must attend the party that Pearl attends.

The logic: If *A*, then either *B* or *C*.

The standard form: The determining factor is the presence of Pearl. If P, then R or L. Note that this cannot be broken into two statements. The existence of Pearl at the party predicts that one or the other of Ramon or Li must attend. Because the statement does not say *but not both,* there is the possibility that both may attend.

4. Pearl must attend the same party that Li attends.

The logic: If *A*, then *B*.

The standard form: Li is the determining factor. If Li, then Pearl.

5. If Sandra attends the first meeting, then Liam attends the meeting immediately after the meeting that Sandra attends.

The logic: If $A = 1$, then $B = 2$.

The statement is already in standard form. It is a variation on If *A*, then *B*.

6. If Morgan does not perform, then Niles performs in the third time slot.

The logic: If $-A$, then $B = x$.

It is in standard form but could be simplified as If –Morgan, then Niles = 3.

Practice Exercise 2

1. Ursula must order the ice cream if she does not order the lasagna.

2. Ursula cannot order cheesecake if she orders spanakopita.

3. Ursula must order flan if she orders enchiladas.

4. If Brad operates on Thursday, then neither Carmen nor Dana operates on Friday.

5. Brad operates on Thursday only if Andrew operates on Monday.

6. Carmen sees patients on Wednesday only if Dana does not.

Answers:

1. Ursula must order the ice cream if she does not order the lasagna.

The logic: If $-A$, then *B*.

The standard form: The determining factor is the absence of lasagna. If –lasagna, then ice cream.

2. Ursula cannot order cheesecake if she orders spanakopita.

The logic: If *A*, then $-B$.

The standard form: If spanakopita, then –cheesecake.

3. Ursula must order flan if she orders enchiladas.

The logic: If *A*, then *B*.

The standard form: If enchiladas, then flan.

4. If Brad operates on Thursday, then neither Carmen nor Dana operates on Friday.

The logic: If $A = x$, then $-B = y$ and $-C = y$.

The standard form: Write as two statements. If Brad = Th, then –(Carmen = Friday). If Brad = Th, then –(Dana = Friday).

5. Brad operates on Thursday only if Andrew operates on Monday.

The logic: If –*A*, then –*B*.

The standard form: The determining factor is the absence of Andrew operating on Monday. This is a typical example of "only if." If –(Andrew = Mon), then –(Brad = Th).

6. Carmen sees patients on Wednesday only if Dana does not.

The logic: If *A*, then –*B*.

The standard form: This is an "only if" statement, as in number 5. However, in this case the "if" statement contains a negative "only if Dana does not." It is the absence of "only if Dana does not see patients." What is the absence of Dana NOT seeing patients? It is "Dana sees patients." If Dana sees patients, then –(Carmen sees patients).

Practice Exercise 3

1. If both Andrew and Dana see patients on Friday, then at least one of them operates on Saturday.

2. Petunias are planted in the front garden if, and only if, the ash tree is removed.

3. No type of flower is planted in both the front and side gardens.

4. Any garden that contains monkshood also contains lobelia.

5. If dahlias are planted in the rear garden, then lobelia is planted in the side garden. Otherwise, lobelia is planted in the front garden.

6. The side garden contains either petunias or monkshood, but not both.

Answers:

1. If both Andrew and Dana see patients on Friday, then at least one of them operates on Saturday.

The logic: If *A* and *B*, then *C* or *D*.

It is already in standard form. The trigger is Andrew and Dana both seeing patients on Friday. The result is that one or the other operates on Saturday.

2. Petunias are planted in the front garden if, and only if, the ash tree is removed.

The logic: If *A*, then *B*. And if –*A*, then –*B*.

The standard form: This statement should be rewritten as two separate statements, one for "if" and one for "only if." If removed, then petunias. If not removed, then not petunias.

3. No type of flower is planted in both the front and side gardens.

The logic: If *A*, then –*B* and If *B*, then –*A*.

The standard form: This expresses a relationship that is mutually exclusive. If front, then not side. If side, then not front.

4. Any garden that contains monkshood also contains lobelia.

The logic: If *A*, then *B*.

The standard form: Note the wording. "Any garden that x . . ." is the same as saying "If a garden has x . . ." If monkshood, then lobelia.

5. If dahlias are planted in the rear garden, then lobelia is planted in the side garden. Otherwise, lobelia is planted in the front garden.

The logic: If *A*, then *B*. If –*A*, then *C*.

The standard form: Note the word *otherwise*. It refers to the negation of "If dahlias are planted . . ." Two statements are necessary. If dahlias in rear, then lobelia in side. If –(dahlias in rear), then lobelia in front.

6. The side garden contains either petunias or monkshood, but not both.

The logic: If –*A*, then *B*. If *A*, then –*B*.

The standard form: For AR purposes, this relationship is best expressed as:

Either side = petunias

Or side = monkshood

Bnb (but not both)

This notation is easier to use in games than the standard form.

Three common if/thens. There are three common if/then relationships with which you should be familiar. The first is the relationship in which two things must go together. If you have pie, you have to have coffee. If you have coffee, you have to have pie. To express a "two must go together" relationship, both of these statements must be made.

If pie → *coffee*

If coffee → *pie*

Just asserting that if you have pie, you must have coffee does not establish that if you have coffee, you have to have pie.

Another common if/then relationship is one in which one or the other player must occur. If John does not go to the meeting, then Susan does.

If –John → *Susan*

The contrapositive indicates that if Susan does not go, then John will. It is also possible that both go to the meeting.

The third common relationship is one in which two players cannot be together. In other words, they are mutually exclusive. If Shanna goes on the field trip, Jason does not.

If Shanna → *–Jason*

It is not necessary to state that if Jason goes, Shanna does not because that is the contrapositive (Jason ∴ –Shanna) of the first statement. It is also possible that neither goes. Table 4.1 summarizes these three common relationships.

Table 4.1 Three Common Relationships

	Standard	Contrapositive	Note
Two must go together	If *A*, then *B* and if *B*, then *A*.	–*B* therefore –*A*, and –*A* therefore –*B*.	The contrapositives say that if *B* is not there, then *A* must not be there and that if *A* is not there, *B* is not there.
One or the other must occur. Both can occur.	If –*A*, then *B*.	If –*B*, then *A*.	The contrapositive captures the second part of this relationship.
The two cannot go together. Mutually exclusive. It is possible that neither goes.	If *A*, then –*B*.	If *B*, then –*A*.	The contrapositive captures the second part of this relationship.

The Diagram

Most games cannot be solved without a diagram. The diagram provides a working space for testing out possible assignments of players. The diagram allows you to fill in information and to spot rule violations.

There is one basic style of diagram that can be used effectively for all games. However, there are many variations on this basic diagram with which you need to become familiar. The advantage of this style of diagramming is that an entire assignment can always be shown on one line.

The diagram represents the fixtures, not the players. The players are assigned to places in the diagram. Therefore, to create the diagram, you must be clear on which elements are fixtures and which players. Do this by creating a sentence on the pattern "blank is assigned to blank," in which the first blank represents the players and the second represents the fixtures.

> ### THE EXCEPTION TO ONE BASIC DIAGRAM
>
> The now-obsolete map games used a different type of diagram. You may see maps on older tests. Maps have not appeared on the LSAT in many years.

SAMPLE SETUP 1

The employees at Baxter Enterprises are John, Kevin, Lainie, Maria, and Nura. Baxter Enterprises has five separate offices situated in a row.

John cannot be in an office next to Maria.

The office that Lainie is in must have at least two offices between it and the office that Nura is in.

Kevin cannot be in the first or last office.

For Sample Setup 1, create a sentence on the pattern "blank is assigned to blank." The correct answer is in the next paragraph. There are only two elements: employees and offices. The trick is to determine which element is being assigned and which element represents the fixed positions (fixtures) to which players are assigned. If you get the relationship backward, you will probably still be able to solve the game but your diagram may not be as effective. People are often players but there are games in which an object is assigned to people, in which case the people are fixtures. As an example, consider a game in which each of four people can receive a hat, a coat, a scarf, and/or an umbrella. Do you see that the people are fixtures and the players are the items of apparel?

The best answer to the previous example is "Employees are assigned to offices." Typically, every fixture has at least one player assigned to it. One or more of the players, on the other hand, may not show up in a particular assignment. Use this fact to help determine which element represents the fixtures.

SAMPLE SETUP 2

Nel, Olga, Pablo, Roger, and Sung will each receive an expense-paid vacation to exactly one foreign country. The possible countries are France, Ghana, Iceland, Japan, Korea, Laos, and Morocco.

Given the above information, create a "blank is assigned to blank" sentence. The answer is in the next paragraph. If you decide that "X is assigned to Y" and then find that the diagram does not seem to be working well, try reversing your sentence and create a diagram in which X represents the fixtures.

The answer to the example above is "Countries are assigned to people." Every person will be assigned a country but two countries will not be assigned. Once you have created the sentence "blank is assigned to blank," you are ready to create a diagram. The diagram lists the fixtures horizontally. Below is a diagram for a game in which the fixtures consist of five offices, numbered 1 through 5.

$$\underline{1} \quad \underline{2} \quad \underline{3} \quad \underline{4} \quad \underline{5}$$

Figure 4.3. Basic diagram for a game with five fixtures

For all games the basic diagram is created by listing the fixtures across the top of the diagram. For more complex games you must modify the diagram.

MULTIPLE ASSIGNMENTS TO EACH FIXTURE

Consider the following variation on a previous example:

SAMPLE SETUP 3

The employees at Baxter Enterprises are John, Kevin, Lainie, Maria, and Nura. Baxter Enterprises has five separate offices situated in a row. Each office receives exactly one chair. The chair can be orange, purple, red, salmon, or tangerine.

John cannot be in an office next to Maria.

The office that Lainie is in must have at least two offices between it and the office that Nura is in.

Kevin cannot be in the first or last office.

The chair in any office cannot be the same color as the chair in any adjacent office.

In the original example, people are assigned to offices. In this example, one chair of a particular color is also assigned to each office. Offices are still the fixtures, but there are now two types of players that are assigned: people and colors of chairs. Figure 4.4 shows how to modify the diagram for this case.

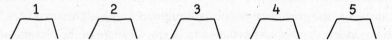

Figure 4.4. A diagram representing two players assigned to each fixture

Each fixture is given branches to show that it can receive multiple players. More complex games may require three, four, or, rarely, five branches.

For games in which there are multiple categories of players (such as *people* and *chairs*), many test takers try to use a grid, such as in Figure 4.5.

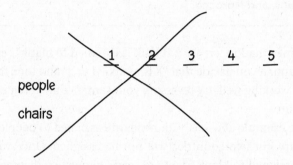

Figure 4.5. Grid. A grid is *not* the most effective diagram.

A grid is *not* the most effective diagram. It takes up too much space vertically. A grid is also more cumbersome for testing multiple possible arrangements, because each arrangement requires two lines. In Figure 4.6, compare the clearer and more compact linear branch approach with the grid approach.

	1		2		3		4		5	
	J	p	M	r	N	o	K	t	L	s
	J	p	M	t	K	o	L	r	N	s

	1	2	3	4	5
people	J	M	N	K	L
chairs	p	r	o	t	s
people	J	M	K	L	N
chairs	p	t	o	r	s

Figure 4.6. The linear branch approach (on top) versus the grid approach (below)

In Figure 4.6, consider the notation in the top diagram. The test taker has decided that the left branch of each pair will represent the person. The right branch represents the color of the chair. In addition, the test taker has capitalized the letters representing people and has used lowercase letters for the colors.

Some games with multiple assignments to each fixture may have only one category of players. For example, consider a game in which there are ten employees and five offices and two employees are assigned to each office. The list of players simply comprises ten employees. The two branches represent two employees. In many games with multiple assignments, however, there is more than one set of players. In the game in Figure 4.6, the players include a set of people and a set of chairs. Figure 4.7 shows the list of players.

People	Chairs
J	o
K	r
L	p
M	s
N	t

Figure 4.7. List of players in two sets

MORE VARIATIONS

Circular Games

You can use as many branches as needed to diagram games with multiple assignments to each fixture. Some games, however, will require additional variations. For example, in some games the fixtures are in a circle.

SAMPLE SETUP 4

Five delegates to a conference—Sami, Tamara, Ursula, Vincent, and Wilbur —are to be seated around a circular table. No one else is seated at their table.

Ursula cannot sit next to Vincent.

Delegates are assigned to five positions. The basic linear diagram still works for this. Consider, though, what happens if Ursula is in seat 1. Can Vincent sit in seat 5? No. In the circle, seat 1 is next to seat 5. The diagram in Figure 4.8 does not show this. By drawing an arc between seat 1 and seat 5, you remind yourself that these are adjacent. A circular diagram would also show this but a circular diagram is much more cumbersome to work with. If you tend to still forget that seat 1 is next to seat 5 despite drawing an arc, you can draw a small supplemental diagram using a circle. However, your working space will still be the linear diagram.

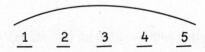

Figure 4.8. Linear diagram showing seating around a circle

Multiple Rows

In some games the fixtures are not in a single row, such as five offices in a row, but rather are in multiple rows.

SAMPLE SETUP 5

Nine passengers on a plane are seated in three adjacent rows, each row immediately behind the row in front of it. The passengers are Penn, Queen, Russell, Sheridan, Thomas, Upton, Vincent, Washburn, and Xerxes.

Penn cannot sit directly behind Vincent.

Russell cannot sit next to Sheridan.

Figure 4.9 shows all nine seats in one row but uses an arc to identify each row.

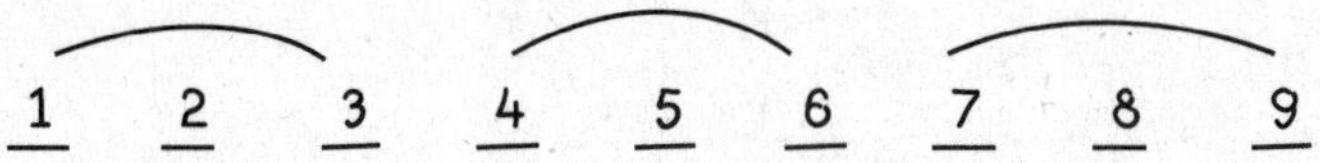

Figure 4.9. Three rows represented by one linear row

Consider the condition *Russell cannot sit next to Sheridan*. If Russell is in seat 3, can Sheridan sit in seat 4? Yes. Seats 3 and 4 are not next to each other. They are in separate rows. If Vincent is in seat 2, in which seat can Penn *not* sit? Do you see why it is seat 5? As with circles, a supplemental diagram can help you remember the orientation of the fixtures. However, the supplemental diagram (Figure 4.10) is not a good working space. Use the linear diagram to test assignments.

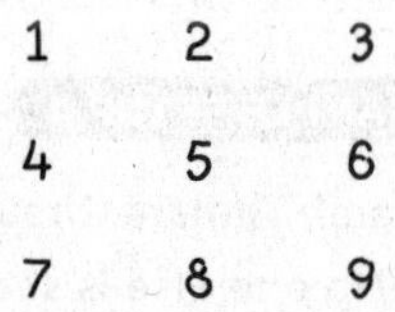

```
1    2    3
4    5    6
7    8    9
```

Figure 4.10. Supplemental diagram for multiple rows

Exclusions

In many games a particular assignment uses only some of the players and leaves the others out. If eight volunteers are assigned to five projects and each project has only one volunteer, then any valid assignment leaves out three of the players. It is helpful to keep track of who is out. You can do this easily by adding a special section to the diagram. Consider Figure 4.11:

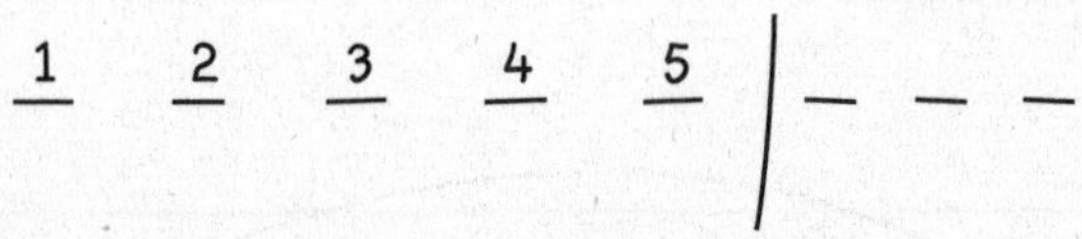

$$\underline{1} \quad \underline{2} \quad \underline{3} \quad \underline{4} \quad \underline{5} \quad \Big| \; \underline{} \; \underline{} \; \underline{}$$

Figure 4.11. A diagram with a section for exclusions ("discard pile")

Notice the line after position 5. The dashes to the right of the line represent the three players who are left out of a particular assignment. The space to the right of the line is the **discard pile** or **out pile**. The space to the left is the **fixture diagram** or the assignment. Avoid using the word *assigned* to refer to the discard pile. Players are either "assigned" (put in the fixture diagram) or "discarded." Consider the following example:

SAMPLE QUESTION 1

On a Saturday afternoon, five community projects will each be assigned exactly one of eight available volunteers: Karen, Lena, Marcel, Nava, Ofune, Peter, Randy, and Shan. No volunteer can be assigned to more than one project. The following conditions apply:

If Lena is not assigned, Marcel cannot be assigned.
Either Randy or Karen must be assigned but they cannot both be assigned.
Either Nava or Shan must be assigned but they cannot both be assigned.

Which of the following must be true?
(A) Ofune is not assigned.
(B) Peter is assigned.
(C) Lena is assigned.
(D) Karen is assigned.
(E) Nava is not assigned.

Solution: The condition *Either Randy or Karen must be assigned but they cannot both be assigned* tells you that one of these two players must be excluded. One place in the discard pile can be labeled R/K (Figure 4.12). Likewise, the condition *Either Nava or Shan must be assigned but they cannot both be assigned* tells you that one of these two must be out. A second place in the discard pile is labeled N/S.

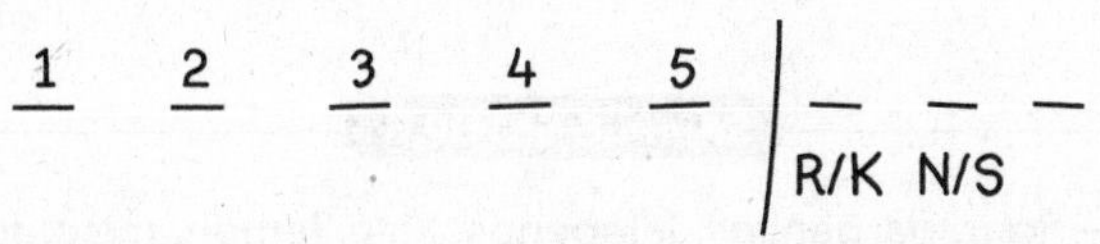

$$\underline{1} \quad \underline{2} \quad \underline{3} \quad \underline{4} \quad \underline{5} \quad \Big| \quad \underline{} \quad \underline{} \quad \underline{}$$
$$\text{R/K} \quad \text{N/S}$$

Figure 4.12. Two places in the discard pile are defined.

Consider the remaining condition: *If Lena is not assigned, Marcel cannot be assigned.* What does this tell you? What happens if Lena is not assigned? She goes in the remaining position in the discard pile. Marcel must also go in the discard pile but there are no discard positions left. Therefore, Lena cannot be discarded. The correct answer is C. Lena must be assigned to a project.

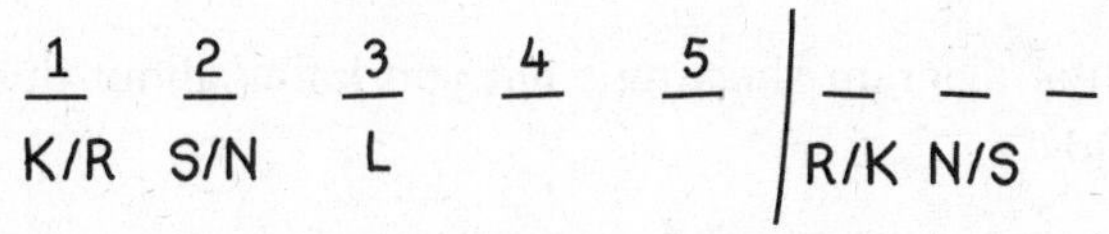

$$\underline{1} \quad \underline{2} \quad \underline{3} \quad \underline{4} \quad \underline{5} \quad \Big| \quad \underline{} \quad \underline{} \quad \underline{}$$
$$\text{K/R} \quad \text{S/N} \quad \text{L} \qquad\qquad \text{R/K} \quad \text{N/S}$$

Figure 4.13. Three slots are shown in the fixture diagram and two in the discard pile.

Because there are no further restrictions on any of the players, Ofune and Peter may or may not be assigned. One of the pair Karen/Randy must be assigned, as shown in position 1, but there is no restriction on which one. The same is true for Shan/Nava. Notice the notation. In the fixture diagram, Karen and Randy are represented as K/R. In the discard pile, they are represented as R/K. This reminds you that if K is in position 1, R is in the discard pile, and vice versa.

There is one important caution you must remember when using a discard pile. The conditions that apply in the fixture diagram do *not* apply in the discard pile. For example, if there is a condition that Lena and Shan cannot both be assigned, it *is* possible for both Lena and Shan to be in the discard pile. Note that once the discard pile is full, all other players must appear in the assignment.

MORE SUPPLEMENTAL DIAGRAMS: SEQUENCES

You learned about two supplemental diagrams in the paragraphs above: a supplemental circle diagram and a supplemental diagram showing multiple rows. A supplemental diagram organizes information in a way that is different from the working diagram. Keep supplemental diagrams small. Sometimes you can use the supplemental diagram to test assignments. The most common type of supplemental diagram organizes a **sequence** of players. For example:

Eight ingredients are added to a soup one at a time.
Seven members of a club joined in different years.
Seven trees have different heights.
Nine cities have different populations.

In these examples, you must determine the relative order in which the ingredients are added or in which the members joined the club. You must determine which tree is tallest, next tallest, and so on. You must determine which city has the largest population, next largest, and so on.

In games with sequences, the number of players is higher than usual in order to make the sequence more difficult to figure out. Consider the following:

SAMPLE SETUP 6

Eight ingredients—flour, garbanzos, jalapenos, kale, lemon, miso, noodles, and onion—are added to a soup, one ingredient at a time. Each ingredient is added exactly once.

Onion is added after garbanzos.
Miso is added after flour.
Jalapenos are added immediately after onion.
Noodles are added last.
Jalapenos are added after miso.

Build a supplemental diagram showing what you know about this sequence. The first condition (Step 1) yields

G – O

Use the convention of moving from left to right. Players on the left come first. The dash between the *G* and *O* is important. It represents the fact that other players could be assigned between *G* and *O*.

The next condition, *Miso is added after flour*, has no relationship to the diagram that you have started. It would have to be diagrammed separately, which is not helpful. Instead, look for another condition that shows a relationship to either *G* or *O*. Use *Jalapenos are added immediately after onion* and add the information to the diagram (Step 2).

$$G - OJ$$

There is no dash between *O* and *J* because the *J* comes immediately after *O*. Which condition should be added next? The condition with miso and flour still has no point of connection with the diagram. The condition *Noodles are added last* can be added (Step 3).

$$G - OJ - N\ //$$

A longer dash between *J* and *N* shows that other players will probably be assigned there, because *N* is at the end of the sequence. The two slashes to the right of *N* indicate the end of the sequence, as well.

The second condition still has no point of intersection with the diagram, so add the condition *Jalapenos are added after miso* to the existing diagram. Jalapenos already appear in the diagram and miso must be to its left, but there is no information indicating where miso occurs in relation to garbanzos and onion. Start a new branch (Step 4), as shown below. Because onion is immediately before jalapenos, the new branch is linked to onion.

$$
\begin{array}{c}
M \\
\diagdown \\
G - OJ - N\ //
\end{array}
$$

You can now add the remaining condition to the diagram (Step 5).

$$
\begin{array}{c}
F - M \\
\diagdown \\
G - OJ - N\ //
\end{array}
$$

There are now two sequences that are known:

$$G - OJ - N$$

and

$$F - M - OJ - N$$

It is critical to note that the relationship between F – M and G – O is unknown. Flour could come before or after garbanzos. Miso could come before or after garbanzos. The key to a sequence is to distinguish what is known from what is unknown.

In a typical sequence game, there is one long string and one shorter string connected to the long string at one player. Most of the questions are relatively easy to answer if you are clear about what is known and what is unknown. For some sequence games, the supplemental diagram is all that you need. In other sequence games you must also use the main (linear) diagram.

The example above uses a supplemental diagram that moves from left to right. In other words, the leftmost player is the player that occurs first in time. For some games, it may be more logical to arrange the supplemental diagram up and down, such as when representing heights of people or objects. It is important that the orientation you use—vertical or horizontal—makes sense to you.

Variations on Sequences

The previous example is a basic sequence. There are a number of common variations of sequences. The section on "Types of Games," starting on page 347, teaches these variations and how to work with them.

Temporary Supplemental Diagrams

As you try to solve a question, you can create temporary supplemental diagrams to organize the information that pertains to that question. For example, if a question says *If kale is added before flour, . . .* you can create a temporary diagram that shows the sequence K – F – M – OJ – N. Be sure to cross out this information before going on to the next question.

PUTTING INFORMATION FROM THE SETUP INTO THE DIAGRAM

To review, the steps for organizing the setup are: Read the setup. Identify the players and the fixtures, using the template "(blank) is assigned to (blank)." Create the diagram. List the players. Going in order, identify each condition and rewrite it in an abbreviated form. Consider the relationships among conditions. Finally, find any information that can be placed directly into the diagram.

There are two kinds of information that go directly into the diagram before you start working on questions: permanent assignments, such as *Alfred is in office 3*, and rules and relationships, such as *Ben cannot go in office 5* or *Only Charlene or David can go in office 1*.

Permanent Assignments

Permanent assignments tell you exactly where a specific player must go. Many games contain permanent conditions.

SAMPLE SETUP 7

The employees at Baxter Enterprises are John, Kevin, Lainie, Maria, and Nura.
Baxter Enterprises has five separate offices situated in a row.
   John cannot be in the first or last office.
   The office that Lainie is in must have at least two offices between it and the office that Nura is in.
   Kevin is in the second office.

The final condition is permanent information. Put it directly into the diagram, as shown in Figure 4.14.

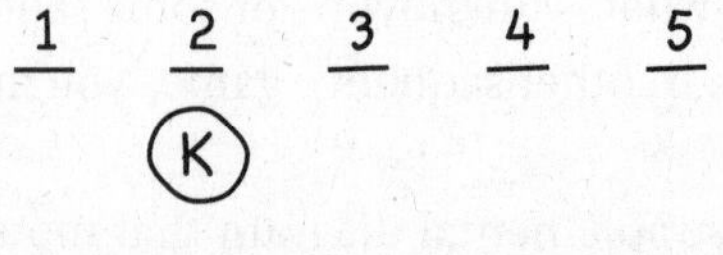

Figure 4.14. Placing a permanent assignment in the diagram

Kevin is placed under office 2. The letter *K* is circled to show that this is permanent information. Every assignment that you test must have Kevin in 2.

Rules and Relationships

Certain rules and relationships can be put directly into the diagram. Unlike permanent assignments, these rules and relationships do not tell you exactly where someone goes. They may, however, indicate where a player cannot go, as in the condition *John cannot be in the first or last office.* Because rules and relationships do not indicate a specific assignment, do not put them below the fixtures in the diagram. Instead, place them above the fixtures, as shown in Figure 4.15.

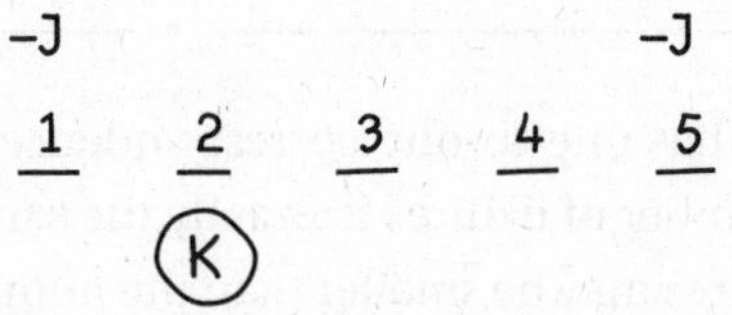

Figure 4.15. Placing rules and relationships in the diagram

Consider the condition *The office that Lainie is in must have at least two offices between it and the office that Nura is in.* There are several ways this can occur. Do not put them into the diagram. Only diagram the concrete information. Many test takers try to work out too many possibilities at the beginning of a game. If you stick only with known facts, your diagramming will be more efficient and more accurate. Do not try to put every condition into the diagram.

Types of Games

You have learned that you can use one type of diagram for all games. In one sense, then, there is only one "type" of game—one in which the relationships can be represented by a horizontal arrangement of fixtures to which players are assigned. You can, however, learn to recognize a number of distinct variations on how the players relate to one another, how the players relate to the fixtures, and how the fixtures relate to one another. It is more accurate to say that a given game consists of a combination of certain game characteristics, which can be thought of as building blocks. There are five main building blocks—or criteria—that you can use to find the essence of any game.

THE MAIN CRITERIA FOR EVALUATING GAMES

1. **One-to-one correspondence.** Is each player used exactly one time or not?
2. **Ordering.** Does the order of the fixtures matter or not?
3. **Sequence.** Do the conditions in an ordered game establish a sequence among at least three players?
4. **Branching.** Do the fixtures have more than one branch or not?
5. **Variability.** Are there a fixed number of fixtures and/or branches or is the number variable?

ONE-TO-ONE CORRESPONDENCE

One-to-one correspondence means that each player gets assigned to one fixture and each fixture (or branch of a fixture) receives only one player. Think of this criterion as a "perfect match" between players and fixtures. Every player gets used exactly once. No one is left over. No one is used more than once. A one-to-one correspondence is a simpler relationship than non-one-to-one correspondence, in which some players may be left over or used more than once. About 70 percent of recent LSAT games have one-to-one correspondence.

Consider the following variation on a previous example:

SAMPLE SETUP 8

Five volunteers—Karen, Lena, Marcel, Nava, and Ofune—are assigned to five community projects on one Saturday afternoon. Each project receives exactly one of these volunteers.

Do you see how this game has one-to-one correspondence? In many one-to-one games the number of players and number of fixtures is exactly the same, as above. In other one-to-one games the number of fixtures may be smaller than the number of players, but the fixtures may be divided into branches in a way that the total number of branches is the same as the number of players.

SAMPLE SETUP 9

Six attorneys—Franchetti, Jordan, Kellogg, Martin, Perea, and Riordan—are to serve as mentors for three debate teams. Each attorney serves on exactly one team and each team has exactly two of the six attorneys as mentors.

Figure 4.16 shows the diagram for this game.

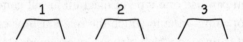

Figure 4.16. One-to-one correspondence with the same number of branches as players

There are exactly six attorneys, each appearing in exactly one of the six branches, even though there are only three fixtures—the three debate teams.

In other one-to-one correspondence games, each player is assigned exactly once, but the number of branches may be larger than the number of players. In some cases, the number of branches that will be assigned a player is unknown.

SAMPLE SETUP 10

Six attorneys—Franchetti, Jordan, Kellogg, Martin, Perea, and Riordan—are the only available attorneys to serve as mentors for two debate teams. Each available attorney serves on exactly one team and each team has at least one and at most four attorneys serving on it.

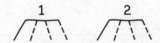

Figure 4.17. One-to-one correspondence with an inexact number of branches

In this game, the number of branches under each fixture is variable, ranging from a minimum of one to a maximum of four. The dotted lines in Figure 4.17 represent branches that *might* hold a player. The solid lines represent a branch that *must* hold a player. There are still exactly six players assigned to exactly six branches, but it is not known which of the total of eight possible branches will actually be used.

Non-One-to-One Games

If a game does not have a one-to-one correspondence between players and fixtures (or branches of fixtures), then the relationship between the players and fixtures is more complex. To understand these complex relationships, use the five criteria below. One-to-one correspondence means each player is used exactly once. Non-one-to-one correspondence means that either (1) some players are left out or (2) some are used more than once. If some players are left out, you need to know whether there is always the same number left out or whether the number left out varies. If players are left out, it may be helpful to use a discard pile.

If no players are left out, it is important to determine whether players are allowed to appear more than once. It is also important to determine whether each player must appear at least once. If so, then no player is left out and there is no discard pile. Finally, if players are allowed to appear more than once, is there a specific number of times that they must appear (e.g., *each player appears exactly twice*) or is the number of appearances variable?

> **NON-ONE-TO-ONE CORRESPONDENCE**
>
> In games that do not have one-to-one correspondence, either:
> 1. Some players are left out, or
> 2. Some players are used more than once.

> **FIVE CRITERIA FOR UNDERSTANDING NON-ONE-TO-ONE CORRESPONDENCE GAMES**
>
> 1. Is there a specific number of players who are left out?
> 2. Is a discard pile helpful in the diagram for this game?
> 3. Are players prohibited from appearing more than once?
> 4. Must each player appear at least once?
> 5. Must each player appear a specific number of times? If so, how many?

Consider the following example.

> **SAMPLE SETUP 11**
>
> Eight volunteers—Karen, Lena, Marcel, Nava, Ofune, Peter, Randy, and Shan—are the only volunteers available to be assigned to five community projects on one Saturday afternoon. Each project receives exactly one of these volunteers, and no volunteer is assigned to more than one project.

This game does not have one-to-one correspondence. Test it using the criteria above. (The answer is in the next paragraph.)

In the example there are eight players and only five fixtures. Each fixture receives only one player. For any assignment there will be exactly three players who are not used. Here are the answers to the criteria questions:

1. Is there a specific number of players who are left out? Answer: exactly three
2. Is a discard pile helpful in the diagram for this game? Answer: probably
3. Are players prohibited from appearing more than once? Answer: yes
4. Must each player appear at least once? Answer: no
5. Must each player appear a specific number of times? If so, how many? Answer: no

When there is a specific number of players who are out in each assignment (question 1), the discard pile is often helpful (question 2).

Evaluate the following non-one-to-one correspondence examples using the five criteria on page 349.

SAMPLE SETUP 12

Five tables at a banquet are to be decorated with flower arrangements. Each table receives exactly one flower arrangement. The flowers that are available are freesias, geraniums, and lobelia. The arrangements must follow these rules:

Any arrangement with geraniums cannot contain lobelia.

Any arrangement with freesias must contain lobelia.

At least one freesia and one geranium must be used.

There must be at least twice as many arrangements with geraniums as there are arrangements with lobelia.

Answers to criteria questions:

1. Is there a specific number of players who are left out? Answer: no
2. Is a discard pile helpful in the diagram for this game? Answer: no
3. Are players prohibited from appearing more than once? Answer: no
4. Must each player appear at least once? Answer: yes. Although the setup does not specifically state this, the third rule states that geraniums and freesias must be used at least once and any arrangement with freesias requires a lobelia.
5. Must each player appear a specific number of times? If so, how many? Answer: no

If each player must appear at least once, no player is discarded, and no discard pile is needed.

SAMPLE SETUP 13

Six tables arranged in a single row at a banquet are to be decorated, each with a vase consisting of a single flower and some greens. The flowers that are available are freesias, geraniums, and lobelia. Each type of flower must be used the same number of times as each other type of flower.

Geraniums cannot be used on a table that is next to a table with lobelia.

Try to answer the five criteria questions for Sample Setup 13.

Answers:

1. Is there a specific number of players who are left out? Answer: no
2. Is a discard pile helpful in the diagram for this game? Answer: no
3. Are players prohibited from appearing more than once? Answer: no
4. Must each player appear at least once? Answer: yes
5. Must each player appear a specific number of times? If so, how many? Answer: two

In this game each player appears exactly two times. Of course, that also means that the answer to question 4 (*Must each player appear at least once?*) must also be "yes." If you find that the answer to the question 5 is "exactly once," then the game actually has one-to-one correspondence.

Memorize the five criteria for non-one-to-one correspondence games. Because one-to-one correspondence games have exactly the right number of players for the fixtures, non-one-to-one correspondence games typically have either (1) too many players or (2) too few players for the number of fixtures. The first and second questions involve cases with too many players (some players are left out). The remaining questions involve cases with too few players, namely, cases in which each player must appear more than once, must appear at least once, or must appear a predictable number of times.

It is quite possible that, even though there are too few or too many players, the number of times that any particular player appears is variable or unpredictable. In these cases the setup does not provide enough information to definitively answer "yes" to any of the five questions. In this situation, work out the relationship between the players and fixtures as you work the game. Evaluating the game in advance for these criteria speeds up your understanding of the game.

> **THE MAIN CRITERIA FOR EVALUATING GAMES**
>
> 1. One-to-one correspondence
> 2. Ordering
> 3. Sequence
> 4. Branching
> 5. Variability

ORDERED VERSUS UNORDERED FIXTURES

Once you have determined whether a game has one-to-one correspondence, consider whether the fixtures in the game are **ordered** or **unordered**. In an ordered game the order of the fixtures matters. In other words, it is important to know whether a player is assigned to fixture 1 or fixture 2, for example. In an unordered game it does not matter to which fixture a player is assigned. A player is simply "in" the assignment or "out" of the assignment. The order in which players are arranged does not matter in unordered games.

Unordered Games

Consider the following unordered game:

SAMPLE SETUP 14

Four members of a committee to plan next year's activities at the local senior center are to be chosen from among eight members of the center—Friedland, Gerhardt, Hong, Kovac, Manning, Neruda, Olsen, and Pappas.

If Pappas is chosen, Gerhardt is not chosen.

If Neruda is not chosen, Manning must be chosen.

Friedland and Hong cannot both serve on the committee.

Figure 4.18 shows the diagram.

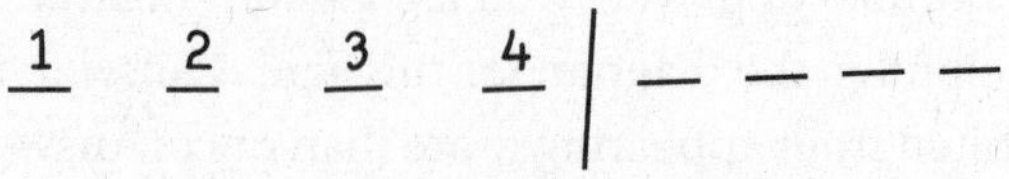

$$\underline{1} \quad \underline{2} \quad \underline{3} \quad \underline{4} \,\Big|\, \text{\_ \_ \_ \_}$$

Figure 4.18. Unordered game with discard pile

Only four of the eight players can appear in any assignment. This is a non-one-to-one game and exactly four players are left out (put in the discard pile). The fixtures are unordered. Even though they are labeled 1 through 4, the order in which the players are assigned to the fixtures does not matter. Look at the conditions. There are none that indicate that one player must come before or after another or that one player must or must not be next to another. There is a condition that says that certain players cannot be on the committee together but that condition does not have to do with the order in which the players appear. An unordered game cannot have a one-to-one correspondence because there is always at least one player left out.

An unordered game is like throwing cards (players) into a hat. If you throw A, D, K, and M into the hat, the order that you throw them in does not matter, nor does the order in which they appear in the hat. The assignment A D K M is the same as K M D A.

In unordered games, nearly all of the conditions are if/then statements. The players are either in or out.

Ordered Games

Only about 10 percent of games are unordered. For the remaining 90 percent, the order in which players are assigned is critical. In other words, the great majority of games are ordered games. Ordered games are more complex than unordered games. Ordered games require you to understand the rules that govern how you assign players to fixtures. You cannot just "throw players into the hat." The rules determine how players relate to the fixtures (*Fontana cannot go in the last office*) and how the players relate to each other—who comes before whom (*Johnson comes before Gomez*); who can or cannot be next to whom (*Martin cannot be in an office next to Olivas. Weichman and Klemm must both be chosen*); and who can, cannot, or must appear if a particular player appears (*If Sheehan is chosen, Franco cannot be chosen*).

Sequences. In a little under 50 percent of the ordered games, the conditions show you a significant part of the **sequence** in which players must appear.

The conditions give clues as to the sequence. As you summarize the conditions, build a supplemental diagram that shows parts of the sequence. The first two conditions have no players in common. They result in two separate relationships:

O – J
P – M

If you look for two conditions that *do* have players in common, as in the first and third conditions, you can start to build a single supplemental diagram (Figure 4.19).

$$\underline{1} \quad \underline{2} \quad \underline{3} \quad \underline{4} \quad \underline{5} \quad \underline{6}$$

MO – J

Figure 4.19. Combine conditions 1 and 3.

The long dash between O and J indicates that there could be other players between them. The fact that there is no dash between M and O indicates that they are adjacent. We define a **sequence game** as one in which the relationship between at least three players is known, as in Figure 4.19.

Now the second condition can be added: Petric is before Melendez (Figure 4.20).

$$\underline{1} \quad \underline{2} \quad \underline{3} \quad \underline{4} \quad \underline{5} \quad \underline{6}$$

P – MO – J

Figure 4.20. Add condition 2.

> **SEQUENCE GAMES: THE WORKING DEFINITION**
>
> Sequence games are games in which the relationship between at least **three** players is known.

At this point the relative order of four of the players is known. You do not yet know how many players appear where the dashes are and you do not know where in the main diagram the sequence P – MO — J will appear.

The fourth condition indicates that N comes after O (Figure 4.21).

$$\underline{1} \quad \underline{2} \quad \underline{3} \quad \underline{4} \quad \underline{5} \quad \underline{6}$$

N
⁄
P – MO – J

Figure 4.21. The fourth condition creates a new branch.

There are now two distinct branches in the supplemental diagram, and there are two sequences of four players.

P – MO – N and P – MO — J

TIP

WHAT YOU DON'T KNOW

Sequences test your ability to recognize *what you do NOT know* in a series.

The most important strategy for sequences is to recognize *what you do not know.* In this case, the relationship between N and J is not known.

Add in the final condition (Figure 4.22).

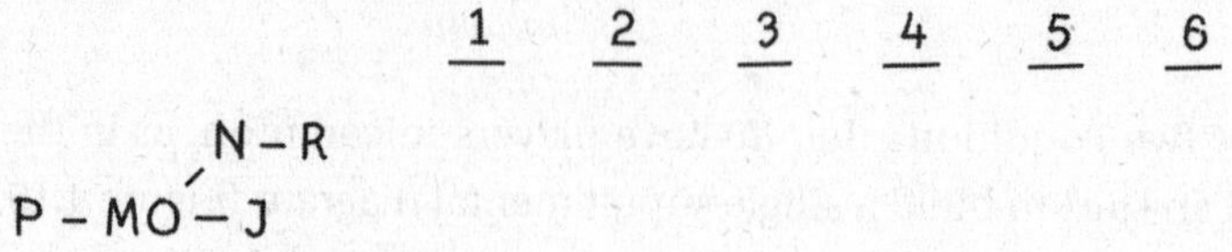

1 2 3 4 5 6
N – R
P – MO – J

Figure 4.22. Add the fifth condition.

There are now two distinct branches, one with five players and one with four. The relationships between J and N – R are unknown. If players are not adjacent and are not connected by a line, the relationship between them is unknown. Look for the positions that are not connected by lines.

TIP

LOOK FOR PLAYERS THAT ARE NOT CONNECTED BY LINES

If nonadjacent players are not connected by lines, their relationship to each other is unknown.

The sequence game above gives you in advance most of the relationships in the sequence and includes all of the players. Many sequence games give only a few relationships and do not include all of the players.

Sequence games are a subset of ordered games. All sequence games are ordered. Unordered games cannot be sequence games. In ordered games, by definition, the players have to appear in a defined sequence. Why, then, are not all ordered games sequences? The conditions for some ordered games only show relationships between two players. Games in which the conditions define the relationships among three or more players function differently from games that do not. By studying games with three or more defined relationships as a distinct type of game—a sequence game—you will be better able to spot these games and solve them.

Non-sequence	Sequence
K – F B – O AO	K – FA

Figure 4.23. Ordered games: non-sequence versus sequence

To be a sequence game, the conditions must create a string that is at least three players long. In the leftmost example, there are several strings but they do not result in a string of at least three players.

THE IMPORTANCE OF SEQUENCE GAMES

Because 90 percent of all AR questions are ordered and 40 percent of these are sequence games, sequences constitute about 35 to 40 percent of the entire AR section!

Non-sequence ordered games. Approximately 60 percent of ordered games are not sequence games. In other words, either the conditions do not describe a string of relationships, or they show one or more strings of two players but no strings of three players. Non-sequence ordered games may have one-to-one correspondence (slightly more than 50 percent) or they may not have one-to-one correspondence (slightly less than 50 percent). By contrast, all sequence games have one-to-one correspondence.

Types of Ordering

The order in which players are assigned to fixtures in an ordered game can be based on many different criteria. Games can be ordered by time (*who goes first, who starts at 2:00 P.M.*), physical location (*who sits next to whom, who is on the first floor*), or any other general ranking (*which costs least, which received the highest rating*). In these examples, the fixtures are on a continuum, such as first to last, least expensive to most expensive, or leftmost to rightmost. It is not necessary, though, for fixtures to be on a continuum.

For example, if the fixtures consist of five different movies, the movies are not necessarily in any order in time, space, or ranking. Fixtures that are not on a continuum might include movies, parks, swimming pools, and zoos.

Ordering in Relation to One-to-One Correspondence

There is a correlation between ordered/unordered games and one-to-one correspondence games. The flowchart in Figure 4.24 shows the possible combinations of one-to-one, ordered, and sequence games. From the top, follow the "Yes" branch of one-to-one correspondence. All such games are ordered. Some are sequences. Some are not.

From the top of the chart, follow the "No" branch. All games in the No branch either leave out some players or use players more than once. There are no sequence games in the No branch. From the label "Ordered," follow the No branch. These are unordered, "throw into the hat" games, in which players are either in or out. Going back to the label "Ordered," follow the Yes branch. These are ordered games without one-to-one correspondence. They cannot be sequence games, which all have one-to-one correspondence, and they function differently from the non-sequence ordered games that are under the one-to-one branch.

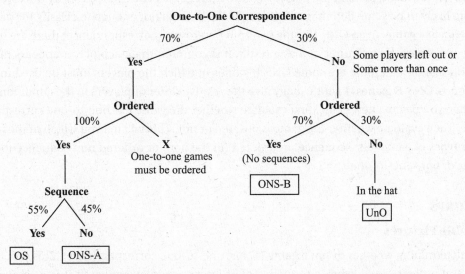

Figure 4.24. Flowchart for one-to-one correspondence, ordering, and sequence games.
OS = ordered sequence; ONS-A = ordered non-sequence (left branch);
ONS-B = ordered non-sequence (right branch); UnO = unordered (in the hat)

All games with one-to-one correspondence are ordered. Because all of the players are assigned, the only factor that the test writers can use to distinguish one assignment from another is the order in which the players are arranged. Similarly, games that are unordered cannot have one-to-one correspondence because only some of the players will be "thrown into the hat." Games that do not have one-to-one correspondence are divided between ordered (70 percent) and unordered (30 percent).

Test yourself using the flowchart. The following categories appear in only one place on the chart. Find the end of the branch that represents:

1. Unordered games
2. Sequence games

The following category appears in more than one place on the chart. Find the three ends (not including the x-ed out branch) of the branches that represent:

3. Ordered games

Find the two places on the chart that represent ordered games that are not sequence games. Do you see that one is in the right branch and one in the left? This means that one place represents non-one-to-one games and the other represents one-to-one games.

Find the four terminal ends of the branches in the flowchart. These represent the four most common categories of games. On the far left are the games labeled OS (ordered sequence) or sequence games (38 percent of all games). On the far right are the games labeled UnO (unordered; 9 percent). These are the *Throw Them in the Hat* games.

The middle two terminal ends are labeled ONS-A (32 percent) and ONS-B (21 percent). Both are ordered non-sequence (ONS) games. Like the sequence games, these two categories are ordered but they do not have the long chains of relationships that are found in sequence games. The two ordered non-sequence types have many similarities but they are different in that the ONS-A games have one-to-one correspondence and the ONS-B games do not. Because of the fact that all of the players in an ONS-A game are assigned exactly once, there is more likely to be some definition of the sequence, though not enough to classify the game as a sequence game. In an ONS-B game (without one-to-one correspondence) there are usually fewer players than fixtures and as a result, it is common that each player appears more than once, although there are some ONS-B games in which the players must be used more than once. ONS-B games do not usually give the relative order of players in the conditions.

When you begin a new game, first evaluate whether the game has one-to-one correspondence. Then evaluate whether the game is ordered or not. This will tell you which of the four major types of game it is: sequence, unordered (in the hat), or ordered non-sequence (one-to-one or non-one-to-one).

FIXTURES

Variable Fixtures

After determining whether or not a game (1) has one-to-one correspondence; (2) is ordered; and (3) if ordered, establishes a sequence of at least three players (i.e., if it is a sequence game), determine whether the number of fixtures is exactly determined (fixed) or varies (variable). Fewer than 10 percent of games have variable fixtures, but be prepared to spot these.

Typically, games with variable fixtures are either:

1. Ordered games in which the players appear more than once but the total number of appearances of players is not known (see Sample Setup 16), or
2. Unordered games (in the hat) in which some of the players are chosen to participate but the total number can vary (see Sample Setup 17).

SAMPLE SETUP 16

Three coworkers—Marta, Nura, and Oliver—have volunteered to visit the parent of a colleague in the hospital on a particular day. Each visit lasts exactly one hour and each coworker visits at least once but not more than twice. Visits do not overlap and, except for the first visit, each visit begins immediately when the previous visit ends. No other coworkers will visit the parent in the hospital on this day. The following conditions apply:

Nura's first visit is some time after Marta's first visit.
Oliver does not visit in any hour immediately after an hour in which Marta visits.
No coworker visits in two consecutive visiting hours.

In this game there must be at least three visits and there cannot be more than six. The number of actual fixtures in a given assignment, then, could be 3, 4, 5, or 6 (Figure 4.25). The diagram uses three dots after fixture 3 to indicate that the additional fixtures may or may not be used in an assignment.

1 2 3 ··· 4 5 6

Figure 4.25. Variable fixtures in an ordered game

SAMPLE SETUP 17

Six children—Lana, Marcus, Nick, Olivia, Patrick, and Rashelle—are eligible to go on a field trip to the natural history museum. No other children are eligible to go. At least one child goes on the trip. The children attend according to the following rules:

If Marcus goes, Nick does not go.
If Olivia goes, Lana does not go.
If Patrick goes, Rashelle also goes.

This game is unordered. Children are either "put in the hat" or not. There is at least one child who goes and the number of attendees cannot exceed the total number of eligible players (six). However, the actual number of children in a given assignment varies. In Figure 4.26, the three dots after fixture 1 indicate that there must be at least one fixture but that the subsequent fixtures may or may not be used. The discard pile is also variable, as there may be up to five players left out. Three dots at the right end of the discard pile help you remember that there may be more slots needed. The three slots that are shown are an arbitrary number.

1 ··· 2 3 4 5 6 | __ __ __ ···

Figure 4.26. Unordered game with variable fixtures and variable discard pile

There is only one significant difference between the above unordered game with variable fixtures and the previous ordered game (Figure 4.25) with variable fixtures. The unordered game has a slightly higher number of players and each player can appear only once (or not at all). The ordered game with variable fixtures has a smaller number of players, some of whom appear more than once.

A game with variable fixtures is unlikely to have one-to-one correspondence because in one-to-one correspondence the number of fixtures (or branches of fixtures) equals the number of players. Variable fixture games are typically found in the right branch of the flowchart—either unordered games or ordered non-sequence non-one-to-one (ONS-B) games.

Branched Fixtures

The setup of a game tells you whether or not the fixtures require branches. Approximately half of all games require branches and branches are found in every game type, though they are rarer in unordered games. Fixtures may require two, three, four, or more branches.

Fixed or variable branches. Just as fixtures can be fixed or variable, branches can also be fixed or variable. In only about 10 percent of games with branches are the branches variable. The rest have fixed branches. A branched game with a fixed number of branches per fixture might be diagrammed as in Figure 4.27.

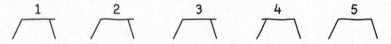

Figure 4.27. Fixed number of branches (two per fixture)

Compare Sample Setup 17 with Sample Setup 18, which has a variable number of branches.

SAMPLE SETUP 18

Eight runners are to be assigned to two teams, the Hares and the Tortoises.
Each team must have at least two members.

The diagram for Sample Setup 18 is given in Figure 4.28.

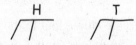

Figure 4.28. Variable number of branches (minimum of two)

Each team must have two members, represented by the solid branches. This accounts for four of the eight possible participants. How many optional branches are there? In theory, one of the teams could receive six runners. Leave space under each fixture to add in additional branches as needed. In some games there may be a maximum of one or two optional branches. Draw these as dotted lines.

SAMPLE SETUP 19

Five runners are to be assigned to two teams, the Hares and the Tortoises. Each team must have at least two members.

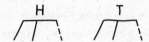

Figure 4.29. Variable branches with a small number of options

With five possible runners, there is only one runner left after the four required slots are filled. At most there can be one additional runner in H or T.

Ordered and unordered branches. If the fixtures are ordered, then determine whether the branches are ordered or unordered. It is very common for the branches of an ordered game to be unordered. If the fixtures of a game are unordered (in the hat game), then any branches will also be unordered.

SAMPLE SETUP 20

Six students—Frances, Gerald, Henry, Jocelyn, Lainie, and Martin—are to be assigned to three volunteer projects: raking, sweeping, and telephoning. Each student participates in exactly one project. Each project receives exactly two volunteers.

Gerald does not volunteer in any project in which Jocelyn volunteers.

If Lainie volunteers for raking, Martin does not volunteer for sweeping.

Henry volunteers for raking.

In this case, the order of the fixtures (raking, sweeping, telephoning) matters (Figure 4.30). Raking must be distinguished from sweeping, sweeping from telephoning, and telephoning from raking. However, it is not important whether a student is assigned in the first or second branch of a fixture. The branches are unordered.

```
   Rake        Sweep        Tele
    /\          /\          /\
   /  \        /  \        /  \
```

Figure 4.30. Unordered branches. The fixtures are ordered but the branches are not.

Consider Sample Setup 21.

Six students—Frances, Gerald, Henry, Jocelyn, Lainie, and Martin—are to be assigned to three volunteer projects: raking, sweeping, and telephoning. Each student participates in exactly one project. Each project receives exactly two volunteers. One volunteer works on Saturday and the other works on Sunday.

Gerald does not volunteer in any project in which Jocelyn volunteers.

If Gerald volunteers for a project on Saturday, Martin must volunteer for the same project on Sunday.

If Lainie volunteers for raking, Martin does not volunteer for sweeping.

Henry volunteers for raking.

In this game, the two branches for each fixture represent Saturday and Sunday, respectively. One of the conditions distinguishes between Saturday and Sunday, so the order of the branches is now important. The branches are now ordered (Figure 4.31).

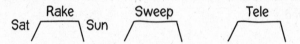

Figure 4.31. Ordered branches. The left branch must represent Saturday and the right branch Sunday.

Examples of Types of Games

You now know the characteristics that make up the four types of games:

Sequence: one-to-one correspondence, ordered, the relationship between at least three players is given

Unordered: "throw the cards in a hat," "in or out," non-one-to-one, unordered

Ordered Non-Sequence Games A: with one-to-one correspondence

Ordered Non-Sequence Games B: without one-to-one correspondence

Within each of these types there are common variations. In the paragraphs below, you will see all the variations and will be able to recognize these variations when you encounter them in practice sections. The examples consist of setups. The setups include representative conditions but not sample questions.

HOW TO USE THIS SECTION

This section is a comprehensive listing of all variations that you will find on actual LSAT AR sections. Trying to read through the whole section in one sitting would be overwhelming. Start by working a few variations for each of the four game types. Do not be concerned if you are not clear on the exact type of the game. It is more important that you feel comfortable with how to set up each game and with how a particular variation is different from other variations. With practice, you will recognize when a game is a sequence, is unordered, or is neither and has or does not have one-to-one correspondence.

You might also find it helpful to skim through the variations at first, getting a general sense of how they differ. This will help you absorb the many diagramming variations. You can come back to the variations later and work through a few at a time more carefully.

Use this section as a reference. Come back to it as you are working practice problems. See if you can identify the game type for the practice question you are working on. Then see if you can find the variation that is closest to it.

We have used the same general setup for most of the examples so that you can easily follow the changes between the various types of games. For each example, try to set up your own diagram before reading the explanation. Then, compare your diagram with the explanation that follows. If you would like to introduce some extra variety into the explanations, try creating your own setup using a different situation and different players. Then diagram your setup.

The in-depth instruction on the problem-solving process appears later in the chapter. For now, simply focus on becoming comfortable with the different types of games. If you already have experience with AR problem solving and are aiming for a superior score, challenge yourself as follows. For each type of game, create a series of six questions, drawing on the various question types, including five possible answer choices. Creating questions and answer choices is an excellent way to test your understanding and to challenge your skills. Then try to solve your own questions, or exchange questions with another superior test taker using this book, and test each other.

SEQUENCE GAMES

All sequence games have one-to-one correspondence. Each player appears exactly once. The order in which the players appear is critical. Sequence games always have a primary diagram—the working diagram—that shows the fixtures. Sequence games usually require a supplemental diagram that summarizes what is known—and not known—about the players. The following samples focus mostly on the supplemental diagrams. Work out the diagrams in each sample for yourself.

Each sample represents a possible variation on sequence games. If you work through each of the samples, you will be prepared for any sequence game. For each variation, consider how it differs from others.

Remember to draw your own diagram first, before reading the explanation. Then compare your diagram with the one presented here.

SEQUENCE SAMPLE 1

Seven singers—Kovac, Larson, Ming, Nieto, Ofune, Parsons, and Rifkin—are to perform in seven distinct time slots at a single concert. Exactly one singer performs in each time slot. Each time slot is fifteen minutes long and time slots start at 7 P.M. and on each subsequent quarter hour. The singers appear according to the following conditions:

Ming performs before Larson.

Nieto performs before Parsons.

Parsons performs immediately after Rifkin.

Ofune performs either immediately before or immediately after Ming.

The strings of relationships that are given in the conditions include:

$$M - L$$
$$N - RP$$

In addition, the M – L sequence must take the form of either OM – L or MO – L. There is no point of connection between the sequences with M and L and the sequence with N, R, and P.

The sequences shown above are supplemental diagrams. The working diagram for the game (Figure 4.32) simply shows the seven time slots.

$$\underline{1} \quad \underline{2} \quad \underline{3} \quad \underline{4} \quad \underline{5} \quad \underline{6} \quad \underline{7}$$

Figure 4.32. Main diagram showing seven slots in the sequence

---

SEQUENCE SAMPLE 2

Seven singers—Kovac, Larson, Ming, Nieto, Ofune, Parsons, and Rifkin—are to perform in seven distinct time slots at a single concert. Exactly one singer performs in each time slot. Each time slot is fifteen minutes long and time slots start at 7 P.M. and on each subsequent quarter hour. The singers appear according to the following conditions:

Ming performs before Larson.

Nieto performs before Parsons.

Ofune performs either immediately before or immediately after Ming.

There are exactly two time slots between Nieto and Rifkin.

The sequences defined are:

$$M - L$$
$$N - P$$

These relationships by themselves are not enough to make this a sequence game but the remaining conditions give us:

$$\text{Either OM} - \text{L or MO} - \text{L}$$

and

$$\text{Either R\_ \_ N} - \text{P or N\_ \_ R and N} - \text{P}$$

$$\text{R \_ \_ N} - \text{P} \quad \text{or} \quad \text{N \_ \_ R}^{\nearrow P}$$

Figure 4.33. R before N or R after N

SEQUENCE SAMPLE 3

Seven singers—Kovac, Larson, Ming, Nieto, Ofune, Parsons, and Rifkin—are to perform in seven distinct time slots at a single concert. Exactly one singer performs in each time slot. Each time slot is fifteen minutes long and time slots start at 7 P.M. and on each subsequent quarter hour. The singers appear according to the following conditions:

Ming performs before Larson.

Nieto performs before Parsons.

Larson performs before Nieto.

Parsons performs at some time after Ofune.

Kovac performs at some time after Ofune.

Figure 4.34 shows the sequences defined.

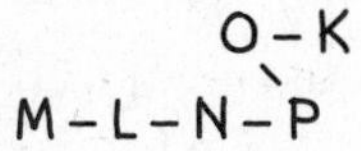

$$O - K$$
$$M - L - N - P$$

Figure 4.34. Sequence sample 3

Notice the string of four relationships, M through P. Notice that the relationship between O and M – L – N is unknown. O could occur either before or after any of these three. The same is true for K. You only know that K appears after O.

SEQUENCE SAMPLE 4

Seven singers—Kovac, Larson, Ming, Nieto, Ofune, Parsons, and Rifkin—are to perform in seven distinct time slots at a single concert. Exactly one singer performs in each time slot. Each time slot is fifteen minutes long and time slots start at 7 P.M. and on each subsequent quarter hour. The singers appear according to the following conditions:

Ming performs before Larson.
Ming performs before Parsons.
If Larson performs third, then Larson performs before Ofune.
If Larson does not perform third, then Larson must perform before Kovac.

The first two conditions do not give a string of three players, the requirement for a sequence game, but the third and fourth conditions do result in a string of three.

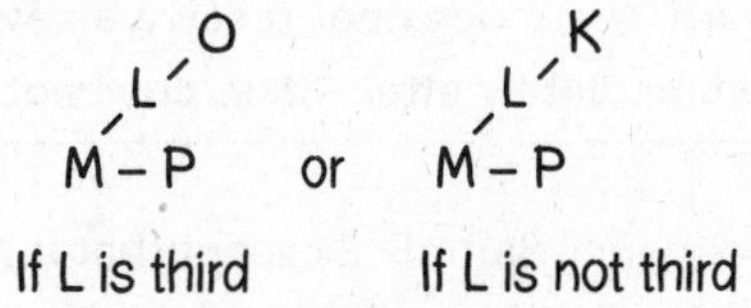

$$\begin{array}{cc} \quad O & \quad K \\ L' & L' \\ M - P & M - P \end{array}$$

If L is third   If L is not third

Figure 4.35. Sequence sample 4

SEQUENCE SAMPLE 5

Seven singers—Kovac, Larson, Ming, Nieto, Ofune, Parsons, and Rifkin—are to perform in seven distinct time slots at a single concert. Exactly one singer performs in each time slot. Each time slot is fifteen minutes long and time slots start at 7 P.M. and on each subsequent quarter hour. The singers appear according to the following conditions:

Both Ming and Rifkin perform before Larson.
Both Ming and Parsons perform before Ofune.
If Ming performs before Rifkin, then Parsons performs before Nieto.
Parsons does not perform in the third slot.

Figure 4.36. Sequence sample 5

Even though five players are represented in the diagram (Figure 4.36), there is not a chain that is at least three players long. Both R and M are before L, but the relationship between M and R is unknown. The last two conditions add additional information but still do not establish a chain of three players. Nevertheless, this game acts more like a sequence game than a non-sequence game, because information is given on nearly all of the players, and should be approached as a sequence.

SEQUENCE SAMPLE 6

Seven singers—Kovac, Larson, Ming, Nieto, Ofune, Parsons, and Rifkin—are to perform in seven distinct time slots at a single concert. Exactly one singer performs in each time slot. Each time slot is fifteen minutes long and time slots start at 7 P.M. and on each subsequent quarter hour. Exactly two singers receive an award. The singers appear according to the following conditions:

Ming performs before Larson.

Nieto performs before Parsons.

Ofune performs either immediately before or immediately after Ming.

There are exactly two time slots between Nieto and Rifkin.

If Ming receives an award, Nieto does not receive an award.

The singer appearing immediately after Rifkin does not receive an award.

This game is identical to Sequence Sample 2 except that it adds another factor—whether the singer receives an award—along with conditions that are related to the award. The award is represented by a second branch on each of the seven time slots (Figure 4.37). The award branch would be assigned either a + or –. In other words, + and – are the two possible players that can be assigned under the award branch.

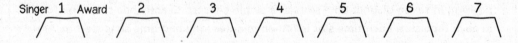

Figure 4.37. Sequence sample 6 showing two branches

Seven singers—Kovac, Larson, Ming, Nieto, Ofune, Parsons, and Rifkin—are to perform in seven distinct time slots at a single concert. Exactly one singer performs in each time slot. Each time slot is fifteen minutes long and time slots start at 7 P.M. and on each subsequent quarter hour. The singers appear according to the following conditions:

Ming performs before Larson and Rifken.

Rifken and Nieto perform before Ofune.

Either Parsons performs before Rifken and Nieto, or both Rifken and Nieto perform before Parsons, but not both.

This sample is similar to previous ones except that the final condition adds two alternatives, each of which is represented by a small diagram of its own (Figure 4.38).

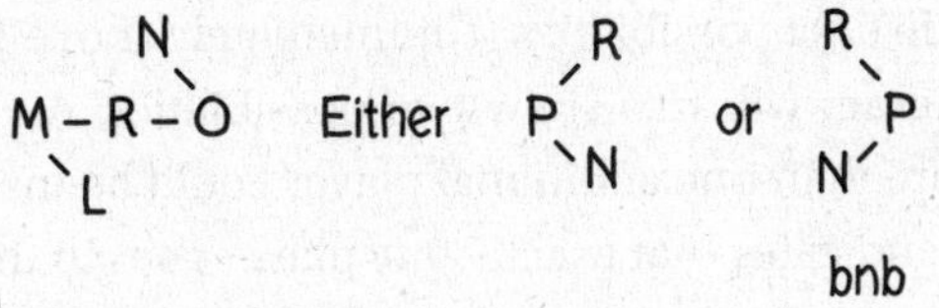

$$
\begin{array}{c}
\quad\ \ N \\
\quad\ \nwarrow \\
M-R-O \quad \text{Either} \quad P \quad \text{or} \quad R \\
\quad\ \swarrow \qquad\qquad\ \ \searrow \quad\ \ \nearrow \\
\quad\ L \qquad\qquad\qquad N \qquad\ N \searrow P \\
\qquad\qquad\qquad\qquad\qquad\qquad\qquad \text{bnb}
\end{array}
$$

Figure 4.38. Supplemental diagram with two parts

Seven singers—Kovac, Larson, Ming, Nieto, Ofune, Parsons, and Rifkin—are to perform in seven distinct time slots at a single concert. Each time slot is fifteen minutes and time slots start at 7 P.M. and on each subsequent quarter hour. The singers appear according to the following conditions:

Ming performs before Larson.

If Ofune performs before Ming, then both Larson and Rifken perform before Parsons.

If Ming performs before Ofune, then neither Parsons nor Larson perform before Rifken.

Here, either the second or third condition must apply. Thus, the first condition can be combined with each of the others to show two possibilities.

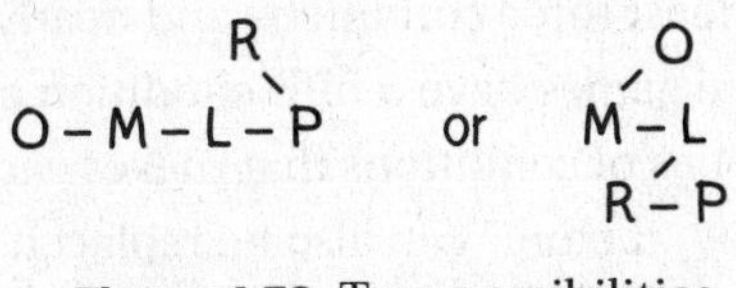

$$
\begin{array}{c}
\qquad R \qquad\qquad\qquad\qquad O \\
\qquad \nwarrow \qquad\qquad\qquad\qquad \nwarrow \\
O-M-L-P \quad \text{or} \quad M-L \\
\qquad\qquad\qquad\qquad\qquad\qquad\quad R-P
\end{array}
$$

Figure 4.39. Two possibilities

A company is assigning departments to the six floors of a new building into which it is moving. Each department takes up exactly one floor and there are six departments: Legal, Management, New Accounts, Payables, Receivables, and Taxation. The following conditions must hold:

   Either Legal is immediately above Taxation or immediately below Payables.
   New Accounts is above Payables but below Taxation.
   There is exactly one floor between New Accounts and Payables.
   Management is on the top floor.

In this game, it is more natural to arrange the players vertically. There are a small but significant number of sequence games that are vertical. Usually vertical sequence games involve floors of a building, layers, or sometimes relative heights of players. In drawing the supplemental diagrams, look for the most concrete information first (Figure 4.40). Because the first condition allows for two distinct possibilities (L immediately above T or L immediately below P), the supplemental diagram will also show two possibilities. A vertical line between two players indicates that more than one additional player could be inserted. A short horizontal line between two players indicates that exactly one player goes in that position.

Figure 4.40. Vertical sequence supplemental diagram

Conditions for Sequences

In the sample setups above you saw many of the common kinds of conditions that are used in sequence games. Below is a more complete list. The most common sequence condition—and by far the easiest to understand—is simply that Player A is before (or after, above, or below) Player B. Almost all sequence games have at least one such condition. Many have two or more and in some sequence games all of the conditions are of this type.

All sequence games have at least three conditions and nearly two-thirds have four conditions. About a third of sequence games have a fifth condition and a few have a sixth condition. It is the combination of types of conditions that makes each sequence game unique.

In the list of conditions below, "before" can also be replaced with "after," or with "above" or "below." The example of receiving an award represents any additional characteristic that can be assigned along with a player, such as being "selected." In some cases players are divided into categories, such as experts and beginners. Here "award" represents the assignment of a category. When a condition also occurs in the negative, the word *not* is included in parentheses.

Use the following list as a reference. You do not need to memorize it. Glance through it now and come back to it as you work on practice sequence questions.

CONDITIONS THAT ARE USED IN SEQUENCE GAMES

- Frank is before Gretchen.
- Frank is before Gretchen but is not first.
- Frank is (not) assigned before the fourth place.
- Frank is before Gretchen but after Howard.
- Frank is immediately before Gretchen.
- Frank is (not) immediately before or immediately after Gretchen.
- Frank is immediately before either Gretchen or Howard.
- Frank is (not) in third place.
- Frank is in third or fifth place.
- Frank is not last.
- Frank receives an award.
- Frank, Gretchen, and Howard cannot be in second, fourth, or fifth place.
- There are at least three players before Frank.
- There are at least two players between Frank and Gretchen.
- Both Frank and Gretchen are before Howard.
- Either Frank and Gretchen are consecutive, or Frank and Howard are consecutive, but not both.
- Either Frank is before Gretchen and Howard, or Gretchen and Howard are before Frank, but not both.
- Either Frank is before Gretchen, or Frank is before Howard, but not both.
- Either Frank or Gretchen is immediately before Howard.
- Either Frank or Gretchen is in fifth place.
- There are (no/exactly two) awards given after Frank performs.
- There are exactly two students between Frank and Gretchen.
- If Frank is before Gretchen, then neither Howard nor Inez is before Jeremy.
- If Frank is before Gretchen, then Howard is before Inez.
- If Frank is (not) in third place, then Frank is (after) before both Gretchen and Howard.
- The award is given to the person in the sixth place.
- The award is given to either Frank or Gretchen and is given to the person in the third or fifth place.
- The expert performs immediately before the beginner.

You can see that the test writers can easily create many variations on the above types. Learn these types but be prepared for new twists.

UNORDERED GAMES ("THROW CARDS IN THE HAT")

In unordered games, you are simply "throwing cards in the hat." In other words, some of the players will be "in," or selected, and the rest will be "out." Because there are always players left out, unordered games do not have one-to-one correspondence. Unordered games also often benefit from using a discard pile. The diagram for an unordered game typically has four to seven fixtures. Number the fixtures in order to distinguish the columns but it does not matter whether a player is assigned under fixture 2 or 5, for example. With occasional exceptions, in most unordered games the fixtures do not have branches. Unordered games may have two or even three categories of players. In some unordered games, the exact number of slots to be filled is variable. The conditions for unordered games are nearly all if/then statements.

For each variation, consider how it differs from other variations. Draw your own diagram first, before reading the explanation. Then compare your diagram with the one presented here.

UNORDERED GAME SAMPLE 1

A student must choose four elective courses to be taken during the next semester. The possible courses include Geography, Japanese, Legal Studies, Mandarin, Native Studies, Oceanography, Phonetics, and Russian. The following conditions apply:

If the student takes Geography, the student cannot take Russian.

If the student does not take Japanese, the student must take Russian.

If the student takes Phonetics, the student must take Mandarin.

If the student does not take Mandarin, the student does not take Native Studies.

Either the student takes Oceanography or Legal Studies, but not both.

This is a common, basic unordered game. The diagram consists of slots 1 through 4 and a discard pile of exactly four slots. The if/then statements represent a number of logical variations, including an "either/or but not both" statement. The students are fixtures and the courses are players.

UNORDERED GAME SAMPLE 2

A student must choose elective courses to be taken during the next semester. The possible courses include Geography, Japanese, Legal Studies, Mandarin, Native Studies, Oceanography, Phonetics, and Russian. The student must choose at least three courses. The following conditions apply:

If the student takes Geography, the student cannot take Russian.

If the student does not take Japanese, the student must take Russian.

If the student takes Phonetics, the student must take Mandarin.

If the student does not take Mandarin, the student does not take Native Studies.

Either the student takes Oceanography or Legal Studies, but not both.

In this game the number of fixtures varies. There must be at least three fixtures. At least one player must be out in an unordered game. As a result, the maximum number of fixtures is seven. It is safe to put seven possible fixtures in the diagram. They may not all be needed. The discard pile is also variable.

$$\underline{1} \quad \underline{2} \quad \underline{3} \quad \cdots \quad \underline{4} \quad \underline{5} \quad \underline{6} \quad \underline{7} \Big| \underline{} \, \underline{} \, \underline{}$$

Figure 4.41. Unordered game with variable
fixtures and a variable discard pile

UNORDERED GAME SAMPLE 3

A student must choose five elective courses to be taken during the next semester. The possible courses include four languages—Greek, Japanese, Lithuanian, and Mandarin—and four humanities—Native Studies, Organizational Management, Phonetics, and Sociology. The following conditions apply:

If the student takes Greek, the student cannot take Sociology.

If the student does not take Japanese, the student must take Sociology.

If the student takes Phonetics, the student must take Mandarin.

If the student does not take Mandarin, the student does not take Native Studies.

If the student takes any language, the student must take Organizational Management.

This game has two sets of players: languages and humanities. You must keep track of them separately because the last rule distinguishes between them. Otherwise, this game functions in the same way as a basic unordered game.

UNORDERED GAME SAMPLE 4

Eight employees—Ferguson, Griego, Handelin, Jong, Kowalski, Levy, Montoya, and Norton—have volunteered to attend a business conference. Each employee who has volunteered falls into exactly one of the following categories: manager, part-time employee, or union representative. Exactly five employees are to be chosen to attend. The following must obtain:

Kowalski is a manager.

Norton attends only if Norton is a part-time employee.

If exactly two managers attend, Kowalski does not attend.

Exactly two union representatives must attend.

This game has two sets of players: the employees and the designations of manager, part-time employee, and union representative. Each fixture must be assigned both a person and a designation. This game, then, requires two branches for each fixture. There are exactly five fixtures and exactly three discard slots.

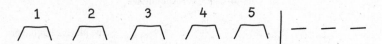

Figure 4.42. Unordered game with two branches

Conditions for Unordered Games

In the previous samples you have seen approximately half of the types of conditions that occur with unordered games. The majority of conditions involve an if/then statement. As with the sequence conditions, the test writers can create many variations. If you master the rules for working with if/thens, you will be able to correctly interpret most of the conditions in an unordered game.

Most unordered games have five conditions. Some have four or six. In the following conditions, players are either "in" or "out." In some games players are grouped by category. The conditions refer to a game in which some players are managers, some are part-time employees, and some are union representatives.

You do not need to memorize these conditions. Use the list below as a reference when you are working on unordered games. Glance through the list now to become familiar with the possible types of conditions.

CONDITIONS THAT ARE USED IN UNORDERED GAMES

- Howard is included only if Leonard is not included.
- Howard is included only if he is a manager.
- Howard is a manager.
- Howard is a manager and is included.
- There is at least one manager.
- There is at least one manager, one part-time employee, and one union representative.
- There are exactly two managers.
- Howard cannot be included if Leonard is included.
- Either Howard or Leonard is included, but not both.
- If Howard is included, then Leonard is included. (=Leonard must be included if Howard is included.)
- If Howard is included, then Leonard is not included.
- If Howard is not included, then Leonard is included. (=Leonard must be included if Howard is not included.)
- If Howard is not included, then Leonard is not included.
- If Howard is included, then neither Leonard nor Penny is included.
- If both Howard and Leonard are included, then at least one is not a manager.
- If either Howard or Leonard is included, then both must be included.
- If there are any managers included, then Howard must also be included.

ORDERED NON-SEQUENCE GAMES WITH ONE-TO-ONE CORRESPONDENCE

The games in this section are the ones labeled ONS-A (ordered, non-sequence, A = left branch, which is one-to-one correspondence) as shown in Figure 4.43.

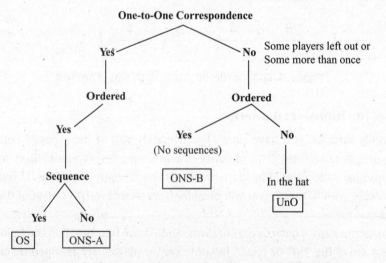

Figure 4.43. The games discussed in this section are ONS-A.

Games with one-to-one correspondence (OS and ONS-A) are all ordered. Because all of the players are used exactly once, it is the order of the players that is important. The first such type are sequence games (OS), which we have defined as establishing strings of relationships among at least three players. Some games have one-to-one correspondence but do not have a string with at least three players. These games (ONS-A) still have some elements of a sequence game but function differently enough that it is worth studying them separately. Study the examples below to find the differences and similarities between the two.

One difference between these two types is that nearly 75 percent of one-to-one non-sequence games (ONS-A) use branched fixtures, with variable branches in about a third of them. By contrast, only 5 percent of sequence games use branched fixtures and the branches are typically not variable. ONS-A games use the small number of fixtures with multiple and often variable branches to create complexity, whereas sequence games are complex because of their long linear relationships.

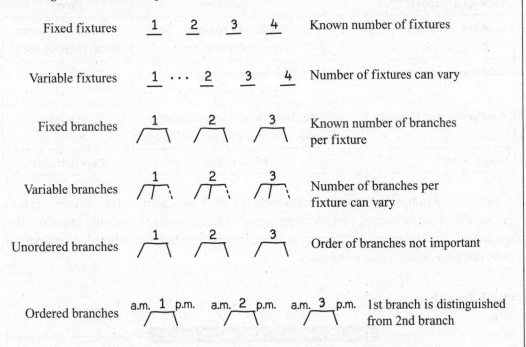

Figure 4.44. Summary of variations for fixtures and branches

In both of these game types each player is used exactly once (one-to-one correspondence), the order of the fixtures is important (ordered), and the number of fixtures is fixed. When the fixtures are branched, the branches—but not the fixtures—can be variable. In addition, the branches can be ordered or unordered.

Whereas in sequence games the fixtures simply represent the order in the sequence (e.g., 1 through 6), in the ONS-A games, fixtures are more likely to represent objects, such as people, presentations, companies, and teams. The players often fall into two or three categories, such as beginners and experts, singers and accompanists. In some games the branches might represent morning and afternoon, or a first presenter and second presenter. It is the relationships between categories of players, characteristics of branches, and fixtures that makes these games different from, and more complex than, sequence games. Table 4.2 summarizes the similarities and differences between sequence games and one-to-one non-sequence games (ONS-A).

Table 4.2. Comparison of one-to-one correspondence, ordered sequence games and one-to-one correspondence, ordered non-sequence games (ONS-A)

	Non-Sequence Games (ONS-A)	Sequence Games
One-to-one correspondence	Yes	Yes
Ordered	Yes	Yes
Strings of relationships	Short or none	Long (three players or more)
Number of fixtures	Fewer	More
Frequency of branched games	75%	5%
Type of branches	Variable	Fixed
Content of fixtures	Objects (people, presentations, etc.)	Places in sequence (first, second, etc.)
Categories of player	Two to three (e.g, singer and accompanist)	Only one
Categories per fixtures	Multiple (e.g., A.M. presentation and P.M. presentation on Day 1)	Only one
Conditions	Many if/then's	Few if/then's

Below are examples of the important patterns of ONS-A games. The patterns include games with fixed branches, variable branches that are unordered, variable branches that are ordered, and no branches. Draw your own diagram first, before reading the explanation. Then compare your diagram with ours.

Fixed Branches

ONE-TO-ONE NON-SEQUENCE SAMPLE 1

Six singers—Kovac, Larson, Ming, Nieto, Ofune, and Parsons—will each perform in one of three shows at a single concert. In each show exactly two of the singers will perform together. Each show lasts thirty minutes and the first show starts at 7 P.M. The shows run consecutively and do not overlap. Each singer performs exactly once. The singers appear according to the following conditions:

If Ming performs in the first show, then Larson performs in the second show.

If Ofune does not perform in the second show, then both Larson and Nieto perform in the third show.

Kovac performs in either the first or third show.

Parsons does not perform in any show that Nieto performs in.

The fixtures are the three shows and each show has two unordered branches, one for each of the two singers. This is a typical ONS-A game, using if/then statements and branches, rather than conditions showing who comes before whom.

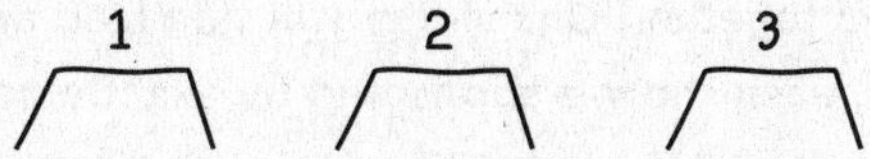

If M = 1 → L = 2

If O ≠ 2 → L + N = 3

K = 1 or 3

If N → –P

Figure 4.45. One-to-one non-sequence with two fixed branches

Six singers—Kovac, Larson, Ming, Nieto, Ofune, and Parsons—will each perform in one of three shows at a single concert. In each show exactly two of the singers will perform together. One singer will sing lead and the other will sing harmony. Each show lasts thirty minutes and the first show starts at 7 P.M. The shows run consecutively and do not overlap. Each singer performs exactly once. The singers appear according to the following conditions:

Either Ming performs in the same show as Larson, or Ming performs in the same show as Nieto.

Ofune sings harmony.

Either Parsons or Kovac sings lead, but they cannot both sing lead.

Kovac must perform before both Ming and Ofune.

This game still has two branches but they are now ordered. One branch represents the lead singer and the other, the person singing harmony. The conditions rely on either/or statements. The last condition is similar to a sequence condition.

Either M = L
 or M = N

O = Harmony

Either P = Lead
 or K = Lead
 but not both

K –< M
     O

Figure 4.46. One-to-one non-sequence with two branches that are ordered

Six singers—Kovac, Larson, Ming, Nieto, Ofune, and Parsons—will each perform in one of three shows at a single concert. In each show exactly two of the singers will perform together. One singer will sing lead and the other will sing harmony. In addition, each show is sponsored by exactly one of three local companies—Stanfield's, Topnotch, and Urban Style—and each company sponsors exactly one show. Each show lasts thirty minutes and the first show starts at 7 P.M. The shows run consecutively and do not overlap. Each singer performs exactly once. The singers appear according to the following conditions:

Ming performs in the show that is sponsored by Topnotch.

Parsons and Nieto do not perform in the same show.

The show sponsored by Stanfield's is after the show sponsored by Urban Style.

Kovac must perform before both Ming and Ofune.

This game introduces a third category of player—the sponsors—and has three branches—lead singer, harmony singer, and sponsor. The branches are ordered and represent different characteristics. The last two conditions show relative orders of players but not enough to make it a sequence game. The third condition gives a relative order of shows, not players, and does so in terms of the sponsors.

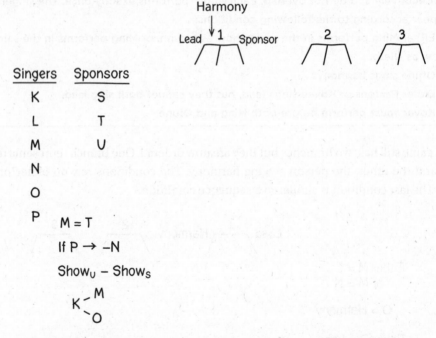

Figure 4.47. One-to-one non-sequence with three ordered branches

Six singers—Kovac, Larson, Ming, Nieto, Ofune, and Parsons—will each perform in one of six shows at a single concert. In each show exactly one singer will perform. Each singer performs either with musical accompaniment or without. Each show lasts thirty minutes and the first show starts at 7 P.M. The shows run consecutively and do not overlap. Each singer performs exactly once. The singers appear according to the following conditions:

Kovac, Larson, and Ming are amateurs.

Nieto, Ofune, and Parsons are professionals.

Larson sings with accompaniment.

Parsons sings without accompaniment.

All of the singers who sing with accompaniment must perform before any of the singers who sing without accompaniment.

Any amateur who sings with accompaniment must perform before any professional who sings with accompaniment.

This game has three categories of player—amateur singers, professional singers, and the characteristic of being accompanied or unaccompanied. However, each fixture (representing one of the six shows) only needs to have a branch for the singer and a branch for being accompanied or not. It is not necessary to have separate branches for amateurs and professionals. The diagram, then, has two ordered branches for each fixture.

This game acts in some ways like a sequence game. The six players are assigned in a one-to-one correspondence to the six shows. The second branch is not the result of clumping players together, as in the previous sample games, but results from adding the characteristic of accompaniment. Unlike in sequence games, the conditions do not show the relationships among the players. Rather, the conditions present a complex set of rules that involve all three categories of players. The last two conditions are particularly complex. Study them carefully.

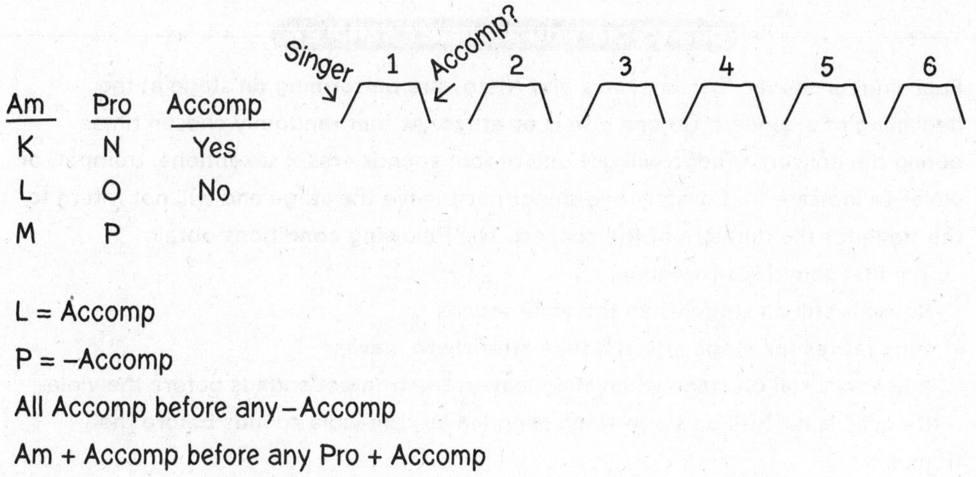

Am	Pro	Accomp
K	N	Yes
L	O	No
M	P	

L = Accomp

P = –Accomp

All Accomp before any –Accomp

Am + Accomp before any Pro + Accomp

Figure 4.48. One-to-one non-sequence with three categories of players and two fixed branches

ONE-TO-ONE NON-SEQUENCE SAMPLE 5

Six singers—Kovac, Larson, Ming, Nieto, Ofune, and Parsons—will each perform in one of three shows at a single concert. In each show exactly two singers will perform, one of whom is an amateur and one of whom is a professional. Each show lasts thirty minutes and the first show starts at 7 P.M. The shows run consecutively and do not overlap. Each singer performs exactly once. The singers appear according to the following conditions:

Kovac, Larson, and Ming are amateurs.

Nieto, Ofune, and Parsons are professionals.

Both Larson and Ming perform before Kovac.

Parsons performs before Nieto.

As in a sequence game, the conditions in this game primarily define relationships among players, but there is no string that connects three or more players. This game acts like a non-sequence game in that it clusters the players into three fixtures (the three shows), each with two ordered branches.

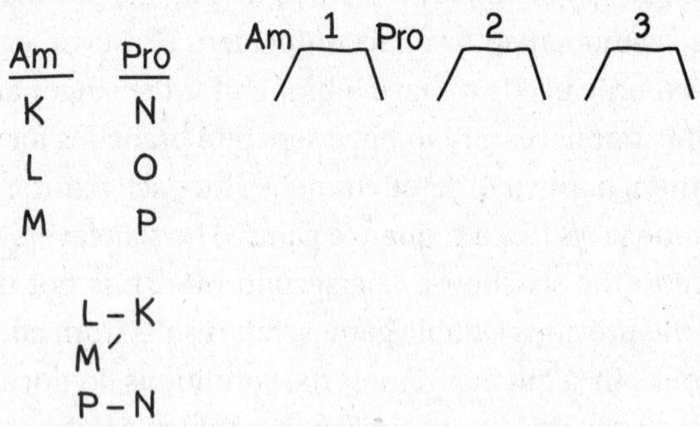

Figure 4.49. One-to-one non-sequence with sequence-like conditions

ONE-TO-ONE NON-SEQUENCE SAMPLE 6

Four singers—Kovac, Larson, Ming, and Nieto—are performing on stage at the beginning of a concert. No one else is on stage. At four randomly chosen times during the concert a judge will use one of four sounds—rasp, saxophone, trumpet, or viola—to indicate that exactly one singer must leave the stage and will not return to the stage for the duration of the concert. The following conditions obtain:

The first sound is saxophone.

Kovac is still on stage when the viola sounds.

Ming leaves the stage at some time after Nieto leaves.

If Kovac is still on stage when Ming leaves, the trumpet sounds before the viola.

If Kovac is not still on stage when Ming leaves, the viola sounds before the trumpet.

This unusual variation (it has only occurred once in recent years) starts with the full cast of players and has them leave one at a time, according to conditions. Think of this as an "unloading" game. The four fixtures, which represent the time at which a sound is played and a player leaves the stage, are divided into two ordered branches, one for the player and one for the sound. One of the last two conditions *must* be true. Notice how the diagram in Figure 4.50 uses the word *else* to show this relationship. S is placed under fixture 1 as permanent.

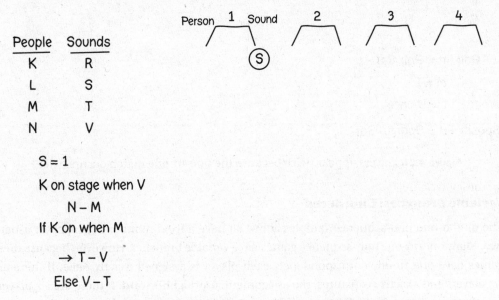

Figure 4.50. One-to-one non-sequence "unloading" game

ONE-TO-ONE NON-SEQUENCE SAMPLE 7

Three singers—Kovac, Larson, and Ming—will each perform in one of three shows at a concert on Friday and again at a concert on Saturday. On each day the shows run consecutively and do not overlap. In each show exactly one singer performs. In addition, each show is sponsored by exactly one of three local companies—Stanfield's, Topnotch, and Urban Style—and each company sponsors exactly one show on Friday and one show on Saturday. Each singer performs exactly once Friday and once Saturday. On Saturday no singer can appear in a show sponsored by the same company that sponsored the show in which that singer appeared on Friday. The singers and sponsors appear according to the following conditions:

Ming does not perform in any show that is sponsored by Topnotch.

Larson must appear in one of the shows sponsored by Urban.

The company that sponsored the show in which Kovac performed on Friday must sponsor the show in which Ming performs on Saturday.

Each of the players—singers and sponsors—appears twice in any arrangement. The game still has one-to-one correspondence. It is simply a one-to-one match that happens twice— once on Friday and once on Saturday.

Singer	Sponsor
K	S
L	T
M	U

Fri: Singer 1 ↘ Sponsor ↙ 2   3

Sat: 1   2   3

Pair Fri ≠ Pair Sat

M ≠ T

L = U once

Spons$_K$ Fri = Spons$_M$ Sat

Figure 4.51. Players appear twice because the one-to-one match occurs twice.

Variable Branches: Unordered

The one-to-one non-sequence samples above all have a fixed number of branches, usually two. Many one-to-one non-sequence games have variable branches. However, because these games have one-to-one correspondence, each player is assigned exactly once. If there are six players and exactly six fixtures, the assignment is straightforward. If there are six players and three fixtures, then the fixtures must have enough branches to make a total of six assignments. With variable branches, the number of branches per fixture varies.

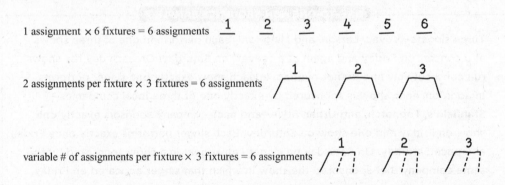

1 assignment × 6 fixtures = 6 assignments   1   2   3   4   5   6

2 assignments per fixture × 3 fixtures = 6 assignments   1   2   3

variable # of assignments per fixture × 3 fixtures = 6 assignments   1   2   3

Figure 4.52. Three ways to assign six players exactly once each: top—one player to each of six fixtures; middle—two players per fixture for three fixtures; and bottom—a variable number of players per fixture for three fixtures

In the following ONS-A game samples, the number of branches is variable and the branches are unordered. The number of fixtures is always fixed.

ONE-TO-ONE NON-SEQUENCE SAMPLE 8 WITH VARIABLE BRANCHES THAT ARE UNORDERED

Six singers—Kovac, Larson, Ming, Nieto, Ofune, and Parsons—will each perform in one of three shows at a single concert. Each show lasts thirty minutes and the first show starts at 7 P.M. The shows run consecutively and do not overlap. Each singer performs exactly once. Each show includes at least one singer. The assignment of singers conforms to the following:

If Ming performs in the first show, Larson also performs in the first show.

Ofune performs in the second show.

Parsons and Kovac do not perform in the same show as each other.

Kovac and Ofune perform in the same show.

There are exactly three shows but the number of branches under each show can vary. Each show must have at least one singer, so there must be at least one branch per fixture. Three players are used up in filling these slots. The three remaining players can be distributed in various ways. Theoretically, the three remaining players could all perform in the same show, resulting in one show with four players and two shows with one player each. The diagram does not necessarily need to show four branches under each fixture. It is enough to show one or two dotted (variable) branches and to know that there may be more branches. In the Figure 4.53 diagram, the line under the number for each show extends past the last dotted line. This helps remind you that there could be more branches. The branches in this game are unordered, meaning that the order in which players are assigned to a show does not matter.

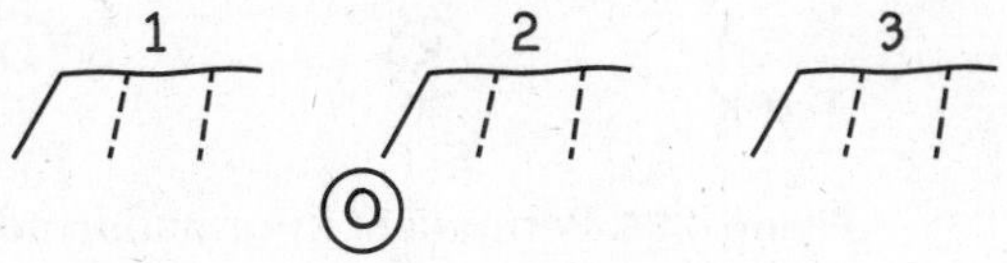

If M = 1 → L = 1

O = 2

P ≠ K

KO

Figure 4.53. One-to-one non-sequence with variable, unordered branches. Ofune is circled under show 2 to indicate that Ofune in 2 is a permanent condition.

ONE-TO-ONE NON-SEQUENCE SAMPLE 9 WITH VARIABLE BRANCHES THAT ARE UNORDERED

Six singers—Kovac, Larson, Ming, Nieto, Ofune, and Parsons—will each perform in one of two shows at a single concert. The shows run consecutively and do not overlap. In the first show up to three singers can perform. In the second show up to five singers can perform. Each singer performs exactly once. The assignment of singers conforms to the following:

Ofune performs in the second show.

Kovac performs in the first show.

Parsons and Kovac do not perform in the same show as each other.

There are only two fixtures—the first show and the second show—but the number of possible branches under each show is different. Unlike the previous sample, this game tells us exactly what the maximum number of branches is for each fixture—three and five, respectively. The setup does not initially state that either of the shows must have at least one performer, so all of the branches are optional at first (represented by dotted lines). If all of the slots in show 1 are filled, there will still be three players that must be assigned to show 2, so show 2 has at least three branches that must be filled. However, it is not necessary to figure this fact out before creating the diagram.

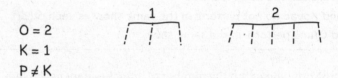

O = 2
K = 1
P ≠ K

Figure 4.54. This represents the initial diagram. It is one-to-one non-sequence, and has two fixtures with different numbers of variable branches. The branches are unordered.

As you work through the diagram in Figure 4.54, players O and K are put into the diagram as permanent (circled) information (Figure 4.55). At that point, change the branches they are under from optional (dotted) to required (solid).

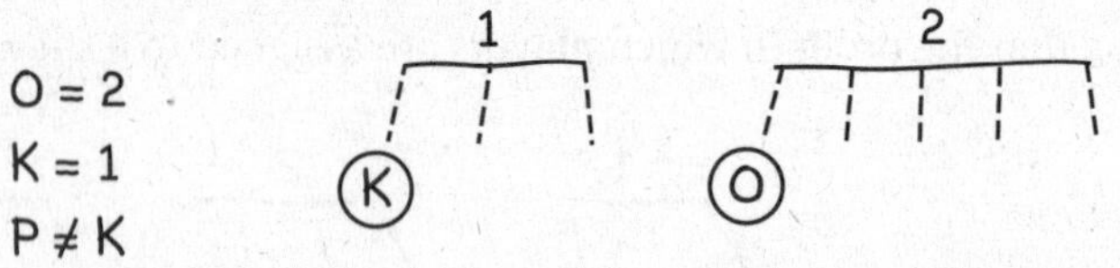

O = 2
K = 1
P ≠ K

Ⓚ   Ⓞ

Figure 4.55. Permanent information added to the diagram and optional branches changed to permanent

---

ONE-TO-ONE NON-SEQUENCE SAMPLE 10 WITH VARIABLE BRANCHES THAT ARE UNORDERED

An archaeological team is excavating three layers—lower, middle, and upper—of an ancient site. Eight archaeology interns—Francesca, Gerard, Hung, Isabella, Jason, Karim, Laila, and Morton—are to be assigned to work on the layers. Up to four interns can be assigned to each layer. Each intern works on exactly one layer. The requirements for assigning the interns are:

    The lower layer must be assigned more interns than the middle layer.

    Gerard must be assigned to the same layer as Isabella.

    Jason must be assigned to a higher layer than Morton.

    Laila must be assigned to the middle layer.

    Karim must be assigned to a layer on which no other interns work.

In this game the fixtures are arranged vertically. Earlier you learned about vertical sequence games. This non-sequence game differs slightly. The eight players are distributed among three fixtures, each divided into branches. Also, in this game there are no long strings of relationships. Long strings are found only in sequence games. About 10 percent of ONS-A games are vertical.

Each of the three layers has up to four branches. The setup does not state that each layer must have any certain number of interns, so the diagram initially shows all branches as optional (dotted lines).

For sequence games you learned to make a vertical supplemental diagram for vertical setups. A supplemental diagram is helpful in sequence games because sequence games are based on long sequences of relationships. For this non-sequence game a supplemental diagram is not applicable. You can represent the relationships among players horizontally. In the diagram below, lower is to the left and upper is to the right. See the rule M – J as an example. Jason is above (to the right of) Morton. The designations of lower, middle, and upper partially overlap with the alphabetical range of the players (G through M). Spell out *low*, *mid*, and *up*.

The first rule has been added into the Figure 4.56 diagram, above the fixtures. The space below the fixtures is used only for assignment of players.

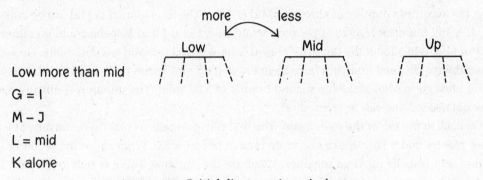

Low more than mid

G = I

M – J

L = mid

K alone

Figure 4.56. Initial diagram. A vertical setup.

The second rule cannot be put directly into the diagram. The third rule shows that Jason must be in a layer above M, so Jason cannot be in the first layer. You can enter –J above Low. The next rule puts Laila into the mid layer. The last rule—that K is alone—tells us that K cannot be in Mid (Laila is there) but also that K cannot be in Low because there must be more players in Low than in Mid. That leaves K in Up. The diagram is now:

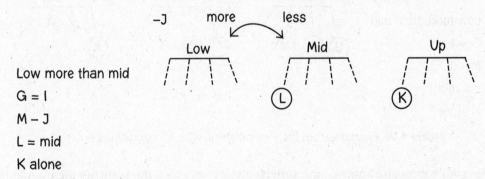

Low more than mid

G = I

M – J

L = mid

K alone

Figure 4.57. The second stage of entering information into the diagram

One branch of Mid and one of Up are now solid lines, with permanent information. Now that there is new information in the diagram (Figure 4.58), go back to the top of the conditions. The first condition indicates that there must be at least two players in Low. Make two branches solid. The second condition still does not go directly into the diagram. The third condition has already been applied. The fourth condition indicates that the last three branches of Up should be crossed out.

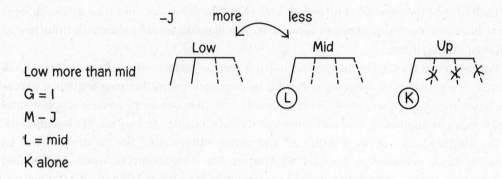

Figure 4.58. The third stage of entering information

Because there is new information in the diagram, go through the conditions again. What are the implications of the first rule? The maximum number of players in Low is four. Therefore, the maximum number of players in Mid is three. The final branch in Mid can be crossed off. It is still not clear how to apply the second rule. Gerard and Isabella could go either in Low or Mid. What about the third rule? Jason cannot go in Low. Mid is a possibility. Up is not a possibility. The final branches have been crossed off and Karim must be alone. Therefore, Jason must go in Mid. Make the second branch of Mid solid. The notation –J above Low is now not needed and can be crossed off.

Go back to the top of the rules again. The first rule now tells us that there must be at least three players under Low. Make one more branch of Low solid. What about the second rule? Gerard and Isabella must go together. What are the options? There is only one space left under Mid and none under Up. They must go under Low. The third rule dictates that M must go under Low. There are six players already accounted for. Two are left—F and H—for which there are no rules. One can go under Low and one under Mid. Make the final branch of Low solid and the third branch of Mid solid.

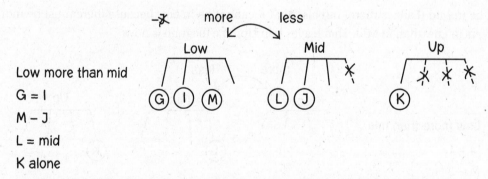

Figure 4.59. Final diagram for vertical game with all conditions entered

Samples 8 through 10 above have variable fixtures in which the branches are unordered. The following samples have variable fixtures in which the branches are ordered. Each branch represents a distinct characteristic and it matters to which branch of a fixture a player is assigned.

Variable Branches: Ordered

Six singers—Kovac, Larson, Ming, Nieto, Ofune, and Parsons—will each perform in one of three shows at a single concert. Each show lasts thirty minutes and the first show starts at 7 P.M. The shows run consecutively and do not overlap. Each singer performs exactly once. Each show includes at least one singer. Exactly one singer in each show must sing lead. The assignment of singers conforms to the following:

Either Ming or Nieto must sing lead in the show in which Larson performs.

Either Parsons or Kovac must sing lead in the show in which Ofune performs.

Ofune performs before Larson.

Kovac and Ofune perform in the same show.

One of the branches of each show represents the lead singer. The other branches are variable. Because three players are accounted for by the three solid branches (lead), there are three remaining players to assign to the variable branches. In Figure 4.60, Show$_L$ refers to the show in which Larson performs.

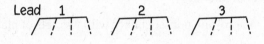

Show$_L$:

Either M = Lead
or N = Lead

Show$_O$:

Either P = Lead
or K = Lead

O – L

K = O

Figure 4.60. One-to-one non-sequence game
with variable branches that are ordered

Six singers—Kovac, Larson, Ming, Nieto, Ofune, and Parsons—will each perform in one of three shows at a single concert. Exactly three accompanists—Thompson, Ulibarri, and Vanh—are available to accompany the singers. Each show lasts thirty minutes and the first show starts at 7 P.M. The shows run consecutively and do not overlap. Each singer performs exactly once. Each show includes at least one singer and exactly one accompanist. Each accompanist is in exactly one show. The assignment of singers and accompanists conforms to the following:

The show with Vanh takes place before the show with Ulibarri.

Vanh accompanies exactly one singer.

The show in which Larson sings takes place before any show in which either Ofune performs or Thompson accompanies.

Kovac cannot perform after any show in which Ming performs.

This game has two sets of players: singers and accompanists. The accompanists cannot be used as fixtures because the order in which they appear matters. The diagram uses the three shows as fixtures. Each show has a required singer and exactly one required accompanist. However, there may be additional singers, shown by the variable branches.

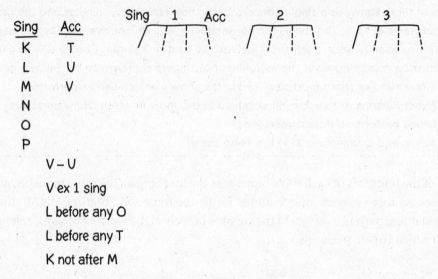

Sing   Acc
K   T
L   U
M   V
N
O
P

V – U

V ex 1 sing

L before any O

L before any T

K not after M

Figure 4.61. One-to-one non-sequence with two sets of players and variable branches

The last two conditions warrant careful attention. To say that Larson appears before any position in which Thompson appears means that once Thompson appears, Larson cannot appear. The final condition has a similar meaning. Once Ming has appeared, Kovac cannot appear.

No Branches

Some ONS-A games have unbranched fixtures, which makes them look like sequence games. These games tend to use fewer if/then conditions than the ONS-A games with branches. Instead, they rely more on conditions that describe who must come before or after whom and who can, cannot, or must go into which fixture, supplemented by some if/then conditions. These features also make the non-branch games more similar to sequences. The primary difference is that there are not the long strings of relationships.

> **ONE-TO-ONE NON-SEQUENCE SAMPLE 13 WITH NO BRANCHES**
>
> Six singers—Kovac, Larson, Ming, Nieto, Ofune, and Parsons—will each perform in one of six shows at a single concert. Each show lasts thirty minutes and the first show starts at 7 P.M. The shows run consecutively and do not overlap. Each singer performs exactly once. The singers appear according to the following conditions:
>
> Ming performs in a show before Larson.
> Ofune performs either immediately before or immediately after Kovac.
> Parsons performs either before Nieto or before Kovac, but not both.
> Kovac performs in either the first or third show.

The six time slots are the fixtures. No branches are needed.

$$
\begin{array}{ccccccc}
 & & -K & & -K & -K & -K \\
\underline{1} & \underline{2} & \underline{3} & \underline{4} & \underline{5} & \underline{6} \\
\end{array}
$$

M – L

OK or KO

Either P – N

   or P – K

   but not both

K = 1 or 3

Figure 4.62. One-to-one non-sequence game without branches

ONE-TO-ONE NON-SEQUENCE SAMPLE 14 WITH NO BRANCHES

Four employees of a company—Ferguson, Gray, Ibanez, and Jordan—are scheduled to each take a paid personal retreat during the first ten days of the upcoming month. Each retreat lasts either two or three complete, consecutive days. Each person takes exactly one retreat and, except for the first retreat, each retreat begins when the previous retreat ends. The first retreat begins on the first day of the upcoming month. The following conditions apply:

The retreats of Ferguson and Jordan last three days.

The retreats of Gray and Ibanez last two days.

Gray's retreat must start on an even-numbered day.

If Jordan's retreat is before Gray's, then Ibanez's retreat is before Ferguson's.

In this game there are four time slots—one for each player—but some slots are two days long and others are three days. In addition, it is important whether a player starts on an even- or odd-numbered day. The fixtures consist of all ten days, numbered from the first of the month through the tenth. Note the possible order drawn into the diagram in Figure 4.63. The dashes represent the number of days taken up for the time slot of the particular player.

$$
\begin{array}{cccccccccc}
\underline{1} & \underline{2} & \underline{3} & \underline{4} & \underline{5} & \underline{6} & \underline{7} & \underline{8} & \underline{9} & \underline{10} \\
I & - & F & - & - & G & - & J & - & - \\
\end{array}
$$

F, J = 3 days

G, I = 2 days

G = even

If J – G →

   J – F

Figure 4.63. Unbranched game with unequal lengths for each time slot

On the LSAT you may also see time slots that start on the hour, half hour, or quarter hour. Some slots could last a half hour and others a full hour, or some a quarter hour and others a half hour.

Three singers—Kovac, Larson, and Ming—are to perform during a concert. Kovac will perform one jazz piece and one rock piece. Larson will perform one folk piece and one modern piece. Ming will perform one swing piece and one tango piece. The performances run consecutively and do not overlap. The order of the performances follows these conditions:

The jazz piece is performed before the modern piece.

The rock piece is performed before the tango piece.

Ming cannot perform immediately after Larson.

At first you might think that this is not really a one-to-one correspondence game because each player appears twice. Notice how the Figure 4.64 diagram simplifies the game by listing the players as Kovac jazz, Kovac rock, Larson folk, and so on. In this way, there are six distinct players. The singers and types of music are not two separate sets of players. They cannot be "mixed and matched." The conditions pair them up for us and that pairing cannot be changed.

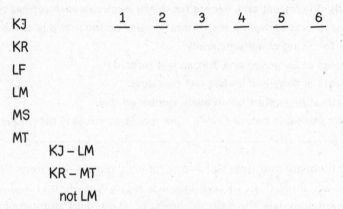

Figure 4.64. Unbranched game with predefined combinations of players and styles

Three types of performers—singers, tap dancers, and musicians—are to perform during the eight time slots in an evening concert. There are exactly three singers, three tap dancers, and two musicians. Each performer performs exactly once. Because the setup for each type of performer is time-consuming, the following rules have been set:

There can be no more than three transitions from one type of performer to another during the evening.

The sixth performer cannot be of the same type as the fifth performer.

There are eight players, each used exactly once, but they do not have distinct designations. There are, for example, three singers but the game does not distinguish between the first, second, or third singer. It is important to keep track of how many singers are available for assigning. This game also introduces the concept of a transition between two different types and a limit on the number of transitions allowed.

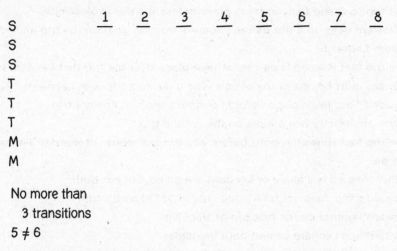

Figure 4.65. Unbranched game with generic types of players

Conditions for Ordered Non-Sequence Games with One-to-One Correspondence

The two tables below show the most common and less common types of conditions for ONS-A games. The test writers can create many variations on the patterns listed here. For the examples below, consider a game in which there are three trips—Grand Canyon, Yosemite, and Zion—and each trip has one guide and two travelers. The order in which the trips take place is important.

**CONDITIONS FOR ORDERED NON-SEQUENCE
ONE-TO-ONE CORRESPONDENCE GAMES**

Most Frequent Conditions, in Relative Order of Frequency

- Howard does not go on the same trip as Leonard.
- Howard goes on the same trip as Leonard.
- Howard goes on the trip to Yosemite.
- Howard's trip takes place before Penny's trip.
- If Howard does not go on the trip to Zion, then Leonard goes on the trip to Yosemite.
- Howard is a guide.
- Howard goes on the trip that takes place second.
- Either Howard or Leonard is the guide on the trip that Penny takes.
- Howard is a guide and is on the same trip as either Leonard or Penny.

```
┌─────────────────────────────────────────────────────────────┐
│              CONDITIONS FOR ORDERED NON-SEQUENCE            │
│              ONE-TO-ONE CORRESPONDENCE GAMES                │
│                    Less Frequent Conditions                 │
```

- Howard does not go on the trip to Zion.
- The trip to Grand Canyon takes place before the trip to Yosemite.
- If Howard goes on a trip before Leonard, Howard goes on the trip immediately before Leonard.
- The trip that Howard is on cannot take place after the trip that Leonard is on.
- Howard must be one of the people who goes on a trip with Leonard.
- Howard's trip takes place before Leonard's trip and Penny's trip.
- There are exactly two people on the second trip.
- The trip that Howard is on is before any trip that either Leonard or Penny are on.
- Either Howard is a guide or Leonard is a guide, but not both.
- Howard's trip does not take place until after Leonard's trip.
- Howard is either on the first trip or third trip.
- Howard and Leonard cannot both be guides.
- The trip that Howard is on has exactly three people on it.
- Either Howard and Leonard are both guides or neither is a guide.
- There are exactly three guides and exactly five passengers.

The following conditions are found on games with certain complex relationships:

- The horse that Sanchez races on Day 1 is raced by Telgarsky on Day 2.
- Any beginner must come before the experts' opening speaker.
- All beginners must come before any experts.
- Tap dancing is on the floor immediately above the floor with an oil painting.
- There cannot be two beginners presenting in a row.

ORDERED GAMES WITHOUT ONE-TO-ONE CORRESPONDENCE

The games in this section fall into the category of ONS-B, as shown in Figure 4.66.

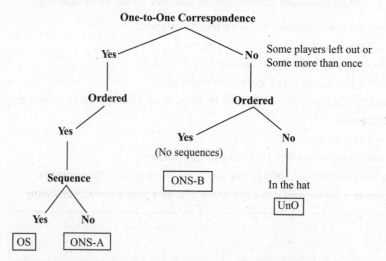

Figure 4.66. The games in this section are in the ONS-B category.

The previous section gave examples of ordered, non-sequence games with one-to-one correspondence (ONS-A). In this section we examine ordered, non-sequence games that are not one-to-one (ONS-B). ONS-B games are similar in many ways to ONS-A games. In the games in the previous section, each player was used exactly once. However, in ONS-B either some players are left out or some are used more than once, and it is important to determine which when setting up an ONS-B game.

ONS-B games may have fixed branches, variable branches, or no branches. Because the number of players in an assignment varies, these games tend to have a higher occurrence of variable branches and may also have variable fixtures.

Draw your own diagram first, before reading the explanation for the samples below.

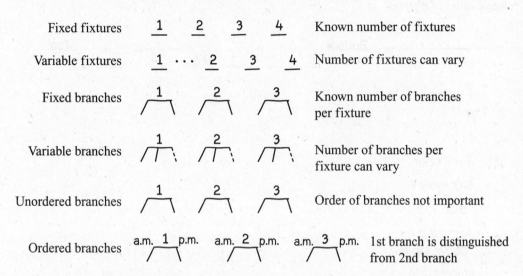

Figure 4.67. Summary of variations of fixtures and branches

No Branches

About a third of ONS-B games have no branches. They may, however, have variable fixtures. If only some of the players are used, the unbranched diagram may include a discard pile, as in the unordered ("throw them in the hat") games.

**NON-ONE-TO-ONE ORDERED GAMES SAMPLE 1
WITH NO BRANCHES AND FIXED FIXTURES**

An office building has seven floors, with floor 1 being the lowest and floor 7 the highest. The seven floors are each occupied by one of seven companies. Each company engages in exactly one of either finance, investment, or management. There is at least one finance, one investment, and one management company in the building. The location of companies is determined by the following conditions:

   The third floor can be occupied only by either a finance company or a management company.

   There are more finance companies on the top three floors than there are finance companies on the lowest three floors.

   At most two investment companies are above the uppermost management company.

   There is at least one management company that is immediately between a finance company and an investment company.

This game assigns types of companies (players) to floors (fixtures). The floors are listed from left to right, which represents bottom to top, respectively. A vertical supplemental diagram is not necessary but might help prevent confusion. Each floor gets exactly one company, so there are no branches. It is not known how many times each of the players is used but there must be a total of seven players, so the fixtures are fixed.

An important aspect of this game is that the players—finance, investment, management—actually represent categories of players. You are allowed to use as many finance companies, for example, as the rules allow. In setting up categories of players, the LSAT uses categories such as types of fruits, colors, and trees.

The conditions in this game include if/then statements along with information about the relative order of players.

Bottom   −I   Top

       1   2   3   4   5   6   7

F

I

M

3 = F or M

5–7 more F
  than 1–3

At most 2 I
  above top M

At least 1 M
  between F and I

Figure 4.68. Non-one-to-one ordered Sample 1. No branches.

NON-ONE-TO-ONE ORDERED GAMES SAMPLE 2 WITH NO BRANCHES AND DISCARD PILE

Five law students—Franticek, Griselli, Hao, Ionescu, and Jones—are available to participate in three sessions of a conference on human rights—the morning, afternoon, and evening sessions. None of the students can attend more than one session and each session is attended by exactly one of the five students. The conference manager must assign the students based on the following conditions:

Either Griselli or Jones, but not both, attends one of the sessions.

If Hao attends any session, Ionescu attends the session that immediately follows.

If Franticek does not attend any session, Griselli attends the evening session.

Jones does not attend the morning session.

In this game only some of the players are used. Exactly three of the five are used and exactly two are discarded. The conditions are primarily if/then statements.

```
                    Morn    Aft    Eve  | __ __
F
G
H
I
J        Either G
           or J
        but not both

      If H  →   HI

      If –F → G = Eve

        J ≠ Morn
```

Figure 4.69. Non-one-to-one game with no branches and with a discard pile

---

**NON-ONE-TO-ONE ORDERED GAMES SAMPLE 3
WITH NO BRANCHES AND VARIABLE FIXTURES**

During his stay in the hospital, Frederick is able to receive at most one visitor
per day from a list that consists of four of his friends: Gerald, Hermione, Inez, and
Jackson. Each friend visits him at least once but no friend visits him more than twice.
The visits are constrained by the following rules:

Hermione visits exactly once out of the first four visits.

The person who visits third is also the last person to visit.

At least once, Inez visits in the next available time after Gerald.

Each player appears at least once but may also appear a second time. The total number of
visits is unknown. The visits—a minimum of four and maximum of eight—are the fixtures.
Therefore, the number of fixtures is variable. Notice how the Figure 4.70 diagram shows the
minimum and maximum number of visits and uses dots to indicate that the exact number is
unknown and variable.

```
G            1    2    3    4  · · ·  5    6    7    8
H
I
J    H = ex 1x
        in 1–4
        3 = Last
      At least 1x
          GI
```

Figure 4.70. Non-one-to-one game with no branches and variable fixtures

Fixed Branches

About two-thirds of ONS-B games have branches. Most of these have variable branches, but a small number have fixed branches.

NON-ONE-TO-ONE ORDERED GAMES SAMPLE 4 WITH FIXED BRANCHES

Three playgrounds—Heights, Midtown, and Uptown—are scheduled to have their equipment repainted. Five colors of paint are available—green, orange, purple, red, and yellow. Each playground is repainted with exactly three colors and each color is used at least once among the three playgrounds. The following conditions apply:

    Red is used at Uptown if, but only if, green is used at Heights.

    At least one playground uses both orange and purple.

    If a playground uses yellow, it also uses green.

    Midtown uses orange.

The number of fixtures is known: three (Heights, Midtown, and Uptown). The number of branches is also known. There are exactly three for each fixture, totaling nine branches. Thus, the branches are fixed. However, it is not known how many instances of each color there will be. Each player is used at least once. The first condition is a complex if/then. It is broken into two statements in the diagram. Orange is entered as permanent information (circled) under Midtown.

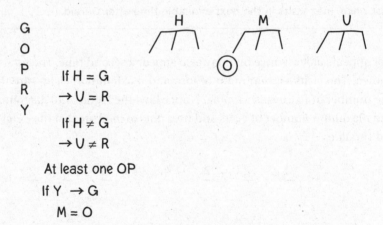

Figure 4.71. Non-one-to-one game with fixed branches

Variable Branches

About half of ONS-B games have branches that are variable. This makes sense because in a game without one-to-one correspondence, it may not be known how many times each player appears.

NON-ONE-TO-ONE ORDERED GAMES SAMPLE 5 WITH VARIABLE BRANCHES

Three playgrounds are scheduled to have their equipment repainted on three consecutive days in respective order: Heights, Midtown, and Uptown, one playground per day. Six colors of paint are available: green, magenta, orange, purple, red, and yellow. Each playground is repainted with at least two colors and each color is used at least once among the three playgrounds. The following conditions apply:

If a playground uses red, then it uses neither orange nor purple.

At least one playground uses both orange and purple.

If a playground uses yellow, it also uses green.

Orange is used in the first playground in which green is used.

The first day on which purple is used is some day before the first day on which yellow is used.

No color can be used on two consecutive days.

In this variation on Sample 4, the number of colors that can be used on a given playground is left variable. There must be at least two colors but there could be up to six colors per playground. Also, the playgrounds are painted in a specific time order. Because of this, the conditions can talk about a player (color) appearing before or after another player or about players appearing consecutively.

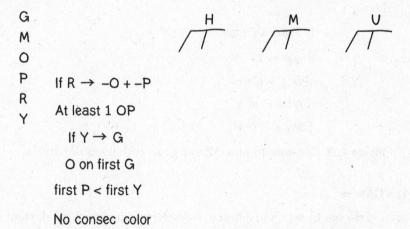

Figure 4.72. Non-one-to-one ordered game with variable fixtures

A club's entry in a parade consists of exactly two parts: a pony and a cart. The parts will be decorated with ribbons, each of which has one color. The only possible colors for the ribbons are green, magenta, orange, purple, red, and yellow. One of the parts will have exactly one ribbon color and the other part will consist of a combination of ribbon colors. The decoration must obey the following rules:

If the pony is decorated with a combination of ribbon colors, there are exactly four ribbon colors in the combination.

No ribbon color used to decorate the pony can be used to decorate the cart.

The cart cannot be decorated with any ribbon that is green or yellow.

The pony cannot be decorated with any ribbon that is magenta or purple.

The players in this game are the colored ribbons, or simply colors. It is unknown whether or not each color must appear at least once. This game is unusual in that the two fixtures—pony and cart—take a different number of branches. One has no branches and the other has multiple branches. In addition, in one arrangement the pony may have no branches and in another, the cart may have no branches. This makes the game more complex. In any arrangement one fixture is unbranched but the other fixture has variable branches.

In the diagram, each fixture has one required branch (solid). The number of other branches is unknown. Rather than using dotted lines to represent possible branches, the diagram in Figure 4.73 leaves room for as many branches as may be needed.

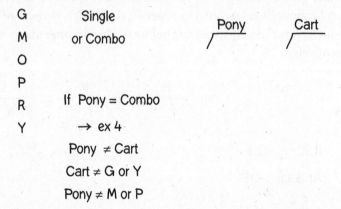

Figure 4.73. Non-one-to-one ordered game with unequal fixtures

Ambiguous Games

Occasionally a game can be set up in different ways depending on which element is considered to be the players and which the fixtures. It is possible that one way results in a one-to-one correspondence game and the other way results in a non-one-to-one correspondence game.

Six dancers—Margolies, Newton, Osaka, Perez, Rafik, and Strong—are each to be ranked on a solo performance. There are four possible ranks—one, two, three, or four pluses, with four pluses being the best. The assignment of ranks is constrained by the following conditions:

Each rank is used at least once but no more than twice.

Strong receives exactly two more pluses than Rafik.

At least one dancer receives more pluses than Perez.

Either Osaka receives the same rank as Perez, or else Newton receives the same rank as Strong, but not both.

This game could be diagrammed in two different ways. Because ranks are being assigned to people, the people could be fixtures—all six listed across the top of the diagram. Doing so results in a non-one-to-one game. However, in this game the ranks—one to four pluses—represent an order. Two pluses is better than one plus and two pluses is greater than one plus by a quantity of one. Ordered elements are usually fixtures. The players are assigned to the ordered fixtures.

In Figure 4.74, the ranks are used as fixtures. Each fixture is assigned at least one and up to two players, so the branches are variable. There is one required branch (solid) and one optional branch (dotted). However, each player is assigned exactly once. When organized this way, the game becomes a one-to-one game. Of course, the game itself has not changed. It is just organized differently. This fact highlights the similarities between one-to-one non-sequence ordered games and non-one-to-one ordered games.

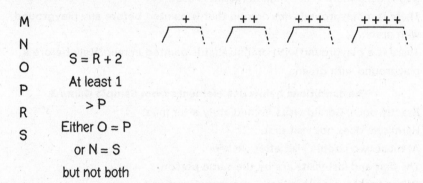

Figure 4.74. Ambiguous game that can be one-to-one or non-one-to-one

Conditions for Ordered Non-Sequence Non-One-to-One Correspondence Games

You have seen many of the common conditions in the samples above. The conditions for these games are different from conditions in the one-to-one games—both sequence and non-sequence—because in the non-one-to-one games, some players are left out or players may be used more than once. Conditions give rules about the first occurrence of a player or about which players are options for a certain fixture. Conditions also define who is used and who is not used. Study the conditions below to understand what relationships between players and fixtures the conditions are conveying. The test writers tend to be creative with conditions for the ordered non-one-to-one games. The ONS-B conditions that you see on actual LSATs will be variations on the patterns in previous tests.

Use the list below as a reference, coming back to it as you work on games. You do not need to memorize the list. Glance through the list now to become familiar with it.

CONDITIONS FOR ORDERED NON-SEQUENCE
NON-ONE-TO-ONE CORRESPONDENCE GAMES

The conditions below use elements from Sample Game 5.

Variations on conditions are listed in parentheses.

- Red is (not) used at Midtown (or at Uptown).
- Uptown uses red if, but only if, Heights uses yellow.
- Yellow is used at the first playground that uses green.
- Green cannot be used at two playgrounds that are painted consecutively.
- Red is used exactly twice.
- Magenta and purple are the only colors that can be used at Heights.
- There are at least two colors but no more than four colors used at Midtown.
- There is at least one playground that uses both magenta and orange.
- There is at least one color that is used at both Heights and Uptown.
- Each color is used at least twice.
- Either red or green is used on any fixture that uses purple.
- Exactly two fixtures use green (and yellow).
- The first use of red is before the first use of green.
- Heights and Uptown have exactly one color in common.
- If red is (not) used at Midtown, purple is (not) used at Uptown (Midtown).
- If red is (not) used, so (neither) is yellow.
- Red is used more times than magenta is used.
- There is a playground with orange that is painted before any playground with green.
- There is a playground with orange that is painted immediately before a playground with green.

The conditions below use elements from Sample Game 3.

- Exactly once, Gerald visits immediately after Inez.
- Hermione does not visit first.
- At most two people visit after Jackson.
- The first and last visits are by the same person.
- Of the first four visits, exactly one is by Hermione.

The conditions below use elements from Sample Game 2.

- Either Franticek attends or Ionescu attends, but not both.
- If Griselli attends in the afternoon, Hao does not attend.
- If Hao attends, Hao attends in the evening.
- If Jones attends, Ionescu attends.
- If Ionescu attends, Franticek attends the session immediately after Ionescu's session.
- If Griselli does not attend, Hao attends in the evening.

The conditions below refer to a game in which only some of eight colors are to be chosen and the colors are divided into primary and secondary colors.

- No more than four colors can be chosen.
- If the third place is a primary color, there are exactly four colors chosen.

UNDERSTANDING THE QUESTION TYPES

Each AR setup is followed by a series of questions. Each question consists of the statement of the question—called the **stem**—and the five answer choices. In this section you will learn all the possible types of questions, starting with the four basic types of questions, along with the variation "EXCEPT." Then you will learn certain special question types.

Refer to the following game to illustrate the question types.

> ### ORIENTING YOURSELF TO THE QUESTION STEM
>
> The first step in solving a question is to take the time to orient yourself to the question stem. Be clear on what it is asking and on how to approach it. Study the question types so that you can orient yourself more quickly and accurately.

SAMPLE SETUP 22

Six geology students—Jones, Kellogg, Lindquist, Ming, Nieto, and Pacheco—are to present papers at a six-day conference. Each student presents exactly one time and only one presentation is given on each day, according to the following conditions:

Jones presents before Ming.

Ming presents before Nieto.

Jones presents either immediately before or immediately after Pacheco.

Pacheco presents before Lindquist.

Either Kellogg presents last or Ming presents before Lindquist, but not both.

The Basic Question Types

The four basic question types are:

1. Could be true
2. Must be true
3. Cannot be true (= Must be false)
4. Could be false

In addition, some of the basic question types can be presented in the form of an EXCEPT statement. The basic questions may sound simple, but it is easy to get confused about what you are looking for, especially after hours of testing. Before you begin trying to solve a question, take time to orient yourself carefully to what the question stem means and how to approach it.

COULD BE TRUE

This question type asks you to select the one answer that could be true, given the conditions. What does this mean about the wrong answers? They violate rules. In this question type, four answers violate rules and one does not. Because there are four rule violations, it is helpful with this type of question to start by going through the rules and looking for answer choices that violate them. About 40 percent of all AR questions are **could be true** questions.

Example: Which one of the following could be the presenter on the third day?

MUST BE TRUE

This question type asks you to select the one answer that *must* be true. In other words, the conditions force certain assignments, for example that G must go in position 3. Be careful to distinguish this from what *could be true*. In a **must be true** question, what do you know about the wrong answers? It is *not* the case that each wrong answer violates a rule. Some of the wrong answers may violate rules, and any answer that does violate a rule is wrong. However, other wrong answers may be valid possibilities. They are simply not *forced* to be true. About 20 percent of all AR questions are **must be true** questions.

> *Example: If Jones presents on Day 3, which one of the following must present after Kellogg?*

CANNOT BE TRUE (= MUST BE FALSE)

This question type asks you to select the one answer that CANNOT be true. (The word CANNOT is always written in all capitals to emphasize that the question is asking for a negation of what the test taker would normally look for.) In other words, the correct answer violates rules. The other answer choices could be true. They do not violate rules. Some of the wrong answers may even be forced to be true. Note the two ways that this question can be worded. Combined, these two wordings account for 18 percent of all AR questions, with 15 percent being **cannot be true** and 3 percent being **must be false**.

> *Example: Which one of the following CANNOT be the presenter on Day 4?*

COULD BE FALSE

This question asks you to find the one answer that could be false. This means that the other four answers cannot be false. They must be (are forced to be) true. The correct answer either has the option of being true or false or is forced to be false. Barely 1 percent of AR questions are **could be false** questions but they are included here because their logic is similar to the other basic questions.

> *Example: If Ming presents before Lindquist, which of the following could be false?*

EXCEPT

TIP

"EXCEPT" AND "CANNOT"

The words EXCEPT and CANNOT, when used in a question stem, are written in all capitals in order to alert you to the fact that the question is based on a negation.

The use of the word EXCEPT (it is always written with all capitals) makes a question logically more complex. If someone asks you to identify all the redheads in a class, you simply look for people with red hair. If someone asks you to identify all the people in the room EXCEPT redheads, you have to keep the criterion "redhead" in your mind and look for the opposite. It is similar to someone telling you, "Think of something that is not an elephant." All you can think of is elephants! With EXCEPT questions, you must (1) identify the criterion, and (2) be careful to remember that you are looking for the *opposite* of the criterion.

In recent LSATs, EXCEPT has been used only in the form of **could be true EXCEPT** and **must be true EXCEPT**. The former accounts for about 5 percent of all AR questions. The latter has only occurred a few times in recent years. In a **could be true EXCEPT** question, four of the answers could be true. The remaining answer is the correct one. It cannot be true. In other words, the correct answer violates one or more rules. In a **must be true EXCEPT** question, four of the answers are forced to be true. The remaining answer is one that is not forced to be true. It may be an answer that could be true or it may violate rules.

> *Example: Each of the following could be true EXCEPT:*
> *Example: If Nieto presents last, each of the following must be true EXCEPT:*

Table 4.3 shows the characteristics of the correct answer and the incorrect answers for each of these basic question types.

Table 4.3. Characteristics of Correct and Incorrect Answers

	Correct Answer	Four Incorrect Answers
Could be true	Does not violate rules	Violate rules
Must be true	Forced to be true	Could be true or violate rules
Cannot be true (= Must be false)	Violates rules	Do not violate rules
Could be false	Could be true or violates rules	Forced to be true
Could be true EXCEPT	Violates rules	Do not violate rules
Must be true EXCEPT	Could be true or violates rules	Forced to be true

Special Question Types

The basic question types, discussed above, account for about 85 percent of AR questions. There are over a dozen special types of questions that appear less frequently but with which it is important for you to be familiar. The special types include many of the more complex and challenging questions. These are the questions that will help you get your maximum score.

COMPLETE AND ACCURATE LIST

Some questions use the wording "complete and accurate list" or sometimes just "accurate list." This wording may simply refer to a complete assignment of players. For example, a complete assignment could be Kellogg, Pacheco, Jones, Ming, Lindquist, and Nieto. This is called a complete list because it does not exclude any player who could appear, and it is called an accurate list because it does not include any rule violations.

The wording "complete and accurate list" can also be used in a different way. Consider the question "Which one of the following is a complete and accurate list of people who could give the first presentation?" In this case the correct answer is not a complete assignment (six players in their specified order). Consider the following answer choices, which refer to **Sample Setup 22**.

(A) Jones
(B) Jones, Kellogg
(C) Jones, Kellogg, Pacheco
(D) Jones, Lindquist, Kellogg, Pacheco
(E) Lindquist, Kellogg, Pacheco

Only Jones, Kellogg, and Pacheco can present first. Only choice C can be the correct answer. Choices A and B are accurate (i.e., everyone in A and B can be first) but are not complete. Choice D is complete (it includes everyone who needs to be in the list) but is not accurate (Lindquist violates rules). Choice E is inaccurate (Lindquist violates rules) and incomplete (it is missing Jones).

In the above example, the complete and accurate list consisted of players. Some questions may ask for a complete and accurate list of fixtures to which a player may be assigned.

EXAMPLE

Which one of the following is a complete and accurate list of positions in which Jones can give her presentation?
(A) 1, 2
(B) 1, 3
(C) 1, 2, 3
(D) 2, 3, 4
(E) 1, 2, 3, 4, 5

Only choice C is both complete and accurate. The other answer choices either include fixtures that would result in rule violations or leave out fixtures in which Jones could present. A similar question might ask for a complete and accurate list of fixtures to which both Jones and Pacheco could be assigned or for a complete and accurate list of players who could be assigned to the third spot if Jones is assigned to the first spot.

COMPLETELY DETERMINED IF

Consider the following question:

EXAMPLE

If Lindquist does not present last, the order in which the students present their papers is completely determined if which one of the following is true?
(A) Lindquist presents fifth.
(B) Ming presents third.
(C) Pacheco presents first.
(D) Jones presents third.
(E) Kellogg presents fourth.

In this question type, when the information in the correct answer is put into the diagram, the rules determine exactly who must be in each remaining position, with no other options. To solve this type of question, test the answer choices by putting the information from that choice into the diagram. Then apply the rules to see if the assignment to every fixture is uniquely determined. The correct answer to the above question is choice D. About 3.5 percent of all AR questions are *completely determined if* questions and these questions appear on two thirds of recent tests.

There are several variations on the wording "completely determined." You may also see "completely resolved," "fully determined," "fully and uniquely determined," and "there is exactly one order if . . ."

Other If Questions

The completely determined questions are based on the consequences *if* each of the answer choices were true. Very rarely there is a question that, rather than asking for a completely determined order, asks for a specific fact that would be true if one of the answer choices were true.

> *Ming presents third if which one of the following is true?*

EQUIVALENT CONDITION

This type asks you to replace a specific original condition with an answer choice that has the same result as the original condition. Consider the following question:

EXAMPLE

Which one of the following, if substituted for the condition that Pacheco presents before Lindquist, would have the same effect in determining the order in which the students present?
(A) Pacheco presents before Kellogg.
(B) Pacheco presents either immediately before or immediately after Lindquist.
(C) Lindquist presents last.
(D) Jones presents before Lindquist.
(E) There is exactly one student who presents between Pacheco and Linquist.

To solve an **equivalent condition** question, you must be sure that your answer accomplishes all of the results of the original condition without adding any additional restrictions. In the above example, choice A does not necessarily result in Pacheco presenting before Lindquist. In choice B, Pacheco and Lindquist are adjacent, so Pacheco might be before Lindquist but might also be after. This answer is not restrictive enough. In choice C, Pacheco is before Lindquist but this answer imposes an additional restriction—that Lindquist presents in position 6—that is, not in the original conditions. The answer is too restrictive. In choice D, Jones presents before Lindquist. Because the only two possible configurations for Jones and Pacheco are JP or PJ, the result is JP – L or PJ – L. In both cases, P presents before Lindquist without any additional restrictions being introduced.

Equivalent condition questions have appeared on every recent test but there is usually only one per AR section, usually the last question in a passage.

HOW MANY

Three minor question types ask you to find the number of possibilities that exist in a certain situation. The answer choices are numbers.

For How Many Can It Be Determined?

Consider the following example:

EXAMPLE

If Kellogg presents last, then for exactly how many of the total students can it be determined in which time slot he or she presents?

(A) two

(B) three

(C) four

(D) five

(E) six

In this question, new information is given—*Kellogg presents last*—and as a result, some players are forced into a specific position. You must calculate how many players are forced into one specific position and how many have options. Theoretically, you could get a question like this without new information.

A slight variation asks for how many players is the choice of fixtures limited to one or two. Both variations are rare. The latter variation has only appeared once in recent years.

How Many Orders Are There?

This question type asks you how many different valid assignments exist. The question may give additional information.

EXAMPLE

If Lindquist is the third presenter, then how many orders are there in which the remaining students could appear?

(A) one

(B) two

(C) three

(D) four

(E) five

This question type is rare but has been introduced recently and may appear again.

How Many Players for a Specific Fixture?

This question type refers to a specific fixture. The question might or might not provide new information. You must determine how many players could be assigned to the specified fixture. This question type does not ask you to identify the players—only to count them.

Exactly how many students are there any one of whom could present sixth?

(A) one

(B) two

(C) three

(D) four

(E) five

The question refers to the sixth fixture. No new information is given. A similar question could ask *If Kellogg presents last, exactly how many students are there any one of whom could present third?* In this case new information is given.

The **how many** questions account for about 2.5 percent of all AR questions. More than half of those are **how many players for a specific fixture**. This type appears in about half of all recent LSATs.

ONE OR BOTH OF A PAIR

In a few special question types the answer choices consist of pairs of players.

At Least One Is In

In the answer choices for this type of question, at least one of the members of the pair must be included in the assignment.

A law professor will choose four law students from a group of eight—Frantishek, Goldstein, Hong, Ibarrez, Jackson, Kelly, Lovato, and Ma—to attend a conference on ethics. The following conditions apply:

If Goldstein is chosen, neither Jackson nor Kelly can be chosen.

If Kelly is not chosen, Hong must be chosen.

If Ma is chosen, Hong is not chosen.

If Jackson is not chosen, then both Goldstein and Frantishek are chosen.

Which one of the following is a pair of students of which the professor must choose at least one?

(A) Goldstein and Hong

(B) Jackson and Lovato

(C) Jackson and Hong

(D) Goldstein and Lovato

(E) Jackson and Kelly

Answer: The key to this question type is to understand that for the correct answer, it is not possible that both members be excluded. This question type is used with a game that has a discard pile. To test an answer, try to put both members of the pair in the discard pile. Test choice C. If Jackson and Hong are both out, then Goldstein is in. If Goldstein is in, Kelly is out. If Kelly is out, Hong must be in. However, Hong is in the discard pile. If a rule violation results, the two members cannot both be out and therefore, at least one of them must be in. Choice C is the correct answer. This question type accounts for slightly less than 1 percent of questions.

Both Can Be Out

In this question type the answer choices represent a pair of players both of whom *can* be together in the discard pile. This is the opposite of the previous type, in which the correct answer is a pair that *cannot* both be in the discard pile. In this type of question, four of the answer choices result in rule violations. One, the correct answer choice, does not result in a violation.

EXAMPLE

A pair of students who are not chosen to go to the conference could be

(A) Jackson and Hong

(B) Jackson and Goldstein

(C) Jackson and Frantishek

(D) Kelly and Lovato

(E) Kelly and Hong

Test each pair by putting it in the discard pile and determining what else must be true. Only Kelly and Lovato can be in the discard pile together. Each of the other pairs results in a rule violation.

Both Fixtures Can Be

In this rare type of question the answer choices also consist of pairs, but the pairs represent fixtures. Consider the following, which refers back to the game introduced in the beginning of the section:

EXAMPLE

Which one of the following is a pair of presentation slots both of which could be taken by Jones?

(A) 1 and 2

(B) 1 and 5

(C) 2 and 5

(D) 3 and 6

(E) 4 and 6

The correct answer consists of a pair of fixtures both of which could have a certain player (in this case, Jones) assigned to them. The pair need not be a complete list of the fixtures to which Jones can be assigned. In other words, choice A is correct even though Jones could also be assigned to slot 3. In the incorrect answers, one or both of the fixtures listed in the pair would result in a rule violation if Jones were assigned to that fixture.

Many other types of questions have pairs in the answer choices. The types explained above are distinctive in that they force you to decide if one or both members of the pair meet a certain criterion.

WHAT IS THE MINIMUM/MAXIMUM NUMBER?

This question type asks for the maximum or minimum number of players that are included in a valid assignment. A **minimum/maximum** question is usually only asked in a game in which the number of fixtures is variable.

SAMPLE QUESTION 3

Judges will choose from among six singers—Robert, Sandra, Tomas, Uma, Vincente, and Yuki—to determine who will be asked to audition for an upcoming performance. At least one singer but no more than five singers must be chosen.
The following rules apply:

If Robert is chosen, then either Uma or Tomas is chosen, but not both.
If Uma is not chosen, Sandra is chosen.
If Yuki is chosen, Tomas is not chosen.
If Vicente is chosen, either Robert is chosen or Yuki is chosen, but not both.

1. What is the maximum possible number of singers who can be chosen?
    (A) five
    (B) four
    (C) three
    (D) two
    (E) one

2. What is the minimum number of singers who must be chosen if Robert is chosen?
    (A) one
    (B) two
    (C) three
    (D) four
    (E) five

Answer: In this game there must be at least one fixture and can be up to five. The first question is based solely on the original conditions. Based on these conditions, there is no combination of five singers that does not violate rules. (Test this by putting one player at a time in the discard pile by itself and testing the set of five remaining players.) The correct answer is choice B, four players. The second question gives new information. If Robert is chosen, Uma or Thomas is chosen. If Uma is chosen, the assignment is complete and accurate, so it is possible to have only two singers. Choice B is correct. **Minimum/maximum** questions account for barely 1 percent of all AR questions and the majority of those are **maximum** questions.

WHAT IS THE EARLIEST/LATEST?

This question type asks you to identify the earliest or latest place in the sequence of fixtures that a player could appear. The example refers to Sample Setup 22.

The earliest Nieto could present is

(A) second
(B) third
(C) fourth
(D) fifth
(E) sixth

The order of players includes the sequences JP – M – N or PJ – M – N. Based on this sequence alone, Nieto cannot present until three other players have presented.

Similarly,

What is the latest time slot in which Jones can present?

(A) sixth
(B) fifth
(C) fourth
(D) third
(E) second

Jones has at least two other players who must follow and based on that alone, choices A and B are eliminated. Testing Jones in fourth place results in a rule violation. Pacheco must go in position 3 and this violates the rule P – L. The correct answer is D.

Earliest/latest questions are very rare. They have only occurred twice—once each—in recent years. However, the concept of earliest and latest position is an important one. In questions such as "Which one of the following cannot present fifth?" you need to calculate the earliest or latest that various players can appear.

New Information

As you read each question stem, determine if the question

1. does not provide new information, or
2. provides new information that can be entered directly into the main diagram, or
3. provides new information that cannot be entered directly into the main diagram, or
4. adds or modifies an original condition.

If there is no new information, answer the question based on the original conditions. New information that can be entered in the diagram includes facts such as *Kellogg presents sixth* that tell exactly to which fixture a player is assigned. Facts such as *Lindquist presents before Ming* give you new information but do not tell you where in the diagram either player goes. For such facts, use supplemental diagrams or temporary rules to keep track of the information.

A question may modify an original condition—for example, *If the original condition requiring Pacheco to present before Lindquist were changed to require Lindquist to present before Pacheco, which one of the following could be true?* A question may also add a new condition, such as *If Jones were required to perform before Lindquist, which one of the follow-*

ing must be true? In both cases, use temporary supplemental diagrams and temporary rules. Cross out these temporary notes before you go to the next question. Remember that new information in a question applies only to that question.

Table 4.4 shows how common or rare each question type is. The first column shows what percentage of all recent AR questions the type constitutes. The second column shows in what percentage of recent tests the type has occurred. The third column shows whether the question type is becoming more common or less common on the most recent LSATs.

Table 4.4. Frequency of AR Question Types

	Percent of All AR Questions	Percent of All Recent Tests in Which the Type Occurs	Current Trends: Is This Type Becoming More Common or Less Common?
Could be true	41	100	No change
Must be true	21	100	No change
Cannot be true (= Must be false)	15	100	No change
Must be false (= Cannot be true)	3	53	Less common
Could be false	0.8	13	No change
Could be true EXCEPT	5	53	No change
Must be true EXCEPT	0.6	13	Less common
Complete and accurate list	1.5	27	More common
Completely determined if	3.5	60	Less common
Equivalent condition	2.3	47	More common
How many?	2.6	40	More common
One or both of a pair	1.5	20	More common
What is the minimum/maximum?	1.2	20	Less common
What is the earliest/latest?	0.6	13	Less common

How Question Types Are Distributed Among Each Type of Game

The question types do not show up equally in all four types of games. For example, a *cannot be true* question with new information that goes in the diagram can appear only in a *sequence* game or an *unordered* game. At the same time, a *cannot be true* game with new information that is *not* in the diagram can appear only in an ONS-A game. Some types of questions do not appear at all for certain types of games. Table 4.5 shows the question types that have such restrictions. You do not need to memorize this information, but these facts may help you orient yourself to a game more quickly. The "New Information" column refers to whether the question type uses no new information, new information that goes in diagram, new information that does not go in diagram, or all three.

Five of the rows below are associated with only one type of game. There are five other rows that are excluded from exactly one type of game. For most of the latter, it is the unordered games in which they cannot appear. Question type and new information combinations not listed below can appear with any type.

Table 4.5. Question Types with Restrictions
on the Game Type with Which They Can Appear

Question Type	New Information?	Cannot Appear With	Only Appears With
One of a pair	All	Sequence, ONS-A, ONS-B	Unordered
Cannot be true	New in diagram	ONS-A, ONS-B	Sequence, unordered
Cannot be true	New NOT in diagram	Sequence, ONS-B, unordered	ONS-A
Could be true	New NOT in diagram	ONS-A	Sequence, ONS-B, unordered
Could be false	All	ONS-A, unordered	Sequence, ONS-B
Could be true EXCEPT	New in diagram	ONS-B, unordered	Sequence, ONS-A
Could be true EXCEPT	No new info	ONS-B, unordered	Sequence, ONS-A
Could be true EXCEPT	New NOT in diagram	Unordered	Sequence, ONS-A, ONS-B
How many	All	Unordered	Sequence, ONS-A, ONS-B
Must be false	New in diagram	Sequence, ONS-B, unordered	ONS-A
Must be false	New NOT in diagram	Unordered	Sequence, ONS-A, ONS-B
Must be false	No new info	ONS-A, unordered	Sequence, ONS-B
Must be true	No new info	Unordered	Sequence, ONS-A, ONS-B
Must be true EXCEPT	All	ONS-A, ONS-B	Sequence, unordered
What is the maximum	All	Sequence, ONS-A	ONS-B, Unordered
What is the minimum	All	Sequence, ONS-A, ONS-B	Unordered
What is the earliest/latest	All	ONS-A, ONS-B, unordered	Sequence

HOW TO SOLVE THE QUESTIONS: A SYSTEMATIC APPROACH

The secret to a perfect score on the games is to develop a systematic approach. Most test takers, when faced with a tough AR question, grasp at straws. They haphazardly put various elements into the diagram. They lose track of what works, what does not, and even of what they have already done. Often test takers go in circles, not getting closer to an answer. Eventually they give up.

With a systematic approach you know what tools you have available. You know when to use each tool, and you know in what order to use your tools. *Every* AR question can be efficiently solved with the right sequence of tools.

The Problem-Solving Tools

There are four major categories of tools for solving AR questions. There are also four supporting tools. Read through this section so that you become comfortable with the tools presented here. Refer back to this section as you work questions.

CATEGORIES OF PROBLEM-SOLVING TOOLS

The Major Categories of Tools

Applying the rules

Working with the answer choices

Using the main diagram

Using supplemental diagrams

The Supporting Tools

Enough to answer the question?

Most restricted players

What rules apply to a given player?

What are the options for a player or fixture?

APPLYING THE RULES

One of the most powerful problem-solving tools is using the rules to evaluate answer choices and diagrams. There are three ways to do this.

Questions with Four Rule Violations: The Typical First Question

For some questions, four of the answer choices violate rules. In fact, in most—but not all—games, the first question in a set has five answer choices that contain possible complete assignments and asks you to find the one answer that could be true. This means the other four answer choices violate rules.

Test takers are often tempted to read through an answer choice and then check the rules to see whether the answer violates any rules. You will get to the answer more quickly if you use a different strategy. Start by looking at the first rule (not the first answer choice). It is important to work systematically. If you start with the rule that pops into your head first, you will have a harder time remembering what you have already tested. Start at the top of your list of rules and work each rule, one at a time, in order, from top to bottom.

When you look at the first rule, identify what a violation of that rule would look like. For example, for a rule *If John is chosen, Mary is not chosen*, a violation would consist of John being in the answer and Mary also being in. Now scan all five answers to see whether any choices violate the rule. Typically, for each rule there is one answer that violates it, although there are sometimes two or more answers that violate it. By carefully going through all the rules, you will quickly eliminate four answer choices, and the correct answer will be revealed.

The advantage of starting with the rules is that you can keep one rule in mind as you scan the answers. If you start with an answer choice and scan all of the rules for a violation, you have to orient yourself to each rule multiple times.

For any question in which there are four answers that violate the rules, start with the rules and look for violations. On the other hand, if only one of the answer choices violates a rule, there are other strategies that are more efficient. These are discussed below.

THE TYPICAL FIRST QUESTION

The first question in a set almost always gives five complete assignments and asks which one could be true. Four of the answer choices violate rules. Usually each rule has one answer choice that violates it, though there can be more than one answer choice that violates a particular rule. Be careful! In some games the first question is not the typical one.

Use the Rules to Fill in Your Diagrams

When a question gives you new information—for example, *Gonzales is in place 3*—your first task is to put that information into the diagram and then fill in anything else that follows from the rules. Start *only* with information that *must* be true. There is a time and place for filling in options, but most test takers confuse themselves by mixing *necessary* information with *possible* information. Put Gonzales in 3. Scan the rules, starting at the top and working down one by one. A rule lower down may jump into your mind first, especially if it has to do with Gonzales. It is all right to work with that rule first, but then go back to the top, to the first rule. For each rule, ask yourself if there is any way in which that rule applies to what is in the diagram. If the rule does not clearly lead to something that must be true, move on to the next rule.

Suppose that there is a rule *If Gonzales is in 3, then Jasper is in 5*. Put Jasper in 5. Now you have new information in the diagram and so you should go back to the top of the rules again. Maybe when you looked at the first rule before, it did not apply, but now that Jasper is in 5, the first rule may give you new information. As you add players into your diagram, go through the rules again until the rules provide no new information.

Test an Assignment for Validity

Another way to use the rules to solve a problem is to test a certain assignment, such as an assignment that is given in one of the answer choices, and apply the rules to that assignment. In that way you can determine whether the assignment you are testing is valid or breaks rules. Consider the following question:

> *Which one of the following is a student who could present third?*
> A. Jones

To test choice A, put J in 3 and then apply the rules to see what else must be true. In order to prove that J can go in 3, you need to fill in the assignment in a way that you believe does not violate the rules. It is easy to make a mistake, so as a double check, once you have filled in an assignment that seems to work, apply the rules to test your assignment. Start with the first rule—at the top—and check it and each subsequent rule carefully against your assignment. If you have inadvertently created a rule violation, this process will find it.

WORKING WITH THE ANSWER CHOICES

The second major problem-solving category is working with answer choices. There are five specific tools you can use to work with answer choices: scanning answers, testing answers, checking answers for violations, checking answers against the diagrams, and checking answers against previous viable assignments.

Scanning Answers

Often one of the first steps is to scan the answer choices. In scanning you are looking quickly at the answers. Scanning may show you an obvious rule violation. It may give you ideas of other strategies you can use. It may give you a sense of what answer choices are most likely to violate rules or to be forced to be true. Testing those answers first can save you time.

Testing Answers

When you test an answer choice, work systematically. It takes time and concentration to do this accurately, so it is important to first identify choices that can be eliminated and then to scan the answers to decide which remaining answers should be tested first. Answer choices can sometimes be eliminated by applying the rules and/or by checking answers against valid assignments that are either in your notes or in previous questions. If you have no clear idea of which answers to test first, start at the top of the remaining answers.

Could be true. If you are testing an answer choice to determine whether it *could* be true, either show that the answer would lead to a rule violation, and thus eliminate it, or use the answer to create a viable assignment.

SAMPLE QUESTION 4

Six students—Jefferson, King, Li, Montoya, Nussbaum, and Olivier—are to present papers, one student at a time, during six consecutive time slots.

   Jefferson presents before King.

   King presents before Nussbaum but after Li.

   Olivier cannot present first.

Which one of the following is a pair of students who could present first and second, respectively?

(A) King, Olivier

(B) Montoya, King

(C) Olivier, Jackson

(D) Jackson, Li

(E) Li, Nussbaum

Answer: Test choice A. Put K in first place and O in second place. Look for a rule violation. This order violates the rule *Jefferson presents before King.* Choice A is out because you have found a clear rule violation. Now test choice D. Put J and L in the first and second places, respectively. Check for a rule violation. Most likely you will not see a violation. At this point you cannot be sure if there is no violation or if you have simply not spotted a violation that exists. In general, if you prove that a certain fact leads to a rule violation, that proof is conclusive. However, if you create an assignment that does not *seem* to violate rules, there is still the possibility that you have missed a violation. For this reason, showing that a certain assignment is possible is never as conclusive as showing that an assignment violates rules. All you can say about a possible assignment is that you "think" it works. For this reason, it is helpful to find all the violations first.

Cannot be true. If you are looking for an answer choice that *cannot* be true, then four of the answer choices are viable assignments. Some may even be required to be true. It is still more conclusive to look for the one violation, rather than to prove that the other answers could be true. As you test an answer, look at it quickly to see if it looks like it might work.

Referring to **Sample Question 4**, consider this question:

EXAMPLE

Which of the following is a pair of students who CANNOT present in the fifth and sixth positions, respectively?
(A) King, Nussbaum
(B) Nussbaum, Montoya
(C) Montoya, Olivier
(D) King, Olivier
(E) Nussbaum, Olivier

Test choice A. Put K in fifth and N in sixth. There are no clear violations. Is it possible to fill in the remaining spaces in a way that creates a viable order? If you try to fill in an order, it will take a lot of time and once you have an order that you think may work, it takes more time to test it. Instead of filling in an order, evaluate whether there seem to be possibilities for creating a viable order. K and N are already assigned at the end of the sequence. J and L will not violate rules no matter where you put them. O and M do not have any restrictions, other than that O cannot go first. There seem to be many options for creating a viable order. It only takes a moment to make this evaluation. You have shown that choice A is *probably* out. Move on to choice B. This strategy is helpful when four answer choices are viable.

When you get to the correct answer (the one that *does* violate a rule) the violation will, hopefully, be clear and you will have saved time. If all of the answer choices seem viable, then you have missed a violation in one of them and have to go back and test each answer choice in more detail. To do that, fill in a complete assignment and then go back to the rules—starting systematically at the top—and check the assignment against all of the rules.

Must be true. If you are looking for an answer that *must* be true, then four of the answers either violate rules or could be true. The correct answer is forced to be true. Testing an answer choice to see if it must be true is tricky. Consider the game with the geology students that was introduced earlier in this chapter.

GAME WITH GEOLOGY STUDENTS

Six geology students—Jones, Kellogg, Lindquist, Ming, Nieto, and Pacheco—are to present papers at a six-day conference. Each student presents exactly one time and only one presentation is given on each day.

Jones presents before Ming.

Ming presents before Nieto.

Jones presents either immediately before or immediately after Pacheco.

Pacheco presents before Lindquist.

Either Kellogg presents last or Ming presents before Lindquist but not both.

If Kellogg presents sixth, which one of the following must be true?

(A) Jones presents first.

(B) Pacheco presents first.

(C) Pacheco presents second.

(D) Lindquist presents third.

(E) Nieto presents fourth.

First, put K in 6. Now apply the rules. If K is in 6, the last rule tells you that L presents before M. M and N must go in 4 and 5, respectively. How would you test choice A? You want to prove or disprove that Jones must present first. What happens if you put J in 1? P must go next to J, which means in 2. There is only one place left for L, in 3. Test this assignment against the rules. There are no violations. Everything works. What have you proven? Only that J *could* go in 1. You have not proven that J *must* go in 1. This is a critical point in working with a *must* question.

To test an answer choice in a *must* question, you cannot simply put the answer into the diagram and show that it works. To prove that J *must* go in 1, you have to show that putting J any place *other* than 1 results in a violation. At this point you have MNK in 4–6. The only other options for J (besides 1) are 2 and 3. Put J in 3. What are the options for L? None. L has to come after J. You have proven that J cannot go in 3. However, you have *not* proven that J must go in 1. You must test J in 2. To show that Jones *must* go in 1 means showing that J cannot go in *any* other slot.

Put J in 2. P goes in 1. L goes in 3. Check this assignment against the rules. No rules are broken. You have proven that J does *not* have to go in 1, because J *can* go in 2.

Test choice D. Put L in any position other than 3. Every slot other than L in 3 violates rules. L *must* go in 3. Choice D is the answer.

Check Answers for Violations

In working with answer choices, you often have to test them for rule violations. Even though you may have started with the rules and eliminated answer choices that violate specific rules, there may be answer choices whose rule violations only show up when you consider more complex combinations of rules.

Four types of trees are to be planted in a new park. The seven available types of trees are Fraxinus, Ginkgo, Juniperus, Kalmia, Larix, Morus, and Poncirus. The trees must be chosen according to the following rules:

   If Fraxinus is chosen, Kalmia is not chosen.

   If Kalmia is chosen, Larix is chosen.

   Either Fraxinus or Morus is chosen but not both.

   If Ginkgo is chosen, either Morus is chosen or Larix is not chosen, but not both.

If Ginkgo is chosen, which one of the following statements could be true?

(A) Fraxinus and Kalmia are chosen.

(B) Kalmia is chosen and Larix is not chosen.

(C) Fraxinus and Morus are chosen.

(D) Fraxinus is chosen and Larix is chosen.

(E) Morus and Larix are both chosen.

Answer: Because four answers violate rules, start with the rules and look for violations. For the first rule, a violation would have F chosen and K also chosen. Choice A violates this. A violation of the second rule would have F chosen and L not chosen. Choice B violates the second rule. A violation of the third rule would have both F and M. Choice C violates the third rule.

A violation of the last rule would have both M chosen and L not chosen. There is no answer choice that specifically says *Morus is chosen and Larix is not chosen*. All the rules have been tested but there are still two choices remaining, D and E. One of the two must contain a violation but that violation is most likely based on a combination of rules. In order to detect a more complex rule, you must check the answer choices for violations.

Test choice D. Create a diagram, putting G in. Put both F and L in. Check the rules to see if a violation has already been created. If F is in, K must be out. Put K in the discard pile. The second rule does not apply because K is not in. Apply the third rule. F is in, so M must be out. Put M in the discard pile. Apply the final rule. M is not in, so the second half of the rule must apply, namely that L must be out. However, L is already in. Answer choice D violates the rules but the violation is not clear without testing the answer choice.

By starting with an answer choice and testing it against the rules, you can spot these more complex violations. The difference between (1) applying the rules to the answers and (2) checking the answers against the rules is a difference of the direction in which you are working.

Check the Answers Against the Diagrams

For many questions, you will create one or more diagrams of partial or complete assignments before you even begin looking at the answer choices. Diagrams represent things that must be true, along with some things that could be true. Once you have finished the diagrams, you can check the answer choices against the diagrams. Some answers may violate the information that must or could be true and these answers can be eliminated. The diagrams can also verify that a particular answer must be correct.

Check the Answers Against Previous Valid Assignments

Consider the following question, which refers to the game with the geology students:

EXAMPLE

If Lindquist presents before Ming, which one of the following is a time slot in which Nieto can present?

(A) first
(B) second
(C) third
(D) fifth
(E) sixth

The condition that L presents before M means that K presents sixth. In an earlier question we created a valid assignment that met that condition: JPLMNK. In that assignment, N presents fifth, so we have proof that N can present in the fifth position. The correct answer is choice D.

In other cases you can use previous valid assignments to eliminate certain answers. For example, consider a question that asks which must be true. If choice A reads *Pacheco presents third*, you can prove that choice A is out because in the valid assignment in the previous paragraph, P did *not* present third.

Because the answer to a typical first question for a game contains a full assignment, you can use that answer to test answers on other questions. (If you often have trouble getting the typical first question correct, do not use this strategy.) Also, use the valid assignments that you create in your diagram. Be careful to cross out any assignments that you try that result in rule violations.

This strategy works best when a question does not present new information. However, if a question does present new information and the answer to the typical first question matches that new information, this tool may help.

USING THE MAIN DIAGRAM

The third category of problem-solving tools is to use the main diagram. The main diagram is your most powerful tool for working through possibilities.

What Must Be True

When you start creating assignments, only put the information that must be true, if there is any. Referring to the geology game:

EXAMPLE

If Lindquist presents third, all of the following must be true EXCEPT:

(A) Nieto presents fifth.

(B) Ming presents fourth.

(C) Jones presents first.

(D) Pacheco presents before Nieto.

(E) Lindquist presents before Ming.

Put L in 3. P must appear before L and J must be adjacent to P. Therefore, M cannot be before L and so K must be in 6. Because L comes before M, there is the sequence L–M–N. M and N must be in 4 and 5, respectively. Check the rules. There is nothing else that must be true. The placement of J and P is optional. Leave the diagram as blank-blank-LMNK. Check the answer choices against the diagram. All answers must be true except C. J could present first but is not required to be first.

What Could Be True

For the above question it was not necessary to deal with the optional information—the placement of J and P. If entering only what must be true does not give you enough information to solve the question, use strategies for systematically showing options that could be true. At every point in the problem-solving process, you should be clear on whether you are looking for optional information or required information. Confusing the two is the cause of many errors. The question below requires entering options.

If Ming presents fourth and Kellogg presents before at least one other student, which of the following could be true?

(A) Pacheco presents first and Kellogg does not present third.

(B) Kellogg presents second and Nieto presents third.

(C) Kellogg presents first and Jones presents third.

(D) Jones presents first and Kellogg presents second.

(E) Pacheco presents first and Jones presents third.

Put M in 4. The rules do not provide the exact location of any of the other players. The last rule does tell us that if K is not in 6, L must come after M. The second rule tells us that N presents after M. There are only two places in the diagram after M so L and N must be assigned to 5 and 6, but we do not know in which order. Notice the notation used in Figure 4.75.

$$\underline{1} \quad \underline{2} \quad \underline{3} \quad \underline{\underset{M}{4}} \quad \underline{\underset{L/N}{5}} \quad \underline{\underset{N/L}{6}}$$

Figure 4.75. Diagram showing options in 5 and 6

The notation L/N indicates that either L or N could appear in 5. In 6, the notation is reversed—N/L. This indicates that if L is put in 5, N is put in 6. It is also fine to call 5 N/L and 6 L/N. It is not necessary to know exactly which players are in 5 or 6. By noting the possibilities, it is clear that J, P, and K cannot go in those slots. For some questions, showing the possibilities is enough to answer the question. For example, if this question had read *Which one of the following is a slot in which Lindquist could present?* then either 5 or 6 would be the correct answer.

Consider the possibilities for J, P, and K. There are a number of options. If you enter them using the slash notation above, the diagram would quickly become difficult to decipher. Instead, use parallel universes.

Parallel Universes

When the possibilities for a diagram become too complex, the diagram can be split into a number of "parallel universes." In the above example, what are the options for K? It seems that K could go in 1, 2, or 3.

You may already have an intuitive insight that one of those options cannot work. However, because it is not possible to *count* on having intuitive insights, use the parallel universe tool. Once you have mastered the tools taught here, you can get the right answer even if the intuitive insights do not come to you.

Using the fact that K's current options seem to be 1, 2, or 3, create three parallel lines in the diagram, one for each possible "universe." All the information other than the placement of K is the same in each universe.

```
 1     2     3     4     5     6
 K                 M    L/N   N/L
       K           M    L/N   N/L
             K     M    L/N   N/L
```

Figure 4.76. Diagram with three parallel
universes based on K

The three parallel universes are based on the three options for K. Now fill in what else is known about each universe. In the top universe, slots 2 and 3 are J/P and P/J. In the bottom universe, J/P and P/J go in 1 and 2. What about the middle universe? If J is in 1, P must be adjacent to it. There are no two slots in which J and P can be adjacent. The middle universe violates rules and is out.

```
 1     2     3     4     5     6
 K    J/P   P/J    M    L/N   N/L
       K           M    L/N   N/L
O/P   P/J    K     M    L/N   N/L
```

Figure 4.77. Diagram with parallel universes.
One violates rules and is crossed out.

The two remaining universes represent all of the possibilities for this question. Each universe contains some optional information but the diagram is now complete enough that the answer choices can simply be compared to the diagrams and the correct answer easily identified. Choice C—K first and J third—appears in the first universe. It can be true and is the correct answer. The other answer choices do not appear as options in either universe. They cannot be true.

When you create parallel universes, do so around the player that has the fewest options. Be cautious about creating more than three universes. Doing so can be time-consuming and can create diagrams that are difficult to use. There are questions, though, in which creating four, five, or even six universes may be the quickest way to solve the question.

Use these diagramming tools in the order that they have been presented here. First enter only what must be true. If that is not sufficient to answer the question, then enter possibilities, using the slash notation (L/N). If that is still not enough, make parallel universes. Even though parallel universes are the most complex to create, they are the most powerful tool for answering a question quickly and accurately.

The great advantage of creating fairly complete diagrams is that the answer choices can simply be checked against the diagrams and the correct answer identified. If the resulting diagram is not complete enough to answer the question, you must test answer choices, which takes more time but is often the only viable strategy.

TIP

PARALLEL UNIVERSES ARE NOT FOR ALL PROBLEMS

Don't try to create parallel universes to solve all problems. For many problems parallel universes take too much time. The alternative is to test answer choices.

USING SUPPLEMENTAL DIAGRAMS

In the earlier section on diagrams you learned how to use supplemental diagrams to represent circular arrangements, multiple rows (such as rows on an airplane), and sequences. Supplemental diagrams are powerful tools for solving questions.

Counting Places in a Sequence

Supplemental diagrams of short or long sequences show how many players must come before or after a particular player.

GAME WITH GEOLOGY STUDENTS

Six geology students—Jones, Kellogg, Lindquist, Ming, Nieto, and Pacheco—are to present papers at a six-day conference. Each student presents exactly one time and only one presentation is given on each day.

    Jones presents before Ming.

    Ming presents before Nieto.

    Jones presents either immediately before or immediately after Pacheco.

    Pacheco presents before Lindquist.

    Either Kellogg presents last or Ming presents before Lindquist but not both.

What is the latest slot in which Jones can present?

(A) sixth

(B) fifth

(C) fourth

(D) third

(E) second

Look at the conditions for this game. They include supplemental diagrams for several sequences.

$$J - M - N$$
$$JP \text{ or } PJ$$
$$P - L$$
$$\text{Either } K = G$$
$$\text{or } M - L$$
$$bnb$$

Figure 4.78. Conditions for game with
geology students (bnb = "but not both")

The first line combines the first two conditions: J presents before M, and M presents before N. To find the latest that J can present, look for the number of players that must come after J. There are two: M and N. P does not have to come after J. Based on the diagram J – M – N, J cannot present in 5 or 6 because M and N must both follow J. Test J in 4 for rule violations. In fact, there is one. As an exercise, try to find the violation.

When you find temporary information in a question, you can create a new, temporary supplemental diagram with the new information and its consequences. This is helpful because new information often cannot be put directly into the main diagram. Cross out temporary diagrams when you are finished with them so that you do not get confused by them in later questions.

If Kellogg presents last, what is the latest that Lindquist can present?

(A) fifth

(B) fourth

(C) third

(D) second

(E) first

If K is last, then L presents before M.

$$PJ/JP - L - M - N - K$$

Figure 4.79. Temporary supplemental diagram

You can read from the diagram that there are three players who must come after L. L can present no later than third. Now test L in 3 to see if any other rules would create a violation. Counting places in the Figure 4.79 diagram also allows you to determine how many players must appear before M, for example.

In addition to counting places, supplemental diagrams allow you to determine which players are options for specific places. In the diagram above, the options for places 1, 2, and 3 are L, P, and J. The diagram also shows required orders, such as P presenting before L, and optional orders, as with J, who may or may not present before P.

Early Versus Late

In Figure 4.79, notice that L tends to come early in the sequence and N, for example, tends to come late. If an answer choice has N presenting before L, there is an increased chance that the answer choice violates a rule. When you scan for answer choices that are likely to violate rules, consider whether players tend to come early or late in the sequence.

The early versus late concept can be applied to a question such as *What is the maximum number of students who can present after Pacheco but before Nieto?* Because you want to find the most possible places between P and N, put P as early as possible and put N as late as possible. To find the smallest number of places between the two, you would choose the latest possible position for P and the earliest possible position for N, as shown in Figure 4.80.

	Earliest P	Latest N
Maximum distance between P and N	← P	N →
Minimum distance between P and N	P →	← N
	Latest P	Earliest N

Figure 4.80. Creating maximum or minimum distances between players

Other Temporary Diagrams and Rules

Some temporary information cannot go into a supplemental sequence diagram but can be written as a new rule or a new sequence. Based on the new rule or sequence, other temporary rules or sequences might follow. All of this information can be helpful in solving the question. Write temporary sequences and rules below the original rules and cross them out when you are finished with them.

Consider a question that adds the condition that P must come after J. Figure 4.81 shows how this condition can be entered as temporary supplemental information. The consequences of the new condition can also be entered.

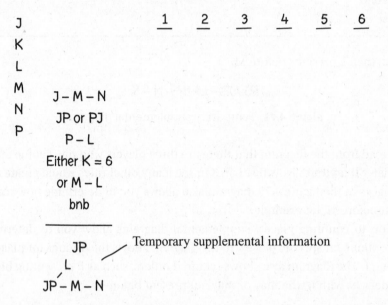

Figure 4.81. Temporary supplemental information. Temporary information should be crossed off after finishing the question to which it applies.

ENOUGH TO ANSWER THE QUESTION?

As you work through a question, it is often not necessary to fill in all possible information in your diagram. Sometimes after one or two steps, you have enough information to solve the question. Stop after every couple of steps to see if you already have enough to answer the question. Check the answers against the diagram. Even if you do not yet have enough to answer the question, you may be able to eliminate some answer choices, which helps you know what to focus on.

MOST RESTRICTED PLAYERS

Players that have the most restrictions on them—meaning that there are a number of rules that govern the player—are more likely to either break a rule or be forced into a certain fixture. As you scan the answer choices, look for players that have the most restrictions. Be aware, though, that a player that has no restrictions is sometimes the one that violates a rule or is forced into a position.

WHAT RULES APPLY TO A GIVEN PLAYER?

This is a rather obvious and simple strategy but it is a powerful strategy that many people forget to use. When you are working through a diagram, look for the rules that apply to specific players. Suppose that you are working on a game in which L and J, among other players, have not yet been assigned, and places 2, 3, and 5 have not yet had players assigned to them. Start with one player. Use L as an example. Check the rules that apply to L. L must come after P. This information helps you determine what the options are for L. You can use the same strategy for the fixtures. Check for rules that apply to fixture 5. J cannot appear in 5.

WHAT ARE THE OPTIONS FOR A PLAYER OR FIXTURE?

Asking yourself what the options are for a particular player or fixture helps you figure out how a question works. In some cases there are only a few specific options for a particular player or fixture, so all of the options can be readily diagrammed and then the answers can be determined directly from the diagrams. If there are only a few options for a player, use them to create parallel universes.

There are two different contexts in which you look for options. You can look for the options for where a particular player can go or you can look for the options for which players can be assigned to a particular fixture.

EXAMPLE

If Kellogg and Lindquist present as far apart from each other as possible, all of the following could be true EXCEPT:

(A) Kellogg presents before Jones.

(B) Kellogg presents immediately before Pacheco.

(C) Ming presents immediately after Jones.

(D) Nieto presents after Kellogg.

(E) Nieto presents after Lindquist.

Try to put K and L into the diagram. What are the options for K and L, given that they must be as far apart as possible? The two furthest positions are 1 and 6. What are the options for fixture 1? Check the rules that apply to fixture 1. Any player who must come after another player cannot be in 1. L must come after P, so L cannot go in 1. There are no restrictions against K going into 1. L cannot present first and so K must present first. There are no restrictions against L being sixth.

1	2	3	4	5	6
K					L

Figure 4.82. Place Kellogg and Lindquist
as far apart as possible.

Which remaining player has the most restrictions? J must come before M and N and must also be adjacent to P. What are the options for J? Count the places in the sequence. J must be followed by two players. What is the latest that J can appear? The latest is 3, because M and N must occupy 4 and 5, respectively. What are all of the options for J? They are 2 and 3. Create a new universe parallel to the existing one.

$$\frac{1}{K} \quad \frac{2}{} \quad \frac{3}{} \quad \frac{4}{} \quad \frac{5}{} \quad \frac{6}{L}$$

$$K \qquad\qquad\qquad\qquad\qquad\qquad L$$

Figure 4.83. The original universe split into two universes

Now create the two options for J.

$$\frac{1}{K} \quad \frac{2}{} \quad \frac{3}{J} \quad \frac{4}{} \quad \frac{5}{} \quad \frac{6}{L}$$

$$K \qquad J \qquad\qquad\qquad\qquad L$$

Figure 4.84. The two possible universes based on Jones

In the first universe, what are the options for M and N? They must go in 4 and 5, respectively. There is only one option for P: 2. In the second universe, there seem to be several options for M and N (ignoring the other conditions)—M in 3 and N in 4, M in 3 and N in 5, M in 4 and N in 5. These are too many to work with. Instead, look for a player with more limited options. What are the options for P? P must be adjacent to J and so it has only one option: 3. Then M and N must be in 4 and 5, respectively.

$$\frac{1}{K} \quad \frac{2}{P} \quad \frac{3}{J} \quad \frac{4}{M} \quad \frac{5}{N} \quad \frac{6}{L}$$

$$K \qquad J \qquad P \qquad M \qquad N \qquad L$$

Figure 4.85. Two universes with all options filled in

The answers can now be compared directly to the diagrams. You can find the correct answer quickly and easily because all possible options are shown.

The Problem-Solving Process

Use the tools that you just learned to systematically work through a question. Below is a general series of steps that you can apply to a question. For each step, the basic tools that you can use in that step are listed and described.

TWO PATHS TO AN ANSWER

There are two distinct paths for getting to a correct answer. The first path is to create a diagram that is accurate and complete enough that the answer can simply be read from the diagram. This is the best problem-solving method but cannot be used on every question. When the diagram path cannot be used, the alternative path is to test answer choices. The two paths are described below.

The Diagram Path

The first path is to create diagrams that are complete enough that the answer choices can simply be compared to the diagrams, eliminating the wrong answers and discovering the correct one. Complete diagrams can consist of (1) a single assignment in which it is determined which player is assigned to every fixture, (2) a single assignment in which it is determined which players are assigned to some fixtures and for other fixtures there is a list of the players who could be assigned, or (3) several assignments (lines) that represent all the possibilities (parallel universes). These can include fixtures to which a specific player must be assigned and fixtures for which there is a list of possible players that can be assigned.

A single assignment, all players determined	$\frac{1}{U}$	$\frac{2}{W}$	$\frac{3}{X}$	$\frac{4}{V}$	$\frac{5}{Z}$	$\frac{6}{Y}$

A single assignment, some options	$\frac{1}{U}$	$\frac{2}{W/V}$	$\frac{3}{X}$	$\frac{4}{V/W}$	$\frac{5}{Y}$	$\frac{6}{Z}$

Parallel universes. Top universe has options. Bottom universe, all are determined.	$\frac{1}{U}$	$\frac{2}{W}$	$\frac{3}{V/X}$	$\frac{4}{X/V}$	$\frac{5}{Y}$	$\frac{6}{Z}$
	U	X	W	V	Y	Z

Figure 4.86. Three types of diagrams that can be used when following the diagram path

The Testing Answers Path

The second path to getting an answer is to test each answer choice. This can be time-consuming, especially if the correct answer turns out to be in the D or E position. Creating diagrams, when it is possible, is a faster and more accurate way to get an answer. However, on many questions there is not enough—or any—information to create a sufficient diagram. On other questions, it would be theoretically possible to show all of the options but it would be too time-consuming or complex. For example, on some questions it would require ten or more parallel universes to capture all of the options.

When diagramming is not practical, you may be able to eliminate some answers by using diagrams, but you then need to test answer choices to get to the correct answer. When testing answers, first eliminate answer choices if possible, and then decide which answer choices to test.

Remember that proving that an answer choice does not violate rules is always tentative. You may have missed a violation. On the other hand, proving that a violation exists is usually accurate.

When you work on a question in which four of the answer choices are viable orders, most of the answer choices may have wide-open options and few restrictions. Often you will have the clear impression that there are a number of ways for creating a viable option. However, it would be time-consuming to actually create an order and then test it. When there are four answer choices that could be true and a particular answer choice seems to have lots of options, it is better to assume that the order is viable (and thus not the correct answer) and move on to test the next answer choice. Hopefully, when you get to the answer choice that breaks rules, it will be clear. If you have made a mistake, all of the answer choices will appear to be viable and you must go back and look at each one more closely.

THE FOUR STEPS FOR PROBLEM SOLVING

There are four steps for problem solving. These steps help you determine which of the two paths you should use and then help you implement the best path.

THE FOUR STEPS FOR PROBLEM SOLVING

STEP 1 **Diagramming.** Fill in as much of the diagram as possible. If this does not provide enough information to answer the question, continue with the next steps.

STEP 2 **Elimination.** Apply strategies to eliminate answer choices.

STEP 3 **Scanning.** Glance at the remaining answer choices to orient yourself.

STEP 4 **Testing answer choices.** Apply strategies to test the remaining answer choices.

Start working on a question by going through the steps in order. Then, you can go back to any of the steps as needed.

Diagramming, eliminating, scanning, and testing answer choices make up your basic problem-solving strategy. This section creates a catalog of the specific tools that you can use for each of the four steps, along with the tools for general problem solving.

Step 1. Create Diagrams

If there is new information in the question stem, the first step is to put that information into a diagram. If the new information can go directly into the main diagram, put it there. Apply the rules in order to enter any other information that *must* be true. If not too complex, put in some information that *can* be true (e.g., L/N and N/L). Look for rules that apply to players in the diagram. Determine which players have the most restrictions. Determine what the options are for the most restricted players and fixtures. If not too complex, create parallel universes.

How much time and effort should you put into making diagrams? Start with what is simple, obvious, and quick. Check frequently to see if you already have enough information to get the answer or at least to eliminate additional answer choices. If you are not sure whether you are doing more work than you need to, move on to the next step. You can always come back and fill in more.

If there is new information that cannot be put into the main diagram, create temporary supplemental diagrams and rules. If there is no new information, go to Step 2.

Below are the specific tools for diagrams. Glance through these now and come back to them as a resource when you are working on problems. It is not necessary to memorize these now.

SPECIFIC TOOLS FOR DIAGRAMS

Diagram—put in new information. Enter new information directly into the main diagram.

Diagram—apply rules, musts. Use the rules to determine what else must be true given what is already in the diagram. When you use this tool, stick with only that which must be true. Do not enter options.

Diagram—apply rules, with options. When you use this tool, you add to the main diagram information that could be true but does not have to be. Keep this tool distinct from the previous tool. Use options to indicate that there are two players, L and R, for example, who could be options for a particular fixture (L/R). Also, when you are trying to create a viable assignment, such as proving that M could go in slot 5, you are entering options. In this case, be sure to check your finished assignment against the rules to make sure the assignment does not create a violation.

Diagram—parallel universes. If you try to enter too many options in an assignment, the assignment can become difficult to work with. Creating parallel universes (multiple lines that show various options) keeps your information clear. Each universe includes information that must be true but can also include information that could be true. If it takes more than three or four universes to cover all possibilities, this tool may be too time-consuming. The alternative is to test answer choices.

Diagram—supplemental diagrams or rules. If a question gives new information but that information cannot be put directly into the diagram, for example, *If Jones presents immediately before Ming, . . .* make temporary supplemental diagrams or write temporary rules to keep track of the information. Check the permanent supplemental diagrams and rules to see if anything else follows from the new information and write down anything that does follow. Be sure to cross out temporary diagrams and rules when you are done with the question to which they apply.

Step 2. Eliminate Answers

If a question does not provide new information, start with this step. Many of your tools allow you to eliminate answers. You can start with the rules and look for violations. This is particularly effective when there are four answers that violate rules, as in *which one of the following could be true.* Alternately, you can start with an answer choice and look for rules that apply to it. Checking previous valid assignments, such as in the correct answer to the typical first question, as well as the valid assignments you create in your diagrams, can sometimes eliminate one or two answers. Checking answers against a diagram, even if the diagram is only partially filled in, can help eliminate answers. You may be able to eliminate answers by using the supplemental diagrams and the temporary diagrams and rules.

Below are the specific tools for elimination. Use these as a resource when you are working on problems. You do not need to memorize these now. Glance through them so that you can start to become familiar with them.

SPECIFIC TOOLS FOR ELIMINATION

Elimination—apply the rules to four violations. This is the main, and often only, tool needed for the typical first question. Start with the first rule. Work the rules in order.

Elimination—apply rules, general. When there are not four violations, apply the rules in a more general way. Start with the rules that are most relevant to the question.

Elimination—check previous valid assignments. Use the answer to the typical first question, as well as any other valid assignments that you have created in your notes, to confirm or eliminate answer choices. This tool is only helpful in about a tenth of the questions. However, when it does work, it saves valuable time by reducing the number of answer choices you need to test. Sometimes this tool leads directly to the correct answer.

Elimination—check answers against the diagram. In nearly half of all AR questions this is the final step that gives you the answer. If you have been able to fill in the main diagram or temporary supplemental diagrams, you can check each remaining answer choice against the diagrams. The answer will be clear unless you have made an error in the diagram. This tool will not give you a definitive answer if there is not enough information to fill in the diagram. However, it may help eliminate some answer choices. In that case you may need to test each of the remaining answers.

Step 3. Scan the Answer Choices

Quickly look through the answer choices to determine what to test. Scanning also allows you to compare answers and to get a sense of what you need to do to solve the question. If it is necessary to test answer choices, scanning helps you determine which choices have the most restrictions on them and are most likely to either break rules or be required to be true. It is not always possible to determine which choices should be tested first. However, this step is an important one because it often saves time.

> **TOOL: SCANNING**
>
> **Scan.** This tool saves time by telling you which answer choices to focus on first.

Step 4. Test Answer Choices

For many questions, creating a diagram and/or eliminating choices leads to a definitive answer and you will be done before Step 4. Before doing Step 4, consider whether it is possible to create a more complete diagram instead. Testing answer choices is not necessarily difficult but can be time-consuming if you have to test many answer choices. On the other hand, testing answer choices is almost always effective. You can get the answer.

When you create a viable assignment, be sure to check it against all of the rules. After testing all answer choices, you will have the correct answer.

Following are the specific tools for testing answer choices. Use these as a reference as you work on problems. Glance through the tools to become familiar with them. It is not necessary to memorize them now.

GENERAL PROBLEM-SOLVING STEPS

There are some general tools that can be used at various stages of the problem-solving process. They are summarized below. Scan them now to become familiar with them. Use the list below as a reference when you are working on problems. It is not necessary to memorize them now.

General—count the possibilities. This tool is used for questions in which you have to determine a number, for example, how many players can be assigned to a particular fixture, or for how many players is the exact assignment determined. (This is not the same as counting places in a sequence.)

General—early versus late. This tool helps you spot answer choices that are likely to violate rules because the choice tries to place a player who tends to be late in the sequence before a player who tends to be early in the sequence. Also use the concept of early versus late to find the earliest or latest that a player can appear.

Below is a decision tree that outlines the common problem-solving paths and tools, as described above. The tree refers to the steps **Diagram**, **Eliminate**, **Scan**, **Test Answers**, and to the **General** tools.

Decision Tree for AR Problem Solving

Is there infomation that goes into the main diagram?

Yes

Diagram
Put in new info
Apply rules, must
Apply rules, option
Parallel universes

↓

Eliminate
Check answers against the diagram

No

Infomation that does not go in main diagram?

Yes

Diagram
Temporary
supplemental
diagrams/rules

↓

General
Option for players
Option for fixtures

↓

Diagram
Parallel universes

↓

Eliminate
Check answers against diagram

↓

Answer?

Yes

No

↓

Scan

↓

Test Answers

No

Eliminate
Apply rules to answers

Check answers against rules

Check previous valid answers

↓

Scan

↓

Test Answers

Strategies for Solving Specific Question Types

By following the previous steps and creatively using the problem-solving tools, you can crack any AR question. In the section below, you will learn strategies for solving specific types of questions quickly and accurately.

The strategies in this section are very in-depth. They represent the tools needed for virtually every AR question that has appeared on recent LSATs. Do not try to memorize these strategies. Read through them to get a sense of how each strategy works. You will get the most out of this section by coming back to it as a reference as you work through questions. For example, as you work on a *must be true* question, go to the sections below that describe the strategies for *must be true* and try to apply the strategies to the question on which you are working. You should also plan to reread this section periodically as you continue to practice. The more you review the strategies and apply them to practice questions, the more natural the strategies will become for you.

The strategies below refer back to the specific tools that were listed in the section above. A particular tool is referred to by its category (Diagram, Elimination, Scan, Testing Answers, or General) as well as the name of the tool. For example, you may see a reference to **Elimination—apply the rules to four violations** or **General—count the possibilities**. If you do not remember what a certain tool does, review it in the lists in the previous section. It takes time and practice to absorb all of the tools, so review them regularly and use the lists of tools as a reference as you work practice questions.

COULD BE TRUE

Could be true questions make up more than 40 percent of all AR questions. There are three main categories of *could be true* questions: those with no new information, those with new information that can be put into the main diagram, and those with new information that cannot be put in the main diagram. The three categories require different problem-solving approaches.

With No New Information

About half of *could be true* questions do not provide new information. Nearly all of these ask you to find a valid complete assignment. These are the typical first question for a game. Because there is no new information, skip the Diagram step and go right to Elimination. These questions can be solved in one step with one tool: **Elimination—apply the rules to four violations**. Start with the first rule. Identify what a violation of that rule would look like and then look for the violation in the answer choices. Review the detailed instructions for this tool earlier in the chapter.

There are some *could be true* questions with no new information that do not ask for a complete assignment. These questions might ask for a partial assignment, which fixtures a player could be assigned to, or any other fact about players. Because there is no new information, diagramming is not likely to help. You may be able to eliminate some answers by applying rules: **Elimination—apply rules, general**. (There are still four violations even though the choices are not complete assignments.) You might also eliminate answers by using **General—count places in a sequence**. The final tool for these questions is testing answers—either **Test answers—create a possible assignment and double check against rules** or **Test answers—prove a violation**. In other words, because four answer choices violate rules and one does not, when you test an answer, you either prove it causes a violation or you prove that it could work.

With New Information That Goes in the Main Diagram

About 30 percent of *could be true* questions provide new information that can be put directly into the main diagram (e.g., *Jones presents third*). In these questions the first step is Diagram and the first tool is **Diagram—put in new information**. The problem-solving process involves applying the rules to find what else must be true (**Diagram—apply rules, musts**). Some questions also require applying the rules to put in some options (**Diagram—apply rules, with options**) and/or creating parallel universes (**Diagram—parallel universes**). By using these tools you create a diagram that is complete enough to answer the question. The final tool is **Elimination—check answers against the diagram**. These questions typically do not require you to test answer choices.

Below are some typical sequences of tools that can be used to solve *could be true* questions with new information that goes into the main diagram. These are sequences that have been used to solve actual, specific LSAT questions. The exact order of steps and the specific steps that are included reflect the unique properties of specific questions. For the questions on which you work, start with the sequences below and then adapt them using the problem-solving tools.

The sequences are similar to summaries of a chess game. They outline the "moves" that you can make to efficiently solve questions. They are not meant to represent the only way to solve a problem. Rather, the sequences show you the thinking process of a skilled test taker. As you work on questions, identify and write down the steps you are using. Then compare them with these sequences.

It is not necessary to memorize the sequences you see here. It is best to use these lists of sequences as a reference, coming back to them later as you work on specific problems. You do not need to understand them thoroughly right now but it may be helpful to glance through them briefly, identifying the similarities and differences among the sequences.

To better understand how these sequences apply, consider an example that uses the first sequence, **Without parallel universes, variation 1**.

GAME WITH GEOLOGY STUDENTS

Six geology students—Jones, Kellogg, Lindquist, Ming, Nieto, and Pacheco—are to present papers at a six-day conference. Each student presents exactly one time and only one presentation is given on each day.

Jones presents before Ming.

Ming presents before Nieto.

Jones presents either immediately before or immediately after Pacheco.

Pacheco presents before Lindquist.

Either Kellogg presents last or Ming presents before Lindquist but not both.

If Ming presents third, which one of the following could be the students who present fifth and sixth, respectively?

(A) Kellogg, Lindquist

(B) Nieto, Kellogg

(C) Jones, Kellogg

(D) Jones, Nieto

(E) Lindquist, Kellogg

Follow the steps in variation 1.

Step 1: Diagram—put in new information. The new information is that Ming presents third. Put Ming in 3 in the main diagram.

Step 2: Diagram—apply rules, musts. Apply the rules that involve Ming. Ming must be after Jones and before Nieto. However, these rules do not give you any information that *must* go in the diagram. Apply the last rule. With Ming in 3, could Ming be after Lindquist? No. Both Jones and Pacheco must come before Ming. Ming appears before Lindquist and, according to the last rule, Kellogg cannot appear last. There is no other information that must be true. Go on to the next step, which looks for information that *could* be true.

Step 3: [Diagram—apply rules, with options]. This step is optional for this sequence. (It is listed in brackets.) This means that the sequence can be used either with or without the third step. In this step, look for information that lists options, because Step 2 exhausted the information that *must* be true. According to the first rule, Jones presents before Ming, so Jones must go in either 1 or 2. According to the third rule, Pacheco and Jones present in adjacent time slots. Enter J/P in 1 and P/J in 2. (It would be equally valid to put P/J in 1 and J/P in 2.) There are three time slots remaining (4, 5, and 6) and three players remaining (Nieto, Lindquist, and Kellogg). Kellogg cannot go in 6, so put N/L in 6. In 4 and 5 put K/L/N. Now each fixture shows either the one player who must go there or the options that can go there.

Step 4: Elimination—check answers against the diagram. This tool involves checking the answer choices against your now complete diagram (which includes options). You can quickly determine from the diagram that choices B through E are not valid options. Only choice A matches the diagram.

The exact sequence of tools that is required by any particular question depends on the specifics of that question. The sequences presented below are common ones and reflect sequences that have been used to solve actual AR questions. As you work through questions, you will find your own variations.

The sequences are presented in the order of how common they are. The sequences at the top apply to a higher percentage of questions than do the sequences at the bottom.

PROBLEM-SOLVING SEQUENCES FOR *COULD BE TRUE* QUESTIONS WITH NEW INFORMATION IN THE MAIN DIAGRAM

When a tool is in brackets, the variation occurs both with and without that tool.

Read the first two examples in each category carefully.

Then skim the others and come back to them as you are working on problems.

Without parallel universes, variation 1

1. Diagram—put in new information
2. Diagram—apply rules, musts
[3. Diagram—apply rules, with options]
4. Elimination—check answers against the diagram

Without parallel universes, variation 2

1. Diagram—put in new information
2. Diagram—supplemental diagrams or rules
3. Diagram—apply rules, musts
4. Elimination—check answers against the diagram

With New Information That Does Not Go in the Main Diagram

Information such as *If Jones presents before Ming . . .* does not tell you exactly to which fixture Jones is assigned. For that reason, you cannot put the information directly into the main diagram. You can, however, put this information into a temporary supplemental diagram or you can create a temporary rule. Sometimes the temporary diagram reveals information that can be put into the main diagram. In addition, even though the new information does not go directly into the main diagram, it may be sufficient to allow you to create parallel universes.

Information that does not go in the diagram is typically not as specific as information that does go in the diagram. In about a third of these questions you can create a diagram that is complete enough that you can check the answers against the diagram, just as you can do for questions with new information that goes in the main diagram. However, for the other two-thirds, you need to test answer choices as your final step.

The general problem-solving process, then, is to create temporary diagrams and rules that may eliminate some choices and will help you test answers more quickly.

MUST BE TRUE

About 20 percent of AR questions ask you to choose an answer that must be true. About half of these provide new information that goes directly into the diagram. A quarter of the questions provide new information that does not go into the main diagram, and the final quarter provide no new information.

No New Information

Four answer choices could be true or may violate rules. Only one answer choice is forced to be true. In these questions there is no new information, which means that something is forced to be true solely based on the original conditions. You may be able to eliminate some answers based on previous valid assignments. For example, if a previous valid order included Jones in 3, then an answer choice that reads *Jones presents fifth* is not an answer that must be true. If previous valid orders do not apply, scan the answers to see what choices are most likely to invoke rules and then test the answer choices by negating them. In other words, prove that the answer does *not* have to be true.

New Information That Goes in the Main Diagram

Because these questions provide new information that can be entered directly into the main diagram, you have more information to go on and it is easier to eliminate wrong answers and spot correct ones. In these questions, start by entering the new information into the main diagram and then applying the rules to find what must be true. In some cases you will need to also enter some options and/or create parallel universes. You then can compare the answer choices to the diagrams and find the correct answer. For some of these questions you can also use temporary supplemental diagrams or temporary rules.

New Information That Does Not Go in the Main Diagram

These questions are more challenging than those that provide information that goes directly in the main diagram. Use temporary supplemental diagrams and rules to organize the new information and to determine what else must be true. You may be able to enter some information in the main diagram, showing what must be true, what could be true, or creating parallel universes. Use the tools for considering what options particular players have or what options can be assigned to particular fixtures. In almost all of these questions your last step is to compare the answer choices to the temporary or main diagram.

Problem-solving sequences. Remember that the problem-solving sequences are meant to be used as a reference as you work on practice problems.

PROBLEM-SOLVING SEQUENCES FOR
MUST BE TRUE QUESTIONS

When a tool is in brackets, the variation occurs both with and without that tool.
Read the first two examples in each category carefully.
Then skim the others and come back to them as you are working on problems.

With no new information:
Variation 1
1. Eliminate—check previous valid assignments
[2. Scan]
3. Test answers—negate a must

Variation 2
1. Scan
2. Test answers—negate a must

With new information that goes into the main diagram:
Variation 1
1. Diagram—put in new information
2. Diagram—parallel universes
[3. Diagram—apply rules, musts]
4. Eliminate—check answers against diagram

Variation 2
1. Diagram—put in new information
2. Diagram—apply rules, musts
[3. Diagram—apply rules, with options]
4. Eliminate—check answers against diagram

Variation 3
1. Diagram—put in new information
2. Diagram—apply rules, with options
[3. Diagram—apply rules, musts]
4. Eliminate—check answers against diagram

Variation 4
1. Diagram—put in new information
2. Diagram—parallel universes
3. Diagram—apply rules, musts
4. Diagram—apply rules, with options
5. Eliminate—check answers against diagram

Variation 5
1. Diagram—put in new information
2. Diagram—apply rules, musts
3. Diagram—parallel universes
4. Diagram—apply rules, musts

5. Diagram—apply rules, with options
6. Eliminate—check answers against diagram

With new information that does not go into the main diagram:

Variation 1

1. Diagram—supplemental diagram or rules
2. General—options for fixture
3. Eliminate—apply rules, general
4. Eliminate—check answers against diagram

Variation 2

1. Diagram—supplemental diagram or rules
2. General—options for fixture
3. Diagram—parallel universes
4. Diagram—apply rules, musts
5. Eliminate—check answers against diagram

Variation 3

1. Diagram—supplemental diagram or rules
2. General—options for player
3. Diagram—parallel universes
4. Diagram—apply rules, musts
5. Diagram—apply rules, with options
6. Eliminate—check answers against diagram

Variation 4

1. Diagram—supplemental diagram or rules
2. Diagram—put in new information
3. Diagram—apply rules, musts
4. Eliminate—check answers against diagram

CANNOT BE TRUE

About 15 percent of AR questions ask you to choose an answer choice that cannot be true. Usually, no new information is given. This means that diagramming is not used very much with these questions. Rely on eliminating and testing answers.

In these questions, four answers could be true. One violates rules. It is difficult to prove that an answer choice could be true because you might overlook a violation. Therefore, it is more efficient to find answer choices that are more likely to break rules and to test them first. You can apply the rules in order to find violations but because there are many rules and only one answer choice that violates them, this is not as efficient as when there are four violations. After eliminating answer choices, you will need to test the answer choices that are most likely to break rules. Test them for violations.

Some *cannot be true* questions can be solved by testing answers to prove a violation. Others are solved by counting places in a sequence.

Problem-Solving Sequences

Following are typical sequences for solving *cannot be true* questions, starting with the most common.

When a tool is in brackets, the variation occurs both with and without that tool.

Read the first two examples in each category carefully.

Then skim the others and come back to them as you are working on problems.

Variation 1

1. Test answers—prove a violation

Variation 2

1. Scan
2. Test answers—prove a violation

Variation 3

1. Eliminate—check previous valid assignments
2. Test answers—prove a violation

Variation 4

1. Eliminate—check previous valid assignments
2. Scan
[3. General—look for most restricted]
4. Test answers—prove a violation

Variation 5 (with new information not in the main diagram)

1. Diagram—supplemental diagram or rules
2. Diagram—parallel universes
3. Diagram—apply rules, musts
4. Eliminate—check answers against diagram

COULD BE TRUE "EXCEPT"

About 5 percent of AR questions are worded *Each of the following could be true EXCEPT*. Four of the answer choices could be true. One choice—the correct response—cannot be true. These questions are logically identical to *cannot be true*. However, the *could be true EXCEPT* questions are equally divided among questions that have no new information, new information that goes in the main diagram, and new information that does not go in the main diagram. As a result, in these questions you can take more advantage of diagramming. Because you create diagrams, your last step is **Eliminate—check answers against diagram**.

PROBLEM-SOLVING SEQUENCES FOR
COULD BE TRUE "EXCEPT" QUESTIONS

Read the first two examples in each category carefully.

Then skim the others and come back to them as you are working on problems.

Variation 1 (new information in main diagram)

1. Diagram—put in new information
2. Diagram—parallel universes
3. Diagram—apply rules, musts
4. Diagram—apply rules, with options
5. Eliminate—check answers against diagram

Variation 2

1. Diagram—put in new information
2. Diagram—supplemental diagram or rules
3. Scan
4. Eliminate—check answers for violation

Variation 3 (new information that does not go in the main diagram)

1. Diagram—supplemental diagram or rules
2. Diagram—put in new information
3. Diagram—apply rules, musts
4. Diagram—apply rules, with options
5. Eliminate—check answers against diagram

Variation 4

1. Diagram—supplemental diagram or rules
2. Diagram—parallel universes
3. Diagram—apply rules, musts
4. Eliminate—check answers against diagram

Variation 5 (no new information)

1. Eliminate—check previous valid assignments
2. Scan
3. Test answers—prove a violation

COMPLETELY DETERMINED IF

About 3 percent of AR questions ask you to find the one answer choice that, if true, would result in the assignment of players being completely determined. In over 90 percent of these questions there is no new information. For most *completely determined if* questions, then, there is nothing to diagram. Because the answer choices do not necessarily violate rules, elimination is usually not helpful either. Your primary tool for these is to test the answer choices. Before testing, scan the answer choices to look for information that forces assignments to happen. To test an answer, put it in the diagram and try to show that it leads to only one, complete assignment. If the answer seems to leave options, move on to another answer.

If there is new information, put it into the main or temporary diagrams. Then continue with scanning and testing answers.

PROBLEM-SOLVING SEQUENCES FOR
***COMPLETELY DETERMINED IF* QUESTIONS**

Variation 1 (no new information)
1. Scan
2. Test answers—create a possible assignment and double-check

Variation 2 (new information in or not in the main diagram)
1. Diagram—put in new information OR Diagram—supplemental diagram or rules
2. Scan
3. Test answers—create a possible assignment and double-check

---

MUST BE FALSE

About 3 percent of AR questions ask you to find the one answer choice that *must be false*. The other answer choices are not forced to be false. They either must be true or could be true. (Note that if an answer choice could be false, it also could be true.) A *must be false* question is logically the same as *cannot be true* and *could be true EXCEPT*.

The *must be false* questions tend to have either no new information or new information that does not go in the main diagram. The questions that do not have new information can be solved in the same way as *cannot be true* questions. Eliminate answers based on previous valid assignments, if possible, and then scan the answer choices and test them, trying to prove a violation.

The *must be false* questions that have new information can be solved in the same way as the *could be true EXCEPT* questions. For those that have new information that goes in the diagram, (1) put the new information in the diagram, (2) apply the rules, (3) create parallel universes if feasible, and then (4) check the answers against the diagram. For those that have new information that does not go in the diagram, (1) create temporary supplemental diagrams or rules, (2) apply the original rules if possible, (3) create parallel universes if possible, and then (4) either check the answer choices against the diagrams, or (5) if there is not enough information in the diagrams, scan and test the answers, trying to prove a violation.

PROBLEM-SOLVING SEQUENCES FOR
***MUST BE FALSE* QUESTIONS**

Variation 1 (new information that goes in the main diagram)
1. Diagram—put in new information
2. Diagram—parallel universes
3. Eliminate—check answers against diagram

Variation 2 (new information that does not go in the main diagram)

1. Diagram—supplemental diagram or rules
2. Diagram—parallel universes
3. Diagram—apply rules, musts
4. Eliminate—check previous valid assignments
5. Scan
6. Test answers—prove a violation

Variation 3 (no new information)

1. Eliminate—check previous valid assignments
2. Scan
3. Test answers—prove a violation

EQUIVALENT CONDITION

About 4 percent of AR questions ask you to find a condition that is equivalent to one of the original conditions. The question stem does not provide new information. Typically, diagramming and eliminating are of little value. Your primary tool is testing each answer choice to see if it creates an equivalent condition without adding any additional restrictions and without leaving out any of the original restrictions. It may help to scan the answer choices to see what to test first.

PROBLEM-SOLVING SEQUENCES FOR *EQUIVALENT CONDITION* QUESTIONS

When a tool is in brackets, the variation occurs both with and without that tool.

Variation 1

[1. Diagram—supplemental diagram or rules]
2. Scan
3. Test answers—other

HOW MANY PLAYERS FOR A FIXTURE

About 2 to 3 percent of AR questions ask how many players could be assigned to a given fixture. Usually this type of question does not provide new information. The sequences used to solve this type of question are a little different from previous sequences. Note the use of the General tools. When there is new information, the strategies shift to creating diagrams and checking answers against them.

FOR HOW MANY CAN IT BE DETERMINED

Fewer than 1 percent of questions ask you to calculate the number of players for whom it can be determined to exactly which fixture they are assigned. One variation asks "For how many players are there exactly two options?" This type of question may give new information or not. If the new information does not go directly into the main diagram, use temporary diagrams or you may be able to create parallel universes that show all the possibilities.

Because you have to count all possibilities, this type of question is difficult to answer if you cannot represent all the possibilities either through parallel universes or through temporary diagrams. Once you have complete diagrams, count how many options there are.

COULD BE FALSE

About 1 percent of AR questions ask you to identify the answer choice that could be false. This means that the other choices cannot be false. They must be true. The remaining (correct) choice does not have to be true.

Because four answer choices are forced to be true, the question has to set up a lot of restrictions. For this reason, *could be false* questions usually give new information that goes in the main diagram. The best strategy is to fill in the main diagram as much as possible and if necessary, create parallel universes. Check the answer choices against the diagrams. This is quicker than testing answer choices.

PROBLEM-SOLVING SEQUENCES FOR *COULD BE FALSE* QUESTIONS

Variation 1 (new information)
1. Diagram—put in new information
2. Diagram—parallel universes
3. Diagram—apply rules, musts
4. Diagram—apply rules, with options
5. Eliminate—check answers against diagram

Variation 2
1. Diagram—put in new information
2. Diagram—apply rules, musts
3. Diagram—parallel universes
4. Eliminate—check answers against diagram

COMPLETE AND ACCURATE LIST

About 1 percent of AR questions fall into this category. Do not confuse this type of question with the typical first question, which presents five complete assignments. The typical first question may use the wording *complete* or *accurate* or *complete and accurate*. The *complete and accurate* question type differs from the typical first question in that the former does not present complete assignments. The *complete and accurate* question presents a complete list of players who can be assigned to a specific fixture (*a complete and accurate list of students who can present third*) or a complete list of fixtures to which a player can be assigned (*a complete and accurate list of slots in which Jones can present*). The word *complete* means that no options are left out of the list. The word *accurate* means that every option in the list belongs there. Four of the answer choices either violate rules or leave out a required element.

This question type can also present a subset of a full assignment (*which of the following could be an accurate list of the students who present third, fourth, and fifth*). When the question asks for a subset of a full assignment, only the word *accurate* is used, not the word *complete*.

The *complete and accurate* questions usually do not provide new information. When there is no new information, eliminate as many answer choices as possible by applying the rules or by using previous valid assignments. Because there is so little diagrammable information in these questions, you must test the answer choices, so it is important to scan the answer choices first to save time and then test the answer choices. When there is new information, put it into the diagram and apply the rules. The diagram helps you eliminate some answers but does not provide enough information to solve the problem. You still need to test the remaining answers.

PROBLEM-SOLVING SEQUENCES FOR
COMPLETE AND ACCURATE **QUESTIONS**

Variation 1

1. Eliminate—apply rules, general
2. Scan
3. Eliminate—check previous valid assignments
4. Test answers—create a possible assignment, double-check

Variation 2

1. Eliminate—check previous valid assignments
2. General—look for rules that apply to player/fixture
3. Scan
4. Test answers—create a possible assignment, double-check

WHAT IS THE MAXIMUM/MINIMUM

This rare type of question historically has asked for the minimum or maximum number of fixtures that there could be. This applies only in a game with variable fixtures. It has also asked for the maximum number of spaces between two players or between two instances of a player. Usually there is no new information.

PROBLEM-SOLVING SEQUENCES FOR
WHAT IS THE MAXIMUM/MINIMUM **QUESTIONS**

Variation 1

1. General—early versus late
2. General—options for player

Variation 2

1. General—look for most restricted
2. General—look for rules that apply to player/fixture
3. General—options for player
4. Diagram—parallel universes

ONE OR BOTH OF A PAIR

This rare type asks you to identify a pair of players of which at least one must be in the assignment. Both could be in but it is not possible for both to be out. In the incorrect answer choices, one or both members *could* be in but do not have to be. This type implies that something *must* be true and some of the questions use the word *must*. Some use the wording *at least one,* as in *Which one of the following is a pair of students at least one of which must present fourth?*

A *one or both of a pair* question is found only in games with a discard pile. There is usually no new information and so little to diagram. Test answers to prove a violation. Put both members of the pair you are testing into the discard pile. Then apply the rules to prove a violation. If an answer choice seems to have many options, move on to the next answer. It is not necessary to work it out thoroughly. When you test the correct answer choice, it does not take much time to spot the violation. If none of the answers seem to have violations, you have missed something. Go back and work them more carefully.

PROBLEM-SOLVING SEQUENCES FOR *ONE OR BOTH OF A PAIR* QUESTIONS

Variation 1
1. General—look for most restricted
2. Test answers—prove a violation

MUST BE TRUE "EXCEPT"

In this rare type, four answer choices are forced to be true. The correct answer is one that could be true or that is false. In order to create four facts that are forced to be true, the question typically presents new information that goes directly in the main diagram. To solve this type of question put the information in the diagram, apply the rules, and then check the answer choices against the diagram.

PROBLEM-SOLVING SEQUENCES FOR *MUST BE TRUE "EXCEPT"* QUESTIONS

Variation 1
1. Diagram—put in new information
2. Diagram—apply rules, musts
3. Eliminate—check answers against diagram

WHAT IS THE EARLIEST/LATEST

This rare question type asks you to find the earliest or latest fixture in which a player can appear. There is usually no new information. Count places in the sequence and consider how early or late the player can appear. If a player must have two other players coming after it, for example, and if there are six fixtures, then the player cannot appear any later than position 4. However, it is possible that there are other restrictions that would prevent the player from appearing in 4, so you have to check the possibilities.

Avoiding Errors

You now have all the tools you need to understand how to set up different types of games, to interpret different types of questions, and to get answers systematically and efficiently. Your final challenge is to learn how to avoid errors.

Even the most skilled master of Analytical Reasoning will make occasional mistakes. To get your absolute best score on AR, you need to:

1. Learn the warning signs of an error.
2. Learn the most common errors.
3. Identify the types of errors you make and develop strategies for avoiding them.

THE WARNING SIGNS OF ERRORS

There are two clear warning signs that you have made an error (short, of course, of looking up the answer). If you have eliminated all five answer choices, you have made an error on one of the choices. If there seems to be more than one answer choice that works, you have made an error. As tempting as it may be to think that the test writers have erred, the odds are against you.

Errors on the AR section are more serious than on either of the other LSAT sections because if you have misunderstood the game, you may have gotten several questions wrong without realizing it. When you do find a question for which no answer seems to work or more than one seems to work, take it very seriously. Do not simply guess in frustration and move on. You need to find what your error was in order to be sure that you have not gotten other questions wrong. This may seem too time-consuming but the alternative is to risk missing nearly every question on a specific game. This has happened to many test takers!

If no answer or more than one answer seems to work, review the question stem to make sure you understood it correctly. Then go back to the conditions and look for any misinterpretations you may have made. Finally, redo your work.

THE MOST COMMON ERRORS

Keep an eye out for the most common errors.

Misinterpreting One of the Conditions in the Setup

Be careful in your analysis of if/then conditions. Be sure you understand the contrapositive of each if/then. Be particularly careful in setting up sequences, as the wording can be misleading. In the condition *George must appear after Henry but before Fred*, the word order of George and Henry is the opposite of their logical relationship. Henry has to come before George. George comes before Fred but alphabetically Fred comes before George. Watch out for the more logically complex conditions, such as *either . . . or . . . but not both*.

If you find yourself misinterpreting your own notations and shorthand, come up with different notation that is less ambiguous. If you cannot come up with a clear abbreviation for a condition, write the condition out in words.

Misinterpreting the Question Stem

Some question stems are logically complex. Be sure to orient yourself to the stem before you begin solving the question. However, orienting yourself at the beginning of the question may not be enough. Many people lose track of what the question is asking part way through solving it. The more complex the logic of the question, the more likely that you will forget what it is asking and find yourself looking for the wrong thing. As you are working a problem, reread the question stem periodically.

Failing to Check All of the Rules

When you test an assignment to see if it is viable, it is important to check all of the rules. If you cut corners on this, you are likely to miss a violation. On the other hand, if you are trying to prove that an assignment violates rules, you only need to find one violation. Once you have found a violation, you do not need to check more rules. Do not confuse these two different processes.

Failing to Consider All the Options

In many questions you need to see all options. For example, in order to answer a *must be true* question, it is helpful if you have written out all the parallel universes. A common error is the failure to include some options. For example, a test taker may assume that George can only appear in position 1 or 2, missing the possibility that George can appear in 3.

Failing to Distinguish What Must Be True from What Could Be True

If you put George into a diagram as a possibility, there is the danger of later assuming that George must be in that position. Develop notation that ensures that you can distinguish necessary information from possible information. Always be clear whether you are working on *must* information or *could* information.

Applying Main Diagram Rules to the Discard Pile

In games with a discard pile, the rules that apply to the main diagram do not apply to the discard pile. For example, the rule *If George is in, then Fred must be in* means that the appearance of George in the main diagram requires the appearance of Fred in the main diagram. However, if you are testing an assignment by putting George in the discard pile, it is *not* true that Fred must go in the discard pile as well.

LEARNING YOUR OWN ERROR TENDENCIES

The best way to perfect your strategy and avoid errors is to carefully analyze every error that you make. When you get a practice question wrong, try to reconstruct how you approached the question and identify exactly where you went wrong. You may not have used effective timing strategy (e.g., feeling too rushed for time to read carefully and work carefully). You may have failed to use the correct strategies or failed to use the correct strategy accurately. However, for some questions your strategy may have been perfect but you may have made an error. Be careful to note when you misinterpret a condition. If you do not understand the conditions, no amount of strategy will get you to the right answer!

It is not accurate enough simply to say that you made a "careless" error. What caused you to make that error? Spend at least as much time analyzing your errors as you do working on questions. Once you have mastered strategies, learning your own tendencies for making errors and developing ways to avoid those errors is the best and fastest way to your absolute top score.

The AR Problem-Solving Troubleshooter

This section describes a process that you can use when you are unsure of the correct answer on an AR question or when you simply cannot find a correct answer at all. As you practice questions untimed, use the troubleshooter to:

- Make sure you get the correct answer.
- Push yourself to master the AR strategies and patterns.
- Internalize the systematic problem-solving process so that you can use it under timed conditions.

For most people, simply working on a question and then checking the answer is not enough for mastering strategy. To get the most out of your practicing, especially when working untimed, look very carefully at each step of the process. When you are confused, uncertain, or unconfident, identifying what is confusing you and learning how to work through the confusion helps you develop powerful problem-solving skills. The troubleshooter walks you step by step through the stages of backtracking through a problem.

When you are working on an AR problem untimed, you should check the troubleshooter every time that:

1. Your level of confidence in your answer choice is less than 100 percent, or
2. You cannot find an answer at all, or
3. More than one answer choice seems to work.

Before you look up the correct answer, ask yourself if any one of the above points is true for the question you are on. If so, use the troubleshooter. It will help you learn more, increase your understanding of AR, and deepen your problem-solving skills. You can even print a copy of the troubleshooter to keep with you, though it is also helpful to have this book handy so that you can review strategies.

THE TROUBLESHOOTER

Step 1

If you have chosen an answer but your level of confidence in your answer is low (less than 100 percent confident), go to Step 1a. If more than one answer seems to be correct, go to Step 1b. If you simply are not sure of the answer, go to Step 2.

Step 1a

- Review the question stem to make sure you have understood it.
- Review your proof of each answer that you are considering.
- Redo the proof from scratch, to make sure you do not repeat an error.
- If you have a proof for more than one answer, there is an error! Go to Step 1b.
- If you have eliminated all answer choices but the remaining answer does not seem defendable, you may have accidentally eliminated the correct answer. Start from scratch, reconsidering all of the answer choices.
- If you still do not have an answer, go to Step 2.

Step 1b

- If more than one answer seems to be correct, or if none of the answers seems correct, you may have misinterpreted a condition. This is a serious error because you may have gotten other questions wrong without realizing it.
- If more than one answer seems correct, double-check your proof for each one.
- If you do not find an error in one proof, reread the question stem, to make sure you did not misinterpret it.
- If no answer seems correct, reread the question stem.
- Go back to the setup and review each condition carefully from scratch. Look for any conditions you may have missed or misinterpreted.
- If any condition is confusing, analyze it carefully. For if/then conditions, review the information in the AR chapter about if/thens. If necessary, review the instruction on if/thens in the LR chapter.
- Check to see if your supplemental diagrams are accurate.
- If you do not find an error in your setup and still do not have the correct answer, go on to Step 2.
- If you have already done Step 2, go on to Step 3.

Step 2

- Review the question stem. Did you understand it correctly? If necessary, identify the type of question stem and review its description in the chapter.
- Review the strategy for solving the particular type of question stem.
- Work the problem again from scratch, applying the strategy for the particular question stem as described in the chapter.
- Create any possible diagrams. If there is no information that can be put in the main diagram, is there information that can go in a supplemental diagram?
- If there is information that can go in the main diagram, first enter *only* the information that *must* be true.

- Now enter options, such as L/P in slot 3. Only enter options for which you have complete confidence. A set of options must not include any elements that cannot go in the slot and they must include *all* elements that can go in the slot. If you are not clear on the options, do not list any.
- Evaluate whether it is feasible to create all the parallel universes that reflect all of the possibilities. If there are fewer than six possibilities, create them. If there are too many possibilities to create in a reasonable time, skip to Step 3.
- Once you have all of the parallel universes listed, you should be able to check each answer against the diagrams and find the correct answer. If you do not find a correct answer, recheck all of your work, or if necessary, redo the work from scratch to avoid making the same error. Review the chapter instruction on creating parallel universes.
- If you still do not find an answer, go to Step 1b to see if you made an error in setting up the passage. Then return to Step 3.

Step 3

- Because there is no or little diagram, you must test the answer choices. Review the chapter instruction on testing answer choices.
- Identify by name the type of question in the question stem. Review the instructions for testing answer choices for the particular question type.
- Carefully test each answer choice. If you are not clear whether the answer is or is not correct, take more time with it.
- If you still do not have an answer, go to Step 4.

Step 4

- Take a short break from the problem and then come back to it and start it from the beginning. Do not use the same setup diagrams or notes. Use clean scratch paper.
- Identify the type of passage. Does it have one-to-one correspondence? Is it ordered? Is it a sequence?
- Create the main diagram. Is the number of fixtures fixed or variable? Are branches required? Is there a discard pile? What are the players and the fixtures?
- Can you make a supplemental diagram?
- Redo your list of the players. Do the players fall into separate categories?
- Redo your list of the rules. If there are rules that you are unclear about, examine them carefully and double-check your interpretation. If you are unclear on an if/then rule, review the if/then instruction in the AR chapter and in the LR chapter.
- Put any permanent information into the diagram. Put any rules, such as T cannot go in 3, above the diagram.
- Rework the question. Be careful of your logic at every step.

Step 5

- Identify exactly what aspects of the problem gave you trouble. Even if you are not able to solve the problem, if you can identify your difficulty, you will increase your problem-solving ability.

PRACTICE GAME WITH EXPLANATIONS

Try the game below untimed and then review the detailed, step-by-step explanations. Be sure to focus on the three fundamental steps for solving games:

1. **THE GAME SETUP:** Create your diagram and carefully summarize the rules and conditions.
2. **THE QUESTIONS:** Carefully orient yourself to each question before you answer. Make sure you understand each question and determine your plan of attack before you evaluate the answers that follow the question.
3. **A SYSTEMATIC APPROACH:** Follow the systematic process described above.

Practice Game

QUESTIONS 1–6

A hiking club has seven members: Frances, Greg, Hang, Luis, Miriam, Nelson, and Ole. The club has agreed to patrol a public open area owned by Placid City and has committed to having exactly one club member hike in the open area on each of the Thursday, Friday, Saturday, and Sunday preceding Memorial Day this year. The members hike according to the following conditions:

No member hikes on more than one day.

If Greg hikes, Luis does not hike.

If Nelson hikes on a given day, Frances hikes on the following day.

Neither Hang nor Frances hikes on the day before or after Miriam hikes.

If Miriam hikes on Saturday, Greg does not hike on any of the days.

1. Which one of the following could be a complete list of members who hike on the four days, in the order in which they hike?
    (A) Nelson, Frances, Miriam, Luis
    (B) Frances, Ole, Miriam, Greg
    (C) Miriam, Greg, Ole, Nelson
    (D) Nelson, Frances, Greg, Miriam
    (E) Greg, Miriam, Ole, Luis

2. Which one of the following CANNOT be true?
    (A) Miriam hikes on the day after Greg.
    (B) Miriam hikes on Saturday and Nelson does not hike.
    (C) Neither Nelson nor Frances hikes.
    (D) Greg does not hike and Frances hikes on Friday.
    (E) Miriam hikes after Nelson but before Luis.

3. If Greg hikes first and Nelson does not hike at all, which one of the following must be true?
    (A) Miriam hikes on either Friday or Sunday.
    (B) Miriam hikes exactly two days before or after Hang hikes.
    (C) Ole is one of the members who hikes.
    (D) Hang, Miriam, and Ole all hike.
    (E) Neither Hang, Miriam, nor Frances hikes on Saturday.

4. Which one of the following is a pair of members at least one of whom must hike?
   - (A) Hang and Miriam
   - (B) Frances and Luis
   - (C) Luis and Ole
   - (D) Hang and Ole
   - (E) Frances and Ole

5. If Miriam hikes on Saturday, then each of the following could be true EXCEPT:
   - (A) Ole hikes on Friday.
   - (B) Luis hikes on Sunday.
   - (C) Frances hikes on Thursday.
   - (D) Ole hikes on Sunday.
   - (E) Luis does not hike.

6. Which one of the following, if substituted for the condition that if Greg hikes, Luis does not hike, would have the same effect on determining which members hike on which day?
   - (A) If Luis hikes, Miriam hikes on Saturday.
   - (B) If Miriam hikes on Saturday, Luis does not hike.
   - (C) If Luis hikes, then Greg does not hike.
   - (D) If Hang hikes on Friday, Greg must hike.
   - (E) If neither Hang nor Frances hikes on either Friday or Sunday, then Greg does not hike.

THE SETUP

Set the game up systematically:

1. Does the game have one-to-one correspondence or not? Answer: No. No player can be used more than once but not all the players have to be used.
2. Is the game ordered or unordered? Answer: Ordered. It matters whether a player appears on Thursday or Friday.
3. Is there a fixed or variable number of fixtures? Answer: Fixed. There are exactly four fixtures.
4. Is each fixture branched or unbranched? Answer: Unbranched. There is exactly one player who is assigned to each fixture.

Create the diagram:

5. What is being assigned to what? Answer: People are being assigned to days of the week. People are the players. Days of the week are the fixtures.
6. Is there a discard pile? Answer: Yes. There are always three players who are left out.

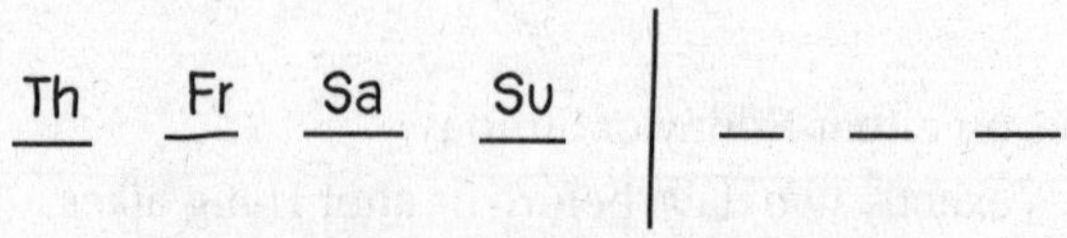

$$\underline{\text{Th}} \quad \underline{\text{Fr}} \quad \underline{\text{Sa}} \quad \underline{\text{Su}} \quad \Big| \quad \underline{\hspace{1em}} \quad \underline{\hspace{1em}} \quad \underline{\hspace{1em}}$$

Figure 4.87. Diagram with discard pile

Next, summarize the conditions. Compare the symbolized rules below with the wording of the conditions in the setup.

No player more than once

If G → –L

If N → NF

–HM, –MH

–FM, –MF

If M = Sa → –G

Figure 4.88. Summary of conditions

Now that the rules have been summarized, ask yourself:

1. Is there anything that can be put directly into the diagram? Answer: No.
2. What elements have the most restrictions? The least restrictions? Answer: Greg and Frances are each involved in more than one condition. Ole is not involved in any rules.
3. Are there any obvious relationships between rules? Answer: Nothing obvious.

TIP

BE FLEXIBLE WITH YOUR NOTATION SYSTEM

It is all right to create your own notation shorthand as long as your notations (1) make sense to you and (2) do not confuse you when you review them later.

THE ANSWERS

1. **(D)** This is a typical first question. One of the answers could be a valid order. The other four break rules. To solve this systematically, use the tool **Eliminate—apply rules, four violations**. The typical first question can usually be solved with this tool alone. When there are four rule violations, it is easier to work with one rule at a time and check it against all five answer choices than to look at each answer choice and check it against all of the rules. Start with the first rule. None of the answers violate the rule that no player can hike more than once.

   Now go to the second rule: If G → –L. Ask yourself "What would a violation of this rule look like?" It would be an order in which G is present but L is also present. Choice E matches this violation.

   Now check the next rule: If N → NF. What would a violation look like? N would appear without F following. Choice C matches this violation.

   The next rule states that neither H nor F can come just before or just after M. Break this down into two statements. Start with H. A violation would have H just before or just after M. No choices match this violation. Now consider F. Choice A matches this violation.

   The final rule states that if M hikes on Saturday, G does not hike. Only choice B has M on Saturday and G hikes on Sunday, violating the rule. Choice D is left as the only answer that does not violate rules.

2. **(E)** This is a *CANNOT be true* question. There is no new information. Apply the following tools.

   Step 1. Elimination—check previous valid assignments. Compare all of the answer choices to the correct answer from question 1. Choice A occurs in the answer to question 1; therefore, it can be true and is out.

   Step 2. Scan. Because there is no new information to put into the diagram, you must test answers. Scan to see which remaining answer choices are most likely to violate rules. At a glance, all of them involve players that have restrictions.

Step 3. Test answers—prove a violation. Start with choice B. Put N in the discard pile and M in Saturday. Apply the rules. G must be out. Even though H and F cannot go on either side of M, there seem to be enough options to create a valid assignment. Go on to choice C. Put N and F in the discard pile. Try putting G in the main diagram. If G is in, L is in the discard pile, which is now full, and all other players must be in. Make a temporary list of the remaining players. They are H, M, and O. Create a possible assignment, being careful to avoid making H and M adjacent and avoid putting M in Saturday. Check this order against all of the conditions. None are violated. Choice C can be true and is out.

Test choice D. Put G in the discard pile and F in Friday. Does G being out trigger any rules? No. In the rule *If G → –L*, the trigger is G being in. The contrapositive of *If M = Sat → –G* is *G ∴ M not Sat* and again it is the presence of G that triggers the rule. The danger in this answer choice is to erroneously think that if G is out, M must be in Saturday, with the result that F cannot be in Friday. Do you see why the absence of G does not lead to the presence of M in Saturday? Avoiding this error, there seem to be multiple options to create a viable order, so go on to choice E.

If M hikes after N but before L, what are the options for N? N must be followed by F. If M comes after N and L comes after M, there must be three players after N. N can only go in Thursday. Put F, M, and L in Friday through Sunday, respectively. Check this assignment against all the rules. It violates the rule that F cannot be adjacent to M. Choice E cannot be true.

		Th	Fr	Sa	Su				
F		___	___	___	___		___	___	___
G	Test of B →			M			N	G	
H	Test of C →	G	H	O	M		N	F	L
L	Test of D →		F				G		
M	Test of E →	~~N~~	~~F~~	~~M~~	~~L~~				
N									
O									

No player more
   than once
If G → –L
If N → NF
–HM, –MH
–FM, –MF
If M = Sa → –G

(Temporary notes)

H, M, O   Note for C

NF – M – L   Note for E

Figure 4.89. Diagram for working through question 2. Note the lines of the main diagram that were used to test choices B, C, D, and E. Below the conditions is an area for temporary notes. Cross these off before going on to the next question.

3. **(C)** This is a *must be true* question. Because the question provides new information that can go directly into the diagram, put as much information into the diagram as possible, including what must be true, what could be true, and if necessary, parallel universes. Then the answer choices can be compared to the diagrams. Remember that if entering possibilities or parallel universes becomes too cumbersome or time-consuming, change your plan. The alternate plan is to test the answer choices.

Step 1. Diagram—put in new information. Put G in Thursday and N in the discard pile.

Step 2. Diagram—apply rules, musts. If G is in, L goes in the discard pile.

Step 3. Diagram—parallel universes. There is only one remaining slot in the discard pile. The possible candidates for that spot are F, H, M, and O. Create a universe for each possibility.

Step 4. Diagram—apply rules, musts. Fill in the universe with F in the discard pile. H, M, and O are the remaining possible hikers. M and H cannot be on adjacent days, so Ole must go between them, in Saturday.

Step 5. Diagram—apply rules, with options. Show that M and H could each go in either Friday or Sunday.

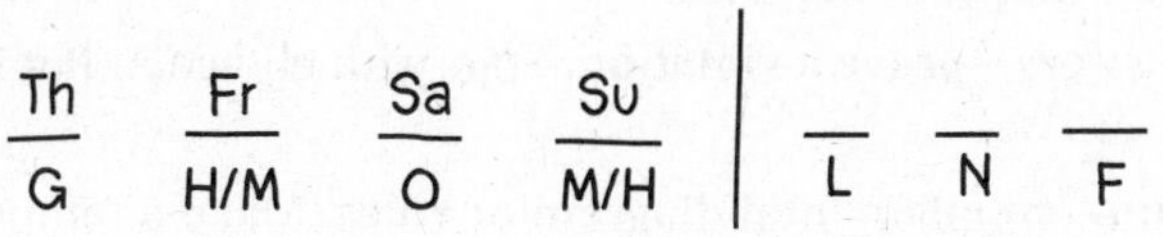

Th	Fr	Sa	Su			
G	H/M	O	M/H	L	N	F

Figure 4.90. One universe showing options

Step 6. Diagram—apply rules, musts. Fill in the universe with H in the discard pile. H has the same restrictions as F, so O must again go in Saturday. Friday and Sunday are listed as F/M and M/F.

(Temporary notes)
Th	Fr	Sa	Su			
G	F/M	O	M/F	N	L	H

F, M, O

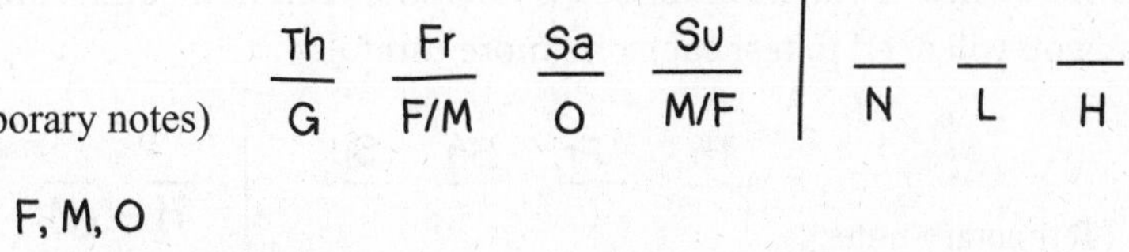

Figure 4.91. Second universe with temporary notes

Step 7. Diagram—apply rules, musts. Fill in the universe with M in the discard pile. Make a temporary list with the remaining hikers —F, H, and O. They have no restrictions. Friday, Saturday, and Sunday are listed as F/H/O.

Step 8. Diagram—apply rules, musts. Fill in the universe with O in the discard pile. Make a temporary list with the remaining hikers: F, H, and M. There is no way to arrange them in Friday, Saturday, and Sunday without putting M next to either F or H. Cross out this universe.

	Th	Fr	Sa	Su			
(Temporary notes)	G	F/M	O	M/F	N	L	H
F, M, O	G	F/H/O	F/H/O	F/H/O	N	L	M
F, H, M	~~G~~				~~N~~	~~L~~	~~O~~

Figure 4.92. Second, third, and fourth parallel universes. The fourth is invalid.

Step 9. Eliminate—check answers against diagram. Check the answer choices against the three valid universes. Only choice C must be true. O must hike. This confirms what you learned in Step 8. If O is out, the rules are violated.

4. **(E)** This is a *one or both of a pair* question in which at least one of the members of the pair must be chosen. Because there is no new information on which to base a diagram, test answers. To test an answer, put both members of the pair in the discard pile and prove that a rule is violated. Look for choices that seem likely to invoke rules. If no such pair stands out, then you must test all choices.

Step 1. General—look for most restricted. No answer choice looks particularly more likely to break rules than another does.

Step 2. Test answers—prove a violation. Start with choice A. Put H and M in the discard pile.

Step 3. Diagram—supplemental diagram or rules. Make a temporary supplemental note that shows that F must hike, because if F were out, N would also have to be out but that would leave four people in the discard pile. The remaining players who can hike are G, N, O, and L, but G and L are mutually exclusive, so write them as G/L, N, and O. This means N and O must hike and one of G and L hikes.

Step 4. Test answers—prove a violation. It looks like there are multiple options for this assignment to work. Rather than spending time proving that it does work, move on to the next answer choice. If you have missed a violation, then none of the answer choices will work and you will need to test each one more carefully.

	Th	Fr	Sa	Su			
(Temporary notes)					H	M	

F – must

G/L, N, O

Figure 4.93. Test of choice A. There are multiple options for this to be valid, so move on to the next answer choice.

Step 5. Test answers—prove a violation. Test choices B, C, and D similarly. Each one seems to have enough options to create a viable assignment.

Step 6. Test answers—prove a violation. Test choice E. Put F and O in the discard pile.

Step 7. Diagram—apply rules, musts. Check each rule against the diagram. How does the rule *If N → NF* apply? If N were in, F would also have to be in. Therefore, N is out and the discard pile is full.

Step 8. Test answers—prove a violation. Because the discard pile is full, all other players must be in. There are too many combinations to diagram. Make a temporary list of the remaining players: G, H, L, and M. Test these against the rules. If G is in, L cannot be in. Putting both F and O into the discard pile leads to a rule violation. At least one of them must hike.

Th	Fr	Sa	Su			
__	__	__	__	F̄	Ō	N̄

(Temporary notes)

G/L, H, L, M

Figure 4.94. Test of choice E. The discard pile is full but one of G and L must also be out. Choice E violates the rules.

5. **(E)** Four of the answer choices are viable. One answer choice violates rules. Because there is new information, the best strategy is to create enough diagrams to represent all options and then simply compare the answer choices against the diagrams. If it is too cumbersome or time-consuming to create diagrams that represent all options, the alternative is to test the answer choices.

Step 1. Diagram—put in new information. Put M in Saturday.

Step 2. Diagram—apply rules, musts. G must go in the discard pile.

Step 3. Diagram—parallel universes. Create parallel universes around F because if F is out, then N is also out. Either F hikes or is out.

Step 4. Diagram—apply rules, musts. For the universe with F out, fill in what else must be true. N is also out. The discard pile is full, so all other players are in. Make a temporary list: H, L, and O. According to the rules, H cannot be adjacent to M, so H must go in Thursday.

Step 5. Diagram—apply rules, with options. In the universe with F in, fill in the options. Friday and Sunday are L/O and O/L.

F
G
H
L
M
N
O

Th	Fr	Sa	Su			
H	L/O	M	O/L	G	F̄	N̄
		M		G		

No player more
than once
If G → –L
If N → NF
–HM, –MH
–FM, –MF
If M = Sat → –G

H, L, O ← Temporary note for universe 1

Figure 4.95. First universe with what must be true and what can be true

Step 6. General—options for player. In the universe in which F hikes, fill in what must be true. What are the options for F? F cannot be adjacent to M and so must go in Thursday. Make a temporary list of the other options: H, L, N, and O. What are the options for H? H cannot be adjacent to M and there are no other places left. H must be out. If N were in, N would have to appear just before F, but F is in the first slot (Thursday), so N is out. The discard pile is full.

Step 7. Diagram—apply rules, with options. The remaining players—L and O—have no further restrictions. Friday and Sunday can be listed as L/O and O/L.

Step 8. Eliminate—check answers against diagram. The answers can now be checked against the two universes. Choice E is the correct answer because L cannot appear in the discard pile in either scenario.

F
G
H
L
M
N
O

Th	Fr	Sa	Su			
H	L/O	M	O/L	G	F	N
F	L/O	M	O/L	G	H	N

No player more
than once
If G → –L
If N → NF
–HM, –MH
–FM, –MF
If M = Sat → –G

H, L, O ← Temporary note for universe 1

H, L, N, O ← Temporary notes for universe 2
L, N, O

Figure 4.96. Full diagram for question 5

6. **(C)** Orient to the question stem. This is an *equivalent condition* question. It does not present new information. Because there is nothing to diagram, you need to test the answer choices. In *equivalent condition* questions testing the answer choices does not mean proving that the answers lead to valid or invalid assignments. Instead, the correct answer has to duplicate the effect of the original condition without adding new restrictions or leaving out original ones.

Step 1. Scan. Look over the answer choices to get an idea of how they are similar or different. They are all if/then conditions.

Step 2. Test answers—other. You are not testing for violations or valid assignments but rather how well the answer choice matches the effect of the original condition. Start with choice A. Using if/then logic, if L hikes, then G does not hike. Though it is true that if M hikes on Saturday, G does not hike, the reverse is not true. (Only the contrapositive would be true—G hikes, therefore M does not hike on Saturday.) Choice A is out.

Step 3. Test answers—other. Test choice B. By adding this rule, if M hikes on Saturday, then both G and L are out. This is not equivalent to saying that if G is in, L is out. Choice B is eliminated.

Step 4. Test answers—other. Test choice C: If L hikes, then G does not hike. Write out the contrapositive. If G hikes, L does not hike. This exactly replicates the original condition. It is not necessary to test choices D and E. However, on questions for which you are not 100 percent confident in your logic, it helps to check the remaining answers quickly.

SUMMARY

This chapter taught you the following skills. There are three necessary skill sets: organizing the setup, understanding the question types, and using a systematic solving approach. Timing strategy for AR requires choosing which games to do, giving each question the time it needs, up to four or five minutes, and marking cold guesses for the remaining questions.

You learned tools for organizing the setup by analyzing the conditions and creating a linear diagram and, where necessary, a supplemental diagram. You learned how to create flexible variations in the linear diagram.

The chapter outlined the components of all games—one-to-one correspondence, ordering, and fixed and variable fixtures and branches. The four types of games are sequence games, ordered non-sequence games with one-to-one correspondence (ONS-A), unordered non-sequence games without one-to-one correspondence (ONS-B), and unordered games.

Basic question types include *could be true, must be true, cannot be true (= must be false), could be false,* and *EXCEPT* questions. Special question types include *complete and accurate list, completely determined if, equivalent condition, how many (for how many can it be determined, how many orders are there, how many players can be assigned to a fixture), one or both of a pair (at least one is in, both can be out, both fixtures can be . . .), what is the minimum/maximum number,* and *what is the earliest/ latest.* Many questions also introduce new information that applies only in that specific question.

The tools for systematic problem solving include *applying the rules (the typical first question, use the rules to fill in diagrams, testing an assignment for validity), working the answer choices (scan, test answers, check for violations, check answers choices against the diagrams, check previous valid orders), using the main diagram (what must be true, what could be true, parallel universes), supplemental diagrams (counting places in a sequence, early versus late, temporary diagrams and rules), enough to answer the question, most restricted players,* and *what rules apply to a player or fixture.*

The steps for systematic problem solving include *two paths to an answer (diagram, test answers), create diagrams, eliminate answer choices, scan, test answer choices,* and various general problem-solving steps. You also learned to apply the problem-solving process to specific question types.

You can avoid errors by recognizing the warning signs of an error and the common error types, *misinterpreting conditions, misinterpreting the question stem, failing to check all the rules, failing to consider the options for players, failing to distinguish what must be true from what could be true,* and *applying main diagram conditions to the discard pile.* You learned to avoid errors by becoming familiar with your own error tendencies.

Time: 35 minutes
23 Questions

> **DIRECTIONS:** The groups of questions in this test section are each based on specific sets of conditions. Making a rough diagram may be useful for answering some of the questions. For each question choose the answer choice that is most accurate and complete. Fill in the space on your answer sheet that corresponds to your answer.

QUESTIONS 1–6

Seven musical compositions—Harvest, Jasmine, Lakeside, Morning, Nightfall, Pastures, and Rainstorm—are to be performed at an outdoor music festival during seven consecutive time slots. No two time slots overlap. The order in which the compositions are played must accord with the following conditions:

    Morning is performed before Harvest.
    Harvest is performed after Rainstorm but before Jasmine.
    If Rainstorm is performed before Lakeside, then Morning is performed after Nightfall.

1. Which one of the following could be the order of the performances from first to last?
   (A) Nightfall, Rainstorm, Morning, Pastures, Harvest, Lakeside, Jasmine
   (B) Morning, Lakeside, Harvest, Rainstorm, Jasmine, Nightfall, Pastures
   (C) Morning, Rainstorm, Harvest, Jasmine, Nightfall, Pastures, Lakeside
   (D) Lakeside, Morning, Jasmine, Rainstorm, Harvest, Pastures, Nightfall
   (E) Nightfall, Rainstorm, Lakeside, Harvest, Morning, Jasmine, Pastures

GO ON TO THE NEXT PAGE

2. If Jasmine is not performed in the sixth or seventh time slot, then which one of the following must be true?
   (A) Morning is performed before Rainfall.
   (B) Rainfall is performed before Lakeside.
   (C) Nightfall is performed before Morning.
   (D) Pastures is performed after Harvest.
   (E) Lakeside is performed after Harvest.

3. If Lakeside is performed last, all of the following could be true EXCEPT:
   (A) Nightfall is performed third.
   (B) Morning is performed second.
   (C) Harvest is performed fifth.
   (D) Nightfall is performed immediately after Pastures and immediately before Rainstorm.
   (E) Nightfall is performed immediately after Pastures and immediately before Harvest.

4. Which one of the following must be true?
   (A) Exactly four pieces are performed before Jasmine.
   (B) If Jasmine is performed last, Harvest is performed fifth.
   (C) If Lakeside is performed after Jasmine, then Nightfall is performed before Harvest.
   (D) If Rainstorm is performed before Lakeside, then Pastures is performed after Jasmine.
   (E) If Pastures is performed before Harvest, then Jasmine is performed last.

5. If Rainstorm is performed first, then which one of the following could be true?
   (A) Morning is performed second.
   (B) Harvest is performed third.
   (C) Pastures is performed immediately before Jasmine.
   (D) Morning is performed immediately before Jasmine.
   (E) Nightfall is performed immediately before Harvest.

6. Which one of the following CANNOT be true?
   (A) Harvest is performed fourth and Jasmine is performed sixth.
   (B) Harvest is performed third and Jasmine is performed fifth.
   (C) Nightfall is performed second and Jasmine is performed sixth.
   (D) Pastures is performed first and Lakeside is performed last.
   (E) Harvest is performed immediately after Rainstorm and immediately before Lakeside.

GO ON TO THE NEXT PAGE

QUESTIONS 7–12

Exactly five employees of a school district are to be chosen to attend a national conference on education. The candidates from whom the attendees will be chosen include three administrators—Franciscus, Gomez, and Jacques—three teachers—Li, McFarland, and Novak—and three support staff—Perea, Rollins, and Woida. The selection of attendees must meet the following criteria:

> If Gomez is selected, then neither Novak nor Rollins is selected.
>
> If Li is selected, then Perea is selected.
>
> Either Woida is selected or Novak is selected, but not both.
>
> At least one administrator, one teacher, and one support staff are selected.

7. Which one of the following could be a complete assignment of employees chosen to attend the conference?
   (A) Gomez, McFarland, Perea, Rollins, Woida
   (B) Jacques, Li, Novak, Perea, Rollins
   (C) Franciscus, Jacques, Perea, Rollins, Woida
   (D) Gomez, Li, Novak, McFarland, Perea
   (E) Franciscus, Li, Novak, Perea, Woida

8. If McFarland and Novak are not selected, which one of the following must be true?
   (A) Gomez is selected.
   (B) Rollins is not selected.
   (C) If Rollins is not selected, Gomez is selected.
   (D) At least two support staff and no more than two administrators are selected.
   (E) Exactly two administrators and no more than two support staff are selected.

GO ON TO THE NEXT PAGE

9. If Woida is not selected, which one of the following CANNOT be selected?
   (A) Franciscus
   (B) Gomez
   (C) Li
   (D) Perea
   (E) Rollins

10. If Gomez is selected, the selection of employees who will attend the convention is fully and uniquely determined if which one of the following is true?
    (A) Exactly one teacher is selected.
    (B) Exactly two administrators are selected.
    (C) Exactly two administrators and one teacher are selected.
    (D) Exactly one support staff is selected.
    (E) Exactly two support staff are selected.

11. If Novak is selected and more teachers are selected than administrators, which one of the following could be true?
    (A) Exactly two administrators are selected.
    (B) Exactly three support staff are selected.
    (C) Exactly one teacher is selected.
    (D) Perea is not selected.
    (E) Li is not selected.

12. Which one of the following, if substituted for the constraint that if Gomez is selected, then Novak is not selected, would have the same effect in determining the selection of the attendees?
    (A) If Novak is not selected, then Gomez is selected.
    (B) If Rollins is selected, then Novak is selected.
    (C) If Woida is not selected, then Gomez is not selected.
    (D) If Woida is selected, then Gomez is selected.
    (E) If Li and McFarland are not selected, then Gomez is selected.

GO ON TO THE NEXT PAGE

QUESTIONS 13–17

A van driver is scheduled to pick up eight passengers, one at a time. The passengers—Oliver, Portman, Quinn, Russell, Shah, Tejeda, Ulibarri, and Vingh—are to be picked up according to the following conditions:

Quinn is picked up before Oliver.
Both Shah and Ulibarri are picked up before Portman.
Oliver is picked up after Shah.
Either Tejeda is picked up before Quinn or Tejeda is picked up before Portman, but not both.

13. Which one of the following could be the order in which the passengers are picked up, from first to last?
    (A) Vingh, Shah, Russell, Portman, Tejeda, Ulibarri, Quinn, Oliver
    (B) Russell, Quinn, Shah, Oliver, Ulibarri, Tejeda, Vingh, Portman
    (C) Russell, Shah, Vingh, Ulibarri, Oliver, Portman, Tejeda, Quinn
    (D) Vingh, Shah, Russell, Ulibarri, Tejeda, Portman, Quinn, Oliver
    (E) Quinn, Russell, Oliver, Tejeda, Shah, Ulibarri, Portman, Vingh

14. Which one of the following CANNOT be true?
    (A) Portman is picked up third.
    (B) Oliver is picked up third.
    (C) Portman is picked up fourth.
    (D) Oliver is picked up third and Portman is picked up fourth.
    (E) Tejeda is picked up after Shah, Ulibarri, and Portman.

15. If Portman is picked up third and Vingh is picked up last, which one of the following could be true?
    (A) Russell is picked up second.
    (B) Oliver is picked up fourth.
    (C) Russell is picked up fourth.
    (D) Quinn is picked up seventh.
    (E) Tejeda is picked up seventh.

16. If Tejeda is picked up seventh, which one of the following must be true?
    (A) Tejeda is picked up before Quinn.
    (B) Shah is picked up before Ulibarri.
    (C) Shah is picked up first.
    (D) Quinn is picked up fifth.
    (E) Portman is picked up eighth.

17. If Quinn is picked up after Portman, then each of the following could be true EXCEPT:
    (A) Oliver is picked up fifth.
    (B) Tejeda is picked up fifth.
    (C) Oliver is picked up eighth.
    (D) Portman is picked up fifth.
    (E) Quinn is picked up seventh.

GO ON TO THE NEXT PAGE

A series of seven lectures on archaeology will be delivered at a conference. The lectures are delivered consecutively and no lectures overlap. There are three professors delivering the lectures—Ofume, Petrick, and Roanhorse. Ofume lectures on the archaeology of Formosa and Ghana. Petrick lectures on the archaeology of Hungary and Moravia. Roanhorse lectures on the archaeology of New Mexico, Texas, and Utah. The following constraints apply to the order in which the lectures are presented:

> The lecture on Texas is presented before the lecture on Ghana.
>
> The lecture on Moravia is presented before the lecture on Formosa.
>
> Roanhorse does not lecture immediately after Ofume lectures.

18. Which one of the following could be a complete order in which the lectures are presented, from first to last?

(A) Petrick on Hungary, Roanhorse on New Mexico, Petrick on Moravia, Roanhorse on Texas, Roanhorse on Utah, Ofume on Ghana, Ofume on Formosa

(B) Petrick on Hungary, Roanhorse on Utah, Petrick on Moravia, Roanhorse on New Mexico, Ofume on Formosa, Roanhorse on Texas, Ofume on Ghana

(C) Ofume on Formosa, Petrick on Moravia, Roanhorse on Texas, Ofume on Ghana, Petrick on Hungary, Roanhorse on Utah, Roanhorse on New Mexico

(D) Petrick on Moravia, Roanhorse on Texas, Petrick on Hungary, Ofume on Ghana, Roanhorse on New Mexico, Roanhorse on Utah, Ofume on Formosa

(E) Roanhorse on New Mexico, Ofume on Ghana, Petrick on Moravia, Roanhorse on Utah, Roanhorse on Texas, Ofume on Formosa, Petrick on Hungary

19. If Petrick cannot present after the lecture on Formosa is presented, which one of the following must be true?
    (A) Roanhorse presents first.
    (B) The lecture on Ghana is presented seventh.
    (C) The lecture on Formosa is presented sixth or seventh.
    (D) Ofume presents fifth and sixth.
    (E) Ofume presents sixth and seventh.

20. If the lecture on Ghana is presented second, which one of the following could be true?
    (A) The lecture on New Mexico is presented seventh.
    (B) The lecture on Formosa is presented third.
    (C) Ofume presents in two consecutive time slots.
    (D) Roanhorse presents in three consecutive time slots.
    (E) Ofume presents fourth and Petrick presents seventh.

21. Which one of the following is a complete and accurate list of the geographical areas the talks on which can immediately follow the talk on Formosa?
    (A) Hungary, Moravia
    (B) Ghana, Hungary
    (C) Ghana, Hungary, Moravia
    (D) Ghana, Hungary, New Mexico
    (E) Ghana, Hungary, Moravia, New Mexico, Utah

22. If Ofume presents in two consecutive time slots but does not present last, which one of the following must be false?
    (A) Petrick presents last.
    (B) Petrick does not present last.
    (C) The lecture on Formosa is presented sixth.
    (D) The lecture on Hungary is presented before the lecture on Utah.
    (E) The lecture on Hungary is presented fourth.

23. If there is exactly one presentation between the two presentations given by Petrick, and if an additional condition were imposed stating that no talk by Petrick can take place after any talk by Roanhorse, which one of the following could be true?
    (A) The final presentation is on Formosa.
    (B) Petrick's first presentation is preceded by a presentation by Roanhorse.
    (C) Roanhorse gives the last three presentations.
    (D) Roanhorse gives the fourth and sixth presentations.
    (E) Ofume gives two consecutive presentations.

STOP If you finish before the 35-minute time period is over, you may go back and check your answers.

ANSWER KEY

1. A		**7.** B		**13.** B		**19.** C
2. D		**8.** D		**14.** D		**20.** A
3. E		**9.** B		**15.** C		**21.** B
4. C		**10.** D		**16.** E		**22.** E
5. C		**11.** E		**17.** A		**23.** D
6. B		**12.** C		**18.** A		

ANSWERS EXPLAINED

QUESTIONS 1–6

The first passage is based on a sequence game. Each player is used exactly once. There are two players who must come before H, so H cannot go in 1 or 2. Similarly, there are three players who must come before J.

```
H              –H –J  –H –J  –J
J              ___  ___  ___  ___  ___  ___  ___
L               1    2    3    4    5    6    7
M
N
P    M – H
R    R – H – J
     M
       `– H – J
     R ´
     If R – L →
     N – M
```

Game 1 setup

1. **(A)** This is the typical first question. To solve it, start with the rules, applying one at a time, and look for answer choices that violate that rule. The first rule states that M comes before H. Rephrase this in terms of what a violation of this rule would look like. "M appearing after H." Looking through the answer choices for this violation, choice E is out.

   The next rule states that H comes after R but before J. Break this down into its parts. Start with H comes after R. What would violate that? H before R. Look for H before R. Choice B is out. Check the second half of the rule. Look for the violation H after J, skipping the answer choices that are already out. Choice D is out.

   The third rule is triggered by R before L. Look for the violation of R occurring before L but N appearing after M. In choice A, R is before L but N is before M. In choice C, R is before L but N is after M. Choice C is out. Choice A is the only answer left.

2. **(D)** This is a *must be true* question with new information that does not go in the main diagram. Use **Diagram—supplemental diagram or rules** to create a supplemental notation that J cannot be in 6 or 7. Use **General—options for player**. What are the options for J? Counting the places in the sequence, there are three players that must come before J. The earliest J can appear is 4. Test J in 4.

With J in 4, H must be in 3, and R/M are in 1 and 2. However, this means that R is before L, which triggers the requirement that N be before M. There is no place for N to come before M. J cannot be in 4. The only remaining place for J is 5. Put J in 5 and use **Diagram—put in new information** to fill in whatever else must be true.

R, M, H, and one other player must be in 1 through 4 but none of them are required to be in any particular spot. First check to see if it is viable to create parallel universes. If not, then it will be necessary to switch to testing answer choices.

Using **General—look for most restricted**, there are only two places that H can go because there are two players that must occur before H. Use **Diagram—parallel universes**. Create two universes, one with H in 3 and one with H in 4. With H in 3, M and R must be in 1 and 2 and the R before L rule is violated again. For H in 4, there seem to be many options. Identify the options by focusing on one player. Either L is before R or L is after R. The only places in which L can be before R are 1 and 2. If L is after R, that can only occur in 6 or 7. If L is in 3, it is after R but there is no room for N before M.

–H –J	–H –J	–J				
1	2	3	4	5	6	7
~~M/R~~	R/M	H		J		
L			H	J		
	L		H	J		
		H	J	L		

Three universes with L before or after R

Create three universes, with L in 1, 2, and 6. L in 6 functions the same as L in 7. With L in 1, places 2 and 3 are M/R and R/M. Places 6 and 7 are N/P and P/N. With L in 2, place 3 must be R, in order not to trigger the R – L rule, and place 1 is M, and places 6 and 7 are N/P and P/N. With L in 6, the R – L rule will be triggered and N must come before M. There are two places for N—1 or 2. Make two more universes. With N in 1, places 2 and 3 can be M/R and R/M. With N in 2, place 1 must be R and place 2 must be M. In both cases, 6 and 7 are L/P and P/L.

–H –J	–H –J	–J				
1	2	3	4	5	6	7
~~M/R~~	R/M	H		J		
L	M/R	R/M	H	J	N/P	P/N
M	L	R	H	J	N/P	P/N
N	M/R	R/M	H	J	L/P	P/L
R	N	M	H	J	L/P	P/L

Four universes representing all options for J in 5

There are now four universes that represent all possibilities. Use **Eliminate—check answers against diagram**. Choices A, B, C, and E could be true. Choice D must be true in all universes.

The alternative method to solve this question, if the process of creating all the universes is too cumbersome, is to test answer choices. The difficulty with testing answer choices is that, although the process may be quick if you test the correct one first, it can be slow if you test the correct one last. It is not difficult to prove that P must come after H. Test it by **Test answers—negate a must**. Putting P before H forces R to be before L but does not leave room for N to be before M. However, this answer choice is in the D position and it might have been more time-consuming to test all the answer choices compared with creating all the universes.

3. **(E)** This is a *could be true EXCEPT* question with new information that goes in the main diagram. Use **Diagram—put in new information** to put L in 7. Nothing follows directly but the R – L rule is triggered so use **Diagram—supplemental diagram or rules** to make a note that N – M, and also to note the string:

$$\begin{array}{c} R \searrow \\ N - M - H - J - L \end{array}$$

It is always important to first consider whether parallel universes can be created. In this case, N is restricted, with four players needing to come after it. N can only go in 1, 2, or 3, so use **Diagram—parallel universes** to make three universes. Once these universes are drawn, it is clear that for each universe, H could go in 4 or 5, and that for each universe with H in 4, J could go in 5 or 6. This results in too many universes. Switch to testing answer choices. The diagrams of the three universes will help test answers.

Reorient to the question stem. Four answer choices could be true. One violates rules. Choices D and E are more complex and thus more likely to break rules. Start with choice C. Test it by trying to show that the conditions described in choice D can occur without breaking rules. Because N needs to come early, rather than late, so that M can come after it, put N as early as possible. P goes in 1, N in 2, and R in 3. M can go in 4 and H and J in 5 and 6, respectively. Test this order against the rules. There do not seem to be violations. Test choice E.

Again putting P in 1, put N in 2 and H in 3. Check the supplemental diagram. H must have R and M before it, which cannot happen in this order. Try putting P later. To make room for R and M, put P in 3. Now R and M can go in either 1 or 2 but the rule N – M is violated. P cannot go in 4 because it needs to be followed by N – H – J – L. All options have been tested. Choice E cannot be true.

4. **(C)** This is a *must be true* question with no new information. The correct answer must be based on the original conditions. There is nothing to diagram, so plan to test the answer choices. In general it is helpful to use elimination to narrow down the choices to test. However, because this is a *must be true* question, it is not necessarily true that any of the answer choices violate rules, so checking the answer choices against the rules is not likely to eliminate any choices.

Start testing the answers with choice A. To test whether A must be true, negate it. Try to show that more or fewer than four pieces can be performed before J. Use **Eliminate—check previous valid assignments**. The correct answer to question 1 establishes that six pieces can be played before J.

Test choice B. In the correct answer to question 1 H *is* performed fifth but to test B, try to put H in any other position. Because H tends to come later, put H in 6. There appear to be many options for creating viable orders with H in 6. For now, assume that H can go in 6 and that choice B does not have to be true.

Test choice C. Put L after J, using the supplemental diagram. R now comes before L, triggering the R – L rule and requiring N – M. Put N in the supplemental diagram before M. It is now clear from the diagram that N *must* come before H. Choice C is the correct answer. Glance quickly at choices D and E to make sure you have not missed anything, but given the clarity of the proof of choice C, it is not necessary to test choices D or E.

5. **(C)** This is a *could be true* question with new information that can be put into the main diagram. Put R in 1. There are too many options for filling out the rest of the diagram. However, a glance at the rules indicates that with R in 1 the R – L rule must apply. Use **Diagram—supplemental diagram or rules** to create a supplemental diagram.

$$R - N - M - H - J$$

Note how powerful this supplemental diagram is. Even though it does not cover all the possibilities, as a full set of parallel universes would, it shows the relationships between five players. Only L and P are not shown. Because four answer choices violate rules, use the supplemental diagram to test the answer choices.

For choice A, M cannot come any earlier than 3. Choice A is out. For choice B, H cannot come any earlier than 4, so choice B is out. For choice C, P is not indicated in the diagram. It could be true. Go on to check the remaining answer choices.

Choice D is out because H must come between M and J. Choice E is out because M must come between N and H. Choice C is the correct answer.

6. **(B)** This is a *cannot be true* question with no new information. There is nothing to diagram, so test the answer choices. Because only one answer choice violates rules, it is better to start with answer choices and test them for rule violations, rather than starting with rules.

Test choice A by trying to prove that it violates rules. Use **Eliminate—check previous valid assignments** to see if choice A occurs in any valid assignments. If it does, you have proven that choice A can be true. Otherwise, try to create an order with choice A. Put H in 4 and J in 6. There seem to be viable options. Go on to choice B. Put H in 3 and J in 5. M and R must go in 1 or 2. This triggers R – L but there is no room for N before M. H cannot go in 3. Choice B cannot be true. Quickly glance at the other answer choices to be sure you have not missed anything, but because of the clarity of the proof that H cannot go in 3, you do not need to test the other answer choices.

QUESTIONS 7–12

This is an unordered game. There are three categories of player—administrator, teacher, support staff. There are four places in the discard pile.

Adm	T	S
F	L	P
G	M	R
J	N	W

1 2 3 4 5 | _ _ _ _

If G → –N, –R

If L → P

Either W or N

    bnb

At least 1 ea

    A, T, S

Game 2 setup. The abbreviation "bnb" means "but not both."

7. **(B)** This is the typical first question. Four answer choices violate rules. Use **Eliminate— apply rules, four violations**. Start with the first rule. There are two parts to it. Select one part to test first. What would a violation look like? G is selected and N is also selected. Choice D is out. Test the second part of the first rule. A violation would have G selected and R also selected. Choice A is eliminated. Test the second rule. A violation would have L selected and P not selected. There are no violations of this rule.

Test the third rule—either W or N bnb—by breaking it into parts. One violation would be no W or N. No remaining answer choices violate this. The other violation would be both a W and N. Choice E violates this. The remaining rule states that there must be one person from each category. A violation would consist of one category not being represented. Scan the remaining answer choices. Choice C is missing a teacher. Choice B is the correct answer.

8. **(D)** This is a *must be true* question with new information that goes in the main diagram. New information in the diagram makes a question easier. Use **Diagram—put in new information** and **Diagram—apply rules, musts** to fill in all of the elements of the diagram that must be true. M and N are in the discard pile. Go through the rules systematically, starting at the top, to see how each rule applies to the information in the diagram. The first rule, *If G → –N, –R* indicates only that G could be in. The rule *If L → P* does not apply yet.

The third rule, *Either W or N bnb*, indicates that W must be in. How does the fourth rule apply? There must be one person from each category. M and N are both from the teacher category. L is the only teacher remaining and must be in.

Now that you have gone through all the rules, there is new information in the diagram, so start the rules again from the top. The first rule still does not apply. The second rule indicates that P must be in. The diagram now is as follows:

$$\underset{W}{\underline{1}} \quad \underset{L}{\underline{2}} \quad \underset{P}{\underline{3}} \quad \underset{}{\underline{4}} \quad \underset{}{\underline{5}} \quad \Big| \quad \underset{M}{\underline{\quad}} \quad \underset{N}{\underline{\quad}} \quad \underline{\quad} \quad \underline{\quad}$$

All of the elements that must be true when M and N are both out

At this point, the two problem-solving options are to create parallel universes that represent all options or to test answer choices against the current diagram, which shows only some options. Creating parallel universes is usually the most accurate strategy but is not practical if there are too many universes. To get a sense of how many options there are, list the players who have not yet been assigned. They are F, G, J, and R. The only rule applying to these players is that G and R cannot both be selected. At least one of them must be out, if not both. This means that one place in the discard pile is assigned to G/R.

$$\underset{W}{\underline{1}} \quad \underset{L}{\underline{2}} \quad \underset{P}{\underline{3}} \quad \underset{}{\underline{4}} \quad \underset{}{\underline{5}} \quad \Big| \quad \underset{M}{\underline{\quad}} \quad \underset{N}{\underline{\quad}} \quad \underset{G/R}{\underline{\quad}} \quad \underline{\quad}$$

Now there is one place in the discard pile for either G or R.

There are still quite a number of options for creating parallel universes, so try testing answer choices instead, using the information in the diagram. For choice A, must G be selected? It does not seem likely. G is one of the options for a place in the discard pile and there do not seem to be any restrictions that would force G to be selected. Mark choice A as improbable (using "?") and go to choice B.

Is there any reason why R could not be selected? This, again, seems unlikely. Move on to choice C. If R is out, does that mean that G must be in? Try putting both G and R out. This puts F and J in, which does not seem to violate any rules.

Test choice D by negating it to see if a violation results. What would violate choice D? A violation would consist of *either* one support staff or three administrators. Test these separately. Is it possible to have an order with one support staff? P and W are both support staff and they must be included. There must be at least two support staff. Test the other half of choice D. Can there be three administrators? Because L, P, and W must be selected, and none of them is an administrator, there are only two slots left. There must be no more than two administrators. All of the statements in choice D must be true. However, because the logic is complex, test choice E as a double check.

Testing choice E, must there be exactly two administrators? Could there be just one? Yes. If R is selected, there would be only one administrator. The first part of choice E does not have to be true and therefore choice E does not have to be true. Choice D is confirmed as the answer.

Note that it was not necessary to prove that choices A through C did not have to be true. It was enough to see that it was unlikely that they had to be true. When the correct answer was tested, it was shown definitively that it had to be true because if it were not, there was a clear rule violation.

9. **(B)** This is a *cannot be true* question with new information that goes in the main diagram. Start with **Diagram—put in new information** and **Diagram—apply rules, musts**. W goes in the discard pile. The rule *Either W or N bnb* indicates that N must be in. The first rule indicates that G cannot be in. This is enough to answer the question.

10. **(D)** This is a *completely determined* question with new information that goes into the main diagram. Put G in the diagram. Use **Diagram—apply rules, musts**. N and R are in the discard pile. The *Either W or N bnb* rule indicates that W is selected.

$$\underset{G}{\underline{1}} \quad \underset{W}{\underline{2}} \quad \underset{}{\underline{3}} \quad \underset{}{\underline{4}} \quad \underset{}{\underline{5}} \quad \Big| \quad \underset{N}{\underline{}} \quad \underset{R}{\underline{}} \quad \underline{} \quad \underline{}$$

All the elements that must follow from Gomez being selected

Consider whether to create parallel universes or test answer choices. There seem to be too many possibilities for parallel universes. Test choice A. Looking at the remaining teachers, L and M, it appears that, if there were to be only one teacher, it could be either L or M. Choice A does not seem to result in a complete order being determined. Put a question mark by it and test B.

For choice B, there is already one administrator selected: G. If there were exactly two selected, it seems possible that it could be either F or J. Put a question mark by choice B. For choice C, if exactly two administrators and one teacher are selected, then G and W are selected but the second administrator can be either F or J.

For choice D, if exactly one support staff is selected, that position is filled by W. P would be out, which also means that L is out. All of the slots in the discard pile are full, so the remaining players must be in. Test the assignment to make sure there are no violations in it. There are none. Choice D appears to be the answer. For accuracy, quickly check choice E. If there are two support staff, they would be W and P. The remaining slot could be L or M. Choice D is confirmed.

11. **(E)** This is a *could be true* question with new information that goes in the main diagram, as well as new information that does not go directly into the main diagram. Use **Diagram—put in new information** and **Diagram—apply rules, musts** to put N in the diagram and to put W and G in the discard pile, based on the first and third rules. Make a temporary supplemental note: more T than A. There are too many options to create parallel universes. Use **General—look for most restricted**. The information about the teachers and administrators is restricting. Organize the options.

Administrators	Teachers
1	2 or 3
2	3
~~3~~	

There must be at least one administrator. Test to see if there can be two. If there are two administrators, there must be three teachers. However, that does not leave room for at least one support staff. There must be exactly one administrator. There can be two or three teachers. This is enough information to eliminate choice A. Also, one of the slots in the discard pile must now be assigned to F/J.

Move on to testing the answer choices. For choice B, if there are three support staff and at least two teachers, there is no room for an administrator. Choice B is out. Test choice C. You have already determined that there must be at least two teachers. Choice C is out.

Test choice D. Put P in the discard pile. The discard pile is now full, containing W, G, F/J, and P. The remaining players are in: J/F, L, M, and R. Check this assignment against the rules. It violates *If L → P*. P cannot be out. Choice D is incorrect.

At this point, choices A through D have definitively been shown to result in violations. Choice E must be the choice that could be true. Check it quickly. Put L in the discard pile. The remaining players must be in: J/F, M, P, and R. Check the assignment for rule violations. There are none. Choice E is confirmed.

12. **(C)** This is an *equivalent condition* question. The condition being replaced is half of the first condition, the part that specifies that *If G → –N*. Because there is nothing to diagram, use **Test answers—other**.

Choice A is logically equivalent to *If –N → G*, the contrapositive of which is *–G ∴ N*. This is not the same as the condition that is to be replaced. Choice B implies that if R is selected, G is not selected and therefore N must be selected. This is the same logic as choice A and is not equivalent to the original.

In choice C, if W is not selected, N must be selected. If it is true that if N is selected, G is not selected (*If N → –G*), then it is also true that *If G → –N*. This is equivalent to the original condition. Choice C appears to be the correct answer. Because the logic is complex, quickly check the other answer choices.

Choice D is equivalent to *If –N (because If W → –N) → G*. This is not equivalent to the original. Choice D results in N being selected and thus states *If N → G*, also not equivalent to the original. Choice C is confirmed.

In choice E, if L and M are out, N must be in because N is the only remaining teacher, and one teacher must be in. This does not, however, relate G and N. To be equivalent, L and M being out would have to have an effect on G.

QUESTIONS 13–17

This is a sequence game. The diagram is shown below.

Setup for Game 3

13. **(B)** This is the typical first question. Four answer choices violate rules. One does not. Use **Eliminate—apply rules, four violations**. A violation of the first rule would have Q after O. Choice C violates the first rule. The second rule has two parts. Start with the part in which S comes before P. Look for instances in which S comes after P. There are none. Look for instances in which U comes after P. Choice A is out.

The next rule is *S-O*. Look for S after O. Choice E is out. Break down the final rule. One violation would be T after both P and Q. Neither of the remaining answer choices violate this. The other violation would be T coming before both P and Q. Choice D violates this. Choice B is the correct answer.

14. **(D)** This is a *cannot be true* question with no new information. One answer choice violates rules based only on the original conditions. Because there is nothing to diagram, use the strategy of testing answer choices. Choices A through C are relatively simple. Check them against the supplemental diagram. Both P and O have two players required before them. Neither P nor O could be in 1 or 2, but slots 3 and 4 are not ruled out. Test choice A. P in 3 requires S/U and U/S in 1 and 2. There seem to be many opportunities for creating a viable order, so put a question mark by choice A and move on. The same is true for both choice B and choice C. Note that you have not *proven* that choices A through C are viable. You simply identified that they are likely to be viable. Continue until you find an answer choice that clearly violates rules, using **Test answers—prove a violation**.

Test choice D. You have already determined that O can probably be in 3 and P can probably be in 4. Choice D, however, requires both to be true at the same time. With O in 3, Q/S and S/Q are in 1 and 2. With P in 4, T is forced to come after both Q and P, which is a violation. Choice D cannot be true and is the correct answer.

The violation in choice D is clear but choice E is complex enough that it is worth-while checking it quickly. Choice E puts T after P and late in the sequence, which risks putting T after Q, as well. A quick check, though, shows that T can be inserted before Q is picked up. Choice D is confirmed as the correct answer.

15. **(C)** This is a *could be true* question with new information that goes in the main diagram. Start with **Diagram—put in new information** and **Diagram—apply rules, musts**. After putting P in 3 and V in 8, there is nothing else that must go in the diagram. Use **Diagram—apply rules, with options** to enter S/U and U/S in 1 and 2.

1	2	3	4	5	6	7	8
S/U	U/S	P					V

Use **General—options for player** to consider the options for Q. Q must be followed by O, so it cannot go in 7. However, T cannot come after both P and Q, so Q cannot go in 4. Q can only go in 5 or 6. Create two universes.

1	2	3	4	5	6	7	8
S/U	U/S	P		Q			V
S/U	U/S	P			Q		V

In the top universe, T must go in 4 and R/O and O/R go in 6 and 7. In the bottom universe, O must go in 7 and T/R and R/T go in 4 and 5.

1	2	3	4	5	6	7	8
S/U	U/S	P	T	Q	R/O	O/R	V
S/U	U/S	P	T/R	R/T	Q	O	V

Two universes with all options

Use **Eliminate—check answers against diagram** to check the answer choices. Only choice C can be true. This question demonstrates the power of parallel universes. Once they are created, the correct answer can be found quickly.

16. **(E)** This is a *must be true* question with new information that goes in the main diagram. Put T in 7 and check the rules that relate to T. T cannot come after both Q and P. Therefore, one of Q and P must come before T and one must come after T. The last place, then, must be for Q or P. Check the rules for P. P has two players who must come before. This does not prevent P from coming last. Check the rules for Q. Q must be followed by O. Q cannot appear last, so it must be P that is in the last slot. This is enough to answer the question.

17. **(A)** This is a *could be true EXCEPT* question with new information that does not go in the main diagram. Use **Diagram—supplemental diagram or rules** to put the new information into a temporary supplemental diagram. Q goes after P, so the sequence Q – O is added to the diagram after P.

$$\begin{matrix} S \\ \quad \searrow \\ \quad\quad P - Q - O \\ \quad \nearrow \\ U \end{matrix}$$

Temporary supplemental diagram

Check the rules to see if any other information can be determined. T cannot appear before both P and Q, nor can it appear after both P and Q. T must appear before one of them and after the other. T, then, can be put into the diagram between P and Q.

$$\begin{array}{c} S \\ U \end{array} \searrow \begin{array}{c} T \\ P-Q-O \\ \nearrow \end{array}$$

Tejeda inserted between Portman and Quinn

Four of the answer choices could be true. One answer choice violates the rules. Use **Test answers—prove a violation** with the supplemental diagram. Even though the diagram is not complete, it may be enough to identify a clear rule violation. Test choice A. Can O be picked up fifth? Use **General—count places in sequence**. There are five people who must be picked up before O. O cannot appear fifth and choice A is a clear rule violation.

Because of the clarity of the violation, the other answer choices do not need to be checked, except as a practice exercise. It can quickly be seen that none of the other answer choices violate the places in the sequence to which they are assigned.

QUESTIONS 18–23

This is a one-to-one correspondence game that is ordered. It is not a sequence game but rather an ONS-A (ordered, non-sequence, with one-to-one correspondence) game. ONS-A games differ from sequence games in that the conditions do not provide long sequences of players. Most ONS-A games have a small number of fixtures with multiple branches. This game does not have branches.

In this game a person is paired with certain topics. The players consist of the seven combinations of person plus topic, such as Ofume–Formosa.

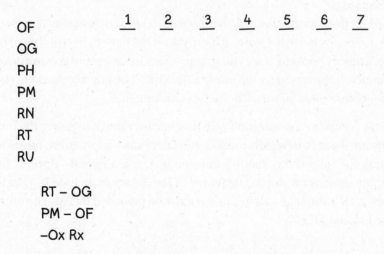

OF

OG

PH

PM

RN

RT

RU

1	2	3	4	5	6	7

RT – OG

PM – OF

–Ox Rx

Game 4 setup. The players consists of seven combinations of people and topic.

18. **(A)** This is the typical first question. Four answer choices violate rules. Use **Eliminate—apply rules, four violations**. A violation of the first rule would have RT after OG. Scan the answers. Choices D and E violate this rule. A violation of the second rule would have PM after OF. Choice C violates this rule. A violation of the third rule would have Roanhorse

immediately after Ofume. Choice B violates this. Choice A is the remaining answer and is correct.

19. **(C)** This is a *must be true* question with new information that does not go in the diagram. Use **Diagram—supplemental diagram or rules** to create a temporary rule:

OF – not P

There is no further diagramming that can be done. Use **General—options for player** to consider the options for the players after OF. The person after OF cannot be P. The only other options are R and O, but R cannot come immediately after O. Thus the only options after OF are OG or no one. In other words, OF could be last or could be followed by OG. If OG comes after OF, what are the options after OG? Because OF comes before OG, OG cannot be followed by P. OG also cannot be immediately followed by R. OF has already presented. There are no options after OG, so OG must be last.

There are two possibilities, then. OF is in last place or OG is in last place and is immediately preceded by OF.

1	2	3	4	5	6	7
						OF
					OF	OG

Two universes

In the bottom universe, any of the remaining players can go in any of the slots. There are no restrictions on the players containing R or P, other than that they present before OG and OF, respectively. For the top universe, there are some restrictions on OG. RT must be presented before OG. OG cannot be followed by R. Other than that there are too many possibilities to diagram. Use **Test answers—negate a must**, working with the above diagram.

Based on the bottom universe, there seems to be no reason why R must be in 1, as in choice A. Go on to choice B. Choice B clearly does *not* have to be true, based on the upper universe. Choice C must be true. The lecture on Formosa cannot go in any slot other than 6 or 7. Choice C appears to be the answer. Confirm it by quickly checking choices D and E. Neither choice must be true. Choice C is confirmed.

20. **(A)** This is a *could be true* question with new information that goes in the main diagram. Use **Diagram—put in new information** and **Diagram—apply rules, musts** to put OG in 2. Applying the rules shows that RT must go in 1. Use **General—options for fixture** to consider the options for slot 3. The player in slot 3 cannot include R. That leaves P and O. However, OF cannot go in 3 because it must be preceded by PM. The only options for slot 3 are PM and PH.

1	2	3	4	5	6	7
RT	OG	PH				
RT	OG	PM				

Two universes

It would require a total of eight universes to diagram all of the possibilities. Try testing answer choices, using the diagrams above. For choice A, putting RN into 7 seems to leave multiple options. The restrictions of RN would only require that O is not in 6, which seems possible. Put a plus by choice A for now and test the others. Because there are four rule violations, four of the answer choices should clearly be out.

Test choice B. According to the diagrams, OF cannot go in 3. Choice B is out. Choice C would require OF to be in either 1 or 3, which are both impossible. Choice C is out. Test choice D. It is impossible because one instance of R is in slot 1. Test choice E. Put OF in 4 in each universe. This results in a rule violation in the top universe because PM must come before OF. In the bottom universe OF cannot be followed by R and the other O is already used. Slot 5 must be PH, so P cannot be in 7. Choice E violates rules and choice A remains as the only answer choice that could be true. Note that it is not necessary to provide absolute proof that choice A could be true. It is enough to see that it seems viable and that the other answer choices clearly violate rules.

21. **(B)** This is a *complete and accurate list* question with no new information. Four of the answer choices either contain an element that cannot immediately follow the talk on Formosa or leave out an element that can follow a talk on Formosa. There is nothing to diagram, so the problem must be solved by testing answer choices. Start with **General— look for rules that apply to player/fixture**, by looking for rules that apply to Formosa. Moravia must appear before Formosa, so any answer choice with Moravia is out. This eliminates choices A, C, and E. Only choices B and D are left and both contain Ghana and Hungary. Therefore, it is only necessary to test New Mexico. If it is not clear that New Mexico is associated with Roanhorse and thus cannot appear after Formosa, which is associated with Ofume, then drawing a complete assignment and testing it will show why New Mexico cannot go after Formosa.

22. **(E)** This is a *must be false* question, which is equivalent to *which one of the following cannot be true*. One of the answer choices violates rules. The others do not violate rules and may even be forced to be true. There is new information that does not go directly into the main diagram. Use **Diagram—parallel universes** to show the options for how O can present consecutively without presenting last. There are two players that must come before the two presentations by O: RT and PM. The earliest that the two presentations of O can begin is the third slot. There are no restrictions on whether OF or OG must go first. List the options as OF/OG, or just as O. There are only three possible universes. The two Os can go in 3 and 4, 4 and 5, or 5 and 6. Use **General—options for fixture** to consider the options for the slot immediately after the second O. It cannot be occupied by any R. Both Os have been used. PM has been presented before the two Os. The only option is PH. PH must appear after the second O.

1	2	3	4	5	6	7
		O	O	PH		
			O	O	PH	
				O	O	PH

Three universes

Check the answer choices to see if this is enough information to either answer the question or eliminate some answers. For choice A, P does present last in the bottom universe but this universe is only partially filled out. It is possible that this universe has some fundamental violation. Because the correct answer is one that will have a clear violation, put a question mark by choice A and move on to choice B.

The logic in choice B is complex. Orient to the meaning of "It must be false that Petrick does not present last." This means that Petrick must present last. As with choice A, it does not appear that P must present last, so move on and look for a clear violation.

For choice C, there does not seem to be any reason why F cannot be sixth. Move on to choice D. The lecture on Utah is given by R and does not have to come before the Os. There does not seem to be any reason why the lecture on Hungary cannot come before the lecture on Utah. Test choice E.

It is clear from the diagram that the lecture on Hungary can only be in slots 5, 6, or 7. It must be false that the lecture on Hungary is presented fourth. Choice E is the correct answer. It was not necessary to spend time proving that choices A through D were possible. It was only necessary to prove that choice E could not be possible. It is easier to prove that a rule is violated than to prove that no rule has been violated.

23. **(D)** This is a *could be true* question with new information that does not go in the main diagram, including a new condition. Consider the new condition. It means that once Roanhorse has given a talk, Petrick cannot give any subsequent talks.

Consider the options for the 2 Ps. They must occur before all 3 Rs. In other words there must be at least 3 places after "P blank P." The two universes for the Ps, then, are in 1 and 3 or 2 and 4.

In the second of these universes, the three Rs are in the last three places. Check the rules. RT must come before OG so this second universe violates this rule. Only the first universe is viable. The Ps are in 1 and 3. Place 2 must be one of the Os. The rule RT before OG indicates that OG cannot be the O in 2, so 2 must be OF. Because PM goes before OF, place 1 must be PM.

Because R cannot go immediately after O, and because there must be one O in the last four places, OG can only go in the final position. The Rs can go in any order in places 4, 5, and 6. We now have a diagram that reads:

PM OF PH Rx Rx Rx OG

It is now possible to test the answer choices against the diagram. Choice A cannot be true as the final presentation must be OG. Choice B cannot be true as no R can appear before a P. Choice C cannot be true as the final slot is OG. Choice D can and must be true. Test choice E as a double check. The two Os cannot be consecutive. Choice D is the answer.

The LSAT Writing Sample (Essay)

5

→ **INTRODUCTION TO THE ESSAY**
→ **THE IMPORTANCE OF THE ESSAY**
→ **AN ORIENTATION TO THE STRUCTURE OF THE ESSAY**
→ **LANGUAGE SKILLS FOR THE ESSAY**
→ **HOW TO CREATE THE ESSAY**
→ **SAMPLE ESSAYS WITH EXPLANATIONS**

This chapter teaches you how to write an LSAT Writing Sample, also referred to as the Essay, that will strengthen your standing with the admissions committee.

INTRODUCTION TO THE ESSAY

The Writing Sample requires you to write a clear and succinct essay in thirty-five minutes. The LSAT writing sample (the **Essay**) is a decision problem that measures your ability to write under actual test conditions. You are given thirty-five minutes to write an essay in which you choose the better of two alternatives, based on two specific criteria. You receive a page and three-quarters of lined and bordered space in which to write your essay. In addition, you receive the equivalent of one page of scrap paper that is divided between two pages, on which you make notes.

Write your essay only within the borders of the lined pages because the LSAC only transmits information to the law schools that is contained within the lined spaces. Only write about the given topic; you *cannot* make up your own topic.

THE IMPORTANCE OF THE ESSAY

Although the Essay is not scored, it is the only spontaneous measure of your essay writing ability to which the admissions committee has access. Because law school exams are typically essays, the Essay affords law schools the opportunity to judge your writing ability and style under test conditions. In comparing you with other applicants who have similar GPAs and LSAT scores, the admissions committee may read your Essay to determine the quality of your writing. Therefore, it is important to use the Essay as an opportunity to demonstrate your superior analytical and writing skills.

ORIENTATION TO THE ESSAY
Essay Components

The Essay includes a page of general directions, scratch space, a page with specific directions, and a prompt. The prompt includes the setup of the topic, the criteria that you must use to determine the better of two alternative courses of action, and a description of the two alternatives.

THE GENERAL DIRECTIONS PAGE

The Essay section begins with a page of **General Directions**, including a place for you to date the form, print your name, and sign. The General Directions, in a paraphrased form, are as follows:

Time: 35 Minutes
General Directions

You will have thirty-five minutes to organize and write an essay on the topic described on the next page. Read the topic and all of the directions carefully. It is generally best to take a few minutes to organize your thoughts before beginning to write. Be sure to develop your ideas fully and leave time at the end to review what you have written. **Do not write on any topic other than the topic given. It is not acceptable to write on a topic of your own choice.**

No special knowledge is needed or expected for this essay. Admission committees are interested in your reasoning, clarity, organization, use of language, and writing mechanics. The quality of what you write is more important than the quantity.

Keep your essay in the blocked and lined area on the front and back of the separate Writing Sample Response Sheet. That is the only area that will be reproduced and sent to law schools. Be sure to write legibly.

Both this topic sheet and your response sheet must be given to the testing staff before you can leave the testing room.

The General Directions are always the same. Read them carefully now so that you understand them and do not need to take time reading them during your test. The most critical information in the General Directions is that you cannot write on a topic other than the one given, that anything you write outside of the blocked area will not be sent to schools, and that you should focus on reasoning, clarity, organization, use of language, and writing mechanics.

THE ESSAY DIRECTIONS

The second page of the Essay section contains the Essay directions, the prompt, and scratch paper space. The Essay directions, in paraphrased form, read:

> **Directions:** The situation described below gives two choices. Either one of the choices can be supported based on the information given. In your essay, consider both choices and then argue in favor of one over the other. Base your argument on the two specified criteria and on the given facts. There is no "right" or "wrong" choice. Either choice can be reasonably defended.

As with the General Directions, the Essay directions are always the same. Familiarize yourself with them now. The most critical information in the Essay directions is that there is no one choice that is "right." You can make a strong case for either choice.

THE PROMPT

The entire description of the Essay topic is called the **prompt**. The prompt starts with a **setup**, then gives a bulleted list consisting of the two **criteria**, and finally includes two paragraphs, each explaining one of the two **alternatives**, which represent the two possible courses of action. The alternatives are sometimes simply called the **choices**.

The Setup

The setup consists of three lines—or, rarely, two or four—that establish the context of the Essay and explain why a choice must be made. The last sentence of the setup is typically something like "Using the facts given below, compose an essay in which you argue in favor of choosing one alternative over the other on the basis of the two criteria below." The setup tells you who must decide which of the two alternative courses of action is best. This chooser may be a person, a family, a city, a corporation, or any other entity. We can call this entity the **decision maker**. In your essay, you speak on behalf of the decision maker, but this does not mean that you yourself should become personally involved in the issue by stating personal opinions or by using the words *I, me, mine, my,* or *myself.* In fact, you must *not* become personally involved. Be sure to identify the decision maker before you go on to the criteria.

The Criteria

The two criteria each contain one or more requirements that you use to select one alternative over the other. The Essay prompt is purposely written so that one criterion favors the selection of one alternative, and the other criterion favors the selection of the other alternative.

The Alternatives

There are only two courses of action that you can choose from and these are described in the two paragraphs below the criteria. Each alternative meets some of the elements in the criteria and does not meet others. It is important to realize that, in terms of meeting the criteria, the two alternatives are equal. It is a waste of time to try to figure out which alternative meets more of the criteria. The prompt is designed so that it is a complete draw. This is what makes the Essay task challenging.

Neither of the two alternatives is necessarily right or wrong, either in terms of logic or in terms of personal values. The subject matter on which the alternatives are based is specifically chosen to be noncontroversial. The people who read your essay are not concerned with which alternative you choose, and, because the topics are not controversial, you do not need

NO RIGHT OR WRONG ALTERNATIVE

There is not a right or wrong alternative. The alternatives are written so as to be equally justifiable.

to worry that you might offend a reader by choosing a certain alternative. Keep in mind that *you* must never introduce any controversial subjects into your essay, either.

Out of fourteen recently published LSAT writing samples, three were about public entertainment, three involved business decisions, two presented educational choices, two discussed travel plans, two were about expansion plans, one concerned expert witness selection, and one addressed writing styles. There is a wide range of areas on which topics can be built.

The Task

The essence of writing the Essay is that you must defend as superior one of two alternatives that are in fact equal in terms of meeting or violating the criteria. The primary way to make one alternative appear superior over the other is to emphasize the strengths of the superior alternative and downplay its weaknesses, while emphasizing the weaknesses of the inferior alternative and downplaying its strengths. Downplaying is not the same as ignoring. It is *not* effective to *ignore* the weaknesses of the superior alternative or to ignore the strengths of the inferior alternative.

LANGUAGE SKILLS FOR THE ESSAY

The kind of language structures that you use on the Essay is at least as important, and sometimes more so, than your actual content. In other words, how you speak is more important than what you say. This section discusses several elements of language that contribute to the impression that your essay will create.

Legal Writing Style

Beyond showing that you can compose an organized and coherent essay, the second most important purpose of the Essay is to show that you have a basic grasp of legal writing style.

When a reader from the admissions committee reads an essay that uses an approximation of legal writing style, the reader will feel comfortable that the essay writer is prepared for law school. If an essay uses language that is very divergent from legal writing style, the reader may be concerned about the student's ability to write law school exams and papers. This general impression could make the difference between being chosen and being passed over in favor of someone who already has legal writing skills.

> **HOW YOU WRITE VERSUS WHAT YOU WRITE**
>
> Your style of writing is at least as important as what you say. Using the elements of legal style writing makes you look like a lawyer!

HEREINAFTER REFERRED TO AS

The first element of legal writing style that you should master is the "hereinafter referred to as" notation. If a certain element of a prompt is referred to by a name, such as Johnson, or Great Tools Factory, it is customary to assign an abbreviation or **acronym** to that element and, after the first reference, refer to the element only by the acronym. Note the punctuation used to do this:

> *The Great Tools Factory ("GTF") chooses Alternative 1 ("A1"). A1 is GTF's superior alternative.*

The first time you refer to an element, state its full name. Follow the name with parentheses, inside of which are quotation marks. Inside the quotation marks is the acronym that you want to assign. The acronym must always start with a capital letter. Notice that the first sentence above includes two elements and that the second time each is referred to, only the acronym is used. The acronym starts with a capital letter but it does not use quotation marks or parentheses once it has been defined.

The use of the *hereinafter referred to as* notation is by itself a strong indication that you have some understanding that legal writing has certain conventions. Be sure to use this notation, even when it may seem unnecessary. Use the notation to refer to each party mentioned in the prompt, as well as to the criteria ("C1") and the alternatives, such as ("Retire") versus ("Work"). If a certain element is already referred to with an initial, you may still be able to use the *hereinafter* notation. For example, if AB Industries is one of the parties, it can be referred to as ("AB"). However, if one party is called simply XY, it is probably redundant to define it as ("XY").

GRAMMATICAL STYLE

Legal writing uses specific types of sentence structures that would sound awkward in nonlegal writing. These structures are used to create clarity within complex material, to avoid ambiguity, to present information in a direct way, and to avoid contaminating logical positions with the personal feelings of the author.

> **THE PARTY OF THE FIRST PART, HEREINAFTER REFERRED TO AS ("P1")**
>
> Be sure to use the *hereinafter referred to as* notation. It shows that you write like a lawyer!

Simple Present Tense Verbs

Legal writing style uses predominantly the simple form of present tense verbs. Compare the pairs of sentences below. Study the change in the underlined verbs in each pair of sentences.

EXAMPLE 1

Normal style: Richardson <u>will</u> probably <u>choose</u> to take the tropical vacation.

Legal style: Richardson ("R") <u>chooses</u> the tropical vacation ("Tropical").

EXAMPLE 2

Normal style: Country X <u>is suffering</u> from a prolonged drought.

Legal style: Country X ("X") <u>suffers</u> from a prolonged drought.

EXAMPLE 3

Normal style: The Jones family <u>should move</u> to the new house.

Legal style: The Jones family ("Jones") <u>moves</u> to the new house ("New").

In legal style the verb is usually reduced to one word. Avoid multiple-word verb structures such as "will go," "can choose," and "should make." Generally, avoid a main verb that ends in -*ing*. *John is going* should be written as *John goes*. If a verb is not the main verb, the -*ing* ending may be acceptable. For example, *John chooses going to the store.* The main verb is *chooses*.

There are cases in which it is appropriate to use the future tense (*If Pleasantville chooses Develop, the forest will disappear within five years*) or other compound verbs (*should, might, may*). However, make an effort to use simple verbs when possible.

Active Voice Verbs

Legal writing uses verbs in the **active voice** rather than verbs in the **passive voice.** Observe how the passive voice verbs below are changed to active voice. The underlined word is the person or agent (the doer) who is performing the action. In an active voice sentence, the doer is the subject. In a passive voice sentence, the doer is identified with a phrase such as ". . . by John."

EXAMPLE 4

Passive voice: The cake is baked by <u>John</u>.
Active voice: <u>John</u> is baking the cake.
Legal style: <u>John</u> ("J") bakes the cake.

EXAMPLE 5

Passive voice: The house should be built by <u>Contractor X</u>.
Active voice: <u>Contractor X</u> should build the house.
Legal style: <u>Contractor X</u> ("X") builds the house.

In a passive sentence, the subject (*the cake*) does not *perform* the action of the sentence but rather *receives* the action. This is why the structure is called passive. The actual performer is given in the phrase "by John." In the examples above, the actual performer is underlined. It is possible to create an **active** sentence by making *John* the subject. To put the sentence into legal style, drop any helping verbs (*should, is*). This may mean that you have to add an "s" to the main verb, as in *should build* versus *builds*.

Avoid Pronouns

One aspect of legal style writing that may seem particularly strange is the avoidance of pronouns.

EXAMPLE 6

Normal style: John Patterson should choose to build a new house. He will have more space for gardening. His family will have more privacy. The new house will save him money and it will last longer than the old one.
Legal style: John Patterson ("John") chooses to build a new house ("New"). John has more space for gardening. John's family has more privacy. New saves John money. New lasts longer than the old house ("Old").

In the legal style, the words *John* and *New* are repeated instead of using the words *he, his, him,* and *it.* The reason for this is that a pronoun such as *he* can sometimes be ambiguous. In the sentence, *John saw Patrick dancing in the street and scratched his head,* the word *his* is ambiguous. Did John scratch his own head or Patrick's? By repeating the name of the party, rather than using a pronoun, legal documents avoid any ambiguity. *Your* reason for avoiding pronouns is to show the admissions committee that you understand this concept of legal writing.

Some sentences can become overly awkward if the noun is repeated multiple times. Rather than writing *PM chooses A1 because it increases PM's chances of impressing PM's customer and ensuring that PM survives long enough to reap PM's benefits,* limit yourself to only two repetitions of the noun in any given sentence.

> **Better:** *PM chooses A1 because it increases PM's chances of impressing its customer and ensuring that it survives long enough to reap its benefits.*

However, if using a pronoun makes the sentence ambiguous, repeat the noun.

> **Best:** *PM chooses A1 because it increases PM's chances of impressing its customer and ensuring that PM survives long enough to reap PM's benefits.*

The word *it* is ambiguous in the above sentence because, the first time "it" is used, "it" refers to "choosing." The word *it* could also refer to "A1."

Short, Direct Sentences

Another element of legal style that you should master is keeping your sentences relatively short and punchy. In the previous example, the legal style changed the sentence *The new house will save him money and it will last longer than the old house* to

> *New saves John money. New lasts longer than the old house ("Old").*

This breaks it into two short sentences. This may sound choppy in normal writing, but in legal writing, shorter sentences make points clearer.

EXAMPLE 7

Normal style: John Patterson hopes he can find a good house that his family will find meets many of their needs that the old house did not meet.
Legal style: John Patterson ("John") seeks a house that better suits John's family.

The legal-style sentence condenses the information. There is not necessarily a right or wrong way to condense or keep sentences short. Do not be so overzealous in condensing that you throw out important information. An excess of short, choppy sentences can be difficult to read. It is fine to incorporate longer sentences as well.

Avoid Unnecessary Adjectives

Keep your use of descriptive adjectives to a minimum. Only use adjectives that are necessary to make your point.

EXAMPLE 8

Normal style: John Patterson should buy a nice, new house. A new house will give him a luxurious amount of space for his hobbies. A large yard will give him a fantastic place to enjoy some refreshing nature and to watch the delightful flight of wild birds. He can go fishing in the idyllic lake behind his tranquil property.

Legal style: John Patterson ("John") buys the new house ("New"). New provides space for John's hobbies. A large yard provides a place for John to enjoy nature and watch birds. John can fish in the lake behind John's property.

Many of the adjectives used in the normal style were not necessary. Legal style reduces the use of adjectives in order to keep essential elements clear and to avoid the impression that the author of the argument has a personal preference. Note that the legal style example says *John can fish* instead of *John fishes*. This is acceptable when the sentence refers to something that clearly describes a potential (he *can* fish as opposed to he *will* fish).

KEEP YOURSELF OUT OF THE ARGUMENT

An important element of legal-style writing is to keep yourself, as a person, out of the argument. Below are three important points to remember.

Avoid Personal Opinions

Another important reason to avoid adjectives is to keep your personal evaluations and opinions out of your argument. You want your argument to be evaluated by others on the basis of logical persuasion. If you insert your own opinions (*Clarkville clearly should promote a wonderfully pristine lake, rather than a cesspool of industrial waste*), you risk having your argument rejected by someone who takes personal offense at your stand. Remove subjectivity by omitting prejudicial adverbs and adjectives, such as *clearly* and *obviously*. In addition to avoiding adjectives, do not introduce personal value judgments in any form.

EXAMPLE 9

Wrong: Clarkville should promote a wonderfully pristine lake, rather than a cesspool of industrial waste. It is clearly immoral to allow a corporation to make money while destroying the natural beauty of the environment.

Better: Clarkville ("C") chooses closing the Bilge Factory ("Closing"). Closing results in a reduction of industrial pollution in the lake. Reduced pollution allows C to introduce game fish. Game fishing provides recreation for citizens of C and revenue for C.

Avoid the First Person

Even though you, the writer of the essay, are responsible for creating a strong argument (on behalf of the decision maker), you as a person should not appear in the argument. Just as you should avoid adjectives that reveal your personal opinion you should not use the words *I, me, my, mine,* or *myself.*

EXAMPLE 10

Wrong: I think John Patterson should buy the new house. It seems like a mistake for him to stay in the old house. Who would want to live in an old house when they can have a new one?

Better: John Patterson ("John") buys the new house ("New"). New provides a more modern living environment.

Avoid Controversial Issues

A corollary of not inserting yourself and your opinions into the essay is to avoid controversial issues. Do not draw on issues that are likely to elicit strong reactions from others. Avoid religious and moral statements, as well as statements that reflect a strong political view.

COMMON ERRORS TO AVOID

There are several common errors that LSAT takers fall into when writing the Essay. Do not attempt to write an essay in the style that you would use in an English class. The Essay is not testing your ability to be clever, creative, entertaining, or unique. Do not try to create a piece of creative writing. Do *not* use flowery, emotive, or elegant adjectives. Adjectives should be used very sparingly and only when necessary.

Do not introduce your essay with an engaging sentence or intriguing quote. Do not try to come up with an innovative way to approach the essay task. Do not use the Essay to show your knowledge of law or your motivation to attend law school. Do not say *I, me, my, mine,* or *myself.*

EXAMPLES AND PRACTICE EXERCISES

Study the following examples:

EXAMPLE 11

Problem sentence: The company <u>will bring</u> new jobs.
Comment: Uses future tense "will bring." Change to present tense "brings."
Better sentence: The company <u>brings</u> new jobs.

EXAMPLE 12

Problem sentence: The city <u>is suffering</u> from lack of employment.
Comment: Uses "is suffering." Simplify to "suffers."
Better sentence: The city <u>suffers</u> from lack of employment.

EXAMPLE 13

Problem sentence: The company <u>is considered</u> by the <u>city</u>.
Comment: Uses a passive structure. Note the word "by." Change to active by making "city" the subject.
Better sentence: The <u>city</u> <u>considers</u> the company.

EXAMPLE 14

Problem sentence: The city hopes to attract a business that is successful enough to help improve the quality of life of the people who live there.
Comment: Avoids the problems in the earlier examples but is too wordy. Simplify and condense.
Better sentence: The city seeks a business that can improve the residents' quality of life.

Practice

Now try changing the following sentences on your own. Use the examples above as models. Answers are below.

Change the following sentences from the future tense to the present tense.

1. Party A will solve the family's problems.

   Answer: _____

2. The mediators will provide guidelines.

   Answer: _____

3. A and B will build ten houses.

   Answer: _____

Change the following sentences from "to be verb-ing" to the simple present tense.

4. The manufacturer is planning a new product line.

   Answer: _____

5. The parties are negotiating a settlement.

   Answer: _____

6. T and M are complementing each other.

   Answer: _____

Change the following passive sentences to active sentences.

7. The offer is submitted by Party A.

   Answer: _____

8. The alternatives are tested by the defendant.

   Answer: _____

9. Accomplishments are listed on the résumé by the applicant.

   Answer: _____

   Try simplifying the following wordy sentences. There is no particular right answer.

10. The business does not really have the kind of income that lets the owners take the time off to have a nice vacation somewhere.

    Answer: _____

11. Given all of the information that I have on hand, I don't see any way to convince the company that it is profitable to lower their prices.

    Answer: _____

Answers

   1. Party A solves the family's problems.
   2. The mediators provide guidelines.
   3. A and B build ten houses.
   4. The manufacturer plans a new product line.
   5. The parties negotiate a settlement.
   6. T and M complement each other.
   7. Party A submits the offer.
   8. The defendant tests the alternatives.
   9. The applicant lists accomplishments on the résumé.
  10. The business does not have enough income for the owners to take a vacation.
  11. The available information is not enough to convince the company to lower its prices.

Handwriting

No amount of logical organization will make up for an essay that the reader cannot read. Poor handwriting creates a negative impression. If your handwriting is naturally difficult to read, practice printing your letters. If necessary, write larger than normal, even if this means that your essay will be shorter. As you write, be careful not to begin rushing and falling into illegible writing. Some people may qualify as having a documentable learning disability based on handwriting. In such a case, the person can request special accommodations, such as extra time to write, being able to use a computer, or even having another person write the essay as you dictate it.

The Mechanics of Writing

While you are writing your essay, if you need to delete something, draw a single line through it. Do not try to erase it or scratch it out. If you need to add something to a section you have already written, use a carat (^) to show the point at which you want to insert your addition. Then write in a neat but condensed way above the line.

CREATING THE ESSAY
Orient to the Prompt

Start by orienting yourself to the prompt. Read the setup. Examine the criteria and determine how they differ. Often one criterion takes a more conservative approach, meaning that it takes less risk but offers less chance of gain. The other criterion, then, does the opposite. It takes more risk but offers the opportunity for a greater gain. In some cases, the difference between the two criteria is a difference between a short-range viewpoint, focused on immediate results with possible future difficulties, and a long-range viewpoint, focused on future results, with possible short-term difficulties.

In order to analyze the relative merits of each criterion, paraphrase and condense each of the two criteria on your scratch paper. Decide which criterion you will defend as the most important. Then, on your scratch paper, write a single sentence that combines the two criteria, stating the most important criterion first. This sentence is the rule that you will use to remind yourself of the basis for your argument. Consider the following:

> *John wants to have his cake.*
> *John wants to eat his cake.*

Your combined sentence might read:

> *John wants to have his cake and to eat it.*

When you begin writing, you might state that *having cake* is the most important of the two criteria because it guarantees a long-term benefit, whereas *eating the cake*, while pleasurable, has only a short-term benefit.

Read the alternatives carefully. If the criteria represent a choice between a more conservative and less conservative approach, or between a long-term and short-term approach, the alternatives will reflect this. Identify the alternative that matches the criterion that you chose as most important.

Choose an Alternative

A distinction between a more conservative (or short-range) alternative and a less conservative (or long-range) alternative is a good basis for choosing the alternative to defend. If you are naturally inclined toward a more conservative approach, it will be easier and more natural for you to defend that alternative, and vice versa.

If a prompt is not based on the distinctions described above, choose the alternative to which you are most naturally drawn. If neither alternative "feels" better, then choose one arbitrarily. There is no "correct" answer. You may have to defend the superiority of an alternative that you do not personally believe is better.

The alternative that you choose to defend should be referred to as the **superior** alternative and the other alternative, the **inferior** alternative. Do not use the terms *best* and *worst*. They imply that there is an absolute right and wrong answer.

Plan Your Defense

As mentioned previously, a defense often consists of merely highlighting the strengths of your choice and downplaying the weaknesses. The way you construct sentences influences whether the reader believes that an alternative is strong. Consider the following:

EXAMPLE 15

Even though some people survived smallpox and gained immunity, the disease killed millions of people in a horrible way.

Does this make smallpox sound good or bad? Now consider the following:

EXAMPLE 16

Even though smallpox killed millions of people in a horrible way, those who did survive were immune to the disease for life.

Does this sound like a positive or negative statement about smallpox? Ignoring weaknesses does not make your argument stronger, as a critical reader will see that you have simply ignored half of the truth. However, by using a sentence structure similar to the example above, you can give the impression that the weakness is minimal and the strength is what is important.

EXAMPLE 17

Even though (severe weakness), the truth is that (moderate strength).

In the case of a choice between a conservative alternative and a more adventurous one, you can use the sentence structure above to either make the potential benefits sound like they are worth the risk or to justify the safety of staying with a plan with few risks. Compare the sentences in Examples 18 and 19.

EXAMPLE 18

Despite the small chance of rain, the tropical island vacation offers the opportunity to see rare birds, swim in the ocean, enjoy the beach, and participate in exotic nightlife.

EXAMPLE 19

Although the tropical vacation offers some opportunities for recreation, the significant chance that the entire vacation would be spent inside because of torrential rains makes staying home the superior alternative.

In the above sentences, a small bit of colorful language helps to make the point. Too much colorful language has the opposite effect. The readers may feel that they have been tricked into an opinion by clever words.

If the essay prompt that you receive is based on a difference between long-term and short-term results, it is very easy for a reader to believe a sentence such as the following:

EXAMPLE 20

While Alternative 1 ("A1") results in a short-term profit, in the long run A1 results in a large loss of income. On the other hand, even though Alternative 2 ("A2") does not bring in much income in the first year, over the long run, A2 results in a steady income stream.

Most readers will naturally see the benefit of a longer-term plan and the drawbacks of a shortsighted plan.

Another approach for defending your alternative, given that every alternative has drawbacks, is to discuss the strengths of your alternative and then explain how any weaknesses can be overcome. When you discuss the inferior alternative, do not address how the weaknesses could be overcome.

EXAMPLE 21

Alternative 1 ("A1") increases City's income significantly after five years. Even though City's income with A1 is less during the first five years than with Alternative 2 ("A2"), the prospect of long-term income attracts bond investments that can improve City's current cash flow. While A2 provides short-term income, in the long term it creates a negative economic atmosphere.

Having planned how to support your alternative, begin composing your essay.

Practice Prompt 1

To illustrate the process of setting up the essay, refer to the following essay prompt.

Lucy Topper, president of a large manufacturing company for nine years, wants to realize her dream of owning a medium-sized bistro in Grometberg. Lucy is considering learning more about either wine or beer making. Using the facts given below, compose an essay in which you argue in favor of choosing one choice over the other on the basis of the two criteria below.

- Lucy is busy and has a limited amount of time to attend classes.
- Lucy wants to offer a wide variety of high-quality, in-house beers or wines.

Vinni's Vintage Emporium is a wholesale grape operation located fifty miles from Grometberg. Vinni's offers wine-making classes twice a year and the next session is for daytime classes, lasts sixteen weeks, and starts in six weeks. Vinni's next nighttime session starts thirty-two weeks from now. Vinni is nationally famous for making outstanding wines, and his students have won medals around the world. Vinni's curriculum is demanding, but Vintage Emporium graduates are well trained, and they typically create great wines from grapes harvested in their own locales.

Bubby's Brew Skool was founded thirty years ago by Bubby Brewster in Hopston, located twenty miles from Grometberg. Bubby brewed beverages from almost every possible combination of grains and fruits and is famous among microbrewery owners for creating an amazing variety of beers, ales, and ciders. Bubby has an endearing charm that almost compensates for his forgetfulness; Bubby simply cannot remember all of his recipes. Even so, Bubby has a stable of twelve recipes that have won medals in beer festivals across the region. Bubby's next nighttime class starts in four weeks and runs for twelve weeks.

Going step by step, first orient to the prompt by examining the criteria. How do they differ? One is conservative. Lucy has limited free time, which she wants to conserve. The other is more expansive. She wants to offer a wide variety of excellent beverages. We will defend the more expansive approach.

Review the alternatives. The first alternative is stronger in terms of quality, which matches the second criterion. The training is more rigorous, the beverages have won awards nationally, and the beverages produced by students have won awards internationally. The second alternative offers the opportunity for a wide variety of beverages but the awards are only regional and there is no mention of whether students have won awards. The training is shorter and is located closer to Lucy. The second alternative, then, meets the conservative need for saving time only slightly better than the first alternative and only weakly meets the need of quality.

The plan of attack will be to present the goal of producing high-quality beverages as Lucy's strongest goal and to defend that goal by saying that the difference in time commitment is minimal and short term compared to achieving her goal of quality.

Compose the Five-Paragraph Essay

Use a basic essay structure consisting of five paragraphs, with each paragraph containing roughly five sentences. The first paragraph introduces the essay and summarizes all of the points that you will cover. The second paragraph analyzes the two criteria and determines which one is most important. The third and fourth paragraphs respectively analyze the superior and inferior alternatives. The fifth paragraph summarizes the entire argument in favor of the superior alternative and concludes.

STRUCTURE OF THE FIVE-PARAGRAPH ESSAY

Paragraph 1: Introduce the essay and summarize the main points.

Paragraph 2: Analyze the two criteria, determine which is most important, and combine them into a single statement that starts with the more important criteria.

Paragraph 3: Analyze and defend the superior alternative.

Paragraph 4: Analyze and attack the inferior alternative.

Paragraph 5: Summarize the entire argument and conclude.

Each sentence has a specific purpose and bears a particular relationship to its paragraph and to the essay as a whole. The structure of each paragraph and sentence is described below.

PARAGRAPH 1: INTRODUCE, SUMMARIZE, AND EXPLAIN THE STRUCTURE

The first sentence of your first paragraph introduces the essay by saying which alternative better meets the criteria. The second sentence says that the decision maker uses two criteria and then paraphrases the criteria. The third sentence says the selected alternative is superior because it meets both criteria. The fourth sentence says the decision maker rejects the inferior alternative because it fails to meet one or both criteria. The fifth sentence concludes by restating the decision maker's selection of the superior alternative on the basis that it meets the criteria better than the inferior alternative.

Referring to Practice Prompt 1 earlier in the chapter, the following is a possible first paragraph. Compare each sentence with the description above.

> Lucy Topart ("Lucy") chooses Vinni's Vintage Emporium ("Vinni") as the superior alternative. Lucy uses two criteria: the need to conserve time and the desire to produce a wide variety of high-quality alcoholic beverages. Vinni is the superior alternative because Vinni has a national and international reputation for high-quality beverages while requiring only a modest investment of time. Lucy rejects Bubby's Brew School ("Bubby") because Bubby's reputation is only regional and involves nearly the same time commitment. Lucy chooses Vinni because of its superior reputation and limited time commitment.

One important purpose of summarizing all of the main points of your essay (namely, which alternative is superior and why) in the first paragraph is that it firmly establishes in the mind of the reader that you have developed a complete argument that is logically sound. This is especially helpful considering that the person reading your essay may have just read thirty or forty other essays and is not likely to have the energy to search through your essay to determine whether your argument is complete and sound. Your first paragraph makes it obvious for the reader and creates a strong first impression.

PARAGRAPH 2: ANALYZE THE TWO CRITERIA AND STATE THEIR RELATIVE IMPORTANCE

The first sentence of the second paragraph introduces the two criteria. The second sentence succinctly paraphrases one criterion and then succinctly paraphrases the other criterion. The third sentence combines the criteria into one statement. The fourth sentence either says why one criterion is more important than the other criterion or says that the two criteria are equally important. The fifth sentence concludes by stating the decision maker's priority is to meet one or both criteria.

Paragraph 2 for Practice Prompt 1 could be as follows:

> Lucy uses two criteria to choose between Vinni and Bubby. Criterion 1 ("C1") requires conserving Lucy's limited time and Criterion 2 ("C2") requires producing a wide variety of high-quality beverages. Combined, the two criteria call for producing a wide variety of high-quality beverages with a minimal time commitment. The need to produce a wide variety of high-quality beverages is more compelling than Lucy's need to conserve time in the long run.

PARAGRAPH 3: ANALYZE AND SUPPORT THE SUPERIOR ALTERNATIVE

The first sentence of the third paragraph states that the superior alternative meets both criteria. The second sentence shows how the superior alternative meets the first criterion. The third shows how the superior alternative meets the second criterion. The fourth sentence demonstrates analytical balance by exposing a minor flaw in the superior alternative, relative either to one criterion or to the inferior alternative. The fifth sentence concludes by restating that the superior alternative is the decision maker's better option because the superior alternative meets both criteria.

The third paragraph for Practice Prompt 1 could read as follows:

> Vinni is the superior alternative because Vinni meets both criteria. Vinni meets C2 because Vinni leads in the ability to produce high-quality beverages that earn national and international awards. Vinni meets C1 because Vinni involves only a modest investment of time. While Vinni does not have a reputation for a wide variety of wines, once Lucy masters Vinni's techniques, Lucy has the option of learning to produce a greater variety. Vinni is Lucy's superior alternative because Vinni meets both the criterion of high quality and the criterion of a minimal time commitment.

PARAGRAPH 4: ANALYZE AND ATTACK THE INFERIOR ALTERNATIVE

The first sentence of the fourth paragraph rejects the inferior alternative. The second sentence shows how the inferior alternative fails to meet one criterion. The third sentence demonstrates analytical balance by stating a single positive attribute of the inferior alternative, relative to either one criterion or to the superior alternative. The fourth sentence negates the single positive attribute of the inferior alternative by restating the inferior alternative's inability to meet both criteria. The fifth sentence concludes by rejecting the inferior alternative relative to the superior alternative.

Paragraph 4 for Practice Prompt 1 could be as follows:

> Bubby is Lucy's inferior alternative. Bubby has earned only regional recognition, compared to Vinni's national and international recognition. Bubby does offer a wide variety of beverages. However, Bubby's quality is not as high as Vinni's and the time commitment is nearly as great and so Bubby fails to meet either criterion. Therefore, Lucy rejects Bubby in favor of Vinni, the superior alternative.

PARAGRAPH 5: RESTATE THE ARGUMENT AND CONCLUDE

The first sentence of the fifth paragraph restates the decision maker's choice of the superior alternative. The second sentence shows how the superior alternative meets one criterion. The third sentence shows how the superior alternative meets the other criterion. The fourth sentence compares the single weak point of the superior alternative against the inferior alternative's failure to meet both criteria. The fifth sentence concludes the essay by restating that the superior alternative meets both criteria better than the inferior alternative.

Paragraph 5 for Practice Prompt 1 could be as follows:

> Lucy chooses Vinni as the superior alternative. Vinni meets C1 by offering training in a reasonable time. Vinni meets C2 by offering high-quality beverages with national and international recognition. The fact that Vinni does not necessarily offer a wide variety is insignificant compared to Bubby's failure to provide high-quality beverages or to save time. Lucy chooses Vinni as the superior alternative because the high quality and reasonable time commitment better meet the criteria than does Bubby.

ABOUT THE FIVE-PARAGRAPH FORM

Note the visual balance among the five paragraphs. None of the paragraphs is so long as to visually intimidate the reader nor is any paragraph so short as to be skipped over. All of the paragraphs and all of the sentences within the paragraphs follow the same pattern: introduction, analysis, analysis, analysis, conclusion. Practice using this writing structure—five paragraphs and five sentences—until it becomes second nature. All Essay prompts are fundamentally the same. Only the details of who the decision maker is, what the specific criteria are, and what the specific alternatives are, change. The essential task of defending one alternative based on the criteria is the same. Once you have refined your Essay skills, you will find that you can easily compose a strong essay with time to spare.

Depending on your analytical approach and writing style, you may use one paragraph more or less and you may use one sentence more or less per paragraph. The important thing is to follow the general structure outlined above.

Though the General Directions state that quality is more important than quantity, a short essay, even if it is a complete argument, probably does not make as strong an impression as an equally good essay that is fleshed out to fill the entire answer sheet.

PROOFREAD

Take 2 to 3 minutes at the end to proofread your essay. Catch mistakes and put a final polish on your essay.

Proofreading

After composing your essay, take several minutes to proofread it. Be careful with spelling, punctuation, and grammar. If your writing is illegible in places, correct it. If there are any flaws in your logic, correct them.

Essay Contingency Plan

If the LSAT Essay section differs from what you have practiced, you can still apply the strategies you have learned. Use the rule of fives: five paragraphs and five sentences per paragraph. Outline your approach on the scratch paper by noting the relationships between the key pieces of information. Think through and finalize your approach in your draft before you start to write your full essay. Write your sentences directly and in the present tense. Use your introductory paragraph to summarize all of your main points. Use the next three paragraphs to analyze the topic. Write a strong concluding paragraph.

Summary of Essay-Writing Steps

1. Orient to the prompt.
2. Choose an alternative to defend.
3. Plan your defense.
4. Sketch out your notes in the scratch space.
5. Compose the five-paragraph essay.
6. Proofread your essay.

SAMPLE ESSAY PROMPTS WITH ANALYSIS OF RESPONSES

The following two prompts are each followed by three sample responses, which range from inferior to average to superior. As practice, improve the inferior and average essays.

Sample Essay Prompt A

> **DIRECTIONS:** The situation described below gives two choices. Either one of the choices can be supported based on the information given. In your essay, consider both choices and then argue in favor of one over the other. Base your argument on the two specified criteria and on the given facts. There is no "right" or "wrong" choice. Either choice can be reasonably defended.

Located in the high Sierras next to famous and beautiful Duck Lake, Lakeburg faces an economic depression because its mines have played out. Lakeburg has evaluated two possible companies to rejuvenate its economy. Using the facts given below, compose an essay in which you argue in favor of choosing one alternative over the other on the basis of the two criteria below.

- Lakeburg is developing a reputation for economic development and avoiding environmental mishaps.
- Lakeburg must find new employers who will provide at least a thousand new jobs as the local mines have all closed permanently.

Big Gun Company has approached Lakeburg as a potential site for a new plant. Big Gun's executives love to hunt ducks and they would like to build a private hunting lodge next to Duck Lake. Big Gun promises to bring two thousand new jobs to Lakeburg that pay high wages compared to the tourist business. Big Gun can build its plant within six months of receiving permission. Unfortunately, Big Gun has a reputation for releasing large amounts of liquid wastes into nearby surface waters. After forty years, the effects of the liquid wastes become irreversible.

Camera Resorts, a famous contributor to the Fund to Preserve Duck Environments, proposes to build a world-class tourist resort near Duck Lake. Camera Resorts will construct the resort in stages over a ten-year period and has made provisions to ensure that no pollution will flow into Duck Lake. Camera Resorts will initially add three hundred new jobs as it builds Phase One. Camera Resorts will cut the three hundred new jobs by half after Phase One is complete. Camera Resorts' proposal calls for a series of such additions and layoffs over the ten-year building program. However, by the tenth year, Camera Resorts will continuously employ over one thousand people at the resort.

SAMPLE ESSAY A RESPONSE 1 (INFERIOR)

I select Big Gun as the better alternative. Big Gun will have an immediate positive economic impact on Lakeburg (Burg). While Camera Resorts ("Camera") presents some attractive benefits, Big Gun gives Burg the opportunity to add two thousand new jobs within six months. In the following paragraph I will analyze the two criteria that Burg must weigh. In the third paragraph I will demonstrate why Big Gun is the superior alternative. In the fourth paragraph I will show why Camera is the inferior alternative. In the final paragraph I will defend my selection and draw my conclusion.

The first criterion says Burg has a long tradition of protecting the environment as it develops its economic base. The second criterion says Burg desperately needs new jobs because the mines have closed. In my opinion, Burg needs to take care of its immediate employment problems before the town dies. If Burg is able to entice a company into town, and if the company brings a substantial number of new jobs, then Burg will give itself enough breathing space to be able to handle adverse environmental impacts as they arise. After all, Burg has a history of effectively dealing with large-scale mining operations. Therefore, the second criterion is more important than the first criterion.

Big Gun can build a plant in Burg in six months. The plant will bring two thousand new jobs. These new jobs will have an immediate positive impact on Burg's economy. While Big Gun is a known polluter, the effects of the pollution do not become irreversible for forty years. Assuming the pollution process can be successfully reversed, Burg will buy the time it needs to survive if it selects Big Gun. Big Gun is Burg's superior alternative because it will ensure Burg's survival.

Camera promises to bring nearly one thousand jobs over time and promises not to pollute Duck Lake. New jobs are attractive to Burg. Camera's promise to keep the environment relatively pollution free is also quite attractive. However, if Burg chooses Camera, the new jobs will come too late to save the town. If Burg is unable to develop new jobs quickly, Duck Lake's beauty will be enjoyed by only a few leftover hermits. Camera is an inferior alternative because it will not ensure Burg's survival.

Burg's dire economic need for immediate new jobs leaves the town little choice. True, Big Gun brings the drawback of its sordid history as well as the promise of new jobs. However, if Burg can properly manage Big Gun, Big Gun's overall economic impact will be sufficiently positive to override Big Gun's potential problems. Camera is the inferior alternative because Camera will fail to bring a positive economic impact soon enough to save the town. In conclusion, Burg should select Big Gun as its best alternative.

Comments on the Inferior Response

Sample Essay A Response 1 is inferior to the following responses because it is too long. The author wastes space by failing to use acronyms (and forgets to use the quotation marks around "Burg"). The author relies on extreme interpretations, such as predicting that the town will fail unless it brings in immediate cash. The author uses the first person as well as many adjectives and adverbs, which subjectively taint the essay and could polarize the admission committee readers.

In the first paragraph, it is not necessary or effective to use wording such as "In the following paragraph I will analyze the two criteria that Burg must weigh." The second paragraph is ineffective in analyzing the criteria. The third paragraph erroneously concludes by saying that the superior alternative will ensure the survival of the decision maker because no alternative will ensure the decision maker's success or failure. The fourth paragraph is adequate. The fifth paragraph is verbose.

SAMPLE ESSAY A RESPONSE 2 (AVERAGE)

Big Gun ("BG") is Lakeburg's ("LB") better alternative. BG will have an immediate positive economic impact on LB. While Camera Resorts ("CR") presents some attractive benefits, BG gives LB the opportunity to add two thousand new jobs within six months. LB must weigh two criteria. BG is the superior alternative based on the criteria. CR is the inferior alternative based on the criteria.

The first criterion says LB has a long tradition of protecting the environment as it develops its economic base. The second criterion says LB desperately needs new jobs because the mines have closed. If LB can entice a company into town, and if the company brings a substantial number of new jobs, then LB will give itself enough space to be able to handle adverse environmental impacts as they arise. Therefore, the second criterion is more important than the first criterion.

BG can build a plant in LB in six months. The plant brings two thousand new jobs. These new jobs have an immediate positive impact on LB's economy. While BG is a known polluter, the effects of the pollution do not become irreversible for forty years. Assuming the pollution process can be successfully reversed, LB buys the time it needs to survive if LB selects BG.

CR promises to bring nearly one thousand jobs over time and promises not to pollute Duck Lake. New jobs are attractive to LB. CR's promise to keep the environment relatively pollution free is attractive. However, if LB chooses CR, the new jobs come too late to save LB. If LB is unable to develop new jobs quickly, DL's beauty will go unappreciated. CR is LB's inferior alternative because CR fails to ensure LB's survival.

LB's need for immediate new jobs leaves LB little choice. True, BG brings the drawback of its sordid history. However, if LB can properly manage BG, BG's economic impact is enough to override BG's problems. CR is LB's inferior alternative because CR fails to bring a positive economic impact soon enough to save LB. In conclusion, LB should select BG as its best alternative.

Comments on the Average Response

Sample Essay A's Response 2 is better than Response 1 because it is more succinct, using fewer words. Response 2 is also more objective because it avoids the first person. The author uses acronyms instead of pronouns, which saves time and space, although the author forgets to introduce the acronym for Duck Lake. This essay is also terse in some areas and tends to wander in others. It also interprets the facts in an extreme way that is unwarranted, in order to make its argument sound stronger.

The first paragraph claims that the alternatives are strong or weak based on the criteria but does not indicate how the alternatives meet or do not meet the criteria. The second paragraph fails to relate the two criteria to each other. The third and fourth paragraphs are adequate. The fifth paragraph skims over the facts, is dramatic, and is therefore subjective.

SAMPLE ESSAY A RESPONSE 3 (SUPERIOR)

Lakeburg ("LB") chooses Big Gun Company ("BG") because BG creates 2,000 new jobs and BG's possible pollution of Duck Lake ("DL") may be mitigated. LB uses two criteria, which are that LB needs new jobs and that LB will avoid undue pollution to DL, to choose between BG and Camera Resorts ("CR"). BG is LB's superior alternative because BG brings many new jobs and likely will not harm DL. LB rejects CR because CR fails to provide as many long-term jobs as BG. Therefore, BG is LB's superior alternative because BG meets LB's selection criteria better than CR.

LB uses two criteria to choose between BG and CR. One criterion is that LB wants to promote economic development while discouraging polluting industries, whereas the other criterion is that LB needs many new jobs because LB's former employers have closed. Combined, the criteria say that LB needs many new jobs and wants to avoid polluting DL. The first criterion is critical because LB may lose population if LB fails to bring in a large employer quickly. The second criterion is important but LB's priority is to recruit a large employer or lose population.

BG is LB's superior choice because BG brings 2,000 new jobs and avoids polluting DL. BG meets the first criterion by bringing 2,000 permanent jobs to LB within six months. BG meets the second criterion because BG's managers love duck hunting and will preserve DL's water quality. While BG's wastes could contaminate DL, LB has forty years to regulate BG's outflow. Therefore, BG is a superior alternative to CR because BG brings many new jobs and probably will not harm DL.

CR is LB's inferior alternative. CR brings only 300 as opposed to BG's 2,000 jobs, and CR's number of jobs ebbs and flows over time. CR supports environmental causes and is committed to protect DL. However, even CR's promise not to pollute DL will not meet LB's economic needs. Therefore, LB rejects CR as LB's inferior alternative.

LB chooses BG. BG brings 2,000 new jobs, which will revitalize LB's economy. BG's managers will preserve their favorite hunting waters on DL. Even though BG could pollute DL, CR is inferior to BG because CR fails to bring enough new jobs to LB. In conclusion, BG is LB's superior alternative because BG better meets LB's need to create a large number of jobs and BG's managers will work to protect DL.

Comments on the Superior Response

Response 3 is superior to the first two responses because it presents a well-balanced argument that is supported by the facts. The author effectively uses *hereinafter referred to as* notation. The first paragraph summarizes all the main points of the essay. The second paragraph analyzes the two criteria and relates them to each other. The third and fourth paragraphs respectively analyze the two alternatives by comparing them to the criteria and then to each other. The fifth paragraph succinctly restates the facts and demonstrates why one alternative is superior to the other when the criteria are applied.

On the whole, Response 3 is fairly objective and takes on the challenge of supporting Big Gun. This task is difficult to achieve in the face of Big Gun's history of emitting pollution.

Sample Essay Prompt B

> **DIRECTIONS:** The situation described below gives two choices. Either one of the choices can be supported based on the information given. In your essay, consider both choices and then argue in favor of one over the other. Base your argument on the two specified criteria and on the given facts. There is no "right" or "wrong" choice. Either choice can be reasonably defended.

Renne Trust inherited the copyrights for a successful series of novels from the late Leslie Banks. Renne Trust is searching for a new author to write a concluding novel in order to generate a large royalty stream. Using the facts given below, compose an essay in which you argue in favor of choosing one alternative over the other on the basis of the two criteria below:

- Renne Trust wants to hire an experienced author with a proven audience.
- Renne Trust is a relatively private charitable organization that purposefully avoids the social spotlight.

Jacque Porsta is a famous fiction writer with a flair for throwing large and wild parties on his yacht. In fact, Porsta has been known to write entire trilogies of pulp fiction in order to pay off his entertainment-related debts. Porsta's paperback novels have an exciting and flowing style that enraptures his large fan base. Porsta's novels are action packed and amusing, and he likes to feature his central character as a cornerstone of each of his novels. Porsta has publicly admitted an unrequited love for Leslie Banks and would dearly love an opportunity to be associated with Banks's work.

Tedori Fino was Leslie Banks's assistant during the final phases of Ms. Banks's writing career. Fino is a quiet and unassuming person who extended Ms. Banks every courtesy during her final years. It is rumored that Fino actually assisted Ms. Banks in writing her last two books and has a profound understanding of Ms. Banks's intentions, writing style, and characters. Fino has a degree in English literature and has authored several comparative literary reviews, one of which is published, and is frequently cited in academic circles. It is rumored that Fino and Banks may have had a romantic, as well as a working, relationship.

SAMPLE ESSAY QUESTION B RESPONSE 1 (INFERIOR)

Jacque Porsta is the obvious choice for Renne Trust. Porsta is likely to produce a positive income stream for them with his wild stories. While Tedori Fino presents some attractive benefits, Porsta brings Renne the money they are looking for. Renne has to consider two criteria but still Porsta comes out on top. Fino does not offer much except the same old status quo.

The first criterion says Renne wants an experienced writer who has a large following. The second criterion says Renne wants to remain out of the spotlight. I do not know how they expect to have their cake and eat it too. Renne needs to take care of its immediate budgetary problems before it dies for lack of financial input. If Renne can engage a well-known author, the probability is Renne will receive enough profit to survive.

Porsta's novel is sure to be a financial success. While Porsta is known for his exuberant personal lifestyle and his bawdy novels, his sensationalism will not damage Renne's reputation forever. In fact, Porsta will probably bring fame to this otherwise stodgy group. They can probably use it.

Fino seems to me like old baggage. Fino's understanding of Banks's work is all well and good, but most likely anything he ever wrote for her was just an imitation of her style. However, if Renne chooses Fino over Porsta for whatever reason, they assume a greater economic risk. It is doubtful that Fino's work would become popular and then Renne will face an uncertain future.

Renne's current need to survive economically leaves them little choice. True, Porsta brings the drawback of his sensationalism. However, if Renne can properly control Porsta's lifestyle and bawdy writing, or at least channel them to their own purposes, his positive economic impact would override his sensational style. There is no real reason why Renne should not go for the gusto.

Comments on the Inferior Response

This response represents a common erroneous approach. It assumes that the task is to find one right answer and one wrong answer. The essay then proceeds to use extreme language to make the "right" answer seem as good as possible and the "wrong" answer seem as bad as possible. This essay also falls into the common fatal flaw of writing in the style of an English composition. The author's opinion is injected into the essay regularly. The effect is that the argument is not based on logic and is not grounded in the actual criteria. An additional misconception of this author is that the purpose of the essay is to entertain or to exhibit clever use of language.

The author's use of pronouns is often ambiguous. The use of the first person seriously hurts the essay. The author fails to use any significant elements of legal writing. The overall effect of this essay on the admissions committee would be concern about whether the applicant was able to construct a valid logical argument. In addition, it would be clear that the applicant did not have any experience with legal writing.

SAMPLE ESSAY QUESTION B RESPONSE 2 (AVERAGE)

Porsta (P) is Renne Trust's ("RT") superior alternative. P is likely to produce a positive economic impact on RT. RT must consider both of the two criteria in order to make a decision. The criteria show why P would be RT's superior alternative and why Fino would be their inferior one.

The first criterion says RT wants to hire an experienced author with a large fan base. The second criterion says RT is proud of its uncontroversial tradition. It seems like it would be hard to meet both criteria. However, the first criterion is more important to RT than the second criterion.

P's novel is sure to be a financial success. P meets the requirement of the more important criterion, which is to ensure RT's financial future. RT's selection of P buys RT some needed time. P is RT's superior alternative because his work ensures RT's survival.

F does not have the fan base or the writing skills to be successful. There is no real reason to choose F.

RT's current need to survive economically leaves RT little choice. P's positive economic impact will benefit them. F is RT's inferior alternative because F does not have anything to offer. In conclusion, RT should select P as its better alternative.

Comments on the Average Response

Sample Essay B Response 2 is somewhat better than Response 1 because the author does not intrude into the essay as much and because it uses legal writing style slightly more effectively. The essay is overly terse because it omits many of the facts needed to support its framework. In the first paragraph, the author uses the *hereinafter referred to as* notation incorrectly (forgetting the quotation marks around "P") and forgets to use the notation for Fino. The phrase "both of the two criteria" is redundant. In the last sentence, legal-style writing would replace "would be" with "is." Logically, it does not help the argument to simply say that the criteria show why one alternative is better.

In the second paragraph, the author correctly summarizes the criteria but then throws in a personal value judgment that is irrelevant. Then the author arbitrarily states that the first criterion is more important without explaining why.

In the third paragraph, the author fails to address the weakness of P. Simply stating only the strengths of one party and only the weaknesses of the other does not make a convincing argument. In addition, the second paragraph uses extreme statements to try to make the case sound stronger than it is.

The fourth paragraph falls into the same trap of dismissing F without addressing F's strengths. The conclusion also relies on pointing out only the good about P and only the bad about F. As a result, the argument is not convincing. A reader would be likely to consider the author deficient in rigorous logical analysis. The elements of legal writing style are used sporadically, sometimes correctly and sometimes not. Certain elements that do not belong in legal writing style, such as the author's personal reflections in *It seems like it would be hard to meet both criteria*, might call into question the author's ability to be objective.

SAMPLE ESSAY QUESTION B RESPONSE 3 (SUPERIOR)

Renne Trust ("RT") chooses Porsta ("P") because P's work generates a large income stream and P might not embarrass RT. RT uses two criteria, which are that RT wants to hire a writer with an established readership and that RT wants to avoid publicity, to select between P and Fino ("F"). P is RT's superior alternative because P's book draws a large audience and P's outspoken love for Banks ("B") is charming, not sensational. F is RT's inferior alternative because F is unknown outside of academic circles, and F's relationship with B possibly could cause a scandal. P is therefore RT's better choice because P better meets RT's selection criteria.

RT uses two criteria to choose between P and F. One criterion is that RT wants to hire an experienced author with a large fan base. The second criterion is that RT wants to preserve its anonymity. Combined, these criteria say that RT wishes to generate income by hiring a well-known author and to simultaneously avoid publicity. RT's goal to generate a large income stream is more pressing than RT's need for anonymity.

P is RT's superior alternative because P already has a large following and P will commit to finishing B's book without incident. P's fan base buys all of his novels, and his previously declared love for Banks is old news and unlikely to create a scandal. Unfortunately, P's penchant for throwing wild parties may create a controversy. However, P is RT's superior alternative because P's established fan base ensures RT's new revenue stream.

F is RT's inferior alternative. F simply does not have the fan base needed to guarantee RT a new income stream. F's secret relationship with B could well bring a scandal to RT's front door. While F has a solid knowledge of B's thoughts and has had some recent literary success, F's lack of readership points to P as RT's better choice. Therefore, RT rejects F as the less desirable alternative.

P is RT's superior alternative. P is more likely than F to generate a new revenue stream. P's former relationship with B brings a romantic ambience rather than scandal to B's final novel. F simply does not bring the economic firepower of P's established fan base. In conclusion, RT selects P because P generates a large number of sales and will behave well in order to protect RT's reputation.

Comments on the Superior Response

This response is superior to the two previous responses. The first paragraph of this response solidly summarizes the main arguments. The second paragraph presents a well-balanced analysis of the two criteria, combines them into a single statement, and then states the governing criteria. The third paragraph builds the argument in favor of Porsta but could be made stronger by using additional facts. The fourth paragraph adequately debunks Fino. The final paragraph concludes adequately.

SUMMARY

The main purpose of the essay is to impress the admissions committee with (1) your understanding of legal writing style, and (2) your ability to present an argument logically and impartially. The committee is much more likely to look at these two elements than to examine the actual reasons that you give for defending an answer. If you have difficulty coming up with a convincing reason that one alternative is superior to the other, simply move forward with composing a well-organized essay, using legal writing elements.

This chapter explained the importance of the Essay and oriented you to the components—the General Directions, the Essay directions, and the prompt (including the setup, the criteria, and the alternatives)—and to the task itself. The language skills necessary for the Essay and for legal writing were discussed, including the *hereinafter referred to as* notation, the use of simple active verbs, avoiding pronouns and adjectives, the use of short sentences, and keeping oneself out of the argument by avoiding personal opinions and the first-person pronoun. Common language errors were described.

The chapter explained how to create the Essay by orienting to the prompt, choosing an alternative, and planning your defense. Instructions were given for composing the five paragraphs of the Essay, in which the first paragraph introduces and summarizes your argument, the second analyzes the criteria, the third analyzes and supports the superior alternative, the fourth analyzes and attacks the inferior alternative, and the fifth restates your argument and concludes. Proofreading was discussed and a contingency plan provided.

SECTION TEST: WRITING SAMPLE (ESSAY)

Time: 35 minutes

GENERAL DIRECTIONS: You will have 35 minutes to organize and write an essay on the topic described on the next page. Read the topic and all of the directions carefully. It is generally best to take a few minutes to organize your thoughts before beginning to write. Be sure to develop your ideas fully and leave time at the end to review what you have written. **Do not write on any topic other than the topic given. It is not acceptable to write on a topic of your own choice.**

No special knowledge is needed or expected for this essay. Admission committees are interested in your reasoning, clarity, organization, use of language, and writing mechanics. The quality of what you write is more important than the quantity.

Keep your essay in the blocked and lined area on the front and back of the separate Writing Sample Response Sheet. That is the only area that will be reproduced and sent to law schools. Be sure to write legibly.

SCRATCH PAPER
Do not write your essay here. Scratch work only.

DIRECTIONS: The situation described below gives two choices. Either one of the choices can be supported based on the information given. In your essay, consider both choices and then argue in favor of one over the other. Base your argument on the two specified criteria and on the given facts. There is no "right" or "wrong" choice. Either choice can be reasonably defended.

Jerry Rodgers, the superintendent of schools in the town of Edburg, is considering whether to continue to utilize the district's in-house Human Resources department or to outsource the district's Human Resources functions to a local employment company, EXL-Pro. All of the other school districts in the region maintain their HR departments in-house. Using the facts given below, compose an essay in which you argue in favor of choosing one alternative over the other on the basis of the two criteria below:

- Jerry wants to preserve the district's tradition of hiring and retaining excellent teachers and staff.
- Jerry needs more funds to upgrade the district's science laboratories, sports equipment, and musical instruments.

Outsourcing the District's HR function to EXL-Pro would allow Jerry to save significant funds and free up administrative resources in order to build new facilities and manage the inflow of new equipment. The district would become a model for innovative administration within the region. There would be higher initial costs associated with migrating databases and hard-copy files to a new HR contractor but those costs would likely be offset by the savings realized over the contract's expected ten-year lifespan. There could be higher teacher turnover and a loss of instructional quality in the event EXL-Pro fails to screen faculty applicants properly. The district's outstanding academic reputation may suffer as a result.

Retaining the district's HR department would be expensive and the costs associated with the department would likely rise over time. The HR department is staffed by senior professionals who pride themselves in building and maintaining the finest faculty and staff in the region. The district's current HR department manages personnel issues in a forthright manner that frees Jerry's administrative time. The retirement of the senior HR professionals could slowly erode the quality of the district's faculty. While the school district is currently experiencing a revenue shortfall, the district is making strides to increase the long-term tax revenues to the schools by recruiting new businesses to town. Jerry knows that local, high-quality educational institutions are an important factor in attracting new businesses to Edburg.

SCRATCH PAPER
Do not write your essay here. Scratch work only.

WRITING SAMPLE RESPONSE SHEET

Use the lined area below to write your essay. Continue on the back if you need more space.

EXAMPLE OF A SUPERIOR RESPONSE TO THE ESSAY

Jerry ("J") retains the HR Dept. ("Retain") because Retain allows J to keep the district's ("District") outstanding faculty and promote District's reputation to increase its tax base. J desires to preserve District's excellent personnel and enhance District's equipment without surpassing District's budget. Retain is J's better choice because Retain keeps District's seasoned professionals and gives J credibility to recruit new businesses to increase District's tax revenues. EXL-Pro ("EXL") is J's inferior alternative because EXL could erode District's faculty and staff and thereby disrupt District's ability to attract new businesses. Therefore Retain is J's better choice because Retain better meets District's long-term faculty and funding needs.

J uses two criteria to choose between Retain and EXL. One criterion says J wants to preserve District's excellent faculty and staff. The second criterion says J needs funds to enhance District's labs, sports, and music programs. These criteria may be conjoined into a single rule that says J desires to keep District's staff and find money to buy new equipment. Overall, J's long-term goal to preserve District's faculty is more important than District's short-term need to purchase equipment.

Retain is J's better choice because Retain allows District to preserve its superior faculty and increase District's tax revenues. District's HR Dept. builds District's staff and manages personnel issues forthrightly. Retain gives J needed credibility to impress new businesses and thereby enhance District's tax base. Unfortunately, District's HR Dept. is expensive and its costs may increase. However, Retain is J's better choice because Retain fulfills District's need to preserve its high-quality faculty and increase its tax revenues.

EXL is J's inferior choice. EXL could erode the quality of District's faculty and staff if EXL fails to correctly screen new candidates. EXL's initial high costs could negate District's plans for new laboratories, sports equipment, and instruments. While EXL could save District money over ten years, in the event District and EXL disagree, it would be difficult for District to replace its HR department. Therefore, EXL is District's less desirable alternative.

Retain is J's better choice. Retain is more likely than EXL to maintain District's quality staff over the long term. Retain will give J credibility to recruit businesses and increase District's tax base. EXL is initially expensive and is a risky alternative. In conclusion, J selects Retain because Retain better serves District's faculty and funding needs over time.

Practice Tests

ANSWER SHEET
Practice Test 1

SECTION I

1. Ⓐ Ⓑ Ⓒ Ⓓ Ⓔ   8. Ⓐ Ⓑ Ⓒ Ⓓ Ⓔ   15. Ⓐ Ⓑ Ⓒ Ⓓ Ⓔ   22. Ⓐ Ⓑ Ⓒ Ⓓ Ⓔ
2. Ⓐ Ⓑ Ⓒ Ⓓ Ⓔ   9. Ⓐ Ⓑ Ⓒ Ⓓ Ⓔ   16. Ⓐ Ⓑ Ⓒ Ⓓ Ⓔ   23. Ⓐ Ⓑ Ⓒ Ⓓ Ⓔ
3. Ⓐ Ⓑ Ⓒ Ⓓ Ⓔ   10. Ⓐ Ⓑ Ⓒ Ⓓ Ⓔ   17. Ⓐ Ⓑ Ⓒ Ⓓ Ⓔ   24. Ⓐ Ⓑ Ⓒ Ⓓ Ⓔ
4. Ⓐ Ⓑ Ⓒ Ⓓ Ⓔ   11. Ⓐ Ⓑ Ⓒ Ⓓ Ⓔ   18. Ⓐ Ⓑ Ⓒ Ⓓ Ⓔ   25. Ⓐ Ⓑ Ⓒ Ⓓ Ⓔ
5. Ⓐ Ⓑ Ⓒ Ⓓ Ⓔ   12. Ⓐ Ⓑ Ⓒ Ⓓ Ⓔ   19. Ⓐ Ⓑ Ⓒ Ⓓ Ⓔ   26. Ⓐ Ⓑ Ⓒ Ⓓ Ⓔ
6. Ⓐ Ⓑ Ⓒ Ⓓ Ⓔ   13. Ⓐ Ⓑ Ⓒ Ⓓ Ⓔ   20. Ⓐ Ⓑ Ⓒ Ⓓ Ⓔ   27. Ⓐ Ⓑ Ⓒ Ⓓ Ⓔ
7. Ⓐ Ⓑ Ⓒ Ⓓ Ⓔ   14. Ⓐ Ⓑ Ⓒ Ⓓ Ⓔ   21. Ⓐ Ⓑ Ⓒ Ⓓ Ⓔ   28. Ⓐ Ⓑ Ⓒ Ⓓ Ⓔ

SECTION II

1. Ⓐ Ⓑ Ⓒ Ⓓ Ⓔ   8. Ⓐ Ⓑ Ⓒ Ⓓ Ⓔ   15. Ⓐ Ⓑ Ⓒ Ⓓ Ⓔ   22. Ⓐ Ⓑ Ⓒ Ⓓ Ⓔ
2. Ⓐ Ⓑ Ⓒ Ⓓ Ⓔ   9. Ⓐ Ⓑ Ⓒ Ⓓ Ⓔ   16. Ⓐ Ⓑ Ⓒ Ⓓ Ⓔ   23. Ⓐ Ⓑ Ⓒ Ⓓ Ⓔ
3. Ⓐ Ⓑ Ⓒ Ⓓ Ⓔ   10. Ⓐ Ⓑ Ⓒ Ⓓ Ⓔ   17. Ⓐ Ⓑ Ⓒ Ⓓ Ⓔ   24. Ⓐ Ⓑ Ⓒ Ⓓ Ⓔ
4. Ⓐ Ⓑ Ⓒ Ⓓ Ⓔ   11. Ⓐ Ⓑ Ⓒ Ⓓ Ⓔ   18. Ⓐ Ⓑ Ⓒ Ⓓ Ⓔ   25. Ⓐ Ⓑ Ⓒ Ⓓ Ⓔ
5. Ⓐ Ⓑ Ⓒ Ⓓ Ⓔ   12. Ⓐ Ⓑ Ⓒ Ⓓ Ⓔ   19. Ⓐ Ⓑ Ⓒ Ⓓ Ⓔ   26. Ⓐ Ⓑ Ⓒ Ⓓ Ⓔ
6. Ⓐ Ⓑ Ⓒ Ⓓ Ⓔ   13. Ⓐ Ⓑ Ⓒ Ⓓ Ⓔ   20. Ⓐ Ⓑ Ⓒ Ⓓ Ⓔ   27. Ⓐ Ⓑ Ⓒ Ⓓ Ⓔ
7. Ⓐ Ⓑ Ⓒ Ⓓ Ⓔ   14. Ⓐ Ⓑ Ⓒ Ⓓ Ⓔ   21. Ⓐ Ⓑ Ⓒ Ⓓ Ⓔ   28. Ⓐ Ⓑ Ⓒ Ⓓ Ⓔ

SECTION III

1. Ⓐ Ⓑ Ⓒ Ⓓ Ⓔ   8. Ⓐ Ⓑ Ⓒ Ⓓ Ⓔ   15. Ⓐ Ⓑ Ⓒ Ⓓ Ⓔ   22. Ⓐ Ⓑ Ⓒ Ⓓ Ⓔ
2. Ⓐ Ⓑ Ⓒ Ⓓ Ⓔ   9. Ⓐ Ⓑ Ⓒ Ⓓ Ⓔ   16. Ⓐ Ⓑ Ⓒ Ⓓ Ⓔ   23. Ⓐ Ⓑ Ⓒ Ⓓ Ⓔ
3. Ⓐ Ⓑ Ⓒ Ⓓ Ⓔ   10. Ⓐ Ⓑ Ⓒ Ⓓ Ⓔ   17. Ⓐ Ⓑ Ⓒ Ⓓ Ⓔ   24. Ⓐ Ⓑ Ⓒ Ⓓ Ⓔ
4. Ⓐ Ⓑ Ⓒ Ⓓ Ⓔ   11. Ⓐ Ⓑ Ⓒ Ⓓ Ⓔ   18. Ⓐ Ⓑ Ⓒ Ⓓ Ⓔ   25. Ⓐ Ⓑ Ⓒ Ⓓ Ⓔ
5. Ⓐ Ⓑ Ⓒ Ⓓ Ⓔ   12. Ⓐ Ⓑ Ⓒ Ⓓ Ⓔ   19. Ⓐ Ⓑ Ⓒ Ⓓ Ⓔ   26. Ⓐ Ⓑ Ⓒ Ⓓ Ⓔ
6. Ⓐ Ⓑ Ⓒ Ⓓ Ⓔ   13. Ⓐ Ⓑ Ⓒ Ⓓ Ⓔ   20. Ⓐ Ⓑ Ⓒ Ⓓ Ⓔ   27. Ⓐ Ⓑ Ⓒ Ⓓ Ⓔ
7. Ⓐ Ⓑ Ⓒ Ⓓ Ⓔ   14. Ⓐ Ⓑ Ⓒ Ⓓ Ⓔ   21. Ⓐ Ⓑ Ⓒ Ⓓ Ⓔ   28. Ⓐ Ⓑ Ⓒ Ⓓ Ⓔ

SECTION IV

1. Ⓐ Ⓑ Ⓒ Ⓓ Ⓔ   8. Ⓐ Ⓑ Ⓒ Ⓓ Ⓔ   15. Ⓐ Ⓑ Ⓒ Ⓓ Ⓔ   22. Ⓐ Ⓑ Ⓒ Ⓓ Ⓔ
2. Ⓐ Ⓑ Ⓒ Ⓓ Ⓔ   9. Ⓐ Ⓑ Ⓒ Ⓓ Ⓔ   16. Ⓐ Ⓑ Ⓒ Ⓓ Ⓔ   23. Ⓐ Ⓑ Ⓒ Ⓓ Ⓔ
3. Ⓐ Ⓑ Ⓒ Ⓓ Ⓔ   10. Ⓐ Ⓑ Ⓒ Ⓓ Ⓔ   17. Ⓐ Ⓑ Ⓒ Ⓓ Ⓔ   24. Ⓐ Ⓑ Ⓒ Ⓓ Ⓔ
4. Ⓐ Ⓑ Ⓒ Ⓓ Ⓔ   11. Ⓐ Ⓑ Ⓒ Ⓓ Ⓔ   18. Ⓐ Ⓑ Ⓒ Ⓓ Ⓔ   25. Ⓐ Ⓑ Ⓒ Ⓓ Ⓔ
5. Ⓐ Ⓑ Ⓒ Ⓓ Ⓔ   12. Ⓐ Ⓑ Ⓒ Ⓓ Ⓔ   19. Ⓐ Ⓑ Ⓒ Ⓓ Ⓔ   26. Ⓐ Ⓑ Ⓒ Ⓓ Ⓔ
6. Ⓐ Ⓑ Ⓒ Ⓓ Ⓔ   13. Ⓐ Ⓑ Ⓒ Ⓓ Ⓔ   20. Ⓐ Ⓑ Ⓒ Ⓓ Ⓔ   27. Ⓐ Ⓑ Ⓒ Ⓓ Ⓔ
7. Ⓐ Ⓑ Ⓒ Ⓓ Ⓔ   14. Ⓐ Ⓑ Ⓒ Ⓓ Ⓔ   21. Ⓐ Ⓑ Ⓒ Ⓓ Ⓔ   28. Ⓐ Ⓑ Ⓒ Ⓓ Ⓔ

Practice Test 1

SECTION I

Time: 35 minutes
26 Questions

DIRECTIONS: The questions in this section are based on the reasoning contained in brief statements or passages. More than one answer choice could conceivably answer the question in some cases. However, you should choose the <u>best</u> answer. The best answer is the response that answers the question most accurately and completely. You should avoid making any assumptions that, by commonsense standards, are implausible, superfluous, or incompatible with the passage. When you have chosen the best answer, fill in the space on your answer sheet that corresponds to your answer.

1. Medical ethicist: If a patient does not report health problems, does not respond to the physician's suggestions for improving the patient's health, and does not ask for the physician's help, the conscientious physician should ask if the patient would prefer to see a different physician.

   Which one of the following principles, if valid, provides the most support for the medical ethicist's argument?

   (A) Unless a patient discusses health issues with a physician, the physician cannot make an accurate diagnosis.

   (B) Unless a patient discusses health issues with a physician, the physician must depend on the reports of the patient's family to make an accurate diagnosis.

   (C) A physician should not force a patient to talk about health issues with which the patient may be uncomfortable.

   (D) If a patient does not discuss health issues with a physician, the problem may be with the physician.

   (E) A physician should not spend time with a patient who refuses to cooperate.

GO ON TO THE NEXT PAGE

2. Ecologists are wary of any nonnative plant species that is accidentally introduced into a natural environment. There are multiple examples of a single nonnative plant species radically disrupting an ecosystem. In some cases millions of dollars have been spent to repair the damage. In other cases the economic loss due to the disruption has been in the millions. Whether or not a nonnative plant species has the potential to disrupt an ecosystem depends on many factors and only rarely can a nonnative species even survive in such a context, let alone become disruptive.

The statements above, if true, most strongly support which one of the following statements?

(A) Ecologists should plan to test a nonnative plant for its potential to cause disruption before introducing it into a natural environment.

(B) Any nonnative plant species that appears in a natural environment should be eradicated, even if the cost of doing so is high.

(C) If the ecology of a natural environment becomes radically disrupted, it is probably because of a nonnative plant species.

(D) If a nonnative plant species survives in a natural environment, it is probable that the species will disrupt that ecosystem.

(E) When a nonnative plant is introduced into a natural environment, it will probably not disrupt the ecosystem.

3. Small business owner: In deciding on a new location for a business, it is a mistake to base the decision on circumstantial information such as whether or not similar businesses exist in the area. Suppose, for example, that someone wants to open a shoe store. If there are no shoe stores in a certain location, does that mean that the location is ripe for a shoe store or that no shoe store has been able to survive there? Similarly, if there are already three shoe stores in the location, does that mean that the location is saturated with shoe stores or that there is a strong demand for shoe stores there?

The claim that in deciding a new location for a business, it is a mistake to base the decision on circumstantial information such as whether or not similar businesses exist in the area plays which one of the following roles in the small business owner's argument?

(A) It is a hypothesis that is used to explain contradictions that are introduced later in the argument.

(B) It is a claim that the argument attempts to defend by pointing to contradictory interpretations of circumstantial information.

(C) It is a premise that the argument shows through examples to be contradictory.

(D) It is the answer to questions that the argument poses later in the passage.

(E) It is a conclusion that describes a causal relationship between the presence of a type of business in a particular location and the probability of a similar business being successful in that location.

GO ON TO THE NEXT PAGE

4. A study of two hundred people attempted to evaluate how easily people adapt to new word processing software. All people in the study had approximately two years of experience using some word processing software and were equally proficient. The study tested the latest version of the word processing program TypeSoFast, which is not yet available to the public. The people in group A had used the previous version of TypeSoFast for at least two years. The people in group B had never used any version of TypeSoFast. Both groups were given a text to type. The group that had previously used TypeSoFast took an average of forty minutes to type the text. The other group took an average of thirty minutes.

Each of the following, if true, helps to explain the findings of the research cited above EXCEPT:

(A) The people in group A relied primarily on typing without looking at the computer screen, whereas the people in group B typed by looking back and forth from the text to the computer screen.

(B) The people in group B had a higher incidence of mistyped words.

(C) The two groups performed their tasks in different rooms in the same research building and on different days.

(D) The new version of TypeSoFast had significant differences from the old version that made it more similar to standard word processing programs.

(E) The copy of the text that group A received inadvertently had some misspelled words in it.

5. Some people have expressed a concern that the city council is not qualified to make an informed decision on the technical feasibility of the proposed solar power plant. Even though none of the city council members is an engineer, each member has shown the ability to intelligently evaluate technical material. With such capable members, the city council is unlikely to make a poor decision.

The reasoning in the argument is flawed in that the argument

(A) infers that something cannot occur on the basis that it is unlikely to occur

(B) assumes that there are no other options in a situation in which there may be other options

(C) infers that something is true of a whole solely on the basis that it is true of each of the parts

(D) accepts something as untrue because it has not been proven to be true

(E) treats information that supports a conclusion as information that proves a conclusion

GO ON TO THE NEXT PAGE

6. Nonviolent resistance as a tool for political change is a misnomer. Even though such resistance is called nonviolent, any political movement that threatens the status quo will serve as a lightning rod for violent reaction. Whereas the political movements spearheaded by Gandhi and Dr. Martin Luther King, Jr., did not result in the amount of bloodshed that the French revolution did, for example, these so-called nonviolent movements resulted, in both cases, in the assassination of a critical political leader, as well as countless episodes of beatings and other violent actions on the part of security forces.

Which one of the following best expresses the conclusion drawn in the argument above?

(A) Some nonviolent movements have resulted in the assassination of important political leaders.

(B) Nonviolent resistance should not be used as a tool for political change.

(C) It is idealistic to believe that nonviolent resistance can change the status quo.

(D) Nonviolent resistance, even though it always involves some violence, may be less violent than other tools for political change.

(E) Nonviolent resistance as a tool for political change involves violence.

7. Horticulturist: Some people describe themselves as "natural gardeners." However, it is not possible to be a gardener without being natural. Gardening by definition involves working with nature. For this reason, people who call themselves gardeners should not call themselves natural gardeners.

The horticulturist's conclusion follows logically if which one of the following is assumed?

(A) Everything in the world is natural in that it is part of nature.

(B) People should not refer to themselves with a term that is inaccurate.

(C) If a quality by which one refers to oneself inherently includes a second quality, one should not use both qualities to refer to oneself.

(D) There is no meaning of the word *natural* that would result in it being possible to be a gardener without being natural.

(E) It is not possible to be natural without also being a gardener.

GO ON TO THE NEXT PAGE

8. People who successfully file for bankruptcy are at least partially relieved of the expense of paying off old debts. At the same time, they are typically offered credit that they previously would not have qualified for by virtue of the fact that they cannot declare bankruptcy again for a number of years. These two facts probably account for why people who have recently completed a successful application for bankruptcy often feel unexpectedly prosperous.

Which one of the following, if true, would most strengthen the reasoning in the argument?

(A) Most people feel relieved after successfully filing for bankruptcy.

(B) Most people do not expect to have their bankruptcy application approved.

(C) In offering new credit to a customer, some credit card companies will absolve the customer of a portion of past credit card debt that was not absolved by bankruptcy.

(D) A credit card company to which a customer continues to owe a balance after successfully filing for bankruptcy will often offer the customer a new credit card once the bankruptcy filing is completed.

(E) Most people are surprised to find that the cost of filing for bankruptcy is far less than they had expected.

9. Student: Our school's debate team is one of the highest-scoring teams in the country. Jessica is on our debate team, so she must be one of the highest-scoring debaters in the country.

The flawed pattern of reasoning in which one of the following is most closely parallel to the reasoning in the student's argument?

(A) Every honor student at our school is a member of the chess club, so the chess club must have the highest percentage of honor students of any club at our school.

(B) The state legislature never approves new funding for recreation. Jeremy is a member of the state legislature, so he must never have voted for new funding for recreation.

(C) Vegetables are good for you. Okra is a vegetable, so okra must be good for you.

(D) Every book in the library annex has been there for at least thirty years, so the library annex must have been there for at least thirty years.

(E) Every flower in the garden is yellow. Marissa planted the garden, so Marissa must prefer yellow flowers.

GO ON TO THE NEXT PAGE

10. If you find a wallet on the street with $100 in it, you should keep it. After all, if your employer offered you a $100 bonus, you would not give it back and say that it probably belongs to someone else.

The argument above does which one of the following in drawing its conclusion?

(A) relies on the advice of an authority in an area in which the authority is not an expert

(B) establishes a cause for an action and demonstrates the effect that results from the cause

(C) infers that a conclusion is correct based on considerations that are irrelevant to the conclusion

(D) proposes that an action is appropriate because the corresponding action in an analogous situation is appropriate

(E) predicts a future action based on an established pattern

11. Physician: Based on my experience with hundreds of patients in the hospital, it is clear that the average food serving that Americans receive at a meal is much too large. I have rarely seen a patient finish all of the food that was served to that patient at a meal.

The reasoning in the physician's argument is flawed in that the argument

(A) infers from the fact that a person's actions had a certain result that the person intended for the result to occur

(B) fails to apply a generalization to all of the cases to which it applies

(C) fails to document whether the size of the sample is large enough to be statistically meaningful

(D) relies on a sample that is not representative of the group that is represented in the conclusion

(E) fails to specify whether the referenced meal is the largest meal of the day

12. Five years ago the number of students graduating from the city's schools who were interested in music was the same as the number who were interested in art. In the past five years, the number of music classes offered in the city's schools has increased, while the number of art classes has decreased. If this trend continues, the number of graduating students interested in music will be significantly greater than the number interested in art.

Which one of the following, if true, most helps strengthen the argument?

(A) The number of students in each music class has stayed the same for five years, as has the number of students in each art class.

(B) The percentage of students interested in music who take a music class has not changed for five years.

(C) Every student who wants to take an art class can get into an art class.

(D) A higher percentage of students interested in art graduate than is true of students interested in music.

(E) There are more music teachers now than there were five years ago.

13. Modern jets are able to transport people quickly to distant destinations. Most jet transportation is relatively inexpensive and comfortable. It is clear that travel by jet provides a service that is indispensable to our modern lifestyle.

The argument's conclusion is properly drawn if which one of the following is assumed?

(A) It is possible for a service that is relatively inexpensive to be indispensable to our modern lifestyle.

(B) Any service that is indispensable to our modern lifestyle is relatively inexpensive.

(C) Most modern forms of transportation are indispensable to our modern lifestyle.

(D) Any service that is indispensable to our modern lifestyle transports people quickly to distant destinations.

(E) Transporting people quickly to a distant destination is a service that is indispensable to our modern lifestyle.

GO ON TO THE NEXT PAGE

14. Psychologist: Most parents do not want to take actions that will cause their child pain in the future. Whereas it is clear which actions may cause pain in the present, it is impossible to know which actions may cause pain in the future. For this reason, a parent should not refrain from an action that does not cause pain in the present based solely on the fear that it might cause pain in the future.

Which one of the following most accurately conforms to the principle put forth by the psychologist?

(A) Only a tiny fraction of fossils contain important information. Nevertheless, it is a paleontologist's biggest fear that a fossil that might have been valuable will be discarded. Therefore, unless there is a reason not to do so, paleontologists should examine every fossil.

(B) I have made my fortune by never investing in a project that loses money. When I am considering an investment, if it is losing money now, I do not pursue it. If it is not losing money now, it might lose money in the future, but, because it is impossible to know whether or not it will lose money in the future, I invest in the project unless there is another reason for me not to do so.

(C) Most animal owners do not want to hurt their pet. It is clear that some punishments hurt an animal in the present. Hopefully, a quick punishment will help the animal avoid punishment in the future. Because it is impossible to know whether a punishment in the present will help an animal avoid punishment in the future, an owner should apply a quick punishment unless there is another reason not to do so.

(D) Most teachers want their students to learn as much as possible. Although it is sometimes obvious that certain students are learning on a particular day, it is impossible to know if all of the students are learning. For this reason, the teacher should continue to teach as much as possible to those students who are learning, unless there is another reason not to do so.

(E) Most people want to be as happy as reasonably possible. It is clear that some unhappiness in the present is because of events that happened during childhood but it is impossible to know the causes of all present unhappiness. For that reason, it is important to get help resolving all present unhappiness, unless there is another reason not to do so.

15. The city council has received proposals from two different architecture firms for constructing the new swimming pool complex. The proposal from Firm X, a local firm, costs $200,000 less than the proposal from Firm Y, a national firm, and yet the plan proposed by Firm X includes all of the same facilities that are included in the plan proposed by Firm Y. Therefore, awarding the contract to the local firm will save the city significant money.

Which one of the following, if true, would most seriously weaken the argument above?

(A) There is already a swimming pool in the city that is open to the public.

(B) Firm X must hire a local subcontractor to build the complex and local subcontractors charge more than nonlocal subcontractors.

(C) Projects constructed by Firm Y typically require less maintenance than similar projects built by Firm X.

(D) Most city residents would be willing to pay extra property tax to fund the new swimming pool complex.

(E) Much of the money that the city will pay to Firm X will go to local residents who will spend their money at local businesses.

GO ON TO THE NEXT PAGE

16. It is well established that infants whose weight is low at birth have a higher mortality rate. It is also established that the children of women who smoke during pregnancy have a higher mortality rate. However, when women who smoke during pregnancy give birth to infants who have a low weight at birth, these infants have a lower mortality rate than other infants with a low weight at birth.

Which one of the following, if true, most helps to resolve the apparent paradox described in the passage above?

(A) If two factors that both lead to a common result are combined, one of the factors will override the other factor.

(B) If factor S leads to result X and factor T leads to result Y, combining factors S and T leads to a result that combines result X and result Y.

(C) If two factors that both cause a specific result are combined, the result will not necessarily occur.

(D) The mortality rates for infants depends on multiple factors that cannot all be predicted.

(E) Women who smoke during pregnancy tend to gain less weight during pregnancy than women who do not smoke.

17. Every star in a galaxy, no matter how distant from Earth, exerts at least a tiny gravitational influence on Earth. Therefore, a galaxy exerts a gravitational influence on Earth that is many times greater than the influence of any one star in the galaxy.

The reasoning in which one of the following arguments is most similar to the reasoning in the passage above?

(A) The influence of a particular political party in a legislature is determined by the number of party members who are legislators. The party as a whole exerts an influence on the outcome of a vote that is significantly greater than that of any particular legislator, whose influence is relatively minor.

(B) Every legislator, no matter how unimportant, exerts at least a small influence on the outcome of a vote. However, the party to which the legislator belongs exerts an influence on the outcome of a vote that is greater than the sum of the influences of all the legislators who are members of that party.

(C) Any piece of legislation cannot pass only with the support of individual legislators. In order to pass, a piece of legislation must have the support of key committee members.

(D) Any individual citizen has only a small influence on how a particular legislator votes. Therefore, if an individual citizen can influence all of the legislators, that citizen can have a larger effect on the legislature than if the citizen had influenced only one legislator.

(E) No political party can hope to pass legislation on its own. Therefore, in order to pass legislation, a political party must coordinate with other political parties, with the result that all political parties can pass more legislation than could have been passed by any one party alone.

GO ON TO THE NEXT PAGE

18. Ferguson, a patient of Dr. Carpenter, had a medical condition that could be corrected equally well by either surgery or physical therapy. Ferguson's spouse told Dr. Carpenter that the most important criterion for deciding which procedure to use was that it be the most reliable procedure possible. Dr. Carpenter recommended surgery.

Which one of the following principles, if valid, most helps justify Dr. Carpenter's recommendation?

(A) If two procedures are equally effective, Dr. Carpenter recommends the most expensive option unless the patient is not insured.

(B) If a patient can be treated equally effectively with both surgery and physical therapy, Dr. Carpenter recommends the procedure that best meets the criteria given by the patient's family.

(C) Dr. Carpenter always recommends the less invasive of two equally effective procedures unless the family of the patient specifically requests the more invasive procedure.

(D) Dr. Carpenter always assumes that if two medical treatments are equally effective, they are also equally reliable.

(E) When a patient's family requests a specific criterion for choosing a medical treatment, Dr. Carpenter recommends surgery if it is one of the options.

19. Engineer: A new technology that attracts potential investors will be economically viable if it has a broad potential market. A new technology that does not offer any improvements over previous technologies still has the possibility of being economically viable as long as it has a broad potential market. The AC Quantum screwdriver is a new technology that does not offer any improvement over previous screwdrivers. However, it does have a broad potential market.

If all of the statements above are true, which one of the following must be true?

(A) The AC Quantum screwdriver attracts potential investors.

(B) If the AC Quantum screwdriver is redesigned to offer improvements over previous screwdrivers, it will be economically viable.

(C) If the AC Quantum screwdriver is economically viable, then it must have added some improvements over previous screwdrivers.

(D) If the AC Quantum screwdriver is economically viable, then it must have attracted potential investors.

(E) The AC Quantum screwdriver will be economically viable if it attracts potential investors.

GO ON TO THE NEXT PAGE

20. Most people believe that we should take steps to stop global warming. This belief assumes that when humans realize that they are harming the environment, they will choose to stop doing so. However, when in human history has this been the case? Even the first cave dwellers must have realized that burning wood in the cave polluted the air and made it difficult to breathe. Yet, they chose the benefits of technology over a healthy environment.

The claim that we should take steps to stop global warming figures in the above argument in which one of the following ways?

(A) It is the claim that the argument is primarily concerned with attacking.

(B) It summarizes the points that are presented in the rest of the argument.

(C) It is a premise that is used to support the main conclusion of the argument.

(D) It answers a question that is posed later in the argument.

(E) It offers a solution to a problem that is exemplified through a specific example from the past.

21. Shortly after a local restaurant expanded its menu to include a wider range of ethnic foods, a greater number of new customers began coming to the restaurant. At the same time, previous customers began coming to the restaurant more frequently than before. It is probable that expanding the menu caused both of these phenomena.

Which one of the following, if true, most strengthens the reasoning in the above argument?

(A) Returning previous customers ordered the new items more frequently than did new customers.

(B) Both new customers and returning previous customers brought more friends with them than had been the case before the menu change.

(C) Most new customers to the restaurant were referred by previous customers.

(D) When the restaurant briefly returned to the old menu for a month, fewer new customers came and previous customers came less frequently.

(E) An influx of new and previous customers from a large, new apartment building across the street from the restaurant motivated the restaurant to expand its menu.

GO ON TO THE NEXT PAGE

22. Roberto: It is true that the Roman Empire imposed the Latin language on people in other areas of Europe. However, even though the Romans used the threat of force to establish Latin in new areas, the people in those areas must have adopted Latin willingly. Otherwise, they would have abandoned Latin after the Romans left.

Margarite: But even two or three generations of an imposed language is enough to cause the original language to become extinct. The Romans maintained their rule for that long. Once the Romans left, the people would not have been able to revive their original language if they had wanted to.

The statements above provide the most support for holding that Roberto and Margarite disagree on which of the following?

(A) The inhabitants of areas in which the Romans imposed Latin did not want to return to their original language when the Romans left.

(B) The inhabitants of areas in which the Romans imposed Latin had the ability to return to their original language after the Romans left.

(C) It is possible that the original language of the inhabitants of areas in which the Romans imposed Latin became extinct.

(D) The Romans used the threat of force to impose Latin on people in some areas of Europe.

(E) Latin was imposed on some people in Europe.

23. If John misses his interview in the next town today, he will not get the new job he is hoping for. John cannot get to his interview unless he gets on the bus that leaves the station in his town at 8:15 A.M. When John arrives at the bus station at 8:15 A.M., the bus that he needs to catch has already left. Therefore, John will not get the new job he is hoping for.

Which one of the following is an assumption required for the argument to be valid?

(A) If John gets to the interview, he will get the new job he is hoping for.

(B) There are no other jobs that John would be willing to accept.

(C) There is no other opportunity further along the route for John to board the bus that left the station at 8:15 A.M.

(D) The bus that John needed to be on left earlier than was scheduled.

(E) John did not have control over the circumstances that prevented him from arriving at the bus station on time.

GO ON TO THE NEXT PAGE

24. Any plant or animal specimen without mineralized tissues cannot become fossilized. A plant or animal that is trapped in mud develops mineralized tissues. Therefore, if an animal is not trapped in mud, it will not become fossilized.

The reasoning in the argument is most vulnerable to criticism on the grounds that the argument

(A) fails to consider that one event is the result of, rather than the cause of, a second event

(B) applies a generalization to an inappropriate instance

(C) infers that because something is unlikely to occur, it will not occur

(D) treats a condition that is sufficient to bring about a result as a condition that is necessary for that result to occur

(E) treats a hypothesis as a fact

25. Principle: The sociological study of an ethnic group should only be undertaken if the majority of members of the ethnic group agree to the study and understand the benefits that the group might derive from the study.

Application: It was appropriate for Anderson to undertake a study of an ethnic refugee community in this city because Anderson first got permission from the majority of members of the group and because the results of the study will be used to build a new community center that the ethnic group has been requesting for years.

Which one of the following, if true, justifies the application of the principle above?

(A) Anderson is a member of the ethnic refugee community that she is studying.

(B) The members of the ethnic group unanimously approved participating in the study.

(C) A similar study of another ethnic group resulted in the group receiving a large donation that had not been anticipated by the researcher or group members.

(D) The new community center will also provide services for other ethnic groups that have participated in recent studies.

(E) Most of the members of the ethnic group understood before approving their participation that the new community center would be built as a result of the study.

GO ON TO THE NEXT PAGE

26. Biologist: An experiment was conducted to test the hypothesis that Canada geese navigate by monitoring electromagnetic radiation. A small plane flying one hundred feet above a flock of migrating Canada geese emitted an electromagnetic field in the range that, according to the hypothesis, would cause the geese to become disoriented. In fact, the geese did become disoriented, which supports the hypothesis.

Which one of the following, if true, most weakens the argument?

(A) When the plane flew one hundred feet above the geese without emitting an electromagnetic field, the geese became disoriented.

(B) When the plane flew two hundred feet above the geese and emitted an electromagnetic field, the geese did not become disoriented.

(C) When the plane emitted an electromagnetic field, the geese slowed down dramatically.

(D) When the plane emitted an electromagnetic field in a range that the hypothesis predicted would not affect the geese, the geese were not affected.

(E) When the plane moved away from the geese while emitting an electromagnetic signal, the geese became reoriented.

STOP If you finish before the 35-minute time period is over, you may go back and check your answers in this section only. You may not work on any other test section.

Time: 35 minutes
23 Questions

DIRECTIONS: The groups of questions in this test section are each based on specific sets of conditions. Making a rough diagram may be useful for answering some of the questions. For each question choose the answer choice that is most accurate and complete. Fill in the space on your answer sheet that corresponds to your answer.

QUESTIONS 1–5

Six activities—fencing, jazz dancing, swing dancing, track, weightlifting, yoga—are to be conducted in three different gymnasiums—1, 2, and 3. The activities all start at the same time and last exactly one hour. Each activity takes place in exactly one gymnasium. Each gymnasium can accommodate up to four different activities and each gymnasium holds at least one of the six activities. The assignment of activities to gymnasiums is subject to the constraints below:

> If weightlifting takes place in gymnasium 1, fencing takes place in gymnasium 2.
> Yoga takes place in the same gymnasium as either jazz dancing or swing dancing, but not both.
> Track and yoga do not take place in the same gymnasium.

1. Which one of the following could be the assignment of activities to gymnasiums?
   (A) Gymnasium 1: fencing, yoga;
       Gymnasium 2: jazz dancing, track;
       Gymnasium 3: swing dancing, weightlifting
   (B) Gymnasium 1: jazz dancing, swing dancing, yoga;
       Gymnasium 2: fencing, weightlifting;
       Gymnasium 3: track
   (C) Gymnasium 1: jazz dancing, weightlifting;
       Gymnasium 2: fencing, track;
       Gymnasium 3: swing dancing, yoga
   (D) Gymnasium 1: track, weightlifting;
       Gymnasium 2: jazz dancing, yoga;
       Gymnasium 3: fencing, swing dancing
   (E) Gymnasium 1: swing dancing, weightlifting;
       Gymnasium 2: fencing;
       Gymnasium 3: jazz dancing, track, yoga

GO ON TO THE NEXT PAGE

2. If swing dancing and track are the only activities in gymnasium 3, which one of the following must be true?
   (A) If jazz dancing is in Gymnasium 2, weightlifting is in Gymnasium 1.
   (B) If fencing is in Gymnasium 2, weightlifting is in Gymnasium 1.
   (C) If yoga is in Gymnasium 2, only one activity is in Gymnasium 1.
   (D) If only one activity is in Gymnasium 2, it is fencing.
   (E) If a gymnasium has only one activity, it must be Gymnasium 2.

3. If weightlifting is the only activity in Gymnasium 1, all of the following could be true EXCEPT:
   (A) Track takes place in a gymnasium in which one other activity takes place.
   (B) Track takes place in a gymnasium in which two other activities take place.
   (C) Exactly two activities take place in Gymnasium 3.
   (D) Exactly three activities take place in Gymnasium 2.
   (E) Exactly three activities take place in Gymnasium 3.

4. If fencing and weightlifting take place in the same gymnasium, which one of the following could be true?
   (A) Fencing takes place in Gymnasium 1.
   (B) Track takes place in a gymnasium in which no other event takes place.
   (C) Yoga takes place in a gymnasium in which no other event takes place.
   (D) Three events take place in Gymnasium 1.
   (E) Four events take place in Gymnasium 1.

5. If track, weightlifting, and swing dancing are the only three activities taking place in one of the gymnasiums, which one of the following must be true?
   (A) Yoga takes place in Gymnasium 3
   (B) Fencing takes place in Gymnasium 2.
   (C) Track takes place in Gymnasium 1.
   (D) There are exactly two gymnasiums in each of which there is exactly one activity taking place.
   (E) Fencing takes place in a gymnasium in which no other activity takes place.

GO ON TO THE NEXT PAGE

QUESTIONS 6–11

A human resources director is scheduling interviews for seven job candidates—Griego, Harris, Jackson, Kristoff, LaPorte, Mink, and Neimann. The seven interview periods run consecutively and do not overlap. Exactly one candidate is interviewed during each interview period. The assignment of interviews is governed by the following constraints:

Mink's interview is before Jackson's interview.

LaPorte's interview is before Neimann's interview.

Jackson's interview is before both Neimann's interview and Griego's interview.

Either Harris or Griego interviews sixth.

6. Which one of the following is an accurate order in which the interviews can be assigned, from first to last?
   (A) Mink, Jackson, LaPorte, Neimann, Griego, Kristoff, Harris
   (B) Mink, Jackson, Neimann, LaPorte, Griego, Harris, Kristoff
   (C) LaPorte, Kristoff, Mink, Jackson, Neimann, Harris, Griego
   (D) Kristoff, LaPorte, Mink, Neimann, Jackson, Harris, Griego
   (E) Harris, Jackson, LaPorte, Neimann, Mink, Griego, Kristoff

GO ON TO THE NEXT PAGE

7. The interview of which one of the following cannot be immediately followed by Griego's interview?
   (A) Harris
   (B) Jackson
   (C) LaPorte
   (D) Mink
   (E) Neimann

8. If Griego interviews third, which one of the following must be true?
   (A) Kristoff interviews fourth or fifth.
   (B) LaPorte interviews fourth or fifth.
   (C) Neimann interviews fourth or fifth.
   (D) Neimann interviews fifth or sixth.
   (E) Neimann interviews seventh.

9. If Mink is interviewed fourth, all of the following must be true EXCEPT:
   (A) Neimann interviews seventh.
   (B) Griego interviews sixth.
   (C) Jackson interviews immediately between Mink and Griego.
   (D) There is at most one interview between Harris's interview and Kristoff's interview.
   (E) LaPorte interviews immediately before or immediately after Kristoff.

10. If Harris interviews before LaPorte, which one of the following could be true?
    (A) Griego interviews fourth.
    (B) Griego interviews seventh.
    (C) Neimann interviews seventh.
    (D) Harris interviews immediately before Neimann.
    (E) Kristoff interviews after Griego but before Neimann.

11. If Mink interviews fourth, which one of the following CANNOT be true?
    (A) Harris interviews first.
    (B) Kristoff interviews seventh.
    (C) Jackson interviews fifth.
    (D) LaPorte interviews first.
    (E) LaPorte interviews third.

GO ON TO THE NEXT PAGE

QUESTIONS 12–17

A wedding cake is to be made with seven layers, layer one being the lowest and layer seven being the uppermost. Each layer has exactly one flavor and the available flavors are peach, raspberry, and strawberry. The cake has at least one layer of each of the three flavors. The order of the layers must conform to the following conditions:

Strawberry is used more times than peach is used.

There can be at most one layer of peach above the uppermost layer of raspberry.

The second layer must be either peach or strawberry.

There is at least one layer of peach that is immediately between two layers of strawberry.

12. Which one of the following could be the order of layers from bottom to top?
   (A) strawberry, peach, strawberry, raspberry, strawberry, raspberry, peach
   (B) raspberry, strawberry, peach, strawberry, strawberry, peach, strawberry
   (C) strawberry, peach, raspberry, strawberry, raspberry, strawberry, peach
   (D) strawberry, raspberry, strawberry, peach, strawberry, raspberry, peach
   (E) strawberry, peach, strawberry, peach, raspberry, peach, strawberry

13. Which one of the following must be true?
   (A) There are more layers of peach than of raspberry.
   (B) There are more layers of strawberry than of raspberry.
   (C) There are at most four layers of strawberry.
   (D) There are at most two layers of peach.
   (E) There are at most three layers of raspberry.

GO ON TO THE NEXT PAGE

14. If the only layer of raspberry is the first layer, and if the second layer is strawberry, which one of the following could be true?
    (A) The seventh layer is peach.
    (B) There are exactly three layers of strawberry.
    (C) There are exactly four layers of strawberry.
    (D) There are exactly two layers of peach.
    (E) There is exactly one layer of peach.

15. Which one of the following CANNOT be true?
    (A) Four layers are raspberry.
    (B) Five layers are strawberry.
    (C) The first, third, and fifth layers are raspberry.
    (D) The first, fifth, and seventh layers are raspberry.
    (E) The first, third, fifth, and seventh layers are strawberry.

16. If the only raspberry layer is the first layer, the assignment of flavors to layers is completely determined if which one of the following is true?
    (A) The seventh layer is not peach.
    (B) Exactly five layers are strawberry.
    (C) The second layer is strawberry.
    (D) The third layer is peach.
    (E) The third layer is strawberry.

17. If there are the same number of layers of raspberry as there are of peach, which one of the following could be true?
    (A) There are four layers of strawberry.
    (B) There are five layers of strawberry.
    (C) The first, fifth, and seventh layers are raspberry.
    (D) The first, fifth, sixth, and seventh layers are raspberry.
    (E) The sixth and seventh layers are peach.

GO ON TO THE NEXT PAGE

QUESTIONS 18–23

Seven scientists—Thomas, Upton, Vincent, Washburn, Xerxes, York, and Zuniga—are to present their research findings during three seminars that are scheduled during a conference. Each scientist presents exactly once. Each seminar lasts one hour. The seminars run consecutively and do not overlap. At least one scientist presents at each seminar. For each seminar exactly one of the scientists is the lead presenter. The assignment of scientists to seminars conforms to the following conditions:

Either Vincent or Xerxes is the lead presenter in the seminar in which Thomas presents.

Upton and Zuniga cannot both be lead presenters.

Thomas presents in a seminar before York.

Washburn cannot present in a seminar after the seminar in which York presents.

18. Which one of the following could be the order in which the scientists present?
- (A) Seminar 1: Washburn (lead), York;
  Seminar 2: Vincent (lead), Thomas;
  Seminar 3: Zuniga (lead), Xerxes, Upton
- (B) Seminar 1: Xerxes (lead), Upton;
  Seminar 2: Vincent (lead), Thomas;
  Seminar 3: York (lead), Washburn, Zenith
- (C) Seminar 1: Upton (lead), Thomas, Washburn;
  Seminar 2: York (lead), Zuniga;
  Seminar 3: Vincent (lead), Xerxes
- (D) Seminar 1: Xerxes (lead), Thomas, Zuniga;
  Seminar 2: Upton (lead), York;
  Seminar 3: Vincent (lead), Washburn
- (E) Seminar 1: Zuniga (lead), Washburn;
  Seminar 2: Xerxes (lead), Thomas;
  Seminar 3: Upton (lead), York, Vincent

GO ON TO THE NEXT PAGE

19. If Washburn is a lead presenter and does not present in a seminar immediately before or immediately after the seminar in which Thomas presents, which one of the following must be true?
    (A) The second seminar has exactly three presenters.
    (B) Either Vincent or Xerxes is lead presenter in the third seminar.
    (C) Either Upton or Zuniga is lead presenter in the second seminar.
    (D) Vincent presents in the first seminar.
    (E) York presents in the third seminar.

20. Which one of the following could be true?
    (A) Xerxes is not a lead presenter and Vincent presents in the third seminar.
    (B) Washburn, Xerxes, and Upton present in the third seminar.
    (C) Neither Washburn, Xerxes, nor York is a lead presenter.
    (D) Vincent is not a lead presenter and Washburn presents before Xerxes.
    (E) Washburn presents in the first seminar and York presents in the first seminar.

21. Which one of the following CANNOT be true?
    (A) Thomas presents in the first seminar and Washburn, Xerxes, and York present in the third seminar.
    (B) Neither Xerxes, York, nor Zuniga is a lead presenter.
    (C) Vincent, Xerxes, and Upton are lead presenters.
    (D) Upton is lead in the first seminar and Zuniga presents in the third seminar.
    (E) Both Vincent and Xerxes present in the third seminar.

22. If York presents in the second seminar and Washburn is a lead presenter, which one of the following must be true?
    (A) Vincent presents in the first seminar.
    (B) Washburn presents in the second seminar.
    (C) Either Upton or Zuniga presents in the third seminar.
    (D) Vincent presents in a seminar before the seminar in which Washburn presents.
    (E) Washburn presents in a seminar before a seminar in which either Upton or Zuniga presents.

23. Which one of the following, if substituted for the constraint that Washburn cannot present in a seminar after the seminar in which York presents, would have the same effect in determining the assignment of the scientists?
    (A) Washburn presents in a seminar before the seminar in which York presents.
    (B) York presents in a seminar after the seminar in which Washburn presents.
    (C) Washburn can present only in a seminar before the seminar in which York presents or the seminar in which York presents.
    (D) Washburn can present only in the seminar in which Thomas presents or the seminar immediately after the seminar in which Thomas presents.
    (E) Washburn cannot present before the seminar in which Thomas presents.

Time: **35 minutes**

25 Questions

DIRECTIONS: The questions in this section are based on the reasoning contained in brief state-ments or passages. More than one answer choice could conceivably answer the question in some cases. However, you should choose the <u>best</u> answer. The best answer is the response that answers the question most accurately and completely. You should avoid making any assumptions that, by commonsense standards, are implausible, superfluous, or incompatible with the passage. When you have chosen the best answer, fill in the space on your answer sheet that corresponds to your answer.

1. Accountant: Some investors have scoffed at the meager return paid by Slow but Steady Industries. However, Slow but Steady has paid dividends every quarter for the past fifty years. In light of this fact, Slow but Steady should be considered an excellent investment.

Which one of the following principles, if valid, most helps to justify the reasoning in the accountant's argument?

(A) An investor should always invest in the best investment that is available.

(B) More investors are concerned with the rate of interest paid by a company than are concerned with the history of the company.

(C) The quality of an investment is based primarily on the total amount of dividends that a company has paid out over its entire history.

(D) The quality of an investment is based primarily on the length of time over which a company has regularly paid dividends.

(E) Any company that has not paid dividends regularly for a long period is not an excellent investment.

2. Biosphere 2 was a completely self-enclosed, experimental environment meant to replicate the conditions of a self-contained colony on another planet. Like a colony on Mars, for example, the participants who were sealed inside were isolated from the rest of humanity and had to depend completely on the balance of natural processes inside the biosphere. Toward the end of the project, oxygen levels dropped dangerously and additional oxygen had to be pumped in.

The statements above, if true, most strongly support which one of the following?

(A) It is possible to create a completely self-sustaining biological system that could support colonists on Mars.

(B) The cause for the drop in oxygen levels was unknown.

(C) The designers of Biosphere 2 did not anticipate a drop in oxygen levels.

(D) The participants in Biosphere 2 had qualities that were similar to the qualities of colonists who might be chosen to live on Mars.

(E) A colony on Mars could face dangers that the participants in Biosphere 2 did not face.

GO ON TO THE NEXT PAGE

3. People today have a wider variety of food products to choose from in the store than did people fifty years ago. At the same time, people today are much more aware of the negative qualities of certain food products. As a result, people today face more frustration when trying to choose which food products to buy than did people fifty years ago.

Which one of the following is an assumption that is required by the argument above?

(A) People buy the same quantity of food today as they did fifty years ago.

(B) Choosing from among a limited variety of food products based on criteria other than negative qualities of the food is not highly frustrating.

(C) When people face a frustrating situation regularly, the degree of frustration lessens.

(D) People fifty years ago knew in advance which food products they would buy when they went to the store.

(E) There are more processed food products today than there were fifty years ago.

4. Sociologist: There is a direct correlation between the number of times per month that a person visits with extended family and the degree of satisfaction with their lives that people report. This correlation holds up regardless of whether the extended family members are parents, cousins, siblings, or in-laws. It seems likely that if people feel dissatisfied with their lives, they can become more satisfied by visiting their relatives more often.

Each of the following, if true, strengthens the sociologist's argument EXCEPT:

(A) People who have no extended family are less satisfied with their lives than is the average person.

(B) The degree of satisfaction with their lives that people report matches closely with measures of life satisfaction that are administered by psychologists.

(C) Many people who started visiting extended family more frequently have reported feeling more satisfied with their lives.

(D) Many people, when they feel particularly satisfied with their lives, like to share their feelings with their extended family by visiting them frequently.

(E) Many people who have lost an extended family member whom they had visited regularly, and who have not begun visiting another extended family member, report feeling less satisfied with their lives.

GO ON TO THE NEXT PAGE

5. Unless an actor rehearses regularly, the actor will forget lines during a performance. When one sees an actor fail to remember a line on stage, it is clear that the actor did not rehearse regularly.

Which one of the following contains flawed reasoning that is most closely parallel to the flawed reasoning in the argument above?

(A) Singers who are extroverted rarely experience stage fright. When one sees a singer showing signs of stage fright, it is likely that the singer is not extroverted.

(B) Comedians who do not take themselves seriously earn the approval of the audience. Therefore, if one sees a comedian who does not earn the approval of the audience, that comedian takes himself or herself seriously.

(C) Only an artist who practices technique can become competent at art. Clearly, Frederick has not practiced technique, because anyone can see that Frederick is not competent at art.

(D) Any dancer who does not exercise regularly will not have the stamina to get through a performance. Julia exercises regularly. Therefore, she will get through tomorrow's performance.

(E) Martin recites poetry to himself every day. Because people who recite poetry to themselves every day will become skilled orators, Martin will become a skilled orator.

6. A doctor has created a strict dietary plan for a young child who is overweight and depressed. The parents have agreed to follow the plan precisely. The plan requires that the parents give the child specific foods and specific amounts of food at each meal, whenever possible. At the same time, the plan requires that the parents not do anything that will upset the child to the extent that the child begins to cry.

The statements above, if true, provide a basis for proving the falsehood of which one of the following claims?

(A) If the child begins to cry when given the specified food for a meal, it is still possible for the parents to comply with the doctor's plan.

(B) If the parents follow the plan, the child can be given only the food that the doctor has approved and in the amounts that have been approved.

(C) The food that the parents give the child will not upset the child to the extent that the child will begin to cry.

(D) The food that the parents give the child is not the same food or the same amount of food that the child would choose to eat.

(E) It is possible that the child may refuse to eat the food that the parents have provided for a specific meal.

GO ON TO THE NEXT PAGE

7. Art critic: Many sculptors, when they have works on exhibit, want people to be able to touch their sculptures. The sculptors claim that touching brings people more intimately in contact with the art. I feel that sculpture is essentially a three-dimensional visual art. It is designed to be best appreciated with the eyes and from enough distance to have a full perspective. When people touch a sculpture, they lose touch with the three-dimensional, visual aspect of it.

The claim that touching a work of art brings people more intimately in touch with it plays which one of the following roles in the art critic's argument?

(A) It is a premise that supports the conclusion of the argument.

(B) It is a false assumption that invalidates the art critic's argument.

(C) It is the conclusion of an argument that the art critic attempts to refute.

(D) It is an assumption that is sufficient to arrive at the art critic's conclusion.

(E) It is a premise that supports an argument that the sculptor attempts to refute.

8. Being able to respond to the needs of others is regarded as a sign of psychological maturity, an ability to go beyond the complete obsession with meeting one's own needs that characterizes the early stages of psychological development. Yet, the skills needed to respond to others are drawn from the skills one has learned in meeting one's own needs. Therefore, people who are not able to respond to others because of being obsessed with meeting their own needs may simply be paving the way to be able to better respond to others in the future.

Which one of the following most accurately characterizes a relationship utilized by the argument?

(A) Learning to respond to the needs of others can help one develop better tools for responding to one's own needs.

(B) An obsession with one's own needs can make a person better able to respond to the needs of others.

(C) Learning to respond to the needs of others is a stage of psychological development that occurs simultaneously with learning to respond to one's own needs.

(D) An obsession with the needs of others is a stage of psychological development that is built on an earlier stage of obsession with one's own needs.

(E) Both the skills for meeting the needs of others and the skills for meeting one's own needs are drawn from skills learned at an earlier stage of psychological development.

GO ON TO THE NEXT PAGE

9. The laws that protect consumers must also protect the legitimate needs of businesses. However, the term *protection* should only refer to protecting an entity, whether the entity is a person or a business, from unfair exploitation. Protection should not mean protecting an entity from being made to pay for its own exploitation of others. For this reason, the current bankruptcy laws should be rewritten to eliminate many of the protections offered to credit card companies.

The reasoning in the argument above is most vulnerable to criticism on the grounds that the argument

(A) fails to provide evidence to support the assertion that the laws that protect consumers must also protect businesses

(B) infers that because the actions of credit card companies led to harming consumers that the credit card companies intended to harm the consumers

(C) fails to consider whether the authors of the bankruptcy laws would accept the definition of protection used in the argument

(D) fails to establish that the current bankruptcy laws include provisions that protect credit card companies from being made to pay for their exploitation of others

(E) falsely applies a characteristic of some companies to all companies of the same type

10. It is clear that the mummified prehistoric animal recently unearthed is an early member of the canine family. The animal walked on its toes, a feature that all modern canines possess, and had a specific ligament that supported the head, which is also a feature found in all modern canines.

Each of the following, if true, weakens the argument EXCEPT:

(A) The teeth of the mummified animal have characteristics that are common to the teeth of modern felines and modern canines.

(B) There are species other than canines that walk on their toes.

(C) The mummified animal's domed head with a short muzzle is a feature found in nearly all modern felines and rarely found in modern canines.

(D) The mummified remains were found in a geographical area in which no other remains of prehistoric canines have ever been found.

(E) The characteristics of a single specimen of a species can be misleading because they may be unique to the individual, rather than representative of the species to which it belonged.

GO ON TO THE NEXT PAGE

11. Public health official: The wave of flu that is sweeping through the country has resulted in the deaths of more than two thousand people over the age of seventy. Given that today's seventy-year-old is probably as healthy as the forty-year-olds of one hundred years ago, we can surmise that this flu is deadly enough to be a serious threat to everyone, even the young and healthy.

Which one of the following is an assumption required for the argument to be valid?

(A) The people over the age of seventy who died from the current flu were not mostly in frail health.

(B) A higher percentage of people in their eighties and nineties died from the current flu than is true for people in their seventies.

(C) A high percentage of people over the age of seventy who caught the current flu died from it.

(D) So far, few people between the ages of five and seventy have died from the current flu.

(E) Most of the people in frail health or with compromised immune systems who have died from the current flu are not over the age of seventy.

12. Because of the large factory that recently opened in the middle of town, the interstate highway that commuters use to return to the suburbs after work has become heavily congested during the 4 P.M. to 7 P.M. rush hour. On several occasions ambulances have been delayed on the highway. Many ambulances have started using the city streets instead of the highway during rush hour, which has resulted in at least one collision between an ambulance and a passenger car.

Which one of the following can be properly inferred from the facts in the passage above?

(A) Before traffic on the highway became congested, ambulances using the highway were not delayed during the evening rush hour.

(B) Many of the workers at the new factory live in the suburbs.

(C) Before the opening of the large factory, evening rush hour traffic was not congested.

(D) There is at least one collision that would have been avoided if an ambulance had not been delayed on the highway during the evening rush hour.

(E) The opening of the large factory contributed to at least one traffic accident.

GO ON TO THE NEXT PAGE

13. The managers of the local branches of Drugstore X and Drugstore Y, two competing drugstores owned by different corporations, have been meeting in private recently to compare the prices they charge for their best-selling items. Since the managers began meeting, the prices for the best-selling items at the two stores have been the same. Although neither manager was aware of laws against price fixing, the two managers should be fired, because their collaboration has unfairly hurt other drugstores.

Which one of the following principles, if valid, most helps to justify the reasoning in the above argument?

(A) Any manager whose actions violate a law should be fired, even if the manager was not aware of the law.

(B) Any manager who meets with a manager of a competing store in order to agree on prices is violating a law and therefore should be fired.

(C) Any manager whose actions hurt a competitor in a way that is unfair should be fired.

(D) Any manager whose actions violate the law and hurt a competitor should be fired.

(E) If two managers conspire to violate a law, both should be fired, even if one manager was responsible for initiating the conspiracy.

14. Physical therapist: Gentle forms of physical exercise, such as yoga or stretching, are healthy in many ways but they do not provide aerobic exercise. Aerobic exercise, such as jogging, stimulates certain important metabolic processes that are not stimulated during activities that are not aerobic. Therefore, if the only form of physical exercise that a person participates in is yoga, that person should _____ .

Which one of the following most logically completes the last sentence of the passage?

(A) also participate in jogging

(B) replace yoga with an aerobic activity such as jogging

(C) increase the amount of time spent doing yoga if the person is not able to do an aerobic exercise

(D) ask a physician if it would be wise to take up an aerobic exercise

(E) consider participating in an aerobic exercise

GO ON TO THE NEXT PAGE

15. Wildlife areas that are not impacted by humans must be left unmanaged but any wildlife area that is impacted by humans must be managed. One form of management simply involves remotely monitoring for adverse changes, such as significant changes in the size of endangered populations. More intensive management can involve the removal or introduction of plants or animals and restrictions on access by humans.

If the statements above are true, which one of the following must be true?

(A) If the population of an endangered species in a wildlife area declines, the area has previously been impacted by humans.

(B) If a wildlife area is impacted by humans, the area must be monitored for signs of adverse changes.

(C) If remote monitoring of a wildlife area does not protect the endangered species in that area, the area must be more intensively managed.

(D) If biologists are monitoring the population of an endangered species in a wildlife area, that area has previously been impacted by humans.

(E) If a new plant species appears in a wildlife area, that area has previously been impacted by humans.

16. For the past ten years, nearly every senior who graduated with honors from City High School has been accepted at a top-ten university. There are five seniors who will graduate from City High School with honors this year. Therefore, there will probably be at least five seniors from City High School who will be accepted at a top-ten university.

The reasoning in the argument above is most similar to the reasoning in which one of the following?

(A) For many years, most of the turtles born in Turtle Pond in the spring have returned to the pond in the fall. A number of turtles were born in the pond this spring. Therefore, most of them will probably return to the pond in the fall.

(B) For the past ten years, most of the people who are residents of the city have attended the state fair. This year there will be a state fair. Therefore, if someone is not a resident of the city, that person will probably not attend the state fair.

(C) For the past ten years, most of the fruit trees by the river have not set fruit. If most of the fruit trees fail to set fruit next year, the city will probably cut them down.

(D) For the past ten years, if it has rained on the Fourth of July, the mosquito population has exploded during the month of July. It is probable that the rain on the Fourth has influenced the breeding conditions for mosquitoes.

(E) For many years, we have vacationed at the lake during the summer. Our regular rental cabin at the lake is not available this year. Therefore, it is probable that we will find a new cabin to rent.

GO ON TO THE NEXT PAGE

17. Business executive: It is impossible to please customers. Our recent survey of one hundred consumers of our breakfast cereals showed that nearly 90 percent of our customers would not buy a product with genetically modified ingredients. Yet these same customers overwhelmingly rated our CrunchOBites cereal as their favorite among ten choices, even though CrunchOBites contains genetically modified corn.

Which one of the following, if true, most helps to explain the apparent discrepancy in the preferences of customers?

(A) Most of the ten cereals that were tested contained genetically modified ingredients.

(B) CrunchOBites is sweeter than any other cereals tested but uses only honey as a sweetener.

(C) The customers who reported that they would not buy foods with genetically modified ingredients did so in the morning when they were not hungry, whereas the customers who rated CrunchOBites as their top choice did so at noon when they were hungry.

(D) Most of the customers in the survey had never eaten CrunchOBites before they were given a sample to rate.

(E) Most customers do not know whether a cereal contains genetically modified ingredients or not.

18. Stephen: Beethoven's music is beautiful and inspiring. I would love to see schools require that children be exposed to his music during the school day but I suppose that we should not force a group of children to listen to music that some of them might not appreciate.

LaShauna: I have to disagree with you. Listening to Beethoven would do a lot of good for many children and should be required in school. Where would schools be if we let children decide what they should be exposed to?

Which one of the following is a point of disagreement between Stephen and LaShauna?

(A) Schools should not require children to be exposed to the music of a specific composer, even if all of the children appreciate the music.

(B) Children in school should be exposed to certain beneficial influences even if not all of the children appreciate the benefits of those influences.

(C) Being exposed to Beethoven's music would be beneficial for some children even if some of them might not appreciate the music.

(D) Beethoven's music holds no particular benefit for today's young people.

(E) Children who listen to Beethoven's music will perform better academically in school.

GO ON TO THE NEXT PAGE

19. Author Vadya Taikon's first novel, *The Good Road*, was reviewed by many critics who felt that it was well written, creative, and had a unique perspective. However, the critics unanimously said it had too much historical detail to sell well, as did all of the literary agents to whom Taikon sent the book. Taikon's second book, *The God in the Cauldron*, has been a top seller and avoids any mention of historical detail. Clearly, the comments of critics and agents caused Taikon to change his writing style.

Which one of the following, if true, most seriously weakens the conclusion of the above argument?

(A) Taikon made a profit from sales of the first book.

(B) Another historical novel published in the same year by a different author contained as much historical detail as *The Good Road* and was a best seller.

(C) Taikon's primary goal in writing novels is to provide entertainment for his family and friends, regardless of how many copies of the book are sold.

(D) Taikon's first novel was intended to be a historical novel.

(E) Taikon's first novel was considerably longer than his second novel.

20. A family in which one person makes all of the decisions without regard to the interests of the other family members may function but it will not be a happy family. Similarly, a society in which a few powerful leaders make decisions without regard to the interests of the public may have economic success but it cannot make its citizens happy.

The argument proceeds by

(A) comparing and contrasting two similar but distinct situations

(B) demonstrating the flaw in one argument by comparing it with another argument that is clearly flawed

(C) showing that two similar situations are different in a significant way

(D) establishing a conclusion for an argument by comparing it to a similar argument

(E) establishing that one thing is not true because something else is true

GO ON TO THE NEXT PAGE

21. Hybrid electric/gasoline automobile engines protect the environment by replacing at least part of the need for nonrenewable fossil fuels with the use of renewable resources, because, in theory, electricity can be generated by renewable means, whereas gasoline cannot. At the same time, a hybrid engine protects the environment by reducing the amount of toxic fumes emitted. People who switch to a hybrid engine, then, are contributing to the well-being of future generations.

The conclusion can be properly drawn if which one of the following is assumed?

(A) If an activity does not contribute to the well-being of future generations, that activity does not protect the environment.

(B) An automobile engine that is not a hybrid does not contribute to the well-being of future generations.

(C) An automobile engine that protects the environment must be a hybrid.

(D) When people switch from an automobile with a gasoline engine to an automobile with a hybrid engine, their previous automobile will be used by someone else.

(E) The process of building an automobile with a hybrid engine damages the environment more than the process of building an automobile with a gasoline engine.

22. A number of visitors to a pet store were asked, on entering the store, if they would like to own a pet. The people who answered yes were handed a puppy to adopt as they were leaving the store. However, nearly all of the people who were handed a puppy gave it back, saying they did not want it. They apparently misunderstood the question that was asked of them when they entered the store.

The reasoning above conforms most closely to which one of the following principles?

(A) Most people are happier with gifts that they buy for themselves than with gifts that are given to them by others.

(B) People often feel differently about a topic at the end of shopping trip than they did at the beginning.

(C) If two responses to a question are contradictory, it is likely that the question was not understood.

(D) People are unlikely to tell strangers how they really feel about an issue.

(E) People who do not understand a question typically refuse to answer it.

GO ON TO THE NEXT PAGE

23. Most journalists try to maintain a high level of objectivity when reporting on news events. When interviewing people as news sources, though, it is difficult for journalists to know if the people are being objective in what they report. In addition, it is difficult for journalists to catch their own subjective evaluations when such evaluations creep into an article. Finally, it can be difficult for editors, who may not know the facts of a situation, to determine when journalists have interpreted events through their own subjective perceptions.

Which one of the following most clearly states the conclusion of the argument as a whole?

(A) Most journalists write as objectively as possible when they report on news events.

(B) People who do not know the facts of a situation are often not objective when reporting on the situation.

(C) Most news articles are not as objective as the newspapers' editors would like.

(D) It can be difficult to create a news article that is completely objective.

(E) It is unlikely that a news article, as finally published, will be objective.

24. Mayor: The city council wants us to put more uniformed police officers on the streets downtown. However, there is evidence that the presence of uniformed officers actually incites people to violence. After all, we have the most uniformed officers on the street in the fourth ward with the result that there is more violence in the fourth ward than in any other part of the city.

The argument is flawed in that it fails to consider the possibility that

(A) people may react more violently to some uniformed officers than others

(B) uniformed officers can be trained to interact with the public in a nonthreatening way

(C) the residents of the fourth ward are more easily incited to violence than are residents of other wards

(D) uniformed firefighters rarely incite violence in people

(E) the violence in the fourth ward is the cause of, rather than the result of, the fact that there are more uniformed officers there than in any other part of the city

GO ON TO THE NEXT PAGE

25. Ethicist: One thousand airline passengers arriving from foreign countries were interviewed before going through customs. The passengers were asked whether or not they thought it was ethical to carry prohibited items through customs if they thought the prohibitions were unrealistic. Nearly 80 percent responded that doing so was ethical. However, a survey of the same passengers, after they had passed through customs, asked if they had carried any prohibited items through customs. This survey revealed that only 8 percent had done so. This confirms my hypothesis that most people report being more willing to push the limits of the law than they are in practice.

Which one of the following most accurately expresses a flaw in the reasoning of the ethicist's argument?

(A) The argument fails to consider the possibility that the people surveyed may not have been representative of all airline passengers.

(B) The argument does not adequately define the meaning of the word *ethical*.

(C) The argument fails to consider that the people being surveyed may have had reasons for not responding to the survey questions truthfully.

(D) The argument draws a conclusion based on premises that presuppose the conclusion.

(E) The argument fails to consider that some people who did not carry prohibited items through customs claimed that they had.

 **STOP** If you finish before the 35-minute time period is over, you may go back and check your answers in this section only. You may not work on any other test section.

Time: 35 minutes

27 Questions

DIRECTIONS: Each set of questions in this section is based on one passage or on a pair of passages. Answer the questions based on what is <u>stated</u> or <u>implied</u> in the passage or in the pair of passages. More than one answer choice could conceivably answer the question in some cases. However, you should choose the <u>best</u> answer. The best answer is the response that answers the question most accurately and completely. When you have chosen the best answer, fill in the space on your answer sheet that corresponds to your answer.

Medical geology is the name given to a relatively new discipline that concerns itself with the effect of geological materials on the health
Line of humans and other animals. There are five
(5) specific goals of medical geology. The first is to determine the existence of potentially harmful, abnormal levels of geological minerals and chemicals in the environment of a particular geographical area. The second is to identify
(10) geological causes of specific health problems and to find solutions or remediations. The third is to identify geological minerals and chemicals that may have a positive health effect. The fourth is to correct misconcep-
(15) tions that the public may have about health concerns related to geological materials or processes. The fifth is to facilitate solutions to geologically related health problems by fostering cooperation between developed and devel-
(20) oping nations.

There are three categories of geological materials with which medical geology is concerned. The first is naturally occurring dusts, which can be generated by mining, fires, earth-
(25) quakes, or wind. The second is the exposure to trace elements, which can include both a deficiency of trace elements and toxic levels of elements. Deficiencies of iodine or selenium, for example, are common causes of health issues
(30) around the world. Typical symptoms of iodine deficiency include goiter, lowered IQ, and birth defects. Selenium deficiency has been linked to muscle abnormalities, reproductive problems,

and premature aging. Overexposure to arsenic
(35) affects millions of people worldwide, with a significant cause being high arsenic levels in drinking water. Fluorine toxicity is even more widespread and is often caused by the release of fluorine when coal is burned in the home.
(40) Over 10 million people in southwest China suffer from fluorine toxicity.

The third category of geological materials studied by medical geology is that of materials with health benefits. Medicinal clays and
(45) other minerals have been used throughout the history of humanity to treat and cure various conditions and to stimulate health.

Unlike most scientific disciplines, medical geology is a collaboration between scien-
(50) tists from several distinct disciplines. Medical geology depends on the cooperation between geologists, biomedical researchers, and public health professionals. In this sense, there are no medical geologists per se. While some may
(55) argue that a discipline without specialists in that discipline cannot be considered a valid area of scientific study, it may well be that medical geology points the way to a new and more effective model of scientific investigation.
(60) Although traditional scientists might argue for the importance of the specialized medical geologist, there are two points of rebuttal. First, for an individual to become highly skilled in all three areas—geology, biomedical research,
(65) and public health—would require a prohibitive amount of time and expense. Second, such a

GO ON TO THE NEXT PAGE

person would most likely not be as skilled in any of the three areas as someone who had specialized in that area. Undoubtedly, as our (70) world becomes more and more complex, the model that medical geology represents offers a new approach to scientific research in many areas.

Adapted from "Medical Geology: A Globally Emerging Discipline," *http://www.geologica-acta.com/pdf/ vol0503a05.pdf* (accessed November 2012).

1. Which one of the following most accurately expresses the main point of the passage?
    (A) Medical geology is a new discipline that offers a new model for scientific research.
    (B) Medical geology is a new discipline combining geology and public health, which has five goals that have to do with toxic exposure to minerals, diseases caused by deficiencies of minerals, and health benefits of minerals.
    (C) Medical geology is a new discipline that addresses critical public health issues but for which there are, as yet, no specialists.
    (D) Despite the effectiveness of the medical geology model, scientists have not yet come up with a research model that can accommodate the increasingly complex interrelationships of factors that affect public health.
    (E) Toxicity from naturally occurring elements such as arsenic and fluorine have the potential to affect hundreds of millions of people unless disciplines like medical geology can find effective treatments.

2. With which one of the following statements about geologists working in medical geology would the author be most likely to agree?
    (A) They are not likely to be knowledgeable enough in biomedical research to make useful contributions to medical geology.
    (B) While they might contribute geological knowledge to medical geology, their contributions would not be likely to lead to actual health improvements for the public.
    (C) They might have trouble collaborating with biomedical researchers unless the biomedical researchers also had a background in geology.
    (D) Their understanding of how geological materials cause certain health conditions would help them determine whether health issues in a particular geographical region were likely caused by geological factors.
    (E) It would be valuable for them to discuss with physicists their method of collaborating with public health officials.

3. In saying that there are "no medical geologists" (line 54) the author most likely means which one of the following?
    (A) The field of medical geology is so new that no one is yet a specialist in it.
    (B) There are no universities that grant degrees in medical geology.
    (C) There are no scientists who are specialists in all three major subject areas that constitute medical geology.
    (D) Medicine and geology are distinct disciplines that study different areas of knowledge.
    (E) Because there are no medical geologists, medical geology is not a valid area of scientific study.

GO ON TO THE NEXT PAGE

4. Which one of the following statements is most strongly supported by the passage?

(A) An immunization program funded by a developed country for children in developing countries would address a goal of medical geology.

(B) It is probable that many people in certain parts of China burn coal in the home.

(C) Overexposure to iodine would most likely be caused by the quality of drinking water.

(D) Geological materials with healthful benefits are the best cures for exposure to geological materials that are toxic.

(E) The more areas in which a scientist is educated, the greater contribution that scientist can make to the public good.

5. Which one of the following would most likely be the response of the traditional scientists in line 60 to the rebuttal, made by the author, of their point?

(A) A discipline without specialists in that discipline can be a valid area of scientific study.

(B) Traditional science has been built on each scientist focusing on one specialized area of interest.

(C) It would be possible for a university to create a degree program that combines geology, biomedical research, and public health.

(D) There are many scientific models that will lead to better science as our world becomes more complex.

(E) Specializing in more than one scientific area improves competence in each of the areas.

6. According to the passage, which one of the following would NOT fall under one of the goals of medical geology?

(A) finding a mineral treatment for lung damage caused by radioactive particles

(B) identifying skin damage sustained by people living in areas in which the ozone layer has become diminished

(C) determining the cause of unusually healthy hair among people exposed to dust from mining

(D) creating a radio ad that explains why the minerals turning drinking water brown are not a cause for concern

(E) organizing a multinational conference on alternatives to burning coal for cooking in the home

GO ON TO THE NEXT PAGE

It can be said that the arguments on both sides of the death penalty debate are emotional ones. Naturally, each side cites statistics Line to support its view, but the mere fact that (5) each side can find supporting statistics demonstrates that the statistics are inconclusive. Fundamentally, then, the reasons for either favoring the death penalty or supporting its abolition are reasons of belief. In other words, (10) they are emotional reasons.

Surely there must be a way to apply logic to the conflicting arguments and beliefs that dominate the debate over the death penalty. Consider the statement by some supporters (15) of the death penalty that, if anything can deter murder, it is the death penalty. This argument is, first of all, logically misleading. The statement tries to convince the listener that the death penalty will deter murder, when (20) an equally valid interpretation of the statement is that nothing, including the death penalty, deters murder. The argument is akin to the statement "No toothpaste gets your teeth whiter than toothpaste X," which attempts to (25) mislead the listener into believing that toothpaste X gets teeth whiter than does any other toothpaste, when the statement could just as validly mean that toothpaste X whitens no better than most other toothpastes.

(30) Secondly, the statement that if anything can deter murder, it is the death penalty, attempts to establish its own truth simply by declaring that truth. Why should we accept such a statement as true? There may well be other social (35) actions, such as improved education, or laws, such as gun control, that might be at least as effective in reducing the number of murders. The statement erroneously implies that the only way to reduce the number of murders is to (40) create deterrence. It also confuses the fact that the death penalty is the most *extreme* method of reducing murders with the assertion that the death penalty is the most *effective* method.

People who have made the above argument (45) have also argued that as long as there is any possibility that the death penalty might prevent a future murder, we should use the death pen-

alty. This argument is based on the assertion that if there is any correlation at all between (50) one event and the prevention of a murder, it is legitimate to act on that correlation. By this logic, anyone who has ever committed a violent crime, even if it did not involve murder, should be put to death. So should anyone from (55) an ethnic group that has a higher incidence of murderers than average. Permanently jailing anyone who has not completed a high school diploma could also be justified. From these examples, it is clear that many people arguing (60) in the debate about the death penalty have not taken care to compose an argument that, when scrutinized carefully, supports their beliefs. Until such people begin to do so, there is no real debate on the death penalty.

7. Which one of the following most accurately expresses the main idea of the passage?
   (A) People who support the death penalty do so with arguments that are based on emotion rather than logic.
   (B) Arguments for and against the death penalty often contain flawed logic and thus do not constitute a real debate.
   (C) It is not logically valid to say that if anything can deter murder, it is the death penalty.
   (D) The death penalty is the most extreme of all possible methods for reducing the number of murders.
   (E) Even though arguments for and against the death penalty are based on emotions, they have been supported by the use of valid logic.

GO ON TO THE NEXT PAGE

8. The main purpose of the second paragraph of the passage is to
   (A) show that it is possible to apply logic to an argument that is essentially emotional
   (B) prove that some arguments in favor of the death penalty are not convincing
   (C) establish that arguments in favor of the death penalty tend to be less convincing than arguments against the death penalty
   (D) demonstrate that it is possible to apply logic to an argument in order to evaluate the argument's logical validity
   (E) provide an example and explanation of a specific logical flaw

9. The passage provides the strongest support for inferring that
   (A) people who have committed violent crimes, even if the crimes did not involve murder, should be considered for the death penalty
   (B) at the time that the passage was written, there was no real debate on the death penalty
   (C) if there is any effective method for reducing murders, the death penalty is the most effective
   (D) there is a correlation between certain events and the commission of murder
   (E) anything that reduces the number of murders is a deterrent

10. Which one of the following phrases most accurately conveys the meaning of the question "Why should we accept such a statement as true?" as it is used in lines 33–34.
    (A) An argument that is purely emotional provides no reason for others to accept it.
    (B) When an argument assumes as true the fact that it is trying to prove, there is no reason to accept the conclusion as true.
    (C) There is no evidence to support that the death penalty can definitely deter murder.
    (D) People who oppose the death penalty are unlikely to accept any argument in favor of the death penalty.
    (E) Logical arguments are unlikely to be convincing to those whose points of view are fundamentally emotional.

11. The passage indicates that the argument at the beginning of the second paragraph and the argument regarding toothpaste are similar in that
    (A) neither attempts to use logic, relying instead on emotions
    (B) both attempt to establish the truth of their conclusions by analogy
    (C) both are arguments that would be made by people on the same side of the death penalty debate
    (D) both are easily interpreted to mean something other than what the logic actually implies
    (E) both confuse preventing something with reducing something

GO ON TO THE NEXT PAGE

12. According to the passage, each of the following is true of people on one side of the death penalty debate or the other EXCEPT:

(A) Their arguments for or against the death penalty are emotional ones.

(B) As of the writing of the article, their arguments do not constitute real debate.

(C) Some of them have confused the fact that the death penalty is extreme with the assertion that the death penalty is effective.

(D) Some who oppose the death penalty believe that nothing can deter murder.

(E) Some who support the death penalty believe that the death penalty should be applied even if there is only a chance that it will prevent a murder.

13. Which one of the following most accurately represents the structure of the second paragraph?

(A) It states a conclusion, provides support for the conclusion through a specific example, points out a possible error in the example, and demonstrates that other people have made similar errors.

(B) It questions a belief, provides a counterexample to the belief, shows the flaw in the belief, and uses a commonplace example to illustrate the belief.

(C) It proposes a hypothesis, provides a test case, demonstrates that the test case draws a conclusion that is not warranted by its logic, and uses an analogous case to further demonstrate the flaw in the test case.

(D) It puts forth a hypothesis and then rejects the hypothesis based on an ambiguous interpretation of a logical statement and on an analogous faulty statement.

(E) It expresses frustration with an issue that has not been resolved, examines an example of faulty logic that has prevented the issue from being resolved, shows that the logic fails to consider a certain option, and clarifies the faulty logic through an analogous argument.

GO ON TO THE NEXT PAGE

Passage A

The early settlement of what is now the country of Liberia has a fascinating history that raises many questions. In 1815, the first
Line Americans to settle in the future Liberia were
(5) free African Americans, led by African American Quaker and entrepreneur Paul Cuffee. Cuffee believed that it was important for African Americans to have a place in Africa where they could "rise as a people," because the con-
(10) ditions for African Americans in America were too restrictive. Cuffee helped a small group of settlers establish themselves along the coast of Sierra Leone.

After Cuffee's initial venture, the concept
(15) of repatriation to Africa was taken up by a different group—a group of prominent, white political and social leaders. The group, called the American Colonization Society (ACS), was formed to encourage free African Americans
(20) to settle in Africa. ACS, however, fostered suspicions among African Americans, who distrusted the predominance of Southerners and slaveholders in the society, as well as the fact that African Americans were excluded from
(25) membership. In addition, the vast majority of African Americans had no interest in abandoning the land of their birth.

In a bizarre replay of the original slave trade in America, ACS placed settlers in swampy,
(30) disease-infested areas, where many died quickly. They remedied the situation by "negotiating" at gunpoint with local tribes for more desirable land. Over a hundred square miles of valuable coastal land was purchased for
(35) $300 worth of goods, weapons, and rum. The ACS settlers moved to the new land, where, far from home and without any resources of their own, they found themselves at the mercy of the authoritarian policies of the ACS governor,
(40) a situation that amounted to virtual, if not actual, slavery.

Passage B

For the many ethnic groups in the world that have ended up far from their original homelands, the concept of repatriation is a
(45) powerful one. At least in theory, the idea of "going back home" has a tremendous draw. It represents the end of marginalization, of being a minority in someone else's land. It represents the end of discrimination and exclusion from
(50) opportunities. It is not surprising, then, that as soon as there were free African Americans with some wealth in America, the notion of returning to an African homeland arose.

When Paul Cuffee, the free African American merchant, first took settlers to what was
(55) later to become Liberia, the contrast between the ideal of a homeland—a land to which one belonged and could return—and the political realities of West Africa became clear. In real-
(60) ity, there was no homeland to which African Americans could return. This was true in two senses. First, the slaves who had been brought to America had come from a multitude of tribes. Second, after multiple generations in
(65) America, African Americans were culturally much more American than African. Though a rich African heritage prevailed among African Americans, the gulf between their culture and the culture of tribal African village life was
(70) vast. It is no wonder that when Liberia gained independence as a country, the native Africans found themselves as second-class citizens among the repatriated African Americans. The road to a true African homeland in Liberia has
(75) been paved with difficulty.

GO ON TO THE NEXT PAGE

14. According to the passages, which one of the following was true about the ACS?
    (A) Even though it was founded by free African Americans to provide an opportunity for African Americans to start a new life in Africa, most African Americans were suspicious of it.
    (B) Slave owners who were members of ACS hoped to earn money from plantations in Africa through the virtual slavery of people who were desperate and had no resources.
    (C) Some of its members had been involved in importing slaves from Africa.
    (D) It sometimes used coercion to gain land for its settlements.
    (E) Its leaders felt that only in Africa could African Americans "rise as a people."

15. The author of Passage A and the author of Passage B would be most likely to disagree over whether
    (A) the founding of Liberia involved hardships and injustices
    (B) many African Americans in the early nineteenth century would have found the concept of repatriation to Africa appealing
    (C) many of the first settlers in Liberia were disillusioned with the realities of life in Africa
    (D) many African Americans were suspicious of the motives of Paul Cuffee
    (E) many early settlers in Liberia were culturally incompatible with the native Africans

16. The passages have which one of the following aims in common?
    (A) documenting the ways in which white Americans controlled the African repatriation movement
    (B) questioning whether Paul Cuffee's motives for repatriating African Americans to West Africa were legitimate
    (C) explaining elements of the current African American experience in the United States through an analogy of the experiences of African American settlers in Liberia
    (D) establishing the historical background of the foundation of Liberia and exploring how the reality of repatriation was more difficult than the ideal
    (E) contrasting the experience of native Africans in Liberia with the experience of repatriated African Americans in Liberia

17. Passage B most strongly supports which one of the following statements about African Americans living in America before the mid-nineteenth century?
    (A) Most of them preferred to stay in the country where they were born.
    (B) Many of them regarded the ACS with suspicion.
    (C) Some of them treated native Africans as second-class citizens.
    (D) They had lost nearly all of the uniquely African cultural elements of their ancestors.
    (E) As long as all African Americans were either slaves or impoverished, it was unlikely that the notion of returning to Africa would have been discussed among them.

GO ON TO THE NEXT PAGE

18. The author of Passage A would be most likely to agree with which one of the following statements?

(A) The ACS was not primarily motivated by the belief that settling in Africa offered African Americans the best chance to "rise as a people."

(B) Most African Americans welcomed the chance to move to a new country that would not treat them poorly.

(C) Repatriation efforts failed because there was no one country that was the original homeland for African Americans.

(D) In its early years, Liberia was important as a safe haven for slaves who had escaped from plantations.

(E) Despite the fact that most were white, the founders of ACS sympathized with the African Americans who they were trying to help.

19. Both passages are concerned with which one of the following questions?

(A) Can people who are not themselves members of an ethnic group be trusted to fairly make decisions about the lives of people who are members of that ethnic group?

(B) Was Paul Cuffee the first person to help African Americans settle in Africa?

(C) Was the repatriation movement beneficial in freeing at least some of the African American slaves in America?

(D) Was the coast of Sierra Leone the actual original homeland of African Americans?

(E) Did the repatriation movement place some African Americans in conditions similar to slavery?

GO ON TO THE NEXT PAGE

Honesty is a universally admired trait. It is the source of trust that binds relationships, the rule of truth that maintains nations. Most people
Line hope that others will be honest with them and
(5) most try in return to be honest. At those times in which we fail, which we inevitably must, we condemn ourselves for our lapse and vow to try harder. Perhaps this is not only unrealistic but also unwise.

(10) Presumably honesty is altruistic. Its alleged purpose is to be fair and considerate to others. This may be true in some cases. If you ask me in which direction the post office lies, I will answer you honestly because I do not want you to be
(15) misled. I have no personal stake in whether you do or do not find the post office and so I naturally am considerate of your time and efforts. This, then, is an example of altruistic honesty.

Most instances of honesty, however, fall into
(20) two other categories. The first is honesty spoken because it is easier to tell the truth than to fabricate a lie, which may then have to be defended with further lying. If I have spent the afternoon in a tavern and you ask me where I have been,
(25) if I say I have been volunteering at the hospital, you may then ask if I saw so and so there, or you may ask how long I have been doing so. The brain must then work at full attention to create answers that are plausible and do not contra-
(30) dict each other. At the same time, the anxiety of being found out becomes stronger, making it more difficult to think clearly. If I tell the truth, I avoid all of this effort.

The second common category of honesty is
(35) honesty spoken in order to influence the actions of others. If you ask me what I did today, I am more likely to say, "I visited my publisher and she was very excited about my new book" than to say, "I finished my laundry." I choose, from
(40) among the honest responses I could make, the one that will most meet my own ends, in this case, to earn your admiration or respect. Some may say that this is a cynical view of honesty, that this kind of self-serving honesty is nearly as
(45) much of a distortion of truth as is an outright lie. This is exactly my point.

If this self-serving honesty erodes the integrity of personal relationships, how much more so does it confound the struggle for integrity
(50) between nations? When ambassadors from two countries sit down to discuss an issue together, their conversation is directed by the three categories of honesty—altruistic honesty, honesty of least effort, and honesty toward an end. How-
(55) ever, the three do not have equal standing. When there is a great deal at stake in the negotiations, will not honesty toward an end predominate? Of the three, it takes the most effort, though not as much as a lie. However, when there is much at
(60) stake, the effort is justified and, in fact, required.

When honesty toward an end predominates, what is said is true but may be misleading. An ambassador who wants to create an impression of military strength might comment that
(65) the government is considering a military draft. This fact may be true. However, the ambassador may choose to leave out the fact that the draft is unlikely to be approved, or that if approved, it will only result in a small increase in the size
(70) of the military. By omission, honesty toward an end leads to a "false truth." Indeed, such honesty is only distinguishable from a lie by the degree of distortion.

20. Which of the following statements best characterizes the main point of the passage?
   (A) True honesty does not actually exist.
   (B) Altruistic honesty does not benefit the person who speaks it.
   (C) Honesty does not always represent the truth.
   (D) Individuals tend to be more honest than nations.
   (E) Few people who want to be honest actually can be.

GO ON TO THE NEXT PAGE

21. Which one of the following would most contradict the author's statements?

(A) In closing a critical sale, a salesperson acknowledges that the product has a known problem, because it is easier to do so than to distort the truth.

(B) A diplomat from one country tells an ambassador of a hostile country that she admires his country's music.

(C) A stranger asks a resident of a city for directions to the train station, and the resident deliberately gives the wrong directions.

(D) The president of a country tells the citizens that there is evidence that another country is planning to attack, without mentioning that the evidence is hearsay, in order to increase the president's approval ratings.

(E) A professor asks a student if the student had studied for the test and the student admits to not having studied.

22. Which one of the statements below would the author most likely agree is a valid explanation for why a person who regularly uses honesty of least effort might be well regarded by others?

(A) People who use honesty toward an end are more clever at flattering others.

(B) Most people do not like to be friends with those whom they perceive as lazy.

(C) People generally feel friendly toward those who try to treat them with fairness and consideration.

(D) People who are not willing to put effort into fabricating a lie are more likely to make statements that seem trustworthy to others, and people are attracted to those who seem trustworthy.

(E) People who have no personal stake with respect to another person are generally well regarded.

23. Which one of the following statements comparing honesty with a lie are consistent with the author's definitions?

(A) Both honesty and a lie may be considerate of others.

(B) Honesty is sometimes as much a distortion of the truth as is a lie.

(C) Lies and honesty are not qualitatively different.

(D) A lie distorts the truth, whereas honesty chooses which truth to state.

(E) Honesty can be misleading but only a lie is a "false truth."

24. Which one of the following would, if true, most support a point that the author makes?

(A) Most people condemn others when others fail to be honest.

(B) In the absence of a vested interest in another person's actions, people are inherently inclined to be helpful.

(C) In some cases it is easier to tell a lie than to tell the truth.

(D) The honesty of least effort is a common type of honesty.

(E) It is unlikely that ambassadors from two countries would use altruistic honesty.

25. The passage most strongly suggests that the author uses the phrase "false truth" (line 71) in order to imply that a statement

(A) conveys a part of the truth that is intended to create a specific impression

(B) conveys information that is not itself true but that approximates the truth

(C) conveys information that is true of one situation but not true of the situation being discussed

(D) embellishes the truth by adding information that is not true in order to create a specific impression

(E) cites a fact that distorts the truth at least as much as a lie would

GO ON TO THE NEXT PAGE

26. The author's primary purpose in the second paragraph is to
    (A) provide an example that demonstrates how honesty is fundamentally self-centered
    (B) establish that there is more than one type of honesty
    (C) describe an interaction that meets the common definition of honesty
    (D) explain why the author personally prefers to be honest
    (E) provide advice for people who have lapsed in their attempt to be honest

27. The passage provides information that most helps to answer which one of the following questions?
    (A) What criterion can a listener use to determine whether a true statement is misleading?
    (B) Which creates more of a distortion—a lie that is based on reality or a lie that is completely fabricated?
    (C) Which is a greater distortion of the truth—honesty of least effort or honesty toward an end?
    (D) How can people avoid condemning themselves for their lapses in honesty?
    (E) Are all three types of honesty equally likely to be used in any situation?

STOP If you finish before the 35-minute time period is over, you may go back and check your answers in this section only. You may not work on any other test section.

WRITING SAMPLE

Time: 35 minutes

> **DIRECTIONS:** You will have thirty-five minutes to organize and write an essay on the topic described on the next page. Read the topic and all of the directions carefully. It is generally best to take a few minutes to organize your thoughts before beginning to write. Be sure to develop your ideas fully and leave time at the end to review what you have written. **Do not write on any topic other than the topic given. It is not acceptable to write on a topic of your own choice.**
>
> No special knowledge is needed or expected for this essay. Admission committees are interested in your reasoning, clarity, organization, use of language, and writing mechanics. The quality of what you write is more important than the quantity.
>
> Keep your essay in the blocked and lined area on the front and back of the separate Writing Sample Response Sheet. That is the only area that will be reproduced and sent to law schools. Be sure to write legibly.

Scratch Paper
Do not write your essay here. Scratch work only.

DIRECTIONS: The situation described below gives two choices. Either one of the choices can be supported based on the information given. In your essay, consider both choices and then argue in favor of one over the other. Base your argument on the two specified criteria and on the given facts. There is no "right" or "wrong" choice. Either choice can be reasonably defended.

Ellen Sanders wants to attend either Marcel University, a large public institution, or Back State College, a small private university. Both schools are located in states away from home and the tuition and related costs are roughly equivalent. Using the facts given below, compose an essay in which you argue in favor of choosing one alternative over the other on the basis of the two criteria below:

- Ellen wants to major in filmmaking and minor in adult recreation.
- Ellen wants to build a network of close friends to share her interests later in life.

Back State College is located in the backwoods of a northern state and has a reputation for its outstanding outdoors recreation program. Back State has a well-known recreation and team-building faculty. To repair the poor reputation of Back State's film department, Back State recently recruited John "Big Bear" Buckough, famous for his nature films and wildlife documentaries, to chair the department. In addition, Back State recently purchased the latest cameras, editing equipment, and software necessary to produce professional-quality digital films. Back State's student body is small and friendly. Their frequent winter wilderness events are legendary, and Back State's alumni reunions are well attended.

Marcel University is a large university located in downtown Large City that is famous for launching the career of the renowned filmmaker, Severna Lakeberg. Lakeberg and several of her colleagues speak at Marcel at least every other year. Many Marcel graduates gain film internships throughout the country. Marcel has a solid but relatively unknown sports and recreation faculty and curriculum. Marcel's large class sizes, numerous course offerings, and competitive atmosphere are not conducive to building long-term relationships. Ellen's closest companions will most likely be her freshman year roommates, who will probably pursue a wide variety of careers.

Scratch Paper
Do not write your essay here. Scratch work only.

Use the lined area below to write your essay. Continue on the back if you need more space.

ANSWER KEY
Practice Test 1

SECTION I: LOGICAL REASONING

1. D	8. C	15. C	22. B
2. E	9. B	16. C	23. C
3. B	10. D	17. A	24. D
4. A	11. D	18. E	25. E
5. C	12. A	19. E	26. A
6. E	13. E	20. A	
7. C	14. B	21. D	

SECTION II: ANALYTICAL REASONING

1. C	8. B	15. C	22. B
2. C	9. E	16. D	23. C
3. E	10. C	17. B	
4. B	11. B	18. B	
5. E	12. A	19. E	
6. C	13. D	20. D	
7. D	14. E	21. E	

SECTION III: LOGICAL REASONING

1. D	8. B	15. D	22. C
2. E	9. D	16. A	23. D
3. B	10. A	17. E	24. E
4. D	11. A	18. B	25. C
5. C	12. E	19. C	
6. B	13. C	20. D	
7. E	14. E	21. A	

SECTION IV: READING COMPREHENSION

1. A	8. D	15. B	22. D
2. E	9. B	16. D	23. C
3. C	10. B	17. E	24. B
4. B	11. D	18. A	25. A
5. E	12. D	19. A	26. C
6. B	13. C	20. C	27. E
7. B	14. D	21. A	

CALCULATING YOUR SCORE

1. Check your answers against the Answer Key on the previous page.
2. Use the Score Worksheet below to calculate your raw score. Your raw score is the total number of questions that you answered correctly.
3. Use the Conversion Table below to convert your raw score into a score on the 120–180 scale. Remember that these scores are approximate.

Score Worksheet

Section	Number of Questions	Number Correct	Number Incorrect	Number Not Answered*
Section I: Logical Reasoning	26			
Section II: Analytical Reasoning	23			
Section III: Logical Reasoning	25			
Section IV: Reading Comprehension	27			
Total:	101			

*You should not leave any questions unanswered. There is no penalty for guessing.

Conversion Table

Raw Score Range	Scaled Score	Raw Score Range	Scaled Score	Raw Score Range	Scaled Score	Raw Score Range	Scaled Score	Raw Score Range	Scaled Score
0–15	120	30	133	50	146	72–73	159	90	172
16	121	31–32	134	51–52	147	74	160	91–92	173
17	122	33	135	53	148	75–76	161	93	174
18	123	34–35	136	54–55	149	77	162	94	175
19	124	36	137	56–57	150	78–79	163	95	176
20	125	37–38	138	58	151	80	164	96	177
21	126	39	139	59–60	152	81–82	165	97	178
22–23	127	40–41	140	61–62	153	83	166	98	179
24	128	42	141	63–64	154	84–85	167	99–101	180
25	129	43–44	142	65	155	86	168		
26	130	45	143	66–67	156	87	169		
27–28	131	46–47	144	68–69	157	88	170		
29	132	48–49	145	70–71	158	89	171		

EXAM ANALYSIS

Every practice section that you take is an opportunity for you to evaluate your testing strategy. If you take a section under timed conditions, that also gives you an opportunity to evaluate your timing strategy. The last section of Chapter 1 (General Strategies) provides a detailed worksheet and plan for reviewing your performance and identifying exactly what strategy error led to each wrong answer. The sections of Chapter 1 on timing explain how to evaluate your timing strategy. Be sure to evaluate your timing strategy for every section that you take under timed conditions.

Use the plan in Chapter 1 to review every question that you answered incorrectly. The plan lists twenty-two specific errors. For each question that you answered incorrectly, you should review the parts of Chapter 1 and the other relevant chapters that cover the strategies with which you had trouble. The key to success is identifying your errors and reviewing again and again.

Use the following chart to summarize your performance based on four main categories of error. Enter the number of incorrect answers in each column. Some questions may fall under more than one category.

Summary of Incorrect Answers

Section	Total Incorrect	Didn't Take Enough Time	Misread Information	Got Down to Two Answers	Didn't Have a Strategy
I: LR					
II: AR					
III: LR					
IV: RC					
Total:					

After you have reviewed your timing strategy, enter the results in the chart on the next page. The questions for which you simply filled in a bubble without working on the question should be counted under Cold Guesses. If you spent more than fifteen seconds working on a question, do *not* count it under Cold Guesses. Under Number Correct and Number Incorrect, do not include Cold Guesses. The number in the Cold Guesses column, then, includes both incorrect and correct answers. In the final column, enter the number of incorrect answers on which you spent under two minutes.

Analysis of Timing Strategy

Section	Number Correct (not cold guesses)	Number Incorrect (not cold guesses)	Cold Guesses	Number of Incorrect Under 2 Minutes
I: LR				
II: AR				
III: LR				
IV: RC				
Total:				

If most of your incorrect answers took under two minutes, you should plan to spend more time on questions. If you have more than two or three questions incorrect—excluding Cold Guesses—you can increase your score by working on fewer questions but spending a little more time on the questions that you do work on. See the example below.

Example of Revised Timing Strategy

Section	Number Correct (not cold guesses)	Number Incorrect (not cold guesses)	Cold Guesses	Number of Incorrect Under 2 Minutes	Total Correct (including cold guesses)
First attempt	11	6	7	5	12
Revised attempt	11 + 2	0	7 + 4	0	15

By guessing cold on four more questions, the test taker in the example above had time to work the remaining two questions correctly. Approximately one out of five Cold Guesses results in a correct answer.

ANSWERS EXPLAINED

Section I: Logical Reasoning

1. **(D)** This is a *strengthens by principle* question. Choice D is a principle that strengthens the argument because the argument describes a patient who does not discuss (*report, respond, ask*) health issues and the conclusion implies that the patient may have a more productive relationship with a different physician.

   Choice A is incorrect because the conclusion is not concerned with making a diagnosis. Choice B is incorrect for the same reason, as well as the fact that the passage is not concerned with the patient's family. Choice C is incorrect because it does not strengthen the conclusion that the physician should ask the patient if the patient would prefer a different physician. Choice E is incorrect because the conclusion is not concerned with the physician wasting time.

2. **(E)** This is a *conclusion—what can be inferred* question. The correct answer must be a statement that can be defended by information in the passage. Choice E is correct because it is rare for a nonnative species to even survive.

   Choice A is incorrect because ecologists do not intentionally introduce nonnative plants. The plants are introduced accidentally. Choice B is incorrect because of the word *any*. According to the passage, most such plants will disappear on their own or will not cause disruption. Choice C is incorrect because the passage does not indicate what percentage of disrupted ecologies are due to nonnative plants. Choice D is incorrect because it cannot be defended that the fact that a plant survives means it will cause radical disruption. The passage leaves open the possibility that some plants might survive for years without causing any damage.

3. **(B)** This is a *role of a claim* question. The claim that is cited in the question stem is the conclusion of the argument. The sentences that follow it support the truth of the first statement. Choice B is correct because it describes the conclusion as a premise that the argument attempts to defend. It correctly describes the questions that point out contradictory interpretations of the "circumstantial information" mentioned in the passage.

   Choice A is incorrect because the cited claim does not explain the contradictions. The contradictions prove the claim. Choice C is incorrect because the cited claim is not contradictory. It is the reliance on circumstantial evidence that is contradictory. Choice D is incorrect because it is not a true statement. Choice E is incorrect. The cited claim is a conclusion but the argument does not propose that there is a causal relationship between the presence of similar businesses and the chance of success. Instead, the argument claims that presence or absence of similar businesses *cannot* be used to predict the success of a new business.

4. **(A)** This is a *resolve a paradox* question in an EXCEPT format. It does not use the words *paradox* or *discrepancy*. Four of the answer choices resolve the discrepancy. One does not. The discrepancy is that the group that had experience with a previous version of TypeSoFast (group A) would be expected to be more familiar with the new version than people who had never used TypeSoFast before (group B), yet in fact it took group A longer to complete the task.

   Choice B resolves the discrepancy by explaining that the people in group B did not take the extra time needed to be more accurate. Choice C resolves the discrepancy by implying that the conditions under which the two groups performed could have been different (noisier or quieter, better light or worse light). Choice D resolves the discrepancy by explaining why the people in group A may have needed more time to adjust to the changes, whereas the features of the new version were more familiar for the people in group B. Choice E resolves the discrepancy by explaining that the people in group A needed extra time to correct errors in the original text.

Choice A remains as the correct answer. Choice A does not resolve the discrepancy because the passage establishes that the two groups were equally proficient, so it is irrelevant that they used two different typing methods.

5. **(C)** This is a *flaw* question. Choice C correctly identifies a flaw in the argument because the arguer defends that each council member (a part of the whole) is capable of making a good decision and then incorrectly concludes that the council itself (the whole) will probably make a good decision.

Choice A is incorrect because the arguer does not infer that a poor decision *cannot* occur, only that it is unlikely to occur. Choice B is incorrect because it does not apply to the argument, which does not have to do with options. Choice D is incorrect because, even though the arguer does not believe the claim that the council cannot make a good decision is true, the arguer's basis for rejecting the claim is *not* that it has not been proven but that there is evidence (the fact that the members are competent) that the claim is false. Choice E is incorrect because the arguer does not claim to have proven that the council will not make a poor decision. The arguer only claims to show that the council will probably not make a poor decision.

6. **(E)** This is a *main conclusion* question. It asks for the main idea of the argument. Choice E is correct. The main conclusion is stated in the first sentence of the passage and expanded upon in the second sentence, which implies that nonviolence always involves some violence.

Choice A is incorrect because, although it is a true statement, it is not the point of the argument. Choice B is incorrect because the arguer does not imply that nonviolence should never be used, only that it should not be expected to be devoid of violence. Choice C is incorrect because the author does not claim that nonviolent resistance cannot affect change. Choice D is incorrect because, though a true statement, it is not the main point.

7. **(C)** This is a *sufficient assumption* question. Choice C is sufficient to make the conclusion true because the quality "gardener" inherently includes the second quality "natural," and the conclusion refers to people who already call themselves "gardener" and thus cannot call themselves "natural."

Choice A is incorrect because it is not sufficient to lead to the conclusion. Choice B is incorrect because the horticulturist does not say that it is inaccurate for a gardener to be called natural, only that it is redundant. Choice D is a necessary assumption. If there were a meaning of natural that was not an inherent part of being a gardener, the argument would fall apart. However, choice D is incorrect because it is not a *sufficient* assumption. By itself, it does not cause the argument to work. Choice E is incorrect because the fact that anyone who is natural must also be a gardener is irrelevant to the argument.

8. **(C)** This is a *strengthen* question. The passage is based on a cause-and-effect argument. The conclusion that is to be strengthened is that the two factors cited in the passage are the cause of people feeling unexpectedly prosperous. Choice C correctly strengthens this

causal relationship by showing that getting new credit can also lead to further reduction in the amount of debt still owed.

Choice A is incorrect because it does not strengthen the cause-and-effect argument, and it is irrelevant to the conclusion that people feel more prosperous. Feeling relieved is not the same as feeling prosperous. Choice B is incorrect for similar reasons. The "unexpected" approval in choice B is not the same as the "unexpected" prosperity in the conclusion.

Choice D is incorrect because it simply restates a premise in the argument that people are offered credit for which they previously did not qualify. Choice D appears similar to choice C but is missing the critical element of choice C in which part of the remaining debt is removed. Choice E is incorrect because it goes in the wrong direction. It indicates a different reason why people might feel prosperous—they saved money on the bankruptcy itself—and thus weakens the argument that people feel prosperous for the reasons given in the passage.

9. **(B)** This is a *parallel flaw* question. The flaw in the original argument is that the student falsely assumes that because a team as a whole has a certain characteristic, every member of the team has that characteristic. Choice B contains the same flaw. Just because the legislature has not approved a measure does not mean that every member of the legislature voted against the measure.

Choice A does not match the original flaw. Its flaw is that even though all of the honors students are in the club, the percentage of honors students could be low if there are many non-honors students in the club. Choice C is incorrect because the logic is not flawed. Choice C states that *all* vegetables are good for you. This is equivalent to saying that all members of the debate team are high scoring, whereas the original argument states that the team as a whole is high scoring. A team can be high scoring and yet have some members who are not high scoring. The logic in choice D is also not flawed. The flaw in choice E is assuming that Marissa only planted flowers that she preferred.

10. **(D)** This is a *type of reasoning* question. The original argument is based on an analogy between finding a wallet with $100 and being given $100 by an employer. Choice D correctly identifies that the conclusion is defended by an analogy.

Choice A is incorrect. It refers to a false appeal to authority. There is no authority cited in the original argument. Choice B is incorrect in that the original argument does not suggest a cause for keeping the $100. Choice C is incorrect because the considerations—how one would respond to a bonus from an employer—are not irrelevant, even if the parallel is not a strong one. Choice E is incorrect because neither keeping the wallet nor getting a bonus is an established pattern.

11. **(D)** This is a *flaw* question. Choice D is correct because the physician bases the conclusion on the actions of patients in the hospital, whose eating habits are unlikely to be representative of Americans as a whole.

Choice A is incorrect because the argument is not based on the intentions of the patients. Choice B is incorrect because the physician does apply a generalization. Choice C is incorrect because it involves supporting a premise. It is not a logical flaw to fail to provide supporting evidence for a premise. Choice E is incorrect because it is irrelevant.

12. **(A)** This is a *strengthen* question. The premises are based on the number of classes but the conclusion is about the number of students. Choice A correctly strengthens the argu-

ment because it establishes that more music classes and fewer art classes also means more music students and fewer art students, because the number of students per class has not changed.

Choice B is incorrect because it does not give a corresponding number for art students. Choice C is incorrect because it does not give the corresponding information for music students. Choice D is incorrect because it weakens the argument. Choice E is irrelevant. It is already known that there are more music classes.

13. **(E)** This is a *sufficient assumption* question. The premises in the passage are

jets transport quickly
indispensable service

To get to the conclusion, it is necessary to link these two statements.

If transport quickly → indispensable service

Choice E provides this statement and the conclusion then must be true.

Choice A is incorrect. It is a necessary assumption. If it were not possible for a service that is inexpensive to be indispensable, the argument would fall apart. However, choice A is not *sufficient* to arrive at the conclusion. Choice B is incorrect because it states

If indispensable → inexpensive

This statement does not lead to the conclusion.

Choice C is incorrect because it is not deductive. Choice D is incorrect because it states

If indispensable → transport

This does not lead to the conclusion.

14. **(B)** This is a *match a principle to a concrete example* question. In this particular question the original setup is a principle but the concrete examples in the answer choices are actually other principles. This question functions like a *parallel reasoning* question based on principles. The skeleton of the argument is

Don't want to cause pain in future
Pain in present is obvious
Pain in future is impossible to know
If not pain in present → go ahead, unless other reasons

In other words, because it is impossible to know if something will cause pain in the future, do not use the *possibility* of causing pain in the future as a reason for avoiding an action. The reasons for avoiding an action are that it causes pain now or that it meets other criteria (that the passage does not specify) for avoiding the action.

Choice B is correct because it has the same structure. The criteria for avoiding an investment are that it is losing money now or other unspecified criteria. The argument states that because it is impossible to know whether a project might lose money in the future, concern that it might do so is *not* a criterion for avoiding the project.

Choice A is incorrect. It states that fear that a fossil might contain valuable information *should* be the criterion applied in every case, unless there are other unspecified conditions. Choice C is incorrect. It differs from the original in that it states that something that causes pain in the present should be used now in the hope of avoiding pain in the future.

Choice D is not parallel to the original. It does not involve a future action and involves focusing on part of a group. Choice E is incorrect because it does not involve a future action.

15. **(C)** This is a *weaken* question. Choice C is correct because it directly weakens the assertion that going with Firm X will save money by showing an area in which Firm X is likely to be more expensive than Firm Y.

Choice A is incorrect because it is irrelevant. Not building the swimming complex is not given as an option. In addition, the swimming complex could contain more than just a swimming pool. Choice B is incorrect because the cost of the project, regardless of what Firm X ends up paying subcontractors, has already been determined.

Choice D is incorrect because the argument is based on the assertion that Firm X's plan is just as good as Firm Y's plan and still saves money. Choice E is incorrect because it strengthens the argument by showing that choosing Firm X has an additional financial benefit for the city.

16. **(C)** This is a *resolve a paradox* question. The paradox is that there are two factors that both lead to a higher mortality rate for infants. However, when the two factors occur together, the mortality rate is lower than for infants with just one of the factors. Choice C correctly resolves the paradox by stating that when two such factors are combined, the results are unpredictable. Although saying that the results are unpredictable may seem vague, it resolves the paradox by establishing that the results in that case may not be the expected result.

Choice A is incorrect. If either one of the factors overrode the other, it would still be expected that the mortality rate for children having both factors would be the same as the rate for children having one factor. Choice B is incorrect because it does not match the setup. The two factors do not lead to two different results.

Choice D is incorrect because, even if there are unknown factors that affect mortality, the two specific factors in the setup are already established as known. Choice E is incorrect because the weight of the mother is irrelevant to the argument. Even if it were argued that lower-weight women give birth to lower-weight babies, it is already established that the infants in question have low birth weight, so choice E does not add any new information.

17. **(A)** This is a *parallel reasoning* question. The original argument states that every member of a group has some influence but the group as a whole has more influence than any one member. Choice A correctly establishes that any one legislator has some influence but the group of legislators from one party has more influence than any one legislator.

Choice B is incorrect because it says the influence of the group is greater than the *combined* influence of all members, rather than the influence of any one particular legislator. Choice C is incorrect because it does not refer to a group. It compares one legislator with key committee members. Choice D is incorrect because it is the individual citizen who has a greater effect in one case than in another. To be correct, the individual citizen would have a greater effect as part of a group than as an individual. Choice E is incorrect because it does not compare one element (political party) with a larger group of which the political party is a member. It simply compares one group alone and one group coordinating with another group.

18. **(E)** This is a *strengthen by principle* question. Choice E is correct. The principle in choice E matches the setup. The patient's family did request a specific criterion, so the principle

is triggered. The result is that Dr. Carpenter recommends surgery if it is an option. Surgery is an option and the conclusion is reached.

Choice A is incorrect because it is not stated that surgery is more expensive. Choice B is incorrect because there is no evidence that surgery best meets the criterion of being more reliable. Choice C is incorrect because there is no evidence that surgery is the least invasive procedure. Choice D is incorrect because it does not lead to Dr. Carpenter choosing surgery over physical therapy.

19. **(E)** This is a *must be true* question. It functions in a similar way to a question that asks what can be concluded. One answer choice is forced to be true based on the original premises. The setup is deductive.

If attract investors AND broad market → viable
If –improvement AND –broad market → –viable

Choice E must be true. Given that *broad market* is a quality of the AC Quantum screwdriver, if *attract investors* is also true, it is inevitable that *viable* will result.

Choice A is incorrect. There is no evidence that *attract investors* must be true. Choice B results in

Improvement AND broad → viable

This is not a valid conclusion, as it results from negating both sides of

If –improvement AND –broad market → –viable.

Choice C is incorrect because it says

Viable ∴ improvement

This is not a valid conclusion.
Choice D is incorrect because

Viable ∴ attract investors

is not a valid conclusion from *If attract investors AND broad market → viable.*

20. **(A)** This is a *role of a claim* question. The arguer disagrees with the claim cited in the question stem and uses the argument to attack it. For this reason, choice A is correct.

Choice B is incorrect because the cited claim is not a summary of the other points but is the target of their attack. Choice C is incorrect because the cited claim does not support the conclusion. Choice D is incorrect because the cited claim does not answer the question of when in history people have stopped doing things that they realized harmed the environment. The implied answer is that people have never done that. Choice E is incorrect. The cited claim is about global warming and so does not match the problem of smoke in caves. Even if the claim were interpreted to mean simply taking care of the environment, offering a solution to the problem of smoke in the cave is not the <u>role</u> of the statement, though it might be a side effect.

21. **(D)** This is a *strengthen* question based on a cause-and-effect argument. The argument states that expanding the menu occurred at the same time as an increase in business from both new and previous customers. The argument concludes that expanding the menu caused both increases. Choice D strengthens the cause-and-effect relationship by showing that when the expanded menu is removed, both increases disappear.

Choice A is incorrect because, if anything, it indicates that new customers may not have come because of the new items, which weakens the argument. Choice B is incorrect because the friends are not necessarily new customers or previous customers who are coming more frequently than before. Because of this, choice B is irrelevant.

Choice C is incorrect because it does not add any new information. It does not strengthen the conclusion that previous customers are influenced by the expanded menu and, if anything, could weaken the argument by showing that new customers are coming because of invitations from friends, not because of the expanded menu.

Choice E is incorrect because it weakens the argument. It indicates that the increase in clientele is not a result of the expanded menu but that the expanded menu is a result of the increase in clientele.

22. **(B)** This is a *committed to agree/disagree* question. Choice B is correct because Roberto is forced to agree with it and Margarite is forced to disagree with it.

Choice A is incorrect because Roberto is forced to agree with it but Margarite is not committed to either the truth or falsehood of the statement. She does not state whether or not people wanted to return to their original language, only that if they had wanted to, they would not have been able to.

Choice C is incorrect because Margarite is forced to agree with it but Roberto does not have an opinion. Choice D is incorrect because Roberto is forced to agree and Margarite does not have an opinion. Choice E is incorrect because both are forced to agree with it.

23. **(C)** This is a *necessary assumption* question. The argument is

$$If -bus \rightarrow -interview$$
$$If -interview \rightarrow -job$$

John misses the bus at 8:15 and the conclusion is that he will not get the job. Choice C is correct because if negated—*There is another opportunity for John to get on the bus*—the argument falls apart.

Choice A is incorrect. It is not a valid statement, and if negated—*If John gets to the interview, he may not get the job*—it does not affect the argument. Choice B is incorrect because its negation—*There is another job that John would be willing to accept*—does not weaken the conclusion that John is not going to get the job he is hoping for.

Choice D is incorrect because its negation—*The bus left on time*—does not affect the argument. Choice E is incorrect because its negation—*John had control over the circumstance that kept him from getting to the station on time*—does not affect the argument.

24. **(D)** This is a *flaw* question that uses the wording *vulnerable to criticism*. The argument is deductive.

$$If\ mud \rightarrow mineralized$$
$$If -mineralized \rightarrow -fossil$$
$$\therefore\ If -mud \rightarrow -mineralized\ \textbf{(invalid logic)}\ AND\ if -mineralized \rightarrow -fossil$$

It does *not* follow from *If mud* $\rightarrow$ *mineralized* **that** *If -mud* $\rightarrow$ *-mineralized*. By definition, this flaw confuses a condition (*mud*) that is *sufficient* to result in *mineralized* with a condition that is *necessary* (*without mud, not mineralized*). Choice D correctly identifies this.

Choice A is incorrect because it refers to cause-and-effect logic. Choice B is incorrect because there is no generalization that is applied inappropriately. Choice C is incorrect because the argument says there will be no fossil because there is no mineralization, not because it is unlikely that there will be a fossil. Choice E is incorrect because there is no hypothesis, only stated if/then conditions.

25. **(E)** This is an *application of a principle* question. The criteria for undertaking a study, as given in the principle, are

> *majority of members agree to the study*
> *majority of members understand the benefits*

The application meets the criterion that the majority of members agreed to the study. It meets the criterion that there *is* a benefit to the group but it does not meet the criterion that the majority of members *understand* the benefit. Choice E is correct because it states that the majority of members understood that the community center is a benefit of participating in the study.

Choice A is incorrect because Anderson's membership or lack of membership in the group is not one of the criteria stated in the principle. Choice B is incorrect because the principle does not require that the approval be unanimous, only that the majority approve, which is already established in the application.

Choice C is incorrect because it refers to an unexpected benefit. Choice D is incorrect because it is irrelevant to the principle.

26. **(A)** This is a *weaken* question based on a cause-and-effect argument. Choice A weakens the argument because it raises the possibility that something other than the electromagnetic field, such as the plane itself, caused the disorientation.

Choice B is incorrect because it could be that the plane was simply too far away for the field to have an effect. Choice C is incorrect because, even though slowing down is not necessarily a sign of disorientation, choice C goes in the direction of strengthening the argument. Choice D is incorrect because it does not provide evidence to either strengthen or weaken the argument, although if anything, it goes in the direction of strengthening the argument. Choice E is incorrect because it does not clarify whether it was the removal of the electromagnetic field that caused the reorientation (which would strengthen the argument) or the removal of the plane (which would weaken the argument).

Section II: Analytical Reasoning

QUESTIONS 1–5

This is a one-to-one correspondence game (which means it is ordered) but is not a sequence game. In other words this is an ONS-A game (one-to-one, non-sequence, in the left branch of the flowchart, meaning it is ordered). There are three fixtures with branches. The branches are variable. There is at least one player assigned to each fixture but there could be as many as four. The optional branches are represented in the diagram by dotted lines. For simplicity, two sets of dotted lines are shown, even though there could be three, plus the solid, required, line.

The branches are not ordered. In other words, if there are several players assigned to a fixture, the order in which they are assigned does not matter. The diagram follows.

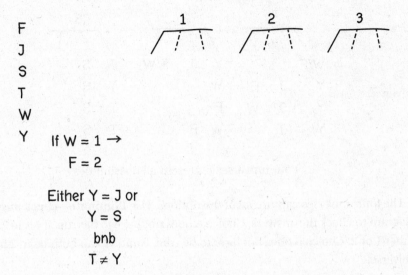

F
J
S
T
W
Y

If W = 1 →
F = 2

Either Y = J or
Y = S
bnb
T ≠ Y

NOTE: Refer to Chapter 4 for an explanation of the problem-solving tools (shown in bold).

1. **(C)** This is the typical first question. Use **Eliminate—apply rules, four violations**. The first rule states that if W = 1, then F = 2. A violation of this would have W in 1 but F *not* in 2. Choice D matches this violation. Break the second rule into two parts. First look for Y without either J or S. Choice A matches this violation. Next look for Y with both J and S. Choice B matches this violation. To check the final rule, look for T and Y together. Choice E matches this violation. Choice C is left and does not violate any rules. Choice C is the correct answer.

2. **(C)** This is a *must be true* question with new information that goes in the diagram. Using **Diagram—put in new information**, put T and S in 3. Using **General—options for player**, consider the options for Y. Y must be with J. They can be either in 1 or 2. Use **Diagram—parallel universes** to create the two universes.

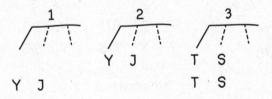

Use **General—options for fixture** to determine what the options are for the required position in 1. It must be either W or F. If it is W, then F must go in 2. If it is F, then W must go in 2, because if W were also in 1, F could not be there. For the top universe, then, W/F goes in the required position in 1 and its counterpart, F/W, must go in 2.

In the bottom universe, the required slot in 2 can be either W or F. The remaining player can go either in 1 or 2. The bottom universe then splits into three universes.

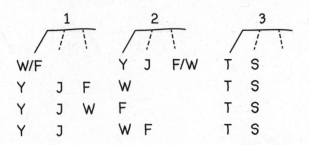

Four universes represent all possibilities

The four universes capture all of the options. Use **Eliminate—check answers against diagram** to check the answers. Choice A does not have to be true. If J is in 2, W can be in either 1 or 2. Choice B does not have to be true. F and W can both be in 2 in the bottom universe.

Choice C must be true. It is clear that with Y in 2, only one activity can be in 1. Quickly check the remaining answer choices to make sure there was not an error in the diagram. Choice D does not have to be true. W can be the only activity in 2. The diagrams also show that choice E does not have to be true. Either 1 or 2 can have one activity. Choice C is confirmed as the answer.

3. **(E)** This is a *could be true EXCEPT* question with new information that goes in the main diagram. Four of the answer choices could be true. One answer choice cannot be true. It violates rules. Use **Diagram—put in new information** to put W in 1. Use **Diagram— apply rules, musts** to put F in 2. Use **General—look for most restricted**. T is a highly restricted player, as it will determine where Y goes. T can go in 2 or 3, so create two universes. If T is in 2, Y is in 3, and vice versa. Applying the rules, wherever Y is, there must be one, and only one, of J or S. The universes are shown in the figure below.

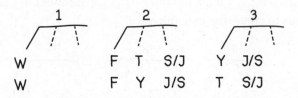

Two universes

The two universes are most likely enough to solve the question, even though they contain some optional information (S/J and J/S). Use **Eliminate—check answers against diagram**. Be careful to orient well to the question stem. Four answer choices could be true. One breaks rules. Choice A could be true if T is in 3. It is out. Choice B could be true if T is in 2. It is out.

Choice 3 must be true. It is out. Choice D also must be true. The remaining answer choice, E, cannot be true because in both universes, Gymnasium 3 has exactly two activities. Choice E is the correct answer.

4. **(B)** This is a *could be true* question with new information that does not go directly in the main diagram. However, it is possible to use two parallel universes to represent F and W being together. FW can be in either 2 or 3. It cannot be in 1 because the presence of W in 1 would trigger F being in 2.

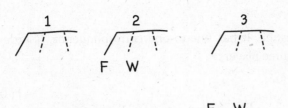

F W

Two universes showing all options for FW together

There are too many ways to fill in the rest of the diagram, so proceed to testing the answer choices. Four choices violate rules. One does not. Use **Test answers—prove a violation**. It is clear from the diagram that choice A cannot be true. For choice B, put T by itself in one of the gymnasiums, such as 1. Then Y could go in 2, with J or S. The remaining S or J could go in 3. There seem to be viable options for choice B, so mark it with a plus and check the other answer choices, because it is more definitive to prove rule violations.

Test choice C. Put Y in a gymnasium by itself. Apply the rules. Y must be with either J or S, so choice C violates rules. Test choice D. With F and W used, there are four elements that remain: J, S, T, and Y. If FW is in 2, for example, then one of the four elements must go in 3. Can the remaining three go in 1? T and Y cannot go together, so put Y in 3. However, Y requires one of J or S, leaving only two in 1. Try putting Y in 1 and putting T in 3. Y must be with J or S but cannot be in both. Thus, it is not possible to have three events in 1. Choice D is out. For the same reason, choice E is out. Choice B is confirmed as the answer.

5. **(E)** This is a *must be true* question with new information that does not go directly in the main diagram. TWS can go in any of the three gymnasiums. Create three universes to show the options. In the universe with TWS in 1, F must go in 2. There are two players remaining, Y and J, and they must go together. Every gymnasium must have at least one activity, so YJ goes in 3.

For the universe with TWS in 2, YJ must go together in one of the remaining gymnasiums and F must go in the final gymnasium. The same is true for TWS in 3.

Another way to consider the situation is that the combination TWS leaves F, Y, and J remaining. Y and J must be considered as a single unit, because they must go together. Because the remaining two gymnasiums must each be assigned something, F must go in one of them and YJ in the other. The options can be diagrammed as in the figure below.

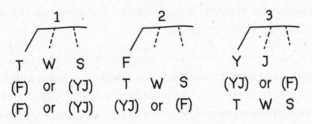

The parentheses represent elements that must be considered as a unit.

Use **Eliminate—check answers against diagram**. Choice A is incorrect because Y could take place in any of the gymnasiums. The same is true for choices B and C. Choice D is incorrect because one of the gymnasiums must have exactly one activity, one has two, and one has three. Choice E must be true. F must be in a gymnasium by itself, regardless of which gymnasium that is. Choice E is the correct answer.

QUESTIONS 6–11

This is a sequence game. It has one-to-one correspondence, is ordered, and provides a sequence of at least three players.

```
                                            H or G
   G                    1    2    3    4    5    6    7
   H                   ___  ___  ___  ___  ___  ___  ___
   J
   K
   L
   M
   N        M – J
            L – N
                 G
            J
                 N

       G = H or G
                 L
       M – J – N
                 G
```

6. **(C)** This is the typical first question. Use **Eliminate—apply rules, four violations**. A violation of the first rule would place M after J. Choice E matches this violation. A violation of the second rule would place L after N. Choice B matches this violation. The third rule has two parts. Check for J after G. No answer choices match this violation. Check for J after N. Choice D matches this violation. Check for someone other than H or G in sixth place. Choice A matches this violation. Choice C is left and is the correct answer.

7. **(D)** This is a *cannot be true* question with no new information. One answer choice violates rules. Use **General—count places in sequence** to review the supplemental diagram and determine who cannot come immediately before Griego. The only clear information from the supplemental diagram is that J must come between M and G. M is an answer choice and must be the correct answer.

8. **(B)** This is a *must be true* question with new information that goes in the main diagram. Use **Diagram—put in new information** and **Diagram—apply rules, musts** to put G in 3 and M and J in 1 and 2, respectively. According to the fourth rule, H must go in 6. Using **General—options for player** and referring to the supplemental diagram, determine the options for N. N must come after L, so the only options for N are 5 and 7. Create two universes.

 In the universe with N in 5, L must go in 4 and K must go in 7. In the universe with N in 7, K and L are interchangeable, so K/L and L/K go in 4 and 5.

H or G

1	2	3	4	5	6	7
M	J	G	L	N	H	K
M	J	G	L/K	K/L	H	N

Use **Eliminate—check answers against diagram** to check the answer choices. Choice A does not have to be true. K can interview seventh. Choice B appears to be required. There is no place other than 4 or 5 to put L. Choice B is a likely answer. As a double check, test the remaining answers.

Choice C is incorrect because N cannot interview in 4. Choice D is incorrect because N cannot interview sixth. Choice E does not have to be true. N can interview in 5. Choice B is confirmed as the correct answer.

9. **(E)** This is a *must be true EXCEPT* question. Four of the answer choices must be true. One either cannot be true or could be true but is not forced to be true. There is new information that goes in the main diagram. Put M in 4. Use **General—count places in sequence** to determine that there are three players that must come after M: J, N, and G. These three will take up all three slots after M. According to the fourth rule, G must go in 6. J comes before N, so N can only go in 7 and J can only go in 5. The remaining players— H, K, and L are assigned to 1, 2, and 3 as H/K/L. H, K, and L can be in any of six orders: HKL, HLK, KHL, KLH, LHK, or LKH.

H or G

1	2	3	4	5	6	7
H/K/L	H/K/L	H/K/L	M	J	G	N

Use **Eliminate—check answers against diagram**. Review the question stem. It is easy to become disoriented on EXCEPT questions. Four answer choices must be true. It is clear that choices A and B must be true. They are out. Choice C also must be true, as M, J, and G are fixed. Choice D must be true because H and K are either adjacent or L is between them. Choice E does not have to be true. H could be between L and K. Choice E is the only answer choice that does not have to be true and thus is the correct answer.

10. **(C)** This is a *could be true* question with new information that does not go directly into the main diagram. Use **Diagram—supplemental diagram or rules** to create a temporary supplemental sequence.

$$H$$
$$\searrow$$
$$L$$
$$M - J - N$$
$$\searrow$$
$$G$$

Use **Eliminate—check answers against diagram** to test the answers. Because the supplemental diagram does not show numbered positions in the sequence, it may help eliminate some answers but probably is not enough to answer the question. The supplemental diagram eliminates choice D, because L must come between H and N. The other answer choices are still options.

Check to see if it is possible to enter any information in the main diagram. Review the rules. Based on the fourth rule, that either H or G must be in 6, and the new information for this question, H cannot be in 6 because it now requires three players after it. Therefore, G must be in 6. Put G in 6 in the main diagram.

Using **General—options for fixture**, determine the options for the final position. Any player who requires another player to follow cannot be in 7. This eliminates H, L, M, and J. G is not an option for 7 because it is in 6. The only remaining options for 7 are N and K. Consider the options for slot 1. No player who requires another player beforehand can be in 1. J, L, N, and G are eliminated. Only H, M, or K can be in 1. There are now two universes. Both have G in 6. One has N in 7 and M/H/K in 1. The other has K in 7 and M/H in 1.

| | | | | | H or G | |
1	2	3	4	5	6	7
H/M/K					G	N
H/M					G	K

Using these universes as templates, test the answer choices. Choices A and B are now clearly out. G must be in 6. Choice C seems to be possible, and thus could be the correct answer. Check the remaining answer choices to prove that they violate rules. Choice D has already been eliminated based on the supplemental diagram. Choice E is out because interviewing after G would put K in the last time slot. Choice C is confirmed as the correct answer.

11. **(B)** This is a *CANNOT be true* question with new information that goes in the main diagram. Using **Diagram—put in new information**, put M in 4. Use **Diagram—apply rules, musts**. J, N, and G must go after M. G must go in 6. Using **General—options for player**, determine the options for N. If N goes in 5, there is no place for the required J before N. N can only go in 7. J must go in 5. Slots 1, 2, and 3 can be assigned H/L/K. There are no restrictions on the relative orders of these three players.

| | | | | | H or G | |
1	2	3	4	5	6	7
H/L/K	H/L/K	H/L/K	M	J	G	N

Check the answer choices against the diagram, looking for one answer that violates rules. Choice A seems consistent with the diagram. Choice C is probably out. Choice B is clearly not possible, based on the diagram. This is probably the correct answer. Double-check the remaining answer choices.

Choice C is out because it must be true. Choice D appears to be a possibility and is out. Choice E appears to be a possibility and is out. Choice B is confirmed as the correct answer.

QUESTIONS 12–17

This is an ordered game that does not have one-to-one correspondence (ONS-B). There are three players, each of which can be used multiple times. The game is set up vertically but the main diagram is horizontal, as usual. In this game there is a fixed number of fixtures (seven) with no branches. This is an exception to the general tendency for ONS-B games to have variable fixtures and to have branches. The setup is shown in the following figure.

P   Bottom   −R   Top

R $\underline{1}$ $\underline{2}$ $\underline{3}$ $\underline{4}$ $\underline{5}$ $\underline{6}$ $\underline{7}$

S

More S than P

   At most 1P

     above top R

   2 = P or S

   At least 1

     SPS

NOTE: The vertical arrangement is indicated by the labels "Bottom" and "Top."

12. **(A)** This is the typical first question. Use **Eliminate—apply rules, four violations**. A violation of the first rule would have either fewer P's than S's or an equal number. Choice E matches this violation. A violation of the second rule would have more than one P above the topmost R. Choice B matches this violation. A violation of the third rule would have R in 2. Choice D matches this violation. A violation of the fourth rule would be the absence of the sequence SPS. Choice C matches this violation. Choice A remains and is the answer choice that is free of violations.

13. **(D)** This is a *must be true* question with no new information. This means the correct answer is something that is forced to be true based on the original conditions. There is nothing to diagram, so test the answer choices, using **Test answers—negate a must**. Testing choice A, try to make an order that has more layers of raspberry than of peach or an equal number. Make a table to calculate the possible numbers of layers of each type. The number of layers of peach must be kept at a minimum so that the number of layers of both raspberry and strawberry are greater. Put 1 for peach. Raspberry can be 3 and strawberry can be 3.

Raspberry	Peach	Strawberry
3	1	3

The total number of layers is seven, as it must be. Choice A does not seem to have to be true. Theoretically, it might not be possible to create a viable order with the numbers above, but it is too time-consuming to test that out at this point. It is enough that there appear to be viable options. When the correct answer is negated, it should be clear that there cannot be viable options.

Negate choice B. Try to create more layers of raspberry than strawberry.

Raspberry	Peach	Strawberry
4	1	2

This seems to be a viable option that does not violate the rules in an obvious way. Go on to choice C and negate it. Try to create five layers of strawberry.

Raspberry	Peach	Strawberry
1	1	5

This order also seems viable. Go on to choice D and negate it. Try to create 3 layers of peach. Three layers of peach would require 4 layers of strawberry. There must be at least one layer of each flavor, so there must be at least one raspberry. However, this totals 8 layers, which is too many.

Raspberry	Peach	Strawberry
~~1~~	~~3~~	~~4~~

It is not possible to create more than 2 layers of peach; thus, choice D is the answer choice that must be true.

14. **(E)** This is a *could be true* question with new information that goes into the main diagram. Put R in 1 and S in 2. Use **Diagram—apply rules, musts**. The first layer is the only R. That means that there can be at most one P after it. Check this information against the answer choices. Choice D cannot be true and is out. Choice E not only could be true but must be true. Choice E is virtually guaranteed to be the correct answer but check the other answer choices quickly as a double check. The seventh layer cannot be P because of the SPS rule. With one P and one R, there must be exactly five Ss. Choices A, B, and C are out. Choice E is confirmed as correct.

15. **(C)** This is a *CANNOT be true* question with no new information. Four answer choices could be true or possibly must be true. One answer choice violates rules based on the original conditions. There is nothing to diagram, so use **Test answers—create a possible assignment, double check** to check the answer choices by trying to establish that the answer choice can be true.

    For choice A, try to create a viable order with four layers of raspberry. There are three remaining layers and more must be strawberry than peach, so exactly one must be peach and exactly two are strawberry. There must be a sequence of SPS and slot 2 must be S or P, so by putting SPS in 2, 3, and 4, respectively, the remaining slots can be raspberry. Because there is only one layer of peach, the second rule is not violated. Choice A is out.

    For choice B, if there are five layers of S, then there are exactly one layer of R and one of P. As long as there is a sequence of SPS and slot 2 is not an R, no rules are violated. Choice B is out.

    For choice C, put R in 1, 3, and 5. There is now no three-slot sequence for SPS. Choice C cannot be true and is the correct answer. As a double check, the remaining choice can be quickly tested. Choice D allows SPS in 2, 3, and 4, respectively, and does not violate the second rule. Choice E allows SPS in 1, 2, and 3, respectively, and does not violate any of the rules. Choice C is confirmed as correct.

16. **(D)** This is a *completely determined if* question with new information that goes in the main diagram. Put R in 1. Use **Diagram—apply rules, musts**. The second rule states that there cannot be more than one P above the uppermost R. Because slot 1 is the uppermost R, there can only be one P. If there is one R and one P, there must be five Ss. Fixtures 2 through 7 can each be either P or S and there only needs to be one sequence of SPS, so there are many options. Because all but one remaining layer is S, the determination of the

complete assignment depends on the position of P. Use **Diagram—supplemental diagram or rules** to make a temporary note that there is one P and five Ss. Test each answer choice to see if the additional information completely determines the assignment.

For choice A, if 7 is not P, it must be S. This does not determine the placement of P. Choice A is out. Choice B is a true statement but it does not determine the placement of P. For choice C, if the second layer is S, P can be assigned to any layer except the seventh. Choice C is out.

Choice D assigns P to 3. This is a valid assignment because the sequence SPS is in 2, 3, and 4, repetively. All of the remaining layers are S. Choice D completely determines the assignment of layers. A quick double check of choice E confirms that choice E does not determine the placement of P.

17. **(B)** This is a *could be true* question with new information that does not go in the main diagram. Four answer choices violate rules. Calculate the options for having the same number of layers of raspberry as peach. If there is one of each, there are five layers of strawberry. If there are two of each, there are three layers of strawberry. If there are three of each, that leaves one layer of strawberry, which violates the rule that there are more layers of strawberry than of peach. Thus, there are only two options. Test the answer choices to see if this enough information to eliminate some choices.

Choice A is out. There can be either three or five layers of S, not four. Choice B appears to be a valid possibility, which makes it a candidate for being the correct answer. Double-check the remaining answers quickly to confirm that they violate rules. Choice D contains too many layers of R. Choice E does not allow for a sequence of SPS. Choice B is confirmed as correct.

QUESTIONS 18–23

This is a one-to-one correspondence, ordered (all one-to-one games are ordered) game that is not a sequence (ONS-A). There are exactly three fixtures. Each fixture has from one to three branches (variable branching) and the order of the branches is important, because one of the branches must represent the lead presenter.

T
U
V
W
X
Y
Z

Lead 1   Lead 2   Lead 3

Either V is lead
with T
or X is lead with T
U, Z not both
lead
T – Y
W not after Y

18. **(B)** This is the typical first question. Four answer choices violate rules. Use **Eliminate— apply rules, four violations** to apply one rule at a time. A violation of the first rule would have someone other than V or X as lead presenter in the seminar with Thomas. Choice C matches this violation. A violation of the second rule would have both U and Z as leaders. Choice E matches this violation. A violation of the third rule would have T presenting in the same seminar as, or a later seminar than, Y. Choice A matches this violation. A violation of the fourth rule would have W presenting in a seminar after the seminar in which Y presents. Choice D matches this violation. Check the remaining choice, B, for violations. There are none. Choice B is the correct answer.

19. **(E)** This is a *must be true* question with new information that does not go in the main diagram. If T and W cannot be in consecutive seminars, then there must be exactly one seminar between them, meaning that T and W are in 1 and 3 or 3 and 1, respectively. Use **Diagram—parallel universes** to create these two universes. Use **Diagram—apply rules, musts** to fill in the universes. The universe with W in 1 and T in 3 violates the third rule, that T presents before Y. The only remaining universe is the one in which T is in 1 and W in 3. Applying the rules, the only position for Y is in 3, as W cannot appear in a seminar after Y but can appear in a seminar with Y. According to the first rule, the lead presenter in 1 is either V or X (V/X). Scan the answer choices to see if this is enough information to answer the question. Choice E must be true. A quick double check of the other answer choices shows that they all represent options that are possible but are not required.

20. **(D)** This is a *could be true* question with no new information. It is different from a typical first question because the answer choices do not represent complete assignments. Four of the answer choices violate rules. As there is no information to diagram, use **Test answers—prove a violation**.

   For choice A, check the rules to find the implications of the information in the answer choice. If X is not lead, then V must be lead with T. Put V and T in 3 and check the rules. This assignment violates the third rule by putting T after Y. Choice A is out.

   For choice B, put W, X, and U in 3. Apply the rules. The fourth rule is violated. The only place for Y is before W.

   For choice C, if W, X, and Y are not leads, V must be a lead. T cannot be a lead and only U and Z are left for the remaining two leads but this violates the rule that U and Z cannot both be leads.

   For choice D, if V is not a lead, then X must be the lead with T. T cannot be in the last position but can be in the second position. Y could then be in 3. W could be in 1. There do not appear to be any rule violations. To be sure you have not missed a violation in choice D, test choice E. If Y presents first, there is no slot for T to present before Y. Y cannot present first, so choice E is out. The occurrence of W in 1 is a distractor and is irrelevant. Choice D is confirmed.

21. **(E)** This is a *CANNOT be true* question with no new information. Four answer choices could be true, or possibly must be true, and one answer choice violates rules based on the original conditions. Finding that an answer choice appears to be valid is not as conclusive as proving that an answer choice violates a rule, so put question marks by answer choices that seem valid and look for the one rule violation.

   For choice A, put T in 1 and W, X, and Y in 3. V must be the lead in 1. There are multiple options for players to present in 2. Checking the rules, there do not appear to be any violations. Move on to choice B. V must be the lead for T. There seem to be many options, so put a question mark by choice B. For choice C, there is no reason why V and X cannot both be leads. There seem to be options for the other positions. For choice D, put U in 1 as lead and put Z in 3. No rules are violated and there seem to be multiple options. For choice E, if both V and X are in 3, one of them must be lead and T must be in 3. However, T in 3 violates the rule that T is before Y. Choice E cannot be true and the other answer choices do not need to be further evaluated.

22. **(B)** This is a *must be true* question with new information that goes in the main diagram, as well as new information that does not go in the main diagram. Put Y in 2 and apply the rules. T must go in 1, with V/X as the lead in 1. Use **General—options for player** to consider the options for W. W cannot go after Y, so W can go in 1 or 2. However, the new information for this question requires W to be a lead. The lead is taken in 1, so W must be the lead in 2. Checking the answer choices shows that this is enough information to answer the question. Choice B must be true. W must be in 2. The other answer choices could be true but do not have to be.

23. **(C)** This is an *equivalent condition* question. There is no new information. The key to answering the question correctly is to understand the original condition that is being replaced. W can appear before Y. W can appear in the same seminar as Y. W cannot appear in a seminar that takes place after the seminar with Y. This is not the same as saying that W must present before Y (choice A) because W and Y can present in the same seminar. For the same reason, choice B is incorrect. Both T and W have restrictions in terms of Y. However, neither choice D nor choice E correctly captures those restrictions. Only choice C correctly captures the relationship between W and Y.

Section III: Logical Reasoning

1. **(D)** This is a *strengthen by principle* question. Choice D is correct because it establishes that Slow but Steady is an investment with high quality (*excellent investment*).

    Choice A is incorrect because the argument does not claim that Slow but Steady is the best investment. Choice B is incorrect because, if true, it would weaken the argument. Choice C is incorrect because the argument is not based on the total amount of dividends—it may not have been much—but rather the length of time over which the company has paid dividends steadily. Choice E is incorrect because it mistakes a sufficient condition (paying over a long time is *sufficient* to make the investment excellent) for a *necessary* condition (if a company does not pay over a long time, it is not excellent).

2. **(E)** This is a *conclusion* question that asks for a statement that can be defended as true based on the premises in the setup. Choice E is correct because if a colony on Mars had a similar dangerous drop in oxygen, there would not be the option to have oxygen pumped in from outside. Completely running out of oxygen would be a danger that the participants in Biosphere 2 did not face.

    Choice A is incorrect because, although possibly true, it cannot be defended from the passage, and the passage implies that Biosphere 2 was not completely self-sustaining over a long period. Choice B is incorrect because it cannot be defended from the passage that the cause of the drop was unknown.

Choice C is incorrect because the passage does not indicate whether or not the designers anticipated the drop. Choice D is incorrect because it cannot be defended as true from the passage, even if it had actually been true.

3. **(B)** This is a *necessary assumption* question. The negation of choice B is that choosing from a limited variety of foods, based on criteria other than negative qualities of foods (which describes the situation fifty years ago) *is* highly frustrating. This destroys the argument because the current situation, then, would not necessarily be more frustrating than the situation in the past.

The negation of choice A is that people do not buy the same quantity of food today as fifty years ago. By itself, this statement does not affect the argument. The negation of choice C is that when people face frustration regularly, the amount of frustration does not lessen. This supports the argument.

The negation of choice D is that fifty years ago, when people went to the store, they did not know exactly what they were going to buy. This is not enough by itself to weaken the argument. The negation of choice E is that there are not more processed foods today than fifty years ago. This does not weaken the argument because the frustration today is not because the food is worse (more processed) but because people are more aware of health issues around food.

4. **(D)** This is a *strengthen* question in an EXCEPT format. Choices A, B, C, and E all strengthen the argument by strengthening the cause-and-effect relationship between visiting extended family and feeling satisfied with life. Choice D weakens the correlation by implying that it is satisfaction that causes people to visit relatives, as opposed to visiting relatives being the cause of satisfaction.

5. **(C)** This is a *parallel flaw* question. The original argument is deductive.

Premise: *If −rehearse regularly → forget*
Conclusion: *Forget ∴ −rehearse regularly* (invalid logic)

The flaw is **that the conclusion switches the two sides of the original syllogism from left to right. This does not create a valid statement. Choice C has the same flaw.**

If −practice → −competent
−competent ∴ −practice

Choice A is incorrect because it is not deductive. It sets up a correlation that implies a cause-and-effect relationship. Choice B is incorrect because it is valid logic. The conclusion is the contrapositive of the first if/then statement.

Choice D is incorrect. The logic in choice D is

If −exercise regularly → −stamina

Exercise regularly → stamina

This is flawed logic but it is a different flaw than the original. The two sides of the first if/then are not switched left and right but rather are negated without switching.

Choice E is incorrect because it is valid logic.

If recite → skilled
Recite ∴ skilled

6. **(B)** This is a *conclusion* question in a rare format that asks you to find the answer choice that can be proven to be false. Choice B can be proven to be false because if the child becomes upset over the food that the parents offer, keeping the child from crying takes precedence over giving the specified food.

Choice A cannot be proven to be false. It is still possible to comply with the plan because preventing the child from crying is an absolute requirement but providing the specified food only must be done "whenever possible." Choice C cannot be proven to be false. In other words, it might be true that the food will not upset the child. Choice D cannot be proven to be false. In fact, it is likely that choice D is true. Choice E cannot be proven to be false. It could be true that the child refuses to eat.

7. **(E)** This is a *role of a claim* question. Choice E is correct because the cited claim supports the conclusion of most sculptors that sculptures should be touched, and the art critic attempts to refute that argument.

Choice A is incorrect because the cited claim does not support the *art critic's* argument, but rather supports the argument of most sculptors. Choice B is incorrect because the cited claim *is* unwarranted, according to the art critic, but this strengthens the art critic's argument.

Choice C is incorrect because the cited claim is not the conclusion, but rather the premise, of the argument that the art critic attacks. Choice D is incorrect because the cited claim does not support the art critic's conclusion.

8. **(B)** This is a rare *identify an element of an argument* question. The element to which this question refers is the relationship between two factors discussed in the passage. Choice B is correct because the passage states specifically that the skills for responding to others are drawn from the skills learned for responding to one's own needs.

Choice A is incorrect because it is the reverse of what the passage describes. Choice C is incorrect because the stage of responding to others comes after the stage of responding to one's own needs. Choice D is incorrect because the passage does not describe a stage of *obsession* with the needs of others. Choice E is incorrect because, although possibly true, the passage does not utilize this relationship.

9. **(D)** This is a *flaw* question that uses the wording *vulnerable to criticism*. Choice D is correct because the argument establishes that a protection is not valid if it protects a company from paying for its exploitations but fails to show that this criterion applies to the protections for credit card companies included in the bankruptcy law.

Choice A is incorrect because failing to provide evidence to support a premise is not a logical flaw. A premise must be accepted as true. Choice B is incorrect because the problem with the protections in the bankruptcy law is not based on intention.

Choice C is incorrect because it is irrelevant whether or not the authors of the legislation agree with the arguer. Choice E is incorrect because it is not true that the arguer specifies the actions of a particular credit card company and then generalizes from that specific case to the case of other companies.

10. **(A)** This is a *weaken* question in an EXCEPT format. The argument uses analogy to defend its conclusion. The characteristics of the prehistoric animal are similar (analogous) to characteristics of modern canines. Choice B weakens the argument by showing that walking on the toes does not guarantee that the animal was a canine. Choice C weakens the argument by showing that the animal had certain features that identify it as

a feline rather than a canine. Choice D weakens the argument because the animal was found in a location where there may not have been canines. Choice E weakens the argument because it indicates that whatever features the specimen had may not be reliable for identifying its species.

The remaining choice, choice A, is correct. It does not weaken the argument because the teeth are consistent with canines. The fact that felines have similar teeth is irrelevant.

11. **(A)** This is a *necessary assumption* question. Choice A is correct because its negation—the people over seventy who died were in frail health—destroys the argument that if healthy seventy-year-olds are dying, we are all in danger.

The negation of choice B is that an equal percentage of people in their seventies died, compared to people in their eighties and nineties. This does not weaken the argument. The negation of choice C is that only a small percentage of people over seventy who caught the flu died from it. This does not destroy the argument because it is likely that for all but the most deadly diseases, it is only expected that a small percentage of people with the disease will die.

The negation of choice D is that a large number of people between the ages of five and seventy have died from the disease. This strengthens, rather than weakens, the argument. The negation of choice E is that those in frail health who have died are mostly over seventy. This is irrelevant because the argument is based on the fact that many healthy seventy-year-olds have died. On the other hand, stating that most of those who died were in frail health destroys the argument, as in choice A.

12. **(E)** This is a *conclusion* question that asks for a fact that can be inferred. Choice E is correct because the opening of the factory caused all of the events that led to the accident.

Choice A is incorrect because it cannot be proven that ambulances were never previously delayed. It is possible that they were delayed for reasons other than the extra traffic from the new factory. Choice B is incorrect because even if all of the factory workers live in the city limits, they would cause congestion by traveling on the highway in the direction of the suburbs.

Choice C is incorrect because the passage states that traffic is now heavily congested. Previously it could have been moderately congested. Choice D is incorrect because the collision was not caused by an ambulance that had been delayed on the highway, but rather by an ambulance that had taken city streets instead of the highway.

13. **(C)** This is a *match a principle to a concrete example* question. The answer choices are principles and the setup is a concrete example. This question functions much like a *strengthen* question except that the answer choices are abstract principles. Choice C best matches the setup. The argument states that the reason for firing the managers is because their actions unfairly hurt a competitor. Breaking the law is *not* one of the criteria that the argument uses to reach its conclusion.

Choice A is incorrect because the argument's reason for firing is not the breaking of the law. Choice B is incorrect for several reasons. It is not clear that the two managers met in order to agree on a common price. It is implied but cannot be proven. In addition, choice B is incorrect because the firing is not based on breaking a law.

Choice D is incorrect because it includes an extra element—violating a law—as a cause for firing, along with correct reason—unfairly hurting a competitor. Choice E is incorrect because it focuses on violating the law.

14. **(E)** This is a *complete the sentence/argument* question. Choice E is correct because the point of the passage is that aerobic exercise has a health benefit that cannot be achieved in any other way.

Choice A is incorrect because it is too specific. The person could do any aerobic activity. Choice B is incorrect because the passage does not imply that it is necessary to stop doing yoga. Choice C is incorrect because doing more yoga is not a substitute for aerobic exercise. Choice D is incorrect because the passage does not imply that it is necessary to discuss exercise with a physician. The passage assumes that aerobic exercise has a unique health benefit.

15. **(D)** This is a *must be true* question, which is a variation on a *conclusion* question. The correct answer is something that must be concluded. Choice D is correct because the passage establishes

$$If-impacted \rightarrow -monitor$$
$$Monitor \therefore impacted \text{ (the contrapositive)}$$

and choice D establishes *monitor*.

Choice A is incorrect because the population can decline for reasons other than human interference. Choice B is incorrect because, although it is true that if an area is impacted, it must be managed, it is *not* true that it must be managed through monitoring. Choice C is incorrect because the passage does not provide any information to support it. Choice E is incorrect because a new plant could be introduced by factors other than humans, such as wind.

16. **(A)** This is a *parallel reasoning* question. The setup predicts the future from an established pattern. Choice A correctly states that a past pattern—turtles returning in the fall—will probably happen, given that there are elements that meet the conditions of the past pattern, namely that there were turtles born in the pond.

Choice B is incorrect because, instead of predicting that most of the residents will attend the fair this year, it gives a different prediction, that people who are not residents will not attend. Choice C is incorrect because, instead of making a prediction about the trees setting fruit, it predicts what will happen if the trees do not set fruit.

Choice D is incorrect because it poses a cause-and-effect argument. Choice E is incorrect because it predicts a new event, rather than the repetition of a past pattern.

17. **(E)** This is a *resolve a paradox* question. Choice E is correct because it explains how the customers could hold to the principle that they would not buy genetically modified products and yet prefer CrunchOBites, namely that they did not know that it contained genetically modified corn.

Choice A is incorrect because it leaves open the possibility that the customers could have chosen one of the cereals with no genetically modified ingredients. Choice B is incorrect because despite the natural sweetness, the customers should have rejected it for its genetically modified ingredients.

Choice C is incorrect because, even though being hungry could conceivably influence someone's food choice, it would not be expected to affect their ethical decision not to buy foods with genetically modified ingredients. Choice D is incorrect because it does not explain why the customers would choose a food with genetically modified ingredients.

18. **(B)** This is a *committed to agree/disagree* question. Choice B is correct because Stephen is forced to disagree with it and LaShauna is forced to agree with it.

Choice A is incorrect because Stephen does not have an opinion about requiring exposure to Beethoven in the case in which all of the children appreciate the music. LaShauna is forced to disagree with choice A. Choice C is incorrect because both arguers agree with it. Choice D is incorrect because both arguers disagree with it. Choice E is incorrect because neither arguer has an opinion. Neither one specifies whether the benefits of Beethoven's music are academic.

19. **(C)** This is a *weaken* question based on a cause-and-effect argument. The argument is that Taikon received certain feedback, after which his writing style changed, and that the feedback must have been the cause of the change. Choice C is correct because the feedback was based on improving sales. If Taikon's primary goal is not sales, this weakens the argument that he changed his style in order to increase sales.

Choice A is irrelevant. Whether or not Taikon made a profit on the first book, he could have made more profit by following the critics' advice. Choice B implies that perhaps the critics were wrong but does not change the fact that their comments caused Taikon to change.

Choice D is irrelevant. The fact that Taikon intended his novel to be historical does not change the fact that the critics' comments changed his approach. Choice E is also irrelevant. The issue is not that the second novel contained a smaller amount of detail (because it was shorter) but rather that it was written in a different style.

20. **(D)** This is a *type of reasoning* question. The setup argues by analogy—a society is like a family. Choice D correctly expresses this.

Choice A is incorrect because the passage does not contrast the two situations. Choice B is incorrect because neither of the two arguments is flawed. Choice C is incorrect because the passage does not emphasize a difference between society and family. Choice E is incorrect. The only aspect of the setup to which it could apply is a family functioning but not being happy. However, the argument does not state that the reason that the family is not happy is because it is functioning.

21. **(A)** This is a *sufficient assumption* question. The logic is

Premise: *If hybrid → protect environment*
Conclusion: *contribute to well-being*

The missing condition needed to arrive at the conclusion is

If protect environment → contribute to well-being

which leads to the conclusion

If hybrid → well-being

Choice A is correct because it states the contrapositive of the missing condition, namely

−contribute to well-being ∴ *−protect environment*

Choice B is incorrect because its logic is

−hybrid → −well-being

which is simply the negation of both sides of the conclusion and is therefore not a valid statement.

Choice C is incorrect because its logic is

$$\textit{If protect environment} \rightarrow \textit{hybrid}$$

This statement switches the original statement from left to right, which does not result in a valid statement.

Choice D is incorrect because it weakens the argument, rather than leading to the conclusion. Choice E is incorrect because it weakens the argument.

22. **(C)** This is a *match a principle to a concrete example* question. The setup is a concrete example. The answer choices are principles. Choice C correctly matches the setup because there are two responses to the question "Do you want a pet?" The first response is a verbal "yes." The second response is a verbal or nonverbal rejection. The two responses are contradictory. The arguer uses this fact to conclude that the question must have been misunderstood.

Choice A is incorrect because, even though it is consistent with the setup, it does not discuss the misunderstanding of the question. Choice B is incorrect for the same reason.

Choice D is incorrect because it is not consistent with the passage. There is no evidence that the customers did not reveal how they really felt. Choice E is also inconsistent with the passage because the customers did not refuse to answer. In addition, both choices D and E fail to address the issue of misunderstanding the question.

23. **(D)** This is a *main conclusion* question, which asks for the point of the passage. Choice D is correct because the passage establishes that objectivity is difficult to achieve.

Choice A is incorrect because the point of the passage is not that journalists try to write objectively but that there are several barriers to doing so. Choice B is incorrect because it is too narrow to encompass the point of the passage as a whole. Choice C is incorrect because it is too narrow and because there is no information about the goals of the editors. They may or may not be as concerned with objectivity as the journalists. Choice E is incorrect because the passage does not state or conclude that it is *unlikely* that an article will be objective, only that there are several obstacles to objectivity.

24. **(E)** This is a *flaw* question that uses the format *fails to consider the possibility*. Choice E is correct. It indicates that the mayor has reversed the cause-and-effect relationship between violence and the number of uniformed officers.

The other answer choices are incorrect because, even if true statements, they are not flaws in the logic of the argument.

25. **(C)** This is a *flaw* question. Choice C is correct because if the people being surveyed felt that they might be arrested for breaking the law, they would be unlikely to admit that they had done so. As a result, the argument would fall apart.

Choice A is incorrect because there is no indication that the one thousand passengers were not representative. Choice B is incorrect because the meaning of "ethical" is not ambiguous. Choice D is incorrect. It refers to circular reasoning, in which the conclusion is contained in one of the premises, which is not the case in this argument. Choice E is incorrect because if people had claimed to carry prohibited items when in fact they had not, this would have strengthened the ethicist's logic because the percentage of people actually carrying prohibited items would be even lower.

Section IV: Reading Comprehension

1. **(A)** This is a *main point* question. Choice A correctly identifies the point of the passage, that the model of medical geology is one that has promise for other disciplines.

   Choice B is incorrect because, even though it includes accurate details of medical geology, it does not mention the importance of the medical geology model. Choice C is incorrect because the fact that there are no medical geology specialists is not the main point of the passage and is not seen by the author as negative.

   Choice D is incorrect because the author considers medical geology to be an effective model. Choice E is incorrect because it leaves out other aspects of medical geology and does not include the importance of medical geology as a model.

2. **(E)** This is an *agree with a view* question. Choice E is correct because the author states that the medical geology model of collaboration between scientists from different disciplines could be helpful in other scientific disciplines as well.

   Choice A is incorrect because the author does not believe that it is necessary to be knowledgeable in all of the subdisciplines in order to make a valuable contribution. Choice B is incorrect because the author believes that each scientist's contribution, even though it might focus on one subdiscipline, is important for the overall outcome of medical geology.

   Choice C is incorrect because there is no evidence that the author believes it. Choice D is incorrect because the author believes that a specialist in geology is not likely to also be a specialist in medicine.

3. **(C)** This is a *use of a word/phrase* question. Choice C correctly captures the author's intent. Choices A, B, and D do not capture the author's intent. Choice E incorrectly attributes to the author an objection that could theoretically be posed by some people.

4. **(B)** This is an *implied fact/inference* question. Choice B is correct because it can be inferred from (1) the statement that many people in southwest China suffer from fluorine toxicity and (2) the statement that much fluorine toxicity comes from burning of coal in the home, that the people in southwest China probably burn coal in the home.

   Choice A is incorrect because an immunization program does not involve geological materials. Choice C is incorrect because there is no information in the passage about *overexposure* to iodine. Choice D is incorrect because the passage does not support this. Choice E is incorrect because the passage says the opposite.

5. **(E)** This is an *extension/application* question. The question stem refers to the two points that the author uses to rebut the possible objection by traditional scientists. Choice E is correct because it is a counterargument to the author's rebuttal that anyone well trained in multiple areas would not likely be as skilled as someone trained in only one area.

   Choice A is incorrect because it addresses a point earlier in the paragraph. Choice B is incorrect because the author's rebuttal is not based on what traditional science has done. Choice C is incorrect because the fact that a university offers such a degree does not affect the author's argument that earning such a degree has two drawbacks. Choice D is incorrect because it addresses a comment later in the paragraph.

6. **(B)** This is a *stated fact* question in a NOT format. Four of the answer choices are based on stated information. Choice B does not fall under the goals because it does not have to do with geological minerals or chemicals. Choice A is incorrect because it falls under goals 2 and 3. Choice C is incorrect because it falls under goal 3. Choice D is incorrect because it falls under goal 4. Choice E is incorrect because it falls under goal 5.

7. **(B)** This is a *main point* question. Choice B is correct because it incorporates the main point that many arguments use invalid logic, as well as the conclusion that lack of valid arguments prevents a real debate.

Choice A is incorrect because it only refers to supporters of the death penalty. Choice C is incorrect because, although consistent with the passage, it is not the main idea. Choice D is incorrect for the same reason. Choice E is not consistent with the passage.

8. **(D)** This is a *function* question that asks for the function of the second paragraph. Choice D is correct because the paragraph begins with the proposition that it is possible to apply logic to certain arguments and then evaluates the argument.

Choice A is incorrect because the argument in the paragraph is not essentially emotional. Choice B is incorrect because it is not the point of the paragraph to judge arguments on one side of the debate only. Choice C is incorrect because the second paragraph does not compare the two sides of the debate. Choice E is incorrect because, even though the paragraph does this, this is not the purpose of the paragraph.

9. **(B)** This is an *implied fact/inference* question. Choice B is correct because the author implies that, as of the time that the article was written, people have not yet begun doing that which is necessary for there to be real debate on the death penalty.

Choice A is incorrect because it is a claim that the author implies is not valid. Choice C is incorrect for the same reason. Choice D is incorrect because it is a statement that the passage considers but does not claim is true. Choice E is incorrect because the passage states the opposite. Something that reduces murders is not necessarily the same as something that deters murders.

10. **(B)** This is a *use of a word/phrase* question. Choice B is correct because the rhetorical question cited in the stem refers to the circular reasoning in the previous sentence, and choice B describes circular reasoning.

Choice A is incorrect because the argument that is being referred to is not purely emotional, even if it has an emotional basis. Choice C is incorrect because the argument being referred to does not claim that the death penalty will deter murder, only that it can deter murder, if anything can.

Choice D is incorrect because the author does not claim to either support or oppose the death penalty. Choice E is incorrect because the author's viewpoint is not fundamentally emotional.

11. **(D)** This is an *analogous situation* question. Choice D is correct because both statements are misleading. Choice A is incorrect because both attempt to use logic, even if the logic is not valid. Choice B is incorrect because it is not true of either argument. Choice C is incorrect because there is no evidence concerning how the people who would make the second argument would feel about the death penalty. Choice E is incorrect because it refers to information in the third paragraph.

12. **(D)** This is a *stated fact* question in an EXCEPT format. Answer choices A, B, C, and E are all stated in the passage. Choice D is correct because the passage does not give any information about the specific beliefs of people who are opposed to the death penalty.

13. **(C)** This is an *identify the structure* question. Choice C is correct because the hypothesis is that it is possible to logically evaluate arguments that are emotionally based. The test case is the statement that if anything can deter murder, it is the death penalty.

The conclusion is that the death penalty can deter murder, and it is unwarranted because the logic only supports that the death penalty might deter murder in some cases. The argument about toothpaste is the analogous case.

Choice A is incorrect because the first sentence is not a conclusion but rather a hypothesis. Choice B is incorrect because the paragraph does not question a belief. Choice D is incorrect because it does not reject the hypothesis that it puts forth. Choice E is incorrect because the first sentence is not an expression of frustration. It is a hypothesis.

14. **(D)** This is a *stated fact* question. Choice D is correct because the passage describes how the ACS used guns to purchase land for a small price.

Choice A is incorrect because ACS was not founded by free African Americans. Choice B is incorrect because the passage does not support it. Choice C is incorrect for the same reason. Choice E is incorrect because it was Paul Cuffee who believed this.

15. **(B)** This is a *disagree* question. It asks for a point of disagreement between the authors of the two passages. Choice B is correct because the author of Passage A states that most African Americans had no interest in moving to Africa, whereas the author of Passage B states that the idea of repatriation had tremendous draw.

Choice A is incorrect because both authors would agree with it. Choice C is incorrect because neither author comments on this. Choice D is incorrect because it was the ACS that they were suspicious of, not Paul Cuffee. Choice E is incorrect because, whereas the author of Passage B would be forced to agree, the author of Passage A has no opinion.

16. **(D)** This is an *in common* question. Choice D is correct because it is true of both passages. Choice A is incorrect because only Passage A mentions this. Choice B is incorrect because neither passage questions Paul Cuffee's motives. Choice C is incorrect because neither passage is directly concerned with the current African American experience. Choice E is incorrect because only Passage B mentions this.

17. **(E)** This is an *implied fact/inference* question. Choice E is correct because the passage implies that it was the presence of free African Americans with some wealth that was required for the notion of repatriation to Africa to arise.

Choice A is incorrect because this is stated in Passage A. Choice B is incorrect for the same reason. Choice C is incorrect because it was African Americans in Liberia, not in America, who treated native Africans as second-class citizens. Choice D is incorrect because Passage B states that a rich African heritage prevailed among African Americans in America.

18. **(A)** This is an *agree with a view* question. Choice A is correct because the author consistently portrays ACS as not representing the real interests of African Americans.

Choice B is incorrect because the author states that most African Americans at that time did not want to move. Choice C is incorrect because it refers to Passage B. Choice D is incorrect because there is nothing to indicate it in the passage and because the passage states that free African Americans first settled in Liberia. Choice E is incorrect for the same reasons that choice A is correct.

19. **(A)** This is an *in common* question. Choice A is correct. It refers to the actions of the ACS in Passage A, and in Passage B it refers to the discrimination against native Africans by African Americans in Liberia.

Choice B is incorrect because neither passage considers this. Choice C is incorrect because the passages do not discuss the effect of the repatriation movement on *slaves,* only on free African Americans. Choice D is incorrect because Passage A does not consider the issue of where the authentic homeland would be. Choice E is incorrect because only Passage A discusses this.

20. **(C)** This is a *main point* question. Choice C correctly identifies the main point as establishing that honesty is not the same as the truth. Choice A is incorrect because altruistic honesty is considered true honesty. Choice B is incorrect because altruistic honesty may unintentionally benefit the speaker. Choice D may be true but is not the main point. Choice E is incorrect because the passage states that people *are* honest but that honesty is not what it seems.

21. **(A)** This is an *extension/application* question. Choice A contradicts the author's proposition that when there is much at stake, honesty toward an end will prevail, because the salesperson uses honesty of least effort.

In choice B it is not possible to determine which type of honesty the statement represents, and therefore the statement does not contradict the author's descriptions. Choice C is not an example of honesty at all and so does not contradict the author's descriptions. Choice D corresponds to the description of honesty toward an end. Choice E corresponds to honesty of least effort.

22. **(D)** This is an *agree with a view* question. Choice D is consistent with honesty of least effort and explains why it would lead to being well regarded. Choice A is incorrect because it talks about honesty toward an end. Choice B is incorrect because, if people considered telling the truth to be lazy, it would lead to *not* holding the person in high regard. Choice C refers to altruistic honesty, as does choice E.

23. **(C)** This is an *implied detail* question. The passage states that the difference between certain kinds of honesty and a lie is a matter of degree, a quantitative difference, rather than a difference of quality. Choice C reflects this.

Choice A is incorrect because the passage does not say whether or not a lie may be considerate of others. Choice B is incorrect because what distinguishes honesty from a lie is the amount of distortion, so honesty must have less distortion than a lie. Choice D is incorrect because according to the passage, both distort the truth. Choice E is incorrect because the passage describes certain examples of honesty as "false truth."

24. **(B)** This is a rare *strengthen* question, which functions in the same way as a *strengthen* question in Logical Reasoning. Choice B is correct because it strengthens the author's assertion in the second paragraph that if the author has no personal stake, the author will naturally be considerate of the other person.

Choices A, C, and E do not strengthen any assertion in the passage. Choice D merely repeats a premise of the argument without adding information that would strengthen it.

25. **(A)** This is a *use of a word/phrase* question. Choice A correctly identifies the author's meaning, namely that by leaving out information and citing only part of the truth, a false impression is created.

Choice B is incorrect because the information in a "false truth" is not false. Choice C is incorrect because it does not match the author's meaning. Choice D is incorrect because a "false truth" does not add false information. Choice E is incorrect because the "false truth" differs from a lie in that it distorts the truth less than a lie does.

26. **(C)** This is a *function* question. Choice C is correct because altruistic honesty matches the common definition of honesty as being free of self-interest.

Choice A is incorrect because self-centered honesty is described in later paragraphs. Choice B is incorrect because the second paragraph introduces only one type of honesty. That there is more than one type of honesty is established in the third paragraph. Choice D is incorrect because, even though the author uses the word *I*, it does not refer to the author. Choice E is incorrect because the second paragraph does not provide advice.

27. **(E)** This is a *helps to answer* question. The passage answers the question in choice E by saying that, when there is much at stake, honesty toward an end will prevail.

The passage does not provide an answer for choices A or D. Choice B is incorrect because the passage does not compare different types of lies. Choice C is incorrect because the passage does not distinguish between the degree of distortion of the two types of honesty.

Writing Sample: Example of a Superior Response to the Essay

Ellen Sanders ("ES") chooses Back State College ("BSC") over Marcel University ("MU") because BSC offers a solid filmmaking education and a strong friendship-building experience. ES uses two criteria, which are that ES wants to major in filmmaking and that she wants to build a network of close friends, to choose between BSC and MU. BSC is ES's superior choice because BSC has shown a commitment to building its film department, and BSC has cohesive alumni. MU is ES's inferior alternative because ES's large system might not be conducive to making close friends. Therefore BSU is ES's superior choice because BSC better meets ES's selection criteria.

ES uses two criteria to choose between BSC and MU. One criterion says ES wants to major in film and minor in recreation. The second criterion says ES wants to develop lifelong friends who will share her interests. These criteria may be combined into a single rule that says ES wants to make long-term friendships and receive a solid education in filmmaking. ES's long-term goal to make close friends is greater than ES's need to attend a famous film school.

BSC is ES's superior choice because BSC's intimate setting affords ES many opportunities to form lifetime friendships through BSC's outdoor recreation programs and wilderness events. In addition, BSC has shown a commitment to film education by hiring Buckough and purchasing new cameras, equipment, and software. Unfortunately, the BSC film department previously had a poor reputation. Even so, BSC is ES's superior alternative because BSC offers ES greater social opportunities and BSC is rebuilding its filmmaking department.

MU is ES's inferior choice. MU's large student population, urban lifestyle, and competitive atmosphere does not help ES form long-term friendships. In addition, MU's recreation department is not well known. While MU's film department has a solid reputation, MU's lack of intimate social opportunities all point to BSC as ES's superior choice. Therefore, ES rejects MU as her less desirable alternative.

BSC is ES's superior alternative. BSC is more likely than MU to help ES form new and long-lasting friendships through its outdoor programs. BSC's new film department chair and equipment provide ES a solid filmmaking education. MU's large size and competitiveness could undercut ES's efforts to form solid friendships. In conclusion, ES selects BSC because BSC will better fit her long-term goals to make excellent friends and films.

ANSWER SHEET
Practice Test 2

SECTION I

1. Ⓐ Ⓑ Ⓒ Ⓓ Ⓔ	8. Ⓐ Ⓑ Ⓒ Ⓓ Ⓔ	15. Ⓐ Ⓑ Ⓒ Ⓓ Ⓔ	22. Ⓐ Ⓑ Ⓒ Ⓓ Ⓔ
2. Ⓐ Ⓑ Ⓒ Ⓓ Ⓔ	9. Ⓐ Ⓑ Ⓒ Ⓓ Ⓔ	16. Ⓐ Ⓑ Ⓒ Ⓓ Ⓔ	23. Ⓐ Ⓑ Ⓒ Ⓓ Ⓔ
3. Ⓐ Ⓑ Ⓒ Ⓓ Ⓔ	10. Ⓐ Ⓑ Ⓒ Ⓓ Ⓔ	17. Ⓐ Ⓑ Ⓒ Ⓓ Ⓔ	24. Ⓐ Ⓑ Ⓒ Ⓓ Ⓔ
4. Ⓐ Ⓑ Ⓒ Ⓓ Ⓔ	11. Ⓐ Ⓑ Ⓒ Ⓓ Ⓔ	18. Ⓐ Ⓑ Ⓒ Ⓓ Ⓔ	25. Ⓐ Ⓑ Ⓒ Ⓓ Ⓔ
5. Ⓐ Ⓑ Ⓒ Ⓓ Ⓔ	12. Ⓐ Ⓑ Ⓒ Ⓓ Ⓔ	19. Ⓐ Ⓑ Ⓒ Ⓓ Ⓔ	26. Ⓐ Ⓑ Ⓒ Ⓓ Ⓔ
6. Ⓐ Ⓑ Ⓒ Ⓓ Ⓔ	13. Ⓐ Ⓑ Ⓒ Ⓓ Ⓔ	20. Ⓐ Ⓑ Ⓒ Ⓓ Ⓔ	27. Ⓐ Ⓑ Ⓒ Ⓓ Ⓔ
7. Ⓐ Ⓑ Ⓒ Ⓓ Ⓔ	14. Ⓐ Ⓑ Ⓒ Ⓓ Ⓔ	21. Ⓐ Ⓑ Ⓒ Ⓓ Ⓔ	28. Ⓐ Ⓑ Ⓒ Ⓓ Ⓔ

SECTION II

1. Ⓐ Ⓑ Ⓒ Ⓓ Ⓔ	8. Ⓐ Ⓑ Ⓒ Ⓓ Ⓔ	15. Ⓐ Ⓑ Ⓒ Ⓓ Ⓔ	22. Ⓐ Ⓑ Ⓒ Ⓓ Ⓔ
2. Ⓐ Ⓑ Ⓒ Ⓓ Ⓔ	9. Ⓐ Ⓑ Ⓒ Ⓓ Ⓔ	16. Ⓐ Ⓑ Ⓒ Ⓓ Ⓔ	23. Ⓐ Ⓑ Ⓒ Ⓓ Ⓔ
3. Ⓐ Ⓑ Ⓒ Ⓓ Ⓔ	10. Ⓐ Ⓑ Ⓒ Ⓓ Ⓔ	17. Ⓐ Ⓑ Ⓒ Ⓓ Ⓔ	24. Ⓐ Ⓑ Ⓒ Ⓓ Ⓔ
4. Ⓐ Ⓑ Ⓒ Ⓓ Ⓔ	11. Ⓐ Ⓑ Ⓒ Ⓓ Ⓔ	18. Ⓐ Ⓑ Ⓒ Ⓓ Ⓔ	25. Ⓐ Ⓑ Ⓒ Ⓓ Ⓔ
5. Ⓐ Ⓑ Ⓒ Ⓓ Ⓔ	12. Ⓐ Ⓑ Ⓒ Ⓓ Ⓔ	19. Ⓐ Ⓑ Ⓒ Ⓓ Ⓔ	26. Ⓐ Ⓑ Ⓒ Ⓓ Ⓔ
6. Ⓐ Ⓑ Ⓒ Ⓓ Ⓔ	13. Ⓐ Ⓑ Ⓒ Ⓓ Ⓔ	20. Ⓐ Ⓑ Ⓒ Ⓓ Ⓔ	27. Ⓐ Ⓑ Ⓒ Ⓓ Ⓔ
7. Ⓐ Ⓑ Ⓒ Ⓓ Ⓔ	14. Ⓐ Ⓑ Ⓒ Ⓓ Ⓔ	21. Ⓐ Ⓑ Ⓒ Ⓓ Ⓔ	28. Ⓐ Ⓑ Ⓒ Ⓓ Ⓔ

SECTION III

1. Ⓐ Ⓑ Ⓒ Ⓓ Ⓔ	8. Ⓐ Ⓑ Ⓒ Ⓓ Ⓔ	15. Ⓐ Ⓑ Ⓒ Ⓓ Ⓔ	22. Ⓐ Ⓑ Ⓒ Ⓓ Ⓔ
2. Ⓐ Ⓑ Ⓒ Ⓓ Ⓔ	9. Ⓐ Ⓑ Ⓒ Ⓓ Ⓔ	16. Ⓐ Ⓑ Ⓒ Ⓓ Ⓔ	23. Ⓐ Ⓑ Ⓒ Ⓓ Ⓔ
3. Ⓐ Ⓑ Ⓒ Ⓓ Ⓔ	10. Ⓐ Ⓑ Ⓒ Ⓓ Ⓔ	17. Ⓐ Ⓑ Ⓒ Ⓓ Ⓔ	24. Ⓐ Ⓑ Ⓒ Ⓓ Ⓔ
4. Ⓐ Ⓑ Ⓒ Ⓓ Ⓔ	11. Ⓐ Ⓑ Ⓒ Ⓓ Ⓔ	18. Ⓐ Ⓑ Ⓒ Ⓓ Ⓔ	25. Ⓐ Ⓑ Ⓒ Ⓓ Ⓔ
5. Ⓐ Ⓑ Ⓒ Ⓓ Ⓔ	12. Ⓐ Ⓑ Ⓒ Ⓓ Ⓔ	19. Ⓐ Ⓑ Ⓒ Ⓓ Ⓔ	26. Ⓐ Ⓑ Ⓒ Ⓓ Ⓔ
6. Ⓐ Ⓑ Ⓒ Ⓓ Ⓔ	13. Ⓐ Ⓑ Ⓒ Ⓓ Ⓔ	20. Ⓐ Ⓑ Ⓒ Ⓓ Ⓔ	27. Ⓐ Ⓑ Ⓒ Ⓓ Ⓔ
7. Ⓐ Ⓑ Ⓒ Ⓓ Ⓔ	14. Ⓐ Ⓑ Ⓒ Ⓓ Ⓔ	21. Ⓐ Ⓑ Ⓒ Ⓓ Ⓔ	28. Ⓐ Ⓑ Ⓒ Ⓓ Ⓔ

SECTION IV

1. Ⓐ Ⓑ Ⓒ Ⓓ Ⓔ	8. Ⓐ Ⓑ Ⓒ Ⓓ Ⓔ	15. Ⓐ Ⓑ Ⓒ Ⓓ Ⓔ	22. Ⓐ Ⓑ Ⓒ Ⓓ Ⓔ
2. Ⓐ Ⓑ Ⓒ Ⓓ Ⓔ	9. Ⓐ Ⓑ Ⓒ Ⓓ Ⓔ	16. Ⓐ Ⓑ Ⓒ Ⓓ Ⓔ	23. Ⓐ Ⓑ Ⓒ Ⓓ Ⓔ
3. Ⓐ Ⓑ Ⓒ Ⓓ Ⓔ	10. Ⓐ Ⓑ Ⓒ Ⓓ Ⓔ	17. Ⓐ Ⓑ Ⓒ Ⓓ Ⓔ	24. Ⓐ Ⓑ Ⓒ Ⓓ Ⓔ
4. Ⓐ Ⓑ Ⓒ Ⓓ Ⓔ	11. Ⓐ Ⓑ Ⓒ Ⓓ Ⓔ	18. Ⓐ Ⓑ Ⓒ Ⓓ Ⓔ	25. Ⓐ Ⓑ Ⓒ Ⓓ Ⓔ
5. Ⓐ Ⓑ Ⓒ Ⓓ Ⓔ	12. Ⓐ Ⓑ Ⓒ Ⓓ Ⓔ	19. Ⓐ Ⓑ Ⓒ Ⓓ Ⓔ	26. Ⓐ Ⓑ Ⓒ Ⓓ Ⓔ
6. Ⓐ Ⓑ Ⓒ Ⓓ Ⓔ	13. Ⓐ Ⓑ Ⓒ Ⓓ Ⓔ	20. Ⓐ Ⓑ Ⓒ Ⓓ Ⓔ	27. Ⓐ Ⓑ Ⓒ Ⓓ Ⓔ
7. Ⓐ Ⓑ Ⓒ Ⓓ Ⓔ	14. Ⓐ Ⓑ Ⓒ Ⓓ Ⓔ	21. Ⓐ Ⓑ Ⓒ Ⓓ Ⓔ	28. Ⓐ Ⓑ Ⓒ Ⓓ Ⓔ

Practice Test 2

Time: 35 minutes
     27 Questions

> **DIRECTIONS:** Each set of questions in this section is based on one passage or on a pair of passages. Answer the questions based on what is <u>stated</u> or <u>implied</u> in the passage or in the pair of passages. More than one answer choice could conceivably answer the question in some cases. However, you should choose the <u>best</u> answer. The best answer is the response that answers the question most accurately and completely. When you have chosen the best answer, fill in the space on your answer sheet that corresponds to your answer.

A patent confers the right for the patent holder to prevent others from making, selling, or otherwise making use of the patented tech-
Line nology without the permission of the patent
(5) holder. In principle, patents benefit society. They encourage innovators to create and perfect new products with the knowledge that the innovator will be able to profit from the results. At the same time, the patent process requires
(10) that the patent holder reveal the details of the innovation so that, after the patent expires, the public will continue to benefit from the product and the technology behind the product.

In practice, the process of issuing patents
(15) has been criticized from numerous perspectives. Whereas informed people might consider the ability for people to own, control, and profit from their work to be the epitome of capitalism, there are those—including the gov-
(20) ernment of the Netherlands in the 1800s—who have believed that patents are inconsistent with capitalistic free trade policy. Presumably,

they would prefer a system in which innovators can try to profit from their work but cannot
(25) stop others from copying or even stealing it.

A more substantial criticism of patents is that many patents are based on improvements to technologies that are already patented, which complicates the issue of ownership.
(30) For example, suppose that Eduardo has been granted a patent on a new type of fishing pole. Sandra then invents a technology that improves the new fishing pole and is granted a patent on it. Sandra's technology is quite likely
(35) useless without Eduardo's technology. This raises the question of whether it is legitimate to issue a patent for a product that cannot be used without the permission of the holder of a different patent. It is also legitimate to propose
(40) that Sandra did not own the right to create an improvement on Eduardo's product.

In the case above, it is not clear who owns Sandra's invention because she cannot use it without coordinating with Eduardo. Because

GO ON TO THE NEXT PAGE

(45) the goal of a patent is to grant exclusive ownership rights to an individual, when a new patent is based on a previous patent owned by a different person, the patent system is not functioning as intended. In this era of rapidly
(50) expanding technologies, it is quite possible that most patents fall into this category.

There is a practical aspect to this theoretical objection to patents. With increasing confusion over the ownership of patents based on
(55) patents based on still other patents, there is an increase in litigation over patent rights. In many cases, the cost of litigation is greater than the value of the patented technology. While the issuing of patents achieves its goals in some
(60) cases, it would be better to eliminate patents altogether. If society were to buy valuable, new innovations outright, the innovators would receive an immediate lump sum payment for their efforts, and society could put the innova-
(65) tion to immediate use.

1. Based on the passage, it can be concluded that the author and the government of the Netherlands in the 1800s would both agree that
   (A) it is the responsibility of a national government to reduce costly litigation when possible
   (B) granting patents can, in some case, confuse the issue of ownership of a technology
   (C) the most substantial criticism of patents is that they are inconsistent with a policy of capitalistic free trade
   (D) a person who has created a new technology should have the right to profit from that technology
   (E) for a person who has created a new technology to own a patent on that technology is not consistent with a policy of capitalistic free trade

2. Which one of the following most directly expresses the central idea of the passage?
   (A) Patents encourage innovators to create and perfect new products, while ensuring that society has access to the technology behind new products.
   (B) Although patents encourage innovators to create new products, patents are not consistent with policies of free trade and should be eliminated.
   (C) While some objections to patents are simply theoretical, there are objections to patents that are based on practical concerns.
   (D) Although patents offer certain benefits, at present patents often do not serve their intended purpose and could be replaced by other approaches for encouraging innovation.
   (E) If society paid innovators a lump sum for their innovations, both the innovators and society would benefit.

GO ON TO THE NEXT PAGE

3. Which one of the following, if true, most seriously undermines the author's criticism of patents for technologies that are based on previously patented technologies?
   (A) When a person obtains a patent for a new technology that is based on a previously patented technology, it is almost never clear who has the right to make decisions about the new technology.
   (B) In many cases of litigation over patented technology, the cost of litigation is not greater than the value of the technology.
   (C) In many cases, patents are owned by corporations, not individuals.
   (D) When a person obtains a patent for a new technology that is based on a previously patented technology, the owner of the previously patented technology is almost always willing to compromise with the owner of the new technology in making any decisions about how the new technology is to be used.
   (E) When a person obtains a patent for a new technology that is based on a previously patented technology, the owner of the previously patented technology almost always allows the owner of the new technology to make any decisions about how the new technology is to be used.

4. Which one of the following is most strongly implied by the passage?
   (A) If an entrepreneur wants to use, for commercial purposes, a patented technology owned by another person, the entrepreneur must agree to disclose the details of the technology once the patent has expired.
   (B) If a merchant wants to sell a product that uses a patented technology owned by another person, the merchant must pay the patent holder.
   (C) If a manufacturer wants to make a product that uses a patented technology owned by another person, the manufacturer must obtain permission from the patent holder.
   (D) A patent is not inconsistent with free trade policy unless a patent holder refuses to allow others to use the patented technology.
   (E) If an innovator creates a new technology and charges others to use it, the innovator's actions are inconsistent with free trade policy.

5. The author's attitude toward the issuing of patents in this modern era can best be described as
   (A) absolute support
   (B) qualified agreement
   (C) complete neutrality
   (D) reserved antagonism
   (E) total disapproval

GO ON TO THE NEXT PAGE

6. Based on the information in the passage, the author would be most likely to agree with which one of the following statements about a later patent—held by one person—based on an earlier patent—held by a different person?

(A) Since the 1800s, most patents have been based on earlier patents.

(B) It is probable that either the holder of the later patent or the holder of the earlier patent will initiate a lawsuit against the other.

(C) The issuing of the later patent confuses the issue of the ownership of the earlier patent.

(D) It is the owner of the earlier patent who actually owns the technology for which the later patent was issued.

(E) It is not clear that the holder of the later patent actually owns the technology for which the later patent was issued.

7. According to the descriptions of the purposes of a patent given in the passage, all of the following would achieve the goals of a patent EXCEPT:

(A) The holder of a patent made a profit from selling the patented technology but only by forcing all competitors out of business.

(B) After receiving a patent on a technology, the holder of the patent borrowed money to manufacture samples of the new technology.

(C) The holder of a patent who never earned a profit from the patented technology published a complete description of the details of the technology.

(D) The holder of a new patent that is based on an earlier patent wins a suit filed by the holder of the earlier patent challenging the new patent holder's exclusive ownership of the newly patented technology.

(E) The holder of a new patent that is based on an earlier patent enters into an agreement with the holder of the earlier patent that allows both patent holders to profit from sales of the newly patented technology.

8. In using the word *legitimate* in line 39, the author of the passage most clearly means that

(A) the assertion that Sandra does not own the right to create an improvement on Eduardo's product is a reasonable one

(B) issuing Sandra a patent for a product that she cannot use without Eduardo's permission does not meet the goals of a patent

(C) there is a legal basis for arguing that Sandra does not own the right to create an improvement on Eduardo's product

(D) there is a legal distinction between receiving a patent and receiving permission to use the patent

(E) it may not be ethical for Sandra to create an improvement on Eduardo's product

Unlike the cities of the Old World, most American cities have evolved around the use of the automobile. With only a few notable excep-
Line tions, public transportation in American cities
(5) has not appreciably reduced private car traffic nor the noise and pollution that go along with car traffic. Because of the spread of American urban areas, even aggressive public transportation initiatives are unlikely to reduce private
(10) car traffic in the future. Cars are simply faster, more flexible, and, in many cases, cheaper than taking the bus.

The most significant drawbacks of car traffic are congested streets, noise, chemical pollu-
(15) tion from car exhaust and from pumped gasoline, and a dependence on petroleum. Dependence on petroleum is a problem because petroleum is a limited resource that, when it runs out, will require a Herculean restructur-
(20) ing of the technologies that currently depend on it. In addition, dependence on petroleum has political implications because it ties our economy to a small number of petroleum-producing countries.

(25) One solution for the problems of heavy car traffic seems appealing, at least at first glance. Electric car technology is quiet and it is clean. A freeway full of electric cars would be, at least in our imaginations, like a breath of fresh air.
(30) While the freeway would not be any less congested, the noise of gasoline engines would be replaced by the sound of wind, and a clean wind at that. The hidden problem with electric car technology is the issue of how and where
(35) the electricity is generated. Even if every car today were replaced with an electric one, if the electric energy to run the cars were generated by gasoline-powered generating stations, the consumption of gasoline would not drop at all.
(40) The pollution from burning fossil fuel would simply be transferred from one location to another.

Electric cars can only reduce the problems associated with gasoline-powered cars if the
(45) electricity needed to run them is generated in clean and renewable ways. One potential source of such energy can be found in the car itself. When the driver of a car applies the brakes, the work performed to slow and stop
(50) the car generates a large amount of kinetic energy. In standard cars, this energy is lost as heat. However, regenerative braking systems capture some of this energy and convert it directly into electricity, which can be stored
(55) in a battery or used directly to power the car. Regenerative braking systems have the potential to generate large amounts of electricity at virtually no cost. In Sweden, massively heavy trains—carrying coal from the coal fields in
(60) the north—that have regenerative braking can generate enough electricity when loaded to return the train, once empty, to its origin. In fact, the trains often have excess electricity that can be pumped back into the power grid.

9. The author's main purpose in the passage above is to
   (A) provide the background of a problem and point out the drawbacks to a solution to the problem
   (B) defend a solution to a problem against criticisms of that solution
   (C) describe a problem, criticize a possible solution, and present an alternate solution
   (D) explain how certain solutions to a problem also solve additional problems
   (E) describe several problems caused by automobiles and consider two alternatives to the use of automobiles

GO ON TO THE NEXT PAGE

10. Based on the passage, which one of the following is the author most likely to believe about automobiles in cities?
(A) They are better than public transportation in several ways.
(B) Despite public transportation initiatives, automobiles will continue to contribute to noise and pollution.
(C) Converting to electric automobiles would reduce the consumption of gasoline by urban car owners.
(D) An automobile in a city causes more pollution than an automobile in the country.
(E) Electric cars using regenerative braking have the potential to reduce congestion in city traffic.

11. It can be inferred from the passage that which one of the following is most likely true of cities of the Old World?
(A) Most cities in the Old World do not have congestion, noise, and pollution.
(B) Some cities in the Old World have been more aggressive about introducing electric cars than have American cities.
(C) More people in cities of the Old World use public transportation than use private cars.
(D) Many cities of the Old World evolved around the use of horses for transportation.
(E) Most cities in the Old World did not evolve around the automobile.

12. Based on the passage, which one of the following scenarios is most similar to the situation of electric cars that use electricity derived from gasoline-powered generators, as described by the author?
(A) In a city that relies on horses for transportation and whose streets are polluted with horse manure, gasoline-powered automobiles are introduced.
(B) In a country with diminishing forests, plastic construction materials are introduced to replace wooden construction materials, but the fabrication of the plastic construction materials requires the burning of wood.
(C) A city buys a new fleet of buses so that taking public transportation becomes faster, more flexible, and cheaper than driving a personal automobile.
(D) A community replaces their coal-burning electricity-generating plant, which had caused serious air pollution, with arrays of solar panels that generate enough electricity that there is an excess that can be sold to neighboring communities.
(E) A city provides a tax credit for residents to buy solar-powered electric lawn mowers to replace gasoline-powered lawn mowers that create noise and pollution, but even with the tax credit, the electric lawn mowers are too expensive for most residents.

GO ON TO THE NEXT PAGE

13. In the first paragraph, the author states that public transportation initiatives are unlikely to reduce private car traffic in the future primarily in order to
    (A) highlight the distinction between Old World cities and American cities
    (B) provide background on the conflict between those who want to increase the role of public transportation and those who want to introduce less-polluting automobiles
    (C) predict that pollution from automobiles cannot be reduced unless public transportation is made a viable option
    (D) suggest that public transportation can reduce congestion but cannot reduce pollution
    (E) emphasize that solutions to the problems caused by automobiles must involve changing the nature of automobiles

14. The author uses the phrase "massively heavy" in the second from the last sentence of the passage in order to suggest that
    (A) regenerative brakes can stop even an extremely heavy vehicle
    (B) the more energy that is required for regenerative brakes to perform their braking function, the more energy they generate
    (C) an empty train requires less energy to operate than a heavily loaded train does
    (D) even a very heavy vehicle can be operated by electricity
    (E) coal is massively more polluting as an energy source than electricity is

GO ON TO THE NEXT PAGE

Passage A

Most people, if asked to give the defining characteristic of fiction, would probably say that a work of fiction is primarily a story that
Line is not true. Some even go on to say that what
(5) predicts that fiction will be entertaining is the *fact* that it is not true, and that the further a story strays from what is true, the more entertaining it can be expected to be.

Undoubtedly there is some correlation
(10) between how imaginative a work of fiction is and how entertaining it is. However, some reflection on this issue leads to the conclusion that the mere fact that a story departs from reality does not, for most people, guarantee
(15) that the people will be entertained by the story. Consider a story in which roads are made of a crushed-brick compound instead of asphalt or concrete or in which peach trees bear fruit in May instead of July. So what? There is noth-
(20) ing inherently entertaining about a fact simply because it does not conform to real life.

What, then, is the quality that turns a compilation of facts that are not true into an interesting work of fiction? The answer, it may be
(25) argued, is in how real the untrue facts are. Consider a story in which a dog talks. Such a story is fascinating, but not because dogs do not really talk. It is fascinating because talking is an intimate aspect of our reality and dogs are
(30) an intimate aspect of our reality. By bringing these two aspects together, a work of fiction creates an entertaining world that is *more* real, not less real, than our ordinary world.

Passage B

How does science fiction differ from other
(35) types of fiction? It is not necessarily in the degree to which the fictional world differs from our ordinary one. After all, the world of the Roman empire, or even the world of Victorian England, is dramatically different from ours but
(40) does not necessarily constitute science fiction. Even the worlds of fantasy literature, which are different from *any* world that has existed on Earth, are not necessarily science fiction.

The key to science fiction does lie in the
(45) imagination but there is another element that defines science fiction. It is the application of imagination to human knowledge. That is to say that science fiction looks into the human mind, into the storehouse of knowledge, of
(50) tools and technologies, and uses imagination to push the human mind into the future. The science fiction writer sees the mind as a movement, from the primitive discoveries of the past toward a distant and unknown future. The task
(55) of science fiction, then, is to show us a glimpse of where we are going, how we are evolving, and what our fate is to be. While science fiction entertains, its primary goal is to allow us to fulfill our destiny, or as science fiction writers
(60) might portray it, the multiverse of possible destinies that unfold just beyond the outer limits of our knowledge. The further that a science fiction story takes us from our current reality, the more entertaining it is.

15. Both passages are primarily concerned with exploring which one of the following topics?
    (A) the distinction in literature between details that are not factually true and details that are factually true
    (B) how writers of certain types of fiction view the human mind
    (C) how accurate most people's definition of certain types of fiction is
    (D) what it is that defines certain types of literature
    (E) the difference between fiction in general and science fiction

GO ON TO THE NEXT PAGE

16. Passage A offers which one of the following as an explanation for what makes a work of fiction entertaining?
    (A) juxtaposing two elements of our reality that are not normally juxtaposed
    (B) pushing the boundaries of human knowledge into the future
    (C) the further a story strays from the truth, the more entertaining it is
    (D) creating a world that is more imaginative than our ordinary world
    (E) drawing on elements that are intimate aspects of our reality

17. Which one of the following is a statement from Passage A that supports the conclusion of the author of Passage B?
    (A) Most people, if asked to give the defining characteristic of fiction, would probably say that a work of fiction is primarily a story that is not true.
    (B) The fact that a story departs from reality does not, for most people, guarantee that the people will be entertained by the story.
    (C) There is some correlation between how imaginative a work of fiction is and how entertaining it is.
    (D) A work of fiction creates an entertaining world that is *more* real, not less real, than our ordinary world.
    (E) Fiction uses imagination to push the human mind into the future.

18. The argument outlined in Passage A and the argument made by the author of Passage B are both put forth by
    (A) showing that details that are untrue are in some ways more real than details that are literally true
    (B) refining definitions that are partially true to make the definitions more accurate
    (C) citing evidence that discredits an erroneous definition
    (D) comparing and contrasting one specific form of fiction with fiction in general
    (E) establishing a definition by eliminating all possible alternate definitions

19. Which one of the following statements is most strongly supported by information given in the passages?
    (A) There are people who consider fantasy fiction to be close to science fiction but not the same as science fiction.
    (B) There are people who would not consider a story based on the Roman Empire to be science fiction.
    (C) There are people who may expect a work of science fiction to be entertaining but are not entertained by it.
    (D) Some people believe that the fact that a story is not true defines it as science fiction.
    (E) There are some people who believe that the primary purpose of science fiction is to entertain.

GO ON TO THE NEXT PAGE

20. Which one of the following most accurately states a relationship between Passage A and Passage B?

(A) The statement in Passage A—that by bringing two aspects of ordinary life together, a work of fiction creates an entertaining world that is *more* real, not less real, than the ordinary world—is relevant to the definition of science fiction in Passage B.

(B) The statement in Passage A—that the mere fact that a story departs from reality does not, for most people, guarantee that the people will be entertained by the story—is inconsistent with the definition of science fiction in Passage B.

(C) The example of a road made of crushed brick in passage A supports the assertion in Passage B that science fiction looks into the human mind, into the storehouse of knowledge, of tools and technologies, and uses imagination to push the human mind into the future.

(D) The conclusion in Passage B expands on the conclusion of Passage A by applying the conclusion of Passage A to a more specific situation.

(E) The statement—that the further a story strays from what is true, the more entertaining it can be expected to be—is questioned by both passages, rejected by Passage A, and forms part of the conclusion of Passage B.

21. The approaches taken by the two authors toward defining their respective areas of literature differ in which one of the following ways?

(A) The author of Passage A does not believe that science fiction meets the definition of fiction, whereas the author of Passage B believes that it does.

(B) The author of Passage A believes that imagination is one element of fiction, but not the most defining element, whereas the author of Passage B identifies imagination as the most key element in defining science fiction.

(C) The author of Passage B supports the conclusion of the passage with logic, whereas the author of Passage A uses only personal opinions to support the conclusion of the passage.

(D) The author of Passage A specifies the goal of fiction, whereas the author of Passage B only hints at the goal of science fiction.

(E) The author of Passage A disagrees with the author of Passage B on whether a work of fiction is more real or less real than the ordinary world.

GO ON TO THE NEXT PAGE

The United States has a two-party electoral system, in which nearly all elected officials are members of one of the two major parties. *Line* The framers of the Constitution may not have (5) deliberately created a two-party system. However, the congressional electoral system has inevitably pushed us toward such a system. The candidate with the plurality of votes in a district wins the right to represent the district, (10) and all other parties, no matter how much of the popular vote they have received, have no representation at all.

By contrast, in a party-proportional representation system, a party that wins 10 percent (15) of the vote wins 10 percent of the seats in the legislature. Such a system encourages the formation of multiple political parties, since each party has a much greater chance of winning at least some representation. The question (20) remains, however, as to which system of representation is actually best—a two-party system or a multiparty system.

Some scholars have suggested that a two-party system such as that in the United States (25) leads to greater political stability, which benefits economic growth, and to a more centrist approach to issues. However, most democracies have multiparty systems. In many cases, there are still two major political parties that (30) dominate the legislature. However, even the presence in the legislature of a few alternative parties can cause the system to function differently than a strictly two-party system.

What are the benefits of a multiparty system (35) that might outweigh the political stability and economic growth of a two-party system? A multiparty system represents a broader range of views than does a two-party system. In a two-party system, voters have only two choices. In (40) a society in which consumers expect at least thirty choices of breakfast cereal, it is strange that consumers are satisfied with only two choices for governing their country.

Beyond simply limiting choices and nar- (45) rowing the political debate, a two-party system has a more insidious danger. It is prone to polarization, to one party or both backing up to an extreme position in order to mobilize supporters. If Party A begins labeling Party B as (50) extreme and evil, voters who believe what they hear have no choice but to commit themselves to Party A. This is not likely to happen in a multiparty system, because many voters may become suspicious of both Party A and Party B. (55) After all, a common first sign of a party that has become extreme is that it calls its opponents extreme.

A simple innovation that has the potential to open a two-party system to more diverse (60) representation and less polarization is instant-runoff voting (IRV). In IRV, voters mark a first, second, and third choice (or more). If any candidate wins a majority of the votes, that candidate wins the election. If not, the candidate (65) with the fewest votes is dropped. For any ballot that had marked the dropped candidate as first choice, that ballot is now counted as a vote for the ballot's second-choice candidate. With IRV, voters can vote for third-party candidates (70) without the fear of wasting their vote or inadvertently aiding the election of a candidate to whom they are opposed. IRV opens the doors to a more representative, multiparty system.

GO ON TO THE NEXT PAGE

22. Which one of the following most accurately expresses the main idea of the passage?

(A) A two-party electoral system is not appropriate for a democracy, and most democracies do not use it.

(B) While a two-party electoral system may have some advantages, it also has disadvantages and can be modified to a better system by means of certain voting innovations.

(C) Both two-party and multiparty electoral systems have disadvantages that can be addressed by instant-runoff voting.

(D) A two-party electoral system leads to a more stable government and a stronger economy, even though such a system has some drawbacks.

(E) A two-party electoral system is more prone to polarization than is a multiparty system.

23. The author mentions the framers of the Constitution in the first paragraph primarily in order to

(A) provide background on the development of the two-party system in the United States

(B) support the assertion that the two-party system is fundamental to the democratic institutions of the United States

(C) counter a possible objection that a multiparty electoral system is unconstitutional

(D) establish that as far back as the time that the Constitution was written, Americans tended to fall into two major political divisions

(E) contrast the American Constitution with the constitutions of other democracies that have multiparty electoral systems.

24. According to the passage, which one of the following is true of a party-proportional representation system?

(A) Voters can mark their first, second, and third choices for an office.

(B) It prevents the domination of politics by two major parties.

(C) Every political party will earn at least some representation in the legislature.

(D) Even a minor political party has a greater chance of winning a seat in the legislature than in the American congressional electoral system.

(E) It offers voters better-qualified candidates than does the American congressional electoral system.

25. The author's descriptions of the drawbacks of the two-party system give the most support for which one of the following generalizations?

(A) A system that is used by fewer people may still be a better system than one that is used by many more people.

(B) When it is not clear which of two systems is better, it is a good idea to blend the two systems.

(C) Most people will not put up with limitations in their political life that are more restrictive than the limitations in their economic life.

(D) People are unlikely to change a political system that has been in place for many years.

(E) When faced with only two choices, consumers are more likely to adopt an extreme viewpoint than when the same consumers are faced with multiple choices.

GO ON TO THE NEXT PAGE

26. Which one of the following is most strongly implied by the above passage?
    (A) Many voters would be willing to have their second-choice candidate win the election.
    (B) Voters in most democracies have chosen to have a multiparty electoral system.
    (C) In the American electoral system, politicians of one party try to consider the views of their constituents who are members of the other party.
    (D) A country with a multiparty electoral system does not have as much economic growth as a country with a two-party electoral system.
    (E) In multiparty electoral systems, votes cast for members of the smaller parties are usually wasted.

27. The passage most helps to answer which one of the following questions?
    (A) In a party-proportional representation system, what is the minimum percentage of the vote that a party must receive in order to earn at least one seat in the legislature?
    (B) What is the reason that people who expect variety when they purchase products do not expect variety when they vote?
    (C) What happens in a multiparty system if one party accuses another party of being extreme?
    (D) Has instant-runoff voting been successful in converting two-party systems into multiparty systems?
    (E) What is a sign that a vote for a third-party candidate may be wasted?

STOP If you finish before the 35-minute time period is over, you may go back and check your answers in this section only. You may not work on any other test section.

Time: 35 minutes
26 Questions

DIRECTIONS: The questions in this section are based on the reasoning contained in brief statements or passages. More than one answer choice could conceivably answer the question in some cases. However, you should choose the <u>best</u> answer. The best answer is the response that answers the question most accurately and completely. You should avoid making any assumptions that, by commonsense standards, are implausible, superfluous, or incompatible with the passage. When you have chosen the best answer, fill in the space on your answer sheet that corresponds to your answer.

1. Lee: Dr. Jansen does not meet the needs of his patients. He was not able to correctly diagnose several patients who turned out to have rare endocrinological disorders.

   Morrison: Dr. Jansen is a general practitioner, not an endocrinologist. If he is not able to diagnose a patient's condition, he refers the patient to a specialist.

   Which one of the following principles, if valid, most helps to justify the reasoning in Morrison's response to Lee?

   (A) A general practitioner should not be expected to meet the needs of all patients.

   (B) Only a specialist can correctly diagnose a rare condition.

   (C) It is up to a patient to decide whether or not to consult a specialist.

   (D) Referring a patient to a specialist meets the needs of that patient.

   (E) Even a specialist cannot meet the needs of all patients.

2. A study conducted by the state government found that 35 percent of the new businesses started in Smithtown over the last three years failed within the business's first year. However, a study conducted by a private group found that only 10 percent of businesses started in Smithtown during the same three years failed within the business's first year.

   Which one of the following, if true, most helps to resolve the apparent discrepancy described above?

   (A) The government study was initiated in order to predict the future tax revenue from new businesses, whereas the private study was initiated specifically to determine the rate of failure of new businesses.

   (B) The government study included Smithtown and three neighboring towns, whereas the private study included only Smithtown.

   (C) There was more funding available for the government study than there was for the private study.

   (D) The people who conducted the government study had never conducted such a study previously.

   (E) The government study and the private study did not use the same definition of "failure."

GO ON TO THE NEXT PAGE

3. When dogs are frightened, they invariably exhibit one of two reactions. They either bark or hide. Recently, when a particularly loud clap of thunder sounded near Marsha's house, her dog raised its ears but did not bark. Instead, the dog walked quickly into another room. It can be concluded, then, that the dog went to the other room in order to hide.

The conclusion is most strongly supported by the reasoning in the argument if which one of the following is assumed?

(A) The dog has been trained not to bark.

(B) Hiding is more comforting to a frightened dog than is barking.

(C) The dog was frightened by the thunder.

(D) If a frightened dog is going to bark, it will do so the moment it is frightened.

(E) It is unlikely that a dog will both bark and hide when frightened.

4. There are many reasons why students often choose online courses over traditional classroom courses. Online courses offer students flexible schedules for reviewing lecture material and for taking exams. Because of the large number of students that can be accommodated by an online course, the course fees are relatively low. Finally, online courses allow students to interact with students from many parts of the country.

The statements above, if true, provide support for each of the following EXCEPT:

(A) Some students enjoy interacting with students from other parts of the country.

(B) Traditional classroom courses do not offer flexible schedules for reviewing lecture material.

(C) Traditional classroom courses accommodate fewer students than do online courses.

(D) Some traditional classroom courses offer flexible schedules for taking exams.

(E) Some students prefer to pay lower fees for courses.

5. Psychologist: Some psychologists claim that when children spend too much time on the computer, the children's behavior becomes more aggressive. However, to date there is no research evidence that supports this claim. Parents can be assured, then, that allowing their children to spend time on the computer will not increase aggressive behavior in their children.

Which one of the following is a questionable technique used in the psychologist's argument?

(A) accepting a claim solely because the opponents of the claim have failed to defend their argument

(B) defending a view by ignoring information that attacks the view

(C) asserting that lack of evidence defending a view is sufficient to prove that the view is incorrect

(D) failing to provide evidence to support the claim that no relevant research exists

(E) citing as an authority a source that is not in fact an authority in the relevant field

GO ON TO THE NEXT PAGE

6. A labor-saving technology is, by definition, a technology that allows a task to be completed with less time input from humans than would have been required without the technology. A piece of equipment that allows a certain person to perform a task in thirty-five minutes, when the same person would have required forty-five minutes to complete the task without the technology, is not a labor-saving technology if _____ .

The argument's conclusion is most strongly supported if which one of the following completes the passage?

(A) some people operating the equipment would require forty-five minutes to perform the task

(B) the person could have saved time by not performing the task at all

(C) other technologies would have allowed the person to perform the same task in twenty-five minutes

(D) the person operating the equipment must spend fifteen minutes cleaning the equipment between tasks

(E) fifteen of the thirty-five minutes is spent in setting up the equipment

7. Regular aerobic exercise reduces blood pressure. Because it is necessary to reduce blood pressure in order to avoid strokes, a person who gets regular aerobic exercise will avoid strokes.

The flawed pattern of reasoning in which one of the following is most closely parallel to the flawed pattern of reasoning in the argument above?

(A) If Sherry completes her term paper, she will pass Dr. Powdrell's course. Any student who completes a term paper gets one hundred bonus points, and Dr. Powdrell only passes students who have gotten one hundred bonus points.

(B) Avoiding carbohydrates lowers total cholesterol. Because lower total cholesterol reduces the risk for a heart attack, a person who avoids carbohydrates reduces the risk for a heart attack.

(C) All great artists experienced personal suffering. Because some people who want to become great artists have not experienced personal suffering, there are some people who will not become great artists.

(D) Any plant that receives adequate nitrogen will grow. Because any plant that grows has received sunshine, any plant that receives adequate nitrogen also has received sunshine.

(E) A society cannot prosper unless all individuals in the society prosper. Because it is true that when society prospers, the greater good is attained, if all individuals prosper, the greater good will be attained.

GO ON TO THE NEXT PAGE

8. Gardener: If the temperature falls below 28 degrees Fahrenheit for at least two hours, the result is a hard frost. I forgot to set out my outdoor thermometer last night, but I know that a hard frost kills tomato plants, and my tomato plants are dead this morning, so the temperature must have been below 28 for at least two hours.

The gardener's reasoning is questionable in that it fails to consider the possibility that

(A) a hard frost kills many types of plants other than tomato plants
(B) if a tomato plant is in a sheltered location, it can survive a hard frost
(C) tomato plants can be killed overnight by a number of conditions other than hard frost
(D) other plants near the tomato plants were not killed
(E) without a thermometer, it is not possible to determine the exact overnight low temperature

9. There are two conditions that are necessary for a manager of a company to approve a new business project. The project must not compete with another of the company's current projects, and the manager must have evidence that the venture can be profitable.

The principle stated above, if valid, most helps to justify the reasoning in which one of the following arguments?

(A) Our manager should approve the new project. The project does not compete with any of our other projects, and there is evidence that the project will generate significant income.
(B) The proposed new project does not compete with any of our other projects. Nevertheless, our manager should not approve the project because the evidence defending the project's profitability is not extensive.
(C) It was a mistake for our manager to have approved the new project. It is true that the project does not compete with any of our other projects, but we have just found out that the facts used to support the project's profitability were inaccurate.
(D) Our manager should not approve the proposed new project. While it does not compete with any of our current projects, all of the evidence indicates that the project would not be profitable.
(E) Even though the evidence supporting the profitability of the new project is impressive, the manager should not approve the project. It is highly likely that the project would compete with other projects that have been proposed.

GO ON TO THE NEXT PAGE

10. The island of Marbay has what most people consider to be an ideal climate. While the island lacks the seasonal variation that many parts of the world enjoy, its temperature is always mild, there is nearly always a light, fresh breeze, and the rain comes only at night. Few other locations offer this combination of climatic conditions.

Which one of the following, if true, most strengthens the argument above?

(A) Many people prefer a climate that does not have seasonal variation.

(B) Most people consider a dry climate to be more ideal than a wet climate.

(C) Mild temperatures, light breezes, and nighttime rain are the primary characteristics of what most people would consider to be an ideal climate.

(D) The island of Marbay is the only location in the world that has this specific combination of characteristics.

(E) What some people consider to be a mild temperature may be considered too hot by other people.

11. While inequities in the law are often obvious, it can take years of legislative research and planning before a remedy for an inequity can be incorporated into existing law. Even though such remedies can correct previous inequities, they frequently introduce new and unanticipated inequities.

Which one of the following is most strongly supported by the information above?

(A) Long-term planning may not reduce the number of legal inequities.

(B) Inequities in the law are not intentional.

(C) The number of inequities in the law increases with time.

(D) The more obvious an inequity in the law is, the longer it takes to remedy the inequity.

(E) Inequities in the law that are not obvious are often ignored.

12. Marissa: Scientific inquiry is both an intuitive and an intellectual activity. Science is unique among human endeavors in that it tests intuition through a rigorous, intellectual process.

Frederick: The problem with science is the intellectuals. Intellectuals are out of touch with the practical needs of people. True science is a practical activity, not an intellectual one.

Frederick's reply to Marissa's argument is most vulnerable to criticism on the grounds that his reply

(A) uses language that is biased

(B) mistakes a cause in Marissa's argument for an effect

(C) uses the word *intellectual* in a way that is different from Marissa's use of the word

(D) assumes that because Marissa has not adequately defended her view that her view is incorrect

(E) uses an unrepresentative group to defend his conclusion

13. The great majority of influenza cases could be prevented by a simple flu shot. The beginning of the flu season coincides with the beginning of the holiday shopping season. It would be an economic boon to our local merchants if everyone were to get a flu shot this season.

The conclusion of the argument is most strongly supported if which one of the following is assumed?

(A) Most people do their holiday shopping even if they are sick.

(B) Anyone who gets a flu shot will not get the flu.

(C) The majority of flu cases occur after the holiday season.

(D) Local merchants lose money when people have the flu during the holiday shopping season.

(E) Nearly all people who get flu shots do so at a local facility.

GO ON TO THE NEXT PAGE

14. A new traffic radar technology for identifying cars that are speeding was tested against traditional traffic radar. Based on cars driven on a track by professional drivers, the study found that every car identified by the new technology as speeding actually was. On the other hand, 20 percent of the cars identified as speeding by the old technology were not in fact speeding. The new technology is clearly superior and should be implemented immediately.

Which one of the following, if true, most weakens the argument?

(A) Neither technology is effective for drivers who have radar detectors.

(B) The new technology is 20 percent more expensive than the old technology.

(C) Thirty percent of the cars identified by the new technology as not speeding actually were speeding, whereas all of the cars identified by the old technology as not speeding were in fact not speeding.

(D) The radar equipment used in testing the old technology was ten years old, whereas the radar equipment used in testing the new technology was new.

(E) The effectiveness of traffic radar technology depends in part on the skill of the person using the technology.

15. The reason that our town does not attract new residents is most likely that potential new residents get the impression that our town is on the decline economically. There are two facts that prove that this is the reason. First, many of our homes have yards that are overgrown and untended. Second, the prospective residents who are shown a copy of the town's economic report, which clearly shows a strong pattern of growth, are much more likely to buy a home here than are prospective residents who are not shown the report.

Which one of the following, if true, most strengthens the reasoning in the argument above?

(A) Many homeowners are so busy with new projects at their jobs that they do not have time to keep their yards up.

(B) Many of the homes with overgrown and untended yards are abandoned because the owners of the homes lost their jobs.

(C) Many people associate overgrown and untended yards with economic decline.

(D) The town's economic report is too technical for most people to understand.

(E) Many prospective residents who saw homes with overgrown and untended yards refused to look at the town's economic report.

GO ON TO THE NEXT PAGE

16. Rancher: Coyotes are the main predator of gophers, helping keep the gopher population down. Over the past several years, wildlife managers have removed most of the coyotes from our ranch. During the same time, though, the gopher population has continued to go down.

Which one of the following, if true, most helps to resolve the apparent discrepancy in the passage above?

(A) There are more coyotes on the ranch now than there were ten years ago.

(B) The coyotes were relocated in order to reduce the gopher population in another area.

(C) The rate of decline in the gopher population has not changed in the past five years.

(D) The populations of other animals on which coyotes prey have increased in the last three years.

(E) Coyotes drive away owls and snakes, both of which are predators of gophers.

17. The five salespeople in our organization have roughly the same sales skills and so have roughly the same odds of winning this year's annual sales competition. However, because Sylvia is the only salesperson who got a head start, she has the best odds of winning. Therefore, Sylvia will win the competition.

The reasoning in the argument is flawed in that it

(A) fails to provide evidence that Sylvia is the only salesperson who got a head start

(B) presumes, without warrant, that no salesperson has better sales skills than Sylvia

(C) ignores the possibility that an event with a higher probability of occurring than other events may still have too low a probability to guarantee its occurrence

(D) attempts to predict the occurrence of an event solely by a comparison of the likelihood of all possible events

(E) assumes, without evidence, that all members of a group are equal

GO ON TO THE NEXT PAGE

18. For a number of years physicians have encouraged their patients to get more physical exercise. However, after several highly publicized events in which people seriously injured themselves doing exercises in which they were not properly trained, some doctors have stopped recommending exercise. This is not right. After all, a small number of people injure themselves every day simply eating fruit or drinking water. This does not mean physicians should stop recommending eating fruit and drinking water.

Which one of the following principles most helps to justify the reasoning in the argument above?

(A) A physician should recommend activities that have the potential to improve the health of a patient.

(B) An activity should be recommended only if the advantages of the activity outweigh the risks of the activity.

(C) It ought to be the responsibility of a patient to decide which recommended activities to do.

(D) Anyone who begins a new exercise program should receive training in performing the exercise.

(E) A physician ought not to refrain from recommending an activity that has health benefits solely on the basis that the activity has the potential to cause harm.

19. Baxter: When new immigrants come to this country, they face two challenges. They must first learn the cultural norms of their new country. Having learned those norms, they must then incorporate those norms into the context of the norms of their native country and arrive at a synthesis of the old and new norms. This same process, then, applies to other minority cultures in our country.

Beardsley: Even though most immigrants are members of minority groups, their experience does not apply to members of minority cultures who were born in this country.

Beardsley's response to Baxter's argument

(A) challenges its assumptions about the experience of immigrants to this country

(B) challenges it by providing an alternative explanation for one of its premises

(C) challenges it by pointing out an inherent contradiction in its premises

(D) challenges the basis on which Baxter argues from a specific situation to a more generalized conclusion

(E) challenges it on the basis that the conclusion would lead to an undesirable result

GO ON TO THE NEXT PAGE

20. Most newspapers today have suffered a significant drop in readership with the advent of the Internet. With this drop in readership, there has been a corresponding drop in revenue from advertisers. Many newspapers have set up their own websites. They must be doing so for the extra revenue they can earn by selling advertising space on their Web pages.

Which one of the following, if true, most weakens the argument?

(A) Advertisements on a Web page bring in less income than similar advertisements in a newspaper.

(B) Most newspapers have found that when people who are otherwise not readers of the newspaper visit the website, they are more likely to become regular readers of the newspaper.

(C) Newspapers that set up websites also typically use social media sites to promote their newspaper.

(D) Some journalists on newspapers began their careers as journalists on websites.

(E) There are no newspapers that have transitioned completely from print to Internet.

21. When top executives at Company X travel for business, they are required to use a corporate jet. No employee who has worked at Company X for fewer than five years is allowed to use a corporate jet when traveling for business. Sarah is a top executive at Company X and has worked at the company for exactly three years.

If the statements above are true, which one of the following statements must also be true?

(A) Sarah sometimes travels for Company X business using a corporate jet.

(B) Sarah never uses a Company X corporate jet.

(C) Sarah sometimes travels for Company X business.

(D) If any employee of Company X uses a corporate jet, it is for Company X business.

(E) If Sarah uses a Company X corporate jet, it is not for Company X business.

GO ON TO THE NEXT PAGE

22. Physicist: The gravitational effect of many astronomical objects cannot be accounted for by the amount of visible matter that the objects contain. Because of this, astrophysicists have postulated the existence of *dark matter*, a type of matter that does not emit light. However, there has never been any direct evidence of dark matter. It is just as likely that gravity simply acts differently on immense astrophysical scales than it does on Earth.

The claim that the gravitational effect of many astronomical objects cannot be accounted for by the amount of visible matter that the objects contain plays which one of the following roles in the physicist's argument?

(A) It is a premise that establishes the truth of the argument's conclusion.

(B) It is an intermediate conclusion that is used as a premise to support the main conclusion.

(C) It is a hypothesis that the argument as a whole rejects.

(D) It is a premise in an argument that the argument as a whole attempts to weaken.

(E) It is a statement that illustrates a principle.

23. Some say that in all things we should strive for simplicity. However, by definition, striving is not simple. The act of striving moves us away from simplicity. Therefore, it is not possible to attain simplicity.

Which one of the following is an assumption that is required by the argument above?

(A) It is not possible to attain simplicity without striving.

(B) There are some forms of striving that are simple.

(C) There is not more than one way to define simplicity.

(D) It is not possible to strive without attaining simplicity.

(E) It is not possible to strive for simplicity in some things.

GO ON TO THE NEXT PAGE

24. Principle: It is not unethical for a judge to rule on a case when the judge has received a large payment of money from one of the parties in the case if the judge is unaware of the payment.

Application: It was not unethical for Judge Clark-Thompson's wife to accept $250,000 from Company Z for a fifteen-minute speech, even though Company Z is the plaintiff in an important case that is being tried by Judge Clark-Thompson.

Which one of the following, if true, most justifies the application of the principle in the above argument?

(A) Judge Clark-Thompson did not rule in favor of Company Z.

(B) Company Z pays all speakers a minimum of $250,000 regardless of the length of the speech.

(C) Judge Clark-Thompson was not aware that his wife had had any contact with representatives of Company Z.

(D) Judge Clark-Thompson's wife put the money into a bank account in the judge's name but did not tell him about either the speech or the payment.

(E) The speech given by the judge's wife took place after the judge had ruled on the case involving Company Z.

25. Astronomers who discover a new comet can become famous but only if they discover a type of comet that is rare. Short-period comets and longer-period comets are relatively common. If an astronomer wants a chance to become famous by discovering a new comet, the astronomer should look for a hyperbolic comet.

Which one of the following most accurately states the overall conclusion of the argument above?

(A) Hyperbolic comets are relatively rare.

(B) If an astronomer wants to become famous for discovering a comet, the astronomer should discover a hyperbolic comet.

(C) Short-period and longer-period comets are not as rare as other types of comets.

(D) An astronomer who discovers a rare comet will become famous.

(E) An astronomer cannot become famous unless the astronomer discovers a rare comet.

GO ON TO THE NEXT PAGE

26. Water-tolerant plant species that cannot grow in more than three inches of water can generally tolerate drought. Water-tolerant plant species that must grow in more than eight inches of water generally cannot tolerate drought. This plant grows in five inches of water, so it may be able to tolerate drought for a short period.

The reasoning in which one of the following is most similar to the reasoning in the argument above?

(A) A bookstore with less than $20,000 in inventory typically cannot make more than $25,000 per year. A bookstore with more than $20,000 in inventory can make more than $25,000 per year. This bookstore has more than $20,000 in inventory, so it can probably make more than $25,000 per year.

(B) A bookstore with less than $20,000 in inventory typically cannot make more than $25,000 per year. A bookstore with over $100,000 in inventory can typically make at least $150,000 profit per year. This store has over $100,000 in inventory and it makes over $150,000 per year, so it must be a bookstore.

(C) A bookstore with less than $20,000 in inventory typically cannot make more than $25,000 per year. A bookstore with over $100,000 in inventory can typically make at least $150,000 profit per year. This bookstore makes over $150,000 per year, so it must have over $100,000 in inventory.

(D) A bookstore with less than $20,000 in inventory typically cannot make more than $25,000 profit per year. A bookstore with over $100,000 in inventory can typically make at least $150,000 profit per year. This bookstore has $60,000 in inventory, so it can probably make a profit of almost $90,000 per year.

(E) A bookstore with less than $20,000 in inventory typically cannot make more than $25,000 profit per year. A bookstore with over $100,000 in inventory can typically make at least $150,000 profit per year. This bookstore has less than $20,000 in inventory, so it can probably make a profit of $15,000 per year.

Time: **35 minutes**

23 Questions

DIRECTIONS: The groups of questions in this test section are each based on specific sets of conditions. Making a rough diagram may be useful for answering some of the questions. For each question choose the answer choice that is most accurate and complete. Fill in the space on your answer sheet that corresponds to your answer.

QUESTIONS 1–6

Seven trees of different species—Larix, Morus, Nyssa, Olea, Poncirus, Robinia, and Salix—are to be planted along a parkway. There are seven specific spots allocated for the trees, and the spots are numbered 1 through 7, from west to east. The assignment of trees to spots must proceed according to the following conditions:

Poncirus is planted to the east of Salix.

Nyssa is planted in either the fifth or seventh spot.

Larix is planted east of Poncirus but west of Nyssa.

If Poncirus is planted in the third spot, Poncirus is planted to the east of Robinia.

If Poncirus is not planted in the third spot, Robinia is planted to the east of Poncirus.

1. Which one of the following is a possible assignment of the trees to the planting spots?
   (A) Olea, Salix, Morus, Poncirus, Robinia, Larix, Nyssa
   (B) Salix, Robinia, Morus, Poncirus, Larix, Olea, Nyssa
   (C) Salix, Robinia, Poncirus, Morus, Nyssa, Larix, Olea
   (D) Salix, Morus, Poncirus, Larix, Olea, Robinia, Nyssa
   (E) Morus, Robinia, Poncirus, Larix, Nyssa, Salix, Olea

2. Which one of the following CANNOT be true?
   (A) Poncirus is in the second spot and Robinia is in the last spot.
   (B) Poncirus is in the third spot and Robinia is in the first spot.
   (C) Poncirus is planted between Robinia and Salix.
   (D) Salix is in the first spot and Robinia is in the second spot.
   (E) Morus is in the first spot and Robinia is in the second spot.

3. If Robinia and Poncirus are planted in adjacent spots, then which one of the following could be true?
   (A) Salix is planted in the third spot.
   (B) Larix is planted in the third spot.
   (C) Salix is planted in the fourth spot.
   (D) Nyssa is planted adjacent to Robinia.
   (E) Nyssa is planted in the fifth spot and Salix is planted in the second spot.

4. If Morus is planted in the first spot, then which one of the following could be true?
   (A) Olea is planted in the fourth spot.
   (B) Olea is planted in the fifth spot.
   (C) Salix is planted in the third spot.
   (D) Robinia is planted in the last spot.
   (E) Poncirus is planted in the third spot.

5. Which one of the following must be true?
   (A) There are at least five trees planted east of Salix.
   (B) There are exactly two spots in which Salix can be planted.
   (C) If Robinia is planted next to Nyssa, Salix is planted in the first spot.
   (D) If Salix is planted next to Morus, Larix is planted next to Robinia.
   (E) If Morus is planted in the seventh spot, Salix is planted in the first spot.

6. Which one of the following must be false?
   (A) Poncirus is planted east of Morus and west of Olea.
   (B) Larix is planted east of Poncirus and west of Robinia.
   (C) Nyssa is planted east of Morus and west of Robinia.
   (D) Morus is planted east of Salix and west of Olea.
   (E) Robinia is planted east of Salix and west of Poncirus.

GO ON TO THE NEXT PAGE

Six members of the university swim team—Paul, Raquel, Shen, Thomas, Uli, and Victoria—will compete in a swim meet next Saturday. Each team member will swim one lap during one of six consecutive time slots. During each time slot, only one member swims. The order in which the members swim must meet the following constraints:

Rachel swims either immediately before or immediately after Victoria.

If Paul does not swim in the third time slot, then Shen swims in the fifth time slot.

Either Rachel swims before Paul, or Rachel swims before Thomas, but not both.

7. Which one of the following could be the order in which the team members swim, from first to last?
    (A) Uli, Shen, Paul, Thomas, Rachel, Victoria
    (B) Uli, Shen, Thomas, Victoria, Rachel, Paul
    (C) Thomas, Rachel, Paul, Shen, Victoria, Uli
    (D) Thomas, Uli, Rachel, Victoria, Shen, Paul
    (E) Victoria, Rachel, Thomas, Paul, Shen, Uli

8. If Paul swims in the first time slot, then which one of the following must be true?
    (A) Thomas swims either fourth or sixth.
    (B) Rachel swims either second or third.
    (C) Uli swims second.
    (D) Thomas swims after Uli.
    (E) Uli swims before Shen.

9. Which one of the following CANNOT be true?
   (A) Rachel swims immediately after Uli.
   (B) Paul swims immediately before Shen.
   (C) Paul swims immediately before Thomas.
   (D) Rachel swims immediately after Thomas and immediately before Victoria.
   (E) Shen swims immediately after Uli and immediately before Paul.

10. For which one of the following are there five possible time slots to which the member could be assigned?
    (A) Victoria
    (B) Uli
    (C) Thomas
    (D) Shen
    (E) Paul

11. If Uli swims before Shen, the order in which the team members swim is fully determined if which one of the following is also true?
    (A) Thomas swims sixth.
    (B) Victoria swims fifth.
    (C) Paul swims third.
    (D) Rachel swims third.
    (E) Shen swims second.

12. If Thomas swims before Paul, which one of the following must be true?
    (A) Paul swims sixth.
    (B) Thomas swims first.
    (C) Shen swims either immediately before or immediately after Paul.
    (D) Uli swims immediately before or immediately after Thomas.
    (E) Either Rachel or Victoria swims fourth.

13. If Paul swims immediately before Shen, then for exactly how many of the team members can it be determined in which time slot he or she swims?
    (A) one
    (B) two
    (C) three
    (D) four
    (E) five

GO ON TO THE NEXT PAGE

Questions 14–18

A radio station plays foreign language news for one hour starting at 8 P.M. every evening. The station's program scheduler must decide which language is assigned for each of the seven days of the upcoming week, beginning with Monday. The possible languages are Norwegian, Polish, Romani, Slovak, Thai, Urdu, and Welsh. Each day exactly one language is used. Each language is used exactly once during the week. The conditions are:

> Romani and Norwegian are both assigned earlier in the week than Polish.
>
> Norwegian and Thai are both assigned earlier in the week than Urdu.
>
> Welsh is assigned to Thursday.
>
> Either Romani is assigned earlier in the week than Welsh, or Thai is assigned earlier in the week than Slovak, but not both.

14. Which one of the following could be the assignment of languages to the days of the week, in order, from Monday to Sunday?
    (A) Slovak, Norwegian, Thai, Welsh, Romani, Polish, Urdu
    (B) Slovak, Thai, Romani, Welsh, Urdu, Norwegian, Polish
    (C) Thai, Norwegian, Slovak, Welsh, Urdu, Polish, Romani
    (D) Romani, Slovak, Norwegian, Welsh, Polish, Thai, Urdu
    (E) Thai, Norwegian, Romani, Welsh, Urdu, Polish, Slovak

15. If there are exactly two days between the day that Urdu is assigned and the day that Romani is assigned, then which one of the following could be true?
    (A) Slovak is assigned on Wednesday.
    (B) Norwegian is assigned on Tuesday.
    (C) Urdu is assigned on Friday.
    (D) Slovak is assigned on Saturday.
    (E) Polish is assigned on Saturday.

16. Which one of the following pairs of languages CANNOT be assigned to Monday and Tuesday, respectively?
    (A) Romani, Slovak
    (B) Slovak, Thai
    (C) Norwegian, Thai
    (D) Thai, Romani
    (E) Romani, Norwegian

17. If Polish is assigned to Wednesday, then which one of the following could be false?
    (A) Slovak is assigned to Friday.
    (B) Thai is assigned to Saturday.
    (C) Urdu is assigned to Sunday.
    (D) Romani is assigned to Monday.
    (E) Welsh is assigned to Thursday.

18. If Thai is assigned earlier in the week than Slovak, then which one of the following could be true?
    (A) Norwegian is assigned to Friday.
    (B) Thai is assigned to Friday.
    (C) Thai is assigned to Wednesday.
    (D) Romani is assigned to Wednesday.
    (E) Urdu is assigned to Wednesday.

GO ON TO THE NEXT PAGE

Questions 19–23

A conference planner must invite at least three employees of Company X to an upcoming business conference. The employees who are available to attend are Fernandez, Gilliam, Hong, Idriss, Jankowic, King, Logan, and Monroe. The selection of attendees must conform to the following conditions:

   If Hong is selected, neither Fernandez nor Logan is not selected.

   King cannot be selected if Idriss is selected.

   Idriss must be selected if Hong is selected.

   Fernandez is selected only if Monroe is not selected.

   If either King or Gilliam is selected, both must be selected.

19. Which one of the following could be the list of the employees who are invited to the conference?
    (A) Hong, Idriss, Jankowic
    (B) Gilliam, Hong, Jankowic, King, Monroe
    (C) Hong, Idriss, Logan, Monroe
    (D) Fernandez, Idriss, Monroe
    (E) Idriss, King, Gilliam

GO ON TO THE NEXT PAGE

20. If Hong is invited, then which one of the following must be true?
    (A) At most four employees are invited.
    (B) At most five employees are invited.
    (C) Monroe is invited.
    (D) Jankowic is invited.
    (E) Jankowic is not invited.

21. If there must be at least four employees who attend the conference, which one of the following is a pair of employees of which the conference planner must select at least one employee?
    (A) Fernandez and Idriss
    (B) Fernandez and Gilliam
    (C) Hong and King
    (D) Idriss and King
    (E) Idriss and Monroe

22. If Fernandez is selected but Jankowic is not, which one of the following could be true?
    (A) Exactly two employees are not selected.
    (B) Exactly five employees are selected.
    (C) Idriss is selected and Gilliam is selected.
    (D) Idriss is selected and Logan is not selected.
    (E) Gilliam is selected and Logan is not selected.

23. What is the maximum number of employees who could be selected to attend the conference?
    (A) four
    (B) five
    (C) six
    (D) seven
    (E) eight

Time: 35 minutes
25 Questions

DIRECTIONS: The questions in this section are based on the reasoning contained in brief statements or passages. More than one answer choice could conceivably answer the question in some cases. However, you should choose the <u>best</u> answer. The best answer is the response that answers the question most accurately and completely. You should avoid making any assumptions that, by commonsense standards, are implausible, superfluous, or incompatible with the passage. When you have chosen the best answer, fill in the space on your answer sheet that corresponds to your answer.

1. Store manager: Our strongest sales are in the evening. Since we changed our store hours last month in order to remain open one hour later in the evening, there have always been customers shopping during the last hour. However, our net profit per day has actually decreased.

   Which one of the following, if true, most helps to explain the decrease in net profit described above?
   (A) People who shop late in the evening tend to buy fewer items than people who shop earlier in the day.
   (B) Most of the people who shop during the last hour of the day would have come to the store earlier in the evening if the store had closed at its original closing time.
   (C) The net profit of any store is lower on some days than on other days.
   (D) Net profit is not the best way to measure the popularity of a store.
   (E) The cost of operating the store for an additional hour is greater than the income from sales during that hour.

2. After Ed suffered a minor heart attack, his physician reviewed Ed's diet, and advised Ed to cut back on certain foods. Like many people in the same position, Ed is not likely to change his eating habits, given that the foods he was advised to avoid were among his favorites. In such circumstances, it is important for family members not to nag the patient about the patient's diet. If, but only if, left alone, most such people begin to make small, healthful changes gradually.

   Which one of the following most accurately expresses the overall conclusion of the above argument?
   (A) Most people who have had a serious health problem eventually begin to make healthful changes.
   (B) Nagging a family member about diet can prevent the family member from making healthful changes.
   (C) Ed's original diet was not as healthy as it could have been.
   (D) If Ed's family nags him about his diet, Ed will probably not make any effort to change his diet.
   (E) Ed's family should accept his decisions about his health because he is reacting in the way that most people in his situation would react.

GO ON TO THE NEXT PAGE

3. There are two widely separated islands in the Pacific Ocean that are both home to a species of flower with a sweet nectar that is located at the end of a long tube. On both islands, there is a butterfly species that has developed an unusually long tongue that allows it to suck the nectar from these flowers. This is an amazing example of two distinct populations independently developing the same adaptive mechanism in response to the same environmental challenge.

The argument's conclusion is properly drawn if which one of the following is assumed?

(A) There has never been any interbreeding between members of the two butterfly species on the two islands.

(B) The two flower species with the long tubes are not genetically related.

(C) If the butterfly species on either island had not developed the long tongue, they would not have had any food source.

(D) There is no other animal that is better adapted than the long-tongued butterflies to suck nectar from the long-tubed flowers.

(E) All of the butterflies on both islands are capable of long-distance flight.

4. Mayor: I have advice for anyone planning to run for mayor after my term is up. When you talk with voters, it is natural for you to want to please them. However, this invariably leads to making promises that you cannot keep. Voters recognize unrealistic promises and are unlikely to vote for you.

Which one of the following is most strongly supported by the statements in the passage?

(A) If a mayoral candidate makes promises that are realistic, the voters are likely to vote for that candidate.

(B) Most mayoral candidates make promises that they cannot keep.

(C) If voters recognize that a mayoral candidate's promises are unrealistic, those voters will be unlikely to vote in the mayoral election.

(D) If a mayoral candidate wants to please the voters, the voters will be unlikely to vote for that candidate.

(E) If a mayoral candidate does not want to please the voters, the voters will be likely to vote for that candidate.

GO ON TO THE NEXT PAGE

5. A new computer programming language, OYSTER, is very powerful because of its highly abstract syntax. Advanced programmers will get better and faster results with OYSTER. However, programmers who are not advanced will find OYSTER harder to work with. Because most computer programs are written by less-advanced programmers, and because programs written by advanced programmers must often be modified by less-advanced programmers, it would be better for advanced programmers to avoid OYSTER.

Which one of the following principles, if valid, most helps to justify the conclusion in the argument above?

(A) A programming language that is very powerful should be used only by those people who will find it to be superior to other programming languages.

(B) A programming language that is very powerful should not be used at all if some of the people who need to use it find it to be more powerful than necessary for their projects.

(C) A programming language that is very powerful should not be used at all if it is harder to work with than other programming languages for some of the people who are likely to need to use it.

(D) A programming language that is better than other programming languages should not be used at all if the people who write programs with the language are more advanced than the people who must modify the programs written in the language.

(E) Programmers who are advanced should not write programs that are so abstract that less-advanced programmers cannot understand or modify the programs.

6. Politician: A recent survey of likely voters showed my opponent to be ten points ahead of me. However, the survey is not likely to be accurate. The survey was conducted by phone. Younger people are much less likely to answer a phone call from an unrecognized number than are older people, and my strongest support is from younger people.

Which one of the following arguments is most similar in reasoning to the reasoning in the argument above?

(A) A recent survey of people visiting an art museum indicated that more of them like classical art than like modern art. The results of the survey cannot be considered meaningful, since the art museum is best known for its collection of classical art and has almost no modern art on display.

(B) A recent survey asked college students to name their "favorite politician." Over 70 percent considered the state's governor to be their favorite politician. The results of the survey, however, can hardly be considered accurate. None of the students responding to the survey asked for a clarification of the term *favorite*. In addition, none of the people conducting the survey explained how the term should be interpreted.

(C) The recent survey of dog owners is flawed. The survey showed that the majority of dog owners like to walk their dogs in the evening. However, the survey was done outdoors during the evening, when people who do not like to walk their dog in the evening would be less likely to be outdoors.

GO ON TO THE NEXT PAGE

(D) A recent survey asked a number of journalists what profession, other than journalism, they most admired. The survey concluded that 80 percent of journalists admire physicians. The results of the survey are, however, not likely to be accurate, because the people surveyed were not themselves physicians.

(E) A recent survey indicated that 75 percent of Americans believe that UFOs exist and that they are flown by extraterrestrials. The survey, however, is unlikely to have any meaning. The mere fact that a high percentage of people believe in a certain phenomenon is not an indication of the existence of the phenomenon.

7. To ensure strong bones, it is important to have an adequate level of available calcium in the body. Because most people get significant amounts of calcium from their diets, they only need to ensure that they get enough vitamin D.

The argument depends on assuming which one of the following?

(A) There are fewer dietary sources of vitamin D than there are of calcium.

(B) Calcium from foods is preferable to calcium from supplements.

(C) It is not possible to have strong bones without a healthy diet.

(D) To ensure strong bones, it is necessary to get as much vitamin D as calcium.

(E) Without enough vitamin D, calcium cannot be made available for the body.

8. Phuong: The primary purpose of a garden is to nourish the spirit. A successful garden may or may not produce vegetables, fruits, or flowers. If, by lovingly tending the garden, the gardener feels relaxed and at home, then the garden has fulfilled its primary purpose.

Jacob: There is no reason to grow a garden other than to nourish the spirit. The spirit is nourished when one's hard labor results in a product that one can enjoy eating or looking at.

Phuong and Jacob disagree with each other over whether

(A) a gardener's feeling relaxed and at home is sufficient to conclude that the garden has served its purpose

(B) the primary reason for gardening is to nourish the spirit

(C) a garden that produces vegetables, fruits, and flowers may have fulfilled its purpose

(D) the primary reason for growing a garden is to produce healthy food

(E) gardening involves hard labor

GO ON TO THE NEXT PAGE

9. In order to discourage speeding, the police periodically increase the number of patrol cars checking traffic with radar guns. Usually, the patrol cars are placed where drivers can see them, as a deterrent. Unfortunately, the conspicuous presence of patrol cars seems to result in an increase in certain kinds of accidents. Apparently, knowing that they are being watched causes some drivers to get into an accident.

Which one of the following, if true, most strengthens the argument above?

(A) Most drivers become nervous when they know they are being watched by the police.

(B) Drivers who are speeding are more likely to cause accidents than are drivers who are not speeding.

(C) Drivers who regularly use radar detectors in their cars are less likely to become nervous in the presence of patrol cars than are drivers who do not regularly use radar detectors.

(D) When a driver becomes nervous, the driver is more likely to switch lanes frequently.

(E) When a driver's eyes focus on the speedometer, the driver's peripheral vision diminishes significantly.

10. A work of art cannot be considered significant unless at least one professional art critic has given the work a positive review. Among those works that have received a positive review from such a critic, it can be said that any work that has been praised by more than one museum curator is certainly a significant work of art.

Which one of the following situations conforms most closely to the principles outlined in the passage above?

(A) Susan's sculpture, *Gull on a Hot Rock*, has been highly praised by all of the visitors to the museum where it is displayed. However, no museum curator has as yet commented on her sculpture. Therefore, *Gull on a Hot Rock*, is not a significant work of art.

(B) Jefferson's print, *Todacheene*, has been praised by each of the five museum curators who recently reviewed it. Even though none of the museum curators is a professional art critic, their praise establishes that *Todacheene* is a significant work of art.

(C) Ruth Anne's print, *Praying Mantis*, recently received significant praise from two museum curators, one of whom is a well-known professional art critic. Therefore, *Praying Mantis* is a significant work of art.

(D) Li's painting, *Delta*, has been highly praised by several professional art critics, one of whom is also a museum curator. Therefore, it is likely, though not definite, that *Delta* is a significant work of art.

(E) Julianna's print, *Blue Chickens*, is not a significant work of art. Therefore, it cannot have received the praise of any professional art critic.

GO ON TO THE NEXT PAGE

11. Attorney: In many jury trials there is circumstantial evidence both for and against the defendant. Often, the only objective evidence is from eyewitnesses, but because members of juries are rarely convinced by testimony from people who they do not consider reliable, eyewitness testimony usually does not convince a jury.

Which one of the following, if assumed, allows the attorney's conclusion to be properly drawn?

(A) People who do not believe that they can reliably report what they have observed at a crime scene usually do not offer to be witnesses.

(B) Eyewitnesses who testify in jury trials often have personal characteristics that cause the members of the jury to doubt the eyewitness's reliability.

(C) People who serve on juries generally do not consider people who have committed crimes to be reliable witnesses.

(D) Most people who serve on juries find circumstantial evidence to be unreliable.

(E) In jury trials in which the circumstantial evidence does not clearly establish the guilt or innocence of the defendant, the jury must rely on eyewitness reports.

12. Even though American public primary education is nearly universally co-educational, with boys and girls in the same class, some educators believe that students would learn more in classes that were either all male or all female.

Which one of the following, if true, would provide evidence against the belief that students would learn better in classes that were all male or all female?

(A) At the primary level, there are usually few male teachers available to teach classes consisting only of boys.

(B) When there are both boys and girls in a classroom, the boys tend to learn more and the girls tend to learn less than if the boys and girls were taught in separate classrooms.

(C) When there are boys and girls in a classroom, the teacher calls on the boys more often than on the girls.

(D) The presence of girls in a classroom reduces the aggressive behavior among boys in the same classroom.

(E) When students know they are being observed by students of the opposite sex, they often want to perform better on tests and quizzes.

GO ON TO THE NEXT PAGE

13. Before the recent citywide election, prominent advertisements warned nearly all residents that the proposed sales tax increase to fund a performing arts center would benefit only middle-class residents. Despite this warning, nearly all of the residents of the city's Old Town area, most of whom have incomes significantly below the middle-class level, voted for the increase.

Which one of the following, if true, best explains the voting pattern of the Old Town residents?

(A) Many city residents who have middle-class incomes voted against the increase.

(B) Nearly all people consider themselves to be middle class, even if their incomes are significantly above or below the middle-class level.

(C) Many people who have middle-class incomes are not in fact middle class.

(D) Many people who would enjoy having a performing arts center nevertheless do not want to pay for one.

(E) The Old Town area has always had a lower sales tax rate than other parts of the city.

14. Surgeon: I will not be able to operate on Edgar tomorrow. Even though Edgar has followed the presurgical protocol perfectly, the protocol does not guarantee favorable conditions for surgery unless the patient is completely free of infection the day before the surgery.

The argument relies on which one of the following assumptions?

(A) Edgar has an infection that cannot be cured by the day of surgery.

(B) Edgar has at least a small amount of infection.

(C) If the conditions for Edgar's surgery were favorable, the surgeon would operate.

(D) The presurgical protocol does not include measures for avoiding infection.

(E) Tomorrow is the only day that the surgeon would be able to operate on Edgar.

GO ON TO THE NEXT PAGE

15. Even though many talented musicians do not know how to read musical notation, there are many advantages to be gained by learning to read music. Just as learning to read English allows a person to "hear" the words of a story when no one is present to tell the story, learning to read music _____ .

Which one of the following most logically completes the final sentence of the above passage?

(A) allows a person to determine the sounds of a composition when no one is present to play the composition

(B) allows a person to write down a piece of music that the person has composed when there is no one present to hear the piece

(C) allows a person to "hear" the emotion that a composer intends to convey when the composer is not present

(D) allows a person to see the notes of which a composition is composed

(E) allows a person to "see" with the imagination when it is not possible to hear with the ears

16. Historian: In comparing the appalling slaughter of combatants during World Wars I and II with the comparatively low mortality rate for combatants in recent wars, some historians have postulated that the difference is because modern politicians have learned lessons from the past. However, a careful analysis of the top political leaders responsible for several modern wars shows that these leaders had almost no understanding of the historical events of the two world wars. Most likely the lower mortality rate for combatants today is due to other factors, including, perhaps, combat technology.

Which one of the following most accurately states the main conclusion of the historian's argument?

(A) Today's lower mortality rate for combatants is due to improved combat technology.

(B) It is possible that modern political leaders have learned important lessons from the history of the two world wars.

(C) The lower mortality rate for combatants today, compared to during the two world wars, is not due to an understanding of history on the part of politicians.

(D) It is possible for wars to become less destructive, whether through improved technologies or through lessons learned from previous wars.

(E) Modern political leaders do not have an adequate understanding of even fairly recent history.

GO ON TO THE NEXT PAGE

17. Rancher: The reintroduction of wolves is a bad thing. Sure, it creates jobs for federal agencies, but the program costs us livestock without giving us anything beneficial in return.

Biologist: That is not true. Reintroducing wolves not only enriches the biological diversity of our ecosystem but also helps cull out weak and unfit livestock in a natural way.

Evaluating the effectiveness of the biologist's response requires clarification of which one of the following issues?

(A) whether the cost to ranchers in terms of lost livestock is less than or greater than the benefit to federal agencies in terms of new jobs

(B) whether either enriching biological diversity or culling out unfit livestock in a natural way benefits ranchers

(C) whether the value of enriched biological diversity is less than or greater than the value of culling out unfit livestock in a natural way

(D) whether the cost to ranchers in terms of lost livestock is less than or greater than the benefit to ranchers from culling out unfit livestock in a natural way

(E) whether enriching biological diversity and culling out unfit livestock have any economic value to ranchers

18. An exit poll of voters at our recent city election showed that those voters who had read a summary of the bond issue for funding a new bridge downtown voted for the bond issue, whereas those voters who had not read the summary voted against the bond issue. The summary must have convinced voters that the bond issue was worth voting for.

Which one of the following, if true, most seriously weakens the argument above?

(A) Once voters decided to support the bond issue, they subsequently wanted to read more about it.

(B) Many voters who opposed the bond issue had decided how they would vote on the bond issue before going to the polls.

(C) There were some people who read the summary of the bond issue and then decided to vote against it.

(D) A high percentage of people who voted in the recent city election did so by absentee ballot and did not go to the polls on election day.

(E) Many voters refused to talk with the people conducting the exit polls.

GO ON TO THE NEXT PAGE

19. Outside of the two-hour rush hour period, the average speed on the highway is 50 miles per hour. During rush hour, the average speed is 30 miles per hour. Cars traveling at an average of 30 miles per hour get better gas mileage than cars traveling at an average of 50 miles per hour. However, stop-and-go driving decreases gas mileage. During the second hour of rush hour, but not the first hour, cars are subject to frequent stop-and-go driving.

Which one of the following can be most properly inferred from the argument above?

(A) Cars on the highway outside of rush hour are not subject to frequent stop-and-go driving.

(B) During the second hour of rush hour, cars on the highway get worse gas mileage than cars on the highway outside of rush hour.

(C) During the first hour of rush hour, cars on the highway get better gas mileage than cars on the highway during the second hour of rush hour.

(D) The maximum speed of cars on the highway during rush hour is less than the maximum speed of cars on the highway outside of rush hour.

(E) The average speed of cars on the highway during the first hour of rush hour is higher than the average speed of cars on the highway during the second hour of rush hour.

20. Attorney: The public should be able to judge the extent to which corporations act ethically. However, because violations of ethics often do not involve violations of laws, the courts have been reluctant to force corporations to report their ethical practices. Unless that changes, it is unlikely that the public will be able to judge the extent to which corporations act ethically.

The reasoning in the argument is most vulnerable to criticism on the grounds that it

(A) presumes, without providing justification, that corporations violate the ethical standards of the public

(B) fails to consider whether public judgment of the ethics of corporations would change the behavior of corporations that are judged to act unethically

(C) presumes, without providing justification, that corporations are unable to judge the extent to which their own actions are ethical

(D) fails to provide a rationale for the claim that violations of ethics are often not violations of laws

(E) fails to consider that there may be other ways to obtain information about a corporation's ethical practices other than a court-ordered report

GO ON TO THE NEXT PAGE

21. With the advent of modern medicine, health care providers have been able to cure diseases and conditions that would have previously been fatal. As a result, the average life expectancy has increased dramatically. As medicine continues to evolve, it will some day be able not just to cure diseases but to protect people from getting the diseases at all. Because a person who has not had a disease is healthier than a person who has recovered from a disease, this new form of medicine will cause the average life expectancy to increase even further.

Which one of the following, if true, most strengthens the argument stated above?

(A) The countries with the best health care have the longest average life expectancy.

(B) Having avoided getting diseases contributes significantly to living a long life.

(C) Modern medicine has completely eradicated certain diseases.

(D) People who have recovered from a serious disease often have antibodies that protect them from similar diseases.

(E) People who have avoided contracting influenza because of a vaccination are typically healthier during influenza season than are people who contracted influenza and recovered from it.

22. The number of sightings of unidentified flying objects has increased dramatically in recent years. At the same time, the attempts to explain these objects as human phenomena have repeatedly failed. Regardless of who or what is piloting these objects, they have clearly begun visiting us more and more frequently in recent years.

The reasoning in the above argument is questionable in that it takes for granted that

(A) the frequency of sightings of unidentified flying objects will continue to increase

(B) the increase in the frequency of sightings corresponds to an increase in the frequency of visitation by unidentified flying objects

(C) something or someone is piloting the unidentified flying objects

(D) there is no explanation for unidentified flying objects that could establish them as human phenomena

(E) unidentified flying objects pose no danger to humanity

GO ON TO THE NEXT PAGE

23. The chances of a new small business surviving for a year are 30 percent. It is a shame that none of the fifteen new small businesses that started up in the last three months are likely to still be in business a year from now.

Which one of the following contains a logical flaw that is most similar to the logical flaw in the argument above?

(A) None of my greyhounds have won more than one race out of four. It is unlikely, then, that any of my six greyhounds will win the race that I have entered them in on Saturday.

(B) Of my ten favorite artists, only one has ever received public recognition. Therefore, it is unlikely that I will see the works of the other nine of my favorite artists when I go to the museum on Friday.

(C) All five of the high schools in our city are governed by our board of education, and all five have excellent academic success. Therefore, the academic success must be the result of the policies of the board of education.

(D) Three separate juries have acquitted the man accused of bribing jurors, so it must be that the man is actually innocent.

(E) Of the employees at Corporation Z, 40 percent have worked there for under a year. Andrea is an employee of Corporation Z, so there is a 40 percent chance that she has worked there for under a year.

24. Ecologist: There is no question that the situation of the Rio Grande silvery minnow is precarious. Its numbers are lower now than when it was first declared endangered in 1994, and it is currently found in only 5 percent of its original habitat. The demise of this fish, which once dominated a 3,000-mile stretch of river, is a sure sign that our entire ecosystem—on which we depend for food, water, and survival—may well be in danger of collapse.

Which one of the following best describes the role played in the argument by the statement that the situation of the Rio Grande silvery minnow is precarious?

(A) It is the main conclusion of the argument and is defended by specific facts.

(B) It is a fact that the argument acknowledges and then attempts to rebut.

(C) It is a premise that supports a conclusion that is then used to support the main conclusion of the argument.

(D) It is a conclusion that is defended by facts and is used as a premise in support of the main conclusion of the argument.

(E) It is a hypothesis that the argument uses to support a conclusion.

GO ON TO THE NEXT PAGE

25. The pursuit of truth is the most noble endeavor of humanity. However, no person can pursue truth if that person is obsessed with finding food and shelter. If society were but to guarantee adequate food and a warm, safe shelter to each and every person, then all of humanity would pursue the most noble endeavor.

Which one of the following most accurately expresses a flaw in the argument's reasoning?

(A) It applies a condition that is true in an individual case to a general case in which the condition is not true.

(B) It presumes, without warrant, that all members of a group have the same characteristic because some members of the group have that characteristic.

(C) It fails to consider that an event that is probable is not inevitable.

(D) It relies on information about a group that is not representative of the population as a whole.

(E) It treats a condition that is necessary for the occurrence of a certain endeavor as a condition that is sufficient to guarantee the occurrence of that endeavor.

Time: 35 minutes

DIRECTIONS: You will have thirty-five minutes to organize and write an essay on the topic described on the next page. Read the topic and all of the directions carefully. It is generally best to take a few minutes to organize your thoughts before beginning to write. Be sure to develop your ideas fully and leave time at the end to review what you have written. **Do not write on any topic other than the topic given. It is not acceptable to write on a topic of your own choice.**

No special knowledge is needed or expected for this essay. Admission committees are interested in your reasoning, clarity, organization, use of language, and writing mechanics. The quality of what you write is more important than the quantity.

Keep your essay in the blocked and lined area on the front and back of the separate Writing Sample Response Sheet. That is the only area that will be reproduced and sent to law schools. Be sure to write legibly.

Scratch Paper
Do not write your essay here. Scratch work only.

DIRECTIONS: The situation described below gives two choices. Either one of the choices can be supported based on the information given. In your essay, consider both choices and then argue in favor of one over the other. Base your argument on the two specified criteria and on the given facts. There is no "right" or "wrong" choice. Either choice can be reasonably defended.

Slotown's city council wants to revitalize Slotown's public transit system because HugeGro Company recently announced that it will locate three or more of its new assembly facilities in different Slotown boroughs. Slotown has narrowed its transportation choices between light rail and buses. Using the facts given below, compose an essay in which you argue in favor of choosing one alternative over the other on the basis of the two criteria below:

- Slotown wants to maximize its transportation flexibility in the event that a HugeGro plant closes or changes location in the future.
- Slotown wants to minimize its fuel costs and hydrocarbon footprint.

RoadRail Corporation offers turnkey packages consisting of light rail trains, tracks, stations, and repair facilities for intracity applications. RoadRail's claim to fame is its recent installation at a major city in the southwestern United States. Officials from that city brag about RoadRail's low fuel costs, high rider capacities, and rapid turnaround times. RoadRail's sales team brags that RoadRail trains are at least thirty times more fuel efficient than buses. RoadRail has a modular track system that could provide flexible passenger routes that can be moved around regular streets once the initial hub and maintenance facilities are built, but the southwestern city officials have been silent concerning this feature.

Green Bus Co. builds natural gas-powered buses for urban use. Green buses are articulated and known for their maneuverability, as well as their large carrying capacities. Green has sold natural gas-powered buses for over twenty years and has refined the buses' efficiencies. Green's salesperson says that both the cost of natural gas and the hydrocarbon footprint of each bus will rapidly decrease in the next few years. Buses are indeed becoming more fuel efficient, but the old axiom that trains use less fuel than buses requires Green to present up-to-date facts and figures to city governments.

Scratch Paper
Do not write your essay here. Scratch work only.

Use the lined area below to write your essay. Continue on the back if you need more space.

ANSWER KEY
Practice Test 2

SECTION I: READING COMPREHENSION

1. D	8. A	15. D	22. B
2. D	9. C	16. A	23. A
3. E	10. A	17. B	24. D
4. C	11. E	18. B	25. E
5. D	12. B	19. C	26. A
6. E	13. E	20. E	27. C
7. E	14. B	21. E	

SECTION II: LOGICAL REASONING

1. D	8. C	15. C	22. D
2. E	9. D	16. E	23. A
3. C	10. C	17. C	24. D
4. D	11. A	18. E	25. B
5. C	12. C	19. D	26. D
6. D	13. D	20. B	
7. A	14. C	21. E	

SECTION III: ANALYTICAL REASONING

1. A	8. A	15. B	22. E
2. E	9. C	16. D	23. B
3. A	10. E	17. D	
4. C	11. B	18. E	
5. D	12. C	19. A	
6. A	13. D	20. A	
7. D	14. D	21. D	

SECTION IV: LOGICAL REASONING

1. E	8. A	15. A	22. B
2. B	9. E	16. C	23. A
3. A	10. C	17. B	24. D
4. D	11. B	18. A	25. E
5. C	12. E	19. C	
6. C	13. B	20. E	
7. E	14. B	21. B	

CALCULATING YOUR SCORE

1. Check your answers against the Answer Key on the previous page.
2. Use the Score Worksheet below to calculate your raw score. Your raw score is the total number of questions that you answered correctly.
3. Use the Conversion Table below to convert your raw score into a score on the 120–180 scale. Remember that these scores are approximate.

Score Worksheet

Section	Number of Questions	Number Correct	Number Incorrect	Number Not Answered*
Section I: Reading Comprehension	27			
Section II: Logical Reasoning	26			
Section III: Analytical Reasoning	23			
Section IV: Logical Reasoning	25			
Total:	101			

*You should not leave any questions unanswered. There is no penalty for guessing.

Conversion Table

Raw Score Range	Scaled Score	Raw Score Range	Scaled Score	Raw Score Range	Scaled Score	Raw Score Range	Scaled Score	Raw Score Range	Scaled Score
0–15	120	30	133	50	146	72–73	159	90	172
16	121	31–32	134	51–52	147	74	160	91–92	173
17	122	33	135	53	148	75–76	161	93	174
18	123	34–35	136	54–55	149	77	162	94	175
19	124	36	137	56–57	150	78–79	163	95	176
20	125	37–38	138	58	151	80	164	96	177
21	126	39	139	59–60	152	81–82	165	97	178
22–23	127	40–41	140	61–62	153	83	166	98	179
24	128	42	141	63–64	154	84–85	167	99–101	180
25	129	43–44	142	65	155	86	168		
26	130	45	143	66–67	156	87	169		
27–28	131	46–47	144	68–69	157	88	170		
29	132	48–49	145	70–71	158	89	171		

EXAM ANALYSIS

Every practice section that you take is an opportunity for you to evaluate your testing strategy. If you take a section under timed conditions, that also gives you an opportunity to evaluate your timing strategy. The last section of Chapter 1 (General Strategies) provides a detailed worksheet and plan for reviewing your performance and identifying exactly what strategy error led to each wrong answer. The sections of Chapter 1 on timing explain how to evaluate your timing strategy. Be sure to evaluate your timing strategy for every section that you take under timed conditions.

Use the plan in Chapter 1 to review every question that you answered incorrectly. The plan lists twenty-two specific errors. For each question that you answered incorrectly, you should review the parts of Chapter 1 and the other relevant chapters that cover the strategies with which you had trouble. The key to success is identifying your errors and reviewing again and again.

Use the following chart to summarize your performance based on four main categories of error. Enter the number of incorrect answers in each column. Some questions may fall under more than one category.

Summary of Incorrect Answers

Section	Total Incorrect	Didn't Take Enough Time	Misread Information	Got Down to Two Answers	Didn't Have a Strategy
I: RC					
II: LR					
III: AR					
IV: LR					
Total:					

After you have reviewed your timing strategy, enter the results in the chart on the next page. The questions for which you simply filled in a bubble without working on the question should be counted under Cold Guesses. If you spent more than fifteen seconds working on a question, do *not* count it under Cold Guesses. Under Number Correct and Number Incorrect, do not include Cold Guesses. The number in the Cold Guesses column, then, includes both incorrect and correct answers. In the final column, enter the number of incorrect answers on which you spent under two minutes.

Analysis of Timing Strategy

Section	Number Correct (not cold guesses)	Number Incorrect (not cold guesses)	Cold Guesses	Number of Incorrect Under 2 Minutes
I: RC				
II: LR				
III: AR				
IV: LR				
Total:				

If most of your incorrect answers took under two minutes, you should plan to spend more time on questions. If you have more than two or three questions incorrect—excluding Cold Guesses—you can increase your score by working on fewer questions but spending a little more time on the questions that you do work on. See the example below.

Example of Revised Timing Strategy

Section	Number Correct (not cold guesses)	Number Incorrect (not cold guesses)	Cold Guesses	Number of Incorrect Under 2 Minutes	Total Correct (including cold guesses)
First attempt	11	6	7	5	12
Revised attempt	11 + 2	0	7 + 4	0	15

By guessing cold on four more questions, the test taker in the example above had time to work the remaining two questions correctly. Approximately one out of five Cold Guesses results in a correct answer.

ANSWERS EXPLAINED

Section I: Logical Reasoning

1. **(D)** This is a rare *agreement between two people* question. Choice D is correct because the policy of the government of the Netherlands allows the innovator to make a profit, and the author's proposal allows the innovator to make a profit (a lump-sum payment).

   Choice A is incorrect because it is consistent with the author's statements but there is no information about the attitude of the government of the Netherlands toward choice A. Choice B is incorrect for the same reason. Choice C is incorrect because the author believes that confusion of ownership is a more substantial issue. Choice E is incorrect because the author does not believe it.

2. **(D)** This is a *main idea* question. Choice D captures the entire context of the passage, including the positive aspects of patents, the negative aspects, and an alternative.

   Choice A is incorrect because it discusses only the positive aspects. Choice B is incorrect because it discusses the positives, one negative, but not the main negative, and does not include the alternative. Choice C is incorrect because it only compares two negatives without mentioning the positives or alternatives. Choice E is incorrect because it only includes the alternative.

3. **(E)** This is a *weaken* question, based on weakening an argument in the passage, similar to *weaken* questions in LR. The author's argument is based on the statement that the goal of a patent is to grant exclusive ownership. Choice E establishes that owners of previous patents on which a new patent depends usually do not interfere with the decisions of the owner of the new patent. Therefore, exclusive ownership is preserved in practice.

   Choice A is incorrect because it supports the author's argument. Choice B is incorrect because even if the cost of litigation is not more than the value, it is still a significant cost, and therefore choice B strengthens the author's argument. Choice C is incorrect because it does not attack the author's premise that patents based on other patents dilute exclusive ownership. Choice D is incorrect because the owner of the older patent, while willing to cooperate, requires compromise, which strengthens the argument that the new patent holder does not have exclusive ownership.

4. **(C)** This is an *implied fact* question. Choice C is correct, and choice B is incorrect, because the passage states that a patent holder can prevent others from making, selling, or using a patented technology without *permission*. Payment is optional. Choice A is incorrect because it is the patent owner who must disclose the technology. Choice D is incorrect because the passage states that some people believe a patent is inherently inconsistent with free trade policy. Choice E is incorrect because it refers only to an innovator, not to a patent owner.

5. **(D)** This is a *tone* question. The answer choices are typically on a continuum, as in this question, ranging from positive without qualifications to positive with qualifications to neutral to negative with qualifications and finally to negative without qualifications. For this question, the author is negative about patents in the modern era but also cites some positive aspects. The correct answer choice is the one that is negative with qualifications, choice D.

6. **(E)** This is an *agree with a view* question. Choice E is correct, based on the statement "In the case above, it is not is clear who owns Sandra's invention . . ." In the passage, Sandra is the holder of the later patent.

Choice A is incorrect because the author states that most patents are based on previous patents "in this era of rapidly expanding technologies." It is not defendable to conclude that that era began in the 1800s. Choice B is incorrect because it is not defendable to say that litigation is probable, only that it is possible. Choice C is incorrect because the author states that it is the ownership of the later patent that is questionable. Choice D is incorrect because the earlier patent confuses the ownership of the later patent, but the passage does not support that the holder of the earlier patent takes over ownership of the later patent.

7. **(E)** This is an *extension/application* question in an EXCEPT format. There are three goals of patents stated in the passage:

1. Patents grant exclusive ownership. This is a necessary condition. Without exclusive ownership, the patent has not met its goal.
2. Patents encourage creating and perfecting a product and allow the patent holder to make a profit.
3. Patents require that the patent holder disclose the details of the innovation.

Choice E does not meet any of these criteria. Because choice E does not confer exclusive ownership, it cannot meet the goals of a patent.

Choice A meets the goal of making a profit. The fact that competitors were forced out of business is irrelevant to the goal of a patent. Choice B meets the goal of creating and perfecting the technology. Choice C meets the goal of disclosing the details. The fact that the patent holder did not make a profit does not detract from meeting the goal of disclosure. Choice D meets the goal of exclusive ownership.

8. **(A)** This is a *use of a word/phrase* question. The word *legitimate* in this instance simply means that the assertion is reasonable, as in choice A.

Choice B is incorrect because it refers to the use of the word *legitimate* in the previous sentence. Choice C is incorrect because the word *legitimate* does not refer to a legal basis for the assertion. Choice D is incorrect because it refers to the previous sentence. Choice E is incorrect because the word *legitimate* does not refer to an ethical basis for making an assertion.

9. **(C)** This is a *main point* or *main idea* question. For this question, the correct answer is not just a summary of the conclusion but rather captures the structure of the argument. Choice C is correct because it includes the beginning of the passage, in which the author describes the problem, the portion of the passage in which the author describes electric cars as a solution but indicates a drawback of electric cars, and the final portion, in which the author presents an alternative to the generation of electricity for cars with fossil fuels, namely regenerative braking.

Choice A is incorrect because it does not include the alternate solution. Choice B is incorrect because no one criticizes the author's solution of regenerative braking. Choice D is incorrect because the fact that regenerative braking solves another problem (generation of electricity for non-transportation uses) is not the author's main point. Choice E is incorrect because the author does not recommend an alternative to automobiles but rather an alternative to gasoline engines.

10. **(A)** This is an *agree with a view* question. The author would most likely agree with choice A. The author lists three advantages of cars over public transportation—fast, flexible, cheap—that are true of all types of cars.

Choice B is incorrect because, even if people continue to use cars instead of public transportation, electric cars have the potential to reduce noise and pollution. Choice C is incorrect because the author believes that some electric cars would consume the same amount of gasoline—in terms of generating the electricity for the car—as current cars. Choice D is incorrect because there is no information in the passage that indicates that a car in the city performs differently than a car in the country. Choice E is incorrect because, although electric cars based on regenerative braking would reduce noise and pollution, the author states that electric cars do not reduce congestion.

11. **(E)** This is an *implied fact/inference* question. Choice E is correct because the passage makes a clear contrast between cities of the Old World and cities in America that "have evolved around the use of the automobile."

Choice A is incorrect because there are many sources of congestion, noise, and pollution other than cars. Choice B is incorrect because there is no information in the passage to support it. Choice C is incorrect because there is no information about the relative percentages of people in Old World cities using cars versus public transportation. Choice D is incorrect because, while it is inferred that these cities did not evolve around the automobile, there is not enough information to defend that they evolved around the use of horses. It is possible that Old World cities did not evolve around transportation at all.

12. **(B)** This is an *analogous situation* question. The role of electric cars that use gasoline-powered electricity is that they appear to be a solution to the use of gasoline but in fact still use gasoline, but in a less obvious way. Similarly in choice B, the plastic materials seem to avoid using wood but in fact use wood in their manufacturing process.

Choice A is incorrect because the automobiles introduce a different kind of pollution, not the same kind in a less obvious way. Choice C is incorrect because it does not involve replacing one technology with a different technology. Choice D is incorrect because the new technology avoids the problems of the old technology. Choice E is incorrect because the problem with the new technology is expense, rather than that it causes the same problem as the old technology in a less obvious way.

13. **(E)** This is a *function* question that asks you to identify the role in the argument of a specific statement. In the statement cited in this question, the author establishes that public transportation is unlikely to be a solution to the problems caused by gasoline-powered automobiles. The only remaining solution is to change the automobiles themselves, as described in choice E.

Choice A is incorrect because the author only mentions the distinction between Old and New World cities as background to discussing the problem of pollution. Choice B is incorrect because the author does not discuss any such conflict. Choice C is incorrect because the author states that public transportation is unlikely to ever be a solution. Choice D is incorrect because the author does not suggest these aspects of public transportation.

14. **(B)** This is a *use of a word/phrase* question. The author states that the train is massively heavy to show that under such conditions, regenerative braking produces large amounts of electricity. The implication is stated in choice B—the heavier the load, the more energy can be generated.

Choice A is incorrect because, although the statement is defendably true, it is not the author's point. Choice C is incorrect because there is no information about the energy required to operate the loaded train. Choice D is incorrect because it is not apparent, or likely, that the loaded train is operated by electricity. Choice E is incorrect because the author does not refer to the polluting quality of coal. Coal is only mentioned because it constitutes the load on the train.

15. **(D)** This is a Comparative Reading *in common* question. It asks for an element that is central to both passages. Choice D is correct because Passage A is mainly concerned with identifying what it is that defines fiction, and Passage B is mainly concerned with identifying what it is that defines science fiction.

    Choice A is incorrect because neither passage is concerned with distinguishing true from untrue details. Choice B is incorrect because only Passage B discusses this. Choice C is incorrect because only Passage A discusses most people's definitions. Choice E is incorrect because Passage A does not compare fiction to science fiction.

16. **(A)** This is a *specific detail (stated fact)* question. Choice A is correct because Passage A specifically states that bringing together two separate elements of our reality (*talking* and *dogs*) is what makes fiction entertaining.

    Choice B is incorrect because it refers to Passage B. Choice C is incorrect because it refers to most people's definition of fiction, with which the author of Passage A disagrees. Choice D is incorrect because Passage A states that imagination is not the sole defining element of fiction. Choice E is incorrect because it is not enough to simply draw on elements of our reality, such as "talking." Elements must be combined in unique ways, as described by choice A.

17. **(B)** This is a rare *element from Passage A supports argument in Passage B* question. Choice B supports the assertion in Passage B that imagination by itself is not enough to make a story science fiction.

    Choice A is incorrect because it is not consistent with Passage B to say that being untrue is enough to make a story effective. Choice C is incorrect because being imaginative is not the defining characteristic of science fiction. Choice D is incorrect because it describes the view of the author of Passage A. Choice E is incorrect because it is not a statement from Passage A, but rather from Passage B.

18. **(B)** This is a Comparative Reading *in common* question that asks you to identify a type of reasoning that is used in both passages. Choice B correctly states that both passages start with definitions that are partially correct and then both passages refine those definitions.

    Choice A is incorrect because it refers only to Passage A. Choice C is incorrect because neither passage includes an erroneous definition, only a definition that is partially correct. Choice D is incorrect because Passage A does not discuss a specific form of fiction. Choice E is incorrect because neither passage eliminates all possible alternatives.

19. **(C)** This is an *implied fact/inference* question that is applied to a Comparative Reading section. Choice C is correct because Passage A states that some people believe that the fact that a work of fiction contains details that are not true predicts that the story can be expected to be entertaining. In the second paragraph, Passage A establishes that, for most people, untrue details do not guarantee that people will be entertained. Therefore, there are some people who may expect a work to be entertaining (based on the fact that it contains untrue facts) and yet not be entertained by it.

Choice A is incorrect because there is no evidence to support that anyone considers fantasy to be close to science fiction, and because the author of Passage B allows for the possibility that certain examples of fantasy could also be science fiction. Choice B is incorrect because there are no people mentioned in either passage who would be committed to believing that a story is not science fiction simply because it is based on the Roman Empire. Choice D is incorrect because the passages only defend that some people believe that the fact that a story is not true defines a work as fiction. Choice E is incorrect because there are no people mentioned in either passage who believe this. The author of Passage B believes that entertainment is not the primary purpose of science fiction.

20. **(E)** This is a Comparative Reading *relationship between passages* question. Choice E is correct in that both passages question the statement in the beginning. Passage A rejects the statement and concludes the opposite, that fiction is truer to life than ordinary life. Passage B incorporates the statement into its conclusion in the final sentence.

    Choice A is incorrect because the statement is not relevant. Passage B does not define science fiction in the same terms. Choice B is incorrect because the statement is consistent with Passage B. Choice C is incorrect because the crushed-brick technology is not necessarily one that "pushes the human mind into the future" and its mention in Passage A does not necessarily support the definition of science fiction. Choice D is incorrect because the conclusion of Passage B is based on different criteria from the criteria used to define fiction in Passage A.

21. **(E)** This is a Comparative Reading *identify the difference between the passages* question. Choice E is correct because Passage A states that a work of fiction is more real than ordinary life, and Passage B states that the further a story takes us from ordinary life, the more entertaining it is.

    Choice A is incorrect because the author of Passage A does not express an opinion about science fiction. Choice B is incorrect because both authors believe that imagination is one element but not the defining element. Choice C is incorrect because the author of Passage B does not use logic to any greater extent than does the author of Passage A. Choice D is incorrect because it is the author of Passage B who specifies a goal, whereas the author of Passage A does not.

22. **(B)** This is a *main idea* question. Choice B correctly incorporates all of the main points of the passage.

    Choice A is incorrect because the passage does not state that a two-party system is inappropriate, only that it has some disadvantages. Choice C is incorrect because IRV does not address the drawbacks of multiparty electoral systems. Choice D is incorrect because it presents a positive view of two-party systems, whereas the passage presents a negative view. Choice E is incorrect because, although a true statement, it is not the main idea.

23. **(A)** This is a *function* question that requires you to identify the function of a certain reference. The author indicates that the framers of the Constitution did not specifically create a two-party system. This provides background for the discussion that follows, explaining how the two-party system in the United States came about. Choice A correctly describes this.

    Choice B is incorrect because the passage does not make such an assertion. Choice C is incorrect because the statement about the framers of the Constitution does not attempt to prove that the Constitution supports a two-party system. Choice D is incorrect because the statement about the framers of the Constitution does not mention that they fell into two major political divisions. Choice E is incorrect because the passage does not do what choice E says.

24. **(D)** This is a *specific detail (stated fact)* question. Choice D is a direct restatement of the facts in the second paragraph.

   Choice A is incorrect because it refers to IRV. Choice B is incorrect because, although party-proportional representation can lead to a multiparty system, a multiparty system is not free from domination by two major parties. Choice C is incorrect because a political party could run a candidate and yet not gain enough votes to earn a seat. Choice E is incorrect because the passage does not support that the candidates in a party-proportional system are any better qualified than in the American congressional system.

25. **(E)** This is a rare *identify a generalization* question. The question asks you to find a generalization that is supported by something in the passage. Choice E is a generalization that is supported by the claim that when there are only two parties, it is easy for the parties to become polarized. In other words, that claim is a specific example of the generalization stated in choice E.

   Choice A is incorrect because the passage supports the opposite view. Most democracies use a multiparty system and the author finds that system superior. Choice B is incorrect because the author does not recommend blending two-party and multiparty systems. Choice C is incorrect because the passage supports the opposite. People expect many choices in breakfast cereal but accept only two choices in candidates. Choice D is incorrect because there is nothing in the passage that supports it.

26. **(A)** This is an *implied fact/inference* question. Choice A is implied because the IRV system assumes that many people have more than one candidate who they would accept.

   Choice B is incorrect because nothing in the passage defends that democracies with multiparty systems have those systems because the voters chose the system. Choice C is incorrect because it contradicts the statement that the party that loses an election has no representation. Choice D is incorrect because, even though the passage mentions a view that two-party systems have stronger economies, there is not enough information to defend that any country with a multiparty system does not have as much economic growth as a country with a two-party system. Choice E is incorrect because it is not supported by the passage. The passage states only that in a two-party system, a vote for a third-party candidate may be wasted.

27. **(C)** This is a *helps to answer* question. Choice C is correct because the passage explains that in a multiparty system, if one party accuses another of being extreme, voters distrust both parties. The other answer choices are incorrect because the passage does not contain information that would answer the questions posed.

Section II: Logical Reasoning

1. **(D)** This is a *strengthen by principle* question. Morrison's argument must address Lee's conclusion that Dr. Jansen does not meet the needs of his patients. Morrison states that Dr. Jansen refers patients to specialists when he cannot diagnose the patient's condition. The principle stated in choice D—that referring patients to a specialist constitutes meeting the needs of the patient—completes the argument.

Choice A is incorrect because Morrison's goal is to show that Dr. Jansen does meet his patients' needs. Choice B is incorrect because it leaves open the possibility that Dr. Jansen is not meeting the needs of his patients. Choice C is incorrect because it does not address whether or not Dr. Jansen is meeting the patients' needs. Choice E is incorrect because it leaves open the possibility that Dr. Jansen does not meet his patients' needs.

2. **(E)** This is a *resolve a paradox* question. The paradox is that the two separate studies seem to have evaluated the same set of businesses and yet found widely different results. Choice E explains the discrepancy because if two different definitions of failure were used, the same set of data would lead to different conclusions.

Choice A is incorrect. Even though it points out a difference between the two studies, the difference does not by itself explain why the results were different. Choices B and C are incorrect for the same reason as choice A. Choice D is incorrect because it does not address a difference between the two studies.

3. **(C)** This is a *sufficient assumption* question. For this particular question, the correct answer is also a necessary assumption. Negating choice C gives *The dog was not frightened by the thunder*. This makes the argument fall apart, which proves that choice C is necessary for the argument to work. From the standpoint of a *sufficient assumption* question, the statement that the dog was frightened by the thunder is sufficient to make the argument work. Often there is no significant difference between a sufficient and a necessary assumption.

Choice A is incorrect. The negation of choice A—*the dog has not been trained not to bark*—does not affect the argument. Choice B does not affect the argument unless it is known that the dog is frightened. Choice D simply confirms that the dog does not bark, which was already established by the passage. Choice E is irrelevant to the situation because the dog did not bark.

4. **(D)** This is a *conclusion* question in an EXCEPT format. Four answer choices can be concluded from the premises in the passage. Choice D is correct because it cannot be concluded from the passage. The passage states that online courses offer flexible exam schedules, but there is no evidence that traditional courses do.

Choices A and E can be concluded because all of the characteristics of online courses that are described in the passage are reasons why students prefer online courses. Choice B can be concluded because, when the passage states that online courses have flexible schedules, the implication is that traditional courses do not. Similarly, for choice C, the statement that online courses accommodate more students implies that traditional courses accommodate fewer.

5. **(C)** This is a *flaw* question. Choice C correctly identifies that the psychologist has assumed the claim about computers is incorrect because there is no proof that it is correct.

Choice A refers to accepting that a claim is correct because there is no proof that it is incorrect. Choice B is incorrect because the psychologist does not ignore information but rather believes that there is no relevant information. Choice D is incorrect because failing to back up a premise with facts is not a logical error. Choice E is incorrect because the psychologist does not cite any authorities in support of his or her case.

6. **(D)** This is a *complete the sentence/argument* question. Because labor saving is defined as saving time to complete a task for the person involved, if fifteen minutes for cleaning

is added to the thirty-five minutes for performing the task, as in choice D, the total time for one task is fifty minutes, which is not a savings of time over the forty-five minutes that the task took to complete without the equipment. There is a difference, then, between the time to perform the task (thirty-five minutes) and the time to complete the task (fifty minutes.)

Choice A does not violate the definition of labor saving because presumably the people who took forty-five minutes to complete the task with the equipment would have taken longer than forty-five minutes to do so without the equipment. Choice B is incorrect because the definition of labor saving does not depend on whether the task is a necessary one. Choice C is incorrect because the definition of labor saving does not depend on whether or not there is a more labor-saving technology available. Choice E does not change the fact that the time to perform the task is thirty-five minutes.

7. **(A)** This is a *parallel flaw* question. The logic in the original passage is:

$$aerobic \rightarrow reduce$$
$$-reduce \rightarrow -avoid\ stroke$$
$$\therefore\ aerobic \rightarrow avoid\ stroke$$

The fallacy in the argument is that it interprets *-reduce → -avoid stroke* as *reduce → avoid stroke*. In terms of A and B, the original argument is:

$$A \rightarrow B$$
$$-B \rightarrow -C$$
$$\therefore\ If A \rightarrow C$$

Choice A correctly parallels this flaw:

$$complete \rightarrow points$$
$$-points \rightarrow -pass$$
$$\therefore\ If\ complete \rightarrow pass$$

Choice B is valid logic:

$$avoid \rightarrow lower$$
$$lower \rightarrow reduce\ heart\ attack$$
$$\therefore\ If\ avoid \rightarrow reduce\ heart\ attack$$

Choice C is incorrect because it is based on a correlation—great artists correlate to personal suffering—not on an if/then statement.

Choice D is logically valid:

$$Nitrogen \rightarrow grow$$
$$-sunshine \rightarrow -grow$$
$$=\ grow \rightarrow sunshine\ \text{(contrapositive)}$$
$$\therefore\ If\ nitrogen \rightarrow sunshine$$

The logic in choice E is similar to the logic in the original passage but is distinct in an important way:

$$-individuals \rightarrow -society$$
$$society \rightarrow greater\ good$$
$$\therefore\ If\ individuals \rightarrow greater\ good$$

Compare the structures of the original and of choice E, in terms of A and B logic.

Original	Choice E
If A → B	If –A → –B
If –B → –C	If B → C
∴ If A → C	∴ If A → C

In the original, it is the second statement that is misinterpreted. In choice E it is the first statement that is misinterpreted.

8. **(C)** This is a *flaw: fails to consider* question. The correct answer is one that, if true, would weaken or destroy the logic in the argument. Choice C is correct because if a condition other than a frost had occurred that was capable of killing the tomato plants, then the conclusion would be invalid.

   The other answer choices, if true, would not affect the conclusion.

9. **(D)** This is a *match a concrete example to a principle* question. The principle is in the setup and the answer choices are concrete examples. Choice D matches the principle. The criterion of evidence of profitability is lacking, so the project should not be approved.

   Choice A does not match the principle. The principle states that if criteria A and B are not met, the project cannot be approved. Choice A states that because criteria A and B have been met, the project should be approved. Choice B claims that because the evidence of profitability is not extensive, the project should be disqualified. However, this goes further than the actual criteria, which state simply that there must be evidence, without specifying how extensive the evidence must be. Choice C does not match because at the time that the manager approved the project, the manager had evidence that supported profitability. Choice E does not match the principle because it talks about competing with future projects, whereas the principle only requires not competing with current projects.

10. **(C)** This is a *strengthen* question based on the matching of terms, which is rare. Choice C is correct because the passage's conclusion is that the climate is ideal, and the only premise is the list of climatic conditions. By adding the statement in choice C—that the stated combination of characteristics constitutes what people consider to be an ideal climate—the conclusion is strengthened.

   Choice A is incorrect because seasonal variation is described as something desirable. The island has an ideal climate despite not having variation. Choice B is incorrect because the passage does not state whether Marbay has a wet or dry climate, so choice B is irrelevant. Choice D is incorrect because Marbay's uniqueness does not add to or detract from the idealness of its climate. Choice E goes in the wrong direction, weakening the argument.

11. **(A)** This is a *conclusion* question that asks for something that can be inferred from the information in the passage. Choice A is correct because the remedy that results from long-term planning to address one inequity may introduce one or more new inequities.

   Choice B is incorrect because, even though inequities introduced through legal remedies may be unintentional, there may be other inequities that were originally intentional. Choice C is incorrect because it does not follow from the passage that the number of inequities will necessarily increase. Even though new inequities may be introduced, there may be a net decrease in the number of inequities. Choices D and E are incorrect because there is nothing in the passage to support them.

12. **(C)** This is a *flaw: vulnerable to criticism* question. Choice C is correct because Marissa uses the word *intellectual* to refer to the use of the reasoning process, whereas Frederick uses the word to refer to a person who is out of touch with practical issues.

Choice A is incorrect because Frederick does not use biased language. Choice B is incorrect because Marissa does not present a cause-and-effect argument. Choice D is incorrect because Frederick's attack on Marissa's argument is not based on her lack of defense for her view. Choice E is incorrect because Frederick does not base his argument on an unrepresentative group.

13. **(D)** This is a *sufficient assumption* question. Choice D is correct because, if local merchants lose money when people have the flu, then reducing the number of people who have the flu leads to the conclusion that the merchants will make more money.

Choice A is incorrect because it goes in the wrong direction. If people shop when they are sick, then preventing people from getting sick will not affect the merchants' income. Choice B is incorrect because it does not lead to the conclusion. Choice C is incorrect because it is irrelevant. There are still enough flu cases during the holiday season to affect sales. Choice E is incorrect because there is no relationship between the local facilities at which people get shots and the local merchants.

14. **(C)** This is a rare type of *weaken* question that is based on a statistical argument. The key to this type of question is the concept of false positive results versus false negative results. The new technology had no false positives. All of the cars identified as speeding actually were. However, the new technology had many false negatives. Many cars that it indicated were not speeding actually were. Weakening the argument depends on pointing this out, as choice C does.

Choices A and E are irrelevant, as they affect both technologies in the same way. Choice B is a factor that might cause a police department to question whether or not to buy the new technology, but choice B does not weaken the logical argument. The argument is based only on the fact that the new technology appears to be better. Weakening an argument requires weakening the logic on which the argument is based. Choice D would strengthen the argument, as it implies that if new equipment had been used for testing the old technology, the results might have been different.

15. **(C)** This is a *strengthen* question based on a cause-and-effect argument. The argument's conclusion is that the impression that the town is declining economically causes people not to move to the town. The first premise to support this cause-and-effect argument is that many yards are overgrown. To support the conclusion, it is necessary to add that overgrown yards create the impression that the town is declining economically. Choice C adds this premise.

Choice A is incorrect because the argument has to do with *impressions* of prospective residents. Prospective residents would not know that the homeowners had good jobs. They would only see that the yards were overgrown. Choice B is incorrect for the same reason. Choice D does not change the fact that there is a correlation between people getting a copy of the report and buying a home in the town. Choice E is incorrect for a similar reason.

16. **(E)** This is a *resolve a paradox* question. The paradox is that, as the coyote population decreased, it would be expected that the gopher population would increase. Instead, the gopher population continued to decrease. Choice E is correct because it states that the decrease in the coyote population resulted in an increase in the population of other predators of gophers.

Choice A is irrelevant to the fact that there are fewer coyotes on the ranch now than there were three years ago. Choice B is irrelevant. Choice C does not explain why the rate of decline has stayed the same. Choice D does not explain the decrease in gopher population.

17. **(C)** This is a *flaw* question. Choice C is correct because Sylvia may have the highest odds—for example, 24 percent—compared to the other four—for example, 19 percent each—but 24 percent odds is not high enough to conclude that she will win. There is a 76 percent chance that Sylvia will not win.

Choice A is incorrect because it is not necessary for a logical argument to provide supporting evidence for a premise. Choice B is irrelevant. The argument has already established that all five salespeople have the same skills. Choice D is incorrect because predicting events based on their odds is not a logical flaw. Choice E is incorrect because the argument does not assume that the salespeople are equal simply because they are members of the same group.

18. **(E)** This is a *strengthen by principle* question. Choice E matches the situation described in the passage and is the correct answer.

Choice A is incorrect because it fails to address the possibility of injury. Choice B is incorrect because the passage's conclusion does not depend on weighing the risks. Choice C is incorrect because it does not strengthen the conclusion. Choice D is incorrect for the same reason.

19. **(D)** This is a *type of logic* question. Baxter generalizes from the specific experience of immigrants to the broader case of all minority groups. Beardsley challenges this generalization by stating that immigrants are different from native-born minorities. Choice D correctly states Beardsley's method of logic.

Choice A is incorrect because Beardsley does not question Baxter's description of the immigrant experience. Beardsley also does not do what is stated in choices B, C, and E.

20. **(B)** This is a *weaken* question. The argument states that the reason for establishing a website is to earn money from advertising on the Web page. Choice B weakens the argument by providing an alternative explanation for how the website generates additional income.

The other answer choices do not weaken the argument.

21. **(E)** This is a *must be true* question. The setup is deductive. The rules are:

If top exec + travel for business → corporate jet
If < five years + travel for business → −corporate jet

Choice E must be true. If Sarah uses a corporate jet, it could not be for business because then both if/then statements would apply, and the result would be a contradiction (both *jet* and *not jet*). Sarah could use a corporate jet for nonbusiness purposes, such as a company-sponsored vacation.

Choice A could not be true. Choice B could be true but does not have to be, as Sarah might use the jet for nonbusiness purposes. Choice C cannot be true, as it would trigger both rules. Choice D does not have to be true. As in choice A, an employee could use a corporate jet for a nonbusiness purpose.

22. **(D)** This is a *role of a claim* question. The claim that is quoted in the question stem is a fact (premise). Based on this fact, astrophysicists have concluded that dark matter exists. The physicist attempts to weaken this conclusion by providing a flaw in it (*no direct evidence*) and an alternate hypothesis. Choice D correctly describes this role.

Choice A is incorrect because, although the quoted statement is a premise, it does not establish the physicist's conclusion. Choice B is incorrect because the quoted statement is neither an intermediate conclusion nor a support for the physicist's conclusion. Choice C is incorrect because the quoted statement is a fact, not a hypothesis. Choice E is incorrect because the quoted statement does not illustrate a principle.

23. **(A)** This is a *necessary assumption* question. Test the answer choices by negating them. If the negation destroys the argument, that answer choice is the assumption. The negation of choice A is that it is possible to attain simplicity without striving for it, which destroys the conclusion that it is impossible to attain simplicity.

The negation of choice B is that there are no forms of striving that are simple, which strengthens the argument. The negation of choice C is that there are many ways to define simplicity, but this does not affect the argument. The negation of choice D is that it is possible to strive without attaining simplicity, which strengthens the argument. The negation of choice E is that it is possible to strive for simplicity in some things. This does not affect the conclusion that doing so does not lead to simplicity.

24. **(D)** This is an *application of a principle* question. Choice D adds the elements that are missing in the application in order to make it match the principle. Namely, for the principle to apply, the money must go to the judge—which is included in choice D—and the judge must not know about the money—which is also included in choice D.

Choice A is incorrect because it is not necessary—in order for the principle to apply—that the judge rule in favor of the party that provided the money. Choice B is incorrect because the principle does not require that the payment be reasonable or usual. Choice C is incorrect because the principle is not based on contact with a party but with a payment from a party. Choice E is incorrect because it does not matter when the speech takes place but rather when the payment takes place.

25. **(B)** This is a *main conclusion* question. You must identify the conclusion that is the main point of the argument. The last sentence of the argument is the conclusion, and is paraphrased in choice B.

Choice A is an unstated premise of the argument, as is choice C. Choice D is not a valid statement. The passage states:

If discover comet and –rare → –famous

In other words, if you discover a comet and it is not rare, you cannot become famous. This is *not* the same as saying that if you discover a comet that *is* rare, you *will* become famous. Choice E is not valid because an astronomer may become famous in a way other than discovering a comet.

26. **(D)** This is a *parallel reasoning* question. The original passage sets up two categories, each with a certain characteristic:

under three inches = drought tolerant

over eight inches = not drought tolerant

The conclusion is that a case that falls between the two categories—*five inches*—has a characteristic that is midway between the characteristics of the original two categories—*somewhat drought tolerant.*

Choice D is parallel:

Under $20,000 inventory = under $25,000 profit per year

Over $100,000 inventory = over $150,000 profit per year

The conclusion is an intermediate case—*$60,000*—and an intermediate characteristic—*$90,000 profit per year.*

Choice A is incorrect because the conclusion is not an intermediate case. Choice B is incorrect for the same reason and, in addition, comes to a different kind of conclusion. Choice C also does not have an intermediate case and argues from the characteristic backward to the case, rather than from the case to the characteristic. Choice E does not have an intermediate case and assigns an arbitrary characteristic—*$15,000 profit per year*—without defending that that amount is proportional to the inventory.

Section III: Analytical Reasoning

QUESTIONS 1–6

This is a sequence game, which means that it must have one-to-one correspondence and be ordered. There are seven fixtures, numbered 1 through 7 from left to right, with left corresponding to west and right corresponding to east. The diagram is as follows:

```
L                    West                          N    East
M                      1     2     3     4     5   6    7
N
O
P
R        S – P
S        N = 5, 7
         P – L – N
      If P = 3  →  R – P
      If P ≠ 3  →  P – R
      _____

         R
         S – P – L – N
      If P = 3
      _____

              R
         S – P – L – N
      If P ≠ 3
      _____
```

Note that there are two possible strings, depending on whether P is or is not in 3.

1. **(A)** This is the typical first question. Use **Eliminate—apply rules, four violations**. The rule S–P is violated by choice E. The rule $N = 5, 7$ is not violated in any answer. The rule P–L–N is violated by choice C. The rule *If P = 3* is violated by choice D. The rule *If P not = 3* is violated by choice B.

2. **(E)** This is a CANNOT be true question with no new information. Because there is nothing to diagram, use **Test answers—prove a violation**. First, though, check the answers briefly against the supplemental diagrams to see which are most likely to violate rules. The two supplemental diagrams are:

If P = 3   **If P not = 3**

Choice A is consistent with the right diagram. Choice B is consistent with the left. Choice C is consistent with the right. Choice D is consistent with the left. Choice E leaves some ambiguity. Test choice E first.

Put M in 1. Put R in 2. Scan the rules, starting with the first rule. No rule gives clear information until *If P not = 3 → P – R*. Because P is *not* before R in the diagram, P must go in 3. Go back to the top of the rules. The first rule is violated. There is no place to put S before P. Choice E cannot be true.

3. **(A)** This is a *could be true* question with new information that is not in the diagram. Use **Diagram—supplemental diagram or rules** to adjust the supplemental diagrams to represent P and R as adjacent.

If P = 3   **If P not = 3**

Comparing the diagrams briefly with the answer choices, choice B is out because L cannot be third in either of the two scenarios. Choice C is out because S must have at least four trees planted to the east of it. Choice D is out because N and R cannot be adjacent. Choices A and E are unclear and must be tested. Theoretically, it would be possible to create parallel universes from the two supplemental diagrams, but because only two answer choices are left, it is faster to test the answer choices.

Test choice A. Putting S in 3 means the rule *If P not = 3* is invoked. So spots 4 through 7 must be PRLN. Spots 1 and 2 can be O or M. There does not appear to be a rule violation. Test choice E. With N in 5, spots 1 through 4 must be either SRPL or SPRL. In both cases, S must go in 1. Choice E violates rules, and choice A is confirmed as correct.

4. **(C)** This is a *could be true* question with new information that goes in the diagram. Put M in 1. In order to fill in more of the diagram, use **General—look for most restricted**. N has only two options. However, P is equally restricted because P's placement affects R's placement. Use **General—options for player** to consider P's options. P cannot go in 2 because there would be no room for S to go before P. Spot 3 is an option. Spot 4 is an option. P cannot go any farther east than 4 because, with P not in 3, R, L, and N must follow P.

Create two universes, one with P in 3 and one with P in 4. Applying the rules, the universe with P in 3 fails, because it requires R before P, and there is no space for R. For the universe with P in 4, create two universes with the two options for N – 5 and 7. The universe with N in 5 violates rules because L must come between P and N. Spots 5 and 6 must be R/L and L/R. Spots 2 and 3 must be O/S and S/O. The answers can now be compared with the diagram.

West   N   East
   1   2   3   4   5   6   7
  ___   ___   ___   ___   ___   ___   ___
   M   O/S   S/O   P   L/R   R/L   N

The only viable universe

5. **(D)** This is a *must be true* question with no new information. Because there is nothing to diagram, use **Test answers—negate a must**. In general, it is sometimes useful to check the answer choices against the supplemental diagrams, but in this case, it does not help.

Test choice A by negating it. Create a diagram in which there are only four trees east of S (S is in 3). Spots 4 through 7 must include P, L, and N, and because P is not in 3, R must also be included. N cannot go in 5, so N must be in 7. R and L can go in 5 and 6 and M/O goes in 1 and 2. There do not seem to be any violations, so choice A does not have to be true.

Test choice B by finding three spots for S. Testing choice A showed that spot 3 is an option. Because S has many players after it, it is likely that S can go in 1 and 2. Two diagrams quickly show that spots 1 and 2 seem viable. Choice B does not seem to need to be true.

Test choice C by putting R next to N and putting S somewhere other than 1. The test of choice A can be used to prove that this is possible. Test choice D by putting S next to M and then trying to place L and R so that they are not adjacent. If P is in 3, S and R must be in 1 and 2. Therefore, to test choice D, P cannot be in 3. Systematically consider the options for P. If P is in 2, S must be in 1 and so cannot be next to M. P cannot go in 1, nor can P go in 5 or 6. Put P in 4. Because P is not in 3, R, L, and N must come after P, just as in the test of choice A. Also, N cannot be in 5 because L must come between P and N, so N is in 7. R/L and L/R are in 5 and 6. Now S and M can be adjacent in 1 and 2 or in 2 and 3. These are the *only* options for S and M to be adjacent and in both cases, R and L are also adjacent. Choice D must be true. For practice, show that if M is in 7, S does not have to be in 1.

6. **(A)** This is a *must be false* question with no new information. Use **Test answers— prove a violation**. Test choice A by diagramming all of the possibilities M – P – O. Use **General—options for player** to consider the options for P. P cannot go in 1, 5, 6, or 7. P can only go in 2, 3, or 4. If P is in 2 or 3, the players for 1 and 2 are determined (S; S/R R/S, respectively). Consequently, M cannot be to the left of P. The only option for M – P – O is with P in 4.

With P in 4, spots 5 through 7 must be L/R, R/L, and N, in that order. There is no place for O to be to the right of P. Therefore, choice A violates rules and must be false. It is not necessary to test the remaining answers, because the rule violation in choice A is clear. For practice, you can show that choices B through E are possible.

QUESTIONS 7–13

This is a one-to-one correspondence game (all one-to-one games are ordered) but it is not a sequence. It is an ONS-A game. There are six fixtures with no branches.

```
P                    1    2    3    4    5    6
R                   ___  ___  ___  ___  ___  ___
S
T        RV or VR
U        If P ≠ 3, →
V            S = 5

        Either R – P
          or R – T
           bnb
```

7. **(D)** This is the typical first question. The RV rule is violated by choice C. The *P not = 3* rule is violated by choice B. The final rule is violated by choice A, in which R is not before either P or T, and by choice E, in which R is before both P and T.

8. **(A)** This is a *must be true* question with new information that goes in the main diagram. Put P in 1 and use **Diagram—apply rules, musts**. The second rule causes S to be in 5. Apply the RV rule. The only options for RV or VR are 2 and 3, or 3 and 4. Use **Diagram—parallel universes**. In the universe with R and V in 2 and 3, T and U are the only unassigned players and can go in either of the remaining slots, 4 or 6, which can be filled in as T/U and U/T.

    In the second universe, with R and V in 3 and 4, T must come after RV or VR and so must go in 6. U must go in 2.

```
 1    2    3    4    5    6
___  ___  ___  ___  ___  ___
 P   R/V  V/R  T/U   S   U/T

 P    U   R/V  V/R   S    T
```

    Use **Eliminate—check answers against diagram** to check the answer choices. Choice B is out because R can be in 4. Choice C is out because U can be in 4 or 6. Choice D is out because T can be in 4 (top universe) and U in 6. Choice E is out because U can be in 6.

9. **(C)** This is a *CANNOT be true* question with no new information. Because there is nothing to diagram, you must use **Test answers—prove a violation**. First, briefly check the answer choices against the rules to see if any choices stand out as likely to violate a rule. There is a relationship between P and T in the third rule, though it may not be immediately clear how to apply the relationship to choice C, so test choice C first. Find all of the options for placing the sequence PT. There are three—in 1 and 2; 2 and 3; or 3 and 4. The pair cannot be placed where one of the members is in 5 because with P not in 3, 5 must be occupied by S.

    Apply the rules to the three universes. With PT in 1 and 2, R/V and V/R must go in 3 and 4. For the universe with PT in 2 and 3, there is no place for R/V and V/R, so that universe is out. For the remaining universe, R/V and V/R must go in 1 and 2. Test the two remaining universes against the third rule. Both violate the third rule, so choice C cannot be true.

$$\begin{array}{cccccc} \underline{1} & \underline{2} & \underline{3} & \underline{4} & \underline{5} & \underline{6} \\ P & T & R/V & V/R & S & \\ \cancel{P} & & \cancel{T} & & \cancel{S} & \\ R/V & V/R & P & T & & \end{array}$$

NOTE: All three universes violate the third rule. The second universe is out because it does not have two adjacent slots for R and V.

10. **(E)** This is a *could be true* question with no new information. Because there is no information to put in the main diagram, you must test answers. Before doing so, check the answer choices briefly against the conditions to see which players are most limited in the number of fixtures to which they could be assigned. It has already been determined in earlier questions that neither R nor V can occupy 1 or 6. Choice A is out. U has no restrictions and so is a likely candidate. S must go in 5 in all cases in which P is not in 3, but it is unclear if that limits S's overall options. It is most reasonable to test U first.

Testing U requires trying U in all six positions to see if there are slots to which U cannot be assigned. Testing the other answer choices will require the same process. This question could potentially take a long time to solve. In testing an answer, look for restrictions that could show in which fixtures a player might cause a violation. Also, consider the fixtures that have restrictions. For example, if P is not in 3, slot 5 is determined. Try putting U in 3. S must go in 5. There is now no acceptable place for RV. To prove that U *does not* have five options, it is necessary to find one more slot to which U cannot be assigned. Try putting U in 5, taking advantage of the fact that 5 is restricted. With U in 5, P must go in 3 and again there is no place for RV. Choice B is out.

Three choices are left to test, but because of the restrictions on S, it is best to consider T or P. Starting with T, put it in 3 to see if the strategy used for U works for T as well. It does. T in 3 means S is in 5 and there is no place for RV. T in 5 has the same result, as it forces P into 3. T is reduced to only four possible slots and is out.

Test P. Putting P in 3 allows S to be anywhere. RV can go in 4 and 5. There does not appear to be a rule violation. Putting P in 5 does result in a rule violation, because the fact that P is not in 3 means that S also has to be in 5. However, it is likely that P can go in any of the remaining five slots.

As a double-check, prove that S has at least two spots into which it cannot go. Because the other answer choices have been ruled out, eliminating S will confirm that P is the answer. Putting S in 3 results in a violation because with P not in 3, S would also have to go in 5. Putting S in either 4 or 6 can be shown to cause a violation.

This is a time-consuming question. You might only have enough time to work through some of the steps and then guess.

11. **(B)** This is a *completely determined* question. There is new information that does not go in the diagram (U-S). There are multiple options for U coming before S, so it is not feasible to make universes. Instead, test the answer choices. Scan the answer choices briefly to see if any choices are more likely to result in enough restrictions that the order is completely determined. P swimming third triggers a specific result—S cannot be in 5.

S swimming second also means that P swims third. V swimming fifth also means that P swims third. Because all three of these require P in 3, choices B and E are more restrictive because they add an additional element.

Test choice E. Put S in 2. Based on the new information in the stem, U is in 1. P is in 3. T must come after R/V and so must be in 6. Fixtures 4 and 5 can be either R or V. The order is not completely determined.

Test choice B. V is in 5. P is in 3. T must come after R/V, so T must go in 6. R must go in 4. U must come before S, so U is in 1 and S in 2. The order is completely determined. As practice, show that choices A and D result in multiple options.

12. **(C)** This is a *must be true* question with new information that does not go directly in the main diagram. Use **General—options for player** to see how many options there are for placing T and P. If there are fewer than five or six, it may be feasible to use parallel universes.

There must be at least two empty slots between T and P (for R/V and V/R). T could go in 1. P could go in 4 at the earliest. This means that P is not in 3, and therefore, S must be in 5. P, then, could go in either 4 or 6. That gives two universes. In the universe with P in 4, R/V and V/R must go in 2 and 3. U must go in the remaining slot, 6. In the universe with P in 6, R/V could either be in 2 and 3 or in 3 and 4. Split this universe into two universes. The placement of U is determined in each.

T could also go in 2. Use **General—options for player** to determine the options for P. There must be two slots between T and P, which leaves 5 and 6 for P. However, because P is not in 3, S must be in 5. With T in 2, the only option for P is 6. S must be in 5. R/V and V/R must be 3 and 4. U must be in 1. There are now four universes that represent all possibilities.

1	2	3	4	5	6
T	R/V	V/R	P	S	U
T	R/V	V/R	U	S	P
T	U	R/V	V/R	S	P
U	T	R/V	V/R	S	P

Use **Eliminate—check answers against diagram** to find the correct answer. Choices A, B, D, and E do not have to be true.

13. **(D)** This is a rare *how many* question, with new information that does not go in the main diagram. Use **General—options for player** to determine the options for placing PS. If P is in 3, S goes in 4. However, if P is in 3, R/V and V/R must go in 4 and 5. Therefore, P cannot go in 3.

If P is not in 3, S is in 5. Therefore, PS must go in 4 and 5. There must be at least two slots between P and T, so T must go in 1 and R/V and V/R go in 2 and 3. U must go in 6. The exact locations of four players are known.

QUESTIONS 14–18

This is a hybrid between a sequence game and a non-sequence game that has one-to-one correspondence. The setup lacks a string of at least three relationships. However, there is information about every player, and the game functions much like a regular sequence game.

N
P
R
S
T
U
W

	M	T	W	Th	F	Sa	Su
	1	2	3	4	5	6	7

(4 is circled with W)

R↘
  P
N↗

N↘
  U
T↗

W = 4

Either R – W
  or T – S
    bnb

R↘
  P
N↗
   ↘
    U
T↗

14. **(D)** This is the typical first question. The first rule is violated by choice C. The second rule is violated by choice B. No choices violate the W = 4 rule. Choices A and E violate the last rule. In choice A, R is not before W *and* T is not before S. In choice E, R is before W *and* T is before S.

15. **(B)** This is a *could be true* question with new information that does not go directly into the main diagram. The new information —*R – – U* or *U – – R* [there need to be 2 dashes between R and P to represent two players]—does not go into the supplemental diagram, either. If this were a pure sequence game, the supplemental diagram would be helpful with this type of question.

In a testing situation, it would not be clear whether it would be faster to diagram all of the universes or to test the answer choices. Because either R or U could be first in the sequence, and because there are multiple options for where the pair can be placed, testing answers would be a reasonable first approach.

Test choice A. Four answer choices violate rules, so use **Test answers—prove a violation**. Put S in 3. Find the options for *R – – U* or *U – – R*. There is only one—slots 2 and 5. Try both universes—one with R in 2 and one with U in 2. With R in 2 and U in 5, there are not enough slots for N and T to come before U. The same is true with U in 2. Choice A violates rules.

Test choice B. Put N in 2. There is only one place for R/U—in 3 and 6. Test both universes. In the universe with R in 3, R is before W, so T must go after S but before U. This means S is in 1, T in 5, and P in 7. Check this order against the rules. There are no violations. This is enough information to prove that N could be assigned to Tuesday.

As an exercise, prove that choices C through E violate rules, and then approach this question by setting up parallel universes, rather than testing answer choices.

16. **(D)** This is a *CANNOT be true* question with no new information. Because there is nothing to diagram, use **Test answers—prove a violation**. Before testing answer choices, though, use **General—count places in sequence** to determine which players cannot appear in either 1 or 2. Both P and U require two players before them. W can only be in 4. Any answer choice that includes P, U, or W is out. However, there are no such choices.

Use **Eliminate—check previous valid assignments** to eliminate choice A, as it appears in the correct answer to question 14. Test choice B. With S in 1 and T in 2, the fourth rule dictates that R must be before W, and thus in 3. Putting N in 5 creates an order that appears valid. Remember that it is not necessary or time-effective to prove absolutely that an order is viable. If an order appears viable, move on. Because the correct answer is one that violates rules, it will be clear when you find it.

Test choice C. N and T in 1 and 2, respectively, means that T is before S and, thus, R is after W. Putting U and P at the end (6 and 7) guarantees that the first two rules are not broken. There appears to be a viable order.

Test choice D. T and R in 1 and 2, respectively, means that R is before W. The last rule dictates that T cannot be before S, but with T in 1, that rule is violated. Choice D violates rules and is therefore the correct answer.

A quick double-check of choice E shows that it appears viable. Because the violation in choice D is clear, it is not necessary to spend much time testing choice E, but it is good strategy to glance at it.

17. **(D)** This is a rare *could be false* question, with new information that goes in the diagram. Four answers choices cannot be false, meaning that they must be true. Use **Diagram—put in new information** to put P in 3. Use **Diagram—apply rules, musts** to determine that R and N must go in 1 and 2. Use **Diagram—parallel universes** to show the two options—R and N in 1 and 2 versus N and R in 1 and 2. The rules indicate that T must come after S, because R is before W. T must also come before U. That means that in both universes slots 5, 6, and 7 must be STU, respectively. The answer choices can now be compared to the two universes. Choices A, B, C, and E all must be true (cannot be false). Only choice D does not have to be true.

M	T	W	Th	F	Sa	Su
1	2	3	4	5	6	7
R	N	P	Ⓦ	S	T	U
N	R	N	Ⓦ	S	T	U

18. **(E)** This is a *could be true* question with new information that does not go directly into the main diagram. However, if T is before S, then the fourth rule dictates that R must be after W. Because R must be before P, there are only two options for R after W—5 or 6. If R is in 6, then P must be in 7. If R is in 5, then P can be in either 6 or 7. This leads to three universes.

T must be before S and also before U, so T must be placed so that there are at least two blank slots after it. There is only one blank slot after W in all three universes. Therefore, T cannot be in 3. The only options for T are 1 and 2.

M	T	W	Th	F	Sa	Su
1	2	3	4	5	6	7
			(W)	R	P	
			(W)	R		P
			(W)		R	P

Partial universes

At this point, pursuing parallel universes would result in over six possibilities. Switch to testing answer choices. Doing so will be easier because of the partially filled-in universes. Test choice A. There is only one universe in which Friday is open, and placing N there violates the *N, T before U* rule.

Test choice B. Placing T in 5 violates the conditions in the question stem (T-S). Test choice C. T in 3 does not allow for both S and U after T. Test choice D. R in 3 is not allowed in any of the universes.

Testing choice E puts U in 3. N and T can go in either order in 1 and 2. S can go in whichever spot is empty after W. Choice E appears to be valid. The other answer choices have been proven to violate rules.

QUESTIONS 19–23

This is an unordered game. There is not one-to-one correspondence. At least one player must be left out. The number of fixtures is variable. There must be at least three people chosen, but there could theoretically be up to seven chosen. For this reason, the number of slots in the discard pile is also variable, from a maximum of five to a minimum of one. It is not necessary to show slots for all five possible discard slots. Simply leave enough room to add players to the discard pile if necessary. Note the use of three dots after fixture 3 to indicate that the first three fixtures are required and the subsequent fixtures are optional.

F
G
H
I
J   If H → –F, –L
K   If I → –K
L   If H → I
M   If M → –F
           If K or G → KG

1 2 3 ··· 4 5 6 7 | _ _ _

19. **(A)** This is the typical first question. The first rule is violated by choice C. The second rule is violated by choice E. The third rule is violated by choice B. The fourth rule is violated by choice D.

20. **(A)** This is a *must be true* question with new information that goes in the main diagram. Put H in the assignment. Apply the rules. The first rule indicates that F and L go in the discard pile. The third rule indicates that I is in the assignment. The second rule now indicates that K is in the discard pile. The fifth rule indicates that G is in the discard pile. The only players not accounted for are M and J. J has no restrictions. M can be in because F is already out. The third, required slot can be taken by either M or J. A fourth slot could be taken by whichever of the two is not in 3.

$$\underset{H}{\underline{1}} \quad \underset{I}{\underline{2}} \quad \underset{M/J}{\underline{3}} \quad \cdots \quad \underset{J/M/\varnothing}{\underline{4}} \quad \underset{}{\underline{5}} \quad \underset{}{\underline{6}} \quad \underset{}{\underline{7}} \quad \Big| \quad \underset{K}{\underline{}} \quad \underset{G}{\underline{}} \quad \underset{F}{\underline{}} \quad \underset{L}{\underline{}}$$

The fourth slot can be J, M, or empty ($\varnothing$).

Use **Eliminate—check answers against diagram**. Choice A must be true. Choice B is incorrect because there cannot be five people chosen. Choice C is incorrect because Monroe does not have to be chosen. Neither choice D nor choice E must be correct, though they could be.

21. **(D)** This is a *one or both of a pair* question, with a new condition that there must be at least four players chosen. The correct answer for this type of question consists of a pair, both of which cannot be out. To test the answer choices, put both members of the pair in the discard pile and try to show that a violation results.

For choice A, F and I go in the discard pile. The rule $H \rightarrow I$ means that H must also be in the discard pile. The absence of F, however, does not trigger any rules. With only three players in the discard pile, there are most likely options for creating a viable assignment of four players. Do not take the time to prove that there is an option. When you find the correct answer, the rule violation will be clear.

Choice B functions similarly to choice A. The absence of F does not trigger any rules. The absence of G means that K is in the discard pile. There are enough players left to create a viable assignment.

For choice C, H in the discard pile does not trigger any rules. Although the presence of H affects many players, the absence of H is not a trigger. The absence of K triggers the absence of G and again there are only three players out.

For choice D, the absence of I triggers the absence of H. The absence of K triggers the absence of G. The remaining players are F, J, L, and M. However, F and M cannot occur together. One slot in the assignment is for one of F and M. Only two players remain, so it is not possible to create an assignment with four players. It is not possible to discard both members of the pair in choice D. One or both of the pair must be chosen.

As a double-check, choice E results in I, H, and M being out. Enough players are left to make a viable assignment.

22. **(E)** This is a *could be true* question with new information that goes in the diagram. Put F in the assignment and J in the discard pile. Apply the rules. The presence of F triggers the absence of H and the absence of M. The discard pile now contains H, M, and J. The assignment contains F. The remaining players are G, I, K, and L. Create two parallel universes based on the presence or absence of I.

In the universe with F and I, the presence of I triggers the absence of K. The absence of K triggers the absence of G. Only L is left. This universe consists of F, I, and L. In the universe without I, K and G must be in. If one of K and G is out, the other is out. If they are both out, there are not three players left (I is out in this universe). K and G, then, must be in, and L might or might not be in.

$$\underset{F}{\underline{1}} \quad \underset{I}{\underline{2}} \quad \underset{L}{\underline{3}} \quad \cdots \quad \underset{}{\underline{4}} \quad \underset{}{\underline{5}} \quad \underset{}{\underline{6}} \quad \underset{}{\underline{7}} \quad \Big| \quad \underset{H}{\underline{}} \quad \underset{M}{\underline{}} \quad \underset{J}{\underline{}} \quad \underset{K}{\underline{}} \quad \underset{G}{\underline{}}$$

1   2   3   ...   4   5   6   7 |
F   I   L   H M J K G
F   K   G   (L)   H M J I (L)

Parallel universes. Parentheses represent optional elements.

Use **Eliminate—check answers against diagram**. Choice A cannot be true because there are always at least four employees not selected. Choice B cannot be true because there can only be three or four employees selected. Choice C cannot be true because the presence of I triggers the absence of K, which triggers the absence of G. The diagram reflects this.

Choice D cannot be true because if I is selected, the only remaining option for a third player is L. Choice E can be true, as is shown in the bottom universe.

23. **(B)** This is a rare *maximum/minimum* question. There is no new information. To find the maximum number of players, try to find the smallest possible number of players in the discard pile. Create two universes, one with H in the discard pile and one with H in the assignment. With H in the discard pile, F and M cannot both be in, so one of them goes in the discard pile (F/M). I and K cannot both be in. If K is out, G is also out, so put I in the discard pile to keep the discard pile as small as possible. The remaining five players can all be in without violating any rules. Choice A is out because there is a viable assignment with more than four players.

In the universe with H in the assignment, F and L are in the discard pile. I and K cannot both be in. Putting I in the discard pile results in three players in the discard pile again. It is not possible to have two or fewer members in the discard pile, so the maximum number of players in an assignment is five, and answer choice B is correct.

Section IV: Logical Reasoning

1. **(E)** This is a *resolve a paradox* question that is worded in terms of explaining a phenomenon, and the phenomenon is a contradiction or paradox. In this question, the paradox is that staying open later, given that there are customers in the store during the additional hour, should bring in more money, and yet the net profit has decreased. Choice E explains how there could be additional sales, but if the cost of operating the store for an extra hour is greater than the sales, there is a net loss.

Choice A is incorrect because, among other reasons, buying fewer items is not the same as spending less. Choice B is incorrect because by itself it does not explain how the net profit decreased. Choice B does go in the right direction, but without including the fact that staying open costs money, as choice E states, choice B does not work. Choice C is incorrect because it is irrelevant and does not explain why there is an ongoing decrease in net profit. Choice D is irrelevant because the issue is not the popularity of the store but rather the net profit.

2. **(B)** This is a *main conclusion* question. It asks you to find the main idea of the passage. Although the passage begins by discussing Ed, its conclusion is about patients in general. For this reason, choices C, D, and E are incorrect. The conclusion is that nagging can prevent or slow down the healthful changes that a patient may make. Choice B correctly states this. Choice A is a premise that supports the conclusion about nagging.

3. **(A)** This is a *sufficient assumption* question. The correct answer is one that, if true, causes the conclusion to be true. The negation of choice A is that there has been interbreeding between the butterfly species on the two islands. This destroys the argument that the long tongues are the result of *independent* adaptation.

   The negation of choice B is that the two flower species are related. This does not affect the argument. The negation of choice C is that, if the butterflies had not developed long tongues, they would not have had any food. This is irrelevant to the conclusion. The negation of choice D is that there is another animal that is better adapted. This does not affect the conclusion that the adaptation of the butterflies is an example of independent adaptation. The negation of choice E is that the butterflies are not capable of long-distance flight. This would strengthen the conclusion, so choice E itself actually weakens the conclusion, by implying that there could have been interbreeding.

4. **(D)** This is a *conclusion* question that asks for information that can be inferred from the premises in the passage. The passage contains a deductive premise:

   If want to please → make unrealistic promises

   It also contains an inductive premise:

   If unrealistic promises → voters unlikely to vote for you

   This is inductive because the conclusion of the if/then statement refers to a probable action, not an inevitable one. Combining these two premises gives:

   If want to please → voters unlikely to vote for you

   Choice D expresses this conclusion.

   Choice A is incorrect because it states:

   If realistic promises → likely to vote for you

   This does not follow from the premise:

   If unrealistic promises → voters unlikely to vote for you

   Choice B is incorrect because, even though the passage implies that it is natural to want to please voters, there is no information to support that *most* candidates want to please voters. Choice C is incorrect because there is no support for the conclusion that voters will not vote in the election at all. Choice E is incorrect because its logic is invalid. The original logical conclusion, as stated in choice D, is:

   If want to please → voters unlikely to vote for you

   The logic in choice E is:

   If –want to please → voters –unlikely to vote for you

   In other words, choice E negates both sides of the actual conclusion, which does not result in a valid statement.

5. **(C)** This is a *strengthen by principle* question. The answer choices are general principles. The correct answer strengthens the argument. Choice C is a principle that matches the argument and strengthens it.

   Choice A is incorrect because the argument is not that only certain people should use OYSTER but that no one should. Choice B is incorrect because the argument is not based on finding OYSTER more powerful than necessary, but rather on finding OYSTER more difficult to use. Choice D is incorrect because the argument is not based on the fact that the people writing the language are more advanced than those modifying programs, but rather that the people modifying programs—as well as people writing programs—will find it harder to use. It does not necessarily follow that a less-advanced programmer will have a hard time working with a program written by a more-advanced programmer. Choice E is incorrect because the argument is not based on less-advanced programmers not understanding OYSTER programming but rather on less-advanced programmers having a hard time working with it. It is possible to understand programming but still have a hard time working with it.

6. **(C)** This is a *parallel reasoning* question. The basis of the original argument is that the sample surveyed is not representative of the population that the survey attempts to evaluate. Choice C establishes that the people surveyed outdoors in the evening were not representative of all dog owners.

   Choice A is incorrect because the sample—visitors to the museum—is the same as the population about which the survey makes a conclusion. Choice B is incorrect because the flaw in the survey is that its terms were not defined. Choice D is incorrect because the survey makes its conclusion about journalists—not about physicians—and the sample consists of journalists. Choice E is incorrect because it criticizes the survey on grounds other than that the sample was not representative.

7. **(E)** This is a *necessary assumption* question. The negation of choice E is that even without vitamin D, calcium can be made available for the body. This destroys the conclusion that people need vitamin D.

   The negation of choice A is that there are as many dietary sources of vitamin D as there are of calcium. This does not affect the argument. The negation of choice B is that calcium from foods is not better than calcium from supplements, which does not affect the argument. The negation of choice C is that it is possible to have strong bones without a healthy diet. This does not affect the argument because the argument is based only on the intake of calcium, not on a balanced diet. The negation of choice D is that it is not necessary to have the same amounts of vitamin D and calcium. This does not affect the argument.

8. **(A)** This is a *committed to agree/disagree* question. Choice A is correct because Phuong is committed to agreeing with it and Jacob is committed to disagreeing with it.

   Choice B is incorrect because both agree with it. Choice C is incorrect because both agree that such a garden *may* have fulfilled its purpose. Choice D is incorrect because both disagree with it (and thus agree with each other). Choice E is incorrect because Jacob agrees with it, and Phuong does not express an opinion about it, thus the two do not disagree.

9. **(E)** This is a *strengthen* question based on a cause-and-effect argument. The argument concludes that being watched causes some drivers to get into an accident. Choice E

strengthens the argument by explaining the mechanism by which being watched leads to an accident, namely that frequent monitoring of the speedometer can block out peripheral vision, which means that drivers are temporarily unaware of the other drivers around them.

Choice A is incorrect because there is no clear reason why nervousness would lead to less-safe driving. Choice B is incorrect because there is no evidence that any drivers are speeding as they pass the visible patrol cars. Choice C is incorrect for the same reason as choice A. Nervousness alone does not necessarily lead to less-safe driving. Choice D is incorrect because it has not been established that the drivers passing the patrol cars are nervous. Choice D would be stronger if it said *Drivers passing patrol cars become nervous and nervous drivers change lanes frequently.* Even then, changing lanes is not necessarily unsafe, whereas losing peripheral vision, as in choice E, inherently cuts the driver off from important information about nearby cars.

10. **(C)** This is a *match a principle to a concrete example* question, in which the passage presents the principle and the answer choices are concrete examples. The principle involves two deductive statements:

If –one positive review from professional critic → –significant
If two or more curators praise AND if one positive review from critic → significant

The first statement establishes that a positive review from a professional critic is *necessary* for the work to be significant. Without the positive review, it is not possible for the work to be significant. However, a positive review from a critic is not *sufficient* for guaranteeing that the work is significant.

The second statement—which requires that the work has received at least one positive review from a professional critic—establishes that the fact that two or more curators have praised the work is *sufficient* to guarantee that the work is significant. Choice C meets both of these criteria, because one of the curators is also a professional critic.

Choice A is incorrect. Its logic is:

If two or more curators praise AND if one positive review from critic → significant
(original condition)
∴ *If –two or more curators praise AND if one positive review from critic → –significant*
(negation of both sides)

Although the occurrence of certain conditions guarantees *significant*, the absence of those conditions does not guarantee the absence of *significant*.

Choice B is incorrect because, even though the situation meets the criterion of two or more curators, it is not known whether it meets the criterion of one professional art critic. Therefore, it cannot be concluded that the work is significant. Choice D is incorrect. It meets the criterion of one art critic but does not meet the second criterion, even though one curator has praised the work. The conclusion is that because the work has met some of the criteria, it has higher odds of being significant. The original principle does not support this conclusion because it does not discuss a partial satisfying of criteria. Choice E is incorrect. Consider what rules are triggered by the fact that the work is not significant. In the first rule,

If –one positive review from professional critic → –significant

the factor *not significant* does not trigger any rules. In the second rule,

If two or more curators praise AND if one positive review from critic → *significant*

the contrapositive is:

–significant → *– (If two or more curators praise AND if one positive review from critic)*

and the factor *not significant* triggers the conclusion that the combination of events shown in parentheses is not true. However, this does not mean that no critics gave the work a positive review. It includes the possibility that some critics gave a positive review but there were not two curators who praised it.

11. **(B)** This is a *sufficient assumption* question. If choice B is assumed to be true—that eyewitnesses often have characteristics that make them seem unreliable—then the conclusion of the argument inevitably must follow—that jurors often do not believe eyewitnesses.

The other choices are incorrect because they do not lead inevitably to the conclusion of the argument. Choice A leads to the conclusion that most eyewitnesses believe they can reliably report what they have seen. Choice C is irrelevant because eyewitnesses are not necessarily people who have committed crimes. Choice D would only lead to the conclusion that jurors ignore circumstantial evidence. Choice E leads to the conclusion that jurors sometimes must rely on eyewitness reports but does not lead to the conclusion that such jurors reject most eyewitness reports.

12. **(E)** This is a *weaken* question. Choice E is correct because it results in all students in a coeducational class performing better on tests and quizzes, and performance on tests and quizzes directly measures the amount that the students have learned.

Choice A is incorrect because the fact that a female teacher teaches a class of boys does not directly influence how much the boys learn. Choice B is incorrect because it is not clear whether there is a net increase in learning. Choice C is incorrect because it does not necessarily lead to an increase in learning. Choice D is incorrect because less-aggressive behavior among boys does not necessarily lead to more learning.

13. **(B)** This is a *resolve a paradox* question that does not use the word *paradox* in its stem. The paradox is that the Old Town voters voted for a measure that they were warned would not benefit them. Choice B is correct because it explains that the Old Town voters considered themselves middle class, even if they did not meet the economic criteria for actually being middle class.

Choice A does not explain why the seemingly non-middle-class residents voted for the measure. Choice C is incorrect because it would only explain why some voters considered middle class because of their incomes might have voted against the measure. Similarly, choice D only explains why some middle-class people might have voted against the measure. Choice E is irrelevant.

14. **(B)** This is a *necessary assumption* question. Choice B is correct because the negation of choice B—that Edgar does not have any infection at all—destroys the argument. The surgeon would then have no reason for not operating.

The negation of choice A is that Edgar's infection can be cured by the day of surgery. This does not affect the argument because the requirement for favorable conditions is that the patient be free of infection the day before surgery. The negation of choice C is that if the conditions were favorable, the surgeon still might not operate. This does not affect the argument. The negation of choice D is that the protocol includes measures for avoiding infection. This does not affect the fact that Edgar has an infection. The negation of choice E is that there are other days on which the surgeon could operate on Edgar. This does not affect the argument.

15. **(A)** This is a *complete the sentence/argument* question. Choice A is correct because it is analogous to hearing the words of a story when there is no one present to tell the story.

    Choice B is incorrect because it would be analogous to writing a story, not to hearing a story. Choice C is incorrect because it is analogous to hearing the excitement or drama behind a story, rather than simply hearing the story itself. Choice D is incorrect because it is analogous to seeing the letters of which a story is composed, rather than reading the story itself. Choice E is incorrect because it is analogous to using the imagination to make up a story, rather than reading the story.

16. **(C)** This is a *main conclusion* question. Choice C correctly identifies the main point of the argument as rebutting the hypothesis that the lower mortality rate is due to an understanding of history.

    Choice A is incorrect because it misses the point that the argument rebuts a hypothesis. In addition, combat technology is only one possible alternative explanation. Choice B is incorrect because it is the point that the argument rebuts. Choice D is incorrect because the fact that modern wars seem less destructive in one way is not the main point of the argument. Choice E is incorrect because it is simply a premise that is used to defend the main point—that knowledge of history is not the cause of reduced mortality.

17. **(B)** This is a *relevant information* question. Four of the answer choices are not relevant to the effectiveness of the biologist's argument. Choice B is relevant because the rancher's argument is that there is no benefit in return for the potential loss of livestock. Clarifying choice B would determine whether or not there was any benefit.

    Choice A is incorrect because it does not compare the ranchers' loss with the ranchers' gain. Choice C is incorrect because comparing the relative values of the two benefits that the biologist names is not relevant to the rancher's argument. Choice D is incorrect because the rancher's argument does not depend on receiving a benefit that is equal to the loss, but simply on receiving any benefit at all. Choice E is incorrect because the benefit to ranchers does not necessarily need to be economic.

18. **(A)** This is a *weaken* question based on a cause-and-effect argument. The argument establishes a correlation between reading the summary and voting for the bond issue and then concludes that the summary caused people to vote for the bond issue. Choice A weakens the conclusion by indicating that the cause-and-effect relationship is the reverse—being in favor of the bond issue caused people to want to read the summary.

    Choice B is incorrect because it is possible that the people had read or not read the summary before deciding how to vote. Choice C is incorrect because the existence of some exceptions to the correlation does not change the fact that there is a strong correlation. Choice D is incorrect because it does not change the correlation that was demonstrated by those who did vote on election day. Choice E would only weaken the argument if many more opponents than proponents refused to talk with pollsters.

19. **(C)** This is a *conclusion* question that asks what can be inferred from the premises in the passage. Choice C is correct because the average speed is the same for cars during the first and second hours of rush hour, but the second hour is subject to stop-and-go conditions that lower the mileage.

Choice A cannot be concluded from the information in the passage. It is possible that stop-and-go traffic occurs at other times. Choice B is incorrect because it is not known whether the reduced gas mileage due to stop-and-go conditions is enough to cancel out the increased mileage from driving at an average of 30 miles per hour. Choice D is incorrect because nothing is known about maximum speed, only about average speed. Choice E is incorrect because it contradicts the information in the passage that states that the average speed is the same throughout rush hour.

20. **(E)** This is a *flaw* question that uses the wording *vulnerable to criticism.* Choice E is correct because, if there were other ways to obtain the information about the behavior of corporations, the conclusion—that if the courts will not order disclosure, there is no way to obtain the information—falls apart.

Choice A is incorrect because the argument does not assume that corporations violate ethics, only that they might. Choice B is incorrect because the argument is not based on changing the behavior of corporations but on simply judging their behavior. Choice C is incorrect because the argument is not concerned with whether corporations can judge their own behavior but rather with the ability of the public to do so. Choice D is incorrect because failing to back up a premise with a rationale is not a flaw in logic.

21. **(B)** This is a *strengthen* question. The argument claims that avoiding disease will help people live longer. Choice B strengthens this conclusion by establishing that avoiding diseases is a significant factor in living longer. It this were not the case, the conclusion would fall apart.

Choice A is incorrect because the conclusion concerns an event in the future, not in the present. The argument has already established that modern medicine has increased life expectancy. Choice C is incorrect because it is irrelevant to the future scenario. Choice D is incorrect because it weakens the argument, suggesting that people who have recovered from a disease may be healthier than people who avoided the disease. Choice E is incorrect because, although it supports the premise that people who have avoided a disease are healthier than people who have recovered from the disease, it does not support the conclusion that people who have avoided diseases will live longer. A statement such as choice B is needed to make the logical leap from healthier people to people who live longer.

22. **(B)** This is a *flaw* question that uses the rare wording *in that it takes for granted.* With this type of question, the argument is flawed because it takes something for granted that may in fact not be true. Choice B correctly points out that the argument assumes that because there have been more sightings of UFOs, there must be more visitations of UFOs. This is not a valid assumption because there could be other explanations for more sightings, such as increased awareness or better reporting of sightings.

Choice A is incorrect because the argument does not depend on an ongoing increase in the frequency of sightings. Choice C is incorrect because, although the argument assumes this, it does not represent a logical flaw. Choice D is incorrect because the argument does not assume this. The argument does not depend on the fact that the UFOs are not piloted by humans. Choice E is incorrect because the argument does not assume that UFOs are harmless.

23. **(A)** This is a *parallel flaw* question that does not use the word *parallel.* The flaw in the original argument is that, even though the odds of any individual new small business

succeeding for a year are only 30 percent, the odds of one out of fifteen surviving are much higher. Choice A contains the same error. Even though the odds of any individual greyhound winning are low, the odds of one out of six winning are higher.

Choice B is incorrect because it is not flawed. Choice C is incorrect because it is a cause-and-effect argument. Choice D is incorrect because its error is in failing to consider the possibility that the man bribed the juries that acquitted him. Choice E is incorrect because it is not flawed.

24. **(D)** This is a *role of a claim* question. Choice D is correct, in that the quoted statement is a conclusion defended by the specific facts in the second sentence. The fact that the silvery minnow is endangered is then used as a premise to support the conclusion in the last sentence.

Choice A is incorrect because the quoted statement is not the main conclusion. Choice B is incorrect because the argument does not rebut the quoted statement. Choice C is incorrect because the quoted statement supports the main conclusion directly, not through supporting an intermediate conclusion. Choice E is incorrect because the quoted statement is not a hypothesis. It is a fact.

25. **(E)** This is a *flaw* question. Choice E is correct because adequate food and shelter is necessary for people to pursue the truth—without it, people cannot pursue the truth. However, the argument concludes that once adequate food and shelter is provided, that people will pursue the truth. That is a logical flaw because people still may not pursue the truth. Food and shelter is necessary but not sufficient.

Choice A is incorrect because there is no individual case given. Choice B is incorrect because the information about the group of people who do not have food or shelter is not based on the characteristics of some people in the group. Choice C is incorrect because it is not necessarily probable that once people have food and shelter, they will pursue the truth. Choice D is incorrect because the argument does not claim that the group of people without food or shelter is representative of the population as a whole.

Writing Sample: Example of a Superior Response to the Essay

Slotown ("ST") chooses RoadRail ("RR") over Green Bus ("GB") because RR affords sufficient routing flexibility while minimizing ST's fuel use and hydrocarbon footprint. ST uses two criteria, which are that ST wants flexibility to make routing changes, and that ST wants to minimize the fuel consumption and hydrocarbon emissions of its public transportation system. RR is ST's superior alternative because RR is more efficient and environmentally friendly than GB and offers a changeable routing system. GB is ST's inferior alternative because GB brings greater fuel consumption and larger hydrocarbon emissions. RR is therefore ST's superior alternative because RR better meets ST's selection criteria.

ST uses two criteria to choose between RR and GB. One criterion says ST wants to minimize fuel use and reduce hydrocarbon emissions. The second criterion says ST wants to maximize its transportation flexibility if a HugeGro factory closes or moves. These criteria may be combined into a single rule that says ST wants to use less fuel and generate minimal pollution, as well as to be able to change routes quickly. Over the long term, ST's goal to reduce its fuel use and hydrocarbon emissions outweighs its needs for routing flexibility.

RR is ST's superior alternative because RR's trains are fuel efficient and emit low amounts of pollutants into ST's atmosphere. RR's modular tracks may be moved around ST's streets to provide routing changes. Unfortunately, the city where RR's tracks are already installed remains quiet about RR's actual routing flexibility. Even so, RR is ST's better alternative because RR uses less fuel and emits fewer hydrocarbons than does GB.

GB is ST's inferior choice. GB's buses are less fuel efficient and therefore emit more air pollution than RR's trains. Over the long term, GB's buses could be more costly to operate than RR's trains. The increased air pollution GB's buses bring could become irreversible. Although GB's buses could provide easy routing changes and are becoming more efficient, GB's greater fuel consumption and harmful emissions point to RR as ST's superior alternative. Therefore, ST rejects GB as ST's inferior alternative.

RR is ST's superior alternative. RR uses less fuel than GB and emits fewer hydrocarbons. RR's modular track system allows GB to make routing changes. GB's buses use more fuel and pollute ST's air more than do RR's trains. Therefore, ST chooses RR because RR is more fuel efficient, emits fewer hydrocarbons, and provides routing flexibility.

General Directions for the LSAT Answer Sheet

The actual testing time for this portion of the test will be 2 hours 55 minutes. There are five sections, each with a time limit of 35 minutes. The supervisor will tell you when to begin and end each section. If you finish a section before time is called, you may check your work on that section <u>only</u>; do not turn to any other section of the test book and do not work on any other section either in the test book or on the answer sheet.

There are several different types of questions on the test, and each question type has its own directions. <u>Be sure you understand the directions for each question type before attempting to answer any questions in that section.</u>

Not everyone will finish all the questions in the time allowed. Do not hurry, but work steadily and as quickly as you can without sacrificing accuracy. You are advised to use your time effectively. If a question seems too difficult, go on to the next one and return to the difficult question after completing the section. MARK THE BEST ANSWER YOU CAN FOR EVERY QUESTION. NO DEDUCTIONS WILL BE MADE FOR WRONG ANSWERS. YOUR SCORE WILL BE BASED ONLY ON THE NUMBER OF QUESTIONS YOU ANSWER CORRECTLY.

ALL YOUR ANSWERS MUST BE MARKED ON THE ANSWER SHEET. Answer spaces for each question are lettered to correspond with the letters of the potential answers to each question in the test book. After you have decided which of the answers is correct, blacken the corresponding space on the answer sheet. BE SURE THAT EACH MARK IS BLACK AND COMPLETELY FILLS THE ANSWER SPACE. Give only one answer to each question. If you change an answer, be sure that all previous marks are <u>erased completely</u>. Since the answer sheet is machine scored, incomplete erasures may be interpreted as intended answers. ANSWERS RECORDED IN THE TEST BOOK WILL NOT BE SCORED.

There may be more question numbers on this answer sheet than there are questions in a section. Do not be concerned, but be certain that the section and number of the question you are answering matches the answer sheet section and question number. Additional answer spaces in any answer sheet section should be left blank. Begin your next section in the number one answer space for that section.

LSAC takes various steps to ensure that answer sheets are returned from test centers in a timely manner for processing. In the unlikely event that an answer sheet is not received, LSAC will permit the examinee either to retest at no additional fee or to receive a refund of his or her LSAT fee. THESE REMEDIES ARE THE ONLY REMEDIES AVAILABLE IN THE UNLIKELY EVENT THAT AN ANSWER SHEET IS NOT RECEIVED BY LSAC.

Score Cancellation

Complete this section only if you are absolutely certain you want to cancel your score. A CANCELLATION REQUEST CANNOT BE RESCINDED. IF YOU ARE AT ALL UNCERTAIN, YOU SHOULD <u>NOT</u> COMPLETE THIS SECTION.

To cancel your score from this administration, you **must**:

A. fill in both ovals here ..... ○ ○
   AND

B. read the following statement. Then sign your name and enter the date.
   YOUR SIGNATURE ALONE IS NOT SUFFICIENT FOR SCORE CANCELLATION. BOTH OVALS ABOVE MUST BE FILLED IN FOR SCANNING EQUIPMENT TO RECOGNIZE YOUR REQUEST FOR SCORE CANCELLATION.

I certify that I wish to cancel my test score from this administration. I understand that my request is irreversible and that my score will not be sent to me or to the law schools to which I apply.

_____
Sign your name in full

_____
Date

FOR LSAC USE ONLY

HOW DID YOU PREPARE FOR THE LSAT?
(Select all that apply.)

Responses to this item are voluntary and will be used for statistical research purposes only.

○ By studying the free sample questions available on LSAC's website.
○ By taking the free sample LSAT available on LSAC's website.
○ By working through official LSAT *PrepTests, ItemWise,* and/or other LSAC test prep products.
○ By using LSAT prep books or software not published by LSAC.
○ By attending a commercial test preparation or coaching course.
○ By attending a test preparation or coaching course offered through an undergraduate institution.
○ Self study.
○ Other preparation.
○ No preparation.

CERTIFYING STATEMENT

Please write the following statement. Sign and date.

I certify that I am the examinee whose name appears on this answer sheet and that I am here to take the LSAT for the sole purpose of being considered for admission to law school. I further certify that I will neither assist nor receive assistance from any other candidate, and I agree not to copy, retain, or transmit examination questions in any form or discuss them with any other person.

_____
_____
_____
_____
_____
_____
_____

SIGNATURE: _____ TODAY'S DATE: __/__/__
                                                   MONTH DAY YEAR

INSTRUCTIONS FOR COMPLETING THE BIOGRAPHICAL AREA ARE ON THE BACK COVER OF YOUR TEST BOOKLET.
USE ONLY A NO. 2 OR HB PENCIL TO COMPLETE THIS ANSWER SHEET. DO NOT USE INK.

USE A NO. 2 OR HB PENCIL ONLY   ● Right Mark   ⊘ ⊗ ⊙ Wrong Marks

A

1 LAST NAME | FIRST NAME | MI

2 SOCIAL SECURITY/ SOCIAL INSURANCE NO.

3 LSAC ACCOUNT NUMBER

4 CENTER NUMBER

5 DATE OF BIRTH
MONTH | DAY | YEAR
Jan, Feb, Mar, Apr, May, June, July, Aug, Sept, Oct, Nov, Dec

6 TEST FORM CODE

7 RACIAL/ETHNIC DESCRIPTION
Mark one or more
1 Amer. Indian/Alaska Native
2 Asian
3 Black/African American
4 Canadian Aboriginal
5 Caucasian/White
6 Hispanic/Latino
7 Native Hawaiian/ Other Pacific Islander
8 Puerto Rican
9 TSI/Aboriginal Australian

8 GENDER
Male
Female

9 DOMINANT LANGUAGE
English
Other

10 ENGLISH FLUENCY
Yes
No

11 TEST DATE
MONTH / DAY / YEAR

12 TEST FORM

Law School Admission Test

Mark one and only one answer to each question. Be sure to fill in completely the space for your intended answer choice. If you erase, do so completely. Make no stray marks.

SECTION 1 | SECTION 2 | SECTION 3 | SECTION 4 | SECTION 5
(questions 1–30, answer bubbles A B C D E)

13 TEST BOOK SERIAL NO.

14 PLEASE PRINT INFORMATION
LAST NAME   FIRST
SSN/SIN
DATE OF BIRTH

TEST 65

Directions: The questions in this section are based on the reasoning contained in brief statements or passages. For some questions, more than one of the choices could conceivably answer the question. However, you are to choose the best answer; that is, the response that most accurately and completely answers the question. You should not make assumptions that are by commonsense standards implausible, superfluous, or incompatible with the passage. After you have chosen the best answer, blacken the corresponding space on your answer sheet.

1. In a recent study of more than 400 North American men and women whose previous heart attack put them at risk for a second heart attack, about half were told to switch to a "Mediterranean-type diet"—one rich in fish, vegetables, olive oil, and grains—while the other half were advised to eat a more traditional "Western" diet but to limit their fat intake. Those following the Mediterranean diet were significantly less likely than those in the other group to have a second heart attack. But the Mediterranean diet includes a fair amount of fat from fish and olive oil, so the research suggests that a diet may not have to be extremely low in fat in order to protect the heart.

Which one of the following, if true, most strengthens the argument?

(A) Research has shown that eliminating almost all fat from one's diet can be effective in decreasing the likelihood of a second heart attack.

(B) Studies suggest that the kinds of oils in the fat included in the Mediterranean diet may protect the heart against potentially fatal disruptions of heart rhythms and other causes of heart attacks.

(C) The patients who consumed the Mediterranean diet enjoyed the food and continued to follow the diet after the experiment was concluded.

(D) Many people who have had heart attacks are advised by their cardiologists to begin an exercise regimen in addition to changing their diet.

(E) Some cardiologists believe that the protection afforded by the Mediterranean diet might be enhanced by drugs that lower blood-cholesterol levels.

2. Florist: Some people like to have green carnations on St. Patrick's Day. But flowers that are naturally green are extremely rare. Thus, it is very difficult for plant breeders to produce green carnations. Before St. Patrick's Day, then, it is wise for florists to stock up on white carnations, which are fairly inexpensive and quite easy to dye green.

Which one of the following most accurately expresses the overall conclusion of the florist's argument?

(A) It is a good idea for florists to stock up on white carnations before St. Patrick's Day.

(B) Flowers that are naturally green are very rare.

(C) There are some people who like to have green carnations on St. Patrick's Day.

(D) White carnations are fairly inexpensive and can easily be dyed green.

(E) It is very difficult to breed green carnations.

3. Millions of homes are now using low-energy lighting, but millions more have still to make the switch, a fact that the government and the home lighting industry are eager to change. Although low-wattage bulbs cost more per bulb than normal bulbs, their advantages to the homeowner are enormous, and therefore everyone should use low-wattage bulbs.

Information about which one of the following would be LEAST useful in evaluating the argument?

(A) the actual cost of burning low-wattage bulbs compared to that of burning normal bulbs

(B) the profits the home lighting industry expects to make from sales of low-wattage bulbs

(C) the specific cost of a low-wattage bulb compared with that of a normal bulb

(D) the opinion of current users of low-wattage bulbs as to their effectiveness

(E) the average life of a low-wattage bulb compared with that of a normal bulb

GO ON TO THE NEXT PAGE.

4. Swimming pools should be fenced to protect children from drowning, but teaching children to swim is even more important. And there is a principle involved here that applies to childrearing generally. Thus, while we should restrict children's access to the soft drinks and candies advertised on television shows directed towards children, it is even more important to teach them _____.

Which one of the following most logically completes the passage?

(A) that television can be a good source of accurate information about many things

(B) that television advertisements are deceptive and misleading

(C) how to make nutritional choices that are conducive to their well-being

(D) the importance of physical activity to health and well-being

(E) how to creatively entertain themselves without watching television

5. In its coverage of a controversy regarding a proposal to build a new freeway, a television news program showed interviews with several people who would be affected by the proposed freeway. Of the interviews shown, those conducted with people against the new freeway outnumbered those conducted with people for it two to one. The television program is therefore biased against the proposed freeway.

Which one of the following, if true, most seriously weakens the argument?

(A) Most of the people who watched the program were aware of the freeway controversy beforehand.

(B) Most viewers of television news programs do not expect those programs to be completely free of bias.

(C) In the interviews, the people against the new freeway expressed their opinions with more emotion than the people for the freeway did.

(D) Before the program aired, over twice as many people were against building the freeway than were in favor of it.

(E) The business interests of the television station that produced the program would be harmed by the construction of a new freeway.

6. Evan: I am a vegetarian because I believe it is immoral to inflict pain on animals to obtain food. Some vegetarians who share this moral reason nonetheless consume some seafood, on the grounds that it is not known whether certain sea creatures can experience pleasure or pain. But if it is truly wrong to inflict needless suffering, we should extend the benefit of the doubt to sea animals and refrain from eating seafood.

Which one of the following most closely conforms to the principle illustrated by Evan's criticism of vegetarians who eat seafood?

(A) I do not know if I have repaid Farah the money she lent me for a movie ticket. She says that she does not remember whether or not I repaid her. In order to be sure that I have repaid her, I will give her the money now.

(B) It is uncertain whether all owners of the defective vehicles know that their vehicles are being recalled by the manufacturer. Thus, we should expect that some vehicles that have been recalled have not been returned.

(C) I am opposed to using incentives such as reduced taxes to attract businesses to our region. These incentives would attract businesses interested only in short-term profits. Such businesses would make our region's economy less stable, because they have no long-term commitment to the community.

(D) Updating our computer security system could lead to new contracts. The present system has no problems, but we could benefit from emphasizing a state-of-the-art system in new proposals. If we do not get new customers, the new system could be financed through higher fees for current customers.

(E) Isabel Allende lived through the tragic events of her country's recent history; no doubt her novels have been inspired by her memories of those events. Yet Allende's characters are hopeful and full of joy, indicating that Allende's own view of life has not been negatively marked by her experiences.

GO ON TO THE NEXT PAGE.

7. Economist: Government intervention in the free market in pursuit of socially desirable goals can affect supply and demand, thereby distorting prices. The ethics of such intervention is comparable to that of administering medicines. Most medicines have harmful as well as beneficial effects, so the use of a type of medicine is ethically justified only when its nonuse would be significantly more harmful than its use. Similarly, government intervention in the free market is justified only when it _____.

Which one of the following most logically completes the final sentence above?

(A) would likely be approved of by the majority of the affected participants

(B) has been shown to have few if any significantly harmful effects

(C) is believed unlikely to significantly exacerbate any existing problems

(D) would do less damage than would result from the government's not intervening

(E) provides a solution to some otherwise insoluble problem

8. The proportion of fat calories in the diets of people who read the nutrition labels on food products is significantly lower than it is in the diets of people who do not read nutrition labels. This shows that reading these labels promotes healthful dietary behavior.

The reasoning in the argument above is flawed in that the argument

(A) illicitly infers a cause from a correlation

(B) relies on a sample that is unlikely to be representative of the group as a whole

(C) confuses a condition that is necessary for a phenomenon to occur with a condition that is sufficient for that phenomenon to occur

(D) takes for granted that there are only two possible alternative explanations of a phenomenon

(E) draws a conclusion about the intentions of a group of people based solely on data about the consequences of their behavior

9. Some paleontologists have suggested that *Apatosaurus*, a huge dinosaur, was able to gallop. This, however, is unlikely, because galloping would probably have broken *Apatosaurus*'s legs. Experiments with modern bones show how much strain they can withstand before breaking. By taking into account the diameter and density of *Apatosaurus* leg bones, it is possible to calculate that those bones could not have withstood the strains of galloping.

Which one of the following most accurately expresses the conclusion drawn by the argument as a whole?

(A) Galloping would probably have broken the legs of *Apatosaurus*.

(B) It is possible to calculate that *Apatosaurus* leg bones could not have withstood the strain of galloping.

(C) The claim of paleontologists that *Apatosaurus* was able to gallop is likely to be incorrect.

(D) If galloping would have broken the legs of *Apatosaurus*, then *Apatosaurus* was probably unable to gallop.

(E) Modern bones are quite similar in structure and physical properties to the bones of *Apatosaurus*.

10. A new process enables ordinary table salt to be fortified with iron. This advance could help reduce the high incidence of anemia in the world's population due to a deficiency of iron in the diet. Salt is used as a preservative for food and a flavor enhancer all over the globe, and people consume salt in quantities that would provide iron in significant amounts.

Which one of the following most accurately describes the role played in the argument by the statement that people consume salt in quantities that would provide iron in significant amounts?

(A) It is the conclusion of the argument.

(B) It provides support for the conclusion of the argument.

(C) It is a claim that the argument is directed against.

(D) It qualifies the conclusion of the argument.

(E) It illustrates a principle that underlies the argument.

GO ON TO THE NEXT PAGE.

11. Inspector: The only fingerprints on the premises are those of the owner, Mr. Tannisch. Therefore, whoever now has his guest's missing diamonds must have worn gloves.

Which one of the following exhibits a flaw in its reasoning most similar to that in the inspector's reasoning?

(A) The campers at Big Lake Camp, all of whom became ill this afternoon, have eaten food only from the camp cafeteria. Therefore, the cause of the illness must not have been something they ate.

(B) The second prototype did not perform as well in inclement weather as did the first prototype. Hence, the production of the second prototype might have deviated from the design followed for the first.

(C) Each of the swimmers at this meet more often loses than wins. Therefore, it is unlikely that any of them will win.

(D) All of Marjorie's cavities are on the left side of her mouth. Hence, she must chew more on the left side than on the right.

(E) All of these tomato plants are twice as big as they were last year. So if we grow peas, they will probably be twice as big as last year's peas.

12. Populations of a shrimp species at eleven different Indonesian coral reefs show substantial genetic differences from one reef to another. This is surprising because the area's strong ocean currents probably carry baby shrimp between the different reefs, which would allow the populations to interbreed and become genetically indistinguishable.

Which one of the following, if true, most helps to explain the substantial genetic differences among the shrimp populations?

(A) The genetic differences between the shrimp populations are much less significant than those between shrimp and any other marine species.

(B) The individual shrimp within a given population at any given Indonesian coral reef differ from one another genetically, even though there is widespread interbreeding within any such population.

(C) Before breeding, shrimp of the species examined migrate back to the coral reef at which they were hatched.

(D) Most shrimp hatched at a given Indonesian coral reef are no longer present at that coral reef upon becoming old enough to breed.

(E) Ocean currents probably carry many of the baby shrimp hatched at a given Indonesian coral reef out into the open ocean rather than to another coral reef.

GO ON TO THE NEXT PAGE.

13. Researchers have studied the cost-effectiveness of growing halophytes—salt-tolerant plant species—for animal forage. Halophytes require more water than conventional crops, but can be irrigated with seawater, and pumping seawater into farms near sea level is much cheaper than pumping freshwater from deep wells. Thus, seawater agriculture near sea level should be cost-effective in desert regions although its yields are smaller than traditional, freshwater agriculture.

Which one of the following, if true, most strengthens the argument above?

(A) A given volume of halophytes is significantly different in nutritional value for animal forage from the same volume of conventional forage crops.

(B) Some halophytes not only tolerate seawater but require salt in order to thrive.

(C) Large research expenditures are needed to develop the strains of halophytes best suited for agricultural purposes.

(D) Costs other than the costs of irrigation are different for halophytes grown by means of seawater irrigation than for conventional crops.

(E) Pumping water for irrigation is proportionally one of the largest costs involved in growing, harvesting, and distributing any forage crop for animals.

14. Principle: If an insurance policy is written in such a way that a reasonable person seeking insurance would not read it thoroughly before signing it, then the reasonable expectations of the policyholder concerning the policy's coverage should take legal precedence over specific language in the written policy itself.

Application: The insurance company should be required to cover the hail damage to Celia's car, even though specific language in the written policy Celia signed excluded coverage for hail damage.

Which one of the following, if true, most justifies the above application of the principle?

(A) Celia is a reasonable person, and she expected the insurance policy to cover hail damage to her car.

(B) Given the way it was written, a reasonable person would not have read Celia's insurance policy thoroughly before signing it, and Celia reasonably expected the policy to cover hail damage.

(C) The insurance policy that Celia signed was written in such a way that a reasonable person would not read it thoroughly before signing it, but Celia did read the policy thoroughly before signing it.

(D) Celia did not read the insurance policy thoroughly before signing it, and a reasonable person in her position would assume that the policy would cover hail damage.

(E) Celia did not read the written insurance policy thoroughly before signing it, and a reasonable person in her position would not have done so either.

GO ON TO THE NEXT PAGE.

15. Researcher: Every year approximately the same number of people die of iatrogenic "disease"—that is, as a direct result of medical treatments or hospitalization—as die of all other causes combined. Therefore, if medicine could find ways of preventing all iatrogenic disease, the number of deaths per year would decrease by half.

The reasoning in the researcher's argument is flawed because the argument fails to consider that

(A) prevention of noniatrogenic disease will have an effect on the occurrence of iatrogenic disease

(B) some medical treatments can be replaced by less invasive or damaging alternatives

(C) people who do not die of one cause may soon die of another cause

(D) there is no one way to prevent all cases of death from iatrogenic disease

(E) whenever a noniatrogenic disease occurs, there is a risk of iatrogenic disease

16. Activist: Any member of the city council ought either to vote against the proposal or to abstain. But if all the members abstain, the matter will be decided by the city's voters. So at least one member of the city council should vote against the proposal.

The conclusion of the activist's argument follows logically if which one of the following is assumed?

(A) If all the members of the city council abstain in the vote on the proposal, the city's voters will definitely decide in favor of the proposal.

(B) The proposal should not be decided by the city's voters.

(C) No members of the city council will vote in favor of the proposal.

(D) If not every member of the city council abstains in the vote on the proposal, the matter will not be decided by the city's voters.

(E) If one member of the city council ought to vote against the proposal, the other members should abstain in the vote on the proposal.

17. Economist: Some critics of the media have contended that negative news reports on the state of the economy can actually harm the economy because such reports damage people's confidence in it, and this lack of confidence in turn adversely affects people's willingness to spend money. But studies show that spending trends correlate very closely with people's confidence in their own immediate economic situations. Thus these media critics are mistaken.

The economist's argument is flawed in that it fails to consider the possibility that

(A) one's level of confidence in one's own economic situation affects how one perceives reports about the overall state of the economy

(B) news reports about the state of the economy are not always accurate

(C) people who pay no attention to economic reports in the media always judge accurately whether their own economic situation is likely to deteriorate or improve

(D) people who have little confidence in the overall economy generally take a pessimistic view concerning their own immediate economic situations

(E) an economic slowdown usually has a greater impact on the economic situations of individuals if it takes people by surprise than if people are forewarned

GO ON TO THE NEXT PAGE.

18. Zoologist: Every domesticated large mammal species now in existence was domesticated thousands of years ago. Since those days, people undoubtedly tried innumerable times to domesticate each of the wild large mammal species that seemed worth domesticating. Clearly, therefore, most wild large mammal species in existence today either would be difficult to domesticate or would not be worth domesticating.

The zoologist's argument requires the assumption that

(A) in spite of the difficulties encountered, at one time or another people have tried to domesticate each wild large mammal species

(B) it is not much easier today to domesticate wild large mammal species than it was in the past

(C) not all of the large mammal species that were domesticated in the past are still in existence

(D) the easier it is to domesticate a wild large mammal species, the more worthwhile it is to do so

(E) of all the domesticated large mammal species in existence today, the very first to be domesticated were the easiest to domesticate

19. Last winter was mild enough to allow most bird species to forage naturally, which explains why the proportion of birds visiting feeders was much lower than usual. The mild winter also allowed many species to stay in their summer range all winter without migrating south, thereby limiting the usual attrition accompanying migration. Hence, last year's mild winter is responsible for this year's larger-than-usual bird population.

Which one of the following, if true, would most strengthen the reasoning in the argument?

(A) Increases in bird populations sometimes occur following unusual weather patterns.

(B) When birds do not migrate south, the mating behaviors they exhibit differ from those they exhibit when they do migrate.

(C) Birds eating at feeders are more vulnerable to predators than are birds foraging naturally.

(D) Birds that remain in their summer range all winter often exhaust that range's food supply before spring.

(E) Birds sometimes visit feeders even when they are able to find sufficient food for survival by foraging naturally.

20. Journalist: Newspapers generally report on only those scientific studies whose findings sound dramatic. Furthermore, newspaper stories about small observational studies, which are somewhat unreliable, are more frequent than newspaper stories about large randomized trials, which generate stronger scientific evidence. Therefore, a small observational study must be more likely to have dramatic findings than a large randomized trial.

Which one of the following most accurately expresses a flaw in the journalist's reasoning?

(A) It casts doubt on the reliability of a study by questioning the motives of those reporting it.

(B) It fails to consider that even if a study's findings sound dramatic, the scientific evidence for those findings may be strong.

(C) It confuses a claim about scientific studies whose findings sound dramatic with a similar claim about small observational studies.

(D) It overlooks the possibility that small observational studies are far more common than large randomized trials.

(E) It fails to rule out the possibility that a study's having findings that sound dramatic is an effect rather than a cause of the study's being reported on.

21. In several countries, to slow global warming, many farmers are planting trees on their land because of government incentives. These incentives arose from research indicating that vegetation absorbs carbon dioxide that might otherwise trap heat in the atmosphere. A recent study, however, indicates that trees absorb and store carbon dioxide less effectively than native grasses. Therefore, these incentives are helping to hasten global warming.

The argument requires the assumption that

(A) trees not only absorb carbon dioxide but also emit it

(B) most farmers do not plant any trees on their land unless there is an incentive to do so

(C) land that has been deforested seldom later sustains native grasses

(D) some of the trees planted in response to the incentives are planted where native grasses would otherwise be growing

(E) few if any governments have been interested in promoting the growth of native grasses

GO ON TO THE NEXT PAGE.

22. Does the position of a car driver's seat have a significant impact on driving safety? It probably does. Driving position affects both comfort and the ability to see the road clearly. A driver who is uncomfortable eventually becomes fatigued, which makes it difficult to concentrate on the road. Likewise, the better the visibility from the driver's seat, the more aware the driver can be of road conditions and other vehicles.

Which one of the following most accurately describes the role played in the argument by the claim that driving position affects both comfort and the ability to see the road clearly?

(A) It is the conclusion drawn in the argument.
(B) It is a claim that the argument shows to be inconsistent with available evidence.
(C) It is used to provide a causal explanation for an observed phenomenon.
(D) It describes evidence that the argument ultimately refutes.
(E) It is a premise offered in support of the conclusion drawn in the argument.

23. Physician: There were approximately 83,400 trampoline-related injuries last year. This suggests that trampolines are quite dangerous and should therefore be used only under professional supervision.

Trampoline enthusiast: I disagree. In the past ten years sales of home trampolines have increased much more than trampoline-related injuries have: 260 percent in sales compared with 154 percent in injuries. Every exercise activity carries risks, even when carried out under professional supervision.

The dialogue provides the most support for the claim that the physician and the trampoline enthusiast disagree over whether

(A) trampolines cause injuries to a significant number of people using them
(B) home trampolines are the main source of trampoline-related injuries
(C) the rate of trampoline-related injuries, in terms of the number of injuries per trampoline user, is declining
(D) professional supervision of trampoline use tends to reduce the number of trampoline-related injuries
(E) trampoline use is an activity that warrants mandatory professional supervision

24. Editorial: One of our local television stations has been criticized for its recent coverage of the personal problems of a local politician's nephew, but the coverage was in fact good journalism. The information was accurate. Furthermore, the newscast had significantly more viewers than it normally does, because many people are curious about the politician's nephew's problems.

Which one of the following principles, if valid, would most help to justify the reasoning in the editorial?

(A) Journalism deserves to be criticized if it does not provide information that people want.
(B) Any journalism that intentionally misrepresents the facts of a case deserves to be criticized.
(C) Any journalism that provides accurate information on a subject about which there is considerable interest is good journalism.
(D) Good journalism will always provide people with information that they desire or need.
(E) Journalism that neither satisfies the public's curiosity nor provides accurate information can never be considered good journalism.

25. Interior decorator: All coffeehouses and restaurants are public places. Most well-designed public places feature artwork. But if a public place is uncomfortable it is not well designed, and all comfortable public places have spacious interiors.

If all of the interior decorator's statements are true, then which one of the following must be true?

(A) Any restaurant that has a spacious interior is comfortable.
(B) Most public places that feature artwork are well designed.
(C) Most coffeehouses that are well designed feature artwork.
(D) Any well-designed coffeehouse or restaurant has a spacious interior.
(E) Any coffeehouse that has a spacious interior is a well-designed public place.

S T O P

IF YOU FINISH BEFORE TIME IS CALLED, YOU MAY CHECK YOUR WORK ON THIS SECTION ONLY.
DO NOT WORK ON ANY OTHER SECTION IN THE TEST.

SECTION II
Time—35 minutes
23 Questions

Directions: Each group of questions in this section is based on a set of conditions. In answering some of the questions, it may be useful to draw a rough diagram. Choose the response that most accurately and completely answers each question and blacken the corresponding space on your answer sheet.

Questions 1–5

A professor must determine the order in which five of her students—Fernando, Ginny, Hakim, Juanita, and Kevin—will perform in an upcoming piano recital. Each student performs one piece, and no two performances overlap. The following constraints apply:

Ginny must perform earlier than Fernando.
Kevin must perform earlier than Hakim and Juanita.
Hakim must perform either immediately before or immediately after Fernando.

1. Which one of the following could be the order, from first to last, in which the students perform?

(A) Ginny, Fernando, Hakim, Kevin, Juanita
(B) Ginny, Juanita, Kevin, Hakim, Fernando
(C) Ginny, Kevin, Hakim, Juanita, Fernando
(D) Kevin, Ginny, Juanita, Fernando, Hakim
(E) Kevin, Juanita, Fernando, Hakim, Ginny

2. If Juanita performs earlier than Ginny, then which one of the following could be true?

(A) Fernando performs fourth.
(B) Ginny performs second.
(C) Hakim performs third.
(D) Juanita performs third.
(E) Kevin performs second.

3. Which one of the following CANNOT be true?

(A) Fernando performs immediately before Juanita.
(B) Ginny performs immediately before Hakim.
(C) Hakim performs immediately before Ginny.
(D) Juanita performs immediately before Ginny.
(E) Kevin performs immediately before Hakim.

4. The order in which the students perform is fully determined if which one of the following is true?

(A) Fernando performs immediately before Hakim.
(B) Ginny performs immediately before Fernando.
(C) Hakim performs immediately before Juanita.
(D) Juanita performs immediately before Hakim.
(E) Kevin performs immediately before Fernando.

5. How many of the students are there any one of whom could perform fourth?

(A) one
(B) two
(C) three
(D) four
(E) five

GO ON TO THE NEXT PAGE.

Questions 6–11

As part of an open house at a crafts studio, three teachers—Jiang, Kudrow, and Lanning—will give six consecutive presentations on six different subjects. Jiang will present on needlework and origami; Kudrow on pottery, stenciling, and textile making; and Lanning on woodworking. The order of their presentations will meet the following conditions:

Kudrow cannot give two presentations in a row.
The presentation on stenciling must be given earlier than the one on origami.
The presentation on textile making must be given earlier than the one on woodworking.

6. Which one of the following could be the order of the presentations, from first to sixth?

(A) stenciling, origami, needlework, textile making, pottery, woodworking
(B) stenciling, origami, pottery, woodworking, needlework, textile making
(C) stenciling, origami, textile making, woodworking, needlework, pottery
(D) textile making, origami, stenciling, woodworking, needlework, pottery
(E) textile making, stenciling, woodworking, needlework, pottery, origami

7. If textile making is presented fifth, which one of the following could be true?

(A) Needlework is presented sixth.
(B) Pottery is presented fourth.
(C) Stenciling is presented second.
(D) Stenciling is presented third.
(E) Woodworking is presented second.

8. If needlework is presented first, which one of the following could be true?

(A) Origami is presented sixth.
(B) Pottery is presented second.
(C) Stenciling is presented third.
(D) Textile making is presented fifth.
(E) Woodworking is presented third.

9. Jiang CANNOT give both

(A) the first and third presentations
(B) the first and fourth presentations
(C) the first and fifth presentations
(D) the second and third presentations
(E) the second and fourth presentations

10. If needlework is presented sixth, which one of the following must be true?

(A) Origami is presented fourth.
(B) Pottery is presented fifth.
(C) Stenciling is presented third.
(D) Textile making is presented first.
(E) Woodworking is presented fourth.

11. Which one of the following CANNOT be the subject of the second presentation?

(A) needlework
(B) origami
(C) pottery
(D) textile making
(E) woodworking

GO ON TO THE NEXT PAGE.

Questions 12–16

The organizer of a luncheon will select exactly five foods to be served from among exactly eight foods: two desserts—F and G; three main courses—N, O, and P; three side dishes—T, V, and W. Only F, N, and T are hot foods. The following requirements will be satisfied:

At least one dessert, at least one main course, and at least one side dish must be selected.
At least one hot food must be selected.
If either P or W is selected, both must be selected.
If G is selected, O must be selected.
If N is selected, V cannot be selected.

12. Which one of the following is a list of foods that could be the foods selected?

(A) F, N, O, T, V
(B) F, O, P, T, W
(C) G, N, P, T, W
(D) G, O, P, T, V
(E) G, O, P, V, W

13. Which one of the following is a pair of foods of which the organizer of the luncheon must select at least one?

(A) F, T
(B) G, O
(C) N, T
(D) O, P
(E) V, W

14. If O is the only main course selected, then which one of the following CANNOT be selected?

(A) F
(B) G
(C) T
(D) V
(E) W

15. If F is not selected, which one of the following could be true?

(A) P is the only main course selected.
(B) T is the only side dish selected.
(C) Exactly two hot foods are selected.
(D) Exactly three main courses are selected.
(E) Exactly three side dishes are selected.

16. If T and V are the only side dishes selected, then which one of the following is a pair of foods each of which must be selected?

(A) F and G
(B) F and N
(C) F and P
(D) N and O
(E) O and P

GO ON TO THE NEXT PAGE.

Questions 17–23

A television programming director is scheduling a three-hour block of programs beginning at 1 P.M. The programs that are to fill this time block include an hour-long program called *Generations* and four half-hour programs: *Roamin'*, *Sundown*, *Terry*, and *Waterloo*. The programs will be shown one after the other, each program shown exactly once. The schedule must meet the following constraints:

　Generations starts on the hour rather than the half hour.
　Terry starts on the half hour rather than the hour.
　Roamin' is shown earlier than *Sundown*.
　If *Waterloo* is shown earlier than *Terry*, it is shown immediately before *Terry*.

17.　Which one of the following could be the order in which the programs are shown, from earliest to latest?

　(A)　*Generations, Roamin', Waterloo, Terry, Sundown*
　(B)　*Roamin', Sundown, Waterloo, Terry, Generations*
　(C)　*Roamin', Terry, Waterloo, Generations, Sundown*
　(D)　*Waterloo, Roamin', Sundown, Terry, Generations*
　(E)　*Waterloo, Terry, Sundown, Roamin', Generations*

18.　If *Waterloo* is the first program, then how many orders are there in which the remaining programs could be shown?

　(A)　one
　(B)　two
　(C)　three
　(D)　four
　(E)　five

19.　If *Roamin'* is the second program, then each of the following could be true EXCEPT:

　(A)　*Sundown* is the third program.
　(B)　*Sundown* is the fourth program.
　(C)　*Terry* is the fifth program.
　(D)　*Waterloo* is the third program.
　(E)　*Waterloo* is the fifth program.

20.　If *Sundown* is the third program, then which one of the following must be true?

　(A)　*Generations* is the first program.
　(B)　*Roamin'* is the first program.
　(C)　*Roamin'* is the second program.
　(D)　*Terry* is the fifth program.
　(E)　*Waterloo* is the fourth program.

21.　If *Generations* is the third program, then which one of the following could be true?

　(A)　*Roamin'* is the second program.
　(B)　*Roamin'* is the fifth program.
　(C)　*Sundown* is the fourth program.
　(D)　*Terry* is the fourth program.
　(E)　*Waterloo* is the second program.

22.　Which one of the following CANNOT be true?

　(A)　*Sundown* is shown immediately before *Generations*.
　(B)　*Waterloo* is shown immediately before *Roamin'*.
　(C)　*Generations* is shown immediately before *Sundown*.
　(D)　*Roamin'* is shown immediately before *Terry*.
　(E)　*Terry* is shown immediately before *Waterloo*.

23.　Which one of the following, if substituted for the constraint that *Generations* starts on the hour rather than the half hour, would have the same effect in determining the order in which the programs are shown?

　(A)　*Generations* is not shown immediately before *Terry*.
　(B)　*Generations* is either the first program or the fifth.
　(C)　*Generations* is neither the second program nor the fourth.
　(D)　If *Generations* is shown third, then *Roamin'* is shown first.
　(E)　If *Generations* is not shown first, then it is shown later than *Terry*.

S T O P

IF YOU FINISH BEFORE TIME IS CALLED, YOU MAY CHECK YOUR WORK ON THIS SECTION ONLY.
DO NOT WORK ON ANY OTHER SECTION IN THE TEST.

SECTION III

Time—35 minutes

27 Questions

<u>Directions</u>: Each set of questions in this section is based on a single passage or a pair of passages. The questions are to be answered on the basis of what is <u>stated</u> or <u>implied</u> in the passage or pair of passages. For some of the questions, more than one of the choices could conceivably answer the question. However, you are to choose the <u>best</u> answer; that is, the response that most accurately and completely answers the question, and blacken the corresponding space on your answer sheet.

In the 1980s there was a proliferation of poetry collections, short stories, and novels published by women of Latin American descent in the United States. By the end of the decade, another genre of
(5) U.S. Latina writing, the autobiography, also came into prominence with the publication of three notable autobiographical collections: *Loving in the War Years: Lo Que Nunca Pasó Por Sus Labios*, by Cherríe Moraga; *Getting Home Alive*, by Aurora Levins
(10) Morales and Rosario Morales; and *Borderlands/ La Frontera*, by Gloria Anzaldúa.

These collections are innovative at many levels. They confront traditional linguistic boundaries by using a mix of English and Spanish, and they each
(15) address the politics of multiple cultural identities by exploring the interrelationships among such factors as ethnicity, gender, and language. This effort manifests itself in the generically mixed structure of these works, which combine essays, sketches, short stories, poems,
(20) and journal entries without, for the most part, giving preference to any of these modes of presentation.

In *Borderlands/La Frontera*, Anzaldúa presents her personal history and the history of the Mexican American community to which she belongs by
(25) juxtaposing narrative sequences and poetry. Moraga's *Loving in the War Years* is likewise characterized by a mixture of genres, and, as she states in her introduction, the events in her life story are not arranged chronologically, but rather in terms of her
(30) political development. According to one literary critic who specializes in the genre of autobiography, this departure from chronological ordering represents an important difference between autobiographies written by women and those traditionally written by men.
(35) *Getting Home Alive* departs even further from the conventions typical of autobiography by bringing together the voices of two people, a mother and her daughter, each of whom authors a portion of the text. The narratives and poems of each author are not
(40) assigned to separate sections of the text, but rather are woven together, with a piece by one sometimes commenting on a piece by the other. While this ordering may seem fragmentary and confusing, it is in fact a fully intentional and carefully designed
(45) experiment with literary structure. In a sense, this mixing of structures parallels the content of these autobiographies: the writers employ multigeneric and multivocal forms to express the complexities inherent in the formation of their identities.
(50) Rather than forcing their personal histories to conform to existing generic parameters, these writers have revolutionized the genre of autobiography,

redrawing the boundaries of this literary form to make it more amenable to the expression of their own
(55) experiences. In doing so, they have shown a strong determination to speak for themselves in a world that they feel has for too long taken their silence for granted.

1. Which one of the following most accurately expresses the main point of the passage?

(A) Certain Latina writers who formerly wrote mostly poetry and fiction have found through experimentation that the genre of autobiography suits their artistic purposes especially well.

(B) Latina autobiographers writing in the late 1980s set aside some standard conventions of autobiography in an effort to make the genre more suitable for the expression of their personal histories.

(C) There is a great diversity of styles and narrative strategies among recent traditional and nontraditional Latina autobiographers.

(D) Through recent experimentation in autobiography, Latina writers have shown that nonfictional narrative can be effectively combined with other genres in a single literary work.

(E) Recent writings by Latina authors have prompted some literary critics who specialize in autobiography to acknowledge that differences in gender and ethnicity often underlie differences in writing styles.

2. According to the passage, which one of the following was a motivating factor in certain Latina authors' decisions regarding the structure of their autobiographical writings?

(A) the importance of chronological ordering to those authors' artistic goals

(B) those authors' stated intention of avoiding certain nonnarrative genres

(C) those authors' preference to avoid overt political expression

(D) the complexities of identity formation faced by those authors

(E) those authors' judgment that poetry should not be a narrative medium

GO ON TO THE NEXT PAGE.

3. The author's discussion of *Getting Home Alive* serves primarily to

(A) distinguish one type of experimental autobiography from two other types by Latina writers

(B) explain how certain Latina autobiographers combine journal entries and poems in their works

(C) demonstrate that the use of multiple voices is a common feature of Latina autobiography

(D) show why readers have difficulty understanding certain autobiographies by Latina writers

(E) illustrate the extent of certain Latina autobiographers' experimentation with form and structure

4. The passage indicates which one of the following about the Latina autobiographies that the author discusses?

(A) Each contains some material that would ordinarily be regarded as belonging to a genre of literature other than autobiography.

(B) Each quotes from previously unpublished private journals or other private documents.

(C) Each contains analysis of the ways in which its content was influenced by its author's cultural background.

(D) Each contains writings that were produced by more than one author.

(E) Each includes explanations of the methodologies that its author, or authors, used in writing the autobiography.

5. Based on the passage, the author's attitude regarding *Getting Home Alive*, by Aurora Levins Morales and Rosario Morales, can be most accurately described as

(A) disappointment in scholars' failure to recognize it as an appropriate sequel to its authors' purely fictional and poetic works

(B) expectation that readers in general might not readily recognize that there is a clear purpose for its unconventional organization

(C) surprise that academic commentators have treated it as having significance as a historical document

(D) confidence that it will be widely recognized by scholars as a work of both history and literary criticism

(E) insistence that it should be credited with having helped to broaden critics' understanding of what counts as autobiography

6. The author most likely intends to include which one of the following principles among the "existing generic parameters" referred to in line 51?

(A) The events presented in an autobiography should be arranged sequentially according to when they actually happened.

(B) When different modes of presentation are combined in one literary work, no one mode should be given preference.

(C) Autobiographical writing should not have political overtones.

(D) Sketches and poems collected together in a single work need not be separated by genre within that work.

(E) Personal experiences can be represented in a compelling way in any literary genre.

7. Which one of the following would, if true, most undermine the author's claim in lines 50–55 about the effect that the Latina autobiographies discussed had on the genre of autobiography?

(A) Few autobiographical works published after 1985 have been recognized for their effective use of chronologically linear prose as a means of portraying the complexities of membership in multiple cultures.

(B) Few critically acclaimed books written by Latina authors have been autobiographical collections consisting partly or wholly of essays, poems, short stories, sketches, and journal entries.

(C) Many autobiographies have been written by authors in the United States since 1985, and some of these present a unified, chronologically linear prose narrative in a single language.

(D) Several nineteenth-century autobiographies that are generally unknown among contemporary critics of twentieth-century autobiography are characterized by generically mixed structure and multiple authorship.

(E) Several multigeneric, nonautobiographical collections consisting at least partly of poetry, short stories, or essays by Latina authors have been published since 1985, and many of these have been critically acclaimed for their innovative structures.

GO ON TO THE NEXT PAGE.

While recent decades have seen more information recorded than any other era, the potential for losing this information is now greater than ever. This prospect is of great concern to archivists, who are charged with
(5) preserving vital records and documents indefinitely. One archivist notes that while the quantity of material being saved has increased exponentially, the durability of recording media has decreased almost as rapidly. The clay tablets that contain the laws of ancient
(10) Mesopotamia, for example, are still displayed in museums around the world, and many medieval manuscripts written on animal parchment still look as though they were copied yesterday, whereas books printed on acidic paper as recently as the 1980s are
(15) already unreadable. Black-and-white photographs will last for a couple of centuries, but most color photographs become unstable within 40 years, and videotapes last only about 20 years.

Computer technology would seem to offer
(20) archivists an answer, as maps, photographs, films, videotapes, and all forms of printed material may now be transferred to and stored electronically on computer disks or tape, occupying very little space. But as the pace of technological change increases, so too does
(25) the speed with which each new generation of technology supplants the last. For example, many documents and images transferred in the 1980s to optical computer disks—then the cutting edge of technology—may not now be retrievable because
(30) they depend on computer software and hardware that are no longer available. And recent generations of digital storage tape are considered safe from deterioration for only ten years. Yet, even as some archivists are reluctant to become dependent on
(35) ever-changing computer technology, they are also quickly running out of time.

Even if viable storage systems are developed— new computer technologies are emerging that may soon provide archivists with the information storage
(40) durability they require—decisions about what to keep and what to discard will have to be made quickly, as materials recorded on conventional media continue to deteriorate. Ideally, these decisions should be informed by an assessment of the value of each document.
(45) Printed versions of ancient works by Homer and Virgil, for example, survived intact because their enduring popularity resulted in multiple copies of the works being made at different historical moments. But many great works, including those of Plato, were
(50) lost for several centuries and are known today only because random copies turned up in the archives of medieval monasteries or in other scholarly collections. Undoubtedly, many important works have not survived at all. The danger now is not so much that some recent
(55) masterpiece will be lost for an extended period of time, but rather that the sheer volume of accumulated records stored on nondurable media will make it virtually impossible for archivists to sort the essential from the dispensable in time to save it.

8. Which one of the following most accurately expresses the main point of the passage?

(A) The increasing volume of information being stored and the decreasing durability of modern storage media are making it more and more difficult for archivists to carry out their charge.

(B) Modern data storage-and-retrieval techniques have enabled archivists to distinguish essential from dispensable information with greater efficiency than ever before.

(C) Many archivists have come to believe that documents and images preserved on conventional storage media are likely to endure longer than those recorded on electronic storage media.

(D) Given the limitations on the capacity of modern storage media, it is increasingly important for archivists to save only those documents that they believe to have genuine value.

(E) Modern electronic media enable us to record and store information so easily that much of what is stored is not considered by archivists to be essential or valuable.

9. The passage provides information sufficient to answer which one of the following questions?

(A) Are there any copies of the works of Homer and Virgil stored on parchment?

(B) Why is information stored on acidic paper more unstable than information stored on digital storage tape?

(C) When were optical storage disks a state-of-the-art storage medium?

(D) Approximately how many of the original clay tablets recording Mesopotamian law are still in existence?

(E) How were the works of Plato originally recorded?

GO ON TO THE NEXT PAGE.

10. The passage most strongly suggests that the author holds which one of the following views?

(A) Archivists have little choice but to become dependent on computer technology to store information.

(B) Archivists should wait for truly durable data storage systems to be developed before electronically storing any more vital information.

(C) The problems concerning media durability facing most archivists would diminish greatly if their information were not stored electronically at all.

(D) Storing paintings, photographs, and other images presents greater overall problems for archivists than storing text does.

(E) Generally, the more information one attempts to store in a given amount of space, the less durable the storage of that information will be.

11. Which one of the following describes the author's primary purpose in mentioning the fact that a wide variety of images and documents can now be stored electronically (lines 19–23)?

(A) to provide evidence to justify the assertion made in the first sentence of the passage

(B) to identify an ostensible solution to the problem raised in the first paragraph

(C) to argue a point that is rejected in the last sentence of the passage

(D) to offer an additional example of the problem stated at the end of the first paragraph

(E) to suggest that the danger described in the last paragraph has been exaggerated

12. The passage provides the most support for inferring which one of the following statements?

(A) Information stored electronically is more vulnerable than information stored on paper to unauthorized use or theft.

(B) Much of the information stored on optical computer disks in the 1980s was subsequently transferred to digital storage tape.

(C) The high cost of new electronic data storage systems is prohibiting many archivists from transferring their archives to computer disks and tape.

(D) Media used recently to store information electronically may ultimately be less durable than older, conventional media such as photographs and videotapes.

(E) The percentage of information considered essential by archivists has increased proportionally as the amount of information stored has increased.

13. The passage most strongly suggests that the author holds which one of the following views?

(A) Future electronic information storage systems will not provide archivists with capabilities any more viable in the long term than those available today.

(B) As much information should be stored by archivists as possible, as there is no way to predict which piece of information will someday be considered a great work.

(C) The general public has been misled by manufacturers as to the long-term storage capabilities of electronic information storage systems.

(D) Distinguishing what is dispensable from what is essential has only recently become a concern for archivists.

(E) Value judgments made by today's archivists will influence how future generations view and understand the past.

GO ON TO THE NEXT PAGE.

The following passages are adapted from articles recently published in North American law review journals.

Passage A

In Canadian and United States common law, blackmail is unique among major crimes: no one has yet adequately explained why it ought to be illegal. The heart of the problem—known as the blackmail
(5) paradox—is that two acts, each of which is legally permissible separately, become illegal when combined. If I threaten to expose a criminal act or embarrassing private information unless I am paid money, I have committed blackmail. But the right to free speech
(10) protects my right to make such a disclosure, and, in many circumstances, I have a legal right to seek money. So why is it illegal to combine them?

The lack of a successful theory of blackmail has damaging consequences: drawing a clear line between
(15) legal and illegal acts has proved impossible without one. Consequently, most blackmail statutes broadly prohibit behavior that no one really believes is criminal and rely on the good judgment of prosecutors not to enforce relevant statutes precisely as written.
(20) It is possible, however, to articulate a coherent theory of blackmail. The key to the wrongness of the blackmail transaction is its triangular structure. The blackmailer obtains what he wants by using a supplementary leverage, leverage that depends upon
(25) a third party. The blackmail victim pays to avoid being harmed by persons other than the blackmailer. For example, when a blackmailer threatens to turn in a criminal unless paid money, the blackmailer is bargaining with the state's chip. Thus, blackmail is
(30) criminal because it involves the misuse of a third party for the blackmailer's own benefit.

Passage B

Classical Roman law had no special category for blackmail; it was not necessary. Roman jurists began their evaluation of specific categories of
(35) actions by considering whether the action caused harm, not by considering the legality or illegality of the action itself.

Their assumption—true enough, it seems—was that a victim of blackmail would be harmed if shameful
(40) but private information were revealed to the world. And if the shame would cause harm to the person's status or reputation, then prima facie the threatened act of revelation was unlawful. The burden of proof shifted to the possessor of the information: the party
(45) who had or threatened to reveal shameful facts had to show positive cause for the privilege of revealing the information.

In short, assertion of the truth of the shameful fact being revealed was not, in itself, sufficient to
(50) constitute a legal privilege. Granted, truth was not wholly irrelevant; false disclosures were granted even less protection than true ones. But even if it were true, the revelation of shameful information was protected

only if the revelation had been made for a legitimate
(55) purpose and dealt with a matter that the public authorities had an interest in having revealed. Just because something shameful happened to be true did not mean it was lawful to reveal it.

14. Which one of the following is the central topic of each passage?

(A) why triangular transactions are illegal
(B) the role of the right to free speech in a given legal system
(C) how blackmail has been handled in a given legal system
(D) the history of blackmail as a legal concept
(E) why no good explanation of the illegality of blackmail exists

15. In using the phrase "the state's chip" (line 29), the author of passage A most clearly means to refer to a government's

(A) legal authority to determine what actions are crimes
(B) legitimate interest in learning about crimes committed in its jurisdiction
(C) legitimate interest in preventing crimes before they occur
(D) exclusive reliance on private citizens as a source of important information
(E) legal ability to compel its citizens to testify in court regarding crimes they have witnessed

16. Which one of the following statements is most strongly supported by information given in the passages?

(A) In Roman law, there was no blackmail paradox because free speech protections comparable to those in Canadian and U.S. common law were not an issue.
(B) Blackmail was more widely practiced in Roman antiquity than it is now because Roman law did not specifically prohibit blackmail.
(C) In general, Canadian and U.S. common law grant more freedoms than classical Roman law granted.
(D) The best justification for the illegality of blackmail in Canadian and U.S. common law is the damage blackmail can cause to the victim's reputation.
(E) Unlike Roman law, Canadian and U.S. common law do not recognize the interest of public authorities in having certain types of information revealed.

GO ON TO THE NEXT PAGE.

17. Which one of the following is a statement that is true of blackmail under Canadian and U.S. common law, according to passage A, but that would not have been true of blackmail in the Roman legal context, according to passage B?

(A) It combines two acts that are each legal separately.
(B) It is a transaction with a triangular structure.
(C) The laws pertaining to it are meant to be enforced precisely as written.
(D) The blackmail victim pays to avoid being harmed by persons other than the blackmailer.
(E) Canadian and U.S. common law have no special category pertaining to blackmail.

18. Based on what can be inferred from the passages, which one of the following acts would have been illegal under Roman law, but would not be illegal under Canadian and U.S. common law?

(A) bribing tax officials in order to avoid paying taxes
(B) revealing to public authorities that a high-ranking military officer has embezzled funds from the military's budget
(C) testifying in court to a defendant's innocence while knowing that the defendant is guilty
(D) informing a government tax agency that one's employers have concealed their true income
(E) revealing to the public that a prominent politician had once had an adulterous affair

19. The relationship between the ways in which Canadian and U.S. common law and classical Roman law treat blackmail, as described in the passages, is most analogous to the relationship between which one of the following pairs?

(A) One country legally requires anyone working as a carpenter to be licensed and insured; another country has no such requirement.
(B) One country makes it illegal to use cell phones on trains; another country makes it illegal to use cell phones on both trains and buses.
(C) One country legally allows many income tax deductions and exemptions; another country legally allows relatively few deductions and exemptions.
(D) One country makes it illegal for felons to own guns; another country has no such ban because it makes gun ownership illegal for everyone but police and the military.
(E) One country makes it illegal to drive motorcycles with racing-grade engines on its roads; another country legally permits such motorcycles but fines riders who commit traffic violations higher amounts than it does other motorists.

GO ON TO THE NEXT PAGE.

As part of an international effort to address environmental problems resulting from agricultural overproduction, hundreds of thousands of acres of surplus farmland throughout Europe will be taken out
(5) of production in coming years. Restoring a natural balance of flora to this land will be difficult, however, because the nutrients in soil that has been in constant agricultural use are depleted. Moreover, much of this land has been heavily fertilized, and when such land
(10) is left unplanted, problem weeds like thistles often proliferate, preventing many native plants from establishing themselves. While the quickest way to restore heavily fertilized land is to remove and replace the topsoil, this is impractical on a large scale such as
(15) that of the European effort. And while it is generally believed that damaged ecological systems will restore themselves very gradually over time, a study underway in the Netherlands is investigating the possibility of artificially accelerating the processes through which
(20) nature slowly reestablishes plant diversity on previously farmed land.

In the study, a former cornfield was raked to get rid of cornstalks and weeds, then divided into 20 plots of roughly equal size. Control plots were replanted
(25) with corn or sown with nothing at all. The remaining plots were divided into two groups: plots in one group were sown with a mixture of native grasses and herbs; those in the other group received the same mixture of grasses and herbs together with clover and toadflax.
(30) After three years, thistles have been forced out of the plots where the broadest variety of species was sown and have also disappeared from mats of grass in the plots sown with fewer seed varieties. On the control plots that were left untouched, thistles have become dominant.

(35) On some of the plots sown with seeds of native plant species, soil from nearby land that had been taken out of production 20 years earlier was scattered to see what effect introducing nematodes, fungi, and other beneficial microorganisms associated with later
(40) stages of natural soil development might have on the process of native plant repopulation. The seeds sown on these enriched plots have fared better than seeds sown on the unenriched plots, but still not as well as those growing naturally on the nearby land. Researchers
(45) have concluded that this is because fields farmed for many years are overrun with aggressive disease organisms, while, for example, beneficial mycorrhiza— fungi that live symbiotically on plant roots and strengthen them against the effects of disease
(50) organisms—are lacking. These preliminary results suggest that restoring natural plant diversity to overfarmed land hinges on restoring a natural balance of microorganisms in the soil. In other words, diversity underground fosters diversity aboveground. Researchers
(55) now believe that both kinds of diversity can be restored more quickly to damaged land if beneficial microorganisms are "sown" systematically into the soil along with a wide variety of native plant seeds.

20. Which one of the following most accurately expresses the central idea of the passage?

(A) The rehabilitation of land damaged by agricultural overproduction can be accelerated by means of a two-pronged strategy aimed at restoring biological diversity.

(B) Restoring plant diversity to overused farmland requires many years and considerable effort.

(C) The damaging effects of long-term agricultural overproduction argue for the modification of current agricultural practices.

(D) Soil on farmland damaged by overproduction will gradually replenish and restore itself over time if left untouched.

(E) Agricultural overproduction tends to encourage the proliferation of disease organisms in the soil as well as problem weeds.

21. Which one of the following most accurately describes the organization of the passage?

(A) A study is described, the results of the study are scrutinized, and the results are judged to be inconclusive but promising.

(B) A hypothesis is presented, evidence both supporting and undermining the hypothesis is given, and a modification of the hypothesis is argued for.

(C) A study is evaluated, a plan of action based on the study's findings is suggested, and conclusions are drawn concerning the likely effectiveness of the plan.

(D) A goal is stated, studies are discussed that argue for modifying the goal's objectives, and a methodology is detailed to achieve the revised goal.

(E) A problem is presented, a study addressing the problem is described, and a course of action based on the study's findings is given.

22. The passage offers which one of the following as an explanation for why native plant varieties grew better when sown on land that had been out of production for 20 years than when sown on the plots enriched with soil taken from that land?

(A) Land that has been farmed for many years lacks certain key nutrients.

(B) Land that has been farmed for many years is usually overrun with harmful and aggressive organisms.

(C) Land that has been farmed for many years has usually been subjected to overfertilization.

(D) The soil that was taken from the land that had been out of production was lacking in fungi and other beneficial organisms.

(E) The soil that was taken from the land that had been out of production contained harmful organisms that attack plant roots.

GO ON TO THE NEXT PAGE.

23. Based on the passage, which one of the following is most likely to be true of any soil used to replace topsoil in the process mentioned in the first paragraph?

   (A) Thistles cannot grow in it.
   (B) It does not contain significant amounts of fungi.
   (C) It contains very few seeds of native grasses and herbs.
   (D) It does not contain large amounts of fertilizer.
   (E) It was never used for growing corn or other commercial crops.

24. The author's reference to the belief that "damaged ecological systems will restore themselves very gradually over time" (lines 16–17) primarily serves to

   (A) introduce a long-held belief that the Netherlands study is attempting to discredit
   (B) cite the justification generally used by people favoring intense agricultural production
   (C) suggest that the consequences of agricultural overproduction are not as dire as people generally believe
   (D) present the most common perception of why agricultural overproduction is problematic
   (E) describe the circumstances surrounding and motivating the Netherlands study

25. In which one of the following circumstances would it be LEAST advantageous to use the methods researched in the Netherlands study in order to restore to its natural state a field that has been in constant agricultural use?

   (A) The field's natural nutrients have been depleted through overproduction.
   (B) The field's topsoil can easily be removed and replaced.
   (C) The field has been heavily fertilized for many decades.
   (D) The field has the potential to support commercial grass plants such as rye.
   (E) The field is adjacent to other fields where corn is growing and will continue to be grown.

26. It can be inferred from the passage that if the disease organisms mentioned in lines 46–47 were eliminated in a plot of land that had been in constant agricultural use, which one of the following would be the most likely to occur?

   (A) Populations of symbiotic mycorrhiza that live in the soil would initially decline.
   (B) Unwanted plant species like thistles would be unable to survive.
   (C) The chance of survival of a beneficial native plant would increase.
   (D) The number of all types of beneficial microorganisms would increase in the long term.
   (E) Populations of other types of disease organisms would increase proportionally.

27. Which one of the following is most analogous to the process, described in the last paragraph, by which the spread of thistles can be curtailed?

   (A) A newspaper works to prevent Party A from winning a majority of seats in the legislature by publishing editorials encouraging that party's supporters to switch their allegiance and vote for candidates from a rival party.
   (B) A newspaper works to prevent Party A from winning a majority of seats in the legislature by publishing editorials defending candidates from a rival party against attacks by certain broadcast journalists.
   (C) A newspaper works to prevent Party A from winning a majority of seats in the legislature by publishing editorials intended to discourage supporters of Party A from voting in the upcoming election.
   (D) A newspaper works to prevent Party A from winning a majority of seats in the legislature by publishing editorials attacking certain public figures who support candidates from Party A.
   (E) A newspaper works to prevent Party A from winning a majority of seats in the legislature by publishing editorials intended to create antagonism between two factions within that party.

S T O P

IF YOU FINISH BEFORE TIME IS CALLED, YOU MAY CHECK YOUR WORK ON THIS SECTION ONLY.
DO NOT WORK ON ANY OTHER SECTION IN THE TEST.

SECTION IV

Time—35 minutes

26 Questions

<u>Directions:</u> The questions in this section are based on the reasoning contained in brief statements or passages. For some questions, more than one of the choices could conceivably answer the question. However, you are to choose the <u>best</u> answer; that is, the response that most accurately and completely answers the question. You should not make assumptions that are by commonsense standards implausible, superfluous, or incompatible with the passage. After you have chosen the best answer, blacken the corresponding space on your answer sheet.

1. When a forest is subject to acid rain, the calcium level in the soil declines. Spruce, fir, and sugar maple trees all need calcium to survive. However, sugar maples in forests that receive significant acid rain are much more likely to show signs of decline consistent with calcium deficiency than are spruces or firs in such forests.

   Which one of the following, if true, most helps to explain the greater decline among sugar maples?

   (A) Soil in which calcium levels are significantly diminished by acid rain is also likely to be damaged in other ways by acid rain.

   (B) Sugar maples that do not receive enough calcium deteriorate less rapidly than spruces or firs that do not receive enough calcium.

   (C) Spruces and firs, unlike sugar maples, can extract calcium from a mineral compound that is common in soil and is not affected by acid rain.

   (D) Sugar maples require more calcium in the spring and summer than they do in the fall and winter.

   (E) Unlike spruces or firs, most sugar maples are native to areas that receive a lot of acid rain.

2. Syndicated political columnists often use their newspaper columns to try to persuade readers to vote a certain way. However, their efforts to persuade voters rarely succeed, for by the time such a column appears, nearly all who will vote in the election will have already made a decision about which candidate to vote for.

   Which one of the following is an assumption required by the argument?

   (A) Syndicated columnists influence the votes of most of their readers who have not yet decided which candidate to vote for.

   (B) The attempts of syndicated political columnists to persuade readers to vote a certain way in an election can instead cause them to vote a different way.

   (C) People who regularly read columns by syndicated political columnists mainly read those written by columnists with whom they already largely agree.

   (D) Regular readers of columns by syndicated political columnists are less likely to be persuaded to vote a certain way by such columns than are people who seldom read such columns.

   (E) People rarely can be persuaded to change their minds about which candidate to vote for once they have made a decision.

GO ON TO THE NEXT PAGE.

3. Travel industry consultant: Several airlines are increasing elbow room and leg room in business class, because surveys show that business travelers value additional space more than, say, better meals. But airlines are overconcerned about the comfort of passengers flying on business; they should instead focus on the comfort of leisure travelers, because those travelers purchase 80 percent of all airline tickets.

Which one of the following, if true, most weakens the reasoning in the travel industry consultant's argument?

(A) Business travelers often make travel decisions based on whether they feel a given airline values their business.

(B) Some airlines have indicated that they will undertake alterations in seating space throughout the entire passenger area of their planes in the near future.

(C) Sleeping in comfort during long flights is not the primary concern of leisure travelers.

(D) A far greater proportion of an airline's revenues is derived from business travelers than from leisure travelers.

(E) Most leisure travelers buy airline tickets only when fares are discounted.

4. Gaby: In school, children should be allowed fully to follow their own interests, supported by experienced teachers who offer minimal guidance. This enables them to be most successful in their adult lives.

Logan: I disagree. Schoolchildren should acquire the fundamental knowledge necessary for future success, and they learn such fundamentals only through disciplined, systematic instruction from accredited teachers.

Gaby's and Logan's comments provide most support for the claim that they disagree about

(A) the way in which schoolchildren best acquire fundamental knowledge

(B) the extent to which teachers should direct schoolchildren's education

(C) the importance of having qualified teachers involved in schoolchildren's education

(D) the sort of school environment that most fosters children's creativity

(E) the extent to which schoolchildren are interested in fundamental academic subjects

5. Judge: The case before me involves a plaintiff and three codefendants. The plaintiff has applied to the court for an order permitting her to question each defendant without their codefendants or their codefendants' legal counsel being present. Two of the codefendants, however, share the same legal counsel. The court will not order any codefendant to find new legal counsel. Therefore, the order requested by the plaintiff cannot be granted.

The conclusion of the judge's argument is most strongly supported if which one of the following principles is assumed to hold?

(A) A court cannot issue an order that forces legal counsel to disclose information revealed by a client.

(B) Defendants have the right to have their legal counsel present when being questioned.

(C) People being questioned in legal proceedings may refuse to answer questions that are self-incriminating.

(D) A plaintiff in a legal case should never be granted a right that is denied to a defendant.

(E) A defendant's legal counsel has the right to question the plaintiff.

6. The calm, shallow waters of coastal estuaries are easily polluted by nutrient-rich sewage. When estuary waters become overnutrified as a result, algae proliferate. The abundant algae, in turn, sometimes provide a rich food source for microorganisms that are toxic to fish, thereby killing most of the fish in the estuary.

Which one of the following can be properly inferred from the information above?

(A) Fish in an estuary that has been polluted by sewage are generally more likely to die from pollution than are fish in an estuary that has been polluted in some other way.

(B) In estuary waters that contain abundant algae, microorganisms that are toxic to fish reproduce more quickly than other types of microorganisms.

(C) Nutrients and other components of sewage do not harm fish in coastal estuaries in any way other than through the resulting proliferation of toxic microorganisms.

(D) Algae will not proliferate in coastal estuaries that are not polluted by nutrient-rich sewage.

(E) Overnutrifying estuary waters by sewage can result in the death of most of the fish in the estuary.

GO ON TO THE NEXT PAGE.

7. The ruins of the prehistoric Bolivian city of Tiwanaku feature green andacite stones weighing up to 40 tons. These stones were quarried at Copacabana, which is across a lake and about 90 kilometers away. Archaeologists hypothesize that the stones were brought to Tiwanaku on reed boats. To show this was possible, experimenters transported a 9-ton stone from Copacabana to Tiwanaku using a reed boat built with locally available materials and techniques traditional to the area.

Which one of the following would be most useful to know in order to evaluate the support for the archaeologists' hypothesis?

(A) whether the traditional techniques for building reed boats were in use at the time Tiwanaku was inhabited

(B) whether green andacite stones quarried at the time Tiwanaku was inhabited were used at any sites near Copacabana

(C) whether reed boats are commonly used today on the lake

(D) whether the green andacite stones at Tiwanaku are the largest stones at the site

(E) whether the reed boat built for the experimenters is durable enough to remain usable for several years

8. Union member: Some members of our labor union are calling for an immediate strike. But a strike would cut into our strike fund and would in addition lead to a steep fine, causing us to suffer a major financial loss. Therefore, we must not strike now.

The union member's argument is most vulnerable to criticism on the grounds that it

(A) fails to consider that a strike might cause the union to suffer a financial loss even if no fine were imposed

(B) fails to define adequately what constitutes a major financial loss

(C) fails to consider that the benefits to be gained from a strike might outweigh the costs

(D) takes for granted that the most important factor in the labor union's bargaining position is the union's financial strength

(E) fails to establish that there will be a better opportunity to strike at a later time

9. Birds and mammals can be infected with West Nile virus only through mosquito bites. Mosquitoes, in turn, become infected with the virus when they bite certain infected birds or mammals. The virus was originally detected in northern Africa and spread to North America in the 1990s. Humans sometimes catch West Nile virus, but the virus never becomes abundant enough in human blood to infect a mosquito.

The statements above, if true, most strongly support which one of the following?

(A) West Nile virus will never be a common disease among humans.

(B) West Nile virus is most common in those parts of North America with the highest density of mosquitoes.

(C) Some people who become infected with West Nile virus never show symptoms of illness.

(D) West Nile virus infects more people in northern Africa than it does in North America.

(E) West Nile virus was not carried to North America via an infected person.

10. In trying to reduce the amount of fat in their diet, on average people have decreased their consumption of red meat by one-half in the last two decades. However, on average those who have reduced their consumption of red meat actually consume substantially more fat than those who have not.

Which one of the following, if true, most helps to resolve the apparent discrepancy described above?

(A) Many more people have reduced their consumption of red meat over the last two decades than have not.

(B) Higher prices over the last two decades have done as much to decrease the consumption of red meat as health concerns have.

(C) People who reduce their consumption of red meat tend to consume as much of other foods that are high in fat as do those who have not reduced their consumption of red meat.

(D) People who reduce their consumption of red meat tend to replace it with cheese and baked goods, which are richer in fat than red meat.

(E) Studies have shown that red meat contains slightly less fat than previously thought.

GO ON TO THE NEXT PAGE.

11. Rolanda: The house on Oak Avenue has a larger yard than any other house we've looked at in Prairieview, so that's the best one to rent.

Tom: No, it isn't. Its yard isn't really as big as it looks. Property lines in Prairieview actually start 20 feet from the street. So what looks like part of the yard is really city property.

Rolanda: But that's true of all the other properties we've looked at too!

Rolanda's response to Tom suggests that Tom commits which one of the following reasoning errors?

(A) He fails to take into account the possibility that there are advantages to having a small yard.

(B) He presumes, without providing justification, that property that belongs to the city is available for private use.

(C) He improperly applies a generalization to an instance that it was not intended to cover.

(D) He fails to apply a general rule to all relevant instances.

(E) He presumes, without providing justification, that whatever is true of a part of a thing is also true of the whole.

12. The best jazz singers use their voices much as horn players use their instruments. The great Billie Holiday thought of her singing voice as a horn, reshaping melody and words to increase their impact. Conversely, jazz horn players achieve their distinctive sounds by emulating the spontaneous twists and turns of an impassioned voice. So jazz consists largely of voicelike horns and hornlike voices.

Which one of the following most accurately describes the role played in the argument by the claim that the best jazz singers use their voices much as horn players use their instruments?

(A) It is the argument's main conclusion and is supported by another statement, which is itself supported by a further statement.

(B) It is the argument's only conclusion, and each of the other statements in the argument is used to support it.

(C) It is a statement for which some evidence is provided and which in turn is used to provide support for the argument's main conclusion.

(D) It is a statement for which no evidence is provided but which itself is used to support the argument's only conclusion.

(E) It is a statement used to support a conclusion that in turn is used to support the argument's main conclusion.

13. Educator: Reducing class sizes in our school district would require hiring more teachers. However, there is already a shortage of qualified teachers in the region. Although students receive more individualized instruction when classes are smaller, education suffers when teachers are underqualified. Therefore, reducing class sizes in our district would probably not improve overall student achievement.

Which one of the following is an assumption required by the educator's argument?

(A) Class sizes in the school district should be reduced only if doing so would improve overall student achievement.

(B) At least some qualified teachers in the school district would be able to improve the overall achievement of students in their classes if class sizes were reduced.

(C) Students place a greater value on having qualified teachers than on having smaller classes.

(D) Hiring more teachers would not improve the achievement of any students in the school district if most or all of the teachers hired were underqualified.

(E) Qualified teachers could not be persuaded to relocate in significant numbers to the educator's region to take teaching jobs.

14. Geographer: Because tropical storms require heat and moisture, they form especially over ocean surfaces of at least 26 degrees Celsius (79 degrees Fahrenheit), ocean temperatures that global warming would encourage. For this reason, many early discussions of global warming predicted that it would cause more frequent and intense tropical storms. But recent research shows that this prediction is unlikely to be borne out. Other factors, such as instabilities in wind flow, are likely to counteract global warming's effects on tropical storm development.

Which one of the following most accurately expresses the conclusion drawn in the geographer's argument?

(A) Tropical storms are especially likely to form over warm ocean surfaces.

(B) Contrary to early discussions, global warming is not the only factor affecting the frequency and intensity of tropical storms.

(C) If global warming were reversed, tropical storms would be less frequent and less intense.

(D) Instabilities in wind flow will negate the effect of global warming on the formation of tropical storms.

(E) Global warming probably will not produce more frequent and intense tropical storms.

GO ON TO THE NEXT PAGE.

15. Copyright was originally the grant of a temporary government-supported monopoly on copying a work. Its sole purpose was to encourage the circulation of ideas by giving authors the opportunity to derive a reasonable financial reward from their works. However, copyright sometimes goes beyond its original purpose since sometimes _____.

The conclusion of the argument is most strongly supported if which one of the following completes the passage?

(A) publication of copyrighted works is not the only way to circulate ideas

(B) authors are willing to circulate their works even without any financial reward

(C) authors are unable to find a publisher for their copyrighted work

(D) there is no practical way to enforce copyrights

(E) copyrights hold for many years after an author's death

16. Critic to economist: In yet another of your bumbling forecasts, last year you predicted that this country's economy would soon go into recession if current economic policies were not changed. Instead, economic growth is even stronger this year.

Economist: There was nothing at all bumbling about my warning. Indeed, it convinced the country's leaders to change economic policies, which is what prevented a recession.

The economist responds to the critic by

(A) indicating that the state of affairs on which the economist's prediction was conditioned did not obtain

(B) distinguishing between a prediction that has not yet turned out to be correct and one that has turned out to be incorrect

(C) attempting to show that the critic's statements are mutually inconsistent

(D) offering a particular counterexample to a general claim asserted by the critic

(E) offering evidence against one of the critic's factual premises

17. Watching music videos from the 1970s would give the viewer the impression that the music of the time was dominated by synthesizer pop and punk rock. But this would be a misleading impression. Because music videos were a new art form at the time, they attracted primarily cutting-edge musicians.

Which one of the following arguments is most similar in its reasoning to that of the argument above?

(A) Our view of pre-printing-press literature can never be accurate, because the surviving works of ancient authors are those that were deemed by copyists most likely to be of interest to future readers.

(B) Our memory of 1960s TV shows could hardly be improved, because so many of the television programs of the era are still rerun today.

(C) Future generations' understanding of today's publishing trends will be distorted if they judge by works published in CD-ROM format, since it is primarily publishers interested in computer games that are using CD-ROM.

(D) Our understanding of silent films is incomplete, because few filmmakers of the time realized that the film stock they were using would disintegrate over time.

(E) Our notion of fashion trends will probably be accurate if we rely on TV fashion programs, despite the fact that these programs deliberately select the most outrageous outfits in order to get the viewers' attention.

18. Hospitals, universities, labor unions, and other institutions may well have public purposes and be quite successful at achieving them even though each of their individual staff members does what he or she does only for selfish reasons.

Which one of the following generalizations is most clearly illustrated by the passage?

(A) What is true of some social organizations is not necessarily true of all such organizations.

(B) An organization can have a property that not all of its members possess.

(C) People often claim altruistic motives for actions that are in fact selfish.

(D) Many social institutions have social consequences unintended by those who founded them.

(E) Often an instrument created for one purpose will be found to serve another purpose just as effectively.

GO ON TO THE NEXT PAGE.

19. Consumer advocate: In some countries, certain produce is routinely irradiated with gamma rays in order to extend shelf life. There are, however, good reasons to avoid irradiated foods. First, they are exposed to the radioactive substances that produce the gamma rays. Second, irradiation can reduce the vitamin content of fresh foods, leaving behind harmful chemical residues. Third, irradiation spawns unique radiolytic products that cause serious health problems, including cancer.

Each of the following, if true, weakens the consumer advocate's argument EXCEPT:

(A) Unique radiolytic products have seldom been found in any irradiated food.

(B) Cancer and other serious health problems have many causes that are unrelated to radioactive substances and gamma rays.

(C) A study showed that irradiation leaves the vitamin content of virtually all fruits and vegetables unchanged.

(D) The amount of harmful chemicals found in irradiated foods is less than the amount that occurs naturally in most kinds of foods.

(E) A study showed that the cancer rate is no higher among people who eat irradiated food than among those who do not.

20. When teaching art students about the use of color, teachers should use colored paper rather than paint in their demonstrations. Colored paper is preferable because it readily permits a repeated use of exactly the same color in different compositions, which allows for a precise comparison of that color's impact in varying contexts. With paint, however, it is difficult to mix exactly the same color twice, and the varying textures of the applied paint can interfere with the pure effect of the color itself.

Which one of the following is an assumption required by the argument?

(A) Two pieces of paper of exactly the same color will have the same effect in a given context, even if they are of different textures.

(B) A slight difference in the color of two pieces of paper is more difficult to notice than a similar difference in the color of two samples of paint.

(C) Changing light conditions have less of an effect on the apparent color of a piece of paper than on the apparent color of a sample of paint.

(D) Observing the impacts of colors across varying contexts helps students to learn about the use of color.

(E) It is important that art students understand how the effects of using colored paper in various compositions differ from those of using paint in those compositions.

21. Philosopher: To explain the causes of cultural phenomena, a social scientist needs data about several societies: one cannot be sure, for example, that a given political structure is brought about only by certain ecological or climatic factors unless one knows that there are no similarly structured societies not subject to those factors, and no societies that, though subject to those factors, are not so structured.

The claim that to explain the causes of cultural phenomena, a social scientist needs data about several societies plays which one of the following roles in the philosopher's reasoning?

(A) It describes a problem that the philosopher claims is caused by the social scientist's need for certainty.

(B) It is a premise used to support a general theoretical claim about the nature of cause and effect relationships.

(C) It is a general hypothesis that is illustrated with an example showing that there is a causal relationship between political structures and environmental conditions.

(D) It is a dilemma that, it is argued, is faced by every social scientist because of the difficulty of determining whether a given cultural phenomenon is the cause or the effect of a given factor.

(E) It is a claim that the philosopher attempts to justify by appeal to the requirements for establishing the existence of one kind of causal relationship.

22. Scientist: Physicists claim that their system of careful peer review prevents scientific fraud in physics effectively. But biologists claimed the same thing for their field 20 years ago, and they turned out to be wrong. Since then, biologists have greatly enhanced their discipline's safeguards against scientific fraud, thus preventing further major incidents. It would be conducive to progress in physics if physicists were to do the same thing.

The conclusion of the scientist's argument is most strongly supported if which one of the following is assumed?

(A) Major incidents of scientific fraud in a scientific discipline are deleterious to progress in that discipline.

(B) Very few incidents of even minor scientific fraud have occurred in biology over the last 20 years.

(C) No system of careful peer review is completely effective in preventing scientific fraud in any scientific discipline.

(D) Twenty years ago the system of peer review in biology was less effective in preventing scientific fraud than the system of peer review in physics is today.

(E) Over the years, there have been relatively few, if any, major incidents of scientific fraud in physics.

GO ON TO THE NEXT PAGE.

23. Biologist: Researchers believe that dogs are the descendants of domesticated wolves that were bred to be better companions for humans. It has recently been found that some breeds of dog are much more closely related genetically to wolves than to most other breeds of dog. This shows that some dogs are descended from wolves that were domesticated much more recently than others.

Which one of the following principles underlies the biologist's argument?

(A) If one breed of dog is descended from wolves that were domesticated more recently than were the wolves from which most other breeds of dog are descended, the former breed may be more closely related to wolves than those other breeds are.

(B) If one breed of dog is more closely related to wolves than to another breed of dog, then the former breed of dog has more recent undomesticated wolf ancestors than the latter breed has.

(C) Any breed of dog descended from wolves that were domesticated is more closely related genetically to at least some other breeds of dog than to wolves.

(D) If one breed of dog is more closely related to wolves than another breed of dog is, then the former breed of dog is more closely related to wolves than to the latter breed of dog.

(E) Any two breeds of dog that are more closely related to each other than to wolves are both descended from wolves that were domesticated long ago.

24. Paleomycologists, scientists who study ancient forms of fungi, are invariably acquainted with the scholarly publications of all other paleomycologists. Professor Mansour is acquainted with the scholarly publications of Professor DeAngelis, who is a paleomycologist. Therefore, Professor Mansour must also be a paleomycologist.

The flawed pattern of reasoning in the argument above is most similar to that in which one of the following arguments?

(A) When a flight on Global Airlines is delayed, all connecting Global Airlines flights are also delayed so that the passengers can make their connections. Since Frieda's connecting flight on Global was delayed, her first flight must have also been a delayed Global Airlines flight.

(B) Any time that one of Global Airlines' local ticket agents misses a shift, the other agents on that shift need to work harder than usual. Since none of Global's local ticket agents missed a shift last week, the airline's local ticket agents did not have to work harder than usual last week.

(C) Any time the price of fuel decreases, Global Airlines' expenses decrease and its income is unaffected. The price of fuel decreased several times last year. Therefore, Global Airlines must have made a profit last year.

(D) All employees of Global Airlines can participate in its retirement plan after they have been with the company a year or more. Gavin has been with Global Airlines for three years. We can therefore be sure that he participates in Global's retirement plan.

(E) Whenever a competitor of Global Airlines reduces its fares, Global must follow suit or lose passengers. Global carried more passengers last year than it did the year before. Therefore, Global must have reduced its fares last year to match reductions in its competitors' fares.

GO ON TO THE NEXT PAGE.

25. Lutsina: Because futuristic science fiction does not need to represent current social realities, its writers can envisage radically new social arrangements. Thus it has the potential to be a richer source of social criticism than is conventional fiction.

Priscilla: That futuristic science fiction writers more skillfully envisage radically new technologies than new social arrangements shows how writers' imaginations are constrained by current realities. Because of this limitation, the most effective social criticism results from faithfully presenting the current social realities for critical examination, as happens in conventional fiction.

Lutsina and Priscilla disagree with each other about whether

(A) some science fiction writers have succeeded in envisaging convincing, radically new social arrangements

(B) writers of conventional fiction are more skillful than are writers of futuristic science fiction

(C) futuristic science fiction has more promise as a source of social criticism than does conventional fiction

(D) envisaging radically new technologies rather than radically new social arrangements is a shortcoming of futuristic science fiction

(E) criticism of current social arrangements is not effective when those arrangements are contrasted with radically different ones

26. Because our club recruited the best volleyball players in the city, we will have the best team in the city. Moreover, since the best team in the city will be the team most likely to win the city championship, our club will almost certainly be city champions this year.

The reasoning in the argument is flawed because the argument

(A) presumes, without presenting relevant evidence, that an entity can be distinguished as the best only on the basis of competition

(B) predicts the success of an entity on the basis of features that are not relevant to the quality of that entity

(C) predicts the outcome of a competition merely on the basis of a comparison between the parties in that competition

(D) presumes, without providing warrant, that if an entity is the best among its competitors, then each individual part of that entity must also be the best

(E) concludes that because an event is the most likely of a set of possible events, that event is more likely to occur than not

S T O P

IF YOU FINISH BEFORE TIME IS CALLED, YOU MAY CHECK YOUR WORK ON THIS SECTION ONLY.
DO NOT WORK ON ANY OTHER SECTION IN THE TEST.

Wait for the supervisor's instructions before you open the page to the topic.
Please print and sign your name and write the date in the designated spaces below.
Time: 35 Minutes

General Directions

You will have 35 minutes in which to plan and write an essay on the topic inside. Read the topic and the accompanying directions carefully. You will probably find it best to spend a few minutes considering the topic and organizing your thoughts before you begin writing. In your essay, be sure to develop your ideas fully, leaving time, if possible, to review what you have written. **Do not write on a topic other than the one specified. Writing on a topic of your own choice is not acceptable.**

No special knowledge is required or expected for this writing exercise. Law schools are interested in the reasoning, clarity, organization, language usage, and writing mechanics displayed in your essay. How well you write is more important than how much you write.

Confine your essay to the blocked, lined area on the front and back of the separate Writing Sample Response Sheet. Only that area will be reproduced for law schools. Be sure that your writing is legible.

Both this topic sheet and your response sheet must be turned over to the testing staff before you leave the room.

Topic Code	Print Your Full Name Here		
103326	Last	First	M.I.

Date	Sign Your Name Here
/ /	

Scratch Paper
Do not write your essay in this space.

LSAT® Writing Sample Topic

Directions: The scenario presented below describes two choices, either one of which can be supported on the basis of the information given. Your essay should consider both choices and argue for one over the other, based on the two specified criteria and the facts provided. There is no "right" or "wrong" choice: a reasonable argument can be made for either.

Two pediatricians are deciding whether to relocate their small practice 10 miles away, to a large medical pavilion downtown, or to keep their present office and also open a second office about 20 miles away across the city. Using the facts below, write an essay in which you argue for one choice over the other based on the following two criteria:

- The doctors want to attract new patients.
- The doctors want to keep their current patients.

The Laurel Medical Pavilion is a new collection of medical office buildings adjacent to the city's major hospital. The pavilion is convenient to public transportation. It offers ample free parking space. Although office space in the pavilion is expensive, it is going fast. The space the pediatricians would lease includes five examination rooms, sufficient office space, and a large waiting area that the doctors would be able to furnish as they like. The pavilion leases space to doctors in a wide variety of fields. It contains facilities for a wide range of laboratory and diagnostic testing.

The space the doctors are considering leasing as a second office is, like their present premises, a 100-year-old Victorian house in a largely residential area full of young families. The house has a large fenced-in yard and off-street parking space for five vehicles. The first floor of the house was recently remodeled to suit the needs of a small medical practice. Like their present premises, it contains three examination rooms, a small waiting area, and ample office space. The second floor has not been converted into suitable working space. The option of doing so is available to the doctors.

WP-S103A

Scratch Paper
Do not write your essay in this space.

Writing Sample Response Sheet

DO NOT WRITE IN THIS SPACE

**Begin your essay in the lined area below.
Continue on the back if you need more space.**

TEST 65

EliteView™ forms by NCS Pearson EM-252259-6:654321   Printed in U.S.A.

Copyright © 2005 by Law School Admission Council, Inc. All Rights Reserved.

TEST 65   723

COMPUTING YOUR SCORE

Directions:

1. Use the Answer Key on the next page to check your answers.

2. Use the Scoring Worksheet below to compute your raw score.

3. Use the Score Conversion Chart to convert your raw score into the 120–180 scale.

Scoring Worksheet

1. Enter the number of questions you answered correctly in each section.

	Number Correct
SECTION I................	_____
SECTION II...............	_____
SECTION III..............	_____
SECTION IV	_____

2. Enter the sum here: _____
   This is your Raw Score.

Conversion Chart
For Converting Raw Score to the 120–180 LSAT Scaled Score
LSAT Form 1LSN091

Reported Score	Raw Score Lowest	Raw Score Highest
180	98	101
179	97	97
178	96	96
177	95	95
176	94	94
175	93	93
174	92	92
173	91	91
172	90	90
171	88	89
170	87	87
169	86	86
168	85	85
167	83	84
166	82	82
165	80	81
164	79	79
163	77	78
162	76	76
161	74	75
160	73	73
159	71	72
158	69	70
157	68	68
156	66	67
155	64	65
154	63	63
153	61	62
152	59	60
151	57	58
150	56	56
149	54	55
148	52	53
147	51	51
146	49	50
145	47	48
144	46	46
143	44	45
142	43	43
141	41	42
140	39	40
139	38	38
138	36	37
137	35	35
136	34	34
135	32	33
134	31	31
133	30	30
132	28	29
131	27	27
130	26	26
129	25	25
128	23	24
127	22	22
126	21	21
125	20	20
124	19	19
123	18	18
122	16	17
121	—*	—*
120	0	15

*There is no raw score that will produce this scaled score for this form.

ANSWER KEY

SECTION I

1.	B	8.	A	15.	C	22.	E
2.	A	9.	C	16.	B	23.	E
3.	B	10.	B	17.	D	24.	C
4.	C	11.	A	18.	B	25.	D
5.	D	12.	C	19.	C		
6.	A	13.	E	20.	D		
7.	D	14.	B	21.	D		

SECTION II

1.	D	8.	E	15.	D	22.	B
2.	A	9.	B	16.	A	23.	C
3.	C	10.	B	17.	B		
4.	E	11.	C	18.	B		
5.	B	12.	B	19.	D		
6.	C	13.	D	20.	E		
7.	D	14.	E	21.	C		

SECTION III

1.	B	8.	A	15.	B	22.	B
2.	D	9.	C	16.	A	23.	D
3.	E	10.	A	17.	A	24.	E
4.	A	11.	B	18.	E	25.	B
5.	B	12.	D	19.	D	26.	C
6.	A	13.	E	20.	A	27.	B
7.	D	14.	C	21.	E		

SECTION IV

1.	C	8.	C	15.	E	22.	A
2.	E	9.	E	16.	A	23.	B
3.	D	10.	D	17.	C	24.	A
4.	B	11.	D	18.	B	25.	C
5.	B	12.	C	19.	B	26.	E
6.	E	13.	E	20.	D		
7.	A	14.	E	21.	E		

EXAM ANALYSIS

Every practice section that you take is an opportunity for you to evaluate your testing strategy. If you take a section under timed conditions, that also gives you an opportunity to evaluate your timing strategy. The last section of Chapter 1 provides a detailed worksheet and plan for reviewing your performance and identifying exactly what strategy error led to each wrong answer. The sections of Chapter 1 on timing explain how to evaluate your timing strategy. Be sure to evaluate your timing strategy for every section that you take under timed conditions.

Use the plan in Chapter 1 to review every question that you answered incorrectly. The plan lists twenty-two specific errors. For each question that you answered incorrectly, you should review the parts of Chapter 1 and the relevant other chapters that cover the strategies with which you had trouble. The key to success is identifying your errors and reviewing again and again.

Use the following chart to summarize your performance based on four main categories of error. Enter the number of incorrect answers in each column. Some questions may fall under more than one category.

Summary of Incorrect Answers

Section	Total Incorrect	Didn't Take Enough Time	Misread Information	Got Down to Two Answers	Didn't Have a Strategy
I: LR					
II: AR					
III: RC					
IV: LR					
Total:					

After you have reviewed your timing strategy, enter the results in the chart on the next page. The questions for which you simply filled in a bubble without working on the question should be counted under Cold Guesses. If you spent more than fifteen seconds working on a question, do *not* count it under Cold Guesses. Under Number Correct and Number Incorrect, do not include Cold Guesses. The number in the Cold Guesses column, then, includes both incorrect and correct answers. In the final column, enter the number of incorrect answers on which you spent under two minutes.

Analysis of Timing Strategy

Section	Number Correct (not cold guesses)	Number Incorrect (not cold guesses)	Cold Guesses	Number of Incorrect Under 2 Minutes
I: LR				
II: AR				
III: RC				
IV: LR				
Total:				

If most of your incorrect answers took under two minutes, you should plan to spend more time on questions. If you have more than two or three questions incorrect—excluding Cold Guesses—you can increase your score by working on fewer questions but spending a little more time on the questions that you do work on. See the example below.

Example of Revised Timing Strategy

Section	Number Correct (not cold guesses)	Number Incorrect (not cold guesses)	Cold Guesses	Number of Incorrect Under 2 Minutes	Total Correct (including cold guesses)
First attempt	11	6	7	5	12
Revised attempt	11 + 2	0	7 + 4	0	15

By guessing cold on four more questions, the test taker in the example above had time to work the remaining two questions correctly. Approximately one out of five Cold Guesses results in a correct answer.

ANSWERS EXPLAINED

Section I: Logical Reasoning

1. **(B)** This is a *strengthen* question. The conclusion is that a diet may not have to be low in fat in order to protect the heart. Choice B strengthens the conclusion by explaining the way in which the fats in the Mediterranean diet protect the heart.

   Choice A goes in the wrong direction, claiming that fat is harmful. Choices C, D, and E do not provide any information that supports fat as a positive factor.

2. **(A)** This is a *main conclusion* question. The correct answer is not just a statement that *can* be concluded but must be the *main point* of the passage. Choice A correctly paraphrases the conclusion of the passage. The other answer choices are all premises that support the conclusion.

3. **(B)** This is a *relevant information* question in a LEAST format. Four of the answer choices are relevant. The correct answer is not relevant. The conclusion of the argument is that low-wattage bulbs are advantageous in some way. Choices A and C are relevant because they address cost. Choice D addresses effectiveness, and choice E addresses the life span of bulbs. These issues are relevant to how advantageous the bulbs are. Choice B—addressing the profits of the manufacturers—has no relevance to whether the bulbs are advantageous to homeowners.

4. **(C)** This is a *complete the sentence/argument* question. The conclusion is based on an analogy with the argument about swimming pools. The pattern of the argument is that it is good to prevent a harmful event, but it is better to teach children positive habits that help them to avoid harmful events. Choice C correctly completes the argument by recommending teaching children how to avoid bad foods.

   Choice A is positive but does not teach about choosing good food. Choice B does not teach a positive habit. Choices D and E are positive but not relevant to food choices.

5. **(D)** This is a *weaken* question. The argument claims that because the interviewees against the project outnumbered those for the project by a two-to-one ratio, the interviews do not represent the views of the public in general. Choice D shows that the ratio does represent the views of the general population.

   Choice A is irrelevant to the conclusion of the argument. Choice B excuses the bias but does not attack the claim that there is a bias. Choice C is irrelevant. Choice E explains why the station might be biased, but to weaken the argument, an answer choice must show that the station's broadcast was *not* biased.

6. **(A)** This is a *match a principle to a concrete example* question. In this question, the principle is in the setup, and the answer choices are concrete examples. The principle is that, in the face of uncertainty, one should extend the benefit of the doubt to others. In choice A, it is uncertain whether the person has already paid the debt, and so the person extends the benefit of the doubt to Farah and pays the debt, possibly for the second time.

   In choice B, the uncertainty is whether owners know their cars have been recalled. To match the principle, choice B would have to say that "we" should inform the owners (acting in their benefit.) Choices C through E do not involve an uncertainty.

7. **(D)** This is a *complete the sentence/argument* question. The conclusion is based on a parallel with the argument that, because medicine has both harmful and beneficial

ANSWERS EXPLAINED

ANSWERS EXPLAINED

TEST 65 729

effects, medicine should only be used when not using it would be more harmful than using it. The conclusion, then, must say that government intervention should be used only when it would cause less harm than not using it. Choice D captures this. The other answer choices are not parallel to the comparison with medicine.

8. **(A)** This is a *flaw* question. The argument shows that two facts are related (a correlation). The flaw is that the argument assumes that fact 1 is the cause of fact 2. This is a flaw because fact 2 might cause fact 1, because some other factor might cause both facts, or because there might be no causal relationship at all. Choice A correctly states the latter. The other answer choices are common types of flaws but are not flaws that occur in this argument.

9. **(C)** This is a *main conclusion* question. The conclusion of the passage is that the claim that *Apatosaurus* galloped is most likely not correct. Choice C captures this. The other answer choices are either stated premises or unstated premises (assumptions) that support the main conclusion.

10. **(B)** This is a *role of a claim* question. The conclusion of the argument is that iron-fortified salt can supply iron requirements. The statement—that people eat enough salt for this to happen—is a premise that supports the argument, as stated in choice B.

   Choice A is incorrect because the cited statement is not the conclusion. Choice C is incorrect because the cited statement supports the conclusion. Choice D is incorrect because qualifying the conclusion means showing an exception to or weakness in the conclusion. Choice E is incorrect because the cited statement is a fact, not a principle.

11. **(A)** This is a *parallel flaw* question. The original passage cites an exclusive correlation—the only fingerprints are those of Mr. Tannisch—that would naturally lead to a conclusion that Mr. Tannisch is the thief, but rejects that conclusion and concludes that there must be another cause of the theft. Choice A similarly cites an exclusive correlation—all campers ate only at the cafeteria—and then rejects the obvious conclusion that the food from the cafeteria made them sick, and concludes that something else must have made them sick.

   Choice B is incorrect because it is a different type of argument and is not flawed. The flaw in choice C is that it makes a false assumption about the group as a whole based on information about each member of the group. Choice D is based on a correlation and cause, but it does not reject a likely conclusion. Choice E is based on an analogous situation.

12. **(C)** This is a *resolve a paradox* question that uses the wording *explain a difference*. The paradox is that shrimp mix freely among the reefs and yet each reef is genetically distinct. Choice C provides a logical explanation—that shrimp mate only with other shrimp that were born at the reef at which they were born. The other answer choices do not resolve the paradox.

13. **(E)** This is a *strengthen* question. The argument is based on cost and one of the premises is that pumping seawater is cheaper than pumping freshwater. Choice E establishes that the cost of pumping water is proportionally one of the main costs in agriculture. This strengthens the argument that switching to pumping seawater would save significant money.

   Choices A and B are not related to cost. Choice C weakens the argument. Choice D addresses cost but does not indicate whether seawater agriculture is more or less costly.

14. **(B)** This is an *application of a principle* question. The principle sets a specific guideline that must be met for its conclusion to apply: The policy is written in a way that a reasonable person would not read it thoroughly. If this is met, then the policy must be interpreted according to *the reasonable expectations of the policyholder*, no matter what is written in the policy. Choice B establishes that the condition for triggering the principle is met and that the policyholder's expectation is that hail damage is covered. Given the information in choice B, the application follows from the principle.

Choice A is incorrect because it does not establish that the condition for triggering the principle is met. Choice C is incorrect because it does not establish Celia's *reasonable expectation*. Choice D is incorrect because it does not establish that the condition for triggering the principle is met. Choice E establishes that the condition was met but does not indicate Celia's *reasonable expectation*.

15. **(C)** This is a *flaw: fails to consider* question. In this type of question, the argument ignores a possibility that would alter or destroy the conclusion. Choice C indicates that many of the people "saved" by preventing iatrogenic disease may well die soon of another cause.

Choice A is incorrect because the argument does not talk about the prevention of non-iatrogenic disease. Choice B is incorrect because it supports the argument, rather than pointing to a flaw. Choice D is incorrect because the argument does not depend on preventing *all* iatrogenic diseases. Choice E does not affect the argument.

16. **(B)** This is a *sufficient assumption* question. For question 16, the correct answer is both a sufficient and a necessary assumption. The negation of choice B is that the proposal should be decided by the voters, which destroys the conclusion of the argument. Therefore, choice B is necessary for the argument to work. From the perspective of a sufficient assumption, the logic of the argument is:

Any member either: against or abstain
If all abstain → *voters decide*
−*voters decide* (**Choice B**) → −*all abstain* (**This is the contrapositive of the above.**)
−*all abstain* → *at least one against*

With choice B added to the logic, the inevitable conclusion is that at least one council member votes against.

The negation of choice A is that if all council members abstain, voters will not necessarily vote in favor. This does not affect the conclusion. The negation of choice C appears at first glance to destroy the argument. However, choice C is incorrect because it is a necessary assumption—without it the argument does not work—but it is not sufficient. Choice C by itself does not result in the conclusion. Choice D does not lead to the conclusion:

Any member either: against or abstain
If all abstain → *voters decide*
−*all abstain* (**Choice D**) → (**No logical conclusion**)

The premise in choice D, −*all abstain*, does not trigger a rule. The conclusion stated in choice D is not logically valid. Choice E is wrong for the same reason. Its premise is −*all abstain* (one member ought to vote against).

17. **(D)** This is a *flaw: fail to consider* question. Choice D shows that the lack of confidence in the general economy predicted by the critics leads directly to the pessimistic view of one's own situation, which the economist acknowledges does affect the economy. The other answer choices do not affect the argument.

18. **(B)** This is a *necessary assumption* question. The argument is based on the fact that in the recent past people were unable to domesticate certain wild mammals, and the conclusion is that today it would still be difficult to domesticate them. The negation of choice B is that it is significantly easier to domesticate wild mammals today than it was in the recent past. This destroys the conclusion.

Choice A is incorrect because the argument does not depend on people trying to domesticate each wild mammal species, only those types that seem worth domesticating. The negation of choice C is that all of the domesticated large mammals of the past are still in existence. This does not affect the argument. The negation of choice D is that the ease of domestication is not correlated with how worthwhile the domestication is. This does not affect the argument. Similarly, the negation of choice E does not affect the argument.

19. **(C)** This is a *strengthen* question. The argument makes its case with two points:

   1. fewer birds at feeders
   2. less migration, so death of fewer birds

For the second point, the argument explains how it leads to the conclusion—that the bird population is higher. However, the argument does not explain how fewer birds at feeders increases the population. Choice C does so, thus strengthening the argument.

Choice A goes in the right direction but "unusual weather patterns" is too vague to clearly apply to the argument. In fact, it is not clear that last winter's weather had an unusual pattern. Choice B talks about a difference but would only strengthen the argument if it led to an increase in population. Choice D goes in the wrong direction, leading to a decreased population. Choice E explains why some birds may still have visited feeders but does not by itself affect the conclusion. Choice E would weaken the conclusion if choice C is also true.

20. **(D)** This is a *flaw* question. The logic in this question is similar to the logic in question 5. The journalist assumes that because there are more reports on one type of situation (small studies) than another type (large studies), the difference is due to an editorial bias (small studies are more dramatic). The flaw is that the journalist overlooks the possibility that the disproportional reporting simply reflects the fact that there are disproportionally more small studies, as pointed out in choice D. Note that choice D is a *fails to consider* answer choice, but some of the other answer choices are not in that format, so this is not a *fails to consider* question. The other answer choices refer to other types of flaws that do not occur in this passage.

21. **(D)** This is a *necessary assumption* question. The negation of choice D is that none of the trees have replaced native grasses. If that is the case, then planting trees has not necessarily increased global warming, and the conclusion is destroyed. Choice D is an assumption necessary to make the argument work.

The negation of choice A is that trees do not emit carbon dioxide. This strengthens the argument. The negation of choice B is that farmers may plant trees without an incentive. This does not affect the argument. The negation of choice C is that deforested land could support native grasses. This does not affect the conclusion. The negation of choice E is that some governments have been interested in promoting native grasses. This does not affect the conclusion that growing trees is worse for global warming than growing grasses.

22. **(E)** This is a *role of a claim* question. The statement—that position affects comfort and ability to see—is a premise used to support the conclusion, as stated in choice E. The argument builds on this premise to show that lack of comfort leads to lack of safety, and that good visibility leads to increased safety. This supports the conclusion that position affects safety.

   Choice A incorrectly calls the cited statement a conclusion. Choice B is incorrect because the cited statement is consistent with the evidence. Choice C is incorrect because the cited statement does not explain a causal relationship. Choice D is incorrect because the argument uses the evidence, rather than refuting it.

23. **(E)** This is a *committed to agree/disagree* question. The question requires you to find a statement that the two arguers are forced to disagree about. Choice E is correct because the physician is committed to the position that there should be mandatory supervision, but the enthusiast is committed to the position that supervision, if it takes place at all, is not mandatory.

   Choice A is incorrect because both arguers would agree with it. Choice B is incorrect because neither arguer expresses an opinion about home trampolines. Choice C is incorrect because the physician does not express an opinion, whereas the enthusiast agrees. Choice D is incorrect because the enthusiast does not express an opinion.

24. **(C)** This is a *strengthen* question based on a principle. The correct answer choices are principles, one of which strengthens the argument because the principle matches the conditions of the argument. Choice C states that meeting the conditions of (1) accuracy and (2) considerable interest is enough to guarantee that the journalism is good. In other words, this is a deductive argument:

$$\textit{If accurate AND considerable interest } \rightarrow \textit{ good}$$

The principle in choice C matches the conditions in the passage and leads to the conclusion that the journalism was good.

   Choices A, B, and E do not match the situation in the passage. The logic in choice D is:

$$\textit{If good } \rightarrow \textit{ interest}$$

The argument in the passage is:

$$\textit{Interest } \rightarrow \textit{ good}$$

These two statements are not the same.

25. **(D)** This is a *must be true* question. The logic is deductive and consists of the rules:

$$\textit{If coffeehouse } \rightarrow \textit{ public}$$
$$\textit{If restaurant } \rightarrow \textit{ public}$$
$$\textit{If well designed AND public } \rightarrow \textit{ probably art}$$
$$\textit{If public AND --comfortable } \rightarrow \textit{ --well designed}$$
$$\textit{If public AND comfortable } \rightarrow \textit{ spacious}$$

Choice D refers to a location that is *public* and is *well designed*. There are only two options for a public place: it is not comfortable or it is comfortable. If it is not comfortable, it is not well designed, but the places described in choice D are well designed, so they must be comfortable. If they are comfortable, they must be spacious, which is the valid conclusion in choice D.

Choice A is incorrect because being spacious is not a trigger. It is possible that a restaurant is spacious and not well designed. Choice B is incorrect because it is possible that many poorly designed public places feature artwork. Choice C is incorrect because, even though it meets the criteria of public and well designed, the applicable rule is not deductive. It only states that most do contain art. Because of this, it is not possible to say that choice C *must* be true, only that it is probably true.

Section II: Analytical Reasoning

QUESTIONS 1–5

This is a sequence game (one-to-one correspondence, ordered). The setup is as follows:

Two supplemental diagrams are shown—one for HF and one for FH. Although these two options could be indicated in one diagram, showing them separately helps avoid errors.

Refer to Chapter 4 for an explanation of the game rules.

1. **(D)** This is the typical first question. The first rule is violated by choice E. The second rule is violated by choice A (K is not before H) and by choice B (K is not before J). The final rule is violated by choice C.

2. **(A)** This is a *could be true* question with new information that does not go directly into the main diagram. Put the new information into a supplemental diagram. Putting J before G results in:

J–G–H/F

K must go before J, which results in:

$$K–J–G–H/F$$

The notation H/F represents either HF or FH. Use **Eliminate—check answers against diagram**. Choices B through E violate the diagram. Only choice A is possible.

3. **(C)** This is a *CANNOT be true* question with no new information. There are too many options to create parallel universes, so test the answers. Although there is no information that can go in the main diagram, the supplemental diagrams are helpful. Choice A appears possible. Do not take time to *prove* that it is possible. Test the other answers, looking for one that clearly violates rules. Choice B appears possible. Choice C violates both supplemental diagrams and must be the correct answer. A quick glance at choices D and E confirms that they appear to be possible.

4. **(E)** This is a *completely determined* question. One answer choice results in the assignment of all players being fully determined. Test each answer by putting it into the main diagram and applying the rules. If there are options, the answer choice is not the correct one.

   For choice A, putting F immediately before H simply results in the second supplemental diagram. Move on to choice B. Putting G immediately before H still allows options for J. For choice C, putting H immediately before J leaves options for G and K. For choice D, there are also options for G and K. For choice E, if K is immediately before F, H must be immediately after F:

$$KFH$$

Check the rules for G. G must go before F and so must go before K. Check the rules for J. J must go after K and so must go after H. The only possible arrangement is:

$$GKFHJ$$

Choice E results in all positions being determined.

5. **(B)** This is a *how many players for a fixture* question. There is no new information. Start by using the supplemental diagrams to find players who cannot appear fourth. G must have at least two players after it, and K must have at least three players after it. Neither can appear fourth. Test the remaining players—F, H, and J—by placing each in 4 in the diagram and trying to create a viable order. Because H and F are interchangeable, it is likely that if one of them can be in 4, the other can as well. Test J first. With J in 4, the adjacent pair H/F has only two options: 1 and 2, or 2 and 3. Neither option allows enough room for both K and G to appear before H and F. J cannot go in 4. H and F are now the only candidates for 4 and because they are interchangeable, there are two players who can go in 4.

   HINT: Game 1 has very limited options. Leaving the order of H and F undetermined, there are only five possible universes. The consecutive pair H/F has to have two players before it, so the only options for H/F and F/H are 3 and 4, or 4 and 5. Writing out all five options would allow each question to be solved more quickly, but it is not intuitively obvious that there are only five options, so the solutions above represent a more reliable strategy.

QUESTIONS 6–11

This game—an ONS-A game—has one-to-one correspondence and is ordered. Although the relative order of some players is given, there is no string of relationships that includes three or more players. For this reason, the game is not a sequence game.

```
J – N
J – O          1    2    3    4    5    6
K – P         ___  ___  ___  ___  ___  ___
K – T
L – W

–KK
S – O
T – W
```

6. **(C)** This is the typical first question. The first rule is violated by choices A and E. The second rule is violated by choice D. The third rule is violated by choice B. Choice C is left as the correct answer.

7. **(D)** This is a *could be true* question with new information that goes in the diagram. With KT in 5, the third rule indicates that LW must go in 6. Slot 4 cannot be another presentation by K, so it must be JO/JN. Slots 1 through 3 are open and there are two presentations by K. They must be separated and so must go in 1 and 3. Slot 2 must be JN/JO.

```
 1     2     3     4     5     6
___   ___   ___   ___   ___   ___
 K   JN/JO   K   JO/JN   KT    LW
```

Use **Eliminate—check answers against diagram**. Choices A, B, C, and E violate the diagram. Only choice D could be true.

8. **(E)** This is a *could be true* question with new information that goes in the diagram. Put JN in 1. Because the Ks cannot be adjacent, there is only one way to distribute them: in 2, 4, and 6. Because both KS and KT must have another player after them, 6 must be KP.

```
 1     2     3     4     5     6
___   ___   ___   ___   ___   ___
 JN    K          K           KP
```

Check the answers against the diagram. For choice A, JO cannot be in 6. For choice B, KP cannot be 2. For choice C, KS cannot be 3. For choice D, KT cannot be 5. Only choice E is possible. LW could be 3 (and 2 would be KT).

9. **(B)** This is a *CANNOT be true* question with no new information. The diagram from the previous question can be used to test choices A, B, and C. If J is in 1, slot 4 must be a K. Choice B cannot be true.

10. **(B)** This is a *must be true* question with new information in the diagram. This question works the same way as question 8, except that JN is at the end, rather than the beginning. The Ks must be in 1, 3, and 5, and the K in 5 must be KP, which is choice B.

11. **(C)** This is a *CANNOT be true* question with no new information. It is necessary to test the answer choices. Use **Scan** to determine if some answer choices are more likely than others to break rules. The Ks are the most restricted players, and KP is forced to appear later in the assignment because the other Ks must each be followed by at least one player. Testing KP in 2 shows that the other two Ks must be in 4 and 6. However, neither of the other two Ks can be in the last position (6). Therefore, KP cannot go in 2.

QUESTIONS 12–16

This is an unordered game, in which players are either in or out, and the order in which they are chosen is not relevant. The game uses a discard pile. The number of fixtures is fixed at five, and as a result, the number of slots in the discard pile is exactly three. The players are divided into three categories—dessert, main, and side. In addition, three players are defined as "hot."

D	M	S
F	N	T
G	O	V
	P	W

1   2   3   4   5 | _ _ _

Hot = F, N, T

At least 1 D, M, S

At least 1 hot

If P $\longleftrightarrow$ W

If G $\rightarrow$ O

If N $\rightarrow$ –V

12. **(B)** This is the typical first question. The rule that there must be at least one D, M, and S is not violated by any answer choices. The rule about one hot food is violated by choice E. The PW rule is violated by choice D. The GO rule is violated by choice C. The NV rule is violated by choice A. Choice B remains as the correct answer.

13. **(D)** This is an *at least one is in* question. The correct answer is a pair, at least one member of which must be included. In other words, for the correct answer, leaving both members of the pair out violates rules. Scan the answer choices to see if any pairs stand out as more likely to violate rules if left out. In this question, no particular answer choice stands out, so it is necessary to test each answer choice.

Test choice A by putting F and T in the discard pile. Use **Diagram—apply rules, musts**. If F is out, then G—the other dessert—must be in. If G is in, O must be in (*If G $\rightarrow$ O*). No other rules are triggered, and there appear to be many options for creating a viable order. Mark choice A as probably out and go on to choice B.

Put G and O in the discard pile. F must be in, but no other rules are triggered. It appears that both members of choice B can be out. For choice C, put N and T in the discard pile. No rules are triggered. Note that (–N) does not trigger the rule *If N $\rightarrow$ –V*.

Test choice D by putting O and P in the discard pile. The remaining main dish, N, must be in. This triggers the rule *If N → –V,* so V is out. The discard pile is now full and all other players must be in. Checking the completed assignment shows that the PW rule is violated. It is not possible to put both O and P in the discard pile and choice D contains the pair at least one of which must be chosen.

14. **(E)** This is a *CANNOT be true* question with new information that does not go directly into the main diagram. The new information, however, can be used to put N and P in the discard pile. Applying the rules, if P is out, then W cannot be selected. The discard pile is full and all other players must be selected. This is enough information to answer the question. W is the player that cannot be selected.

15. **(D)** This is a *could be true* question with new information that goes in the diagram. Put F in the discard pile. Apply the rules. At least one dessert must be chosen, so G is in. The GO rule means that O is also in.

$$\frac{1}{G} \quad \frac{2}{O} \quad \frac{3}{} \quad \frac{4}{} \quad \frac{5}{} \quad \Big| \quad \frac{}{F} \quad \frac{}{} \quad \frac{}{}$$

There are too many options to create parallel universes, so each answer choice must be tested. First scan the choices to see if any are obviously out. Choice A is out at a glance because O is also a main dish. The other choices are unclear. Test choice B, using **Test answers—prove a violation**. Put T in 3 and put the other side dishes—V and W—in the discard pile. The discard pile is full, so all other players are in. Test this assignment against the rules. The PW rule is violated. Choice B is out.

Test choice C by putting both N and T in the diagram. With N in, V must be out. The remaining players are P and W but there is only one space left. Putting either P or W in that space violates the PW rule.

Test choice D by putting N and P in. With P in, W must be in, and the assignment is complete. Checking the assignment against the rules shows that there are no violations. Choice D looks like the correct answer. However, because it is possible to miss a violation, check choice E. Putting T, V, and W in the assignment completes the diagram, but the PW rule is violated. Choice E is out and choice D is confirmed as the correct answer.

16. **(A)** This is a *must* question with new information that is in the diagram. T and V are in. With V in, N must be out. This is the basic setup for this question. Given this setup, the correct answer is a pair, both of which must be in. Be sure to distinguish this from the type of question in 13, in which the correct answer is a pair at least one of which must be in. For this question, it is possible to create all parallel universes. Given the basic diagram, create two universes around the fact that either F or G must be in.

For the universe in which G is in, O must also be in. Only one space is left, so neither P nor W can be in. P and W go in the discard pile. The only remaining player is F.

Break the universe with F into two. In one, P and W are both in. In the other, P and W are both out. For the universe with P and W in, the assignment is complete, with G and O out. For the universe with P and W out, the assignment is also complete, with G and O in. This final universe is identical to the universe that was based on G being in because the order in which players are "thrown into the hat" does not matter.

$$
\text{Identical} \begin{cases}
\begin{array}{ccccc|ccc}
\underline{1} & \underline{2} & \underline{3} & \underline{4} & \underline{5} & \overline{N} & \overline{P} & \overline{W} \\
T & V & G & O & F & N & P & W \\
\end{array} \\
\begin{array}{ccccc|ccc}
T & V & F & P & W & N & G & O \\
T & V & F & G & O & N & P & W \\
\end{array}
\end{cases}
$$

Three universes for question 16. The top and bottom universes are identical.

Choice A is the only pair—F and G—both of which are chosen in each universe.

QUESTIONS 17–23

This game has one-to-one correspondence and is ordered (ONS-A) but is not a sequence. Because there is a distinction between programs that start on the half hour and programs that start on the hour, the three hours must be broken into six half-hour fixtures. G is the only program that lasts for a full hour. G occupies the half-hour fixture to which it is assigned, as well as the half-hour fixture that immediately follows it.

G
R
S
T   G = 1 hr
W   G on hr

T on $\frac{1}{2}$ hr

R – S

If W – T

→ WT

	1:00	1:30	2:00	2:30	3:00	3:30

17. **(B)** This is the typical first question. The first three rules have to do with the length of the programs and whether they start on the hour or half hour. These rules are difficult to apply without entering the answer choices in the diagram, so first apply the other rules. The RS rule is violated by choice E. The WT rule is violated by choices C and D. Choices A and B are left and must be tested against the first three rules. For choice A, G starts on the hour and lasts an hour. Therefore, R starts on an hour, W on a half hour, and T on an hour, which is a violation. Choice B remains as the correct answer.

18. **(B)** This is a *how many orders* question with new information that goes in the diagram. Put W in 1. Applying the rules, T must go immediately after W, in 1:30. Create two universes based on the options for G, which are 2:00 and 3:00. Because the half-hour slot after G is also taken by G, there are only two slots left in each universe—for R and S—those players must go in the order RS.

1:00	1:30	2:00	2:30	3:00	3:30
W	T	G	——	R	S
W	T	R	S	G	——

These are the only two universes, so the correct answer is choice B.

19. **(D)** This is a *could be true* question in an EXCEPT format with new information that goes in the diagram. This means that the correct answer is one that violates rules. R is the second program, so put R in 1:30. Use **General—options for fixture** to consider the options for 1:00. There is not enough space for G to go in 1:00. S must go after R, so cannot go in 1:00. Only W and T are left. W cannot go in 1:00 because T would have to go in 1:30. Only T is left, but T cannot go in 1:00 because T starts on a half hour. There are no options for R in 1:30. The wording of the question states that R is the "second program" but the second program does not necessarily start at 1:30. If G is in 1:00, the second program starts at 2:00. Put R in 2:00.

With R in 2:00, create three universes around the options for S—2:30, 3:00, and 3:30. In all three universes, the remaining players are T and W. For the universe with S in 2:30, T can only go in 3:30 (the half hour). For the universe with S in 3:00, the remaining two slots are both half hours, but W cannot be before T, because S is between them. T must be before W, in 2:30. For the universe with S in 3:30, T can only go in 2:30. All three universes are completely determined.

1:00	1:30	2:00	2:30	3:00	3:30
G	——	R	S	W	T
G	——	R	T	S	W
G	——	R	T	W	S

In comparing the answer choices to the diagram, remember that the third program is not the same as the third time slot. Choice D is the only answer choice that cannot be true in any of the universes and thus is the correct answer.

20. **(E)** This is a *must be true* question with new information in the diagram. Create two universes with the two options for S—either G comes after S and S is in 2:00, or G comes before S and S is in 2:30. For the universe with S in 2:00, G must go in 3:00 (the only remaining hour) and the players left to assign are T and W. Break this universe into two universes based on R—one with R in 1:00 and one with R in 1:30. For the universe with R in 1:00, because there are not two consecutive slots, W cannot come before T. T must go in 1:30 and W in 2:30. For the universe with R in 1:30, W again cannot go before T but T cannot go in 1:00 (an hour). The universe with S in 2:00 and R in 1:30 is not valid.

For the universe with S in 2:30, G must be in 1:00. (If G were in 2:00, S would be the fourth program.) R must go in 2:00. W must go in 3:00 (T cannot go there because 3:00 is an hour) and T goes in 3:30.

1:00	1:30	2:00	2:30	3:00	3:30
R	T	S	W	G	—
~~R~~		~~S~~		~~G~~	~~—~~
G	—	R	S	W	T

Two valid and one invalid universe. The middle universe
is crossed out to indicate that it is not valid.

Use **Eliminate—check answers against diagram** to evaluate the answer choices. Only choice E must be true in both universes. The other answer choices *could* be true but do not have to be.

21. **(C)** This is a *could be true* question with new information that goes in the diagram. The only place where G can be the third program is in 2:00. It is possible to create parallel universes to represent all possibilities. Doing so requires six universes, which approaches not being time-effective, but two of the six turn out not to be viable. With the remaining four universes, it is very easy to find the correct answer.

Put G in 2:00. The 2:30 slot is also occupied by G. Create three universes based on the options for S—in 1:30, 3:00, and 3:30. With S in 1:30, the order is completely determined. R is in 1:00 and W and T are in 3:00 and 3:30, respectively.

With S in 3:00, create two universes based on the options for R—1:00 and 1:30. With R in 1:00, T must go in 1:30 and W in 3:30. With R in 1:30, neither T nor W can go in 1:00, so this universe is not valid.

With S in 3:30, create three universes based on the options for R—1:00, 1:30, and 3:00. With R in 1:00, T must go in 1:30 and W in 3:00. With R in 1:30, there are no options for 1:00, so this universe is not valid. With R in 3:00, W and T must go in 1:00 and 1:30, respectively.

1:00	1:30	2:00	2:30	3:00	3:30
R	S	G	—	W	T
R	T	G	—	S	W
~~R~~		~~G~~	~~—~~	~~S~~	
R	T	G	—	W	S
~~R~~		~~G~~	~~—~~		~~S~~
W	T	G	—	R	S

Four valid universes and two invalid universes.

In testing the answers, be careful to determine which slot corresponds to which program. Choices A, B, D, and E cannot be true. Only choice C—S as the fourth program (the 3:00 slot)—can be true.

22. **(B)** This is a *CANNOT be true* question with no new information. Because there is nothing to diagram, each answer choice must be tested. However, first use **Eliminate— check previous valid assignments**, because any answer choice that has been used in a valid assignment cannot be the correct answer. Choice A is found in the diagrams for

question 18. Choices D and E are found in the diagrams for question 19. Choice C is found in the diagrams for question 21. This leaves choice B as the correct answer.

If you do not have reliable diagrams for the earlier questions, it is necessary to test each answer choice. If you start with choice A, then, when you test choice B and find that it cannot be true, you can stop without testing the other answers. Choice B cannot be true because T must come before W. The only slot for T is 1:30. Putting T at 2:30 does not leave enough room for WRS. With T in 1:30, W can be in either 2:00 or 2:30. In each instance, there is no sequence of two consecutive slots for G.

23. **(C)** This is an *equivalent condition* question. *Equivalent condition* questions do not contain new information. Typically, for this type of question, each answer choice must be tested. Choice A is based on the rule that T must be assigned to a half hour, but choice A, then, goes in the direction of *not* putting G on the hour. Choice A is also too vague to capture the original condition, because there are a number of slots that are not immediately before T.

Choice B results in G beginning on the hour but is more restrictive than the original condition because it does not allow G to start at 2:00. Choice C eliminates two of the three half-hour slots—1:30 and 2:30. Because the rule that G takes a full hour is still in effect, the third half-hour slot—3:30—is also eliminated. The effect is exactly the same as saying that G can only start at 1:00, 2:00, or 3:00. Choice C is the correct answer. Choices D and E do not eliminate the possibility that G is shown at 1:30 or 2:30.

Section III: Reading Comprehension

1. **(B)** This is a *main point* question. Choice B fully captures the essential points of the passage.

Choice A falls short because it does not address the setting aside of standard conventions of autobiography. Choice C is incorrect because the passage does not focus on the difference between Latina autobiographers but on the difference between these women as a group and traditional autobiographers. Choice D is incorrect because it misses the point that the use of different genres, along with alternative structures, sets these autobiographies apart from traditional autobiographies. Choice E captures only a part of the main point but misses the emphasis on the difference between these women's autobiographies and traditional autobiographies.

2. **(D)** This is a *specific detail (stated fact)* question. Choice D is specifically defended by the information in lines 48–49.

Choice A goes in the wrong direction. Some of the authors rejected a chronological ordering. Choice B likewise goes in the wrong direction, as the authors embraced many genres. Choice C is incorrect because some authors specifically included political development. Choice E is incorrect because the authors used poetry as part of their narrative.

3. **(E)** This is a *function* question. The function of the discussion of *Getting Home Alive* is described by choice E. Choice A is incorrect because the author does not emphasize that *Getting Home Alive* is distinct from the other two examples. The author's point is that it is similar to the other two and expands on some aspects in the other two. Choice B is incorrect because combining journal entries and poetry is a characteristic of all three examples. Choice C is incorrect because the author indicates that the use of multiple

voices is unique, not common. Choice D is incorrect because, although the author refers to the possibility that some people may find the style confusing, this is not the main point of the author's discussion.

4. **(A)** This is a *specific detail (stated fact)* question. Choice A is correct because the passage specifically mentions essays, sketches, short stories, poems, and journal entries, in lines 19–20. Choice B is incorrect because the passage does not state that the journal entries were private or previously unpublished. Choice C is incorrect because the passage does not mention this. Choice D is incorrect because only one work included more than one author. Choice E is incorrect because the passage does not contain what choice E describes.

5. **(B)** This is a *tone* question. Choice B can be defended as correct by lines 42–45. Specifically, the clause *while this ordering may seem fragmentary*, shows that the author anticipates that readers may have trouble with the unconventional organization. The second half of the sentence shows that the author expects that readers may not understand that the organization is purposeful.

   Choice A cannot be defended by anything in the passage. The same is true for choice C. Choice D is incorrect because it is not clear that the author believes the work contains history or literary criticism, and because, even if the author does believe that, the author's confidence that it will be recognized as such is not mentioned in the passage, and thus is not defendable. Choice E is incorrect because, even though it is likely that the author believes that the work has helped broaden critics' understanding, there is nothing in the passage that defends that the author "insists" on this.

6. **(A)** This is an *extension/application* question. The cited phrase—existing generic parameters—refers to traditional guidelines that the authors of *Getting Home Alive* do *not* want to follow. Choice A is an example of a traditional guideline—events arranged sequentially—that the authors do not follow. The other answer choices are all examples of strategies that the authors use.

7. **(D)** This is a *weaken* question. You are asked to weaken the claim made in lines 50–55. The claim is that the authors of *Getting Home Alive* have "revolutionized the genre of autobiography." Choice D weakens this argument because it shows that autobiographies in the previous century contained some of the same "innovations," and thus the innovations in *Getting Home Alive* did not revolutionize the genre. Choice A is incorrect because, even though it refers to works with some of the innovations in *Getting Home Alive*, the works it refers to were written after *Getting Home Alive*, and thus do not detract from the revolutionary quality of *Getting Home Alive*.

   Choice B is incorrect because, if anything, it highlights the uniqueness of *Getting Home Alive*. Choice C is incorrect for the same reasons as choice A. Choice E is incorrect because it does not refer to autobiographies, whereas the original claim specifically refers to autobiographies.

8. **(A)** This is a *main point* question. The main point of the passage is stated in the last paragraph—that there is a danger that because of (1) the volume of material and (2) the limited durability of the media, it will not be possible for archivists to sort the essential from the inessential. Choice A captures all of these elements.

   Choice B is incorrect because it is the opposite of what the passage states. Choice C is incorrect because, even though it is consistent with the passage, it is not the main point.

Choice D is incorrect for the same reason as choice C. Choice E is incorrect because it is not the main point of the passage.

9. **(C)** This is a *helps to answer* question. Choice C is answered in lines 27–29. The questions posed by the other answer choices are not answered in the passage.

10. **(A)** This is an *implied fact/inference* question. It can be defended that the author holds the belief in choice A. Although the author admits that some archivists may be hesitant to rely on computer technology, the author states that time is running out. This implies that archivists must rely on technologies that are available now. This is further defended by the statement in lines 37–40 that computer technology may be able to meet durability requirements.

Choice B is incorrect because the author believes that time is running out. Choice C is incorrect because there is no evidence that the author recommends nonelectronic storage. Choice D is incorrect because there is no information to defend that the author believes this. In lines 19–23, images and texts are referred to as having similar requirements. Choice E is incorrect because the author does not specify that it is the amount of information per storage area that determines the durability. The only correlation stated in the passage is in lines 23–26, which correlates the pace of technological changes with decreasing durability.

11. **(B)** This is a *function* question. The cited passage documents that large amounts of information can be stored in a small space and that this fact would appear to be a solution to the degradation of large amounts of printed material. Choice B captures this function of the cited passage.

Choice A is incorrect because the assertion in the first sentence is that the potential for losing information is great. The cited passage is not a justification of that fact but rather appears to be a solution. Choice C is incorrect because the cited passage is factual information that is not rejected. Choice D is incorrect because the cited passage is a solution, not a problem. Choice E is incorrect because the cited passage supports the conclusion by showing that even though more information can be stored in smaller spaces, the problem of degradation is worse.

12. **(D)** This is an *implied fact/inference* question. The statement in choice D can be inferred from the passage by statements such as line 18 and lines 31–33. The other answer choices cannot be defended by any information in the passage.

13. **(E)** This is an *implied fact/inference* question. Choice E is defendable by the information in the passage that states that archivists must use their judgment to decide what to save, and that what was saved in the past has affected our understanding of history.

Choice A is incorrect because the passage contradicts it in lines 38–40. Choice B is contradicted by the author's statements that archivists should decide what is most worth saving. Choice C is incorrect because there is nothing in the passage to defend it. Choice D is incorrect because the passage defends that certain ancient works have survived because they were considered essential.

14. **(C)** This is a *main point* question applied to a Comparative Reading passage. It asks you to identify the point that is central to both passages. Both passages are primarily concerned with how blackmail is handled in certain legal systems, as described in choice C.

Choice A is incorrect because only Passage A mentions triangular transactions. Choice B is incorrect because free speech is a secondary issue, not the main issue. Choice D is incorrect because, even though the two passages together give a picture of blackmail across time, neither passage individually discusses the history of blackmail. Choice E is incorrect because Passage B does not discuss ambiguity in the definition of blackmail.

15. **(B)** This is a *use of a word/phrase* question that refers exclusively to Passage A. Choice B is correct because the blackmailer's position depends on the fact that the state is interested in finding out about crimes committed in its jurisdiction. Choice A is incorrect because presumably the blackmailer already knows that an action committed was a crime. Even though choice A hints at the state's role, it is not accurate in the way that choice B is.

Choice C is incorrect because the crime has already occurred. Choice D is incorrect because the passage does not imply that the state relies *exclusively* on private citizens. Choice E is incorrect because the blackmailer's position is not based on the knowledge that the blackmailer will be forced to testify.

16. **(A)** This is an *implied fact/inference* question that is applied to both passages. Choice A can be inferred because Passage A supports the fact that the primary paradox of blackmail is a result of the right to free speech. Passage B states that no special category of blackmail was necessary in Roman law. There is no mention of the right to free speech conflicting with Roman law in regard to blackmail.

Choice B is incorrect because it is not defendable by information in the passage. Choice C is incorrect for the same reason. Choice D is incorrect because it is Roman law that is concerned with reputation. Choice E is incorrect because Passage A mentions the state (public authority) has an interest in certain information being revealed.

17. **(A)** This is a Comparative Reading *disagree* question. The correct answer is true in the context given in Passage A but not true in the context given in Passage B. Choice A is correct because Passage A specifically states that this is true in Canadian and U.S. law, and Passage B states that under Roman law, the legality of actions was not the main concern.

Choice B is incorrect because blackmail is triangular by definition in both systems. Choice C is incorrect because the statement is not true of Canadian and U.S. law. Choice D is incorrect because it is true in both systems. Choice E is incorrect because it is not true of Canadian and U.S. law.

18. **(E)** This is an *extension/application* question applied to both Comparative Reading passages. This differs from question 17 in that it requires you to evaluate hypothetical situations, which is a characteristic of *extension* questions. Choice E is correct. It would be illegal under Roman law because it harms the reputation of an important person and does not involve an offense that would be of interest to public authorities. The action would be legal under Canadian and U.S. law because it is not given that the person who revealed the information tried to get money for not revealing the information.

Choice A is incorrect in part because it is not an example of blackmail and so neither passage covers it. However, it is clearly an example of an illegal act in Canada and the United States. Choices B and C are incorrect for the same reason as choice A. Choice D is incorrect because it would not be considered illegal under Roman law.

19. **(D)** This is an *analogous situation* question. In choice D, the fact that there was no need for a special category for blackmail in Roman law is analogous to the fact that there is no need for a special gun law category for felons.

Choice A is incorrect because it would be analogous to Roman law not finding blackmail punishable in any circumstances. Choice B is incorrect because it would be analogous to Roman law expanding on the Canadian and U.S. definitions of blackmail. Choice C is incorrect because it would be analogous to Roman law having a more restricted definition of blackmail than Canadian and U.S. law have. Choice E is incorrect because it would be analogous to Roman law allowing blackmail but having severe penalties for blackmailers who also commit another crime.

20. **(A)** This is a *main point* question. Choice A captures the main idea of restoring land by fostering diversity both aboveground and underground. Choice B is incorrect because it ignores the measures that can accelerate rehabilitation. Choice C is incorrect because the passage is not concerned with changing agriculture but with giving land a break from agriculture. Choice D is incorrect because it ignores the article's emphasis on ways of accelerating the restoration process. Choice E is incorrect because it ignores the article's emphasis on recovering from the effects of agriculture.

21. **(E)** This is an *identify the structure* question that asks you to find the structure of the passage as a whole. Choice E correctly describes the three sections of the article. Choice A is incorrect because the results of the study are not found to be inconclusive. Choice B is incorrect because, if the hypothesis is that lands can restore themselves, there is no evidence that undermines the hypothesis. Choice C is incorrect because there is no discussion of the likely effectiveness of the plan. Choice D is incorrect because, although a general goal is outlined in the beginning of the passage, there is no discussion of modifying the goal or of a methodology for achieving a modified goal.

22. **(B)** This is a *specific detail (stated fact)* question. Choice B is correct and is defended by lines 44–50. Choice A is defendable as a fact specified in the passage but does not address the question in the stem. Choice C is incorrect for the same reason. Choices D and E are contrary to what is stated in the passage.

23. **(D)** This is an *implied fact/inference* question. The replacement topsoil is defined in contrast to the depleted soil, which has the characteristics:

depleted of nutrients
overfertilized
encourages thistles
discourages native plants

The replacement topsoil can be inferred to have qualities opposite to the above. Choice D is a clear opposite to *overfertilized*. Choice A is incorrect because replacement topsoil is only expected to be less conducive to thistles. Choice B is incorrect because the replacement topsoil would be expected to have beneficial fungi. Choice C is incorrect because the replacement topsoil would be expected to have seeds of native plants. Choice E is incorrect because it is not known that the replacement soil was never used for commercial crops.

24. **(E)** This is a *function* question. The Netherlands study was designed to test whether there were methods of speeding up the process alluded to in the cited statement. Choice E captures this. Choice A is incorrect because the study was not designed to discredit the statement. Choice B is incorrect because the author does not refer to people who justify intense agricultural practices. Choice C is incorrect because it is not the author's

purpose to justify agricultural overproduction. Choice D is incorrect because the author is concerned with remediating agricultural land, not with discussing the problems of agricultural overproduction.

25. **(B)** This is an *extension/application* question in a LEAST format. In four of the answer choices, the methods tested in the Netherlands study would be beneficial. In the correct answer, they would not. Choice B is correct because the passage states that replacing the topsoil is the quickest way to remediate the land if it can be done easily. The other answer choices are either examples of problems that can be remediated by the methods in the study (choices A and C) or are irrelevant (choices D and E).

26. **(C)** This is an *implied fact/inference* question. The passage says that the disease organisms are the direct cause for the native plants not growing as well as native plants on more natural soil. Thus, the most direct implication is that without the disease organisms, the native plants would grow better, as in choice C. Choice A is incorrect because the beneficial fungi would be expected to increase, not decrease. Choice B is incorrect because it is too extreme. Thistles could survive but would not thrive. Choice D is incorrect because, even if it is true, it cannot be inferred as directly as can choice C. Choice E is incorrect because other disease organisms would probably decrease under healthier conditions and because choice E cannot be directly inferred from the passage.

27. **(B)** This is an *analogous situation* question. Choice B is analogous because it tries to discourage Party A (thistles) by promoting the preferred party (native plants), specifically by defending it against attacks by an opponent (harmful bacteria). Choice A is incorrect because it would be analogous to somehow directing the nutrients in the soil only to the native plants. Choice C is incorrect because it would be analogous to preventing the nutrients in the soil from being used by any plant. Choice D is incorrect because it would be analogous to attacking the thistles directly. Choice E is incorrect because it would be analogous to somehow creating an incompatibility between thistles and native grasses.

Section IV: Logical Reasoning

1. **(C)** This is a *resolve a paradox* question that uses the word *explain* rather than the word *paradox*. The paradox is that three species are all affected by lack of calcium but one species, sugar maples, shows more serious decline. Choice C provides a difference between sugar maples and the other two species that explains why sugar maples are more affected.

    Choice A is irrelevant. Choice B goes in the wrong direction, implying that sugar maples should decline less rapidly. Choice D does not explain the difference between sugar maples and the other two species. Choice E does not explain why sugar maples act differently than the few spruces and firs that are in the same location.

2. **(E)** This is a *necessary assumption* question. The negation of choice E is that once people have decided for whom to vote, they can be persuaded to change their mind. This destroys the argument.

    The negation of choice A is that columnists do not influence the votes of undecided readers. This strengthens the argument. The negation of choice B is that the attempts of columnists to persuade readers to vote one way cannot cause them to vote the other way. This does not weaken the argument. The negation of choice C is that people do not just read the columns of columnists with whom they agree. This does not weaken the argument. The negation of choice D is that regular readers and occasional readers are equally likely to be persuaded. This does not weaken the argument.

3. **(D)** This is a *weaken* question. The argument is based on the fact that 80 percent of ticket buyers are leisure travelers and only 20 percent are business travelers. Choice D weakens the conclusion by establishing that more than 50 percent of revenue comes from business travelers.

Choice A is incorrect because it is irrelevant to the issue of which group generates more income. Choice B is incorrect because it assumes that the argument is correct and that airlines should also accommodate leisure travelers. Choice C is incorrect because it does not attack the argument that the leisure travelers are more important to revenue than are the business travelers. Choice E goes in the right direction by hinting that revenues from leisure travelers are not what the statistics imply, but does not go far enough—unlike choice D—to indicate that business travelers account for a greater percentage of revenue.

4. **(B)** This is a *committed to agree/disagree* question. In this case, the two arguers must be committed to disagree about a fact. Choice B is correct because Gaby is committed to the view that teachers should offer only minimal direction, and Logan is committed to the view that teachers should offer disciplined, systematic instruction.

Choice A is incorrect because Gaby is not committed to an opinion about how children learn fundamental knowledge. Choice C is incorrect because both arguers agree that teachers should be qualified (*experienced* or *accredited*). Choice D is incorrect because neither arguer discusses creativity. Choice E is incorrect because neither discusses whether children are interested in fundamental knowledge.

5. **(B)** This is a *strengthen by principle* question. Question 5 functions like a *sufficient assumption* question. If choice B is true—that each defendant has the right to have his or her own legal counsel present—then the argument follows logically: for one of the defendants who shares a common legal counsel, it will be unavoidable that the legal counsel for a codefendant (namely, the same legal counsel) will be present.

Choice A is incorrect because there is nothing in the argument that requires the legal counsel to disclose information. Choice C is incorrect because it is irrelevant. Choice D is incorrect because the argument does not grant a right to the plaintiff that is denied to a defendant. Choice E is incorrect because the argument does not involve the defendant's legal counsel questioning the plaintiff.

6. **(E)** This is a *conclusion* question that asks for a statement that can be inferred. The logic in the argument is:

$$If\ overnutrified \rightarrow algae$$
$$If\ algae \rightarrow toxic\ microorganisms$$
$$If\ toxic\ microorganisms \rightarrow kill\ most\ fish$$

Choice E follows this logic by stating:

$$If\ overnutrified \rightarrow kill\ most\ fish$$

Choice A is not defendable by any information in the passage. Choice B is incorrect because it is not defendable that the toxic microorganisms multiply more quickly than other microorganisms. Choice C is incorrect because there is no information to defend that sewage has no other harmful effect. Choice D is incorrect because it states:

$$-overnutrified \rightarrow -algae$$

This is a negation of both sides of an original premise but such a negation does not necessarily result in a true statement.

7. **(A)** This is a *relevant information* question. Choice A is correct because if the traditional techniques used now had *not* been in use at the time Tiwanaku was inhabited, then the experiment does not prove that reed boats could have been used.

   Choice B is incorrect because the hypothesis is that the stones were brought by boat, and the fact that the stones were used at sites near the quarry does not strengthen or weaken the hypothesis. Choice C is incorrect because whether the boats are common now does not affect the hypothesis. Choice D is incorrect because it is irrelevant whether there are stones other than green andracite that are bigger than the andracite stones. Choice E is incorrect because the hypothesis does not require that the boats were used for several years.

8. **(C)** This is a *flaw* question with the wording *vulnerable to criticism*. Choice C is correct because the argument does fail to consider the benefits, and considering the benefits might lead to a different conclusion.

   Choice A is incorrect because it still results in the conclusion that the strike has negative results. Choice B is incorrect because failing to define a term in a premise is not a logical flaw. Choice D is incorrect because the argument does not assume that the union's financial strength is its most important bargaining position. Choice E is incorrect because the argument is not based on the fact that there will be a better time for a strike.

9. **(E)** This is a *conclusion* question that asks for a statement that can be inferred. Choice E is correct because, if West Nile virus was brought to North America by an infected person, it could not have been transmitted to a mosquito. If it could not have been transmitted to a mosquito, it could not have been transmitted to a bird or mammal, including other humans.

   Choice A is incorrect because there is nothing in the passage that leads to the conclusion that West Nile will never be common among humans, even though it may not be common in North America. Choice B is incorrect because, even though it is consistent with the argument, it cannot be defended. It may be that West Nile is more common in other parts of North America. Choice C is incorrect because it cannot be defended by the passage. Choice D is incorrect because, although likely to be true, it cannot be defended by information in the passage.

10. **(D)** This is a *resolve a paradox* question. The paradox is that people have reduced their consumption of red meat in order to reduce their fat intake but actually consume more fat than people who did not reduce their consumption of red meat. Choice D explains that people who reduce their red meat consumption do so by eating more of foods that are even fattier.

    Choice A is incorrect because it does not address the paradox. Choice B is incorrect for the same reason. Choice C is incorrect because it should still lead to the conclusion that people who have reduced their red meat consumption are taking in less fat. Similarly, choice E also leads to the conclusion that reducing red meat consumption should lower fat intake.

11. **(D)** This is a *flaw* question. It requires you to find the flaw in Tom's argument. Tom's error is that all properties are equally affected by the twenty-foot inset, so the house on Oak Avenue still has the largest yard. Choice D describes this error as failing to apply a general rule (the twenty-foot inset) to all relevant instances (all of the houses that they have looked at, as opposed to just the house on Oak Avenue). The other answer choices are types of logical errors that do not appear in this argument.

12. **(C)** This is a *role of a claim* question. The conclusion of the argument is stated in the last sentence. The cited statement is put forth, supported with evidence, and then used to support the conclusion, as described in choice C.

    Choice A is incorrect because the cited statement is not the main conclusion. Choice B is incorrect because the cited statement is not the only conclusion. Choice D is incorrect because evidence is provided for the cited statement. Choice E is incorrect because the cited statement is used directly to support the main conclusion.

13. **(E)** This is a *necessary assumption* question. The negation of choice E is that qualified teachers from other areas could be persuaded to relocate to the educator's region. This destroys the argument.

    The negation of choice A is that class sizes should be reduced even if doing so does not result in improved achievement. This does not affect the argument. The negation of choice B is that no qualified teachers could improve the quality of their classes if class sizes were reduced. The educator's argument—that reducing class size will not improve achievement—is based on the assertion that reducing class size will require hiring underqualified teachers. For this reason, choice B is irrelevant to the argument. Likewise, choice C is irrelevant because it does not address the need to hire underqualified teachers. Choice D is incorrect because the argument does not assume that there will not be any students at all who do not improve.

14. **(E)** This is a *main conclusion* question. The conclusion of the argument is simply that global warming is not likely to increase the frequency and intensity of tropical storms. Choice E captures this.

    Choice A is incorrect because it is a premise of the argument. Choice B is incorrect because it is a premise that supports the conclusion. Choice C is incorrect because the argument does not state this, and the argument implies the opposite. Choice D is incorrect because it is a premise that supports the conclusion.

15. **(E)** This is a *complete the sentence/argument* question. The stated purpose of copyright is to allow authors to profit from their work financially. The blank requires an example of something that goes beyond the purpose. Choice E is correct because if the copyright continues beyond the author's death, the copyright has gone beyond its purpose.

    Choice A is incorrect because it does not go beyond the purpose of the copyright. Choice B is incorrect because it does not require a copyright. Choice C is incorrect because the author still has the opportunity to profit, even if the author has not yet realized that opportunity. Choice D is incorrect because, even though this is a drawback of copyrights, it is not an example of the copyright going beyond its purpose.

16. **(A)** This is a *type of logic* question. Choice A correctly points out that the economist's prediction was based on conditions that did not occur.

Choice B is incorrect because it refers to a different type of argument. Choice C is incorrect because the economist does not claim that the critic's premises are inconsistent. Choice D is incorrect because the critic does not assert a general claim. Choice E is incorrect because the economist does not question the critic's premises. The critic correctly describes the economist's prediction and correctly states that the economy did not go into a recession. It is only the critic's conclusion—that the economist bumbled—that is incorrect.

17. **(C)** This is a *parallel reasoning* question. The essence of the argument is that the distribution of genres that are published in a certain medium is not proportional to the distribution of genres in general because there is a specific reason some genres are represented in the medium more than others. Choice C captures this.

In choice A, it is true that the existing copies are not representative of all that was originally written, but this is because of choices made by copyists, not by authors. The parallel to choice A would be that certain types of music were not represented on video because the video manufacturers refused to make copies of certain types of music. Choice B is incorrect because it does not deal with an unrepresentative sample. Choice D is incorrect because the unrepresentative sample is caused by degradation of the medium. Choice E is incorrect because it deals with a representative sample, not an unrepresentative sample.

18. **(B)** This is a *match a principle to a concrete example* question in which the setup is the concrete example and the answer choices are principles. Choice B matches the setup exactly. The organization has the property of being selfless even though many of its members are not selfless.

Choice A is incorrect because it compares one organization with another organization, but there is only one organization in the setup. Choice C is incorrect because the setup does not state that any of the members of the organization claim to be altruistic. Choice D is incorrect because the setup does not mention the intentions of the founders. Choice E is incorrect because the setup does not state that the organization was founded for a different purpose than its current purpose.

19. **(B)** This is a *weaken* question in an EXCEPT format. Choice B is correct in that it does not weaken the argument. The argument is that X causes Y. Choice B claims that other things can cause Y. This does not weaken the argument.

Choice A weakens the premise that radiolytic products are found in irradiated food. Choice C weakens the premise that irradiation reduces vitamin content. Choice D weakens the premise that irradiated food contains harmful chemicals. Choice E weakens the premise that irradiated food is associated with cancer.

20. **(D)** This is a *necessary assumption* question. The argument is:

Colored paper → compare impact of color in varying contexts

?

Colored paper → learn about use of color

In the above argument, the question mark represents a missing step, which is the assumption. By replacing the question mark with choice D, the argument works:

Colored paper → compare impact of color in varying contexts
Compare impact of color in varying contexts → learn about use of color (choice D)
Colored paper → learn about use of color

If choice D were negated, the argument would not work. The other choices do not connect the two original premises in the correct way. Note that the correct answer to this question is both necessary (without it the argument does not work) and sufficient (it alone is enough to make the argument work).

21. **(E)** This is a *role of a claim* question. Choice E is correct. The cited statement is the conclusion (a claim that the arguer attempts to justify) and is supported by the rest of the argument. In addition, choice E correctly describes the logic of the argument. The argument recommends proving that X causes Y by showing that every instance of X results in Y, and that every instance of Y is preceded by X. The other answer choices miss both the logic and the fact that the cited statement is the conclusion.

22. **(A)** This is a *sufficient assumption* question. The argument is:

Current system → fraud
?
current system → deleterious to progress

The question mark represents a missing if/then condition. If the question mark is replaced with choice A, the argument works:

Current system → fraud
Fraud → deleterious to progress
current system → deleterious to progress

The other answer choices do not properly connect the two original premises.

23. **(B)** This is a *strengthen by principle* question. The key to this question is that the original argument starts with an observed fact (a premise) and comes to a conclusion. The correct answer must start with the same fact. In the original argument the premise and conclusion are:

If some breeds of dog are more closely related to wolves than
dogs → descended from more recently domesticated wolves

Choice B exactly matches the argument.
　　Choice A is incorrect because it states:

If descended from more recently domesticated
wolves → more closely related to wolves

Choice C is incorrect because it states:

If descended from domesticated wolves → more closely
related to some breeds of dogs

This is clearly a different argument than the original. Choice D is incorrect because it states:

> *If one breed of dog closer to wolves than another*
> *breed is* → *first breed is closer to wolves than to other breed*

Choice E is incorrect because it states:

> *If two breeds more closely related to each other than to*
> *wolves* → *descended from wolves domesticated long ago*

24. **(A)** This is a *parallel flaw* question. The logic of the original argument is:

> *If Paleo* → *acquainted with publications of all Paleos*
> *Acquainted with publication of one Paleo* ∴ *Paleo*

This argument is somewhat more complicated than the more usual version:

> *If X* → *Y*
> *Y* ∴ *X*

In question 24, the second half of the first if/then involves all members of a category, and the first half of the second if/then involves one member of the category. In other words, the argument in question 24 takes the form:

> *If X* → *all Y*
> *One Y* ∴ *X*

Choice A follows the same pattern:

> *If first flight delayed* → *all connecting flights delayed*
> *One connecting flight delayed* ∴ *first flight delayed*

Choice B is incorrect because its structure is:

> *If one agent misses* → *all others work harder*
> *–one agent misses* → *–all others work harder*

Choice C is incorrect because its structure is:

> *If fuel price decreases* → *expense decreases and income unchanged*
> *Fuel price decreased* → *profit*

Choice D is incorrect because its structure is:

> *If one year or more* → *can participate in retirement plan*
> *One year or more* → *participates*

Choice E is incorrect because its structure is:

> *If competitor reduces fare* → *Global reduce or Global lose passengers*
> *Global more passengers than before* ∴ *reduced fares to match competitor*

25. **(C)** This is a *committed to agree/disagree* question in which the correct answer is one that the two arguers are committed to disagreeing about. Choice C is correct because Lutsina is committed to the belief that futuristic science fiction is a better source of social criticism than conventional fiction, and Priscilla is committed to the opposite belief.

Choice A is incorrect because Lutsina agrees but Priscilla does not have an opinion. Priscilla's opinion concerns radically new technology. Choice B is incorrect because neither arguer has an opinion. Choice D is incorrect because neither arguer is committed to this. Priscilla believes that radically new technologies are a shortcoming but does not express an opinion about radically new social arrangements. Lutsina believes that radically new social arrangements are positive but does not express an opinion about technologies. Choice E is incorrect because neither arguer expresses an opinion.

26. **(E)** This is a *flaw* question. The argument has two flaws. One is that it attributes the qualities of the members of the team to the team as a whole. However, the correct answer is not based on this flaw. The second flaw is that the argument assumes that because an event is the most likely of all events, it is more than 50 percent likely to occur. To understand why this is a flaw, consider the following example of a game with five players, each of which has distinct odds of winning.

Person	Odds
Person S	15%
Person T	10%
Person U	30%
Person V	27%
Person W	18%

Person U has the greatest odds of winning. However, it is logically flawed to conclude that Person U is more likely to win than not. There is a 70 percent chance that someone else will win. Choice E correctly identifies the flaw. The other answer choices refer to possible logical flaws that do not occur in this argument.

Writing Sample: Example of a Superior Essay

The two pediatric doctors ("Doctors") choose the Victorian House ("VH") over the Laurel Medical Pavilion ("LMP") because VH offers an office that is conveniently located to new patients and allows Doctors to continue practicing in their current location. Doctors use two criteria, which are that Doctors want to attract new patients and keep their current patients in order to choose between VH and LMP. VH is Doctors' superior choice because VH is located in a residential area filled with young families, and VH allows Doctors to keep their current space. LMP is Doctors' inferior alternative because moving to LMP forces Doctors to close their current location and move to LMP's risky facility located far away from Doctors' current patients. Therefore, VH is Doctors' superior choice because VH better meets Doctors' two selection criteria.

Doctors use two criteria to choose between VH and LMP. One criterion says Doctors want to gain new patients. The second criterion says Doctors want to retain their current patients. These two criteria may be combined into a single rule that says Doctors want to increase the size of their practice by retaining their old patients and gaining new patients. Doctors' long-term goal to increase the size of their practice is greater than Doctors' need to relocate into a new office.

VH is Doctors' superior choice because VH's location near a large number of young families affords Doctors the opportunity to increase the size of their practice while still retaining their current location and keeping their ongoing patients. In addition, VH has a fenced yard for children to play in, sufficient parking space, is recently remodeled, and has room for Doctors to grow their practice by remodeling the upstairs. Unfortunately, VH is not located near the city's major hospital. Even so, VH is Doctors' superior alternative because VH offers Doctors greater opportunity to build the size of their practice while minimizing their business risk.

LMP is Doctors' inferior choice. LMP is located ten miles away from Doctors' current practice, is expensive and risky, and its large size means that LMP may house competitors. In addition, LMP is a collection of new buildings that might not be well constructed. While LMP's location next to a hospital and laboratories make LMP somewhat attractive, LMP forces Doctors to possibly lose their current clients, which points to VH as Doctors' superior choice. Therefore, Doctors reject LMP, as LMP is their less desirable alternative.

VH is Doctors' superior alternative. VH is more likely than LMP to help Doctors build the size of their practice over the long term. VH's location in a residential area filled with young families provides Doctors with a stream of new patients and allows Doctors to retain their current patients. LMP's new location is risky because Doctors would have to close their current location, and LMP is expensive. In conclusion, Doctors select VH because VH better fits Doctors' long-term goal to increase the size of their practice while minimizing their business risk.

Index

by undermining an apparent
counterexample to a general claim,
172
Regular set, 261
Rejecting a view because it has not been
proven, 165, 201
Relationship between passage
questions, 279–280
Relevant information questions, 221
Role of a claim questions, 212–215
Rushing, 108, 110

Scoring, 3–5
Section, 261
Self-confidence, 120, 128
Sentences
active, 484
complex, 294
diagramming of, 288
short, direct, 485
Sequence
conditions for, 366–367
counting places in, 418–419
description of, 352–354
Sequence games
conditions for sequences, 366–367
definition of, 353
description of, 353–354, 361–366
one-to-one correspondence, 361
Set, 261
Set arguments, 139–142
Setup, for analytical reasoning
definition of, 319, 324
description of, 325–326
information from, included in
diagram, 346–347
organizing the, 323–324
Short, direct sentences, 485
Signal words, 287
Similar situations to the current
situation, inferences from, 169
Skimming of passages, 271–272, 288
Specific detail questions, 284, 293, 296
Statistical arguments, 160, 182–184
Strategy
definition of, 114
mastering of, 103–104
selection of, 128
timing. See Timing/timing strategy
Strengthen arguments by applying a
principle
overview of, 179–180
wording variations for, 180
Strengthen arguments by conclusion
cause-and-effect arguments, 174–177
matching terms, 177

miscellaneous logic types, 177–179
Strengthen questions, 281–282
Stretching, 127
Study plan, 6–7
Sufficient assumptions, 189–190, 192
Sufficient conditions, 150–151, 161–162,
199
Sufficient premise, 213
Support a generalization question, 282
Supported information treated as
information that proves the
conclusion, 170
Survey arguments, weakening based on,
182–184
Syllogism, 152–153

Takes for granted flaw question, 199,
202
Tautology, 160
Temporary supplemental diagrams,
344
Test anxiety, 104, 127
Testing strategy
analyzing of, 127
perfect, 110
Thinking
big-picture, 118–120, 128
detail, 118–120
Three-month study plan, 6–7
Time
tracking of, 105–106
watch for tracking, 105–106, 113
writing down, 112
Timing/timing strategy
for all sections, 109
for analytical reasoning section, 108,
320–323
application of, 112–113
description of, 104–105
evaluation of, 110–112
importance of, 103
improvements in, 110–112
for logical reasoning section, 133–135
perfect, 110
power of, 110
for reading comprehension section,
108, 262–263
summary of, 113–114
understanding of, 106–110
Tiredness, 127
Tone questions, 282–283
Treats one element as something else,
169–170
Triggers, 147–150
True of the parts must be true of the
whole inference, 162, 199

Two-labeled arguer format, of logical
reasoning questions, 223–224
Type of reasoning questions, 220–221

Undermining an apparent
counterexample to a general claim,
172
Undesirable results, challenging an
argument by showing that its
conclusion would lead to, 172
Unjustified assertion treated as an
intentionally false assertion, 170
Unordered branches, 359–360
Unordered games
conditions for, 369–370
description of, 351–352, 367–368
sample types of, 368–369
with variable fixtures, 358
Unreliable source, 164, 200
Unrepresentative sample, 163, 200
Use of a word or phrase questions, 273,
275, 297

Valid arguments
deductive arguments. See Deductive
arguments
inductive arguments. See Inductive
arguments
Valid logic, 137
Variable branches
ordered, 383–384
unordered, 378–382
Variable fixtures, 356–358
Visual aids, 116–118, 230–231
Vocabulary
for analytical reasoning games, 324
for reading comprehension, 261, 289
Voice, 125, 484

Watch, 105–106, 113
Weaken arguments
analogy, 185
cause and effect as basis for, 180–182
description of, 180
miscellaneous logic types, 185–186
statistical or survey arguments, 182–
184
wording variations for, 187
What can be inferred conclusion
questions, 193–194
Which conclusion can be rejected?, 196
Word or phrase questions, 273, 275, 297
Writing sample section
description of, 2
essay. See Essay
Wrong answers, 129

LSAT CD-ROM
SYSTEM REQUIREMENTS

This CD is intended to run on systems meeting the minimum requirements below.

Windows®

2.33GHz or faster x86-compatible processor,
or Intel® Atom™ 1.6GHz or faster processor
for netbooks
Microsoft® Windows® XP (32-bit), Windows
Server® 2003 (32-bit), Windows Server 2008
(32-bit), Windows Vista® (32-bit), Windows 7
(32-bit and 64-bit), Windows 8 (32-bit or 64-bit)
512MB of RAM (1GB of RAM recommended
for netbooks); 128MB of graphics memory
CD-ROM drive
1024 × 768 color display

Mac OS®

Intel Core™ Duo 1.83GHz or faster processor
Mac OS X 10.6 or higher
512MB of RAM; 128MB of graphics memory
CD-ROM drive
1024 × 768 color display

Installation Instructions

The software is not installed on your computer; it runs directly from the CD-ROM. Barron's CD-ROM includes an "autorun" feature that automatically launches the application when the CD is inserted into the CD-ROM drive. In the unlikely event that the autorun feature is disabled, follow the manual launching instructions below.

Windows®

1. Click on the Start button and choose "My Computer."
2. Double-click on the CD-ROM drive, which will be named **LSAT**.
3. Double-click **LSAT.exe** application to launch the program.

Mac®

1. Insert the CD-ROM.
2. Double-click the CD-ROM icon.
3. Double-click the **LSAT** icon to start the program.